Praise for *Decolonizing Anarchism*

Maia Ramnath offers a refreshingly different perspective on anticolonial movements in India, not only by focusing on little-remembered anarchist exiles such as Har Dayal, Mukerji and Acharya but more important, highlighting the persistent trend that sought to strengthen autonomous local communities against the modern nation-state. While Gandhi, the self-proclaimed philosophical anarchist, becomes a key figure in this antiauthoritarian history, there are other more surprising cases that Ramnath brings to light. A superbly original book.

—Partha Chatterjee, author of *Lineages of Political Society: Studies in Postcolonial Democracy*

"This is a stunningly impactful and densely researched book. Maia Ramnath has offered a vital contribution to our understanding of the long historical entanglement between liberation struggles, anticolonialism, and the radical movement of oppressed peoples against the modern nation-state. She audaciously reframes the dominant narrative of Indian radicalism by detailing its explosive and ongoing symbiosis with decolonial anarchism."

—Dylan Rodríguez, author of *Suspended Apocalypse: White Supremacy, Genocid*

DECOLONIZING
ANARCHISM

AN ANTIAUTHORITARIAN HISTORY OF INDIA'S LIBERATION STRUGGLE

Decolonizing Anarchism: An Antiauthoritarian History of India's Liberation Struggle by Maia Ramnath

ISBN 978 1 84935 082 2 | Ebook: 978 1 84935 083 9
Library of Congress Number: 2011936326

Cover Design and Interior: Josh MacPhee/Justseeds.org

Illustrations: Favianna Rodriguez/Favianna.com/Justseeds.org
Printed in the USA on 100% recycled, acid-free paper by union labor

AK Press, 674-A 23rd Street, Oakland, CA 94612
www.akpress.org | akpress@akpress.org | 510.208.1700

AK Press UK, P.O. Box 12766, Edinburgh EH8 9YE
www.akuk.com | ak@akedin.demon.co.uk | 0131.555.5165

Institute for Anarchist Studies, P.O. Box 15586, Washington, DC 20003
www.anarchist-studies.org | info@anarchiststudies.org

At least 50 percent of the net sales from each title in this series are donated to the Institute for Anarchist Studies, thanks to the generosity
of each author.

DECOLONIZING ANARCHISM

AN ANTIAUTHORITARIAN HISTORY OF INDIA'S LIBERATION STRUGGLE

Maia Ramnath

AK Press / Institute for Anarchist Studies   2011

Anarchist Interventions:
An IAS/AK Press Book Series

Radical ideas can open up spaces for radical actions, by illuminating hierarchical power relations and drawing out possibilities for liberatory social transformations. The Anarchist Intervention series—a collaborative project between the Institute for Anarchist Studies (IAS) and AK Press—strives to contribute to the development of relevant, vital anarchist theory and analysis by intervening in contemporary discussions. Works in this series will look at twenty-first-century social conditions—including social structures and oppression, their historical trajectories, and new forms of domination, to name a few—as well as reveal opportunities for different tomorrows premised on horizontal, egalitarian forms of self-organization.

Given that anarchism has become the dominant tendency within revolutionary milieus and movements today, it is crucial that anarchists explore current phenomena, strategies, and visions in a much more rigorous, serious manner. Each title in this series, then, will feature a present-day anarchist voice, with the aim, over time, of publishing a variety of perspectives. The series' multifaceted goals are to cultivate anarchist thought so as to better inform anarchist practice, encourage a culture of public intellectuals and constructive debate within anarchism, introduce new generations to anarchism, and offer insights into today's world and potentialities for a freer society.

Contents

Introduction

The impulse for this intervention was twofold: to bring an anarchist approach to anticolonialism, and an anticolonial approach to anarchism. I tackle the first by addressing practices of historiography and active solidarity. Both interventions are linked through the need to know other histories besides the familiar European/North American one. Furthermore, recognizing those other histories as relevant to the anarchist tradition means seeing anarchism as *one* instance of a polymorphous engagement with certain key questions and issues, as *one* manifestation of a larger family of egalitarian and emancipatory principles.

The seeds for this writing were planted over a decade of involvement with global economic justice, antiwar, and Palestine solidarity work, all framed as part of an anti-imperialist analysis, and then fertilized during the better part of a year spent studying in India, 2006–7. It wasn't my first trip to my father's country of origin, and it wouldn't be my last, as I hoped eventually to spend a significant amount of time there each year. With this in mind I set out to try to find my closest political counter-parts and get a sense of where I might someday fit in the terrain of social movement activity. It quickly became clear that there was no simple one-to-one correspondence with the radical spectrum familiar to me in the United States. The histories and contexts were too different; the trajectories of the vocabulary too weighted with mutu-ally illegible baggage. Sub- and countercultures as well as oppositional movements only have meaning when em-bedded in and against their respective hegemonic main-streams, which are in turn deeply embedded in history, geography, and global political economy. This renders direct translation impossible.

Thus there was no group or formation that would be a perfect match for my U.S. political profile, and in any case it would be misguided—colonialist, you could say—to expect one. So the question shifted from "Where/who are my political counterparts?" to "What political niche makes sense for me here (as the half-breed, rootless-cosmopolitan, déclassé-intelligentsia, self-described anarchist daughter of a thoroughly acculturated, diasporic professional)?" My relationship to this context was that of a peculiar travel-ing cousin, neither an outsider nor a native, enjoying ac-cess but not total belonging. Based on the questions being asked and analysis made, issues raised and stances taken, organizing principles espoused and critiques rendered of the mainline Left party (or parties), I found some aspects of affinity with some sectors, and other aspects with oth-ers. These sectors would never see eye to eye with each other, however, and indeed are often positioned as radical opponents, never the twain to meet. Yet the seeming polarity was in reality masking a range of critical variants being voiced within each category. To me the synthesis seemed perfectly logical because of my idiosyncratic angle of vision, free of entanglement in the intermovement dynamics that seemed to overdetermine any statement so that a critique of entity X would by implication align you with entity Y, within a fixed arrangement of alternatives.

In India, when I hear people use terms like anarchism, anarchist, and anarchistic, they are usually referring either to violent, nihilistic chaos or competitive, free market individualism. It stands to reason, then, that the terminology is used disapprovingly by leftists and Left-liberal progressive types, and approvingly by postmodern academics and self-indulgent, capitalist entrepreneurs. The implied opposite is top-down centralized state planning of the sort that was instituted through the Nehruvian social democracy that officially dominated Indian society until the liberalization of the early 1990s (though already undermined by the Emergency period of authoritarian crackdown in the mid-1970s). Despite its stated goals of redistributive justice, this system became in practice a byword for inefficiency and unwieldy bureaucracy.

If engaged in an appropriately complex yet amicable political discussion, I might point out that the contrary of top-down organization and concentrated power is not the absence of organization but rather a different form of decentralized, participatory organization in which power is dispersed. I might suggest that the alternatives to a state-controlled economy include not just neoliberal free market capitalism (which far from representing an escape from the state, actually depends on favorable state policies) but also some form of nonstate socialism built on an overlapping network of self-run syndicates and collectives.

Most often, though, there doesn't seem to be much point in quibbling. Why force my vocabulary into a place where it doesn't make sense, using words that will inevitably trigger referents and associations that are far from what I am trying to communicate? Even in explaining this project to people in Indian social movement and scholarly contexts I've hesitated to use the words, because whenever I did, due to an accepted sediment of meanings and associations, it led directly into miscomprehension of what I was trying to do. If the concern is with content and meaning rather than with labels, it is better to scrap any attachment I have to a terminology from another context and seek a different shared vocabulary for the principles to be discussed, the problems to be solved.

And what are these principles, these problems? My political, ethical, and intellectual worlds have long orbited a binary star of anarchism and anticolonialism. The attempt to explain their relationship has a double implication: in how an anarchist perspective affects our understanding of a history of anticolonialism, and in how an anticolonial perspective affects our understanding of a history of anarchism.

Regarding the first, standard nationalist history tells one story of decolonization. There are others, and they are still unfolding. In these stories, the achievement of a national state was not the endpoint of liberation, and its inherited institutions not the proper vehicle. The elimination of the British government left incomplete the task of ending injustice and inequity. The postcolonial state, insufficient at best, at its worst actually perpetuated the same kinds of oppression and exploitation carried out by colonial rule, but now in the name of the nation.

I should emphasize that what I am *not* doing here is looking for anarchism in South Asia (although I do sometimes find it), staking out territorial claims with a red-and-black flag. Rather, I am exploring a slice of South Asian history through the lens of an anarchist analysis. In doing so, what becomes visible or legible, what is foregrounded or emphasized, that may otherwise seem to defy logic or simply be overlooked? What in India's counterhistory does this shed light on—what forgotten but not lost possibilities? Where and in what form do I recognize certain questions being asked, certain concerns being addressed, that I as an anarchist share—for example, regarding the role of the state, the nature of industrial development, or attitudes toward modern rationalism? How and in what terms do people embedded in *this* particular history generate theory and praxis regarding those questions and concerns? Where do I see intersections, articulations, or direct points of contact with the Western anarchist tradition? Why is there a recurring linkage made (in praise and condemnation alike) between anarchism and certain elements of an Indian social movement history, such as the militant wing of the freedom struggle from 1905 to the 1930s, or the postindependence offshoots of Gandhism? Without either taking the equation at face value (given the questionable usage of the word) or dismissing it as groundless (given its persistence), can we identify just what affinities and analogies are being sensed whenever the linkage is made?

This leads to the second implication, which has to do not just with anarchism's role in decolonization but also with decolonizing our concept of anarchism itself. That means that instead of always trying to construct a strongly anarcha-centric cosmology—conceptually appropriating movements and voices from elsewhere in the world as part of "our" tradition, and then measuring them against how much or little we think they resemble our notion of our own values—we could locate the Western anarchist tradition as one contextually specific manifestation among a larger—indeed global—tradition of antiauthoritarian, egalitarian thought/praxis, of a universal human urge (if I dare say such a thing) toward emancipation, which also occurs in many other forms in many other contexts. Something else is then the reference point for us, instead of us being the reference point for everything else. This is a deeply decolonizing move.

This is perhaps where I need to make a distinction between the concept of anarchism and the Circle-A brand. The big *A* covers a specific part of the Western Left tradition dating from key ideological debates in the mid-nineteenth century and factional rivalries in the International Working Men's Association. It peaked worldwide in the early twentieth century among radical networks that consciously embraced the label while nevertheless encompassing multiple interpretations and emphases within it. Genealogically related to both democratic republicanism and utopian socialism, the big *A* opposed not only capitalism but also the centralized state along with all other systems of concentrated power and hierarchy. It bore echoes of earlier radical egalitarian, libertarian, and millenarian movements as well, with their carnivalesque upendings of rank and social norms, and upholding of a pre- or noncapitalist moral economy. These in turn resonated through later Romantic reactions against an excess of Enlightenment positivism, bemoaning the psychic disenchantment as much as the material exploitation wrought by industrial capitalism.

With a small *a*, the word anarchism implies a set of assumptions and principles, a recurrent tendency or orientation—with the stress on movement in a direction, not a perfected condition—toward more dispersed and less concentrated power; less top-down hierarchy and more self-determination through bottom-up participation; liberty and equality seen as directly rather than inversely proportional; the nurturance of individuality and diversity within a matrix of interconnectivity, mutuality, and accountability; and an expansive recognition of the various forms that power relations can take, and correspondingly, the various dimensions of emancipation. This tendency, when it becomes conscious, motivates people to oppose or subvert the structures that generate and sustain inequity, unfreedom, and injustice, and to promote or prefigure the structures that generate and sustain equity, freedom, and justice.

These tendencies, culturally inflected, are certainly present within South Asian history. There is a long tradition, for instance, of radical egalitarianism and subversion of authority, celebrated in the (Muslim) sufi and (Hindu) bhakti movements immortalized through mystical poetry since the thirteenth century. Sikhism was originally founded as an attempt to counter caste hierarchy and religious division through synthesis and egalitarian social relations. The birth and evolution of Buddhism too (along with certain branches of Vedanta) placed a rational and antihierarchical philosophy at the heart of India's intellectual heritage, countering the Orientalist portrait of Indian culture as *essentially* defined by hierarchy, autocracy, and unreason.[1]

In this case, those seeking counterparts or solidarities might be guided not by Anarchism but instead by that broader principle, tendency, or orientation of which Western anarchism is one derivation or subset. The Liberty Tree is a great banyan, whose branches cross and weave, touching earth in many places to form a horizontal, interconnected grove of new trunks.

Some of the touchdown points are in the mutually informing three sections that organize this book. The first section further explores some of these theoretical issues at the nexus of anarchism and anticolonialism. The second is a series of historical chapters focusing on intersections between the Western anarchist tradition and the tapestry of Indian anticolonialism. Such crisscrossings occurred during the peak of propaganda of the deed, a popular tactic for anarchists, nihilists, and radical nationalists alike; at the international high point of syndicalism, linking issues of immigrant labor to an analysis of colonial relationships; and in the presence of critical voices within the development of organized world Communism until defined out by schism or purge. My hope is that the specifics of this history may be one point of access to more generally applicable questions.

The sketches I offer of an alternate history of anti-colonialism aren't complete and certainly don't solve all problems. This narrative is still dominated by the over-whelming presence of male, upper-caste voices, whereas any truly antiauthoritarian, antihierarchical history of India—whether writing or enacting it—has to confront the malignant realities of caste and patriarchy. Yet this is not a history of caste or patriarchy, or the movements to dismantle the structures of oppression based on them. So for the purposes of this project, it seemed better to offer what is actually there rather than to simply condemn or discard the record on account of what isn't there—and then continue the efforts it chronicles to broaden and deepen liberation, *in practice*. (It is crucial to remember that no would-be emancipatory movement, regardless of its primary focus, can afford *not* to take ubiquitous caste inequities into consideration in its own goals and process, in much the same way that North American movements have to maintain their awareness of race.)

The third section's intervention is an attempt to con-tribute to the conversation on how we go about prac-tices of solidarity. This section also changed considerably during the writing process. As I said, one motivation for this book was the quest for counterparts, for affinity. This means asking, even if the form of anarchism I practice and speak doesn't necessarily translate. Who is addressing the issues that anarchists address, identifying the structures of power that anarchists identify, utilizing methods and processes that anarchists recognize? How does one behave toward them? How does one participate in global anticolonial struggles? In this sense, the third section is a series of proposals, and an invitation to others to elaborate on them.

Finally, I need to offer a note on geographic limits. I originally meant to define this project as South Asian rather than merely Indian. But as most of the material I was working with pertained to India, it seemed better to call it what it was than to subsume the whole region within an unacknowledged Indian hegemony—which often happens, a primary example of postcolonial neocolonialism. It would be ideal to expand my exploration to a truly South Asian scope, but that effort will take a lot longer. In the meantime, I focus here on India. When I'm speaking of India during the colonial period, however, this also includes areas that later became part of Pakistan and Bangladesh. Nevertheless, I continue to use the term India when referring to the independence struggle before the partition, as both efficient and period appropriate.

Acknowledgments

Special thanks to Joshua Stephens and Jude Ortiz for astute comments on early drafts; Cindy Milstein, Josh MacPhee, and Favianna Rodriguez for the gift of your skills; Jai Sen, Subah Dayal, Suzanne Schultz, Tyler Williams, Lex Bhagat, and the members of the organizing collectives of South Asia Solidarity Initiative, Adalah-NY, and New York City's Anarchist People of Color (APOC), for inspiring me and catalyzing my thinking in some ways you intended, and many other ways that you probably didn't expect—for which I take full responsibility. Finally I owe a debt to Raymond Williams, for eternal guidance on the importance of thinking through words and meanings.

DECOLONIZATION

The Highest Form of Anarchism

Given that colonization is one of the most concentrated forms of power in history, incorporating extreme modes of domination, dispossession, and racial hierarchy, the categorical imperative of resisting it or acting in solidarity with those doing so should require no justification to any anarchist. Yet anarchists in the global North often feel conflicted by the sense that opposing colonialism requires supporting national liberation struggles. This in turn implies compromising their own principles to allow for a provisional alignment with nationalism, with all its distasteful corollaries of statism, chauvinism, and patriarchy. This is precisely why an anarchist approach to anticolonialism is needed: to sketch out a more comprehensive emancipatory alternative to the limited nationalist version of liberation.

It begins, perhaps, with distinguishing between the negative (much simpler) and positive aspects of liberation.

Resistance is by definition a negative project, aimed at the removal of that which obstructs equity and emancipation. Such a goal may be held in common—even if for different reasons—among many who share nothing else. The positive counterpart is the prefigurative project of creating the conditions that generate equity and emancipation. Many anarchists emphasize this as a distinguishing feature of their praxis; here limitless variation is possible among divergent visions of an idealized future. Of course we insist that even in the midst of struggle, the visions can't be postponed, since the route we choose determines where we end up. But since resistance is the common denominator, clarifying the nature of the enemy is a logical place to start. In redefining what we're for, it always helps to understand what we're against.

Anticolonialism ≠ Nationalism

The words colonialism and imperialism are often used interchangeably, although there are some nuances. Imperialism is the projection of power by a political entity beyond its territorial jurisdiction, whether through economic or military means, hard power or soft, or some combination thereof. It may take the form of direct occupation along with some degree of administrative control, though strategically located bases or concessions are cheaper, easier, and demand less responsibility for the residents. Colonization, which originally denoted settlement within metastasizing enclaves, has more recently come to imply hegemony through the export of culture.

In the national liberation context, using the terminology of imperialism as opposed to colonialism suggested an analysis of global capitalism, which was thus more radical than simply opposing foreign rule or presence per se. In the corresponding metropolitan context, anti-imperialism was a term used on the Left to add an anticolonial component to a domestic anticapitalism focused solely on localized (and ethnically bounded) class struggle.

The goal of modern imperial power projection is the accumulation of capital, considered necessary for the strengthening of the colonizing state relative to other states. Capitalism in the north, particularly in its industrial form, required "underdeveloped" areas in order to continue expanding and stave off periodic crises in its wealth-generating system, constantly renewing the founding act of primitive accumulation along new frontiers of dispossession. By seizing resource-rich areas, enlisting the resident populations as cheap labor and a captive market, a "great power" could externalize its costs on to its colonies while enabling a massive extraction of surplus. In this way, colonialism embodied the symbiosis of global capital with the interstate system, underpinned by the crucial legitimizing ideologies of cultural and racial supremacy. Colonialism was in fact instrumental in generating the logics and structures of capitalism, nationalism, and racism during their formative periods.

Nationalism developed in tandem with the period of high imperialism in the second half of the nineteenth century, leading to what's often termed the first round of globalization at the turn of the twentieth. The logic was that a great nation needed a strong state, and a strong state needed a colonial empire in order to secure an advantageous balance of financial and military power against its rivals. Furthermore, in the escalating paranoia of realpolitik, maintaining autonomy became equivalent to achieving supremacy. World War I was the inevitable result of imperial competition running up against its material limits, combined with the increasingly vehement and organized objections of these empires' subject peoples.

A restive or insurgent colony was even better than a pacified one as a laboratory for states to develop their military, bureaucratic, disciplinary, policing, and surveillance capabilities. Here administrators tested new techniques for future application to domestic security in the metropole. In the later stages, coercion came to the fore as sporadic revolt swelled into irrepressible resistance, but earlier—initial conquests aside—colonizers attempted to consolidate their control (and claim moral legitimacy) by training the racialized "primitive" through the ideological apparatus of both liberal and religious civilizing missions. The "white man's burden" was the onus of enlightening the ungrateful savage, the heathen, the eugenically challenged—while doomed never to be appreciated for this selfless effort. Hence, some of the most pernicious and persistent aspects of colonization involved not just military occupation, political domination, and economic superexploitation but also the systematic assault on cultural integrity, languages, lifeways, and ethnic identities. But are these always defined as *national* identities?

So far I've been referring to the nationalism of the colonizers, not the colonized. Is the widespread instinct that one is good and the other bad as simple as the difference between overlords and underdogs? While nationalism lies at the root of many evils, its emotional force and historical significance for freedom fighters cannot be ignored, and so the notion of national liberation struggle requires some attention.

Indian Marxist literary theorist Aijaz Ahmad took Perry Anderson to task in an essay for stating that "all third world literature is nationalist literature."[1] The same objection could be made regarding the historiography, not just the literature, of the global South. Periodized in terms of precolonial, colonial, and postcolonial, a nationalist narrative moves from primordial purity to unjust enslavement to destined redemption. A cycle of restoration and rebirth, combined with a linear progression toward teleological fulfillment, results in a triumphal spiral toward statehood: the destination for the nation's journey, sign of its legitimacy, and guarantor of its autonomy and well-being.

The fundamental assumption of nationalism is that in order for a people to be recognized as holders of collective rights and freedoms, it must be constituted as a nation duly manifested in a state: an exclusive institution defined by its monopoly on sanctioned force and revenue extraction. A state is, in the starkest terms, a mechanism designed to accumulate wealth in order to make war, to make war in order to protect its wealth, and to make laws to facilitate its functioning, meaning to protect its own stability. This includes the maintenance of a reasonable degree of contentment among its members; the liberal or social democratic state adds the requirement of legitimation either by formal mechanisms of consent for its members or its claim to serve the members' common welfare. Therefore, the only

anticolonial militance retroactively recognized as a legitimate freedom struggle (violence by an anticipated future
state) rather than a crime (nonsanctioned violence within a
state) or terrorism (as extrastate violence) must be nationalist. The nationalist fairy tale culminates in the marriage of
(spiritual) nation and (physical) state, where the people live
happily ever after.

By this circular logic, without a state a group is merely
a marginalized minority, hoping at best to exist on suffer-
ance as outsiders within someone else's jurisdiction where
safety and success cannot be guaranteed. This logic became
particularly important in South Asia, where the movement
for a separate Pakistani state emerging from the Indian
national liberation movement depended on the argument that the Muslims of the subcontinent constituted an
ethnically distinct nation defined against the numerically
dominant Hindus, correspondingly framed as the quintessence of a more monocultural Indian state—never mind
the immense variety of regional and linguistic identities
that crosscut either religious identity, or their centuries-old
coexistence and cultural cross-fertilization.

The same fractal pattern has been repeated many times
since independence from British rule, by separatist movements objecting to the domestic practices of postcolonial
national states, exercising forms of "internal colonialism"
on border areas and hinterlands (for whom internality was
exactly the question) and deploying the same forms of governmentality. In seeking to replicate the techniques of colonial rule by institutionalizing states rather than abolishing
them, the nationalist goal diverged from that of substantive

decolonization. If the colonial regime's structures of oppression were not simply to be reopened for business under new local management, yielding a new generation of authoritarian dictatorships and cultural chauvinists, a different logic of anticolonial struggle was imperative.

But should we object to a group's self-identifying as a nation per se?

Where ethnicity is brutalized and culture decimated, it is callous to discount the value of ethnic pride, asserting the right to exist as such—not forgetting that cultural expression must include the right to redefine the practices of one's own culture over time, in dialogue with multiple internal and external influences, rather than sanctifying a fixed tradition. In the colonial context, the defense of ethnic identity and cultural divergence from the dominant is a key component of resistance, with the caveat that it's equally crucial to pay attention to who's dictating the "correct" expression of culture and ethnicity. No culture is as homogeneous or static as the invented traditions of nationalism. Precolonial reality was dynamic, multifarious, and also horrible for some people. The decolonization of culture shouldn't mean rewinding to a "pure" original condition but instead restoring the artificially stunted capacity freely to grow and evolve without forcible outside interference to constrict the space of potential.

In any case it's possible to concede a strategic identity politics, evoked by the context of resistance, where the assertion of collective existence and demand for recognition functions as a stand against genocide, apartheid, systemic discrimination, or forced assimilation to a dominant norm.

Of course, defining any group as a nation is not without its own risks as the political stakes of identification rise, even if a community is culturally, linguistically, and genealogically distinct, with shared historical experience and aspirations. But here too it's the specter of stateness—the pressure to establish your own, or to resist the aggression of someone else's—that calls forth the enforcement of internal conformity, elimination of elements who fail or refuse to conform, and relentless policing of boundaries, including those of hereditary membership, for which task the control of female bodies, sexuality, and reproduction is essential.

What about the geographic boundaries? Aside from the unambiguous wrong of dispossession, indigenous land claims constitute an argument for a way of relating to place and biosphere that counteracts the ecologically destructive logic of late capitalist consumer society. Statehood aside, calls for sovereignty in this sense can amount to a way of securing spaces in which other logics can prevail and other modes of existence can be protected. Even if we hypothetically establish a connection between territory and ethnic identity, establishing a qualitative relationship of people to places, and places to identities, does not by definition require enforcing the separation of homogeneous categories of people assigned to fixed, exclusive plots of land.

Could collective demands for self-determination then be distinguished from the demand for a state? Nation-statehood was only one possible form that shared memories, visions, and social/place relations could take. In practice, "nation" has also been used as a blazon of symbolic solidarity, a committed choice of ethical affiliation. That it's such a freighted word attests to the overriding force of nationalism, conceptually locking nation to state. The devil's in the hyphen.

Is it possible then to conceptualize the liberation of nation from state, along with the liberation of people from occupation and exploitation? This is what classical anarchist thinkers such as Mikhail Bakunin and Gustav Landauer attempted to do during the late nineteenth and early twentieth century, respectively. It's also something contemporary solidarity activists may need to think about.

Bakunin saw Pan-Slavism as a vehicle of liberation against dynastic autocracy, imbuing a transnational identity with certain values that could resist tyranny and subjugation. Poland was then the democratic-republican battleground, and Russia's village terrain the spiritual heartland. In the same way, radical democrats and antiauthoritarians were Francophiles in the 1790s and 1871, and Hispanophiles in the 1930s. In all these cases devotees of a principle embraced the people who were fighting for that principle, acknowledging their location on the shifting front line of an ongoing global struggle, while also imputing to them inherent ethnocultural traits that made them fit bearers of the struggle. But this would be to miss the moon for the finger pointing at the moon: a people could betray an ideal as well as defend it, and others, when their turn came, would then become the defenders.

For Bakunin, while rejecting the state, nationality remained an essential trait, both a "natural and social fact," given that "every people and the smallest folk-unit has its own character, its own specific mode of existence, its own way of speaking, feeling, thinking, and acting; and it is this idiosyncrasy that constitutes the essence of nationality."[2] In contrast, Rudolf Rocker argued that it was positional and contingent: "nation is not the cause, but the result of the state. It is the state that creates the nation, not the nation the state." Moreover, he warned, in any talk of nationalism,

> we must not forget that we are always dealing with the organised selfishness of privileged minorities which hide behind the skirts of the nation, hide behind the credulity of the masses. We speak of national interests, national capital, national spheres of interest, national honour, and national spirit; but we forget that behind all this there are hidden merely the selfish interests of power-loving politicians and money-loving business men for whom the nation is a convenient cover to hide their personal greed and their schemes for political power from the eyes of the world.

What he described was the state hijacking the credulous masses through the method of nationalism.[3]

Later Landauer tried to differentiate the folk or people, viewed in an almost spiritual sense, from the institutional mechanisms of the state.[4] The dangers here (as Rocker surely guessed) are obvious: it's a slippery slope from the praise of a *völkisch* spirit to a mysticism of blood and soil, to chauvinism and fascism—especially when the state to be distinguished from the organic soul of the people was identified with modern bureaucracy and a liberal intelligentsia—likewise anathema for today's populist right wing. But to transmute into fascism, a folk idea such as Landauer portrayed would have to augment its integral sense of connection to place and community with racial exceptionalism, supremacism, and xenophobia, and moreover to lure its nation back around to the cult of the state, to be embodied in its virile leader, its military strength, and the order and discipline through which its people were taught to find honor in serving it—all of which Landauer detested.

In the 1930s, anticolonial activists drew explicit parallels between the fascism on the rise within Europe and the imperialism that had long been exercised outside Europe's borders. Both used the same authoritarian methods of supremacy, racializing a population in order to classify it as outside and below the paragon of the human. Elaborate hierarchies of being were necessary to justify systematically excluding groups from full status as rational agents, thereby protecting the principles of liberalism or Christianity from being forced into revealing their apparent contradiction with the imperial enterprise. Racialist logic provided the final, crucial ingredient in the toxic assemblage of capitalism plus state; without racism, the imperial project would have been insupportable according to the logic of the empires' own domestic populations. But the dehumanization could remain far away, unobjectionable until carried out on internal populations.

If colonization—to be dehumanized and forcibly incorporated into a global cycle of accumulation, by subjection to a parasitic regime of surplus extraction under the control of a hypertrophied state mechanism unmistakably external to society—is a neat paradigm of everything anarchists abhor, does that mean that the most fully developed form of anticolonialism should be something that resembles anarchism?

Anarchism ≈ Decolonization

Indian anticolonial radicals overseas after the turn of the twentieth century sought out active collaborations in cosmopolitan cities with anarchist networks whose tactics and principles they saw as applicable to the needs of their cause.

In fact until the mid-1930s, the traits that differentiated anarchism from other sectors of the Left were also those that gave it affinities with contemporary anticolonial struggles—for example, the perception of the government itself as an evil and the state as clearly extraneous to society, so that the primary sites of resistance were the defining mechanisms of state function, including both disciplinary and ideological apparatuses. In British India, military installations, infrastructure, legal and educational systems: all were targeted for raids, sabotage, boycotts, or noncooperation. For some, this externality implied that the problem could be solved through decapitation, sidestepping the need for deep systemic change, and stoking a taste for propaganda of the deed.

Furthermore, classical anarchism was often associated with primary resistance to the onset of industrialization, as opposed to the Marxian and syndicalist assumption that the transition had already occurred, and that revolution would be organized from within industrial society. For many anarchists and anticolonialists (and later for India's Maoists), agrarian peasants rather than industrial proletarians represented the leading edge of struggle. Therefore it was more than just a matter of co-opting an already-existing mode of production, changing its relations while retaining its means and instruments; it meant challenging the establishment of capitalism and modern governmentality, sometimes even opposing the structures of thought on which they were based. Either way, the result was that the ground of struggle, conditioning the modality of resistance, was primarily non- or preindustrial. Given the enforced role of nonindustrial dependency within the classical colonial relationship, the structural comparison to the situation faced by Britain's South Asian subjects at that time was clear.

Finally, cultural practices, language, education, and everyday life in the colonial context constituted a major dimension of oppression, and therefore a major field on which resistance played out. Here there was no question of base and superstructure. Colonization functioned on multiple levels, through several interlocking modalities of hard and soft power, from the structural to the psychological. Economically it was accumulation by dispossession; politically it was authoritarian state control; militarily it was occupation and counterinsurgency; ideologically it was cultural hegemony leaving its stamp through linguistic retraining and epistemic violence. Striving for total decolonization would mean working on all these levels in addition to (but not instead of) tackling capitalism and the state, without reducing the struggle to either the material or ideological/discursive plane.

Thus some of the differences between the Left antisystemic movements of a colonized agrarian region and those of a heavily industrialized one were analogous to those between classical anarchism and early Marxism—for example, critiques of the latter's (real or perceived) overemphases on developmentalist teleology, instrumental reason, class reductivism, and analysis of political economy without a comparable analysis of power. This resonance arose because anarchist and anticolonialist traditions were responding to analogous conditions: a collision with the leading edge of capitalism and the state at a crucial transition point into their modern forms.

Modernity = Coloniality?

Historians identify several processes definitive of the modern condition:

- The expansion of the rationalized state, functioning through mechanisms of surveillance, policing, discipline; governmentality exercised through bureaucratic enumeration and management of populations, resources, and so on; and the recognition of such a state as one unit among a mutually reinforcing system of units
- The incorporation of more and more goods, commons, natural resources, land, water, labor, time, space, minerals, crops, genetic information, cultural materials, raw materials, manufactured/processed products into the logic of a global capitalist economy, subject to quantification as alienable and

exchangeable commodities on the world market rather than local use values

- An exponential increase in technology, industrialization, scientificity—especially with regard to communication and transport—and the fossil-fuel-based energy regime

The processes entailed in colonization are recognizable as a particularly traumatic, violent acceleration of the frontier of modernization, here experienced as an assaultive external force that shredded the existing sociocultural fabric rather than incrementally modifying it. This is not to paint the inhabitants of such a region as identical, passive victims; many participated in these projects, and some significantly benefited. This is one reason why resistance always entails internal conflict as well as a defensive front; many an anticolonial effort has segued into civil war.

Moreover, without colonial incursion, modernization may well have emerged on its own; some argue that colonization itself is what prevented this from happening. But Asian, African, and Latin American modernities unaffected by European intervention are a counterfactual speculation in our historical reality. The fact is that every dimension of modernity as we know it was built on colonial history. Modern European and North American material prosperity along with cultural consumption and production at every level owed an immense debt to its colonial relationships with Asia, Africa, and elsewhere, from the plantation slave labor driving the Industrial Revolution, to the silver and gold mines financing military might, whereas modernization in India and elsewhere was experienced through the medium of colonization. The Latin American subalternists, inspired by but diverging from the South Asian Subaltern Studies Collective, actually theorize coloniality as the other face of modernity.[5]

Despite their close interrelation, however, colonization and modernization are not interchangeable terms. What distinguished the process of colonization from any other instance of coercive modernization, legitimating and masking it, was the dimension of racism in all of its iterations (including Orientalism), whether as a religious and cultural myth, or a scientific and biological one. This is also what makes antiracism such an important component of mobilizations in solidarity with anticolonial movements.

The key to manifesting an anarchist anticolonialism (a point shared with third world feminism as well as what Chela Sandoval calls the methodology of the oppressed, among other analogous terms) lies in the intersectionality of those dimensions.[6] This is exactly where twentieth-century antisystemic movements in decolonizing regions—the "tricontinental" of Asia, Africa, and Latin America—had critiques to offer their counterparts in the Western, northern, and/or colonizing world: isolating class struggle in practice and rhetoric did not sufficiently address the fundamental global structures of imperialism, nor the realities of racism and colonization.

Meanwhile, systemic analysis allowed for the relating of Left internationalism to national liberation struggles and other transnational anticolonialisms. The power grid of race both reinforces and complicates that of capitalism, especially when we add the dimension of spatiality at the global scale—and there we have imperial geopolitics. But as is still true today, the counterpart of a globalization of power systems is a globalization of antisystemic resistance.

The question of orientation to modernity underlies both the anarchist and anticolonial discourses. This question fuels the perennial debate on the nature of anarchism, the genealogy of its intellectual tradition, and its relationship to other radicalisms on both the Left and Right. It also refracts the spectrum of intellectual and political differences within Indian anticolonialism.

If the processes of colonization correlate to those of modernization, then does anticolonialism have to be antimodern? No, and this largely has to do with sloppy language use. Modernity, modernization, and modernism are all words too often used in confusing, contradictory ways. There are the material processes associated with modernization, a project never fully realized and never proceeding evenly without frictions and obstructions; there are also shifts in perception and consciousness that make up our experience of these new conditions—of which multiple effects and affects, interpretations and evaluations, are possible—all of which are modern, but not all modernist. Modernism reveals a third level, which is a conscious aesthetic, philosophical, political, epistemological stance manifested in art, literature, architecture, and so on. But the description of modernity as an existential condition consists of the full package of contradictions and contradictory vectors on all these levels, a complex agglomeration of causes, effects, and responses to them.

Under the harsh stamp of racialization it became difficult (on both the material and epistemological levels) for
Indians to develop without conflict an alternate, indigenous modernity out of the materials already available,
or freely exchanged through their transnational contacts
with other activists and intellectuals. Yet even within the
given circumstances, responses to the projects and conditions of modernity ranged from complete rejection to
complete embrace, with all variants of critical and selective
adaptation in between. For example, liberal reformers
such as Rammohan Roy, Dwarkanath Tagore, or Sir Syed
Ahmad Khan objected to their exclusion from the liberal
Enlightenment paradigm of republican democracy and
humanist rationalism, but not to that paradigm itself.[7]
They saw it as a universal that was theirs by right, no less
than anyone else's (not Westernness masquerading as universalism but rather universalism only masquerading as
Westernness).[8] Others rejected the whole paradigm as anti-
thetical to their particular ethnocultural natures, embracing
with pride an Orientalist binary logic that had been jointly
formalized by Western scholars and Asian clerical elites.

Both the universal and binary were false, of course. The
existential condition of colonialism facilitated a flattening
out or repression of the range of internal variation on both
sides. A state of war tends toward extreme polarization; colonialism is a permanent state of war, whether in the low-inten-
sity register of prolonged occupation, or the hotter moments
of conquest, reconquest, pacification, and counterinsurgency.
Accordingly, coloniality tends to generate Manichaean
binaries, as Frantz Fanon and Albert Memmi observed.

Non-Western, Oriental, or so-called primitive cultures, including the Celtic, were portrayed as the polar opposite of the modern, occupying the space of the spiritual, the not-yet-disenchanted, the unilluminated—whether that was seen as a sign of danger and backwardness (as for the Utilitarian reformers, who tried to make India over with railroads and Shakespeare in the 1820s–30s) or salvation for the world (as for the theosophists, who took dictation from Buddhist "hidden masters" and added their force to the Indian nationalist movement in the 1900s–1910s). Whether the Enlightenment logic was evaluated as good or bad, or a little of each, depended on how you felt about mechanization, rationalization, and so forth, or whether you lived in England, Ireland, India, or the Ottoman Empire.

It bears mentioning that the words progressive and reactionary—in their most literal sense—entail relative direction, not necessarily political content or ideological value. One means to go forward in the direction of change, and the other means to generate friction, stoppage, or reversal. But what is the particular change we're talking about, and what was the status quo? It seems more pertinent to ask what a specific vision of utopia looks like—what its content is—than which direction we need to move in to reach it from where we are now—whether we envision it as having existed in a prelapsarian past or as the destination of future redemption. The legacy of utopian thought contains both kinds of narrative.

Neither an across-the-board improvement nor unmitigated ruin, modernization was rather a radically destabilizing rearrangement in the status quo, which benefited some and harmed others. A critique of modernism (or colonialism) or any of the phenomena of modernity (or coloniality) is not necessarily a bid to "go back" but instead an attempt to seek a different way forward that doesn't destroy beneficial aspects of an existing fabric, while improving on those aspects that were detrimental to the expansion of freedom and equality. Far from being reactionary, as an orthodox Marxist teleology would deem it, anticolonial critique of modernity was not necessarily an attempt to halt progress—as if the only options were to go forward or backward along a narrow track—but rather to choose a different direction—oblique, perpendicular, or spreading in a skewed delta of potential alternatives. In other universes, with other histories, maybe they are what modernity looks like. Resistance thus contains a range of adaptive, subversive, redirectional, or dialectically synthetic responses not just to halt or reverse modernity but also to generate alternate modernities or countermodernities.

Anarchism = Modernity?

And what about anarchism? In its attempt to solve the problems of oppression and exploitation, is it inherently modernist or antimodernist? Rationalist or Romanticist? This debate has implicitly structured much of the past and current terrain of Western anarchism. It also underlies a pervasive confusion among those who, in the effort to define anarchism historically, give up and dismiss it as incoherent and contradictory.

The crux is this: if by asking "Is anarchism modern or antimodern?" we mean "Is anarchism really part of the rationalist or Romanticist tradition? Is it a child of the Enlightenment or its counterrevolution? Does it do the work of Dionysus or Apollo?" then we fail to grasp that the cultural profile of modernity itself is not wholly identifiable with either side. Rather, its very fabric is woven from the dialogic counterpoint of both, as a play of energies that exists within the field of material conditions symptomatic of modernization. Generated in response to these conditions, anarchism is part of modernity, and like the rest of modernity, partakes in the same interplay of energies.

What's unique about the anarchist tradition among Western political discourses is its continuous struggle for a synthesis between the two polarities, rejecting neither. Taken as a whole, it's a cumulative attempt to find a balance by making contextually appropriate adjustments along the spectrum. Nowhere is it a reduction to one or the other, and indeed a quest for balance implies a critique of such a reduction at either end. True, even within the broadly drawn boundaries of anarchism, there are those who have staked out positions near to one or the other. But to argue over which pole truly represents the tradition is to hear only half the conversation. We might ask, for example, whether in a specific context the source of oppression is an excess of either instrumental reason or superstition, whereas the existence of rationality itself is neither disease nor cure. I like to use a lemonade metaphor: depending on the circumstances and what's already been mixed, you might need to increase or decrease your ratio of lemon juice to sugar to reach the perfect balance. Without both, your lemonade is going to suck.

Is it meaningless—or unanarchistic—to try to identify boundaries? I don't think so; on the contrary, refusing to do so makes the conversation meaningless. Maybe a more relevant way of putting this is that the anarchist tradition is a discursive field in which the boundaries are defined by a thematic, not a problematic, as Partha Chatterjee puts it in a famous essay on the conceptual difficulties of an Indian nationalist historiography. According to this formulation, it is necessary to distinguish two parts of a social ideology: "the thematic . . . refers to an epistemological as well as ethical system which provides a framework of elements and rules for establishing relationships between elements; the problematic, on the other hand, consists of concrete statements about possibilities justified by reference to the thematic." The problematic includes an ideology's "identification of historical possibilities and the practical or programmatic forms of its realization," and the thematic "its justificatory structures, i.e., the nature of the evidence it presents in support of those claims, the rules of inference it relies on to logically relate a statement of the evidence to a structure of arguments, the set of epistemological principles it uses to demonstrate the existence of its claims as historical possibilities, and finally, the set of ethical principles it appeals to in order to assert that those claims are morally justified."[9]

Anarchism is a thematic larger than any of its myriad manifestations, all of which can be considered anarchism if they refer to that thematic—if they are part of the anarchist conversation. This is also analogous to contrasting *langue* as "a language system shared by a given community of speakers"—that is, anarchists—with *parole*, "a concrete speech act of individual speakers"—that is, what's said or done by any type of anarchist.[10] The totality of the conversation generated by a particular set of ethical questions and concerns can't be identified solely with any one utterance, or any one answer to its defining questions.

The anarchist tradition is a continuously unfolding discourse—meaning not just the writings and rhetoric of anarchism but also its body of practices and history of performative acts. And the content of this discourse—the thematic that defines its boundaries—is the quest for collective liberation in its most meaningful sense, by maximizing the conditions for autonomy and egalitarian social relationships, sustainable production and reproduction. The tradition consists at the same time in the argument over what anarchism is, and the argument over the proper balance between a whole constellation of key pairs: freedom and equality, liberty and justice, the individual and the collective, the head and the heart, the verbal and the sensual, power relations and economic relations. India's anticolonial history represented a similar conversation. Here too the totality of the discourse is characterized by a shared thematic of defining and attaining liberation, through a dialogic counterpoint of the modernist/rationalist lineage (exemplified in the twentieth century by Jawaharlal Nehru, B. R. Ambedkar, and the People's Science Movement) and its variously positioned critics.

It is a crucial and delicate issue, however, to recognize that some of these critical positions have included fascism and fundamentalism. Furthermore, wherever the terminology of anarchism appears in the Indian context, right-wing elements frequently crop up as a menacing shadow not far away. This does not mean that there is any inherent affinity between anarchism and the reactionary Right, contrary to the conflation sometimes made by sectors of the mainline Indian Left. What it does indicate is that certain situations create common openings for both.

The same could be said in general of the worldwide radical ferment in the fin de siècle moment before World War I—a moment of equal significance for the rise of anarchism and the emergence of radical anticolonialism—when multiple potentialities were held in combustible suspension. Georges Sorel offers some clues here, in his writings about revolutionary syndicalism during the same period, when anticolonialists were meeting anarchists in Paris and London. Sorel was a French civil servant born in 1842, an engineer by training and a disciple of philosopher Henri-Louis Bergson. He produced the bulk of his difficult-to-categorize work on social theory in the last decade of the nineteenth and first of the twentieth centuries, after his professional retirement. As an advocate of labor syndicalism, he abhorred bureaucracy and parliamentary armchair socialism, favored total revolution over piecemeal reform, and touted worker militance and direct action to seize control of production. He also despised the state, particularly in its bourgeois capitalist incarnation. Yet the premises of his analysis were quite different from those of the socialist branch of the Enlightenment project. Antirationalist and antiliberal, his top imperative was seeking a workable, living revolutionary myth capable of revitalizing and reinspiring an alienated, moribund modern society.

As the bearer of libidinal energy or Bergsonian élan vital, the myth, in Sorel's view, must recharge the potency of the heroic revolutionary class through militant struggle. Sorel had no doubt that the needed revitalization must come about through violence, which he differentiated from force, meaning the physical dominance of the state that was inherent in its foundation and the institutions of its preservation. Either class struggle or external threat would do the trick, though the latter would more sharply stimulate the national myth and the former the social, in which case the mythic icon of the general strike would serve to motivate the working class, while icons of the counterrevolution for which the workers' opening move was the stimulus would rouse the bourgeoisie from its decadent stupor. Regardless of who won, the struggle would have done its work. This is why the Sorelian logic of prewar revolutionary syndicalism bore within it the seeds of both the Right and Left radical movements of the 1920s. It didn't really matter what that myth might be; it only mattered that it did the job.

But of course, it does matter quite a lot to the outcome. From this perspective the significance of these moments of dual potentiality is not that anarchism converges with the Right but precisely that it does *not*. At a crossroads, choices matter most; here is where ethical orientation and content make the difference. What determined whether the myth of right-wing populist rhetoric or libertarian socialism would prevail? The key distinction is in the prefigurative content of the emancipatory vision, not in the simple fact of opposition to the state. It's not enough to call for small government or the elimination of a foreign regime without also articulating a critique of capitalism, race, and power. This is equally true of the difference between national supremacism and radical (and potentially nonstatist) anticolonialism.

ECHOES AND INTERSECTIONS

The Propagandists of the Deed

By the first decade of the twentieth century, Indian revolutionists had established a worldwide presence through labor diasporas and educational circuits, often converging on the same cosmopolitan cities as their radical counterparts from East and Southeast Asia, Egypt, Turkey, and Ireland. Their tasks overseas were twofold: to organize insurrectionary activities, and to spread information and propaganda.

The Swadeshi (autonomy; literally "one's own country") movement was a flash point of unrest sparked in 1905 by the administrative partition of Bengal. It took heart from the Japanese victory over Russia in the same year, setting the rapturous precedent of an Asian nation defeating a European power. From the moment of the movement's emergence, police intelligence reports and newspaper accounts anointed its militant wing as anarchists. Accurate or not, the label dogged them at home and abroad.

In a 1916 newspaper article Ram Chandra, one of the leaders of the Ghadar Party founded by Indian anticolonial militants in the United States, objected to a remark in the London *Times* that "just as Ireland still has her Sinn Fein extremists, so has India still her anarchists and her fanatical bombthrowers." Chandra retorted, "The truth in this statement is that India has her Sinn Feiners. The falsehood lies in the implication that the Hindu revolutionists are a forlorn hope of intransigents. They are not 'anarchists'; they are nationalists; and hence the whole nation is and is growing to be, with them."[1]

Such disclaimers were meant to defend the revolutionaries' legitimacy. To be called an anarchist in the rhetoric of the day meant being seen as a purveyor of meaningless violence; to be dubbed a nationalist meant being seen to serve a just cause—democratic self-determination in the face of imperial tyranny and the looting of one's country. Precisely because of their claim to the justice of their cause, they objected far more to the label of anarchist than terrorist, a term then used matter-of-factly without any particular moral condemnation to describe a tactic of extralegal, conspiratorial deployment of propaganda of the deed.

The most obvious factor in the pinning of the anarchist tag on the Swadeshi militants was their willingness to express their hatred of the British colonial government through violent means. The Indian radicals' penchant for dramatic, symbolic bombings and assassinations linked them in the public eye to an international spate of attacks on establishment figures, applying to them the caricature of the bearded desperado cradling a sphere with a guttering fuse under his coat.

Ideological anarchism, of course, is not to be equated with violence and irrationality. But the traits that made the link plausible went deeper than that. Besides the philosophical and tactical orientation toward propaganda of the deed (not to mention a quasi-mystical fascination with the bomb), they shared with certain contemporary strands of the Western anarchist tradition a voluntarist ethic of individual action, militant romanticism, disregard for conventional standards of law and propriety in the face of what they saw as greater truths, a frictional relationship with bourgeois materialist society, and a marked antigovernment stance. Although in this context the objection was to the British colonial government specifically, by the simple dropping of an article many of their statements were virtually indistinguishable from anarchist ones regarding government in general.

In the end the question we need to ask, in examining the praxis of the Swadeshi militants as they became links in a wider nexus stretching from Calcutta to London and Paris, is not "Were the Swadeshi extremists anarchists?" or even "What kind of anarchists were they?" An even better question is, "Where do they fit into the revolutionary family tree of which anarchism and its various cousins are also scions?"

Bengal

Since the 1870s there had been a proliferation of social and religious reform societies (*samitis*), athletic or "physical culture" clubs (*akharas*), and cultural nationalist

groups, including both open and secret "student organizations inspired by the Carbonari and [Giuseppe] Mazzini's
Young Italy," which is to say by the form of mid-nineteenth-
century romantic republicanism that played such a prominent role in the development of international revolution.
The newly politicized Anusilan Samiti emerged around
1902 or 1903 from a consolidation of several akharas, with
Aurobindo Ghose as one of the key movers. Born and
educated in England, Ghose idolized figures like Mazzini
and Charles Stewart Parnell, the hero of Irish home
rule. Philosophically, he morphed over the years from
agnosticism to spiritual leadership as a Hindu mystic.

After the Bengal partition, he along with his younger
brother Barindra Kumar Ghose and a few of their friends
began energetically recruiting and training young men
in *lathi* (wooden staff) and martial arts, swimming, and
horseback and bicycle riding. Students also received lectures on political and military history including such topics
as the Sikh Khalsa, the French Revolution, and the Italian
Resorgimento. Anglo-Irish transplant Sister Nivedita (born
Margaret Noble) lectured on "patriotic feelings and a sense
of duty to the country," and donated her library, including a
well-known Mazzini biography, whose chapter on guerrilla
warfare was extensively copied and circulated.[2]

Nivedita also introduced a conscious connection with
ideological anarchism. She had followed the famous sage
Swami Vivekananda to India intending to work at the
Ramakrishna Mission, but once there threw herself into
the cause of Indian national liberation, eventually separating herself from the mission in order to pursue her political

commitments without compromise. But Vivekananda was not her only philosophical inspiration; she had also discovered Peter Kropotkin en route, becoming fiercely excited about his ideas, which she claimed "confirm[ed] me in my determination toward Anarchy." When she met Kropotkin in London in 1902 after some correspondence, she decided that he knew "more than any other man of what India needs."[3] Given her close association with Aurobindo's circle, it seems likely that Kropotkin's ideas entered the mix.

The group's militancy soon intensified in a program of targeted assassinations, bombings, sabotage, and political *dacoity* (social banditry) to obtain weapons and funds. There were raids on police stations, armories, British treasuries, tax collections, and even expropriations of wealthy Indians, some of whom were presented with certificates declaring them holders of a debt to be repaid after the revolution by the treasurers of a Free India. Besides arms and ammunition, funding went toward printing costs and legal expenses. *Bande Mataram* was founded in 1906 as an English-language daily paper targeting the educated elite, as companion to the *Yugantar*, "the paper for the masses" in colloquial Bengali.[4]

The revolutionary headquarters was an empty house and grounds on Calcutta's outskirts, known as Maniktola Garden. There in idyllic seclusion, they set up bomb-making and arms-storage facilities along with a library, on the principle of revolutionizing minds in order to achieve revolutionary goals. Bullets and bombs, they knew, were only a quick fix; deeper, lasting change would require the education of consciousness through integrated physical, political, and spiritual training.

The curriculum included economics, history, geography, and the philosophy of revolution. There was also technical training in departments such as that "referred to in Upen's notebooks as 'Ex+Mech+An,'" which historian Peter Heehs interprets as "explosives, mechanics and anarchism." Heehs reports that one fifteen-year-old recruit recalled, "'In the garden Upen Babu used to teach us Upanishads and politics and Barindra Babu [taught Bhagavad] Gita and History of Russo-Japanese war and Ullas Babu delivered lectures on explosives.' Indu Bhusan Roy spent his time 'studying Gita and preparing shells.'"[5]

What they took from this text, Krishna's prebattle advice to the warrior Arjuna, was that one should act in accordance with dharma without overly worrying about the results. If the actions themselves were righteous, then the results could not be otherwise. Karma yoga—the way of action in the world of material causality—was one of the recognized paths to liberation, as much as the ways of meditation or devotion.

Among the other incendiary texts that the Criminal Investigation Department found when it raided the Maniktola Garden library were *Ananda Math*, Bankimchandra Chatterjee's famous novel of warrior monks that later became part of the Hindu nationalist canon; Aurobindo's *Bhawani Mandir* ("temple of the goddess," or Kali, manifest as pure *shakti*, force, or power), a blueprint for a utopian community; *Sikher Balidan*, extolling Sikh martyrdom; and *Raja ke*, questioning the institution of monarchy.[6] Many of these texts expressed the pursuit of national liberation in the idiom of intense religiosity.

Others combined pragmatic how-to instructions with philosophical justifications for militant activity.

Mukti Kon Pathe ("which way lies salvation?") mainly contained excerpts from the *Yugantar* on topics such as "Battalion Drill Made Easy" and "Field Exercises." Its author noted that particularly for Bengalis, cultivating muscular development was important, referring to the British colonial taxonomy that classified them as a feeble "non-martial race." Yet even if they were not able to achieve the requisite physical training by the time action became imperative, they nevertheless might find "consolation in the thought that not much muscle is required to kill a European with a revolver or a rifle, or to kill many Europeans with a Maxim gun. It does not take much strength to pull a trigger; even a Bengali can do that."[7]

The author also systematically outlined the other items required for organizing insurrection. Under the heading "Revolution" were subtopics such as "Building Up Public Opinion," which listed newspapers, music, literature, and "secret meetings and associations." On the matter of clandestinity, he observed: "Secret societies are necessary since it is impossible to talk of freedom openly because of bayonets and guns. If one wants to talk of freedom publicly, he must necessarily do so in a roundabout way. It is precisely for this reason that a secret place is necessary where people may discuss 'What is truth?' without having recourse to hypocrisy. But it must be a place that the tyrant cannot see." As examples of models for good covert practice, the author pointed to the Russian revolutionists and the militant ascetics of *Ananda Math*.[8]

The text listed three ways to obtain arms:

1. By preparing weapons silently in some secret place. In this way, the Russian nihilists prepare the bombs. Indians will be sent to foreign countries to learn the art of making weapons. On their return to India they will manufacture cannon, guns, etc., with the help of enthusiastic youths.
2. By importing weapons of all kinds from foreign countries.
3. Through the assistance of native soldiers.

In August 1907, the *Yugantar* suggested that "much work can be done by the revolutionists very cautiously spreading the gospel of independence among the native troops," thereby at once gaining both weapons and mutineers. The textbook assured the revolutionist that soldiers too were human beings, despite their role as mercenaries to a tyrant, and would therefore surely join their arms with the revolution once the situation was fully explained to them by "the clever Bengali."[9]

The *Yugantar* often published on the justification and need for violence in resisting the systemic violence of colonial oppression. In other words, it was not the revolutionists who had introduced force into the dialogue. "The laws of the English are based on brute force. If we want to liberate ourselves from those laws, it is brute force that is necessary. . . . There is no other door of admission into life but death."[10] An article headed "Away with Fear" declared that British supremacy was an illusion, which if once challenged, must crumble away. If Indians would conquer their own fear and take initiative, victory and liberation would be easy.

> What we want now is a number of men who will take the lead in giving a push and thus encourage the masses and infuse hope in the minds of those who are almost dead with fear and dread. . . . They must be shown by deeds done before their eyes that the work is not impossible exactly to the extent that they think it to be.[11]

Hence, the *Yugantar* strengthened the perception of anarchism by its emphasis on taking a complete antigovernment stance, as opposed to collaboration or participation of any kind. *Bande Mataram* too came under frequent attack for its "seditious" content as well as plain "intention of bringing the Government into hatred and contempt."[12] This was a misreading, though, of such statements as this one:

> [Indian secretary of state] Mr. Morley has said that we [Indians] cannot work the machinery of our Government for a week if England generously walks out of our country. . . . [But] did it not strike Mr. Morley that if, instead of walking out the English were by force driven out of India, the Government will go on perhaps better than before, for the simple reason that the exercise of power and organisation necessary to drive out so organised an

> enemy will in the struggle that would ensue teach
> us to arrange our own affairs sufficiently well.[13]

This passage called for the takeover, not the abolition, of government, while suggesting that it was in the crucible of revolutionary action that people learned autonomy—a foreshadowing of Fanon.

The other "principle revolutionary textbook" was *Bartaman Rananiti* ("modern art of war"), a 1907 Bengali version of Jan S. Bloch's *Modern Weapons and Modern War*.[14] The book contained information on weapons, army organization, and guerrilla tactics, recommended as "the mode of fighting adopted by a nation which is weak, disarmed and oppressed by conquerors, but resolved to break the bondage of slavery." In such a war, the author predicted that the native troops and mountain tribes would be sure to join in; irregular warfare would forge the country's youths into heroes, leading ultimately to popular uprising on a much larger scale; and a protracted conflict could only benefit the people while wearing down the enemy.[15]

But *Bartaman Rananiti* also drew on the concept of karma yoga. An early chapter was a reprint of an October 1906 *Yugantar* article that stated, "'War is the order of creation.' After explaining that destruction is creation in another form"—a rather Bakuninesque sentiment—"the writer proceeds, 'Destruction is natural and war is, therefore, also natural.'" Gangrenous body parts, he pointed out, must be removed to save the whole. Therefore "war is inevitable when oppression cannot be stopped by any other means whatsoever, when the leprosy of slavery corrupts the blood of the body of the nation and robs it of its vitality."[16] The article went on to invoke Krishna, Rama, and Kali as exemplars of divine sanction for an avenging (and purifying) destruction—making this too a potential seed text for both anarchist- and Hindu nationalist–inflected radical rhetorics.

Significantly, in the process of a dedicated practice by which the vanguard's hearts were to be forged and tested, while rousing and inspiring the people, conventional morality became irrelevant: for "A nation yearning for freedom . . . the power of discriminating between right and wrong is gone. Everything is sacrificed at the feet of the goddess of liberty."[17]

The author of *Mukti Kon Pathe* claimed that if the revolution was being brought about for the welfare of society, then it was perfectly just to collect money from society for the purpose. Admittedly theft and dacoity are crimes because they violate the principle of the good of society. But the "political dacoit" is aiming at the social good: "so no sin but rather virtue attaches to the destruction of this small good for the sake of some higher good. Therefore if revolutionists extort money from the miserly or luxurious wealthy members of society by the application of force, their conduct is perfectly just."[18]

Beyond levying "donations" from the rich, the final stage of the funding plan called for robbing government treasuries. "This also is justified because, from the moment the kingly power tramples upon the welfare of the subjects, the king may be regarded as a robber from whom it is perfectly right to snatch away his stolen money." For the social bandit, apparently, property was theft, and redistribution a function of a moral economy—although in this case, the text somewhat mysteriously added, "to defray the expenses of establishing the future kingly power."[19] Again two tendencies coexist. Which would prevail? Or would they diverge?

Thus prepared, the Maniktola Garden gang launched a series of bombings, dacoities, and assassination attempts between 1906 and 1908.[20] Harsh punitive reaction then enforced a lull in militant activities, effectively muzzling the radical press, preventing meetings, and accelerating convictions and deportations. All of this, by making open dissent so difficult within British India, simply increased clandestine activity and injected fresh blood into the radical community overseas.

London

Oxford lecturer and sometime-theosophist Shyamaji Krishnavarma had founded the Indian Home Rule Society in London a mere six months before the partition of Bengal.[21] He stated three official objectives for the organization: to secure Indian home rule (obviously), carry on propaganda in the United Kingdom for this purpose, and spread among the people of India greater knowledge of the advantages of freedom and national unity.[22] An important element of this enterprise was the notoriously "seditious . . . penny monthly"[23] the *Indian Sociologist*, which Krishnavarma founded and edited with the aid of long-term ally Henry Mayers Hyndman, a "high-minded English gentleman" and prominent socialist. Printed in English as "an organ of freedom, and of political, social, and religious reforms," the periodical's intent was "to plead the cause of India and its unrepresented millions before the Bar of Public Opinion in Great Britain and Ireland," striving "to inculcate the great sociological truth that 'it is impossible to join injustice and brutality abroad with justice and humanity at home." It was also meant as a tool for developing the revolutionary student movement, on the presumption that the well-educated young rebels would likely hold prominent and influential positions on their return home.[24]

In Highgate, Krishnavarma also set up a headquarters dubbed India House to serve as a boardinghouse and training center for neophyte revolutionaries. With financial help from wealthy patriot Sardar Singh Revabhai Rana, a Paris-based pearl merchant, he made several attempts at funding fellowships to bring Indian students to London for a political awakening. Fellows were required to spend a minimum of two years in Europe or the United States studying a profession of their choice, living at a home or hostel on an allowance of sixteen shillings per week. On returning to India, each was to "solemnly declare" that he would never accept any "post, office of emoluments, or service under the British Government."[25] Scholarship recipients began arriving in 1906, just as Swadeshi activities were picking up in Bengal.

In contrast to the fervid Swadeshi papers, the *Indian Sociologist* had a plain affinity with the progressive libertarian thinking of the time. Quotations from Herbert Spencer crowned the masthead: "Every man is free to do that which he wills, provided he infringes not the equal freedom of any other man"; "Resistance to aggression is not simply justifiable but imperative. Non-resistance hurts both altruism and egoism."[26] Eschewing links with any political party, Krishnavarma expanded on these ideas in an introduction to the first issue: "The British people . . . can never succeed in being a nation of freemen and lovers of freedom so long as they continue to send out members of the dominating classes to exercise despotisms in Britain's name upon the various conquered races that constitute Britain's military Empire." Spencer, he said, had proven that "all despotisms, whether political or religious, whether of sex, caste, or of custom, may be generalized as limitations to individuality, which it is the nature of civilization to remove."[27] Hyndman stated in the same issue that "Indians must learn to rely upon themselves alone for their political salvation, i.e., the forcible expulsion of the British rule from India and not hope for anything from the changes of governors and governments."[28]

Every Sunday, meetings and discussions open to all Indians took place, focusing on issues of independence, and often featuring patriotic speeches, lectures, songs, and magic lantern projections of martyred resistance heroes. Scholarship winner Vinayak Damodar Savarkar read weekly excerpts from his historical work "The Indian War of Independence of 1857," and a commemoration was held on May 10, 1907, the fiftieth anniversary of the uprising.

Meanwhile, more serious activities were unfolding in the shadows. Since August 1906, arms trafficking occurred under cover of Nitisen Dwarkadas and Gyanchand Varma's Eastern Export and Import Company in Gray's Inn Place.[29] In June, a Dr. Desai who was studying at London University "gave a lecture at the India House on the making of bombs, justifying their use and explaining what ingredients were required. He reportedly said, 'When one of you is prepared to use a bomb at the risk of his life, come to me and I will give full particulars.'[30]

By then the India House community also functioned as a recruiting ground for a more exclusive inner circle dominated by Savarkar, the Abhinava Bharat. Although one of the young militants recalled that "under [Savarkar's] direction we were training ourselves as propagandists of revolutionary nationalism," the special intelligence branch assigned to them described them yet again as "the anarchist gang." The young men were also under constant surveillance from Scotland Yard. A pair of detectives followed each one, and some even grew to be on friendly terms with their escorts.[31] By spring 1908, informants were reporting that "the policy of assassinations was advocated at regular Sunday meetings." Some of the Abhinava Bharat inner core had taken up target practice at a shooting range on Tottenham Court Road. On July 1, 1909, one of the budding sharpshooters, a student called Madan Lal Dhingra, successfully targeted William Curzon-Wyllie, aide to the secretary of state for India. Dhingra was hanged, then lauded as a revolutionary martyr with the aid of a much-republished courtroom speech, in which he expressed regret not for his deed but rather for having just one life to lose for his country.[32]

Meanwhile back home, Savarkar's brother Ganesh had been prosecuted for sedition and sentenced to transportation for life. Documents found at Ganesh's home and in the hands of accomplices during the proceedings "indicate[d] that the association aimed at some sort of organisation founded upon the model of revolutionary societies in Russia," including Thomas Frost's *The Secret Societies of the European Revolution, 1776–1876*, a book "in which is described the secret organisation of the Russian Nihilists, consisting of small circles or groups affiliated into sections, each member knowing only the members of the circle to which he belonged. This may explain the existence of various small groups of young men who are found in this case to have been working for the same objects and drawing weapons from the same source without personal acquaintance with the members of other groups."[33]

Enraged at his brother's conviction, Savarkar called for the murder of English people in India as reprisal. He sent a consignment of twenty Browning pistols and ammunition back to India concealed in a false-bottom box in the luggage of Govind Amin, India House's resident chef and ammunition buyer. These pistols were then used in the assassination of a district magistrate in Maharashtra. Savarkar was quickly implicated in the killing, thought to be a dual act of revenge for Dhingra's death and Ganesh's imprisonment. Demonstrating its transnational perspective, the *Indian Sociologist* commented, "Allowing for the difference in the longitudes of Paris and Nasik the time of our writing to sympathise with the members of the family of Mr. Savarkar synchronized almost to a minute with that of the assassination avenging the sentence of transportation passed on him. There is a sort 'poetic justice' in all this which will, we doubt not, strike the imagination of our readers."[34]

Savarkar fled to Paris in 1910. Heedless of warnings not to return to London, he did so anyway and was arrested on arrival at Victoria Station under the Fugitive Offenders Act, then deported by ship to India with a stopover in Marseilles. There he attempted to escape by leaping from a porthole into the harbor and swimming to shore, only to be snatched by police waiting on the pier. (One account has it that the comrades who were supposed to meet him and spirit him into concealment had lingered at a café and arrived too late.)

To no avail, high-profile supporters among the British and French Left took up the case. London anarchist Guy Aldred formed a Savarkar Release Committee as soon as he himself got out of jail. He also featured the case in his own fiery paper *Herald of Revolt* and produced an appeal on the matter in August 1910 addressed "To the English proletariat."[35]

When the *Indian Sociologist* was proscribed and its publisher, Arthur Horsley, convicted for printing sedition, Aldred offered his own shoestring Bakunin Press to continue publication. He made it clear that while he did not agree fully with the paper's content, being an advocate neither of political violence and assassination nor "nationalism, and . . . the Statism it implied," he did believe in free speech, freedom as a general principle, and resistance to imperial rule.[36] His meager combined office and living quarters were searched, and when three hundred copies of the paper (though no trace of a press) were found, he too was convicted for sedition and sentenced to a year in prison.[37] Printing then shifted to Paris, and the paper continued to appear until 1914, despite several more enforced relocations.

Paris

After the Dhingra incident, London abruptly became too hot for Indian radicals to function freely, though a few did try to maintain an active presence. Now the primary center of Indian overseas radicalism moved to Paris. The political expatriate community there was already well established, centered around Rana and Madame Bhikaji Rustomji Cama, both of whom maintained close ties with the London community.

Besides carrying the cachet of its revolutionary history, France had the advantage of lying outside British jurisdiction. Ironically, France's own colonial outposts inside India offered them this functional free zone: French Pondicherry became a key location for moving weaponry and literature into the country, and "the great importance of both Pondicherry and Chandernagore from the point of view of the anarchists," said the officiating director of Criminal Intelligence Department, lay in their independent postal connections with European countries.[38]

Paris was also an unparalleled hub for cross-fertilization among Chinese, Japanese, Turkish, Egyptian, Lebanese, and Filipino modernist, liberal and Left, anarchist, nationalist, and internationalist movements, hosting exiles from countries throughout East Asia and the Ottoman Empire. The Indians formed particularly strong bonds with the Egyptians.

It was the large population of Russian political exiles, though, whom the Bengali revolutionists looked to as their most significant source of inspiration as well as technical and organizational mentorship. They admired the efficacy of their fellow revolutionists, whose uncompromising calls for emancipation from imperial autocracy they understood to be analogous to their own. These particular Russians were of the maximalist faction of Socialists-Revolutionaries, bearing the mantle of the late nineteenth-century People's Will Party (Narodnaya Volya). The group was associated with Bakunin's hyperviolent protégé Sergey Nechayev. It also had been linked to the assassination of Czar Alexander II in 1881—an act that the Swadeshi militants warmly approved. The most recent wave of exiles had arrived after the postrevolutionary crackdown in 1905; by 1907, the Paris police reported "some 1500 Russian 'terrorists'" resident there, among them Vera Figner, Vera Zasulich, Vladimir Burtsev, Victor Serge, and Nikolai Safranski, who was regarded as the ringleader and remained under heavy surveillance.

Back in November 1907, Har Dayal had written in the *Indian Sociologist*, "Every Indian must be convinced that if Russian methods are carried on in our country rigorously by our oppressors, the so-called British rulers, we must meet it with measure for measure."[39] He repeated the argument for learning "the art of organising secret societies and insurrections" from the Russians in the next issue, December 1907: "It seems that any agitation in India now must be carried on secretly, and that the only methods which can bring the English Government to its sense are the Russian methods vigorously and incessantly applied until the English relax their tyranny and are driven out of the country."[40] In August 1908, he added, "As to the ethics of dynamite, it may be laid down in a general way that where the people have political power there is no need for the use of explosives. It only promotes reaction. But where the people are utterly defenceless, both politically and militarily, then one may look on the bomb or any other weapon as legitimate. Its employment then becomes merely a question of expediency. We hope to discuss this question, particularly with reference to India, in an early issue."[41]

Back in Maniktola Garden, Hem Chandra Das (Kanungo) had grown impatient with a string of botched bombing and assassination operations followed by a year of relative inactivity. So he took the initiative to seek more advanced revolutionary techniques through an apprenticeship with the Russians in Paris.[42] Funded by Rana ostensibly to study chemistry—often a convenient route to the science of explosives, it would appear—Kanungo was joined by his Maharashtrian friend Pandurang Mahadev Bapat.[43] Das and Bapat were reported to be in contact with a female anarchist from the United States in Paris who Heehs suggests (rather implausibly, I think) could have been Emma Goldman. Whoever she was, she introduced them to a mysterious figure known as PhD, identified only as a leading figure in a French socialist organization. PhD and one of his comrades, "a former officer belonging to his party," offered them instruction in "history, geography and economics, along with socialism, communism, etc.," along with notes on the organization of secret societies, and after some initial hesitation, "got a member of their party to instruct Hem and Bapat in explosive chemistry and demolition." French police reports are vague on which of these was Safranski, since he was both a former "brilliant" officer in the Russian army, and enrolled in l'Ecole des Langues Orientales.[44]

Another student was Miss Perin Naoroji, granddaughter of the renowned parliamentarian Dadabhai Naoroji, best known for his book on the economic drain theory of British colonial rule. The "Grand Old Man" had her educated in Europe along with her three sisters. Since Perin's boardinghouse was on Cama's street, the Boulevard Montparnasse, intelligence surmised the girl had "learned politics from her." Crossing the English Channel to visit one of her sisters in London, she was with Savarkar at the time of his arrest. She followed his case with interest, visiting him in jail and then returning to Paris after it was over. Thereafter she could be found "working hard in the Extremist ranks," and within a few months she was reportedly being tutored in bomb making by W. Bromjevski, described as "a young Polish engineer, believed to be an anarchist, who visited her and her sister constantly at their flat for months." The sisters returned to India at the end of the year, yet remained in communication with Cama, "with whom [Perin] had arranged a simple but effective cipher before she left Paris."[45]

What of the local French anarchists? Soon after arriving in Paris, Kanungo had been introduced to Albert (Joseph) Libertad, founder of the journal *L'anarchie*, as someone who might be able to provide expertise in explosives and clandestine organization. According to Kanungo's memoir, when Libertad invited him to attend anarchist meetings, Kanungo went, under the impression that "anarchism was just another word for revolution."[46] But once he realized what they were talking about, he withdrew. Libertad was an exponent of illegalism, an amoral and extreme individualist school of thought. *L'anarchie*'s rhetoric favored criminality as an antinomian lifestyle and expressed antipathy to all forms of organization. None of this interested Kanungo, dedicated as he was to a militant cause with a focused goal. The reason he had become so frustrated with his Swadeshi comrades in the first place was what he saw as their aimless ineffectuality; this was not the remedy he sought. Ironically, the fabled rampage of the Libertad-inspired outlaw Bonnot gang in 1911–12 may have borne some resemblance to the Samiti's dacoities, albeit more purely nihilist in their hatred of the bourgeoisie, lacking the additional motive of funding an anticolonial struggle.[47]

When French law enforcement officials got wind of the rumor that the notorious "Russian anarchist [Safranski was] instructing natives of India . . . in manufacture of explosives," they were quick to inform their British counterparts.[48] But the detectives arrived too late; the suspect was gone, and the information successfully transmitted to India and the United States. Their prize was "a single cyclostyled copy of a manual of explosives" whose opening sentence declared, "The aim of the present work is to place in the hands of a revolutionary people such a powerful weapon as explosive matter is."[49]

Full Circle

In late 1907 or early 1908, with their training complete, Kanungo and Bapat left to bear their new skills and information back to India. Thereafter the Criminal Investigation Department recorded, "Special emissaries . . . moved from time to time between India and Europe for arms and bomb manuals."[50] Kanungo's manual contained three sections: preparation of explosive substances, fabrication of shells, and use of the finished products. In the estimation of James Campbell Ker, assistant to the director of Criminal Intelligence,

> The subject is exhaustively and scientifically treated; the amount of attention given to detail may be gathered from the fact that the composition and manufacture of thirty different explosives of one class only, namely those containing salts of chloric and chlorous acids, are described. The reason why it is necessary to be able to make explosives of various substances is given as follows: "In revolutionary practice we have often to use not the explosives we should like to use, but those which we can prepare with the materials at hand. . . . Again in the time of armed conflict the expenditure of explosives is considerable, and it is necessary to expropriate pharmaceutical shops (just as armouries are expropriated) and out of useful substances to prepare what is needed."[51]

The remainder of the manual, Ker explained, gave specialized instructions for making percussion and fuse bombs, with fuses ranging from instantaneous detonation through lengths of seconds or minutes, up to eight or nine hours. Possible uses for the results of such handi-work included street fighting, assassination, and destroying bridges or buildings. Heehs too goes into some detail about the explosives used (picric acid, sulfuric acid, fulminate of mercury, and nitroglycerine) and construction of bombs: shells made of forged spheres, or cleverly concealed in hollowed-out bedposts or books, as in the instance of the deadly but maddeningly unexploded Cadbury cocoa tin packed with detonators and explosive material, all encased in a copy of Herbert Broom's *Commentary on the Common Law*, intended to kill Chief Presidency Magistrate Douglas Kingsford in 1908.[52]

Above all else, it was the use of the bomb that drew the Bengalis into focus as anarchists in the colonial govern-ment's eyes. More than just a tactical instrument, at times it manifested for them as the focus of a viscerally intense cult of devotion to annihilation that shaded imperceptibly into sacrificial devotion to the mother goddess-as-nation. The bomb was also personified as the "benefactor of the poor . . . [which] has been brought across the seas. Worship it, sing its praises, bow to it. Bande Mataram."[53]

The quotation is from Har Dayal's "Shabash! In Praise of the Bomb," a pamphlet written from San Francisco on the occasion of a grenade blast heard by Indian expatriates around the world—namely, the attempt on Viceroy Lord Hardinge's life during his elephant-borne ceremonial en-trance into Delhi to reinaugurate the city as the seat of em-pire in December 1912.[54] Maniktola Garden veteran Rash Behari Bose had masterminded the attack. But the actual bomber was a young man named Basanta Kumar Biswas, to whom Bose had imparted both the "political indoctrination and practical training he would need to carry out his mission."[55] Disguised as a woman with the significant alias of Lakshmibai (the rani of Jhansi, heroine of the 1857 mutiny), Biswas flung the bomb from a balcony overlooking the parade route. Although the blast seriously wounded the viceroy, it did not kill him; the Indian attendant riding behind him was less fortunate.

Cama commented in the *Bande Mataram* of January 1913, "The enemy entered formally Delhi on the 23rd December 1912, but under what an omen? . . . This bomb-throwing was just to announce to the whole world that the English Government is discarded, and verily, whenever there is an opportunity the Revolutionaries are sure to show their mind, spirit and principle in Hindustan!"[56] Cama's comments made it clear that whether or not the target had been killed or injured was irrelevant; its message exceeded the bomb's immediate effect. The catalyzing act to rouse the laggard and latent to action was at the heart of the ideal. Sure enough, the spectacular deed ignited a new series of murders and attempted murders carried out by both the major groups in Bengal.

Many socialists and nationalists considered the adoption of this kind of action a sign of impatience—the voluntaristic belief that a single autonomous will could jumpstart the change rather than waiting for its conditions to ripen through the slower processes of parliamentary modification, mass education, molecular shifts, or structural impasse. It also indicated an analysis that saw oppression as stemming from an external source, relatively easy to

excise, rather than from internal and systemic contradictions, which would require a more profound transformation to correct. Such an externalization of oppression was
particularly easy to adopt under conditions of colonial rule.

Anarchism?

A special police unit had tagged Shridar Vyankatesh
Ketkar (later sociologist and historian) as a member of the
Savarkar brothers' old group, which had "carried out experiments in explosives, and entered into correspondence with
the anarchists of Bengal." He later traveled to the United
States to study, and wrote a letter from there in June 1909
"to a high official in India suggesting that Government
should deal with the anarchist youths through the extremist leaders" to whom he claimed to have access. He said he
had "discussed the subject of nihilism" with nationalist
firebrand Bal Gangadhar Tilak, "nearly two years before
the first bomb outrage. I had advocated nihilism while Mr.
Tilak condemned it outright as injurious to the interest of
the country."[57]

What did he mean by nihilism? What uses would he
have associated it with? In one sense it was reminiscent of
the French illegalists' utter rejection of social norms and institutions. But in Russia, nihilism was associated primarily
with urban students and intellectuals. While they likewise
rejected the governmental, educational, legal, and disciplinary institutions then existing in their society, they also
proposed a more positive alternative vision for what might

come after or alongside the ecstasy of destruction. The nihilists' Narodnik or populist outgrowth began to idealize the peasantry as not only the revolutionary class but also the bearer of the true spiritual essence of the Russian people and maintainer of its preindustrial organic social and economic formations. As the argument ran, there was no need to pass through the prescribed stages of capitalism only to end up, after much suffering, back where they had started, with some form of romanticized stateless socialism based on the village commune or mir. Furthermore, to the Narodnik Slavophile, the true soul of Russia was in effect an *Asian* village soul, and many of the same mystical stereotypes that Indians bore were attributed to it. Such a true Russian felt the czar's enforced modernization as an alien Western encroachment no less than the Indian villagers did their modernization at British hands. In this too the urban intellectual Swadeshists resembled the Russian Slavophiles.

In the meantime, Criminal Investigation Department director William Cleveland had another, more menacing take on the true nature of the Indian soul. In his introductory remarks on "anarchism," written for his assistant Ker's 1919 documentary compilation *Political Trouble in India*, he diagnosed the "psychology of the politico-criminal activities of Indians" as none other than a fervidly intense religious nationalism.[58] To characterize this, he enlisted the aid of an extended quotation from John Nicol Farquhar's *Religious Nationalism*, published in 1912.[59]

Farquhar identified this new trend (in contrast to the thin, bloodless old politicism) as a species of religious nationalism indicating the maturation of "racial" confidence,

which produced greater independence of thought as
well as greater demands for full political independence.
Marked by its commitment to a comprehensive revitalization of national life, it was "fired" by deep devotion and
self-consecration "to God and India." And he claimed that
"finally, whether in anarchists or men of peace, the new
nationalism is willing to serve and suffer. The deluded boys
who believed they could bring in India's millennium by
murdering a few white men were quite prepared to give
their lives for their country; and the healthy movements
which incarnate the new spirit at its best spend themselves
in unselfish service." Here he pointed to a divergence between anarchists and Hindu revivalists, for whom, given
their possession of such a plainly superior civilization, it
was "a religious duty to get rid of the Europeans and all the
evils that attend him."[60]

But Farquhar nevertheless identified "a general attitude . . . common to the revivalists and the anarchists. It is
clear as noonday that the religious aspect of anarchism was
merely an extension of that revival of Hinduism which is
the work of Dayananda, Ramakrishna, Vivekananda and
the Theosophists." Farquhar was thus setting up an unprob-
lematic equivalence between anarchism and the religious
nationalism that would later spawn a noxious Indian vari-
ant of fascism, while actually misrepresenting both sides of
the equation.

This distorted characterization of Hinduism was not
new. Cleveland's descriptions of a cult of "furious devotion
to some divinity of hate and blood" recall in nearly identical terms those of the Thuggee and Dacoity Department's

sensationalized obsession with Kali-worshipping bandits dating from nearly a century earlier—an obsession enshrined as a timeless trope from William Sleeman's books in 1815 to *Indiana Jones and the Temple of Doom* in 1984. The Thuggee and Dacoity Department was reconstituted in 1903 as the Criminal Investigation Department with a new focus on seditious activity. Granted, the revolutionists did not help matters with passages such as this one from the *Yugantar* of May 2, 1908:

> The Mother is thirsty and is pointing out to her sons the only thing that can quench that thirst. Nothing less than human blood and decapitated human heads will satisfy her. Let her sons, therefore, worship her with these offerings, and let them not shrink even from sacrificing their lives to procure them. On the day on which the Mother is worshipped in this way in every village, on that day will the people of India be inspired with a divine spirit and the crown of independence will fall into their hands.[61]

Like many Orientalist fantasies, this was a cocreated myth.

Times editor Valentine Chirol, by extolling the civilizing effect of British rule as the best thing that ever happened to a benighted, squalid land, could then argue that the causes of Indian unrest were not really political or economic grievances. Such would be rational. Indian resistance was not rational, since despite an understandable tendency to become irritated or vexed by the presence of a foreign power, which Chirol did somewhat indulgently acknowledge, British rule was on the whole, he repeated, beneficial and salubrious for India. The true root of the unrest must therefore be the perverse, bloodthirsty nature of Brahminic religion itself.

Nevertheless, despite their obtuse misreading, Farquhar, Cleveland, and Chirol—whether or not they knew it—were responding to an undeniable antirationalist element common to a certain strand of religious politics and a certain strand within the anarchist tradition, to whom an erotically charged millenarian sensibility was mutually legible in ways that escaped rationalist liberals and socialists. The political significance came whenever millennial escape was transposed into the impulse to create a rupture not between this world and a transcendent one somewhere else, but rather between the existing society and a future one based on an ethical or moral order enacted in this world.[62]

Furthermore, what in mid-nineteenth- to early twentieth-century Europe took the form of a rejection of certain (rational, industrial, or disciplinary) elements of modernity, became for Indian extremists and Russian populists a proudly self-essentializing rejection of Western elements. For both, a hatred of the modernizing/colonizing state was paramount and class analysis was minimal. This affinity continued to echo in the mutually reinforcing statements of European Romanticist and cultural Pan-Asianist antiliberal critics of modernity.

This was a crucial evolutionary node, from which Right and Left branchings were possible. Already within the Swadeshi movement distinctions could be made between the Calcutta-based *Yugantar* group and the Anusilan Samiti in Dhaka. The former had more international connections with activists who would later move into Left formations. By cultural default strongly Hindu, upper caste, and educated, the *Yugantar* group did not make any of this foundational to its ideological identity. But the less socially progressive Dhaka group actively recruited its leadership based on distinctions of class, caste, and English education, and explicitly excluded Muslims from membership.[63]

One way leans toward dangerous cultural chauvinism, while the other uses the cultural materials at hand to reach conclusions compatible with, but not derivative of, something else. Where is the line between these shadings?

Let's take the path of karma yoga as expounded in the Bhagavad Gita and central to the applied Swadeshi philosophy, since its emphasis on the value and meaning of action is an explicit point of affinity with turn-of-the century propagandists of the deed. On the occasion of Khudiram Bose's execution for the Muzaffarpur bombing, the *Bande Mataram* commented that "he not only read the Gita but also acted on it."[64] Such a focus on action as its own justification was still not the same as the reveling in destruction that was liable to be associated with nihilism, however—or with the similar characterization of Bengali shaktism. Among the Bengali militants, it was typical to fixate on the climactic moment of sacrifice itself rather than on the tactical outcome or mode of social organization to come afterward. But there was nevertheless a tactical goal: to use the symbolic violence to rouse quiescent popular consciousness, by punching a hole in the complacent functioning of an intolerable system.

The *Indian Sociologist* wrote of the "Indian propagandists and the physical force party, with whose implacable hostility, it admits, the English will probably always have to reckon."[65] This physical force partly alluded to precisely that tendency the British identified as anarchist. A chain of correspondence had been activated by which physical force equaled shakti equaled power equaled energy equaled the bomb—that is, the pure manifestation of such energy; or by an alternate route, physical force equaled karma yoga equaled action in the world equaled direct action equaled propaganda of the deed . . . equaled the bomb.

Another passage read, "An immense and incalculable revolution is at hand, and its instruments must be themselves immense in their aspiration, uncalculating in the self-immolation." Following further calls to self-sacrifice for the greater good, the author concluded that "the fair hope of an orderly and peaceful evolution of self-government, which the first energies of the new movement had fostered, are gone forever. Revolution, bare and grim, is preparing her battlefield, mowing down the centres of order which were evolving a new cosmos, and building up the materials of a gigantic downfall and a mighty new creation. We could have wished it otherwise, but God's will be done."[66]

Here is the aesthetic of apocalyptic rupture, blasting a gateway to the new world. This association of anarchism with insurrectionary nihilism would prove a lasting one, overshadowing later points of contact with other strands within the anarchist tradition, even though this was a definition originally elaborated by hostile colonial police, who arguably misunderstood both Hindu karma yoga and anarchism.

Savarkar became a founding hero of the Hindu far Right, while other Abhinava Bharat members like Har Dayal, Mandayam Parthasarathi Tirumal Acharya, and Virendranath Chattopadhyaya (aka Chatto) became leaders of the dissident Left. From that crossroads, this is the path that we take now.

The Anarcho-syndicalists

In the years between two seismic events—geologic in 1906, geopolitical in 1914—the San Francisco Bay Area rivaled Paris in its plenitude of international revolutionaries and progressives of all sorts. It was a milieu suffused by various aspects of individual as well as social anarchism that brought together bohemian counterculture, artistic and spiritualistic experimentation, efforts toward women's suffrage, reproductive rights and sexual freedom, and militant labor activity. This was the headquarters of the Indian expatriate Ghadar movement, which bonded migrant laborers and radical students—including some Swadeshi and India House veterans—into a revolutionary anticolonial force from 1913 onward.

In "What Hindus Want" (in the contemporary U.S. context, "Hindus" referred generically to Indians of all faiths), Chandra, editor of the Ghadar's eponymous news and propaganda organ from 1914–17, divided the anticolonial mobilization into three parties: moderates who wanted self-rule within the empire like the Canadians and

Australians; extremists who "want[ed] independence and separation through passive resistance," who didn't "believe the promises of the Government. They want[ed] their own Government and [didn't] care what kind whether Monarchical or Democratic"; and Ghadar, which wanted "total autonomy and absolute freedom through revolution (nothing can be achieved by begging the Government, or passive resistance.) They [sought] to establish the free Republic of the United States of India" as a decentralized, subcontinental federation.[1]

Among the proponents of that vision were two young scholars: Dhan Gopal Mukerji and Har Dayal, theorist and propagandist of the early Ghadar movement.[2] Mukerji was the cousin and brother of prominent anticolonial activists in India and the United States.[3] While a student at the University of California in Berkeley, he gravitated to socialist, anarchist, and Wobbly friends. He later formed long-term close associations with radical writers like Will and Ariel Durant, Roger Nash Baldwin, and Romain Rolland. Through his encounters with a succession of mentor/informants (an ultra-individualist voluntary hobo, a syndicalist labor veteran, and an extremist Indian nationalist), Mukerji's picaresque autobiography can be viewed as both an allegory of persistent debates within the anarchist discourse—between social and individual, rationalist and antirationalist, and insurrectionary and organizational strains—and a microcosm of the Indian movement in that context. There is no evidence that he knew Har Dayal personally, although given their shared context, it seems improbable that they didn't at least know one another by reputation.[4] Then again, circa 1912, there were few people in Bay Area political circles who would not have known Har Dayal by reputation.

Har Dayal

Har Dayal was born in Delhi in 1884 or 1885. A gifted student from an early age, he embarked on a stellar academic career that took him to the National College in Lahore and then to Oxford on scholarship in 1905. Both Indian and English mentors predicted a great role for him in the affairs of his country as a lawyer or civil servant. All were equally shocked when just months short of completing his degree, Har Dayal wrote a letter to the British secretary of state for India renouncing his scholarship and leaving the university on the grounds that he could no longer in good conscience accept aid from a government whose presence in India was illegitimate. In an abrupt shift from "young Englishman" to homespun patriot, he threw himself into "the study of the history of the free, parliamentarian institutions, the tenacity with which the British people fought for and defended their individual liberties." Why, he charged, should the desire for national and individual freedom, considered "the supreme social virtue" among the English, be called "madness and sedition" when evinced by an Indian? His mind, "always an enormous and readily absorbing sponge, became filled with the unrest of the New Century," that encompassed "nationalisms of all subject peoples (Irish, Polish and what not), revolutionism against native despots

(Russian, Turkish, etc.), the movement for votes for women, labour and socialistic developments."[5] In between India House meetings and Abhinava Bharat activities, Har Dayal also met Kropotkin and George Bernard Shaw.[6]

When Har Dayal returned to India in early 1908, his personal life was overtaken by the vocation of ascetic revolutionary sage, at the expense of his relationship to his wife, Sundar, who had married him at seventeen and accompanied him to England against the wishes of her family.[7] Setting up a house in Kanpur, he gathered a clique of "disciples," who studied "revolutionary books ... from Europe: on the Russian revolution (against the Czar), Irish Nationalist Movement, the Italian movement of Mazzini, [Giuseppe] Garibaldi, [Conte] Cavour, the German Nationalist Movement and the making of the German Empire by Bismark [*sic*], Egyptian Nationalism, Young Turkism, the Rise of Japan, Polish Nationalism, the French Revolution." In short, Har Dayal had worked his way through the Enlightenment and the democratic republicanism of the "Long Nineteenth Century." "Sometimes he would recite and act out passages from some book on the French Revolution, concerning [Georges-Jacques] Danton or Napoleon or some other fighting revolutionist. He would discuss the teachings of [Jean-Jacques] Rousseau, whose 'Social Contract' he carried around, or of Voltaire."[8] As this curriculum illustrated, he had no objection to Europe or modernity; but his rejection of Britain and its institutions was unequivocal—a distinction he noted in an essay.

His cohort of "nationalists and revolutionaries of all ages" spent their evenings enjoying the cool breezes along the sands of the Jumna, swathed in khaddar and carrying lathis, talking about ways to fight their colonial rulers or how to set up a national state. By this time Har Dayal had also come to admire Buddha, whose biography *Light of Asia* by Edwin Arnold he often recited from beginning to end. After a while he moved to Lahore, where he published articles in English and Urdu urging complete noncooperation and disengagement from British educational and governmental institutions. But he was no less scathing about the weaknesses of his own people. In one piece for Calcutta's *Modern Times*, titled "Social Conquest of the Hindu Race," he argued that by placing its victims in a constant position of existential inferiority, psychological colonization led a people in effect to collaborate in its own subordination.

Har Dayal seemed poised to emerge as a rival to other nationalist leaders within the country, until he was targeted in the vicious police crackdown unleashed by the Maniktola bomb case in 1908. Tipped off about a warrant for his arrest, he managed to get a train south, sail from Ceylon to Italy and from there to Paris to join Cama, Rana, and company. His daughter was born only a few days before he left the country. He never saw her; nor did he ever see Sundar again.

Once more he predictably grew "engrossed in the study of the philosophies and methods of great revolutionary and reform movements of history."[9] Almost immediately, Cama tapped him as editor of the new *Bande Mataram*, which she and Rana had intended as a more overtly revolutionary alternative to the increasingly cautious *Indian Sociologist*. It was in these pages that Har

Dayal began systematically to articulate the principles of "Hardayalism," a program for change based on the idea of three successive stages through which "an enslaved people must pass . . . before it can again establish itself as a member of the community of nations": education, revolution, and reconstruction (shorthanded in the phrase "after Mazzini, Garibaldi; after Garibaldi, Cavour," alluding to key figures in the Italian unification). The first was "moral and intellectual preparation. During this period the workers must elevate the character of the people and instruct them in the principles that govern an efficient social organization." The people must be purged of all cowardice, selfishness, and greed; "the spirit of the slave must disappear before slavery can be ended." He continued, "The second stage is that of war. The way must be declared for the establishment of a free and sovereign state managed by the people. The debris of the old regime must be removed. And the only agent that can accomplish this work is the sword. No subject nation can bring freedom without war . . . with its alien rulers." And finally, "After the war the work of reconstruction and consolidation commences."[10] It's clear that he was still thinking in classically nationalist terms. Yet even here he was starting to suggest that not just a transfer of political power but also a comprehensive social, psychological, and cultural transformation was the goal.

Less than a year later, in July 1910, Har Dayal decided to leave Paris. He tapered off his writing for the *Bande Mataram*, ceasing after 1911. Various writers have speculated about his motivations: despair at Savarkar's arrest perhaps, mingled with general philosophical/political malaise. Biographer Emily Brown suggests that Har Dayal was having trouble squaring his more overtly Hindu ideals with Cama and Rana's focus on international socialism.[11] Based on his writings of the time, though, it appears he was himself struggling with what content he wished to express through a spiritual idiom, and doubting whether that idiom could be a vehicle for what he found himself wanting to say. Aldred's evaluation of Har Dayal's ideological development was that

> he now proclaimed his belief in the coming republic, which was to be a church, a religious confraternity, based on an ideal, on freewill and mutual cooperation. Its motto was to be: Atheism, cosmopolitanism and moral law. This republic would not be a state, because the latter represented force and persecution. No modification of its activity, no tinkering with parliaments and senates and parties, could bring up the republic. The latter must grow up by the side of the state, which it would undermine finally.

Aldred added that Har Dayal "also asserted the superiority of woman, declared for anti-patriotism and repudiated the race idea as a relic of barbarism."[12] If this is an accurate reflection and not simply Aldred's own projection, Har Dayal's new "religion" was a self-consciously modernist and unmistakably anarchistic utopian vision.

Har Dayal first relocated to Algiers, where he planned to live ascetically in a climate kinder to his fragile health, but was no more contented there than in France. His next

choice was Martinique, another French colony. This is
where Bhai Parmanand, an old comrade from London and
Lahore who was then working as an Arya Samaj mission-
ary to the Indian indentured laborers of British Guiana
and elsewhere in the Caribbean, found him absorbed in a
bare-bones routine of study and meditation, sleeping on
the floor, and subsisting on boiled grain and potatoes. Har
Dayal explained that he intended to offer the world a new
philosophy. Parmanand tried to dissuade him. Surely the
world didn't need another creed. Why not go to the United
States and teach people about one of the existing schools
of Hindu philosophy—some of which were atheistic and
rationalistic, if that's what he was after?

Har Dayal agreed to give it a try. He went first to
Harvard University, where he met the Sikh priest and
scholar Teja Singh. This West Coast community leader invited him to come to California, where he said there were
"thousands of Sikhs and other Punjabi laborers working in
fields or factories . . . who lacked leadership in their struggle
for social acceptance and economic equality."[13] Har Dayal
accepted, but only after a stint in Hawaii living in a cave
on Waikiki Beach, "where Japanese Buddhist fishermen,
who regarded him as a Buddhist sage, fed him and lent him
their ears." He was reportedly capable of discussing many
aspects of this philosophy at great length, but at the same
time he was also studying Kant, Hegel, and Marx.

He arrived in Berkeley early in 1911, and then was
hired at Stanford as a lecturer in Indian philosophy for academic year 1912–13. After only a few months, however,
he resigned over his public stances on controversial topics

such as British rule, anticapitalism, and most scandalous of all, free love. But as he continued to lecture in Oakland, Berkeley, and Palo Alto, he and his cause began to attract prominent progressives in the area, including Jack London, Clarence Darrow, and literary critic Van Wyck Brooks.[14] He also drew the attention of the *San Francisco Bulletin*'s editor Fremont Older, who introduced him to a wider circle of "reformers, labour leaders, intellectuals," and "fighters for social justice and so forth." Soon Har Dayal was regarded as a leader among the "free thinkers called 'radicals' of San Francisco, the Bay Cities, Palo Alto, and the whole region."[15]

Overall, the radical energy and intellectual dynamism of the Bay Area was a refreshing stimulant for Har Dayal, whose political convictions had flagged amid the lull in the nationalist movement that followed Savarkar's arrest. In fact, between his return to California in 1911 and the end of 1912, he was more engaged in the city's radical milieu than with the Indian community, with whom he had relatively little direct involvement during this period.[16]

Har Dayal spent summer 1912 making plans for a propaganda magazine and a lecture series on sociology. He continued a series of articles for *Modern Review* between 1911 and 1913 on the condition of the Indian community in North America, in which it was plain that his ideas for a total social and cultural transformation went far beyond simply eliminating foreign rule.[17] Attacking the caste system and archaic educational approaches, and discounting both nation and religion as meaningful categories of affiliation, he argued that Indian progressives ought to be concerned with "the great ideas of social equality and personal dignity, of scientific research and rationalism, of economic freedom and organisation, of public spirit and political principle, of popular government and social progress."[18]

Instead of their preoccupation with "transcendental nonsense," Indian intellectuals should concentrate on the fact that in the face of famine and pestilence, "there is not a single decent representative institution, technical institute, laboratory or library in the whole country." It was imperative, Har Dayal said, for young people to read Rousseau, Voltaire, Plato, Aristotle, Ernst Haeckel, Spencer, Marx, Leo Tolstoy, John Ruskin, and Auguste Comte as well as to study ethics, science, sociology, economics, and politics rather than the Vedas.[19]

In "Barabari da Arth" (The Meaning of Equality), he noted that since the Vedic Aryan conquest, Hindu philosophy and society had been based on inequality, although things were different in pre-Vedic times, and he would like them to be different again. But equality had to be practiced, not just lauded, in its full and true meaning, which included first economic equality, then equality of opportunity, and then equal distribution of wealth by the people working on the land and in the factories. Wealth could not exist except by depriving or exploiting someone else. All people must have autonomy, which was also a form of equality.

In another piece on the Indian peasant, written in May 1913, Har Dayal argued that the caste system had it upside down; the laboring classes—in his scheme comprised not of an industrial proletariat but instead of peasants, artisans, and menial workers—were the source of all value, wealth, and life, and the true masters of society. In order to achieve this, society as a whole along with each individual within it would require a psychological change. India's existing national literature exalted materially unproductive parasites: ancient epics glorified nobles and warriors, while the medieval literature featured spiritual ascetics. Now, even the nationalist "Extremists" gave no thought to the peasant or artisan, aiming for a hierarchical government with princes and parliamentary houses. Others, "if they are wiser and more democratic, they talk of a Republic, with representative government, which would mean the rule of the educated classes and the landowners, bankers and manufacturers," while the Indian people were still left out. "Our imagination stops at the border-line that separates the clean and literate classes from the dirty and illiterate masses. Where we stop, there humanity begins. We waste our lives in the service of false gods."[20]

Meanwhile to his U.S. audience, he advised renunciation and asceticism as the path to humanity's salvation, recommending a holistic amalgam of the theories of Saint Rose, Saint Francis, Rousseau, Voltaire, Marx, Bakunin, Mazzini, and Haeckel as the ideal.[21] In other words, he did not fully jettison spiritual concerns but rather transposed them into the sphere of concrete ethical action in society.

His *Modern Review* article "Marx: A Modern Rishi" in March 1912 was thought (by first Communist Party of India [CPI] General Secretary Puran Chand Joshi no less) to have been the first Indian article on Marx. But the author's interpretation of Marx's significance was far from orthodox. Like other Indian readers, Har Dayal respected Marx first and foremost as a moral exemplar of dedication and personal sacrifice, ranking him with Christ and Buddha as a "benefactor of humanity." He approved of the ideas of equal economic distribution and abolition of money, yet also insisted that materialism alone was insufficient. Choice and volition must not be disregarded; civilization did not proceed mechanically through inevitable teleology but was also affected by "a product of personal influences." Finally, Har Dayal wanted to modify the notion of class struggle by rejecting what he called "class-selfishness" in favor of "social cooperation based on the appreciation of a higher ideal."[22]

Despite the degree to which he had "[become] very busy with Americans" during this period, he also managed to earn the loyalty of many Indian students at Berkeley and Stanford. But his rival as charismatic mentor was Jatindra Nath Lahiri, a veteran of the Bengali movement best known for carrying out an assassination in 1905, who provided a direct conduit for the philosophy and training methods of the Bengali akhara.[23] The basis for the ideological conflict between Lahiri and Dayal, said Darisi Chenchiah, one of the Berkeley students and later a Ghadar activist, was the role of religion in political revolution. Was it a distraction, substitute, or inspiration? Another point of contention was Lahiri's claim that Har Dayal was a coward and hypocrite for having left India when the political situation grew precarious in 1908, and instead speaking out from the safety of twelve thousand miles' distance. Har Dayal's retort was that he was following in the footsteps of luminaries such as Mazzini and Sun Yat Sen, who worked from peripatetic exile. Lahiri further charged that Har

Dayal was damaging the freedom movement by "wasting his eminent revolutionary qualities in lecturing on anarchism, free love and comparative philosophy in USA," when all around him, going to seed, was the best of "human material [available] for you to inspire them with patriotism."[24] In a nutshell, the friction between the two leaders was indicative of the transfer from Swadeshi to Ghadar. Lahiri was attempting to replicate or continue the previous movement, imported intact from a political context specific to Bengal. Har Dayal was participating in the construction of a new, more expansive one, rooted in the oppositional communities of the West Coast.

Moreover, he had begun making overtures to the more than five thousand "young Sikhs" around Stockton who worked "in field, factory and small shop [workshop] operations."[25] Despite their habitual distrust of educated elites, these workers responded well. Perhaps this was because of Har Dayal's evident integrity, through a consistent effort "to live what he preached," suggested Chenchiah. By now a self-avowed anarchist, Har Dayal didn't believe in money, Chenchiah asserted, and so gave away whatever his wife still sent him while maintaining a "proverbial" simplicity of lifestyle. As he had done in Martinique and Hawaii, Har Dayal was "living like a saint or fakir" in a bare room, sleeping on the floor, eating bread and milk. The *San Francisco Examiner*'s version of his living arrangements were that he ate only fruit and slept on a board, claiming that "by denying himself all things in life but the satisfaction of his anti-social ideas he would concentrate all his physical and mental powers" toward the ultimate goal of "overthrow[ing] society."[26]

Meanwhile, he continued voraciously to process additional material into the mix of what he both practiced and preached, having "developed a great respect for and sympathy with the teachings of Count Tolstoy, then known as one of the world's leading 'philosophic anarchists.'"[27] Har Dayal declared himself a supporter of Ricardo Flores Magón and his anarcho-syndicalist Partido Liberal Mexicano, and quietly assisted in the cross-border mobilization to liberate Mexico from the clutches of northern capitalists and rival comprador warlords. Ghadar's designated military coordinator, Pandurang Khankhoje, also became friends with Magón and even for a time contemplated sending Indians from California to train with Mexican revolutionaries. Khankhoje later spent many years in Mexico, and made significant contributions as an agricultural scientist through the strains of high-yield corn he developed. His friend Diego Rivera depicted him in a famous mural, distributing bread with a benevolent smile.[28]

Brooks recalled that Har Dayal had held a gathering at Brooks's home in 1912 during which he "boldly affirmed that the international social revolution was his only interest."[29] Brooks later described his friend in light of

> Bakunin's definition of a revolutionist as one who "has no interests, no affairs, no feelings, no attachments of his own, no property, not even a name," having broken with the codes and conventions that govern other people and having only "one thought, one passion: revolution." . . . For, whether as an Indian nationalist or an anarchist internationalist,

> he was a revolutionist at every moment with a
> shrewd psychological knowledge of the value of the
> martyr's role for attracting and retaining disciples
> to carry out his work. . . . [His mind] seemed to
> combine in a curious way the opposite types of the
> "yogi" and the "commissar."[30]

According to Chenchiah, Har Dayal was well known "among the numerous foreign revolutionary societies which were then functioning in . . . San Francisco which was the headquarters of many of these organizations." Russian, Irish, Japanese, Turkish, and Chinese groups regarded Har Dayal as a "great friend, philosopher and guide," and sought him out "as a political revolutionary [who] worked for the liberation of many countries, from the clutches of feudalism and imperialism." He in turn invited foreign leaders to lecture and teach. As in France, "the most spectacular [were] the Russians who used to escape from their exile in Siberia and manage to arrive in USA," wrote Chenchiah. From them "we learnt many lessons not only about printing, publishing and distributing secret revolutionary literature, but also the method of recruiting, training and organizing youths."[31]

Har Dayal continued to lecture to progressive intellectual gatherings and labor organizations, at venues including the monthly William Morris Circle, International Radical Club (as the founder and secretary), and Industrial Workers of the World (IWW) (as the secretary for the Oakland branch). The Radical Club (or as Har Dayal's former Stanford boss called it, the

"International-Radical-Communist Anarchist Club," and the intelligence officers keeping an eye on it, "an assemblage of 'Russians, Poles, and Socialists'") met monthly for dinner—often at one of San Francisco's many excellent Italian restaurants, noted Govind Behari Lal—and to discuss a variety of subjects, led by distinguished experts on topics in the natural or social sciences. Here was a platform for "dissenters from the establishment in any social, political, or intellectual area" to "work off steam" or "vent [their] feelings."[32] The club had no formal political affiliation or party line, but each week Har Dayal produced some notable speaker (on one occasion, John Reed), after which "there were questions and discussions, and everybody ate and drank and called each other 'comrade' [as the] burning themes of the changing human relationships and ideologies of the first decade of the 20th century were tossed about," from the "equality of women, equality of races, equality of nations, equality of labour etc." to free love, or the desirability of political bombings and assassinations.[33]

Har Dayal's other enterprise as entrepreneur of radicalism and inventor of religion was the Fraternity of the Red Flag. A month after resigning from Stanford, he published an invitation to "all Radical Comrades" over the age of twenty to join this group, whose stated object was "the service of the Radical ideal of life." The rules for achieving this required that aspirants sign up for a one-year "novitiate" of "moral and intellectual preparation" under the guidance of an existing member, after which they would vow poverty and homelessness, humility, "purity (but not celibacy)," service and propaganda. The vow meant specifically that the member "renounces all wealth, promises not to earn money or be a parent at any time, repudiates all other social ties and obligations, and live[s] a life of simplicity and hardship. (Since neither celibacy nor parenthood was recommended, presumably Har Dayal was familiar with the work of Margaret Sanger, perhaps through mutual colleague Agnes Smedley.) Anyone was free to leave the fraternity at any time.[34]

Finally, initiates would pledge to uphold "the eight principles of Radicalism," of which the first three concerned personal development, and the last five a revolution in social institutions, the latter of which suggest a combination of anarcho-syndicalism, rationalist secularism, and contemporary fads. These were:

> 1. Personal moral development through love and self-discipline
> 2. Personal intellectual development through education and self-culture
> 3. Personal physical development through hygiene and eugenics
> 4. The establishment of communism, and the abolition of private property in land and capital through industrial organization and the General Strike
> 5. The establishment of free fraternal cooperation, and the ultimate abolition of the coercive organization of Government
> 6. The promotion of science and sociology, and the abolition of religion and metaphysics

7. The establishment of Universal Brotherhood, and the abolition of patriotism and race feeling

8. The establishment of the complete economic, moral, intellectual, and sexual freedom of woman, and the abolition of prostitution, marriage, and other institutions based on the enslavement of woman[35]

Echoing his nod to Francisco Ferrer above, Har Dayal stated that the fraternity in the United States, Europe, and Australia would "devote its effort chiefly to the establishment of Modern Schools, and the promotion of industrial organization and strikes (in cooperation with the I.W.W. and Syndicalist movements). In Asia and Africa, it will further the movements of progress and revolt in various countries." He signed and dated the document "Ferrer's Day, October 13, 41 P.C., 1912 A.D."[36]

Shortly afterward, he received a "windfall" in the form of a real estate parcel: a house on six acres of farmland near Oakland that he described as having a lovely view from a hill sloping down to the sea. It was donated by a woman who had volunteered to teach gratis in the "modern school and training institute for anarchist propagandists" to be founded there. Har Dayal named it the Bakunin Institute and envisioned it as the order's first "monastery." He wanted it to have a good library and serve as a place of hospitality for all wandering lecturers regardless of their party. Described by the *San Francisco Chronicle* of May 12, 1914 as a "socialistic affair," it functioned for about two years but lost cohesion after Har Dayal's departure.[37]

British-born Magónist William Owen was another project participant. A close collaborator of the Magón brothers, from 1910 he was in charge of the English-language page of the Los Angeles edition of their organ *Regeneración*.[38] Described as an "American anarchist," Owen was mentioned addressing an enthusiastic crowd at a Ghadar meeting in early 1914.

At the time, Har Dayal seems to have been indifferent to invitations to lead the local Indian community in its struggles with anti-immigrant legislation, explaining later that he had been too "caught up in the labor movement and the social revolution" to think much about Indian nationalist politics.[39] By this he presumably meant the particularity of eliminating British colonial rule; but in a larger sense, with hindsight, what could be more key to the U.S. labor movement and social revolution than the condition of a racialized, low-income workforce in the United States?

All this changed with the news of the Hardinge bomb. Lal remembered Har Dayal as being "tremendously excited" on hearing about it.[40] Speaking vehemently about it at an Indian students' meeting Har Dayal insisted on the right to struggle for independence and equality by any means possible. He dashed off a circular saluting the bomber, under the title "Yugantar." Then the news arrived from India that some of his "closest friends had been drawn into the net of the 'bomb conspiracy,'" and that according to the Indian newspapers, British authorities believed that Har Dayal was connected in some way to the attack on the viceroy. At this point he "knew that he could never go back to India. Now he must do everything from abroad."[41]

On the first anniversary of the event, he published the notorious "Shabash!" pamphlet exhorting, "Don't sit there. Death hovers near—kill or be killed, do a great deed before you pass on." In other words, why not die for a cause, since one dies anyhow: "Blessed is the death of the man who suffers martyrdom for the sake of freedom."[42]

The bomb, he rhapsodized, had several advantages. It got immediate results, flashing an unmistakable signal for the enemy, as well as a beacon by night for the lost traveler. Dawn would follow darkness; clouds were gathering toward the impending downpour. In short, violence was a universal language. "Punishing" nondemocratic rulers by killing and wounding them was a surefire, direct remedy for ending oppression. Only violence goaded the powerful into reform, concession, or amelioration. The bomb would apply the "whip of fear" to induce the government to reform itself, if only to stave off a mutiny that would annihilate it.

He continued to switch between registers and pull eclectic themes together, while also betraying the lingering inconsistencies in his awareness of gender politics. The only civilized and free nations with a measure of honor, he insisted, were those that could demonstrate a "warlike, bold and manly spirit." Belying a glorious past, Indians now were mistreated as slaves in all nations because of their own cowardice. So then regain some courage, he declared: throw a bomb! And thereby refuse to accept the "ignoble and contemptible" existence of a slave.

For comparison, he pointed to Sun Yat Sen's successful republican overthrow of an empire from a diasporic base just a year earlier; the West Coast Indians could do the same. As for the Russians, they "daily shoot Governors, police commissioners, spies, etc., like little birds of prey and the people applaud. . . . [T]he Indians should become disciples of the Russians." He reserved special praise for women like Sophia Perovskaya and Vera Zasulich, "who were worshiped like goddesses by the people." Har Dayal also drew eclectically on Hyndman, Kropotkin, and sacred poet Matthew Arnold to legitimate the distinction between an act of murder and one of justice, and offered a litany of regicidal heroes, including the anarchist assassins of King Umberto of Italy, President William McKinley, and Czar Alexander II.[43]

Indian revolutionaries could not afford to wait around for Germany and Britain to come to blows, as they were bound to do eventually, he insisted. In the meantime, "in Asiatic countries the appearance of the bomb is the advance guard of complete liberty."

Ghadar member Rattan Singh and Ghadar historian Harish Puri (among many other Left critics of propaganda of the deed) later called this vanguardist approach a symptom of the "desperation" that springs from the yawning absence of a mass revolutionary movement. What changed circa 1912 was precisely the emergence of an opportunity to organize such a movement. The several thousand Indian agricultural and lumber workers on the West Coast were dry tinder ready for a spark, as they began to articulate the links between the racial discrimination they faced in California, and the colonial status of their country of origin. Har Dayal wrote to Aldred in December 1913, reporting on "his work on the Coast, especially among the

Hindu working men there," among whom he was gaining three to four hundred new "converts" each week to "the economic ideals of the Revolutionary Party of India—the Ghadr Party," and also asked Brooks to forward Aldred some of the Ghadar literature.[44] The movement's takeoff was meteoric; but that story must be told elsewhere.

On March 25, 1914, just as it was picking up steam, a warrant went out for Har Dayal's arrest and deportation. After Leon Czolgosz killed President McKinley in 1901, a law had been passed allowing deportation within three years of entry to the United States, of any anarchist alien for whom there was "local evidence of belonging to any revolutionary society."[45] The Ghadarites' nemesis William Hopkinson, a Canadian undercover agent with police experience in Calcutta—allegedly he could pass as a Sikh—suggested this strategem, since Har Dayal's views and associations were well known.

The evidence for his deportation case included letters written in his hand, purportedly discovered among Alexander Berkman's and Goldman's personal effects. Any real connection is apocryphal, although Har Dayal did at least attempt to make contact. Later, two letters he posted from Netherlands in 1916 to Berkman were used as proof in the wartime Hindu-German conspiracy case, even though these had been deployed less to link Har Dayal to anarchists than to link Goldman and Berkman to Germany. Goldman herself dismissed the letters, and when confronted, claimed to remember Har Dayal vaguely only as a "great idealist" and "Tolstoyan" whom she had met in California.[46]

Har Dayal had written,

> Dear Comrade: I am well and busy. Can you send
> some earnest and sincere comrades, men and wom-
> en, to help our Indian revolutionary party at this
> juncture? They should be persons of good charac-
> ter. . . . Kindly also send me names and addresses
> of the prominent anarchist comrades in Spain,
> Denmark, France, Sweden, Norway, Switzerland,
> Italy, Germany, Austria, and other European coun-
> tries. Please also send letters of introduction for
> me to them from Emma or yourself, if you know
> them. With love and respect, Yours for the cause,
> Har Dayal.

In the second letter a couple of days later, he was still "well
and busy," but also "sad," because "we have lost some very
brave comrades in the recent skirmishes . . . we are fighting
against heavy odds." He repeated the request for aid and
reinforcements, suggesting the "real fighters, I.W.W.s or
anarchists" who might be found in New York or Paterson,
New Jersey.[47]

But guilt by such indirect association was not enough.
Confident that deportation would be easy if he could only
come up with damning evidence of anarchist convictions,
Hopkinson set out to find it—such as the "large stock
of anarchist literature" (unspecified) that police found
in the possession of Ram Nath Puri, one of the early Bay
Area radicals with whom Har Dayal was in communication. After a year of attending Har Dayal's public lectures,

Hopkinson declared his quarry to be without a doubt the most dangerous of the Indian agitators he had yet evaluated in the United States, and warned ominously of the dangerous impact someone of Har Dayal's "knowledge and influence and declared Anarchistic tendencies, is bound to wield . . . on the young boys at the University."[48] The *San Francisco Chronicle* reported that as Har Dayal embarked under escort to the Angel Island immigration center for his interrogation, two hundred highly demonstrative Indians flanked him.[49]

The answers provided in the course of his three-hour grilling may have been as illuminating as one of the public lectures haunted by Hopkinson.[50] The first line of questioning picked up on a speech Har Dayal had given on the Russian Revolution and important lessons to be gained from it. He considered himself a "disciple" of the movement and its literature, and felt the revolution had been "justified essentially and necessary for civilization."[51]

The questioner pounced: A disciple? What did he mean? Har Dayal responded: "The word discipline has so many meanings. I am a student of it; I have derived inspiration from it. I know personally many leaders of the Russian revolution." Presumably he meant the exiled Socialists-Revolutionaries in Paris. Pressed more closely on his endorsement of violence, he claimed that each case had to be considered in context, and that where violent action was the only means available for changing an unacceptable government, and if it would "help the progress of civilization and freedom," then he would condone it. The Russian situation fit his criteria: "That is my opinion as a student."[52]

And India? While reiterating his conviction that "the British Empire is sucking the life blood of millions of people in Ireland, India, and Egypt," he stated that he didn't think violence was the most constructive option currently available in the Indian context. The revolutionary nationalist movement was still "in a stage of infancy and should devote all its energy to propaganda."[53] In a country such as India, rendered "backward" by despotism, he predicted that the preparatory phase of education and propaganda would need to be lengthy.

What about the United States? He stated for the record that he did not "believe [in] or advocate the overthrow by force or violence" of the U.S. government, or of any government and form of law. He refrained from categorically disavowing the assassination of public officials, repeating that it depended on the specific situation, but that a mass uprising was generally preferable. He made a distinction between collective movements and individual acts of "terrorism," or "direct action," 99 percent of which he dismissed as unproductive or even retrogressive, though he would not condemn those who acted in the integrity of their conscience.[54]

A related line of questioning pursued Har Dayal's thoughts on U.S. labor militance. Commenting on labor leaders accused of illegally transporting dynamite, he opined that "no person should be heavily punished for the social phenomena in which we are involved," and suggested that the steel trust officials bore culpability for the "horrible conditions" in their mills, so destructive of "the lives and health and manhood of American citizens." As for his views on the state, would he say that he was "at variance with most of the present forms of government in the administration of the judicial and . . . executive branches of government"? He replied: "I am a critic, but I should not say I am entirely at variance. . . . I certainly think that the social organization of what is called government is very liable to be perverted from its proper operation when there is a great difference of economic conditions in a community, because in a community where there is a small class of very rich people, they generally manage to control these institutions." Har Dayal continued that in some countries, the situation could be rectified by the gradual "persuasive abolition" of the institutions in question, but that in others, the only possibility was through "upheavals called revolutions."[55]

His answers regarding his intentions in the United States clarified his dual role and dual audience. One of his tasks was to raise the Indian people's revolutionary consciousness: in this context, he considered himself an active participant in the social/political struggle and "an organizer of a movement." But in the U.S. context, the role he had assigned himself was more as a "thinker and philosopher, if I may be so vain as to use that word, than as an agitator participating in any temporal social movement. I always lecture from the academic and educational standpoint to the white people in this country, because, being a foreigner, I cannot directly influence social movements."[56]

In the end, the case for deportation hinged on proving that Har Dayal had been a confirmed anarchist at the time of entry and had come to the United States with the premeditated intention of violently overthrowing the British government of India. F. C. Isemonger and J. Slattery of the Punjab police were at pains in their official report on the Ghadar movement to determine, based on letters written between 1905 and 1906, that these were long-standing aims that remained unchanged when Har Dayal began his activities in the United States. "Two quotations from these letters," they assured readers, "will make this clear": Har Dayal wrote, "Our object is not to reform the Government but to reform it away, leaving, if necessary, only nominal traces of its existence." And

> The more I think the more I realise that half measures are of no use. . . . We must lay the axe at the root of the tree. The people can never understand the figment of loyalty to the Sovereign and hostility to his Viceroy. This is a European conception, which cannot be assimilated by us. . . . "Constitutional Government," "Colonial Self-Government," "Autonomy," etc., are terms borrowed from the western political phraseology which convey no meaning to our people. Place a clear issue before the people: "Such is your state; this is the cause; remove the cause."[57]

Context is needed to assess such statements, and there is no doubt Har Dayal was always a slippery talker. In this case, his words could be taken either as self-consciously anarchist or simply radically anti-British. He himself professed the latter. This was the defense often used by earlier expatriate revolutionaries, exonerating themselves of the charge of anarchism by assuring their host countries that they had no interest in overthrowing that government, just the colonial regime back home, and so there was no reason to expel them since they posed no threat.

Chandra, for instance, pointed out that "England called American Revolutionists 'Anarchists'" in 1776, and the Indians as republicans and nationalists were no different in 1914; "the yearnings of the oppressed for a measure of political freedom always appear 'anarchistic' to the oppressor." (It should be mentioned that Chandra was on the more conservative end of the Ghadar spectrum in its post–Har Dayal era schism and not popular among those associated with the original Yugantar Ashram collective. For example, in the immigration debates of the 1910–20s, he pushed for extending Caucasian/Aryan status to high-caste Indians seeking U.S. citizenship, rather than opposing the racist policies that barred non-Caucasians, including Indians of low caste.)

Har Dayal insisted that "at the time of my entry into the United States I had not taught much on conclusions of government in general. My two chief interests were Buddhism and its efficiency and the nationalist movement in India. As time passed my interest in Buddhism has waned and the modern labor movement has taken its place, while the nationalist movement in India retains the same hold on my affection."[58]

Chenchiah implied that both accusations were applicable and had to be differentiated. Har Dayal was arrested for preaching anarchism, he said, not for serving the Indian national cause. And although he, Chenchiah, identified himself strictly as a "Nationalist and a Revolutionary," he nevertheless held Har Dayal in the highest regard as "the greatest intellectual exponent of the anarchist philosophy in San Francisco," after giving what Chenchiah considered the best speech at an annual conference of anarchists, socialists, syndicalists, communists, and national revolutionaries held there in 1913.[59]

True to form, Har Dayal was released from his interrogation in time to make it back to the IWW hall for one of his regularly scheduled Radical Lecture Course talks that very day, on "The Problem of Unemployment."[60] But though the government had insisted that Har Dayal was not going to be deported, his lawyer was skeptical, and the client ducked quietly out of the country on his own accord shortly afterward, notwithstanding the five hundred dollar bail paid by the Ghadar office and the eight hundred dollars that the Indian community had raised for his defense. After assuring himself that the San Francisco operations were in capable hands, Har Dayal resurfaced in Switzerland to take up a brief yet prominent role among the Indian revolutionaries in Berlin and Istanbul. His local and international supporters did not remain quiet; from London, Aldred penned, "Stop this Infamy!" in *Herald of Revolt*, in Har Dayal's defense.

Even on the run, Har Dayal's intellectual energy did not flag. Indeed it long outlived his activism. In a letter to Brooks in April 1914, he expanded on an idea for a book he hoped to write "on 'The Time-Spirit,'" in which he would "trace the different tendencies of XIX century civilization making for progress, finishing with the synthesis that I approve of. It will be a kind of survey (from the Anarchistic standpoint) of XIX century history, descriptive and critical, having for its central theme the dissolution of medievalism and the introduction of Anarchism (in its broad sense)."[61]

Incidentally, this plan brings to mind a similar opus envisioned by Aldred. Biographer and associate John Taylor Caldwell reveals some of Aldred's thinking circa 1908, toward an ambitious compendium of social philosophy in the form of a projected series of books and pamphlets. "One was a book containing the biographies of ten radicals, among them such varied characters as Richard Carlisle, Jonathan Swift, Theodore Parker, Robert Owen, Bishop Colenso, and Michael Bakunin. . . . This would be the first of a series of books . . . under the general title of The Library of Synthetical Iconoclasts. . . . The term 'Synthetical' did not refer to the character of the biographical subjects," explained Caldwell, but to Aldred's theory that "every aspect of dissension (iconoclasm) from right to left, whether in religion, politics, art or science, was the forward-urging of the first principle of change, of becoming . . . . This dissenting articulation should be brought together, synthesized, in a general concept."[62]

Another of his intended projects, *Organisation*, was supposed to include sections on Marx, the Communist International, and the International's failure and supplanting by Lassallean social democracy; "the development of Capitalist Imperialism, and the subsequent industrial development of the native races towards the stage of International Working Class Solidarity, the specific examples taken being India and Africa"; the history and theory of "Working Class Industrial Organisation" culminating in Aldred's recently founded Industrial Union of Direct Action; political and educational struggle; bourgeois culture; and sexual relationships as they pertained to the class war. (Aldred, like Har Dayal, believed in free love.) In general, Aldred's intellectual link with what Caldwell terms the "early Victorian radicals" who represented the "liberal-radical tradition" of republicanism prior to the "socialist turn within Secularism" in England also sounds quite similar to Har Dayal's definition of radicalism in prewar San Francisco.[63]

Har Dayal's book was never realized, and within a few years he had abandoned the revolutionary movement. His comrades viewed his shocking political recantation and avowal of British loyalism at the war's end (partially explainable, though not excusable, by the disillusionment evinced in his memoir/exposé *Forty-Four Months in Germany and Turkey*) as a harsh betrayal, tantamount to apostasy.

He ended his days in London, where he continued his studies of science and philosophy, earned a long-delayed PhD at the School of Oriental and African Studies with a dissertation on Buddhism, and opened the Modern Culture Institute for Rationalism, Socialism, and Self-Culture (Physical, Mental, Aesthetic, and Ethical). Its elaborate program and statement of precepts were weirdly reminiscent of a reformed Bakunin Institute. He was still aiming for a utopian holism, which was perhaps his truest and most consistent life's quest; as Lal insightfully observed, his Ghadar work "was just one application" of this.[64] Jack London remarked after Har Dayal's death in

1939 that the "two stars" he followed were the emancipation if India and elaboration of a "synthetic philosophy for the world." Another eulogy acknowledged that the goal of liberating his homeland from colonial rule was a subsidiary albeit urgent component of his ultimate ambition of a "philosophical synthesis," drawing the best elements from both Eastern and Western thought. This in turn would lead to the "moral, spiritual, and intellectual perfection of man ... [in] a world of love, mutual trust, and respect among all people, where colonialism and nationalism would both disappear in a true internationalism of peace and prosperity for man in his beatitude."[65]

What is one to make of Har Dayal? He was a creative thinker and voracious learner. He was trying to create a new map toward total liberation. Furthermore, like Aurobindo Ghose before him and Mohandas Gandhi after, Har Dayal identified himself as a karma yogi, fixated always on the manifestation of principle through dynamic action. The social anarchism of the fin de siècle, when he encountered it, seemed to him to express what he was seeking. His interests and activities in San Francisco aptly reflected the ferment, language, and progressive trends of his day. His complexities also are a reflection of the counterpoint between rationalism and romanticism; he virtually encompassed within himself the whole discourse over time. Har Dayal's ideas illustrated the ease with which revolutionary anticolonialism could shift between opposition to a particular government deemed illegitimate, and the determination to replace that very conception of government with other political, economic, and social forms.

Mukerji

In 1908 or 1909, Mukerji left India for Japan due to a combination of educational and political reasons.[66] After a stint
of technical training, odd jobs, and some revolutionary support work, he made his way to San Francisco in 1910. But in
the scramble for menial work to support himself in Berkeley,
the erudite young scholar suffered unaccustomed daily racism and exploitation. He showed up for one job armed with
"my bundle and one book, [Ralph Waldo] Emerson's *Self-
Reliance*," but was fired in a day when it became clear he had
no clue how to wash dishes. He was finally hired to serve
meals and make beds at a boardinghouse.

Unfortunately, the University of California seemed
to him much less intellectually stimulating than the
University of Calcutta, where there had been

> hot discussions with my fellow students regard-
> ing the state, society, and the future of man. And a
> very large majority believed, with me, that profes-
> sors were not allowed to teach the truth because
> it was dangerous. So whenever we were assigned a
> dangerous topic such as the French Revolution, or
> civil war in England under [Oliver] Cromwell, we
> read up more books on the subject than were pre-
> scribed. We did it for the purpose of contradicting
> the professor and finding out the truth.

Here, it seemed to him, the students just took notes
passively and never questioned anything in depth. Then an

Irish-born U.S. student called Leo who was staying at the boardinghouse where Mukerji worked befriended him, having noticed him in classes. By the way, inquired Leo casually, "Do you know anything about anarchism?" Mukerji replied that he did, and was a believer in Kropotkin's communism. To which his new friend sneered, "That's not anarchism. That's mush." Leo then launched into a diatribe on the "difference between . . . Kropotkin's mush and Tolstoi's mush. And he ended with a tremendous defense of [Pierre-Joseph] Proudhon's Anarchism which was anti-mush." Mukerji commented, "Of course I had heard of these gentlemen, though I had not read them all. Tolstoi I knew by heart, Proudhon only by name." Leo then showed Mukerji the pictures on his wall: Adam Smith, Tolstoy, Bakunin, Kropotkin, Marx, Victor Hugo, and Jesus Christ. Leo was a disenchanted ex-Jesuit-in-training whom socialists had lured to the creed of Charles Darwin and Spencer. But socialism too had disappointed him. "To make a long story short," he said,

> I began to speak from soap boxes for the Socialists
> on different street corners, but as I associated with
> them I began to see that the majority of them had
> perfectly ragged minds. . . . [I]n order to overcome
> the system of the church, the Socialists gave me the
> system of social order, and that seemed even more
> gruesome . . . so I threw over the whole Socialist
> regime and took to individualistic anarchism.

He continued, "I read Tolstoi, Kropotkin and a lot of others. This suited my temperament. It substituted 'no system' for 'system,' liberty for authority, and personality for social gregariousness." But his family was not happy with his apparent aimlessness, and promised him a monthly allowance if he would go to college and study law.

Mukerji was intrigued by Leo's ideas. The two new friends decided to move out of the boardinghouse and share cheaper lodgings. Preempting university classes, they now applied themselves with "feverish" dedication fourteen hours a day to their chosen course of independent study. They liked Walt Whitman, glanced at Shaw, discarded Plato, and were "delighted" with Henry David Thoreau, Proudhon (particularly the suggestion that "property was theft"), and Friedrich Nietzsche (especially the notion that "God was dead"). When Leo flunked out and Mukerji barely scraped by in his exams, they blamed "the capitalist system," which they also identified as the root of Mukerji's lack of shoes, "petty larceny" of an exploitative boss, and presence of factory workers and prostitutes wandering rainy Oakland streets at night. On leaving school, Leo vowed never to work and thereby never to further enrich the capitalist system. Luckily for him his roommate did not take the vow. Mukerji accepted a job at another boardinghouse while supplying Leo with philosophy texts from the university; Leo summarized the chapters for his humble benefactor after Mukerji got off work. Sometimes Mukerji would pass the hat while Leo soapboxed.

One night Leo decided it was time to take Mukerji to see his friend Jerry, the "ideal anarchist." When they sat down to talk, Jerry asked, "What makes you so interested in anarchism?" The starstruck Mukerji answered, "Why, it's the vision of the future."

After chiding him for grandiose phraseology, dead giveaway of bourgeois thinking, Jerry narrated his own background. He, like Leo, had emigrated from Ireland as a child. Exemplifying Leo's aspirations, Jerry had not done a lick of work in twenty-seven years. He attributed this fact to a life-changing experience at Haymarket Square on the day of the famous explosion, catalyzed as it was by a struggle over work conditions. Since that day, Jerry said, "I vowed to myself that I'd never help the capitalist system with the slightest exertion of a single muscle." He lived off charity, simultaneously despising other people for their pity, and himself for taking it. But he embraced the indignity, because for a true anarchist there could be "no pride nor humility, no matter what happens."

Mukerji asked whether Jerry still believed in a better future for humanity if he despised humankind. Jerry answered: "I despise the common herd, but I cannot despise the individual man. Whenever he stoops to pity I think of the common herd, but whenever he flays me with his insolence I think of the individual man." Mukerji was delighted, but Jerry rebuffed him.

First, he did not think Mukerji would be able to face jail and beatings, or handle the hard life of beggary, here criminalized rather than venerated as in India. Second, what did the traveler need anarchism for? "Why don't you go back to India?" challenged Jerry. "Your ancestors found the truths you are seeking thousands of years ago; Buddha was the greatest of all anarchists."

Mukerji asked if Jerry had ever visited his homeland. "No," Jerry admitted, "but one can fathom India. I can feel them, those old Hindus. Once in a while I have read a scrap of their writings, and I have felt then that they were the primordial anarchists. Isn't it one of your ancestors who said, 'This world is not, is not, is not?'" In other words, to Jerry's mind, "those old Hindus" were primordial nihilists, achieving the apotheosis of negation and rejection that he himself somewhat inconsistently aspired to. Jerry was revealing here an idea of liberation that resembled not collective social utopia but instead *moksha*, release from material existence and restraint of any kind.

In a later discussion of Henrik Ibsen, Shakespeare, and Sophocles, Jerry again alluded to the notion that Asian civilization already possessed the secrets to a utopian countersociety without needing to pass through the steps of industrialization and modernization: "But, Mukerji, your ancestors knew all this and never were troubled about it. It is strange that you should come to us to find out what you had at home. It's time for you to go back." Again he hectored, "Why in hell do you want to be an anarchist? I am an anarchist because I am a leader. I am not an anarchist because I am an example."

"What do you lead us into?" Mukerji probed.

"Into a greater sense of social danger," Jerry replied. "I want to lead you from security to bravery." Jerry's and Leo's was an individualist interpretation of anarchism, each rejecting any authority over himself without rejecting authoritarianism in principle. This was an unshackling of ego rather than (a Swadeshi militant's) annihilation of ego, with a whiff of the *Übermensch*'s disgust for the herd. There was another acquaintance present, a socialist (though

Mukerji's individualist anarchist friends were generally quite contemptuous of his ilk), who scoffed, "Bah! Oriental stories. You many convince an Easterner like Mukerji. . . . But I want logic."

Jerry retorted, "Mythology is the logic of the imaginative races, as logic is the mythology of the dull races." After which the socialist "left us, furious." Jerry and the others had cast their friend as the mystical Oriental even as Mukerji pushed them on rationalist modernity.

Mukerji's next discussion with "the boys" addressed the question, "What is the relation of man to society?"

Jerry: "The basis of the relation of man to society is fear."

Leo: "The basis of the relation is ignorance. The more you know, the more unsocial you are."

Mukerji then reflected that in actuality, neither of them had any idea about people's relation to society—or at least, neither had any experience of the delicate negotiations required by the economic imperatives and behavioral restraints of that relation when one was a dark-skinned recent immigrant trying to make ends meet. For example, later that night Mukerji was threatened with violence by the drunken son of his employer ("You damned heathen, I'll smash your head!") and quit the job after his boss dismissed his concerns. Thus, Mukerji recalled, "began the most difficult part of my life."

Mukerji worked a series of odd jobs—boardinghouses during the school year and picking crops during the summer—and still soapboxed with Jerry and Leo, whose harangues invariably concluded with the tagline, "Now my Hindu comrade will pass the hat." They shared beds on a rotating basis, and before long were sharing fleas. Mukerji earned their keep, while the others read, philosophized, and ranted.

At one point, the IWW local allowed them to sleep on the floor of its hall in exchange for four weekly street corner lectures. Mukerji carried the box. But while Leo and Jerry proved brilliant at holding forth on the abolition of church and state, it seemed Jerry could or would not comply with the IWW request that he "insist in his speeches on industrial control by the workers." Rather, Jerry "insisted that even industrial control should not be in the hands of the workers, because that would be a violation of individualism." So the IWW withdrew the offer, and the trio was again on its own.

Yet that was not the end Mukerji's encounter with syndicalism—an idea personified for him by Frank Bonnington. Whereas Jerry epitomized the refusal to engage society in any way, Bonnington was committed to engaging with, contributing to, and transforming it.

Bonnington was the scion of a southern patrician ex-slaveholding family and a graduate of the University of Virginia. But he had rejected that life for vagabondage, walking across the country, sleeping under the stars, and eating out of garbage cans. Bonnington told them, "I had no desire to love humanity. I had no desire to do good; I had no desire even to improve myself. But a sudden vision seized me and compelled me to believe that a higher social order is essential for the growth of the free spirit. I believe that there will be a dissolution of church, state and society in a higher human organism. I believe in freedom so heartily that I am enslaved to my dream of freedom."

He had later gone to Australia, where he "led two syndicalist strikes and put a factory 'on the blink'" before stowing away in a boat leaving Sydney to evade arrest. To Mukerji's question about any "extraordinary experiences in the course of his work," Bonnington answered that he had had his "skull broken in two places once and another time I had to stand watch over a troup of women and children, whose husbands had been arrested. The most terrible part of it all was that the children cried for milk and the women cried for food and I had nothing to give them. The only thing that tided us over was the singing. We sang the 'Marseillaise' so that in the delirium of it we forgot everything about hunger." This sounded more like the constructive goal that Mukerji himself was seeking.

Bonnington now stepped in to help Mukerji as breadwinner, supporting all four of them on the monthly salary of eighty dollars he drew for editing a socialist weekly—lavish compared to Mukerji's twenty-five cents per hour doing inventory at a socialist bookstore, or the monthly ten dollars plus room and board he had earned at his last boardinghouse job. Bonnington even loaned Mukerji money to continue his education and warned him against aspiring to the hobo's life that Jerry so embraced.

"To be a hobo . . . means that you lose your greatest asset—you have no faith in anything, even in your own greatness," said Bonnington. But hadn't Bonnington himself endured it? Mukerji challenged. How? "You put all of your life out of yourself," he answered. "You think and live in a far future when man will be as the Titans. Since you live in the far off, you don't mind the here and the now."

The next leg of Mukerji's political-intellectual journey intersected with the world of Ghadar through contact with Indian fieldworkers, both Sikh and Muslim, and with Hindu nationalist students.

Working in the fields during his Berkeley summer vacation, Mukerji's first impression of these Indians of such a different class and regional background from his own was that they labored so hard for incomparably long hours, yet lived on so little that native-born white workers were "agitating against Hindu immigration on the ground that my countrymen were pulling down the wages and getting all the jobs."

He described the physical ordeal of picking asparagus and celery from predawn to dusk, at ten cents a full box. He also noted the rampant alcoholism and occasionally homicidal jealousy over women induced, he believed, by the harshness of the working and living conditions (rather than by moral contamination of Western decadence, as the religious bodies claimed). Gradually Mukerji learned the tricks of the trade, picking apples and hops: how to pace oneself, slowing down whenever the foreman wasn't nearby, and posting a lookout in the apple trees; how to use "misunderstandings" through details deliberately lost in translation; and how to fudge the number of workers in the record book to more than were actually present on the crew in order to inflate the wage.

He also put his English-language education to use as interpreter for groups of his fellow workers. One humorous scene describes his wry rendition of a Salvation Army delegation's attempts to reach the heathen farm laborers, who were astounded to hear the missionaries explained as those who "represent the Militarism of Nirvana." The workers took up a collection simply to induce this nuisance, "ambassador of the Son of Bibi Miriam," to go away.

Back at the university in fall 1912, Mukerji now found that all the Indian students he encountered there—more than there had ever been—were nationalists. "They wanted to free India. As if a politically free India meant an India traditionally and uniquely herself!" But despite his own family history, he quarreled bitterly with many of these radical students, who "thought that if India had factories and a government as well as an army and navy of her own, she would be one of the civilized countries of the earth."

Here is Mukerji's portrayal of his encounter with the quintessential Indian radical nationalist, a person he said many would still remember in San Francisco, though here unnamed:

> He wanted to cut the throat of every English official just as he wanted to cut the throat of every Indian traitor. He meditated such a gigantic slaughter that he seemed to me like an epic poet of death. He contemplated vast holocausts as magnificent offerings to the god of Patriotism. He devised ingenious plans to blow up garrisons of English soldiers as a disinfectant and a preventive of political hells, and once in a while he would grow lyrical about the joy of belonging to a free people. He imagined very suave massacres, and delicate assassinations.

Mukerji one day challenged this revolutionist, "Look here, why should we supersede British massacres by our own, except that our own may be a little more radical? Theirs are only practical and utilitarian." The answer was that the English massacres were continuous; their own would be economical and a temporary necessity—a little hurt to create a giant benefit.

Mukerji declared himself weary of such "hygienic" and "mathematical" conceptions of violence, for which the nationalist accused him of slave mentality "tainted" by Western influence. He decried the British charge "that rebellion is unholy, and a destructive profanity," when it was the colonists' "soulless railroads piercing through the sacred places throughout India" that had called it forth. Mukerji agreed this far: "It is true that this industrialization of Asia is terrible. . . . It is sucking out the life blood." But he made a crucial distinction between culturalist and economic paths of resistance, correcting his interlocutor: "Your quarrel is not with the British nation, but with Western capitalism."

The nationalist disagreed: If it was their own people running the army and exploiting the natural resources, he insisted, at least the wealth and benefits would be going back into the country. Mukerji, though, vehemently rejected this sort of nationalism as being virtually indistinguishable from imperialism in its greed and crudity. Instead, he suggested, why not "think in terms of two classes, the possessing class and the dispossessed classes, throughout the world? These two marching against each other are to my mind the forces of the conflict. I cannot make out much difference between imperialism and nationalism."

"To this his rejoinder was that I talked like a soulless Socialist." Mukerji denied this category as well. "'I am not a socialist,' I said. 'I hate Socialism. Socialists only want to create a new authority in the place of an old one. What I want is to create a sense of freedom in people's souls. Then all will be well.'" So he sounded like a social anarchist after all, even while ultimately moving away from active involvement toward a more spiritual-philosophical approach.

They parted on poor terms. In a conversation with another newly arrived student, Mukerji expressed the idea that India's salvation lay in its spiritual resources and rich intellectual tradition, and that the way to create beneficial change in the world was to change one's own heart and consciousness. The other replied,

> I agree with you that we have a spiritual wealth which is more important than our material wealth. The material wealth that we have underground in India combined with the cheap labor that lies above the ground is the thing that attracts Western exploitation. Western capitalism finds in those two factors enough inducement to come to India and to tear up the whole system of personal relationship founded on domestic industry, substituting in its place this terrible Western "civilization." Peasants are driven from their fields where they worked eight hours a day to other people's factories where they work twelve hours a day. When a peasant breaks the ground he sings, when he works in a factory he spits and swears.

To which Mukerji reiterated that "if we free ourselves from ourselves first"—that is, transform our own West-imported "gregarious gluttony"—then Indians would "be able to save Asia from the West, I think, almost automatically."

But this interlocutor was not sanguine about the ability of a subject people to influence the spirituality of the world from that position; who would give credit to a conquered race? "The West will never accept the spirituality of the east until by force we free ourselves from any Western domination. In order to give the spirituality of India to the modern barbarism of Europe we must beat them at their own game. We must go through the necessary step of nationalism and nationality. Until we have a victorious India free from all foreign control and domination no proud Western nation will ever care to listen to our spiritual talk." In other words, philosophical and spiritual influence could only come from a place of material strength and sovereignty.

By this point, having critiqued nationalism, imperialism, capitalism, and socialism, Mukerji admitted, "My zest for anarchism was coming to an end. I began to see that there was nothing to do but to find a new philosophy, something that had little concern with the material future of mankind. It was during this period that I began to rediscover India," where at that time "things, both political and otherwise, were fermenting." As Mukerji witnessed the trickle of Indian students grow to a steady stream crossing the ocean in search of "knowledge and wisdom, the more I grew convinced that they were coming through a desert to slake their thirst with the waters of a mirage."

Although Mukerji retreated from active politics to literary and spiritual pursuits, perhaps he became even more of an apolitical, philosophical anarchist in the way that Jerry would have strived for: seeking liberation not through social organization but instead at the level of the individual mind.

The Critical Leftists

The three people featured here, like the two in the last chapter, were creative, flexible, and eclectic freethinkers, rather than systematic followers of a watertight body of philosophy. But they were also pragmatic in their commitment to a concrete goal—the end of colonial rule in India—and consistent in the set of concerns they were trying to address—the existence of injustice, oppression, and exploitation, and the nature of a liberated society. As contemporaries in the 1920s, they were all inspired by revolutionary socialism. Yet each, for his own reasons, was uncontainable within the Communist Party orthodoxy then crystallizing rapidly. So it was perhaps inevitable that in forging an alternate path, each of them encountered aspects of the anarchist tradition. Through these encounters, Acharya, Ranchhoddas Lotvala, and Bhagat Singh sharpened their critiques of a formal left wing that they identified with in spirit, if not always in letter.

Acharya

Among radical nationalist revolutionaries, none made their identification with the international anarchist movement more explicit than Acharya. Born in 1887, this "somewhat remarkable youth" was labeled early on as a "seditious character." By the time he was twenty, he was working on two newspapers in Madras: the Tamil *India* and the English *Bala Bharat*. Over several months he "copied out . . . most of the English version of V. D. Savarkar's book on the Mutiny" of 1857 for serial publication. When the editor was arrested in July 1908, Acharya took the reins.[1]

On the retrospectively ironic date of August 15 the *India* office and press were raided, articles seized, and the paper charged with sedition. To evade further searches Acharya finally moved operations to French Pondicherry, transferred formal ownership to a cousin (who thought him "very enthusiastic and very daring"), and boarded a steamer to Marseilles, where he hoped to apprentice with a process engraver. Finding no prospects in Marseilles, he then wrote to Varahaneri Venkatesa Subramaniam Aiyar in London. Aiyar had been a correspondent for *India*; among his writings were an article on Rousseau's *Social Contract* and a Tamil history of Garibaldi. He was also a part of the radical core at Krishnavarma's India House, where he now invited Acharya to come and live for free. British intelligence first spotted Acharya at a meeting in London in January 1909, after a stop in Paris along with a nameless Bengali (who was in town "to learn the art of making noiseless bombs" from a M. Etienne). Aside from Aiyar,

Acharya's closest associates included Chatto, a prominent figure among the revolutionists in Europe who was himself tagged with the anarchist label despite his later ties to the Russian Communist Party (whereas Indian Communists dismissed him for nationalist deviation).[2]

As part of the Abhinava Bharat inner circle, Acharya was involved with firearms training as well as the publication of the papers *Talwar* and *Bande Mataram*. Copies of these flowed back to Pondicherry for distribution inside British India, along with Krishnavarma's *Indian Sociologist* and the *Gaelic American* from the United States.[3] When Dhingra shot Curzon-Wyllie, Acharya was by Savarkar's side in court to protest the resolution condemning Dhingra to death, and when a barrister called Palmer "boxed [Savarkar] in the eye," Acharya retaliated by hitting Palmer with a stick, and added insult to injury by penning "A Straight Indian Lathi" as a rejoinder to Palmer's letter "A Truly British Blow" in the London *Times*.[4] It was reported around this time that "Savarkar and others were urging" Acharya to follow Dhingra into martyrdom, perhaps by returning to India to carry out another assassination.[5]

He went instead to Paris, but soon after attempted to reach Morocco along with another comrade, Sukh Sagar Dutt (younger brother of Ullaskar Dutt, the original Maniktola Garden bombing instructor). Their intent was to gain militant experience by joining forces with Abdul Karim's Rif rebellion against Spain. But at Gibraltar, customs seized some suspicious items from their luggage: a rifle, a revolver, and three hundred rounds of ammunition. Acharya nevertheless made it to Tangier, only to find that the "good friend" serving as his guide there was actually an agent who was informing on him and handing over his letters. He dodged police spies back to Paris, then went with Aiyar to Amsterdam, then Rotterdam (where the *Talvar* was published) to learn engraving and printing, then onward to Munich and Berlin.[6] He also met Egyptian nationalists in Brussels and Young Turks in Constantinople.

The steamer *Argentina* brought him to New York in July 1912, where Irish republican George Freeman, editor of the *Gaelic American* and longtime friend to Indian revolutionists, received him. Almost immediately, though, the U.S. and Canadian immigration departments began efforts to get this undesirable alien "of a most desperate and dangerous type being prominently connected with the London-Paris group of revolutionary East Indians" out of the country. Just as they would do two years later in the case of Har Dayal, they sent special agent Hopkinson— who had been dogging the steps of Indian radicals in North America for almost as long as Freeman had had their backs—to seek out "any documentary evidence . . . to show that [Acharya] belongs to the revolutionary class, and is closely allied with anarchists."[7]

Acharya managed to reach Berkeley, where he attended Ghadar meetings and attempted to apply for a naturalization certificate. But he left the country of his own accord when the war started and returned to Berlin along with most of his political compatriots abroad. He served in several missions to Egypt and Mesopotamia, cosponsored by the Berlin India Committee and German Foreign Office in its initiatives to weaken the British Empire by promoting mutiny among the South Asian soldiers who formed the bulk of its army in the Middle East.

As German patronage dried up in 1917, Acharya accompanied Chatto to Stockholm, where they set about mastering Swedish as well as equipping a reference library and propaganda center. In spring 1919, the Criminal Investigation Department intercepted a letter from Acharya to Aiyer. "I have been alright these years and working in both continents on either side of the Atlantic up to San Francisco and Baghdad," Acharya wrote. "I trust you have also been well. For the last two years, I . . . have been in Sweden. . . . All our friends are well in France and Germany—and very hopeful and cheerful in spite of the differences . . . . I have seen here our friend [French socialist Jean] Longuet and everyone is interested in us. I hope everything will go on well in a few years if not months, and we will see each other as soon as things are in order here and there."[8]

But Yusuf Ali, the British Foreign Office's designated Indian mouthpiece for loyalist propaganda, dismissed their efforts as not representing the Indian national cause on the grounds that the so-called Indian Committee, he scoffed, really consisted of "just two anarchists." Aside from the customary use of the term to isolate and discredit "seditionists" regardless of their actual political views, the further implication of Ali's slight was that what British rule provided in India was the quintessence of modern governance, otherwise lacking; and thus that the only idiot who could possibly reject such a thing would have to be an anarchist.[9]

Chatto and Acharya published a rebuttal in a Swedish paper in which Chatto—like Chandra—insisted that on the contrary, their Indian Committee was "a revolutionary body, similar to the Irish Sinn Fein, striving for the independence of India."[10] And yet Chatto had blurted in response to an earlier allegation in 1909,

> If it is anarchism to be thoroughly ashamed of being ruled by a handful of vile alien vandals, if it is anarchism to wish to exterminate them with the noble desire of establishing our national freedom upon the basis of popular sovereignty, of justice, of mercy, of righteousness, and of humanity, if it is anarchism to rise for the sanctity of our homes, the integrity of our life, and the honour of our God and our country, and to slay every individual tyrant, whether foreign or native, that continues the enslavement of the great and noble people, if it is anarchism to conspire ceaselessly to take human life with the only object of emancipating our beloved Motherland, then we say, Cursed is the man that is not an anarchist![11]

Of course, god and country are not generally within the vocabulary of Western anarchism, but it's worth noting where the salient sites of oppression and resistance appear in this context.

In 1919, the pair made their way to Moscow. From there Lenin sent Acharya to Kabul as part of a mission to establish contact with the "Provisional Government of India," which had been set up there by a wartime German-, Turkish-, and Ghadar-backed expedition. Following a difference of opinion with the government officers regarding anti-British strategy, Acharya—who favored a more overt alliance with the Bolsheviks—relocated to Tashkent in July of 1920 with his colleague Abdur Rab to cofound a separate party called Inqilab-e-Hind (Indian Revolutionary Association), the precursor to the CPI associated with M. N. Roy.[12]

He attended the second and third congresses of the Third International in Moscow with consultative status. During his two years in Russia, he married an artist called Magda Natchmann. (Long forgotten, apparently, was the woman to whom his parents had married him before he ducked out of the country over a decade prior.) He contributed articles to Russian journals, including a monthly report for the *Foreign Office Review* and *Herald NKID* on revolutionary developments and movements in India. Meanwhile, he maintained contact with tribes along the Indo-Afghan frontier (what is now Pakistan's Khyber-Pakhtunkhwa region) in the continued attempt to move arms across the border. This had always been an important part of the Provisional Government's agenda, as a prerequisite for the cherished dream of sparking an uprising.

By 1921, Acharya was referring to himself as a "confirmed communist." But a factional split pitted Acharya and Chatto against Roy, who wanted sole leadership of the fledgling Indian Left to be organized in a party whose doctrine and direction he alone was to determine. Acharya had always been part of the less orthodox faction, and his true ideals, at least in his colleagues' view, leaned in an antiauthoritarian direction. By the time he left Moscow,

Acharya's differences with Roy had developed into "differences with the Communist International and with the Communist regime in Russia itself. We are not against Communism," he had stated (presumably on behalf of the Indian Revolutionary Association) on December 5, 1920, "and we do not make a distinction between a Communist revolutionary or just a revolutionary. All we object to is forcible conversion to Communism," at least in the form dictated by Roy and the Comintern.[13]

CPI founding member Muzaffar Ahmad mentioned in his memoir that both Acharya and Chatto were "in contact with the Anarcho-communist Party" in France, and that Acharya had insisted on the inclusion of anarcho-syndicalists at the early congresses in Moscow. On growing disenchanted with the way things were developing in the USSR, said Ahmad, Acharya reverted to "his former anarchism, and described himself thereafter as an 'Anarcho-Syndicalist'—though also reportedly 'a member of the Trotskyist Fourth International.'"[14]

The pair returned to Berlin in late 1922 or early 1923, and worked together in the office of the League of Oppressed Nationalities, forerunner to the League against Imperialism (backed by the Communist International). Struggling as usual to remain solvent, Acharya did secretarial, steno, and typing work for the league and the Indian Independence Committee; intelligence reports commented that he was quite good at it. He also undertook the task of sending assorted political texts to the Comintern's mailing list inside India, including anarcho-syndicalist literature on his own initiative.[15]

When Indulal Yajnik met Acharya in Amsterdam in 1930–31, he was attached to the "School of Anarchist-Syndicalism" there.[16] He kept tabs on emerging trade union activity in Madras, and wrote to one of the key figures in the Labour-Kisan Party there in July 1923 concerning the New International Workmen's Association, which unlike the Comintern he described as "anti-political and federal. It is an improvement far ahead of the Third International with which I am at loggerheads after cooperating with hope for a whole year. I know all the personalities there well including Lenin, whom I had met twice. I am fighting them all in every writing and talk and everywhere."[17] He also mentioned a Russian anarcho-syndicalist paper called *Way of the Worker*, which he supplied with items on the Indian labor movement.[18]

Chatto, meanwhile, returned to the USSR in 1931, dedicating himself to a life as a scholar and Soviet citizen until he was shot in a Stalinist purge in 1937. He had found a brief happiness (after a tumultuous, and mutually damaging relationship with Smedley in the early 1920s) with a Russian woman named Lidia Karunovskaya, who headed the Indonesian section of the Institute of Anthropology and Ethnography in Leningrad, where he worked as a linguist.[19]

Meanwhile in 1935, Acharya finally overcame a long-standing ban on his entry into India. He had been trying since 1926, only to be repeatedly denied a passport or threatened with arrest on arrival. Now he scratched out a living as a journalist in Bombay, contributing a series of eight articles for the *Mahratta* called "Reminiscences of a Revolutionary," a series of autobiographical pieces for Lotvala's *Praja Mitra Kesari*, an English weekly in Poona, and yet another series on the activities of Chatto, Cama, and other revolutionaries abroad. He also wrote for the *Bombay Chronicle*, *Free Press Journal*, and *Harijan*. Magda kept painting and even gained some recognition in her new hometown, but must have passed before her husband, for when Acharya died in 1954 he was alone and destitute.[20]

His *Harijan* editor Mashruwalla memorialized him in that paper, writing that

> Acharya was a total believer in the doctrine of philosophical anarchism. He believed in the message of Gandhiji's non-violence and Sarvodaya. This belief he had come to hold as a result of his long and arduous campaigning in foreign lands for the cause of India's freedom. He stood for a free and decentralised social order based on complete liberty, equality and dignity of true human personality.[21]

Long before his death, he had emptied himself of any "sympathy or tolerance" for "the politics of any kind of Party or Government," and was "a convinced anti-Bolshevik."[22] Yet he remained engaged in the perusal of anarchist writings, declaring himself "after all this study," according to Ahmad, to be "a Libertarian Socialist; I do not know what the thing is."[23] Daniel Guérin or Noam Chomsky might have explained to the Marxist-Leninist Ahmad that "the thing" was their very definition of an anarchist.

Lotvala

Even if Acharya introduced the term libertarian socialism to India, as an institution it must be associated with one idiosyncratic (and problematic) figure who was its dedicated patron: Acharya's mentee and correspondent, Lotvala. Yajnik, Lotvala's biographer as well as Krishnavarma's, situates his early years against the backdrop of a vigorously simmering period in the social and political life of the Bombay Presidency, punctuated by outbreaks of plague and famine that catalyzed "agrarian and popular discontent," and swirling with new energies of nationalist activity both through the secular Indian National Congress (INC) and the religious, social reform-oriented Arya Samaj.

Born in 1875, Lotvala was one of twelve children of a successful Bombay flour trader. He took over the family business when his father died in 1894; his mother had died when he was quite young. Soon revealing a keen entrepreneurial talent, he managed to expand the business during the famine of 1899–1900, and made a tidy profit thanks to his stocks of wheat and flour while all the while earning a reputation for integrity. At twenty-five, the budding tycoon then bought up a mill with its adjacent land and buildings. But Yajnik claimed that what redeemed young Lotvala from either decadence or cutthroat profiteering was his education—a fruitful synthesis of spirituality and rationality. He had devoured the writings not only of John Stuart Mill and Spencer but also the teachings of Arya Samaj founder Dayananda Saraswati. Yajnik thought this enabled Lotvala to "integrate the new doctrines of political liberty and social equality with passionate love for the religion and land of [India]," thereby saving him from the dreadful fate of alienated Westernization as "a cynical atheist or social rebel . . . uprooted from the land of his birth and cut away from the mass of the people." Instead, he was able to connect "the modern rational cult of human equality and social reform" with an indigenous intellectual tradition.[24]

But this enthusiastic fellow was not content with theory, said Yajnik; he must have praxis. He blossomed first as a propagandist and lecturer for the Bombay Arya Samaj as well as a generous funder thanks to his business success. Impelled to reach out to the masses, his next step was to branch into journalism, publishing a Gujarati-language weekly to which he also contributed "a series of articles on the vexed social questions of the day." As he moved further away from the spiritual toward the material aspects of "the grim realities of human suffering and social injustice," he joined the struggle against untouchability, capping his efforts at the abolition of the caste system with a series of "cosmopolitan dinner[s] . . . intended to deal a practical death-blow to the institution" by uniting members of the intelligentsia, social luminaries, reformers of varied ages and genders, and "notables of the depressed (untouchable) classes" all at one table. The enterprise generated massive public hostility, however, and in the end broke down over irreconcilable differences on the issue of menus: veg versus nonveg.[25]

Soon afterward, seeing the need for "a daily paper which could serve as an effective vehicle of modern social and liberal ideas," Lotvala rescued a struggling Gujarati daily, *Akhbar i Soudagar* (Business News), which he renamed

Hindustan. He began to recruit writers, including a young Fabian socialist lawyer named Narshinhadas Vibhakar. Taking Vibhakar's advice, Lotvala visited London in 1913, where "he began to devour [the Fabian Society's literature] with a new born zeal" and "cultivate personal relations" with leading Fabians. He returned home fortified with a fresh interpretation of his old concerns: now he had the language to articulate that "the grinding poverty of the vast masses, the root cause of their hunger, malnutrition, bad housing and high death-rate . . . were . . . the direct result of this exploitation of labour by those who had monopolised land, factories and banks—all the instruments of production, distribution and exchange." This could not be solved through any "crumbs of charity, private or Governmental." The only solution was expropriating the means of production, and "vesting these in Government or local authorities." He now began to interpret caste through the lens of class, not to mention the social position of women, on whose freedom the "innumerable restrictions" could be "easily traced to the latter day growth of the joint family system which enshrined the economic and physical mastery of man."[26]

Hindustan's circulation continued to expand throughout the war years. Although the paper initially endorsed Gandhi on his return from South Africa, it soon turned to condemn his "reactionary social ideas," particularly his "stale views in favour of idolatry and caste." Instead, Lotvala anointed Vithalbhai Patel for his demonstrated commitment to fighting untouchability, audacity in spurning all manner of orthodoxies, and "irreverence toward all authority." The two became close friends and allies. At Patel's request, Lotvala traveled again to London on a mission to build popular support for the INC in England, attempting to counteract ignorance and prejudice by appealing directly to the people rather than to the government.[27]

When he returned in late 1919, he and Patel were disgusted by new turns in the national movement. They disagreed with the call to boycott all law courts and legislative bodies, suggesting that these very courts could be used "to harass the Government and defend the rights of the people," though they had no objection to the boycott of taxes. And they deplored Gandhi's "fatuous" obsession with the spinning wheel, which they feared would "distract the people from their rightful path of political agitation," and that for Lotvala, symbolized the worst of Gandhi's "irrational, superstitious and suicidal traits."[28] The pair particularly opposed his support for the Khilafat movement, which they viewed as theocratic folly.

But was this the antireligious sentiment of a rationalist or the anti-Muslim sentiment of a Hindu? Although Yajnik's account is a bit inconsistent on this point, the distinction is a significant one, with troubling implications. Lotvala had earlier identified progress, reform, and rationalism with the Arya Samaj program—that is, as the purified heart of true Hindu thought—only to clothe them in a socialist reading later. Given the idiosyncrasies and inconsistencies of his own mode of thought—which Yajnik sometimes chalks up to Lotvala's anarchistic freethinking, sans content—no conclusions can be drawn from this that anarchism had any inherent link to later Hindu Right politics.

However, the pattern has yet again to be acknowledged and confronted wherever a duality of possible paths occurs.

In February 1922, after the collapse of the Noncooperation/Khilafat movement wave, Lotvala penned an indictment of the Gandhian program. His paper lost circulation thereafter through its championing of unpopular ideas, but in the end Lotvala preferred loss of income to ideological compromise. Meanwhile, he had acquired a new enthusiasm: the Russian Revolution. He now pored over the full works of Marx, Lenin, Reed, and Roy, and built up a formidable collection of leftist literature in the Nityanand Library, including books on socialism and socialist newspapers from abroad. Here he welcomed all workers, students, and other "young enthusiasts who flocked every day" for serious study of "discourses on all shades of Marxism."[29] Forming the Lotvala Trust for advancing socialism in India, he also turned his attention to the plight of the proletariat.

Yajnik recalled the stimulating atmosphere of the *Hindustan*'s editorial offices in the 1920s and 1930s: the egalitarian Lotvala joined journalists, college students, politicians, and workers with the Labour and Kisan parties for lively arguments over chai on matters of "various shades of reform and communism, Stalinism and Trotskyism, Gandhism and anti-Imperialism and all other vexed questions of the day." The *Hindustan*'s other major concern was advocating for workers' rights in the Bombay textile mills, publicizing a series of massive strikes in the 1920s. The paper covered meetings, demonstrations, and world affairs, putting forth a consistently rationalist, progressive line on social issues, trumpeting the scientific and bemoaning the superstitious or traditional approach to political mobilization. The paper approved the CPI role in the independence struggle, championing its constituency of workers, peasants, and "the underdog" even while often criticizing the party and its actions.[30]

In 1922, Lotvala was responsible for the first-ever publication of the *Communist Manifesto* in India.[31] In that same year, a section of the English and Marathi printing apparatus was set aside as the Labour Press, on which Shripat Amrit Dange put out one of the first Marxist weeklies in India, the *Socialist*.[32]

The Labour Press also published a rather eclectic Socialist Series ranging from Kropotkin's "An Appeal to the Young" to Karl Kautsky's "Working Class," to Paul Lafargue's "Religion of Politics" and Delisle Burns's "Politics of Oil." Through his Liberty Publications, Lotvala issued pamphlets on scientific socialism to augment "the meagre sources of knowledge and scientific socialism available to the English-educated intellectuals of those days."[33] Lotvala supported Dange's study and writing until 1929, when Dange was tried and jailed in the Meerut conspiracy case, which by rounding up India's most prominent leftist activists put the whole movement back for several years.

By the early 1930s, Lotvala had evolved into a Trotskyist. During his annual sojourns to London, he lent his aid to this faction while shunning previous associates; Stalinism, he had decided, was a betrayal of Marxism and socialism, and a danger to world revolution. He staunchly opposed the policies of Stalin's regime, denouncing as "worthless propaganda" all the "literature emanating from

Russia and orthodox communist parties."[34] His disenchantment with the Soviet dream—along with his perennial
anti-Gandhism—facilitated a new friendship with and
sponsorship of Subhash Chandra Bose, who he met in
Europe in 1932 around the time of Patel's death.[35]

It also led to his formation of the Indian Institute of
Sociology. Increasingly distancing himself from "militant,
economic and political movements of the day," he shifted
focus once again to the consolidation of a "comprehensive
body" for facilitating discussion and doing research on "all
progressive, economic, social and sociological studies and
activities" that might light the way toward "a new order of
society in which economic equality would be harmonised
with individual freedom" of thought and action. He was
against "all totalitarian systems, whether fascist or communist," in which equality could be secured only by sacrificing
freedom.[36] Lotvala intended the institute to join together
all the scattered discourses he felt were better addressed in
conjunction with each other, such as "eugenics, poverty and
individual freedom."[37]

It was around this time that he met Acharya, in
Germany, circa 1932–33. Lotvala was "profoundly impressed" by what the veteran revolutionary had to report
about his Soviet experience, confirming his own anti-
Stalinist inclinations. After Acharya returned to India
in 1935, the two spoke together regularly about "the
anarchist and syndicalist theories in which he was deeply
interested." Under Acharya's influence, "the economic theories of philosophical anarchism wormed their
way gradually into [Lotvala's] mind. Individual liberty,

economic and political, was now rooted in his mind as the alfa [*sic*] and omega of all human efforts." His new mentor also seems to have convinced him "that central-ised economic and political power would inevitably tend to totalitarian autocracy and oppression whether fas-cist or communist." Instead of the "centralised power . . . generally visualised as the high objective, by Socialists and Communists," he now began to favor the promotion of small industries and workers' cooperative societies as "the most democratic bodies of the age and dreamt of the cooperative commonwealth as the best economic organ-isation [to] give plenty to the toilers while according the fullest individual liberty to them."[38] But he never ceased "ridiculing" the Gandhian hand-loom production model. Furthermore, Yajnik tells us, in what sounds like a con-tradiction of what he has just endorsed, "Lotvala could not however stomach the doctrine of communist social order implicit in the anarchist theory. The cooperative commonwealth and the workers' syndicates were alright as economic bodies. But how could they take the place of the modern State?"[39] After all, without a state, how could they fight off British rule in a war-torn world?

By the 1940s, Lotvala had experienced another dra-matic conversion; Yajnik was "dumb-founded" to find his old friend had "not only [given] his support to Gandhi's political fight but moreover waxed eloquent over his prefer-ence for the rural over the urban life, for the small over the big industries, and for all-round decentralisation . . . over the present system of centralisation in all walks of life."[40] What had happened?

After the upheavals of the Quit India movement and Bose's tragic defeat, Lotvala developed "even closer relations with Acharya," from whom Lotvala "imbibed [even] more of the anarchist gospel" through the recommended reading of Bakunin, Kropotkin, Rocker, and Proudhon (his particular favorite). His "conversion to the creed of philosophical anarchism" as he understood it, after a magpie path, was nearly complete.[41]

In 1945, the appointed secretaries of the Institute of Indian Sociology, K. N. Phadke and Shanta Bhalerao, resigned from their long-standing arrangement with the Lotvala Trust. Though they had been producing articles on labor and women's rights to supplement the *Hindustan*, and holding discussion meetings on current topics, they could not support the new anarchist trend. Lotvala appointed Acharya and two others as the institute's new Managing Committee, tasked with redrafting its constitution under the new name of the Libertarian Socialist Institute to reflect the "socialist opinions" of its members. On August 7, 1947, a week before India proclaimed its own independence, they announced the institute's mission statement: to promote interest, gather and disseminate information about its way of thinking, run a library and eponymous journal, generally develop the discourse around libertarian socialism, and "facilitate the study of natural and social sciences," which it linked to human happiness.[42]

> Historically, governments are found to rest on force, maintain injustice, curtail freedom, cause

poverty and breed wars. Moral character of man is the product of his environment. . . . The most considerable environmental influence is "government" in the sense of all the social and political forces to which the individual is subjected. These forces are nearly all evil, the worst being the vast inequality of property, giving rise to the insolence and usurpation of the rich, and the toil, penury and servility of the poor. The causal connection between political power and economic privilege, [which also constrained] freedom of the mind is a major evil.[43]

The writer elaborates on the minimization of government—even if pragmatically speaking, its total elimination were not possible—but anticipates the ideal of a stateless, classless society to be "worked for here and now," by guiding an association "for the sake of mutual assistance and not so much . . . for the struggle of existence."[44]

The way to "regain paradise" would be through the use of reason, improvement of education systems, and interpretation of natural law. Furthermore, "such rationality leads one inevitably away from the narrowness of patriotism to cosmopolitanism. . . . A wise man will be ready to exert himself in the defence of liberty wherever it exists . . . but his attachment will be to the cause and not to his country as such. . . . Always he returns to freedom."[45]

Is it Acharya's hand we detect in the attached statement? This certainly sounds—though here unattributed—like the stance of a seasoned veteran of the revolutionary movement abroad, plausibly reflective of Acharya's experiences and leanings. Lotvala's personal interpretation sounds slightly different, however.

In his own version of what the institute was selling, the "watchwords" were to be "Free Land, Free Money, Free Industry and Free Trade," meaning the abolition of individual land ownership and the removal of cash flow from the control of banks. Lotvala retained some use for the state, which he felt should "limit its activities to defence of the people from foreign enemies and from anti-social forces within the country," while in all other ways—but particularly the economic—leaving the "government of society to be managed by the people themselves without any let or hindrance."[46] This will ring largely familiar to the U.S. ear; in fact, it sounds a bit as though libertarianism outweighed socialism in the foundation of Lotvala's Libertarian Socialist Institute. Lotvala had his origins in the system of free enterprise, with his mill "[laying] the solid foundations of his worldly fortunes which ensured his social and economic freedom and which secured him the leisure and the latitude to think and act untrammelled in all walks of life," and making possible his journalistic endeavors and financial contributions. Indeed, Yajnik's description of his subject's mental composition makes him sound quite the paragon of a Weberian Protestant ethic—wedding his "innate asceticism" and thrift to an aversion to "inherited superstitio[n] . . . stimulat[ing] his active mind to think more freely and fully on the vexed problems of religion, morality and social life."[47]

Does this imply that unrestricted individual autonomy of thought and action, and a reputation for pragmatism, freethinking, and an aversion to dogma such as Lotvala's, is a luxury reserved for the industrious and prosperous? If so, perhaps it is not surprising that in later years, the notion of libertarian thought in India seems to have become restricted to individualist consumer aspiration and free market capitalism, posited as the natural and only antithesis to a crushingly restrictive state apparatus. Lotvala's intellectual trajectory seems superficial, fickle, and self-serving, as if he seizes on the notion of "free thought" as an excuse for inconsistency. If he had worked fully through the logic of libertarian socialism, perhaps he might have seen fit to scrap both the state and free market in favor of a decentralized federation of small-scale free enterprise and collectives of producers, consumers, and service providers.

Bhagat Singh

One revolutionary who might have been capable of persuasively elaborating such a synthesis died too soon to do so. Bhagat Singh was perhaps the greatest of the anarchistic thinkers of the independence struggle era. Atheist, socialist, republican, and militant, he read voraciously from Kropotkin to Lenin, hung a portrait of Bakunin on the hall of the Naujavan Bharat Sabha headquarters in Lahore, and wrote a series of articles on anarchism for the *Kirti*, a Punjabi monthly founded by returned Ghadar revolutionaries in the mid-1920s.

Marxist-Leninists proudly claim that he saw the light shortly before his execution at the age of twenty-three, giving a clear indication that had he lived, he would have embraced the proper orthodoxy; it is therefore safe to celebrate him as one of the fold, rehabilitated and approved. Although the British imperialists had labeled Singh and his comrades as "anarchists" or "terrorists" in order to "defame them in the eyes of the Indian people," Communist contemporary Sohan Singh Josh insisted that they were "not terrorists or anarchists as those terms were known in Europe," although they "accepted some of the political views" associated with that denomination.[48] On the contrary, he explained in their defense, they were nationalist revolutionaries, "the most self-sacrificing, most honest and selflessly dedicated to the cause of liberating India. They hated exploitation of the working class and the Indian people by the bloodsucking British imperialists and their allies, and were willing to make any sacrifice for the upliftment of the working class."[49]

This characterization was true, whatever name it was given. It is also true that Singh spent his time on death row engaged in a serious study of Marxist texts. Had he lived, he likely would have incorporated the new insights of his reading of Marx, Friedrich Engels, and Lenin into his own ever-evolving, flexible, innovative synthesis, as he had been doing for years with everything else he read; but based on his available writings, it is hard to imagine him limiting or reducing his thinking to them, let alone to the mandates of some party claiming to speak in their name.

Every detail of Singh's short life and meteoric political career is familiar through several popular films and numerous biographical accounts ranging from painstaking scholarship to hagiographic excess.[50] His writings have been collected and commented on in multiple editions.[51]

Singh was born in 1907, to a political family—both his father and uncle were committed radicals, with tight Ghadar movement links. He idolized the revolutionaries who frequented their home, and resolved early on to emulate them. Eagerly he joined in the first great wave of mobilizations of the mature freedom movement, the Noncooperation movement kicked off by Gandhi in 1920 in coalition with the Khilafat movement.

But Gandhi called a halt on the growing resistance when protesters burned a police station in a small town in northern India, resulting in the death of twenty-three officers. For Gandhi, a movement marred by violence was not worth continuing, even though as rank-and-file activists well know, then and now, it is the police who most often make the first move when a protest "turns violent." In this case, a few people had acted in retaliation for police firing on a demonstration, killing three and wounding others. Gandhi's willful postponement (as Singh and many young noncooperators saw it) of independence in 1922 prodded protesters in more militant directions. Those dissatisfied with the meekness of Congress, yet bound by political principle to reject religiously framed mobilization, began forming "small, compact groups" for "revolutionary action." Singh was a member of one such group, along with some friends he met while studying history and politics at the National College in Lahore. (Bhai Parmanand was one of his mentors there, as he had earlier been Har Dayal's.)

Fleeing school in 1924 to escape the confinement of an unwanted arranged marriage, he joined a radical circle in Kanpur around journalist and activist Ganesh Shanker

Vidyarthi, and through this milieu, began his connection
to the Hindustan Republican Association. He traveled
around northern India forging links among radical groups,
leafletting at *melas* and fairs, and presenting educational
magic lantern shows.

Singh returned to Lahore in 1926, just as some of the
returned veterans of the Ghadar movement were building a
new formation known as the Kirti group, a worker-peasant
organization that was in effect a rogue Communist Party.
The party's founders came from the same faction as Acharya
and Chatto, and maintained their autonomy from CPI di-
rectives. Beyond the factional rivalry with Roy that dated
from the international meetings in Moscow in the early
1920s, they differed also in temperament and approach:
"Kirti communism" tended to be more agrarian and rooted
in actual militant experience, as opposed to the more urban
intellectual profile of the CPI. The Kirti group also harbored
a tendency in the eyes of the latter toward romanticism and
individual adventurism (in a word, "infantile").

Kirti began publication in 1926, edited by Sohan
Singh Josh. Bhagat Singh wrote for the journal under the
nom de plume of Vidrohi ("rebel") in 1927–28 on a variety
of topics related to the history of the revolutionary movement in India, the importance of revolutionary methods,
and why youth should prefer the movement to Congress
and mainstream leadership.[52]

Between May and September 1928, he also produced a
serialized essay for *Kirti* on the history of anarchism, commenting, "The people are scared of the word anarchism
. . . [which] has been abused so much that even in India

revolutionaries have been called anarchist to make them unpopular." He pointed out that if anarchism was defined as the absence of any form of government, there were also Indian philosophical equivalents to the concept: "I think in India the idea of universal brotherhood, the Sanskrit sentence vasudev kutumbakam etc., have the same meaning." Singh offered a brief introduction to the Western tradition: "The first man to explicitly propagate the theory of Anarchism was Proudhon and that is why he is called the founder of Anarchism. After him a Russian, Bakunin worked hard to spread the doctrine. He was followed by Prince Kropotkin etc." He then explained his attraction to the philosophy: "The ultimate goal of Anarchism is complete independence, according to which no one will be obsessed with God or religion, nor will anybody be crazy for money or otherworldly desires. There will be no chains on his body or control by the state. This means that they want to eliminate: the Church, God and Religion; the state; private property."[53] His essay culminated in a reference to Auguste Vaillant's bomb attack on the French Chamber of Deputies on December 9, 1893; just before Vaillant was executed for this act, he proclaimed, "Death to the bourgeoisie! Long live anarchy!"—the same words that Singh would use a few years later after his own act in the Legislative Assembly.

Singh also served briefly as the editor of *Kirti*'s Urdu edition, but went underground after three months.[54] The two editorial styles and distinct political leanings of Singh and Josh reveal two strands coexisting within the movement. Singh's faction met at a house in Lahore, which Josh described as "well decorated and neatly kept with pictures of Kropotkin and Bakunin hanging on the walls." In Josh's opinion, this group, with its insistence on immediate action instigated by small groups or individuals, lacked the patience needed for the long maturation of revolutionary conditions through mass organizing. "Bhagat Singh wanted to do something very quick, through the use of bombs and pistols, in order to awaken the slumbering youth and students who had forgotten their duty toward their motherland, something spectacular that would make them sit up and do some thinking about the soul-crushing enslavement of India and come forward to make sacrifices for the cause of freedom."[55]

Ajoy Ghosh (Bhagat Singh's comrade and coaccused, later prominent in the CPI) said that for them at the time,

> As for the most important question, however— . . . [of how] the fight for freedom and socialism was to be waged—armed action by individuals and groups was to remain our immediate task. Nothing else, we held, could smash constitutionalist illusions, nothing else could free the country from the grip in which fear held it. When the stagnant calm was broken by a series of hammerblows delivered by us, at selected points and on suitable occasions, against the most hated officials of the government and a mass movement unleashed, we would link ourselves with that movement, act as its armed detachment and give it a socialist direction.[56]

This insurrectionary tactical logic was that "one deed brings forth another, opponents join the mutiny, the government splits into factions, oppression intensifies the conflict, [and] revolution breaks out."[57]

Of his own thinking at this time, with the hindsight of his later Marxist-Leninist orthodoxy, Josh admitted that back then even he "did not know much of Marxist theory. I knew only what I had read and learnt from [Charles T. Sprading's book] *Liberty and the Great Libertarians*, which also contained some excerpts from the writings of Marx, Engels and Lenin. Hence, whatever I knew was eclectic, anarchistic and communistic all mixed together and unsystematic." (Sprading's anthology also contained writings from Thomas Paine, Thomas Jefferson, William Godwin, Mill, Emerson, Thoreau, Tolstoy, Kropotkin, Max Stirner, Josiah Warren, Benjamin Tucker, Lysander Spooner, George Bernard Shaw, Oscar Wilde, and Ferrer.) Since the only person he felt could have guided him—Santokh Singh, the California-returned Ghadar leader who had shepherded the organization to its postwar Marxist reincarnation—was extremely ill and not to be disturbed on strict doctor's orders, Josh said he had to fend for his own ideological education. Given the official prohibition on importing Marxist literature into India, he assessed his own youthful writings as "progressive and leftist no doubt, but, strictly speaking, not Marxist."[58]

Josh ruefully criticized his own early articles in retrospect as "betray[ing] individualism," revealing that he had still been "very far from . . . knowledgeable in the theory and practice of Marxism, of the Marxist principles of

organisation."[59] Yet these were the same writings for which
Santokh Singh had expressed approval before his death,
suggesting that although Josh made no small contribution
to Ghadar-Kirti's Marxist-Leninist reorientation, perhaps
it was Bhagat Singh's less orthodox philosophical synthesis
that had more continuity with Ghadar's earlier manifestation. In any case, what he described sounds very much like
the mélange of ideological ingredients that had informed
Ghadarite writings prior to the war, as he himself would
not have denied; like Bhagat Singh, he was then "under the
spell of the Ghadar Party ideology and [Ghadar martyr]
Kartar Singh Sarabha was the common hero to both of us."
While Josh might have considered this a sign of political
immaturity, it could also be interpreted as an illustration
of a consistent alternative sustained over a long period.
To Josh's dismay, even after he himself had abandoned it,
"some Kirti poets . . . remain[ed] anarchist."[60]

Singh had played a founding role in a Lahore-based
youth group, the Naujawan Bharat Sabha, whose main goal
was the establishment of an independent peasants' and
workers' republic in India. In 1928, at historic meetings in
Amritsar and Delhi, the Sabha joined forces with the Kirti
group as well as the United Provinces–based Hindustan
Republican Association (established in 1924), which
simultaneously renamed itself the Hindustan Socialist
Republican Association (HSRA). The boundaries between
the three now more or less dissolved. Sixty people attended
the first meeting, including "rural and urban middle-class
youth" along with "Singh's group of individual activists,"
from which they adapted the Sabha's name.[61] At the same

time, they made a move toward internal democratization by introducing elections and collective leadership, and seeking consensus for decisions.[62] These modifications in form and outlook reflected the conclusion—for which Singh was probably the most articulate spokesperson—"that it is not enough to simply 'free mother India from the chains of foreign slavery,' it was important to understand, and fight, the larger system that produces slavery in the first place."[63]

Singh took charge of ideological work while Chandrashekhar Azad was elected commander in chief of militant activities. Designed for political education and activist recruitment, the revamped group would also provide a gateway through which promising members might join the more clandestine inner circle. While not calling immediately for armed resistance, Josh said, "We ... despised everything that created hurdles in the way of achieving freedom," including "communalism, liberalism, Gandhian non-violence, etc. Our first priority was freedom of the country, everything else was subordinate. 'Freedom by all possible means' was our motto."[64] The HSRA located its central office in Delhi, but set up an explosives workshop in Agra, for training in the manufacture and proper use of bombs and firearms, after which the association would disperse to reproduce operations elsewhere.[65] (Kanungo's famous manual lived on.)

The Sabha launched a tract society to put out political pamphlets. One of its first pieces "urged the youth of the country to follow the example set by the young men of Ireland, Turkey, Japan and China in their struggle for independence," and encouraged them to study Communist movements as well as "doctrines of freedom and equality, democracy and self-determination, which alone could bring self-government and economic freedom."[66] The series also included a pamphlet by Har Dayal emphasizing the importance of the peasants.

Propaganda secretary Bhagwati Charan Vohra stated in the Sabha's new manifesto that "without going into details we can safely assert that to achieve our object thousands of our most brilliant young men, like the Russian youth, will have to pass their precious lives in villages and make the people understand what the Indian revolution would really mean. . . . A revolutionary does not necessarily mean a man of bombs and revolvers." Vohra's manifesto also urged its readers to look for worthy models, demanding, "Do you not know the wonders worked by the Turks? Do you not daily read what the young Chinese are doing? Was it not the young Russians who sacrificed their lives for Russia's emancipation?" rather than eschewing such risks for elite privilege. He finished, "The future programme of preparing the country will begin with the motto 'Revolution by the masses and for the masses.' In other words Swaraj for the 98%."[67]

In December 1928, the HSRA carried out one such dramatic action. The plan was to assassinate police superintendent J. A. Scott to avenge the death of venerated nationalist leader Lajpat Rai, who had died as the result of a beating from police lathis at a demonstration against the Simon Commission. But they killed the wrong man, when assistant superintendent J. P. Saunders walked into the trap set for his superior officer. At least it was a step, commented

Singh to Josh, at whose house he had sought refuge when escaping the crime scene—maybe not the right officer, but a British officer nonetheless. While this sounds callous, his point was that the true target was not the man but the system. Accordingly, the next day a red leaflet was posted, announcing that the HSRA had avenged Rai's murder:

> Today the world has seen that the Indian people are ever watchful of the interests of their country and no cost is too great for them to defend its honour. ... We regret to have had to kill a person but he was part and parcel of that inhuman and unjust order which has to be destroyed. In him, an agent of British rule has been done away with. Shedding of human blood grieves us but blood shed at the altar of revolution is unavoidable.[68]

The next major action was planned for April 8, 1929, to take place in the central Legislative Assembly in Delhi, where discussion was scheduled on the Public Safety and Trades Disputes Bills. These were seen as direct attacks on anticolonial dissent and labor organizing, respectively. A majority in the House rejected the two bills, but the viceroy had determined to go over its head and announce the enactment of the bills in this assembly session.

When the president of the assembly rose to announce the ruling, Singh and Batukeshwar Dutt threw two bombs down from their vantage point in the public gallery. Amid the smoke and fumes filling the hall, the two bombers then scattered a flurry of leaflets and shouts of "Inqilab

Zindabad!" (Hindi/Urdu for "viva la revolución"), "Down with British Imperialism!" and "Workers of the World, Unite!" Rather than trying to escape, they submitted willingly to arrest; the plan all along had been to use the subsequent trial "as a forum from which to proclaim their programme to the nation and rouse it to action."[69]

During the trial, the defendants freely acknowledged throwing the bombs, but insisted that their intentions could be amply shown by the results: no one was injured beyond "slight abrasions in less than half a dozen cases. . . . Loaded with an effective charge of potassium chlorate and sensitive picrate, the bombs would have smashed the barriers and laid many low within some yards of the explosion. Again, had they been loaded with some other high explosive with a charge of destructive pellets or darts, they would have sufficed to wipe out a majority of the members of the Legislative Assembly."[70] The level of detail in the statement seems calculated to demonstrate that they could have constructed a maximally lethal bomb had they so chosen, but did not, just as they had aimed their throws carefully behind the president's bench to avoid human targets. So while echoing the philosophy of propaganda of the deed, they had gone well beyond the fetishization of the blast evident in Har Dayal's 1912 pamphlet. The often-quoted leaflet distributed in the assembly along with the bombs proclaimed, "It takes a loud voice to make the deaf hear. With these immortal words uttered on a similar occasion by Vaillant, a French anarchist martyr, do we strongly justify this action of ours."[71]

Indeed movement participant Shiv Varma claimed that of the HSRA group at Lahore, "Bhagat Singh and

Sukhdev in particular" were still more under the influence of Bakunin than of Marx. In addition to Bakunin's tactical thinking, Singh had also been influenced by his ideas on religion in *God and the State*, which were among the ingredients of Singh's famous essay "Why I Am an Atheist."

Somewhat predictably, much of the HSRA personnel was rounded up and incriminating materials seized in the ensuing crackdown, including bomb cases, chemicals, explosives formulas, small arms manuals, a live bomb, a pistol, and most combustible of all, the open letters written in the HSRA's name.

One of these letters was pasted on Lahori Gate on April 15, 1929. Under the heading "Loud voice to make the deaf hear," it threatened to take out more police officers than just Saunders if illegal police actions continued. Another letter was sent to the police superintendent in Delhi on April 21:

> God Soviet guide our way [*sic*]. You arrested our brethren but we repeat, you can kill men, not ideas. Our movement is not backed by a few. We are many. . . . A general meeting of our Association is going to take place at Delhi . . . where we are going to chalk out a plan to blow up all Government places and offices. Therefore, beware. If the Government is proud, let it accept the challenge. Beware, beware.[72]

Is this the work of the HSRA, or of an agent provocateur or copycat? Is there any way to know? The language

sounds far cruder than that seen in the usual HSRA documents, whose writers were quite politically sophisticated.
Movement chronicler Gurdev Singh Deol notes that the
writer(s) of "many letters of that type . . . received both by
the Government officials and prominent members of the
public" were never traced.[73]

During his final two years in jail, from April 1929 until he was hanged on March 23, 1931, Singh did not await
death quietly. In addition to continuing his activism within
the walls and honing the messaging to be spread from the
trial's public platform, he was busy reading, writing, and
making preparations for four intended manuscripts: on the
personal side, an autobiography and a soliloquy titled "At
The Door of Death," plus a more general "History of the
Revolutionary Movement in India" and an essay called "The
Idea of Socialism." It is unknown how far he got in making
notes toward these projects. A friend destroyed many documents in 1938 to prevent these works from falling into the
hands of police, although other writings were smuggled out
and published both before and after Singh's death.

His *Jail Notebook*, a collection of quotes and nota-
tions, offers a window into his preoccupations and thought
processes. He was in a sense a brilliant autodidact, indepen-
dently pursuing many of the same concerns that one would
expect to find within any zone where iterations of libertarian socialism and antiauthoritarian Marxism converge. One
request he made in July 1930 for library books for his reading list survives in a letter to his old friend Jaidev Gupta.[74]
It included *Militarism* by Karl Liebknecht, *Why Men Fight*
by Bertrand Russell, *Soviets at Work, Collapse of the Second*

International, Left-wing Communism, Kropotkin's *Mutual Aid* and *Fields, Factories, and Workshops,* Marx's *Civil War in France, Land Revolution in Russia,* Nikolay Ivanovich Bukharin's *Historical Materialism,* and—for fun—the 1920 novel *The Spy* by Upton Sinclair.[75]

The interconnected themes in the notebook include theories of law along with its nature and purpose, the idea of natural rights, and the role of force; theories of government and the state; and notes toward a history of the political philosophy of the state and its institutional forms from Plato, Socrates, and Aristotle, to Thomas Aquinas, Benedict de Spinoza, Hugh Grotius, John Milton, John Locke, Thomas Hobbes, and Rousseau—specifically his *Emile* and the *Social Contract.* It's clear that Singh was extremely critical of all state forms that had existed so far; it's possible he would have put the Communist workers' state into an exceptional category, yet these notes may also be taken to contain a warning to the workers' society not to fall into the traps of previous powerholders.

He indicated justifications of revolutionary tactics, insurrection, and extralegality, combined with a developing analysis of organization, and an increasing appreciation for the pragmatic benefits of a disciplined mass party ("as opposed to sudden and unorganised or spontaneous change or breakdown") and seizing political power in order to bring about economic liberation.[76] In addition to Marx, Lenin, and Engels, he was reading Trotsky, Morris Hillquit, Eduard Bernstein, and Kautsky.

He also pursued these thoughts in the posthumously published statement "To Young Political Workers," plainly a Marxist-Leninist influenced document. Singh stated unequivocally that workers' revolutionary aim must be to achieve power, snatching "the state, the government machinery" away from its use as "a weapon in the hands of the ruling class to further and safeguard its interest," and toward "utilis[ing] it for the consummation of our ideal, i.e., the social reconstruction on new, i.e., Marxist, basis." What forms would the new dispensation take? He posed some sharp questions without venturing to give definitive answers, though he did caution against institutions of top-down, centralized power. In calling for a dedicated cadre of professional party workers, Singh urged them to "crush your individuality first" in the total dedication to the cause. The question is how this hard line fits within the context of all his other writings.[77]

On freedom and a just society, he drew inspiration from—among others—William Wordsworth, Whitman, Thomas Paine, James Russell Lowell ("If there breathe on earth a slave, / Are ye truly free and brave?"), Fyodor Dostoevsky, Hugo, Eugene Debs ("While there is a lower class, I am in it. While there is a criminal element, I am of it. While there is a soul in jail, I am not free."), Charles Fourier, Spencer, Wat Tyler, Maxim Gorky, London, and Ibsen ("Away with the State! Undermine the whole conception of a state, declare free choice and spiritual kinship to be the only all important conditions of any union, and you will have the commencement of a liberty that is worth something").[78]

Singh included this Sinclair quotation: "The Anarchists and the apostles of insurrection are also represented; and if some of the things seem to the reader the mere unchaining of furies, I would say . . . let him blame himself, who has acquiesced in the existence of conditions which have driven his fellowmen to extremes of madness and despair."[79] He copied down inspiring lyrics ranging from the *Internationale* to *Charge of the Light Brigade*.

Singh also compiled demographic and economic statistics about the United States—an interest perhaps not surprising given his Ghadar links—and most poignantly, scraps of the words of revolutionary martyrs and political prisoners such as Patrick Henry, Figner, Nikolai Alexandrovich Morozov, and Ferrer, for solace in his present circumstances.[80] Legend has it that when the executioners arrived at Singh's cell to escort him to the gallows, he was sitting absorbed in a book, attempting to finish Lenin's biography before he died.

The point here is not to cherry-pick scraps that support a slender thesis on Singh's true political stance while ignoring those that imply something else. In fact, he copied down many quotations that he plainly did not agree with, but valued as food for thought. Cherry-picking is anyway impossible in his writings; no excerpt is sufficiently representative without locating it in the complexity of the whole. What does seem clear is that through all his study, and the huge range of writers he quoted, he was trying to balance the imperatives of liberty and equality, socialism and democracy, always in pursuit of the meaning of justice and freedom.

While Singh is one of the most beloved heroes of the freedom struggle, it is hard to speculate about what role he would have played if he had lived longer, or how his ideological position would have developed. Although it is clear that Marx, Lenin, and related theorists had exerted a compelling influence on his thinking, it's difficult to imagine him adopting any party line uncritically, based on what he wrote, said, and did.

In his notebook, he cites the words of Wendell Phillips: "If there is anything that cannot bear free thought, let it crack."[81] Singh was in all likelihood engaged in building a dialectical synthesis that while exceeding leftist orthodoxy in its actually existing, codified form, nevertheless incorporated Marx's and Lenin's insights on economics and organizing resistance into all the other wide-ranging sources that his voracious mind never ceased processing. In this sense, rather than being recuperated by Communism— seeing the light before he died—perhaps he himself might have recuperated Communism, allowing it to develop into another actualized form more emancipatory in its theory and practice.

The Romantic Countermodernists

The hegemonic political discourse during the latter decades of the freedom struggle and early decades of independence, including Nehru's Fabian-influenced socialism and Ambedkar's Buddhist-influenced rationalism, tied the achievement of substantive liberation to a model of industrial development based in centralized state planning—meaning liberation not just from foreign rule but also from an oppressive past, the flaws in which had led to being colonized in the first place.

Gandhi and Rabindranath Tagore were both culture heroes of the Indian freedom struggle, beloved as spiritual as well as political figures. They were also outspoken critics of modern industrial society, with deep misgivings about nationalism and the state. Both were radical pacifists, designers of utopian communities, and liberation philosophers whose closest counterparts were Tolstoy and Kropotkin.

The traditional Left, in its passionate devotion to economic materialism, secularism, and modernization, rejected Gandhian thought as reactionary. Their deep anxiety about deviating from the principles of science and rationality is quite understandable, given what they were positioning themselves against—the bloodbaths of communalism, the religiously sanctioned degradation of the caste system, and recently the growth of religious politics both Hindu and Islamic. Yet this made the entire category of the spiritual or nonrational out of bounds for progressive politics, ceding it to the Right rather than allowing it other modes of expression.

The bifurcation between the Marxist and Gandhian schools of thought—sometimes coding for the rationalist/modernist and its antithesis—has been one of the major influences shaping the Indian radical spectrum, both during and after the independence struggle. Applying an anarchist lens here allows for the possibility of conceptually straddling the line.

Tagore

Most renowned as a writer of poetry, novels, and plays, and the first non-European winner of the Nobel Prize in 1913, Tagore was also a musician, painter, educational innovator and social reformer, generally regarded as having revolutionized Bengali culture. In 1901 he founded an ashram in Shantiniketan, linked to his Institute for Rural Reconstruction and later to an alternative university that he opened in 1921. Its philosophy aimed at replacing rote learning with holistic, creative pedagogy, featuring outdoor classrooms, individualized mentorship, training in the arts, and a global rather than national focus. (He was also knighted, but publicly rejected the honor in protest of the British massacre of unarmed demonstrators in Jalianwala Bagh in 1919.) Although he is the writer of the lyrics adopted for two national anthems—India's and Bangladesh's—and despite his staunch anticolonialism, Tagore was highly critical of the nationalist movement. He raised his objections explicitly in his book *Nationalism*, first published in 1917, and more subtly in his fiction and drama.

Tagore's critiques of colonialism and nationalism were of a piece with his diagnosis of modernity's ills. Commerce and state were the deadly symptoms, but the criticism was sociocultural rather than socioeconomic in origin. The emphasis is on greed and consumption, not on class exploitation, and Tagore's objections to industrial modernity are primarily moral, spiritual, and aesthetic—decrying selfishness, materialism, and utilitarianism. Unlike artisanal work, industry is ugly, defiling landscape and behavior; according to his moral aesthetics, beauty is an accurate index of the right and the true.

Tagore's terminology of the "Nation" versus the "Spirit" of the people is reminiscent of Landauer's distinction between state and nation. Nation, for Tagore, is a machine, an engine of oppression that crushes what is best within humanity. "I am not against one nation in particular, but against the general idea of all nations," he insisted. In its greed and aggression, the existence of any nation in the world is a terrible danger to all peoples.[1] That which encourages divisive, narrowly national interests is destructive to the good of humanity. This is why patriotism is a bad idea from the perspective of the spiritual evolution of humankind.[2]

"What is the Nation?" he challenged.

> It is the aspect of a whole people as an organized power. This organization incessantly keeps up the insistence of the population on becoming strong and efficient. But this strenuous effort after strength and efficiency drains man's energy from his higher nature where he is self-sacrificing and creative. . . . He feels relieved of the urging of his conscience when he can transfer his responsibility to this machine. . . . By this device the people which loves freedom perpetuates slavery in a large portion of the world . . . where whole peoples are furiously organizing themselves for gaining wealth and power.[3]

But through the very institution organized to procure them, such wealth and power endangered even those on the receiving side. Tagore compares the "government by the Nation" to a pair of shoes encasing feet walking on a gravelly terrain. If snugly fitting, as in modern times, perhaps no gravel could get in, but it was "a closed up system, within which our feet have only the slightest liberty to make their own adjustments." Previously the feet might have encountered more gravel, but had room "to adjust themselves to the caprices of the inhospitable earth." The problem was

> not the numerousness of the outside obstacles but the comparative powerlessness of the individual to

cope with them. This narrowness of freedom is an evil which is more radical not because of its quantity but because of its nature. And we cannot but acknowledge this paradox, that while the spirit of the West marches under its banner of freedom, the nation of the West forges its iron chains of organization which are the most relentless and unbreakable that have ever been manufactured in the whole history of man.[4]

He warned,

When this organization of politics and commerce, whose other name is the Nation, becomes all powerful at the cost of the harmony of the higher social life, then it is an evil day for humanity. . . . When [society] allows itself to be turned into a perfect organization of power, then there are few crimes which it is unable to perpetrate. . . . When this engine of organization begins to attain to a vast size, and those who are mechanics are made into parts of the machine, then the personal man is eliminated to a phantom, everything becomes a revolution of policy carried out by the human parts of the machine, requiring no twinge of pity or moral responsibility.[5]

There is yet hope for society if it can find some wiggle room beyond the mechanisms of the modern state. "When the humanity of India was not under the government of the Organization, the elasticity of change was great enough to encourage men of power and spirit to feel that they had their destinies in their own hands. The hope of the unexpected was never absent, and a freer play of imagination, both on the part of the governor and the governed, had its effect in the making of history." But within nation's domain the exercise of creativity and moral choice has been destroyed:

> For every single individual is completely in the grip of a whole nation. . . . At the least pressing of its button the monster organization becomes all eyes, whose ugly stare of inquisitiveness cannot be avoided by a single person amongst the immense multitude of the ruled. At the least turn of its screw, by the fraction of an inch, the grip is tightened to the point of suffocation around every man, woman and child of a vast population, for whom no escape is imaginable in their own country, or even in any country outside their own.
>
> It is the continual and stupendous dead pressure of this unhuman upon the living human under which the modern world is groaning. Not merely the subject races, but you who live under the delusion that you are free, are every day sacrificing your freedom and humanity to this fetich [*sic*] of nationalism, living in the dense poisonous atmosphere of world-wide suspicion and greed and panic.[6]

Tagore is describing the panopticon of modern governmentality: not the character of Western civilization—whose achievements he also honored—but instead the machinery of state and commerce, which would be the same if exercised by Indians. "This government by the Nation is neither British nor anything else; it is an applied science and therefore more or less similar in its principles wherever it is used. It is like a hydraulic press, whose pressure is impersonal and on that account completely effective." Despite the differences in power between engines, ranging from hand-driven to many-horsepowered heavy machinery (that is, different colonial governments), they all function according to the same principle.[7]

Tagore's own nationalism was separate from the political arena, the space of the state. Although calling for political and economic autonomy, the nation itself had more to do with a cultural aura that not only pervaded the social fabric of India but also extended beyond the subcontinent to an "organically interlinked" Pan-Asian sphere. Its self-rediscovery would lead not just to emancipation for Asian colonized countries but the spiritual redemption of the modern world as a whole, functioning as a rebuke to the capitalist-imperialist world order. Tagore's vision of *swadeshi samaj* (autonomous society) was built on the "key elements . . . [of] the organization of cooperative enterprises, the critique of consumption practices, the emphasis on labor practices oriented toward the accumulation of spiritual and material shakti (power), the forging of rural grass-roots development projects, and mass education schemes through received folk media."[8] Again, this was primarily a moral and aesthetic critique, not a material analysis of capitalist exploitation.

A liberated culture and psyche would no longer be subject to crippling alienation through enforced imitation of Western thought forms or institutions, not even the forms of resistance and liberation. Tagore proclaimed in many an address that colonial subjects need not look outside for models, need not "imagine ourselves to be dream-made Mazzinis, Garibaldis and Washingtons," nor in economic life need they be "caught in the labyrinth of imaginary Bolshevism, Syndicalism or Socialism."[9] All that was required could be discovered within their own cultural inheritance. For Tagore, decolonization would not occur through the construction of divisions between parties and nations but rather in the integration of new inputs with any traditions conducive to maximizing freedom, equality, and holistic social, psychological, and ecological health.

After spending his later years as a universal celebrity, lecturing and meeting notables, intellectuals, and artists throughout the world, Tagore died at the age of eighty in 1941. He himself would never have claimed a connection to anarchism. His own use of the term equates it to pure individualism: "Then look at those who call themselves anarchists, who resent the imposition of power, in any form whatever, upon the individual. The only reason for this is that power has become too abstract—it is a scientific product made in the political laboratory of the Nation, through the dissolution of the personal humanity."[10] Yet there were plain affinities in his analysis, and those attitudes toward modern society recognizable as typical of the Romantic impulse, that is one component of the anarchist tradition.

Gandhi

It's not necessary to repeat the details of Gandhi's life and political career here. But it is important to draw attention to the anarchistic facets of his thought. It was not unusual during his lifetime for Gandhian ideas to be described as anarchistic—usually by hostile opponents, although also in some cases "positive, or at least neutral, when coming from a friendly critic." When made sympathetically, an anarchist reading of Gandhi could function as an attempt to "make Gandhism intelligible within (though not compatible with) the framework of socialist thinking" by articulating it with socialist debates.[11]

Economist J. C. Kumarappa was a close associate of Gandhi, the major public interpreter of Gandhian economic thought, a theorist of rural development, and cofounder in 1935 of the All India Village Industries Association aimed at poverty reduction and self-sufficiency. After independence, he resigned from the Congress National Planning Committee because of his skepticism concerning the INC's emphasis on big industrialization. A critic of the All India Village Industries Association scoffed at its approach, calling it "a cloak of tattered patches" that stitched Kumarappa's "economic notions" together with "elements of Ruskin, William Morris, Proudhon, Bakunin and Tolstoy . . . [to] try to furnish a swadeshi alternative to the imported ideas of socialism."[12] On the anarchy of Gandhism, Kumarappa claimed neutrality while "admitt[ing] that 'certain aspects of our reasoning can be paralleled from anarchists and others but that is not sufficient cause to hang us.'"[13]

In 1949 Lotvala (by then described as "a retired anarchist, of the Libertarian Socialist Institute, Bombay") concluded, based on conversations he had with Kumarappa's brother, that Gandhi's basic positions could be summed up as "1) India being an agricultural country, priority should be given to rural development. 2) Decentralisation. 3) Man should be non-economic. 4) State being a class organisation to be replaced by voluntary cooperative associations." Lotvala and Kumarappa "agreed that these were 'predominantly Anarchistic ideas'; and added, 'Fundamentally, Anarchist position is humanistic and so man has been made herein the centre of all rational and moral values. Gandhism is very near to it.'"[14] (As historian Benjamin Zachariah also points out, recommending a grain of salt, Lotvala illustrates the possibility for "selective and creative readings" of Gandhi.)[15]

Nirmal Bose, another sympathizer, defended Gandhi from accusations by the Hindu chauvinist wing of the INC that excluded socialists and Gandhians in the article "Is Gandhi a Nationalist?":

> The Nationalists want to build a state that supports industries and culture of India. But Gandhi does not discriminate among humanity that way by class or nation. For him, humanity is one. In this respect, his sympathies are more with the Socialists than the Nationalists.
>
> But Gandhi is not a Communist. . . . Gandhi is in fact a philosophical anarchist. But as a practical idealist, he aims at building up little village states, as

well as a feeble confederation of them in the form
of a centralised State. That requires a certain use
of violence, which he thinks, is unavoidable under
the circumstances. He is eager to drop even that
centralisation as early as possible. As such, Gandhi's
Varnashrama, in its practical form, is another form
of Socialism, but approaching Anarchism more
closely than most prevalent forms of Socialism.
It approaches Kropotkin's idea of an anarchistic
socialism more closely than anything else.[16]

In addition to his well-known skepticism of the merits
of modern Western civilization, Gandhi harbored a deep
distaste for the institution of the state, and distrusted any
nationalism that sought to lay instrumental claim to unified
top-down power. Unlike Nehru and the INC, he had no
desire to adopt rationalized techniques of administration
and production; rather, Gandhi's vision of liberation called
for spiritually fulfilled, nonalienated lives of material self-
sufficiency through artisanal efforts within a decentralized
federation of autonomous village republics.

He founded several intentional communities run
as collective farms, such as Phoenix Settlement in South
Africa and Sabarmati Ashram in Gujarat. The autonomous
village republic was the building block of Gandhi's vision
of a just society, and a recurring theme among those critical not just of colonialism's foreignness but of the rational/
industrial system that nationalists too embraced. Although
the authenticity of this trope remains controversial, it
seems less important whether or not such a thing had ever

existed in the past than that the idea of it was welcomed as a desirable future.

Gandhi's utopia was influenced by his readings of Ruskin, Thoreau, Morris, Kropotkin, and most particularly Tolstoy, with whom he corresponded, and whose antimilitarist, socially emancipatory version of Christianity was not unlike Gandhi's version of Hinduism.[17] Of course, his culturally specific religiosity gives his thought and practice quite a different guise from anything generally associated with anarchism in the West.[18] It was precisely his religiosity, along with antimodernism and refusal to endorse class war or repudiate the caste system, that led the Indian Left to angrily reject him, holding him accountable for the festering canker of communalism within the Indian national movement and Indian society's persistent attachment to archaic structures of oppression. Instead of stoking dialectical conflict, he called for social harmony, counseling a benevolent, paternalistic relationship between landlords and peasants.

The paradigm for decolonization that prevailed during the mid-twentieth century pegged socialism and secularism to modernization, development, and scientific knowledge. To Gandhi, technology and industry were components not of emancipation but rather of spiritual and cultural damage, which is yet another reason why many leftists denounced him as a reactionary. He emphatically rejected post-Enlightenment reason, preferring a premodern condition, although not in the form of stasis or regression. Gandhi also at times fell into the trap of cultural superiority, which paradoxically made it possible for anarchistic content to coincide with an "extreme nationalist position." Nevertheless there was room within the discourse for Left Gandhians and Gandhian socialists as well as Gandhian traditionalists and cultural conservatives. Furthermore, while it's possible to reject Gandhian discourse for reasons that can be linked to anarchism, it doesn't follow that one must then reject anarchism itself. More precisely, one rejects the Gandhian form of anarchism—as did his historical contemporaries, militant anarcho-communists Acharya and Singh.

The closest thing we have to a Gandhian manifesto is "Hind Swaraj," an essay he wrote in 1909 while on a ship sailing from London to South Africa, where he lived and worked at the time. In this imaginary question and answer between himself as "Editor" and an imagined "Reader" of the *Indian Opinion*, he lays out his ideas on the state, modernity, industrialization, technology, the ideal village community, and the way to free India.

"The removal of the cause of a disease results in the removal of the disease itself," he said, and his diagnosis of what ailed his country was stark: "It is my deliberate opinion that India is being ground down, not under the English heel, but under that of modern civilization. It is groaning under the monster's terrible weight. . . . Civilization is like a mouse gnawing while it is soothing us." One after the other he panned lawyers, doctors, railroads, machinery, factories, English education, and the profit motive. "[The English] hold whatever dominions they have for the sake of their commerce. Their army and their navy are to protect it. . . . They wish to convert the whole world into a vast market for their goods."[19] Violence was another symptom of everything that was wrong with Western civilization.

The essay was influential and was translated into many languages. Gandhi also spoke on his alternative vision on several public occasions:

> [January 1939:] Political power, in my opinion, cannot be our ultimate aim. . . . The power to control national life through national representatives is called political power. Representatives will become unnecessary if the national life becomes so perfect as to be self-controlled. It will then be a state of enlightened anarchy in which each person will become his own ruler. He will conduct himself in such a way that his behaviour will not hamper the well-being of his neighbours. In an ideal State there will be no political institution and therefore no political power. That is why Thoreau has said . . . that that government is the best which governs the least.[20]

> [April 1946:] Independence should be political, economic and moral.
> "Political" necessarily means the removal of the control of the British army in every shape and form.
> "Economic" means entire freedom from British capitalists and capital, as also their Indian counterparts. . . .
> "Moral" means freedom from armed defence forces. My conception of Ramarajya excludes replacement of the British army by a national army of occupation. A country that is governed by even its national army can never be morally free.[21]

[July 1946:] Independence must begin at the
bottom. Thus, every village will be a republic or
Panchayat having full powers. It follows, therefore, that every village has to be self-sustained and
capable of managing its affairs even to the extent of
defending itself against the whole world. . . .
[U]ltimately it is the individual who is the unit.
This does not exclude willing help from neighbours
or from the world. It will be a free and voluntary
play of mutual forces. . . .

In this structure composed of innumerable villages, there will be ever-widening, never-ascending
circles.[22]

But as independence approached—and soon after it,
the end of Gandhi's life—he was shunned and politically
isolated by those who had been happy to tap into his mass-
mobilizing power, but had no use for his antistate and anti-
capitalist social vision.

States and Village Republics

For the first few decades after independence, Nehru's secular socialist democracy was the normative referent for the
notion of the redistributive state. This paradigm for decolonization equated liberation with state-planned modernization and development, which was in turn equated with
large-scale industrialization.

Both Tagore and Gandhi denied that the modern state was the most natural or desirable form for an emancipated, "regenerated" Indian society to take, and warned against the dangers of centralized authority, which they felt would threaten self-sufficiency at the local level. For them, the anticolonial commitment to self-determination ran deeper than the transfer of political power.

Historian Rajat K. Ray writes,

> They shared the conviction that the essence of Indian civilization lay in the self-regulating character of society. This social autonomy was rendered feasible by the peripheral existence of the state insofar as the inner life of the community was concerned. . . .
>
> Tagore's concept of "self-strength" (Atmashakti') and Gandhi's notion of "self-rule" (Swaraj') were both anti-state in tendency, one stressing the autonomy of the community and the other the self-sufficiency of the village. Neither of these prophets of Indian regeneration gave primacy to the political movement in their doctrine of self-help. The aim was to make society self-sufficient again, so as to render the state irrelevant.[23]

According to the theorists of South Asian state formation, the unitary, centralized state was a late addition to the subcontinental repertory of political formations.[24] Prior to the nineteenth-century imposition of British paramountcy—the doctrine that all subcontinental power must be subject to one overarching authority—there was instead a range of overlapping, segmentary, sovereign units oriented toward different centers. Ray describes this as a cellular "beehive" structure.

> For centuries, the various communities and the villages had lived in their demarcated spheres, secure in the autonomy of their local and communal concerns from the interference of the [center].... [T]he self-regulating units of society were forced into dependence as an alien government broke into concerns hitherto regulated within the village and the community. The British made state power central to the life of the people, and thereby profoundly disturbed the balance between the various cells.[25]

Still, while decentralized and pluralistic, with a near-endless capacity to accommodate new cells and be "enriched" by any new arrivals willing to be incorporated without attempting to overhaul the whole, this society was also hierarchical. Tagore, says Ray, "deprecated the inequality but valued the multiplicity" of the traditional cellular society; for him, India's community of sentiment was that of a civilization, but not of a modern nation-state.[26] In contrast, Nehru's democratic vision was uniformly egalitarian but also centralized. Would visionaries invested in the shape of decolonized India have to choose between the priorities of freedom and equality?

The village republic idea is sometimes dismissed as an invention of East India Company ideologues such as Charles Metcalfe and Henry Maine, who deployed it as a way to perpetuate Orientalist dualisms of tradition versus modernity, the timeless East versus the dynamic West, or later as a way to theorize subaltern spaces as external to the modern political arena.[27] Yet whether or not it had ever really existed in such a pure form, such a republic occupied the radical imaginary of those within the freedom movement who sought an alternative to the centralized industrial state—especially if it could be claimed as indigenous, not imported.

The idea also circulated in the movement overseas between the world wars. Surendranath Karr, editor of the *Independent Hindustan*, the New York–based organ of the heterodox Left Hindustan Ghadar Party, wrote eloquently "On the Village Republics of India" in the March 1921 issue.[28]

"In view of the revolutionary movements that are so rampant in India at the present day," Karr began, "and of the decision of the Indian people to set up an independent government of their own in accordance with the wishes of the people," there was much speculation regarding "the plans and programs of the revolutionaries who are directing the forces to destroy British imperialism." What did they envision?

First, Karr commented on the curious fact that humanity tends always to "look backward to find the basis of our present day activities, perhaps in the unconscious mind or dream of the past. A new thing we want to create, no doubt; but a great deal of energy is being spent in collecting the materials." This was a quest for usable precedents. His intention in seeking hints of the possible shape of the "New India" was not "to delve into the discovery of whether the

Hindu genius evolved out of a conception of the present
Soviet system existing in Russia or not, but to stimulate
a desire among those who may, through close and careful
study, find that India's soul is very fertile for transplantation
of the ideas which have already shaken the very foundations of the political, economic and social theories." Even
so, he compared the Russian proverb "What the Mir has
settled is God's own judgment" with the Indian one "There
is God in the Panch" (that is, the traditional five-person local decision-making council). Just as the "mir is the mother
of the Soviet," Karr predicted, "the Panchayat is going to be
the parent of the future Indian polity."

These were the village councils wherein the reclaimed
traditions of the republic, "repository of rights and liberty
of the peoples," could provide the political foundations for
their future. "Industrial socialism may not be known to the
people," he argued, "but agrarian communism is a natural
system in which the people have been accustomed to live,"
although with "the advent of the British capitalistic system,
the communistic principles have been shattered to pieces."

In this indigenous utopia of village republics, Karr
claimed, there was no caste divide: intermarriage prevailed,
along with free choice of occupation based in trade and
craft guilds. Industry was "controlled by the public," with
the means of production such as common looms and utili-
ties such as wells and channels collectively owned. "Dignity
of labor was duly recognized," and there was no conflict
between work of brain and brawn. A village assembly held
sessions in a sort of town hall, with legislation made by
directly elected representatives. Six standing committees

were tasked with "Animal, Garden, Tank (Irrigation), Gold, Justice and Panchvara" duties. Committee membership was open to all men and women between thirty-five and seventy years old who owned an amount of taxable land roughly equivalent to five acres, lived in a house on its own site, were well educated (an education could trump the property requirement), honest in business dealings, and had not committed any crimes.

The public offices that Karr cited as examples of non-hereditary occupations in a Madras village included an executive, accountant, security and border guards, superintendent of tanks and watercourses, priest, schoolmaster, astrologer, smith, carpenter, potter, washer, barber, cowkeeper, doctor, dancer, musician, and poet. Education was paramount and knowledge treasured, until colonial rule "ruthlessly destroyed the indigenous national system of education." This widespread "village republican educational system" had always been "secular and democratic in the strictest sense of the term," and Hindu, Sikh, and Muslim schools in all regions "possessed identical constitutions, and methods of management and instruction." It should be a priority for revolutionaries, counseled Karr, in boycotting English education to revive their own people's intelligence.

He closed with the words of Dr. Radhakumud Mookerji, on whose work the article drew heavily:

> It is often forgotten that a great deal of socialism and communism (representing advanced democratic ideals of the modern age) is held in solution in the Indian social system. Appropriate expression

is found through various institutions which all
imply strong collectivist or communistic sense
and intuitions in the people, combined with a due
restraint of that aggressive individualism and proprietary instinct . . . emphasizing private property
and the sacredness of creditors' rights over those of
the debtors, have given, in the opinion of the most
thoughtful sociologists and political philosophers,
a somewhat wrong direction to the development of
nations and states in Europe.[29]

Mookerji was an eminent historian who had published a book in 1919 titled *Local Government in Ancient
India*.[30] In his preface, Mookerji explained, "The present
work aims at a systematic presentation of . . . the exuberant
vitality and manifold growth of self-governing institutions
among a people characterized by a genius for social experiments and constructions." His introduction "put forward,
as a tentative suggestion, the hypothesis about the peculiar relations between the state and society in ancient India
which has, to my mind, the merit of explaining some of the
paradoxes in its history and throwing light on some of its
obscure aspects or chapters." Namely, he felt that "a proper
presentation of Hindu culture in all its aspects and phases
should take into account these diverse developments . . .
the many manifestations of the democratic principle which
that culture represents. In the present work an attempt will
be made to trace one particular line of that development, to
dwell upon the workings of the democratic principle in one
particular sphere": local self-government.[31]

It was to this trait that Indian society owed its resilience despite years of crises and upheavals, he claimed, quoting Metcalfe:

> The village communities are little republics, having nearly everything they can want within themselves, and almost independent of any foreign relations. They seem to last where nothing else lasts. Dynasty after dynasty tumbles down; revolution succeeds to revolution ... but the village community remains the same. ... This union of the village communities, each one forming a separate little state in itself, has, I conceive, contributed more than any other cause to the preservation of the peoples of India, through all the revolutions and changes which they have suffered, and is in a high degree conducive to their happiness, and to the enjoyment of a great portion of freedom and independence.[32]

We might see here not static timelessness but rather continuity and survival in the face of great change.

Mookerji observed:

> The fact is that India presents the rare and remarkable phenomenon of the state and the society co-existing apart from, and in some degree of independence of each other, as distinct and separate units or entities, as independent centres of national, popular, and collective life and activity. Both of them were independent organisms with distinct

and well-defined structures and functions of their own and laws of growth and evolution. The limits of state-interference were accordingly so defined and fixed as not to encroach upon the sphere of the activities of the social organization. A policy of non-interference was recognized as the ideal policy of the state, the functions of which were ordinarily restricted to "the irreducible minimum," vis. the protection of life and property and realization of the revenue for the proper execution of that duty.[33]

This created a stark contrast between India and the West, where

the predominant tendency has been towards a progressive extension of state interference and state control so as to bring within its limits all the main departments of social life and national activity until the ideal is attained of a complete nationalization or socialization of all the means and processes of life itself. The state, beginning as an agent of society, becomes its master and representative; society is merged in the state to which it surrenders its functions, dropping its independent life.[34]

Even if in the "advanced" countries of the West the people's main interface with power was through local not central bodies, these were still the creations and tools of the central government, "the wheels of a common machine," whereas in ancient India the local bodies had originated outside the state, which only later incorporated or super-imposed itself on them.[35] In fact, pragmatically speaking, in the absence of any means of fast long-distance communication or travel by which to administer a far-flung empire, the smartest thing was to take advantage of existing institutions.[36] Such consolidation was only possible

> because it did not cherish the ambition of setting up a centralized government consciously legislating for and controlling the life of every part of that vast whole, but aimed only at an elastic system of federalism or confederation in which were incorporated, along with the central government at the metropolis, as parts of the same system, the indigenous local administrations. The essence of this imperial system was thus a recognition of local autonomy at the expense of the authority of the central government, which was physically unfit to assert itself except by its enforced affiliation to the pre-existing system of local government.[37]

The practical interest of this study lay in its applicability to current questions of administration and administrative reform. Of two rival schools of thought,

> [one] seeks to introduce self-government "from above" and the other "from below." . . . [I]t may, perhaps, be pertinent to point out that any form of provincial or central government which is organized merely "from above," however mechanically

perfect it may be, will fail to take a real root or gather to itself that vital force without which it will be a mere lifeless machine, a cog upon our national development, unless it is grafted in some way or other upon the spontaneous groupings of the people themselves as represented by their local self-governing institutions and based upon these natural foundations of all government. . . .

[A] people cannot be deemed to be essentially self-governing and enjoying the blessings of free institutions if they are without the right of themselves administering their local affairs and interests, on which their daily well-being depends. Besides, local government is itself the best school of political training for the masses living in the villages who cannot take part in the provincial or the central government except through their few representatives, and it is also to be cherished as a school of social service and a most efficient factor of social progress.[38]

Finally, Mookerji wanted to remind his readers that ancient Indian "[Hindu] society was suffused with the democratic principle. The numerous self-governing, 'kingless' states in ancient India, the existence of which is attested by sober history," contrasted with the usual assumptions that it was only all about "respect for tradition and authority and blind faith, rather than discriminating judgement."[39] And like Tagore, he suggested that not only was this model beneficial for India, it also offered answers applicable to the whole world.

Sarvodaya

Two postcolonial institutions have roots in the village republic ideal: the *panchayat* system, and the *bhoodan* or land grant movement. The panchayat system, sanctioned by the constitution since 1993, calls for seven-person village councils (originally five) democratically chosen for five-year terms at the village, block, and district levels, tasked with settling land disputes and civil disagreements, providing for water supplies, clinics, and schools, and implementing economic development and social justice. All villagers are supposed to be able to express their opinions as decisions are made. In practice, the system is far from emancipatory; critics point out that functional control often remains in the hands of petty tyrants among local landholders and caste elites, and that women who hold seats are frequently chosen more for their potential as puppets than as leaders.

Of course, restoring self-sufficiency and autonomy to village communities doesn't in itself erase existing oppressions any more than calling for "states' rights" eliminates racism. Even if an anarchistic logic holds that decentralization and local control are goods in themselves, it can never assume that changing the formal relations of governmentality is enough without also reweaving the very fabric of culture and society at every level. Har Dayal wrote in his *Modern Times* articles of the necessity for breaking the chains of tradition that shackled, subjected, and saddled women to patriarchy, subject "untouchables" to a toxic caste hierarchy, and saddle all with the corrupt and parasitic priesthoods of organized religion.[40]

The bhoodan (and the related *gramdan* or village grant) idea evolved out of the work of Gandhi's disciple Vinobha Bhave, and then Jayaprakash Narayan (or JP, as he was commonly called). The Sarvodaya movement (taking its name from Gandhi's translation or "paraphrase" of Ruskin's *Unto This Last*) aimed to persuade landowners to follow the dictates of an evolved conscience, and bequeath parcels of their holdings to peasant collectives to be self-managed in perpetuity with an emphasis on self-sufficiency, equitable distribution of resources, and individual freedom. Gramdan continued Bhoodan: landowners in a village would agree to renounce ownership though retaining occupancy, donate a portion of their land to the landless, and donate a portion of produce annually to the village.

The saintly Bhave convened the first meeting of a Sarvodaya Samaj soon after Gandhi's death, to carry on the social mission that he wasn't able to complete. The Bhoodan land distribution project began in 1951, followed by the more extensive Gramdan program in 1952. This was intended not just as an ownership arrangement but a whole way of life. Bhave explained,

> Sarvodaya does not mean good government or majority rule, it means freedom from government, it means decentralization of power. We want to do away with government by politicians and replace it by a government of the people, based on love, compassion and equality. Decisions should be taken, not by a majority, but by unanimous consent; and

they should be carried out by the united strength of the ordinary people of the village.

If I am under some other person's command, where is my self-government? . . . It is one mark of swaraj not to allow any outside power in the world to exercise control over oneself. And the second mark of swaraj is not to exercise power over any other. These two things together make swaraj—no submission and no exploitation. This cannot be brought into being by government decree, but only by a revolution in the people's ways of thought.[41]

"The fact is that people do not really need a government at all. . . . The ultimate goal of sarvodaya is freedom from government." Bhave then took care to distinguish this from "absence of government," meaning the absence of any kind of order and structure, wherein "anti-social elements" would have free rein. Rather, he said, the administrative authority for a harmonious, stateless society "rests in the villages."[42]

This must come about not through a period of totalitarianism, as the Communists said; it should happen through an ongoing process of decentralization until "in the final stage there would be no coercion but a purely moral authority. The establishment of such a self-directing society calls for a network of self-sufficient units. Production, distribution, defence, education—everything should be localized. The centre should have the least possible authority."[43]

Still, the achievement of this form was dependent on individual acts of enlightened paternalism without requiring true systemic socioeconomic change. A fear was that bhoodan actually helped to stabilize rather than subvert the system, due to its ameliorative effects. In fact, after India attained independence it seemed that people had gotten all the more dependent on the central state, expecting it to do everything for them. Laws offered band-aids without enabling the self-strengthening necessary for a true "politics of the people" (*lokniti*) to replace a "politics of the power-state" (*rajniti*).[44] The Bhoodan movement, Bhave claimed, as an attempt to weave comprehensive change in the fabric of society without recourse to the state, could produce such strengthening:

> In our modern conditions a powerful state can bring nothing but slavery. Therefore sarvodaya stands for an immediate reduction in the power of the state. . . . In our social structure we must accept the principle that the welfare of one group is not opposed to the welfare of another.
>
> In such a social order the need to use force would be eliminated. . . . Such a society would be truly self-governing.[45]

In the mid-1960s, Bhave retreated into a life of spiritual contemplation, dying at his ashram in 1982. After Bhave, JP was the movement's most prominent figure. The concerns and goals that motivated JP in the attempt first to bridge socialism and Gandhism, and then in his shift from Marxism to Sarvodaya, resonated with the concerns and goals expressed in anarchist critiques of the dominant Marxist tradition.[46]

A native of Bihar, JP left Patna College just shy
of finishing his science scholarship to join Gandhi's
Noncooperation movement in 1921. After that revolution was aborted, he traveled to the United States for
further study from 1922 to 1929, because his decision to
avoid educational institutions sanctioned by the colonial
government ruled out higher education in India. While
working in "fields, factories, restaurants and slaugh-
ter houses," he attended universities in California, Iowa,
Ohio, and Wisconsin, achieving a masters in sociology in
1929. In Madison, Wisconsin, he fell in with some local
Communists and embraced Marxism.

During his long absence, his wife, Prabhavati, had been
staying with Gandhi and his wife, Kasturba; on JP's return
to rejoin the national movement they welcomed him as a
son-in-law. Family obligations kept him busy during the
first round of the Civil Disobedience movement, but he
was active in the second round, and with most of the senior
leaders under lock and key, was named acting INC General
Secretary in 1932.

During this period he was shocked by the
Communists' attitude of hostility toward the INC as a
"bourgeois" nationalist movement. His own thinking was
that it was imperative for socialism and the freedom struggle to inform one another. To this end, he helped to found
and lead the Congress Socialist Party (CSP) in 1934.

In his 1936 pamphlet "Why Socialism?" he laid out
the CSP's ideology. "The immediate task is to develop the
national movement into a real anti-imperialist movement
aiming at freedom from the foreign power AND the native

system of exploitation. For this it is necessary to wean the anti-imperialist elements in the Congress away from its present bourgeois leadership, and to bring them under the leadership of revolutionary socialism."[47]

At this point he still viewed Marxism as the one true theory of socialism. Although acknowledging differences in tactics and approaches, it remained hard to refute the apparent success of the Russian Revolution. He also still assumed the necessity of seizing power to effect change. JP elaborated a program for economic liberation completely compatible with the then-dominant paradigm for Nehruvians and Communists alike: state-planned and controlled development, the socialization of critical industries, and the redistribution of land. Since inequality stemmed from the appropriation of natural resources and means of production by individuals for their own ends, private ownership had to be abolished. So did state support for distinctions of caste, religion, or gender.

But JP was already expressing a preference for pastoral communities over urban concentrations. His land redistribution plan was not based on massive collective farms but instead on evenly dispersed village cooperatives, with mixed agricultural and industrial economies, to be reorganized gradually through persuasion, not immediately through coercion.[48]

When World War II broke out, JP toured the country calling for noncooperation with the war effort. For this he was imprisoned for nine months in 1940, then arrested again immediately on release and put into a special camp in Deoli along with other leftist leaders. He tried to send a letter via Prabhavati to "chosen comrades of the CSP, advising them to go underground, collect arms and money and prepare for an armed struggle against the British."[49] But the jail staff intercepted the letter, and the government publicized it in hopes that it would ruin JP's reputation among Gandhians. It had quite the opposite effect on his standing in popular opinion, however.

After a successful monthlong fast for the demands of Deoli political prisoners, including repatriation to their home provinces, he was sent to a prison in Bihar. In 1942 he and five others broke out by scaling a wall under cover of holiday revelry—another boost to his reputation as a freedom fighter. He established contact with others, and wrote several morale-building letters for revolutionaries, in which he described not just the need for resistance but also the kind of society to be built afterward, already thinking beyond the seizure of power to the work needed throughout all levels of society. The desired goal was *gramraj*—"self-governing village[s] or . . . village republic[s]," which would be "centres of struggle and resistance during a revolution and would constitute the bricks with which the structure of the free Indian republic could be built."[50]

Along with Ram Manohar Lohia, another CSP founding figure, JP tried to organize a guerrilla force dubbed Azad Dasta in north Bihar, near the Nepali border. He and six others were arrested during officer cadre training, but freed by their trainees. Before there was much time to build the organization though, he was arrested again, this time subject to solitary confinement, torture, and interrogation at Lahore Fort, and then held together with Lohia in Agra

Central Jail. By the time both were released in 1946, the war was over and arrangements for the British transfer of power were under way.

During the 1940s, JP began to have increasing doubts about the Soviet model, compounded by his disillusionment with the CPI and its tactics. In "My Picture of Socialism," in 1946, he emphasized that Marxist principles could not be applied uniformly or dogmatically, without taking into consideration India's specific history and conditions as well as the changes in the world since Marx's death.[51]

In 1947, he cautioned in "From Socialism to Sarvodaya" that "in a society where it was possible for the people by democratic means to bring about social change it would be counter-revolutionary to resort to violence" or coercion. Socialism, for its existence, required the presence of democratic freedoms. The dictatorship of the proletariat therefore had to be abandoned on the grounds that it created "in effect . . . the dictatorship of a bureaucratic oligarchy."[52]

In his 1950 pamphlet "Democratic Socialism: The Ideal and Method," JP argued for the significance of human values in "any scheme of socialist reconstruction." Socialism, he insisted, "could not be equated with mere nationalisation of industry and collectivisation of agriculture. It should mean the end of exploitation, injustice, oppression and insecurity, equality of opportunity, and an equitable distribution of the good things of life." And "if under such an economy all political and economic power is concentrated in the hands of a party oligarchy, irreplaceable and self-perpetuating, there can be no socialism but its suppression, no revolution but reaction." True, socialism "ultimately aims at creating a stateless society, but it wishes to make the State all-powerful by making the social revolution itself dependent upon State action. Gandhism too, like Socialism, aims at a stateless society," the creation of which "begins here and now, and is not relegated to a remote and imaginary period in the future."[53]

Instead of Marxism, he now began referring to a "Democratic Socialism" that in his mind entailed a synthesis of Gandhian, socialist, and liberal ideas, such as guarantees for basic individual and civil rights, cultural and religious freedoms, and a mode of expression for the people's will, while maintaining that the guiding principles for the political and economic organization of the state should be social justice and economic freedom, with large-scale production collectivized, combined with small-scale production by individuals and cooperatives "for the equal benefit of all concerned." The public good had to be defined not solely in terms of providing for material comforts but also in the creation of "conditions for healthy living and the moral and intellectual development of the individual."[54]

> Democratic socialists had no doubt talked vaguely of the decentralization of power.... But in practice I found that their entire concern was, and still is with the capture of power.... Decentralization cannot be effected by handing down power from above to people ... whose capacity for self-rule has been thwarted, if not destroyed, by the party system and concentration of power at the top.... The process must be started from the bottom. A program of self-rule

and self-management must be placed before [them],
and by a constructive, non-partisan approach they
must be helped to translate it into practice.[55]

He then went a step further; in questioning the
political system,

> fundamental questions arose in my mind as to the
> place and role of the State in human society, partic-
> ularly in relation to the goals of social life that had
> fixed themselves before me. . . . Though I had given
> up the basic postulates of Marxism, because they
> did not promise to lead me to my goals, I contin-
> ued to feel strongly that human freedom could be
> fully and wholly realized only in a stateless society. I
> was, and am, not sure if the State would ever wither
> away completely. But I am sure that it is one of the
> noblest goals of social endeavour to ensure that the
> powers and functions and spheres of the State are
> reduced as far as possible. . . . The test of human
> evolution for me became man's ability to live on
> amity, justice and cooperation with his fellow men
> without outward restraints of any kind. That is why
> I have considered the human and social problem to
> be at bottom a moral problem.[56]

To the bourgeois state's monopoly of political power,
JP noted, the socialist state added the monopoly of economic power, which made it even more dangerous, and
would require even stronger checks and balances than a

constitution could provide. Could this be the function of trade unions, cooperatives, and consumers' associations? Possibly, but "the democratic socialist State remains a Leviathan that will sit heavily on the freedom of the people." The remedy, then, would be Sarvodaya. "Speaking as a socialist, I would put it thus: the remedy is to create and develop forms of socialist living through the voluntary endeavour of the people rather than to seek to establish socialism by the use of the power of the State," which would be both a truer socialism and a truer democracy, characterized by the values of "co-operation, self-discipline, sense of responsibility," to enable "self-government, self-management, mutual co-operation and sharing, equality, freedom, brotherhood," which were best "practiced and developed . . . in small communities."[57]

This would further require a blending and balance of nature and culture, green space and urban space. Science and technology could help. Indeed, departing from Gandhi here, JP believed that the problem wasn't science and technology but rather the destructive uses to which governments and profiteers had put them. (JP had high hopes for nuclear energy.)

Nevertheless, his 1951 article "Socialism and Sarvodaya" defended the Gandhian legacy against charges of "wishy washy sentimentalism." It was a "concrete programme of basic social revolution," combining attention to morality and ethics with unprecedented tactics of resistance (with the corollary that ends do not justify means; means create ends), and "[insisting] on decentralisation—economic and political." Although "in leftist circles, this is characterised as antediluvian," JP insisted that "this aspect of Gandhism . . . does not necessarily mean the rejection of modern science and technology; though it does mean that the modern techniques of production are neither used as means of exploitation nor as means of domination."[58]

In 1952 he broke with Marxism. The questioning that had started with news of Russian purges led him now to abjure materialism as a philosophy of historical and political change. From his reading of Erich Fromm while in prison, JP had learned to focus on the humanistic as opposed to the economistic side of the Marxian tradition, with its emphasis on alienation. Drawing on Fromm, he noted that while "socialisation of production means bureaucracy and manipulation of the individual . . . [a] balanced system . . . must be evolved so as to reconcile large-scale planning with freedom for the individual."[59]

In the same year, despite pressure to seek office in the first general elections of independent India, he abruptly walked away from the game of electoral power. He then immersed himself in Vinoba Bhave's Bhoodan movement, facing bitter reproaches for giving up on politics. He retorted that he hadn't: he had only abandoned rajniti, "the politics of parties, elections, parliaments and governments," not lokniti.[60]

In his 1959 "A Plea for Reconstruction of Indian Polity," JP called for counteracting the alienation of modern industrial society by cultivating integrated, meaningful communities based on "a feeling of unity in the midst of diversity; a sense of freedom within the framework of accepted social responsibilities; differentiation of functions converging to the single goal of the good of the community and its members." The base units for this hypothetical social structure would be "neither so small that a balanced development of communal life and culture becomes difficult, nor so large that life in them becomes impersonalized. They will be neither rural nor urban, but . . . based on a balance of agriculture and industry, making full use of science and technology to serve their ends." They would be "self-governing, self-sufficient, agro-industrial, urbo-rural communities."[61] These would then federate at the district, provincial, and finally national levels, from the base upward.

If possible, large cities would be reorganized into smaller federated communities. In each village the gram sabha would consist of all adult members, from which the five-member gram panchayat council would be chosen by consensus. Their duties would be to make sure that all village members had access to food, clothing, shelter, education, and medical care. Most things would be taken care of by those immediately involved. As responsibilities moved up the levels by indirect election from panchayat samitis to district councils and state assemblies, the national parliament would deal only with defense, foreign relations, interstate coordination, and currency.[62]

Again, it's crucial to note that JP acknowledged the innovation of such an arrangement: it was not a return to the past (as right-wing antimodernists might wish, restoring a time of Brahminic/patriarchal supremacy). These were "communities of the future."[63]

JP continued to elaborate these ideas in the 1961 "Swaraj for the People," which dealt with the transition to the new system and how to enable people "to participate in the management of their affairs as far as possible."[64] This in turn entailed a criticism of the actually existing panchayati raj—yes, it was decentralized, but it would not be a truly participatory democracy until people were educated, competitive elections were abolished so that no one could use the panchayat as a launching pad for power, and all adults had a voice in the gram sabha, with the panchayat functioning as no more than an implementer of decisions.

He spent the 1950s and 1960s on speaking tours, writing, and taking stands on sometimes controversial or apparently hopeless causes. He took the unpopular position of advocating for Kashmiri and Naga efforts at greater autonomy from Indian central government. Then in the early 1970s, he began to move back toward conventional political engagement, sensing that Bhoodan-Gramdan was not proving sufficient to bring about the social revolution. In 1970, he threw himself into the mobilization led by leftists in Bihar to peacefully occupy land exceeding the legal ownership allotment ceiling. He also got involved in the Bihari youth movement, supporting students' demands to disband the Bihar ministry and legislative assembly, while urging the dismantling of the caste-based hierarchical structures utilized to maintain the feudal landholding regime.[65]

By 1974, aged seventy-two and in fragile health, JP was again facing assaults, lathi blows, and solitary confinement as in his early days of radicalization. He was released from prison in 1975, with failing kidneys, just in time for the Emergency period of authoritarian rule Indira Gandhi imposed from 1975–77.

JP was now promoting the idea of "total revolution" (Sampoorna Kranti). He sent "messages to the workers for the cause of total revolution that they must prepare for a long struggle"—a struggle that was permanent in duration, but always changing in form. The times called for a Second War of Independence (Doosri Azaadi)—this time to free the Indian people from the dictatorship of the postcolonial state.

For JP as for many others, the Emergency period was a turning point. Fearing that the vision of freedom and justice for India that he had worked for his whole life was falling apart, JP sent Indira Gandhi an impassioned letter imploring her not to destroy her father's ideals. In 1977, he finally reentered the electoral battlefield to persuade leaders of all major non-Congress and non-Communist parties to form a coalition as the new Janata Party to oust Gandhi, in an election framed as a fight between dictatorship and democracy. The new party coalition was victorious but short-lived, quickly fragmenting into its Left and Right components whose only shared goal had been opposition—this time not to British, but to Congress raj.[66]

Historian-diplomat Bimal Prasad stresses that, although Indian freedom was a lifelong motivation for JP, his ideal of liberation was more universal and comprehensive than that: "freedom of man everywhere and from every sort of trammel . . . freedom of the human personality, freedom of the mind, freedom of the spirit. . . . This freedom has become a passion of life and I shall not see it compromised for bread, for power, for security, for prosperity, for the glory of the State or for anything else."[67]

Although the Left parties criticized JP harshly—
for the sins of romanticism, utopianism, and escapism
from politics—in his own mind he was faithful to the
Communist ideal. His anti-Communism referred to actually existing Communist parties in India, China, and the
USSR, which he saw as damaging oppressors that were not
promoting the goals of true socialism. For him, Sarvodaya
was "a higher form" and fuller expression of socialism's ultimate principles, and a better road to its goals.[68] But the
parties each equated their own institutional identity with
the universal ideal, seeing any opposition as tantamount to
a betrayal of socialism itself. Moreover, since JP was identified with the Gandhian tradition, he was tarred with the
same reactionary brush. But his propositions were not reactionary, if that meant clinging to the old against modern
change. His proposals were new ones, simply calling for a
different kind of transformation.

On Reaction and Progress

It can't be overlooked that when Gandhi, Tagore, Lotvala, or
Mookerji connected anarchist principles to a refurbished "indigenous" tradition, they cast this tradition in Hindu terms.
The hackles this raises for modern progressives in the face of
a still-powerful Hindutva are therefore unsurprising.[69] Even
when done by default as reflective of a majority, without
hostile intent or ideological commitment, this was a risk.

But no outcome can be projected backward as inevitable. Moreover not all criticisms of modernity are

antimodern, and not all antimodernisms are the same, though a certain kind of anti-antimodernist discourse tends to equate postmodernism, Hindutva, and anarchism as identically reactionary, and virtually interchangeable.

For example, the anarchistic dimension of Gandhi's thought is sometimes misidentified as his "postmodern" aspect.[70] But neither anarchist thought nor decolonizing theory is the same as postmodernism, although there are postmodernist forms of each. Indeed, recent assessments of postcolonial theory and subaltern studies have proposed a synthesis by which the interventions of various forms of oppositional knowledge (such as poststructuralism, critical race theory, and feminist and queer theories), if used in a nuanced fashion, can be seen as a necessary critique, enriching rather than negating Left thought and practice by using an intersectional, holistic strategy and analysis to better suit changes in the social, cultural, and economic shape of the world since the 1970s.[71]

As for the taint of reaction where tradition is defended, each situation needs to be evaluated for its content, not just its provenance. Where tradition is a source of oppression, it must be opposed; where it plays an emancipatory role, it should be retained. The same is true of elements of modernity, including instrumental reason. Where do science and technology, say, humanize and promote justice? Where do they dehumanize and promote injustice? Each old or new practice or belief gets the same evaluation relative to a chosen goal—in this case, maximizing freedom and equality. But it's misplaced to call something bad or good simply because it is either modern or traditional.

Simply, is it bad or good by the standards in question? That's all we need to know, as there are bad and good elements in both the modern and the traditional.

If there can be reactionary modernism—a description attributed to fascism in certain contexts—perhaps conceptually, there could also be a progressive antimodernism, or a critical alternative modernity restoring submerged or excluded principles whose submersion or exclusion contributed to the destructive imbalances we have experienced.[72] In effect, what each of these political thinkers tried to do was to draw on the cultural resources they had as a source of emancipatory alternatives to the destructive forms of modernity they knew. The village republic had never existed as they imagined it. The key thing is that they did imagine it. They wanted to create it anew.

The New Social Movements

A crucial effect of looking at decolonization through an anarchist lens is that the story changes from the formation of a nation-state to the ongoing process of deconstructing hierarchies and exploitative power relationships, no matter who the perpetrator.[1] But it didn't take an anarchist to see that. On the recognition of formal independence, it was obvious to anyone Left of the INC that the visions of freedom that had inspired generations of revolutionaries had not been fulfilled in the new nation-states of India and Pakistan. The most radical elements among South Asian freedom fighters (including Ghadar, Kirti, and the HSRA) declared that their work would not be done simply by eliminating British rule; not until there was economic and social justice for all, not just the elite interests represented in the mainstream nationalist movement. After the handover of power, the new South Asian nation-states inherited the colonial state's army, bureaucracy, revenue extraction mechanisms, and disciplinary techniques. These then had to be confronted on the grounds of their character and function, regardless of who was running them.

Furthermore, the revolutionaries' horizon of liberation was transnational: there must be no enslavement of peoples anywhere in the world, not just in India. No one was free until and unless everyone was free, they wrote; until then, the system(s) of oppression were still functional. This required taking the analytic step from opposing a foreign government in a particular context to contesting imperialism in general; from resisting foreign capital in one locality to fighting global capitalism as a whole.

Thus from the anticolonial (as opposed to the national) standpoint, the work of liberation was not completed in 1947. The post-British era might then be considered a period of continuing antisystemic struggle against both neocolonialism and internal colonialism as the new nation-state redefined its relationship to global capitalism, and its own dispossessed and marginalized peoples.

Activists and political theorists Nivedita Menon and Aditya Nigam read the movement history of late twentieth-century India in terms of a contradiction, not between capital and labor or colonizer and colonized, but more broadly between "power and contestation." From the perspective of what Menon and Nigam identify as the Indian New Left, "power is the axis constituted by Nation and Capital, while contestations are of two kinds—one demanding inclusion within, the other running counter to these entities."[2] (Plainly the anarchist preference would be for the latter.)

The following chapter scans the terrain of Indian social movements since 1947 to see what's visible to an eye accustomed to applying the stereoscopic lenses of anarchism and anticolonialism. Whether the two views intersect remains to be seen.

The Postcolonial State

Even on purely nationalist terms, the handover of power on August 15, 1947, wasn't an unambiguous victory. Not all who aspired to inclusion in the nation were incorporated on equal terms; while some who didn't want to be included were strong-armed into joining. Some other areas might have been included—Afghanistan and Nepal—if the British had ever succeeded in conquering them. Partition broke the colonial unit into three pieces—India, West Pakistan, and the former East Pakistan, now Bangladesh—igniting a traumatic multidirectional transfer of populations tantamount to ethnic cleansing in some areas. By some estimates, between 500,000 and 1 million people died, and 14.5 million were made refugees during this crisis.

The unitary nature of these states proved no less precarious over time. When writing their constitutions, both the Indian and Pakistani government-forming bodies debated whether to enshrine a more centralized locus of power or a looser federal model with greater regional autonomy. Some argue that had a more decentralized federal structure been adopted from the start, the bloody plunge to partition might have been averted, as would the repeated pattern of separatist movements.

Yet both new states have forced an escalation in separatist movements by even further concentrating power, while enforcing discipline in the peripheries through draconian special legislation to empower brutal paramilitary forces. Through this vicious cycle, what began as initiatives for greater autonomy and representation within India's federal structure—protests against the "increasing concentration of power and wealth, [and] the extraction of surplus" in areas whose populations accuse the central government of plundering their mineral wealth, raw materials, and cheap labor, or in short, replicating the colonial relationship in the name of national progress—then hardened into demands for separate sovereign entities.[3]

This pattern came to a head in the 1980s in the northeastern regions of Manipur, Assam, and Nagaland, and in the northwest with the Sikh demand for Khalistan as an independent homeland. At its peak in the early to mid-1980s, this conflict claimed between fifteen and twenty thousand lives. In Pakistan, the country's eastern wing rebelled and then split to form independent Bangladesh in 1971, leaving a still-undetermined number (between one and three million) dead. Today separatist unrest is echoed in its far west, Baluchistan. To the south the Tamil separatist movement and Sri Lankan civil war raged from 1983 to 2009, killing over thirty-eight thousand. And of course, there is the perpetual tragedy of Kashmir. Despite UN calls for a plebiscite on independence—hanging in perpetual limbo since 1948—both India and Pakistan continue to lay violent claim to a territory with separatist aspirations. At least fifty-six thousand have died since the insurgency emerged in 1989, with no end as yet on the horizon.

From the perspective of a regional separatist movement, calling the central state's behavior "internal colonialism" is already contentious, since the boundaries or sovereignty are precisely what's at issue. It's colonialism, plain and simple, complete with the illegal occupation of territory. But these death tolls are yet another indication that ethnonationalism does not solve the problem of colonialism, internal or otherwise.

Activist, sociologist, and social movement scholar Gail Omvedt writes, "The common denominator" among these various "assertions of autonomy," whether in border regions or interior hinterland areas, "was not simply 'identity politics' but the drive by the inhabitants of a geographically delimited area to control its economic and political life in a situation where they were increasingly coming under the domination and exploitation of a centralized state-industrial machine of capital accumulation."[4]

Yet the Indian state was originally founded as a socialist democracy, seen as a leader among the nonaligned movement of decolonizing nations. This endowed it with the lingering aura of standing for emancipation, anti-imperialism, and anticapitalism in the immediate postcolonial decades. Under the "Nehruvian consensus," it had a mandate for progressive development toward economic autonomy and redistributive justice. Assumptions about its fundamental legitimacy were common sense, even when subject to criticism for being ineffectual and corrupt in practice. The ideal was intact, and the problems lay in not living up to it.

Such assumptions were irreparably damaged when then Prime Minister Gandhi declared the Emergency period of dictatorship in 1975. Aimed ostensibly at stabilization, law, and order under threat from the militant Left, but in reality a move to shore up her slipping political control against charges of ethical violations, the Emergency made explicit the government's dictatorial, repressive nature. To some radical critics, this was no aberration—not a state of exception, but rather a state revealing its true face. In Partha Chatterjee's words (echoing Ranajit Guha's well-known formulation of Indian nationalism), there was now truly dominance without hegemony—that is, no component of consent, but only force. Recalling his leftist student days in the early 1970s, Chatterjee says, "The phenomenon we were always concerned with was the fundamentally authoritarian character of the postcolonial state. Why did it have to be authoritarian in this way, if in fact the national movement was what it claimed to be, which was a movement of the people against an authoritarian, colonial state?"[5]

The Emergency period was reversed in 1977, but the unraveling of the Nehruvian consensus could not be halted. During the 1980s, the territorial integrity of the nation seemed liable to fragment in multiple directions. Meanwhile—a foreshadowing of the liberalization to come—India accepted its first International Monetary Fund loan in 1981. These loans increased along with their structural adjustment demands throughout the decade.

After the cold war, the developing/decolonizing societies of Asia, Africa, and Latin America had to readjust. India lost the Soviet Union as ally and military patron. With the neoliberal transformation of the Indian economy in the early 1990s, the state reoriented itself toward global capital along the familiar lines of the Washington Consensus, abandoning the previous protectionist, redistributive model, with the Indian capitalist class now aspiring to move from being comprador junior partner to major economic power in its own right. In the process, an unprecedented middle class with first world consumerist aspirations was spawned. The traditional Left, at the same time, was widely seen as no longer viable, while new forms of political consciousness were emerging on the basis of caste identity, a potential demographic tidal wave of long-submerged aspirations and justified rage. The resulting cultural anxieties and economic destabilizations fed the reemergence of the far Right Hindutva movement politically marginalized since the time of Gandhi's assassination by a right-wing extremist in 1948.

After the 1980s, Menon reminds us, the axis of debate among political scientists was not along a "simple Liberal/Marxist divide" in which both tendencies "took for granted the legitimacy of the nation-state's pre-eminent role in setting the agenda for development and social transformation/modernization." Now it was along the very "conception of the nation-state—its role and its legitimacy." Within this debate, those "who question 'the agenda-setting presuppositions and legitimizing myths of state-directed development led by a 'rational,' 'modern' elite," such as Chatterjee, Ashis Nandy, Guha, and in his later phase, Rajni Kothari, were (negatively) characterized as intellectual "anarcho-communitarians." India's contemporary social problems, "ecologically unsustainable development, regional inequalities, and the growing control of the economy by global capital . . . are not trends that have emerged despite the nation-building project of Indian elites, but precisely are what 'anarcho-communitarians' point to as the result of that project."[6]

Of course, these alleged anarcho-communitarians are intellectuals, and the context is a highly charged academic discourse that spills into other social science disciplines as a feud between Marxist and poststructuralist theoretical approaches. So maybe this debate has nothing to do with actual political struggles, social movements, and grassroots resistance. Yet the distance between the academic debates of activist scholars and their real-world political implications is far less in India than it is in the United States. Such debates affect the very recognition and validation of movements—how struggles are framed and carried out, who leads and takes part in them, and whose interests and beliefs are represented or left out of political space.

Once the ideal type of the Nehruvian developmental welfare state was discarded in 1991, other models replaced it: state as vehicle for neoliberal capital accumulation or violent ethnoreligious chauvinism. Either of these orientations made it less and less feasible for the organized Left to strategize a role within it. Not only had it failed in its original stated goals but it had then actively abandoned these goals altogether. The function previously ascribed to the state was as a defender against imperialism and military-backed capital accumulation with a British face. Now it was the promoter of the same, with an Indian face. It could be condemned now for what it was trying to be, not just for what it was failing to be. The key questions for new social movement formations then became: If the state model had forfeited its credibility as a medium for representing the will of the people, and delivering on what they asked of it, what other routes to social transformation lay beyond it? If the political party model had failed as vehicle of emancipation, then what other forms of mobilization could be imagined?

The Nontraditional Left

It's a cliché to note that in India, old things don't disappear; new things just get added, juxtaposing computers with rustic squat toilets, and SUVs with bullock carts. This may have much more to do with the acute maldistribution of wealth than the persistence of tradition, but in any case you could say it was true of the Indian Left, where the Old Left never really disappeared; it was simply joined (sometimes in actual battle) by the New Left.

In 1962, the Communist Party of India (Marxist), or CPI(M), broke off from the CPI (founded in 1924), following the Sino-Soviet split. (The CPI stayed loyal to Moscow; the CPI(M) sided with China.) In 1969, the Maoist Communist Party of India (Marxist-Leninist), or CPI(ML), peeled away from its Left flank along with an insurgent wing commonly known as the Naxalites (after the Bengali village of Naxalbari, site of a police firing on a peasant demonstration in 1967). As in many other places around the world, the late 1960s' revolutionary upsurge crested into the early 1970s only to collapse in a round of lethal repression, crushing defeats, disillusionments, and major world-system shifts—and the way forward had to be reconsidered. Nevertheless, the array of militant groups shorthanded as Naxalite has reemerged from decades of quiet persistent growth throughout the "red corridor," a north-south axis through the central forested areas from Nepal to Andhra Pradesh. A merger of the major militant factions in 2004 produced the CPI (Maoist)—which the prime minister and home minister have repeatedly called India's greatest internal security threat (except when it's the Muslims, as the joke goes).

The CPI(M) has remained the dominant party and a relatively significant force in electoral politics. It held power in the provinces of West Bengal and Kerala for over thirty years, and at several junctures was an influential player in national coalition politics. Adept in the pragmatic compromise required in the game of parliamentary power, it favors industrialization above all—which ironically has put it at odds with the further Left and its own rural constituency, especially given harsh recent conflicts around acquisitions of agricultural land for industrial projects.

It also identifies itself as the only true and representative voice of the Left. Yet critics had been challenging the CPI(M)'s attempts to claim its own institution and party line as synonymous with the Left itself for many years. As was the case worldwide, the critiques and correctives applied by the New Left to the Old Left tended to tilt it in more antiauthoritarian, flexible, and intersectional directions—which is to say, more anarchistic elements would be present in its commonsense form and content. Incidentally, Omvedt comments that in the earliest stages of the New Left upsurge, "the Naxalite movement . . . combined orthodox Marxist-Leninist language with what many saw (with a good deal of validity) as 'ruralist anarchism.'"[7] (Of course, depending on who those "many" were, this was of a piece with other criticisms and self-criticisms, such as "infantile," "adventurist," and "ultra-left.")

Several Delhi-based progressive scholars wrote a statement in May 2011 after the defeat of the CPI(M)-led Left Front governments that had governed West Bengal and Kerala since 1977, proclaiming that the death of the Left had been (yet again) greatly exaggerated, because the Left is not the CPI(M); and not only because the coalition, while losing its majority, had actually held on to a significant percentage of votes.

> Votes have never been a real marker of the strength
> of a political movement and its culture. Indeed, the
> Left Front parties now have a historic opportunity
> to transform themselves, starting with a conscious ef-
> fort to introduce more democracy in their ranks and
> a culture of open debate. . . . [I]t is clear that as long
> as Indian democracy survives . . . in its broken state
> as a system unable to nourish the mass of its popula-
> tion or live without violence and the subjugation
> of whole communities, the Left outside parliament,
> the left as a culture of democracy and resistance, a
> network of movements and organisations, and a
> new more vigorous set of campaigns, will continue

to flourish. A younger, more radical generation
will undoubtedly be attracted to it and to its values
of solidarity, equality, freedom and opposition to
capitalism both in India and worldwide.[8]

Until his death in 2009, Kandalla Balagopal was one of
the most highly respected voices within critical leftist circles.
He left his position as a professor of mathematics in 1985 to
work full time as a civil liberties and human rights activist,
and later became a lawyer. After serving as general secretary
of the Andhra Pradesh Civil Liberties Committee for fourteen years, he broke away in 1997 to form the Human Rights
Forum.[9] The split was due to a disagreement on the militant
methods of the Naxalites. While unquestionably a man of
the Left (and erstwhile Maoist sympathizer), he was unwav-
ering in his criticism of violence and violations of human
rights, no matter who perpetrated them.

"My own understanding of the human rights move-
ment is that it is essentially a moral concern," said Balagopal
in an editorial in the *Human Rights Bulletin* shortly before
his death. "This is where many of my friends disagree; they
believe it is a political concern. It all depends on how you
define politics, but my only point is that essentially it is a
question of . . . asserting certain values other than the values
of domination, power and oppression."[10] In the 1990s, he
had a strong influence on student Left activities in Delhi.
Menon recalls that "for many of us politicized during this
period, Balagopal stood for something that many dedicated human rights activists/intellectuals found difficult
to do: to respond to changing realities and not hesitate

to unflinchingly argue against even the (revolutionary) stream—from within—if that is where his analysis of realities took him."[11] In the discussions inspired by Balagopal and the People's Union for Democratic Rights (PUDR), they began moving beyond mode of production debates and "the traditional left questions," such as "semi colonial/ semi feudal or capitalist; parliamentary/mass based politics or armed struggle," by linking class analysis to other issues and structures, such as gender- and caste-based injustices, communalism, and regional autonomy.

Apart from the issue of violence, Balagopal's critiques also had to do with the recognition of all kinds of rights violations on the basis of unequal power relations. The legitimacy of the political cause never lets you off the hook for acts of rights violation on your own account, he stressed. Those could and must be criticized even (or even more) when the cause is one you supported. Similarly, Balagopal pointed out the importance of the distinction between the political issues behind a militant struggle, which are primary and must be addressed, and the legal/ criminal aspect, which should be dealt with separately (assuming the rule of law was recognized as just—perhaps a surprisingly optimistic view of the law on his part). Therefore, even if the political issues could be resolved in favor of what the movement is fighting for, the movement would then still have to pay for the consequences of its own crimes against democracy and human rights. This begs the question, What overarching rights framework and enforcement regime was Balagopal pointing toward? If it was one that existed both before and after the new dispensation, was this then not a total revolution but instead a more localized reform?

"Can we turn to the law to make governance answerable to popular disapproval other than at election time? Constitutional democracy as we know it in India gives little scope for such a hope," he wrote on India's Republic Day in 2009. Although many activists seemed to look to Public Interest Litigation cases (PILs, comparable to class action lawsuits) as magical remedies, Balagopal was more skeptical of the system. "Desperation can be the only reason for these illusions. Less excusable is the ignorance of the sociology of adjudication. Judges, taken as a class, are at one with most of the political and economic tendencies since liberalisation for no more subtle reason than that they belong to the social class that has benefited and will benefit much more from these tendencies."[12]

In the face of this kind of intractability,

> There is no option but to devise ways of stopping the system in its depredations. Since Indian democracy has not learnt to respect reasoned criticism unless it is armed with the strength to physically prevent the execution of the policies criticized, ways of achieving such strength must be sought by agitational movements. In principle the best method is to mobilize the people likely to be affected in large numbers and physically sit in the path of the State and Capital.[13]

Activists must resist the temptation of shortcuts, whether by PIL or taking up arms.

It all came back to the principle that ends never justified means; prefiguration was essential.

> When the violence attaches itself to a political path that is mediated by establishment of political and social domination at each level, as in the case of communists in general and the naxalites in particular, it raises more questions for the human rights movement. A defining characteristic of the human rights movement is its attitude of suspicion towards all power and authority, whether political or social. It may be utopian to believe that human society will at any time be fully free of all power and authority. And moreover, the human rights movement has positively welcomed the use of the authority of the law for ameliorative purposes in the context of social and economic deprivation. Yet it cannot be again said that a major and quite necessary concern of the human rights movement is to reduce the quantum of authority and power in society to the strictly necessary level. . . . [14]

This meant that activists could never relax their vigilance against

> the consequences that spring from a political strategy of "liberation" through establishment of the authority and power of the "right" agents, whether the rightness is defined in moral terms or "scientific" terms. It cannot be content with the assumption

that when power is exercised by the "right" people, there can be no occasion for human rights concern. Most of us do not need to be told this about putative benevolent dictators, but we do not find it equally obvious about communist dictators, whether in power in the State or in power over local society preliminary to such ascendance. How can the Human Rights movement not look at how this power is being established, . . . what norms it is following, how democratic the norms are, how accountable this power is to the people in whose name it is exercised, and so on? Can the fact that the purported final aim of the authority is total liberation of us human beings from all oppression render one blind to these questions?[15]

For Balagopal, of course, the answer was no.

Another formation conscientious of prefigurative methods (although they probably wouldn't have put it in those terms) was the Shramik Mukti Dal in rural Maharashtra, one of the "post-traditional communist" groups that developed throughout the 1980s. Bharat Patankar, one of its founding activists, said, "Now, revolution means . . . the beginning of a struggle to implement a new strategy regarding the relationship between men and women and between people of different castes and nationalities. It means alternative ways of organizing and managing the production processes, alternate concepts of agriculture and of agriculture/industry/ecology, and alternative health care."[16]

He also insisted that the goal was no longer to encourage the working class to take over the state and industrial system but rather to reconceptualize and reconstruct the very nature of political and economic systems. According to the Shramik Mukti Dal's manifesto, "The basis of this conception is a total transformation in all fields including the relations among human beings, the means of human production and the relations of production, the relations of humans with nature." This would be a revolution that "creates a new ecologically balanced, prosperous, non-exploitative society," not as a single event, but instead a daily "process of creation," by "striking one blow after another against the roots of the established capitalist, casteist, patriarchal, social-economic structure."[17] Rather than solely focusing on class, the means, process, and organization of production had to be understood as based also in the systems of caste and patriarchy. Furthermore, environmental sustainability could not be forgotten, nor the fact that (in Patankar's words) within the "symbiotic and harmonious balance existing in nature . . . [h]umankind could only advance on the basis of . . . the healthy development of these interrelationships" between themselves and "the atmosphere, water, rain, trees, jungles, rivers, hills, other animals, birds, insects, worms, germs, the sun, the moon, the solar system, and so on."[18]

"In order to create a new society of human liberation," therefore, "'revolution' cannot be simply a matter of the toiling classes taking of control of the means of production created by capitalism." Renewable resource based production, while not guaranteed to be carried out in a just way, could at least, unlike the production method instituted by capitalism, be "undertaken in a decentralized fashion under the cooperative control of the toiling people."[19]

Finally, it was not part of the Shramik Mukti Dal's agenda to replace the current state with a new state power; instead,

> destroying the power of the current state and in its place bringing in the organized network of decentralized and ecologically balanced agro-industrial centers and, the development of the whole society is the all-round development of every individual as a precondition for the people's new democratic society, this is the revolutionary alternative. From its very beginning, "for a principled transformation the people's parallel power" will be established from the "revolutionary process of the toilers." . . . The power that has been known as the state will be ended and a new communal cooperative society will be established in this world.[20]

Jogin Sen Gupta, another ex-sectarian Communist, was disgusted by parties but still committed to movements. Through participation in various struggles during the 1980s, he found himself learning from feminist and indigenous perspectives, and proclaiming himself heartened rather than depressed by the disintegration of the iron curtain, concluded that "autocracy—whatever be its color—stands for curbing the bottom peoples' right to associate, assert and build up their power. So a movement against authoritarianism—whatever its color—is building up people's capacity for socialism." To him it was "not van-guardist tendencies, but informal networks; not armed 'liberation struggles' but popular upsurges; not the purely political, but the daily-life-based cooperative practices [that] were the keys to the future. This process of coopera-tion and democratic action by ordinary people in everyday life was . . . the 'primary' social movement, the force behind the others."[21]

The Nonparty People's Movements

Other new manifestations of antisystemic resistance posi-tioned themselves completely outside the contentious fami-ly tree of Left parties and guerrilla groups. This critical New Left perspective called for a more intersectional analysis, with a strong social ecology component as opposed to the Nehruvian dirigiste developmental orthodoxy. Just as the debate over post-Enlightenment reason was the implicit backdrop to the spectrum of Indian anticolonialism, the principle of the developmental state placed its stamp on the mainstream Left—pinning the task of liberation on state planning and science, with industrial development as the key to freedom and equity. There were also critical alternate interpretations, however, that argued for the need to con-ceptualize a nondevelopmentalist paradigm while simulta-neously questioning their relationship to existing political institutions and the very meaning of democracy.

In the environment of advanced global capitalism, an entirely new notion of revolution and emancipatory mobilization was essential—one that would address those sectors subject to "particular forms of exploitation not recognized in traditional class analysis" and yet more salient than ever at the present stage—namely, the women's, peasant, environmental, and Dalit movements. The other stream of resistance to the structures of neocolonialism and internal colonialism since the 1990s came from the new social movements and "non-party people's struggles," as intellectuals and activists grew more aware of the necessity of incorporating the registers of caste and patriarchy as well as ecological concerns into their analysis of power.[22]

Interestingly, one theme among the variously situated economic struggles that Omvedt identifies is that they are "directed against the state, rather than against the holders of private property; that is, the 'decentralizing' or 'antistatist' thrust, is economic as much as it is political." She draws on Immanuel Wallerstein's linkage between the political and economic decentralizing moves of "emphasizing democratic participation . . . 'eroding the state' rather than attempting to take state power," and "retaining 'local' control over surpluses." This movement orientation, though, is not apolitical but instead "an effort to redefine political action, to find ways of reconstructing politics."[23] Foregrounding these dimensions called for a more comprehensive "unified" analysis of capitalism that could recognize manifold sites of surplus extraction—not limited to wage labor but rather falling everywhere along a complex and distended chain of accumulation—from appropriation of land and minerals, to reproductive labor, through a string of value-added transactions.

One of the first sustained analytic alternatives to the traditional Left approach came from the members of the Lokayan ("dialogue of the people") group, founded by Rajni Kothari and D. L. Sheth in 1980.[24] Lokayan's stated mission was to create a nonvanguardist "action-research project" that sponsored dialogues and workshops among intellectuals and activists on topics covering the gamut of new social movement concerns, including Dalit and tribal struggles, gender, ecology, communalism, and civil rights. The goal was

> to evolve a systematic critique of the established models of development and the state, and also to promote political action drawing upon the large variety of micro-initiatives that are engaged in the struggle for a just society. . . . [T]o build a body of knowledge, opinion and concrete strategies of intervention at the "macro" level that will promote a decentralised democratic order and enhance respect for the cultural and social diversity of marginalised sections of society . . . [thus] helping to unify the various movements for egalitarian change.[25]

The prolific writings of its key members, in the *Lokayan Bulletin* and other publications, made "the overall Lokayan perspective almost hegemonic in the wider circles of those who were attracted to the new movements and the issues they raised."[26] But they ultimately stopped short of advocating a true alternative, turning back toward a reformation of the structures they were critiquing. (Lokayan's ambiguous relationship to foreign funding also under-scored the wariness many activists came to feel toward transnationally connected NGOs in their subtle depoliticization of radical struggles.)

In dozens of articles, Kothari proclaimed the failure of most of the previous political institutions and systems associated with the postcolonial state alongside the failure of previous forms of resistance, revolutionary parties, and organization. This was partly their own fault, for losing touch with the people, their needs and aspirations; but the harsh backlash "perpetrated both by the State and by private vested interests" was not their fault. This took place in

> a context where . . . the process of marginalisation is spreading, technology is turning anti-people, development has become an instrument of the privileged class, and the State has lost its role as an agent of transformation, or even as a mediator, in the affairs of civil society. It is a context of massive centralisation of power and resources, centralisation that does not stop at the national centre either and makes the nation State itself an abject onlooker and a client of a global "world order."[27]

Menon notes that "for Kothari, the crises of 'ecocide, ethnocide and militarization' [were] inevitable outcomes of processes unleashed by the three dominant projects of the state—Development, Secularism and Security." This resulted in "a kind of development driven by the needs of global capital, which is destroying the resource base of the country, its sustainability as well as people's access to it."[28] The state that once upon a time "had so confidently joined in Third World struggle against hegemonic powers, had been a pillar of the non-aligned movement, and had followed a model of self-reliance based on a measure of de-linking from the world capitalist system, has today fallen so easy a prey to the doctrines of . . . integration into the world market, and to the homogenising spread of high tech, high consumerism, ecological destruction and ethnic genocide."[29] In other words, it was being re- or neocolonized.

Furthermore, Kothari contended, its repressiveness was directly related to its increasing alienness and separateness from society: lacking hegemonic consent or a sense of legitimate representativeness, the only recourse was to force. He concluded one article by saying that

> our overview is of the decline of the state as a legitimate instrument of social will and its being sidetracked by new constellations of power and resources—corporate capitalism with its global reach, communal and ethnic formations . . . also leading to its growing decline as an authoritative organ of civil society which was at one time supposed to possess a monopoly of coercive power and violence. What remains of the state is, of course, being turned over to agents of violence and terror, all the way from police and the military to mafia criminal gangs. . . . There is taking place a growing breakdown of authority of the state in the wake of its being challenged by a growing incidence of revolts and

rebellions on the one hand and delegitimisation
through new managerial doctrines like privatisation
on the other. Perhaps the fault lay in adopting this
very conception of the state as the sole repository of
power and authority.[30]

After all, this concept had emerged in the Europe of the late
Middle Ages. Why should anyone assume it was identically
applicable in the modern third world?

All the changes on the international and domestic
terrain, brought on by the turbulence of a new phase of
globalization, called for new nonparty forms of popular
resistance more appropriate to the conditions. These grassroots movements could be understood as signs of a sense of
the bankruptcy "of States. Of parties. Of other party-like
organisations. Of the organised economy. Of leadership.
Of democratic institutions. Of NGOs and voluntary agencies," observed Kothari. "They are based on deep stirrings of
consciousness . . . as a response to the incapacity of the State
to hold its various constituents in a framework of positive
action, its growing refusal (not just inability) to deliver the
goods and its increasingly repressive character."[31]

Yet their implications were on the macro scale. They
also had "to be seen as part of the democratic struggle at
various levels, in a radically different social context than
was posited both by the incrementalists and the revolutionaries, at a point of history when existing institutions
and the theoretical models on which they are based have
run their course . . . when large vacuums in political space
are emerging thanks to the decline in the role of the State

and the virtual collapse of 'government' in large parts of rural India."[32]

In Kothari's view, the nonparty organizations and

> movements for regional autonomy and decentrali-
> sation [were] intended to take the avenues of politi-
> cal participation closer to the people, to be carried
> out in an idiom and mode of communication and
> around issues that intimately relate to them....
> The "regional" phenomena in India, combining in
> its force a rejection of the authoritarianism of the
> Centre; the dominance of the metropoles (and
> their imperial patrons), the cultural hegemony of
> bourgeois cosmopolitanism and the political econ-
> omy of corruption ... the chauvinist drives of the
> national elite, has to be understood as part of the
> larger democratic struggle [that will] reorder the
> distribution of power in favour of the lower reaches
> of society.[33]

Kothari, however, then made a 180-degree recupera-
tive turn, apparently contradicting his own description.
Although the movements he has just portrayed so positively "were to be seen as attempts to open alternative political spaces outside the usual arenas of party and government," he then insisted that they were not really outside
the state, which he had just depicted so negatively. They
instead should be seen as potential "new forms of organisation and struggle meant to rejuvenate the State and to make
it once again an instrument of liberation from exploitative

structures (both traditional and modern) in which the underprivileged and the poor are trapped." With apparently no justification to be deduced from anything he had just said, he wanted to use "the democratic idea as a means of rendering the state into a socially purposive instrument" whose legitimacy and indispensable authority would be clear to all.

But who are the underprivileged and poor?

No antiauthoritarian history (or revolutionary social transformation) of India could overlook the issue of caste, one of the most toxic systems of social hierarchy ever instituted in the world, comparable in its entrenched effects to the foundational racism of the U.S. state—a comparison not lost on the Dalit Panthers, who modeled themselves on the Black Panthers, combined with a splash of Naxalism and a generous infusion of Ambedkarism, when they formed their group in 1972. The Dalit's new political visibility after the Mandal Commission's report in 1980 was one of the features identified as transforming the terms of the Nehru-era political discourse.[34] "To this new brand of vernacular leaders," Menon and Nigam write, "the ideological battles between Left and Right might have appeared . . . as insubstantial differences within a modernist bloc of privilege."[35]

Yet Dalit movements weren't necessarily antiauthoritarian, although some were indeed radically egalitarian. (Some weren't even that, seeking not an end to the hierarchy but instead a better rung on the ladder for a particular group.) From the anarchist perspective, Dalit and feminist movements may be objectively, even if not subjectively, revolutionary in their efforts at dismantling interlocked, hierarchical structures of oppression and exploitation. The greatest legacy of Ambedkar, Dalit leader, legal scholar, and primary drafter of the Indian constitution, was as a republican in the best Enlightenment sense of the word. His ideology combined the values of the French Revolution with the egalitarianism and rationalism of Buddhism. Hinduism, as a dominant feature of Indian culture, had to be judged like any ideology or system by the "test of justice" and "test of utility," declared Ambedkar. It failed on both counts. True liberty, he argued, required social equality, economic security, and the availability of knowledge. After Ambedkar, though, in Omvedt's regretful estimation the Dalit movement tended to lack ideological content; while the latter-day Panthers sorted themselves into Ambedkarite/ Buddhist, Marxist, and urban gangsterish ("we didn't read the manifesto, we only knew—if someone puts their hand on our sister, cut it off!") tendencies.[36]

Dalit movements did not necessarily see themselves as part of an anticolonial struggle, unless in the implicit sense that the Brahminic master narrative proudly claims the mantle of conquest along with the identity of primordial Aryans, enshrining an origin myth in which they entered the subcontinent from the northwest in ancient Vedic times, bringing their dominion and civilizational advancement to the primitive (and supposedly darker-skinned) prior inhabitants. During the anti-British mobilizations, Ambedkar and his followers were more apt to be British loyalists, blaming Gandhi and the INC for the discrimination, exclusion, and brutality they routinely faced within a conservative Hindu-dominated society.

On the other hand, the contemporary Adivasi narrative of resistance clearly evokes the dynamics of colonization. This is particularly true in the regions of Jharkhand and Chhattisgarh—the mineral-rich, heavily forested areas in the center of India, carved out of Bihar and Madhya Pradesh in 2000—where Adivasis are the bulk of the population.

In these as in many other regions of India today, the issue of land acquisition is possibly the most urgent frontier of resistance to neoliberal capitalism, with the Indian state seen as its agent. And the major legal instrument by which the Indian state commandeers land from agrarian and forest-based communities to give to mining and manufacturing corporations is still the Land Acquisition Act of 1894, put in place by the British colonial administration. The law was ostensibly a way to transfer private land to "public use"; in practice in the liberalized economy, it is quite the opposite. Nowadays, "private" can mean the commons of a village or tribal community, while "public" can mean a multinational corporation's mining concession or designated Special Economic Zone. These zones are tax-free, duty-free areas that in effect function as foreign territory, exempt from compliance with domestic labor and environmental laws.[37] This arrangement sounds uncannily like the colonial-era concessions and extraterritoriality agreements by which the East India Company was able to set up shop even prior to formal sovereignty.

Resistance to land acquisition became big news with the Narmada Valley Development Plan, which sparked a massive mobilization against the submersion of villages that threatened the displacement of over a quarter million people. The

Narmada Bachao Andolan (Save the Narmada movement) was established in 1985, and grew to be an international cause célèbre, catalyzing an unprecedented alliance of environmental, peasant, human rights, and other organizations. But this target was still a remnant of the Nehruvian state model; dams were his great "temples" of modernity and the modern nation-state. In the more recent mobilizations, the enemy is more directly transnational capital.

In 2006, the villages of Singur and Nandigram in West Bengal, respective sites of a proposed Tata car factory and an Indonesian-owned (Selim Group) chemical plant, became volatile flash points for resistance and violent repression as well as widespread solidarity action, as did the Pohang Iron and Steel Company (POSCO), a Korean corporation, in the Indian state of Orissa in 2011. Such contestation is simultaneously an intervention in the logic of commerce and profit, and a primary defense of the lives and livelihoods of the people affected—thus addressing both aspects of "postcolonial" colonialism at once: global and internal. Yet the two are closely tied. Grassroots mobilizations that focus on manifestations of transnational corporate capitalism, engaged in the unmasked act of accumulation by dispossession, also function as implicit indictments of the neoliberalized state. So land acquisition struggles can easily be seen as continuing resistance to colonization, or at any rate to the economic processes included historically within the colonial package. This is what enclosure of the commons looks like.

Similarly, the Indian state utilizes the logic of insurgency and counterinsurgency to guarantee the security of capital accumulation in these areas, through various army, police, and paramilitary bodies as well as a state-backed citizens' militia, the Salwa Judum, as a counterweight to Naxalite militance. It is not coincidental, as many progressive activists and scholars point out, that the Indian government sensationalizes the threat in order to justify the militarization and extralegality by which it controls unrest in these regions of great potential wealth extraction as well as endemic local poverty. Simply by slapping on the Naxalite label, any human rights activist or reformer who works in those areas can be accused of sedition—that is, any sort of criticism of the Indian government, which is again a move taken directly from the British colonial playbook of the early twentieth century—and made vulnerable to lengthy imprisonment or extrajudicial killing.[38]

Acknowledging the need to incorporate ecological awareness on the long march to socialism, Archana Prasad, a researcher known for her work on forest policy and tribal issues, has criticized environmentalists for equating modernization with colonization. The difference, she argues, is that colonization means development for someone else's benefit; current development is for Indians' own benefit.[39]

But this contention is somewhat misleading. First, we can't reduce modernity simply to development and/or industrialization. It's possible, as many have already done, to criticize industrialization while proposing an alternate modernity. This is a genuine point of disagreement between the new social movements and the CPI(M): if industrialization is the road to revolution and progress, because it will generate the revolutionary class, then the priority must be to develop an indigenous industrial base; but if industrialization is part of the problem, then an alternate mode of socially and ecologically sustainable production must be sought.

Second, the tribal and regional separatist movements are saying precisely that they are undergoing development for someone else's benefit, for extraction and incorporation into the capital accumulation process. The attribution of classical colonial practices to the central state is in this case aptly applied. In fact, only according to a nationalist logic is it possible to limit the differences between a collective "you" and a collective "someone else" to nationality. Such differences can also be based in class, gender, region, and minority status. But the nationalist logic equates "your nation's benefit" with "your benefit," even if it asks you to sacrifice personally.

Many of these mobilizations have been linked—at least communicationally, if not operationally—through loose networks of the National Alliance of People's Movements, defined in 1992 as an emerging "process" in the context of the dual trends of intensified liberalization and the rise of the Hindu right wing. It was formalized in 1996 as

> an alliance of progressive people's organisations and movements, who while retaining their autonomous identities, are working together to bring the struggle for primacy of rights of communities over natural resources, conservation and governance, decentralised democratic development and towards a just, sustainable and egalitarian society in

the true spirit of globalism. We stand against corporate globalisation, communalism and religious
fundamentalism, patriarchy, casteism, untouchability and discrimination of all kinds. We believe
an alliance emerging out of such a process with
shared ideology and diverse strategies can give rise
to a strong social, political force and a National
People's movement.[40]

The characteristic analysis—as summed up by Biju
Mathew, referring to a conversation he moderated between
Medha Patkar, a cofounder of the National Alliance of
People's Movements and the Narmada Bachao Andolan,
and political geographer David Harvey—true to its global
South base, is rooted in a consciousness of anticolonialism, thereby challenging the Eurocentrism of traditional
Marxist analysis.[41] This analysis also expands on the category of class, using a more multilevel concept of community at multiple scales that cut across classes. It favors the
revitalization of agriculture, but without romanticizing the
collective return of land to the tiller or an Edenic agrarian
life. As in the case of the panchayat system, while immediate control of resources by a local community may be struc-
turally desirable, this in itself does not guarantee that the
community will choose to use the resources in an equitable
and sustainable way, unless the communities themselves are
redefined from the bottom up.

Finally, as the early twentieth-century anticolonial
activists found affinity and sought solidarity amid the international radical networks of the metropoles, some late

twentieth-century people's movement activists came into contact with the network of resistance from below known as the global justice or alter-globalization movement. This in turn provided opportunities at both moments for points of encounter with Western anarchists, or activists who at least partake of a movement culture pervaded by the influence of Western anarchism.

Many groups participating in the National Alliance of People's Movements were also associated with the People's Global Action, an international coordinating framework initiated in 1998 in response to a call put out by the Zapatistas. Representatives from grassroots movements of seventy-one countries met in Geneva, including a large (200,000) delegation from India's Mazdur Kisan Sangram Samiti farmers' movement. The People's Global Action hallmarks manage to comprehensively catalog the essential features of multiple facets of oppression and exploitation, while aiming for universal relevance without cultural particularism. In this sense, it is both antiauthoritarian and anticolonial.

Some of these linked campaigns have also maintained their dialogue with the alt-globalization movement through participation in the World Social Forum process, though not without controversy. When the forum was held in Bombay in 2004, it provided an opportunity to crystallize some of the major contemporary debates around means and ends of antisystemic struggle in South Asia. Multiple counterconvergences organized by the traditional Left parties denounced it as a tool of imperialism for derailing struggles, "putting a human face on neoliberal globalisation," and being a hotbed of counterrevolutionary "anarchists, Trotskyists, postmodernists," and proponents of the "Seattle tradition."[42] It also drew valid critiques of the forum's complicity with corporate funding agencies in the global North, relative inaccessibility to nonelites, and general ineffectiveness on account of its refusal to shut down its treasured multivalence by committing itself to programmatic action. This indicated a tension between conflicting ideas of the forum's function: "Open Space or Organisation? Event or Process?" Movement or festival?[43]

The concept of open space has been the subject of extensive critical commentary anchored by the Delhi-based India Institute for Critical Action: Centre in Movement, which has played an active role in the World Social Forum process, and even more so in the evolving critical assessment of it.[44]

Director Jai Sen articulates open space as a complex term with multiple meanings and implications. For Sen, this includes a maintenance of possibilities and resisting closure; emergence, indeterminacy, and ambiguity; a condition of "networking, the apparent horizontality of social relations," which not only social movement activists but also corporate, military, and civil society entities have embraced as a "natural and normal way . . . to behave and organise things"; "the idea and practice of . . . a generalised, widespread, non-centralised and autonomous political-cultural phenomenon"; networking "in the material means of information exchange and communication and also of international travel"; an unstructured zone of "freedom, liberty, safety, a place where we can . . . exchange and learn more freely, the possibility of unexpectedness and therefore of unboundedness, and the possibility of another world." Open space, accordingly, "challenges and subverts the idea that structure and organisation are necessarily vertical or programmed," or hierarchical by definition. Yet Sen also stresses the importance of contextualization and accountability. Such a space is never "inherently neutral, open or equal," since it "lives in dialectical tension with its surrounds," and may have been created through "displacement and appropriation." It represents potentiality, not utopia. Therefore it must be "conceived, perceived, and practiced as struggle; as critical action. Open space—and opening spaces—must be seen as an insurrectionary act; as an insurrection."[45]

The task at hand is to keep an eye out for where antiauthoritarian and decentralizing tendencies are visible while also noting where resistance to neocolonialism, most obviously in the form of neoliberal capitalism and accumulation by dispossession, is visible, and asking whether there is any logic by which these two elements should have anything do with each other.

In the context of post-cold war neoliberal globalization, the Indian state reneged on its social contract and renounced its previous institutional persona, betrayed often in practice yet still cherished in the abstract, as emancipator and benefactor. Now that the state was aligned with colonizing forces rather than against them, as its redistributing mechanisms channeled wealth upward, not downward, an anticolonial (or neocolonial) orientation would by default have to involve opposition to the state. But did this materialize as a principle, and not just a situational tactic? For some, perhaps, yes.

In the words of Menon and Nigam, "What began with dissatisfaction over formal institutionalized politics, and the consequent search for more 'people-oriented' kinds of political structures and institutions, eventually moved toward a realization that it was not just the authoritarian-bureaucratic nature of development that was problematic. There grew a recognition of the more fundamental problem with the very ideology of development, centrally tied as it was to the idea of the nation-state's sovereignty over its domain."[46]

But again, this is an exploratory observation stemming from the analytic framework of this book, not an attempt to attribute this interpretation to anyone else. None of the movements discussed here is anarchist with a capital *A*; that word lacks resonance for them, and indeed conjures up quite different associations than it does in North America and Europe. Yet the questions, themes, conflicts, and issues involved—such as, How do you see the role of the state in relation to social movements? To global capitalism? To society? How do you relate to concentrated power? How do various forms of social hierarchy relate to class? What roles do technology, rationalism, and spirituality play in either liberation or oppression? What is "progress"? How do you articulate ecological sustainability with social justice?—are analogous to those that have characterized the anarchist problematic and lowercase *a* motif.

They are not anarchists, but some of them—for example, Vandana Shiva and Arundhati Roy—are people whom anarchists appreciate. Their commitments are intersectional, antiauthoritarian, nonhierarchical, and framed mainly in connection with a principle of social ecology whose genealogy may be traced through a selective synthesis of Gandhian and socialist thought—that is, the best of the rationalist-progressive and the romantic-countermodern tendencies.

All of this reinforces the conviction that liberation never meant the handover of institutions of governmentality and surplus extraction from foreign to local rulers. Instead, it means the dismantling of those institutions entirely, and the replacement of their functions and the systems of relationships they are based on with other systems of relationships. In this way, the warp and weft of the ongoing process of South Asian decolonization beyond formal independence on into the twenty-first century are tantalizingly analogous to those of the Western anarchist tradition.

PURNA SWARAJ

On Solidarity

Now for some practical applications, for this book isn't intended simply for theoretical or historical interest. The study of anticolonial activity is never just theoretical, and can never be disembedded from its still-unfolding history.

The historical reference point for my exploration of anarchism and anticolonialism tends to be South Asia. But the reference point for current political activism relevant to this conjuncture tends to be Palestine. This jump would seem strange if the motivation was a particularist interest in an exceptional region, but not if it is the principle of anti-imperialism. Besides, whenever I ask myself—as I often do—what the historical subjects I admire would do if they were around today, it's not hard to speculate that they would be continuing their efforts at social and economic justice by fighting against neocolonialism and neoliberalism in India, defending civil rights and racial justice in the United States, supporting political prisoners, and lending their solidarity and aid to any anticolonial struggles extant in the world—more or less exactly what they were doing fifty, seventy, or a hundred years ago.

In the memoir *Lucknow ki Panch Raaten* (Five Lucknow Nights), Ali Sardar Jafri paints a picture of himself and his Progressive Writers' Association comrades as young radicals in the 1930s, perpetually on fire with poetry and revolution. The fourth night is a dark and stormy one in 1941. Jafri and his friends have gathered at somebody's house after midnight, still on a collective high from a *mushaira* at All India Radio (a traditional high-culture form infused with new radical energy into something like an elevated spoken-word poetry slam). On the wall above the fireplace hangs a portrait of a *mujer libre* of Spain, below which is written "To Death." Jafri ardently describes the free woman's clenched fists, her heaven-raised face, her lips taut with fierce emotion, and the swelling breast that her warrior's garb could not conceal. (These are young guys, remember; amid the passions of global solidarity, they still had some work to do on the patriarchy front.)

"In a way," Jafri writes, "the picture was the translation of our romantic and our revolutionary emotions; we too wanted to be warriors unto death. We considered Spain to be our own country, because it was fighting against fascism for freedom and the beautiful dreams of humanity. Spain's freedom was our freedom, and on this night, the warrior woman was included in our party and advancing our courage in the intoxication of India's freedom."[1] (And possibly wine, he adds.) His buddy Faiz Ahmad Faiz offers up a poem he just heard, and they continue to trade couplets.[2] "This music was a new signal-bell in Faiz's soul, which in his later life would bring him to the tents of the Palestinian mujahidin. This warrior woman of Spain, and Yasser Arafat of Palestine, are two names for the same united front."[3] So too their struggle against imperialism in India. (From there he segues into a story about a Ku Klux Klan riot at a Paul Robeson concert in Peekskill, New York, and the power of song and poetry.)

During the first half of the twentieth century, India was the most prominent front in the global struggle against imperialism. A strategic linchpin for British imperial power, it was also a focal point for Western activists involved in movements comparable to those that in a later era (after the 1955 Bandung conference) would be described as third world solidarity. Following World War II and South Asian decolonization this front shifted in the 1950s to Algeria, Cuba, and Vietnam, joined throughout the 1960s by a wave of African decolonization struggles as well as New Afrikan, Puerto Rican, and Native American movements within the United States in the 1970s, and then by U.S. involvement in Central America in the 1980s. In the 1990s, Chiapas was most prominent; in the 2000s, the biggest flashpoint among extant anticolonial struggles and solidarity movements has probably been Palestine, along with indigenous movements throughout the Americas. (This, of course, is not an exhaustive list of all the sites of anticolonial resistance, which are legion, but just a quick sketch of a moving front line.)

Inevitably, questions about the ethics and effectiveness of solidarity work come up in any situation in which a relatively privileged outsider is coming into contact with a less privileged community, whether within or across political borders, and whether defined in terms of race, class, or anything else. It should be obvious that the first issue in relating to someone else's struggle is to avoid the Scylla of paternalist charity and Charybdis of appropriation, both exacerbated by the savior complex. Second, the recognition of analogies, affinities, and systemic connectivity—all of which may facilitate solidarity—has to be distinguished from simply claiming equivalence; "related" doesn't mean "identical." We can articulate connections and parallels by applying the language of colonization to various instances of expropriation, commodification, encroachment, enclosure, and subordination, without thereby trivializing the significance of actual historical colonization, located at a particular intersection of the racial power grid with the configurations of capitalism and state power.

I'm going to take a cue here from Gandhi, who wrote his manifesto *Hind Swaraj* in 1909, on a boat from England to South Africa, in the form of an exchange between himself and an imaginary interlocutor. The following composite exchange reflects years of internal and external dialogues, and countless workshops, events, and panels that I have attended or taken part in. These include most recently speaking on a panel exploring "anarchist solidarity" at the 2011 Left Forum along with Can Baskent and Matt Houston, and developing a workshop on boycott, divestment, and sanctions against the Israeli occupation for the 2011 anarchist book fair in New York along with Ethan Heitner, Samia Shafi, and Alexis Stern.

I hope this conversation continues, along with the effort to practice critical solidarity with those in struggle for any form of decolonization—including both neocolonialism (read neoliberal globalization) and the persistent legacies of previous colonization (read U.S.-backed authoritarian regimes).

You say you're an anarchist. Yet you're supporting X national liberation movement. How can you support a demand for statehood?

I don't support demands for statehood, per se. I do support people's struggle for self-determination and the space to determine the conditions of their own lives. It's not the task of an ally to decide what the best alternative is; in order to remain consistent with our own principles, anarchist allies of anticolonial struggles have to recognize that the people in question must decide for themselves.

But isn't that kind of a naive cop-out, knowing that they plan to create a state?

Well, the fact remains that they're forced to operate within a world of states. The reason anticolonial resistance struggles feel the need to institute sovereignty is because at any scale, a "liberated" area—whether an autonomous zone, *quilombo*, *caracole*, reservation, or any space run on decentralized and nonhierarchical principles—is still embedded in nonliberated space. It has boundaries inside of which these principles prevail, and outside of which they do not. It needs ways to mediate or transition between the two. That is, a zone in which its right to set the terms of how things will go is recognized and enforceable, where another law or power can't interfere.

An area that has fought off colonial rule still exists within the interstate system. If a newly decolonizing area doesn't gain recognition by that system, it has to fear reconquest or incorporation into someone else's nation-state or empire. This has always been the case for places with fuzzy borders or in border marches. Independent statehood was at least a nominal guard against that, even if only to establish external boundaries by the terms of international law. The logical conclusion to this dilemma is that in order for a decolonizing area to truly adopt a "no-state solution," we would have to dismantle the interstate system as a whole and create anarchism everywhere. There can be no postcolonial anarchism in one country! No doctrine of peaceful coexistence, but continuous world revolution!

Whoa, you're freaking me out! For a while there I was thinking you sounded sort of like a Maoist, but now. . . . Are you some kind of Trot?

No. I'm putting you on—sort of. Maybe. At least about the Trot part.

Seriously, though, how do you feel about standing next to or under a national flag? In an era when media images are so powerful, you have to be aware of what it means to link yourself visually to an icon like that.

Yeah, I do pay attention to that—say, to where I'm standing during a rally. The same goes for some sectarian organizations back home. But since you brought up visual meanings: flags and such are powerful symbols for many groups, including nations and states. Still, the symbolism of any given flag in a particular context is also layered with other complicated meanings and associations. We need to pay attention to the messages being communicated. Where is it shorthand for "freedom," "revolution," or "self-determination," and where is it read as an icon of state power?

Yeah, about that idea: your principle about respecting other people's self-determination raises more questions, and not just about states. What are the limits within which you can say, "This isn't my business; they can organize themselves as they want to," and beyond which you have to say, "This is abhorrent to my principles; I cannot stand with this struggle"?

Look, we all know that the enemies of our enemies aren't always our friends. Especially given the emphasis we place on the importance of means and process as a prefigurative path to the desired outcome, anarchists engaged in solidarity-based resistance can't postpone the problem or write it off as tactical. So one clue is whether someone else who's opposing a particular empire—the United States, let's say—is categorically anti-imperialist, or if they're just pulling for a rival power to get the advantage, supporting some unsavory character simply because they're anti-American. There are a lot of false binaries presented to us.

Well then, let's be more concrete. If you can't separate means and ends, the negative and positive fights, how can you support uncritically a group of people who are—oh, I don't know—reactionary, misogynistic, authoritarian, anti-Semitic, chauvinistic, or super religious?

I don't. For one thing, be careful not to equate a whole culture or society with any of those adjectives. But I take your point, and the thing is, relationships of solidarity should not be uncritical from either side. If practiced on a level ground of mutual respect and two-way dialogue, there should be neither romanticizing nor paternalism. Your partners are not saints, noble savages, or charity cases. If I hate imperialism, then it's in my own interest to work against it from any angle I can. I'm not doing it as a favor to anyone. If we have (at least some of) the same goals and enemies, agreement in the need for resistance is not a stretch. And along the way you're learning from and changing each other. Pay attention. You gain trust by showing integrity and commitment over time. Then maybe someday, you'll have earned the right to intervene as an insider.

Sure, be respectful, listen, learn. OK. Still, how can you remain committed to your own core anti-oppression principles regarding things like gender and sexuality, or animal rights, without perpetuating the subtle (or not-so-subtle) colonialism of trying to "improve" someone else's culture? Can you refrain from imposing your own ideas on someone whom you're supposed to be supporting, if that means condoning ideas that go against your convictions regarding pure anarchist principle?

You mean, why can't we just persuade the Arab world to go vegan?

Very funny. But I mean really: is this an insurmountable paradox? On the other hand, is "taking leadership" just another cop-out, an abdication of principles?

It's important to recognize the internal debates within any society and its dynamic changes through time. Nothing is monolithic. It's virtually guaranteed that not all members of the putative nation are in total agreement about their social visions. Chances are that among these elements, you'll recognize counterparts with whose principles, strategies, tactics, and methods you do feel affinity. That's who you "take leadership" from.

I guess I feel comfortable enough with all that. So let's say I'm ready to get involved. What do I do? What is the job of a relatively privileged, mobile activist from the global North in relation to those resisting oppression on their own behalf in the South?

There are two answers to that. First of all, have you been invited to do something, and if so, what? Has someone put out a call for action? Who? What sort of action? Are there resources and capacities that are available to you as a first world dweller or northern passport holder that you can usefully leverage? Great, use that.

The second answer is deeper. It's pretty simple to see solidarity as the expression of support, whether symbolic or directly material, to a current resistance movement. But there's a deeper recognition of systemic, structural, and historical interrelationships that goes beyond that. A guy in the West Bank once said to some members of an International Solidarity Movement delegation, "We appreciate you all being here. It means a lot. But really, the best thing you can do to help is to go back home and end U.S. imperialism. Liberating ourselves is *our* job. Ending

U.S. imperialism is *your* job. You're in the belly of the beast." He was right. We've got the corporations and command systems all here, so what are we waiting for? If we recognize colonialism as an interconnected global power system in which we're all differentially located, then we're all engaged in a multifronted battle to dismantle and replace that system. Each particular site of exploitation and oppression requires resistance appropriate to that location. The key is to consciously link these sites and their particular struggles up with each other.

So how do they link up?

I knew you were going to say that. Aside from the military and monetary (thank you, Gil Scott Heron), I think perhaps the most obvious point of connection for anticolonial solidarity activists in the North during the last century has been the domestic struggle against racism. Antiracism in the metropolis is always profoundly interconnected with anticolonialism in the global South, since both depend on the same logic and are effects of the same historical causes. In fact, you could even say they're mutually constitutive. Accordingly, an APOC perspective or tendency makes an important theoretical contribution to anarchist praxis by foregrounding colonialism as a primary category of analysis as well as primary structure of oppression. This works in two directions: emphasizing antiracism with regard to North American society, including within its countercultures, such as anarchist milieus, and second . . .

Wait, aren't anarchist milieus already antiracist by definition?

Of course. They're also antipatriarchal. Therefore there is no manifest racism, sexism, ableism, ageism, homophobia, or other oppressive behavior within any anarchist space, project, collective, or community that I have ever seen. Nor is there any hegemonic orthodoxy about cultural practices and attitudes. That would be against our principles. So we're all set.

Now are you putting me on?
Yes.

And what was the second direction?

The second direction is emphasizing antiauthoritarian and nonnationalist modes of anticolonial struggle with regard to colonized peoples. This is what I meant before, about making decolonization a far more comprehensive liberation than the problematic concept of the nation-state can achieve. The meaning of freedom has to keep expanding to incorporate more categories of being, more dimensions of existence—I suspect I'm drawing that notion from Angela Davis.

Linking up these two dimensions, then, means viewing contemporary racial issues through the lens of colonial history and politics—not only in the ways we address native sovereignty claims and black civil rights, for example, but also in the ways we understand U.S. military doctrine and immigration policy. Occupying a hinge position, an APOC-oriented politics can create an intervention concerning precisely the question of the relationship between anarchism and anticolonialism. It's a shift in emphasis, calling for large-scale contextualization in both space and time—an argument for the centrality of decolonization to emancipatory praxis.[4]

OK, OK, calm down, you're basically preaching to the choir here. But you've just said a whole lot of stuff. What do you really want me to take from this?

I'm glad you asked. To sum up, decolonizing anarchism means making anarchism a force for decolonization, and simultaneously dismantling colonial assumptions within our own understanding and practice of anarchism. That requires us to see anarchism as one locally contextualized, historically specific manifestation of a larger antiauthoritarian tradition.

This does two related things. For one, it enables us to recognize processes of decolonization and practices of anticolonial struggle as analogous or parallel to the anarchist tradition (or at least to its aspirations), but without seeing them as imitations of anarchism, and without trying to claim them or pressuring them to take on our mantle. Questions about power, industrialization, and alienation that have been at the heart of the struggle for a postcolonial future have the capacity to shed light on the similar dilemmas that have marked out some of the debates central to the Western anarchist tradition, and vice versa.

The second is that it makes colonialism—as a system constructed from state institutions, global capitalism, and profound racism—a primary component of all our analysis and strategy. Much of this logic is common to the anti-imperialist politics of the 1970s' radical Left, but with the crucial amendment of antiauthoritarian means and ends. Efforts to facilitate nonstatist concepts of anticolonial liberation along with attempts to dismantle and discredit the racial inequities on which Western empires were built, and by which their resultant societies continue to function, are then two fronts in the same epic emancipatory struggle.

Meaning, in practical terms . . .
That if someone puts out a call that you have the capacity to answer, then go, but only if you're willing to be engaged consistently over the long term. And if you're able to do so with empathy and respect, without abandoning your critical awareness. Above all look to your own house; work at and from your own sites of resistance. While you do that, connect the dots; make the connections explicit. Fight racism. Undermine neoliberal capitalism. Interfere with war making. Resist gentrification and displacement. Subvert norms. Decolonize your mind.

Wait, didn't you forget one?
Oh yeah. Smash the state.

Notes

Introduction

1. See, for example, Adi Doctor, *Anarchist Thought in India* (Bombay: Asia Publishing House, 1964).

Highest Form of Anarchism

1. Aijaz Ahmad, *In Theory: Classes, Nations, Literatures* (London: Verso, 1992), 69.

2. Cited in Robert Cutler and Robert Baird, eds., *The Basic Bakunin: Writings, 1869–1871* (Amherst, NY: Prometheus Books, 1996), 175–77; see also Alfredo Bonanno, *Anarchism and the National Liberation Struggle* (Elephant Editions, 2002), 20–21. Many other classic texts on this theme can be found at http://theanarchistlibrary.org. More recent texts of interest include Steven Hirsch and Lucien van der Walt, *Anarchism and Syndicalism in the Colonial and Postcolonial World, 1870–1940: The Praxis of National Liberation, Internationalism, and Social Revolution* (Boston: Brill, 2010); Jason Adams, *Non-Western Anarchisms* (Zabalaza Books, 2003).

3. Rudolf Rocker, *Nationalism and Culture* (Montreal: Black

Rose Books, 1997), 252–53; Bonanno, *Anarchism*, 22–24.

4. Gabriel Kuhn, ed., *Revolution and Other Writings: A Political Reader* (Oakland, CA: PM Press, 2010).

5. See, for example, pieces by Walter Mignolo, Anibal Quijano, and Enrique Dussel in *Coloniality at Large: Latin America and the Postcolonial Debate* (Durham, NC: Duke University Press, 2008).

6. See Chela Sandoval, *The Methodology of the Oppressed* (Minneapolis: University of Minnesota Press, 2000).

7. In the 1820s, Roy and Tagore founded Brahmo Samaj, a liberal social reform movement that in essence redefined Hinduism; Roy is also sometimes called "the father of modern India." Khan did much the same for Islam, as a modernizing reformer and founder of Aligarh University in 1875.

8. This theme recurs throughout Cemil Aydin, *The Politics of Anti-Westernism in Asia* (New York: Columbia University Press, 2008).

9. Partha Chatterjee, *Nationalist Thought and the Colonial World* (Minneapolis: University of Minnesota Press, 1986), 38. Chatterjee is drawing on Louis Althusser here.

10. Ibid., 39.

The Propagandists of the Deed

1. Tilak Raj Sareen, *Select Documents on the Ghadr Party* (Delhi: Mounto Publishing House, 1994), 136. From the *Springfield Republican*, August 11, 1916.

2. Peter Heehs, *Nationalism, Terrorism, Communalism: Essays in Modern Indian History* (New York: Oxford University Press, 1998), 33–34.

3. Cited in ibid., 27.

4. James Campbell Ker, *Political Trouble in India, 1907–1917* (Calcutta: Superintendent Government Printing, 1917), 62–65.

5. Heehs, *Nationalism*, 112–13.

6. Rowlatt Sedition Committee Report (Calcutta: Superintendent Government Printing, 1919), 21–24.

7. Cited in Ker, *Political Trouble*, 51; paraphrase.

8. Cited in ibid.

9. Rowlatt Sedition Committee, 22, citing *Yugantar*, April 11, 1907.

10. Cited in Ker, *Political Trouble*, 66.

11. Cited in ibid., 67.

12. Cited in ibid., 75–76.

13. Cited in ibid., 78.

14. Ibid., 47; Heehs, *Nationalism*, 112. According to Nirode K. Barooah (*Chatto: The Life and Times of an Indian Anti-imperialist in Europe* [New Delhi: Oxford University Press, 2004], 40, 45), *Bartaman Rananiti*'s authorship was attributed to Abhinash Chandra Bhattacharya. Bloch's book appeared in 1900. A banker and railway magnate of humble Polish origins, Bloch served briefly as adviser to Czar Nicholas II. The book, which still appears in military curricula, was an indictment of modern industrial war as prohibitively destructive, annihilating the loser and economically crippling the winner, whose resources would be far better put toward pragmatic, constructive investment. It analyzed in detail military technology at that point, and predicted an emphasis on defensive positioning and guerrilla tactics rather than mobilization of massive conventional land armies.

15. Ker, *Political Trouble*, 49, 50.

16. Cited in ibid., 50.

17. Cited in ibid., 51–52.

18. Cited in ibid., 52; see also Rowlatt Sedition Committee, 24–25.

19. Cited in Ker, *Political Trouble*, 52.

20. The most famous of these were the attempted assassination of Superintendent Bampfylde Fuller; efforts to mine the railroad tracks on which the lieutenant governor's train would be passing; and several attempts to use bombs to assassinate Presidency Magistrate Douglas Kingsford, resulting in the "Muzaffarpur Outrage" when two Englishwomen were killed departing from his Muzaffarpur home in a carriage.

21. Indulal Kanailal Yajnik, *Shyamaji Krishnavarma: Life and Times of an Indian Revolutionary* (Bombay: Lakshmi Publications, 1950).

22. Home Political file 35A, October 27, 1908; Indian Home Rule Society (February 1905), *Indian Sociologist* 1, no. 3 (March 1905), in Arun C. Bose, *Indian Revolutionaries Abroad, 1905–1927: Select Documents* (Delhi: Northern Book Centre, 2002), 6.

23. Ker, *Political Trouble*, 156; Rowlatt Sedition Committee, 5.

24. Home Dept. A, September 27, 1905; Pran Nath Chopra, ed., *Indian Freedom Fighters Abroad: Secret British Intelligence Report* (New Delhi: Criterion Publications, 1988), 88–91.

25. Britain and France Sedition Committee Report, Bengal Secretarial Press, Calcutta, 1918, in Bose, *Selected Documents*, 3–5; Arun C. Bose, *Indian Revolutionaries Abroad, 1905–1922: In the Background of International Developments* (Patna: Bharati Bhavan, 1971), 16–17.

26. Cited in Brown, *Har Dayal*, 26. Brown notes the sources of these quotations as, respectively, *Principles of Ethics*, section 272, and *The Study of Sociology*, chapter 8.

27. Cited in ibid., 26.

28. Cited in Bose, *Indian Revolutionaries Abroad, 1905–1922*, 15.

29. See Bose, *Indian Revolutionaries Abroad, 1905–1922*, 18; Chopra, *Indian Freedom Fighters*, 69–70.

30. Home Political file, Secret 3, March 1909, 148–50, in Bose, *Selected Documents*, 28–30.

31. Letter from Sukh Sagar Dutt to Arun C. Bose, March 30, 1958, in Bose, *Selected Documents*, 38–39. For details on the intelligence operations, see Richard Popplewell, *Intelligence and Imperial Defence: British Intelligence and the Defence of the Indian Empire, 1904–1924* (London: Frank Cass, 1995).

32. Secret Prog. 49, DCI Simla 14.8.1909, B. September 1909, 47–54; DCI 31.7.1909, B. August 1909, 120–29; Prog 110, DCI 4.9.1909, B. October 1909, 110–17—all in Bose, *Selected Documents*, 32–38. See also Rowlatt Sedition Committee, 8. On other propagandists of the deed, see Chaman Lal Azad, *Bhagat Singh aur Dutt ki Amar Kahani* (New Delhi: Satya Prakashan, 1966); Sohan Singh Josh, *My Meetings with Bhagat Singh and on Other Early Revolutionaries* (New Delhi: Communist Party of India, 1976).

33. Cited in Ker, *Political Trouble*, 168–69.

34. Cited in ibid., 99.

35. In June 1912, Aldred published another article about Savarkar in the *Freewoman*, Dora Marsden's weekly suffragist journal. In fact, commented Ker (*Political Trouble*, 176–77) with some surprise, the Indians' main source of English sympathy, if not substantive support, was now among "the Socialists, and even . . . the Women Suffragists." Ker, with prim distaste, expresses some suspicion of Aldred's motives for doing so, since Ker sees no logical

reason why such an article should appear in "a magazine mainly devoted to sex questions which the lady editor permitted to be discussed with an amount of freedom usually confined to medical journals." Leela Gandhi doesn't find this surprising, however. On affinities between anticolonial movements and counterhegemonic groups within the empire whose oppositionality stemmed from other sources, see Leela Gandhi, *Affective Communities: Anticolonial Thought, Fin-De-Siècle Radicalism, and the Politics of Friendship* (Durham, NC: Duke University Press, 2006).

36. John Taylor Caldwell, *Come Dungeons Dark: The Life and Times of Guy Aldred, Glasgow Anarchist* (Glasgow: Luath Press, 1988), 95. See also, in general, the work of Ruth Kinna, such as "Bridging Differences through Revolutionary Action: Aldred on Anarchism and Marx" (paper presented at Cooper Union, New York, March 15, 2008); cf. DCI 11.9.1909, B. October 1909, 110–17, in Bose, *Selected Documents*. Indian radicals warmly recalled him later as the only Englishman to have stood up for them at the time, although Caldwell (*Come Dungeons Dark*, 213) notes that the only hint of socialist sympathies his Indian colleagues evinced occurred incidentally, "on the common ground of opposition to imperialism."

37. Caldwell, *Come Dungeons Dark*, 96. Aldred was later to return to prison as a conscientious objector to World War I.

38. Confidential, A. August 1909, 44–52, "Notice on Pondicherry and Chandernagore as Centres of Seditious Agitation," in Bose, *Selected Documents*, 70; evidence is given here that French Chandernagar was a conduit for arms and ammunition being moved from Paris to Bengal: "It is my strong impression that Chandernagore constitutes the arms depot of the Calcutta anarchist group."

39. Cited in Brown, *Har Dayal*, 30.

40. Cited in Ker, *Political Trouble*, 97; Bose, *Indian Revolutionaries Abroad, 1905–1922*, 22. In this connection, see also Bruce Marks, *How Russia Shaped the Modern World* (Princeton, NJ: Princeton University Press, 2003).

41. Cited in Ker, *Political Trouble*, 97.

42. Heehs, *Nationalism*, 89.

43. Chopra, *Indian Freedom Fighters*, 13–14.

44. Peter Heehs, *The Bomb in Bengal: The Rise of Revolutionary Terrorism in India, 1900–1910* (New York: Oxford University Press, 2004), 90–91. Another suspect in the instruction of the Indians is "the Russian revolutionary Mirinow—an exiled military engineer and a Sanskrit scholar" (Heehs, *Nationalism*, 91).

45. Chopra, *Indian Freedom Fighters*, 112.

46. Cited in Heehs, *The Bomb in Bengal*, 181.

47. See Richard Parry, *The Bonnot Gang: The Story of the French Illegalists* (London: Rebel Press, 1987)

48. Heehs, *Bomb in Bengal*, 90–91. See also Marks, *How Russia Shaped the Modern World*; Paul Avrich, *The Russian Anarchists* (Princeton, NJ: Princeton University Press, 1971).

49. Cited in Ker, *Political Trouble*, 55.

50. Cited in Bose, *Indian Revolutionaries Abroad, 1905–1922*, 21. On other bomb trainees in the course of the next year or so (1908–9), see Chopra, *Indian Freedom Fighters*, 1, 26.

51. Ker, *Political Trouble*, 56.

52. Heehs, *Bomb in Bengal*, 134.

53. The phrase means literally "hail to the mother" or motherland—one of the national liberation movement's main slogans.

54. Har Dayal, "*Shabash!* or *Yugantar* Circular," *Hindustan*

Ghadar (San Francisco), 1913, box 2:2, Bancroft Library, South Asians in North America Collection, Berkeley, CA (hereafter SANA).

55. Heehs, *Bomb in Bengal*, 256.

56. Cited in Ker, *Political Trouble*, 106.

57. Cited in Chopra, *Indian Freedom Fighters*, 78–79.

58. Ker, *Political Trouble*, xii.

59. John Nicol Farquhar, *Modern Religious Movements in India* (Macmillan, 1915), 354–86.

60. Ker, *Political Trouble*, xiii, xvii.

61. Cited in ibid., 71; cf. 92.

62. This is a common theme. On various aspects of it, see, for example, James Joll, *The Anarchists* (London: Eyre and Spottiswoode, 1964); James Billington, *Fire in the Minds of Men: Origins of the Revolutionary Faith* (Piscataway, NJ: Transaction Publishers, 1999); George Katsiaficas, *The Imagination of the New Left: A Global Analysis of 1968* (Boston: South End Press, 1987); Yves Fremion, *Orgasms of History: Three Thousand Years of Spontaneous Insurrection*, trans. Paul Sharkey (Oakland, CA: AK Press, 2002).

63. See Rowlatt Sedition Committee, 93–96; Heehs, *Nationalism*, 243. In actuality, the name Yugantar Gang referred to a larger, looser community that after the breakup of the "Maniktola Garden gang" in the Alipore bomb case, reconvened informally at the *Yugantar* publishing offices as well as various rendezvous points around Calcutta and environs, and was distinct from the Dhaka formation.

64. Cited in Heehs, *Nationalism*, 152.

65. Cited in Ker, *Political Trouble*, 100.

66. Ibid.

The Anarcho-syndicalists

1. Tilak Raj Sareen, *Select Documents on the Ghadr Party* (New Delhi: Mounto Publishing House, 1994), 153.

2. In this account I am primarily drawing on the words of Gobind Behari Lal, a member of Ghadar's original inner circle, included in Sareen, *Select Documents*; Emily Brown's comprehensively detailed biography *Har Dayal: Hindu Revolutionary and Rationalist* (Tucson: University of Arizona Press, 1975). See also Dharmavira, *Lala Har Dayal and Revolutionary Movements of His Times* (New Delhi: India Book Company, 1970).

3. His cousin Bengali revolutionary leader Jatin Mukherjee was part of the Maniktola Garden group and later killed by police during a Germany-backed insurgency attempt during World War I; his brother Jadu Gopal Mukherjee was active in the alliance of the postwar Hindustan Ghadar Party and Friends of Freedom for India, based on the U.S. West and East coasts, respectively.

4. Gordon H. Chang, introduction to *Caste and Outcast*, by Dhan Gopal Mukerji (Stanford, CA: Stanford University Press, 2002), 8.

5. Lal, cited in Sareen, *Select Documents*, 23–25.

6. Brown, *Har Dayal*, 21.

7. Ibid., 50.

8. Lal, cited in Sareen, *Select Documents*, 26–27.

9. Ibid., 29.

10. Indulal Yajnik, *Shyamaji Krishnavarma: Life and Times of an Indian Revolutionary* (Bombay: Lakshmi Publications, 1950), 275.

11. Brown, *Har Dayal*, 81.

12. Ibid., 83, citing Aldred's "Stop this Infamy!" *Herald of Revolt* 4, no. 5 (May 1914).

13. Brown, *Har Dayal*, 85.

14. Brooks, a Stanford literature professor best known for his work on American transcendentalism, became a long-term intellectual confidante. See Van Wyck Brooks, *An Autobiography* (New York: E. P. Dutton, 1965).

15. Lal, cited in Sareen, *Select Documents*, 30, 38.

16. Brown, *Har Dayal*, 129.

17. Ibid., 7–126.

18. Har Dayal, "Some Phases of Contemporary Thought in India," *Modern Review*, August 1911, cited in Brown, *Har Dayal*, 92. See also *Writings of Lala Hardayal* (Benares: Swaraj Publishing House, 1923); *Barabari ka Arth* [The Meaning of Equality], 1913, box 1:33, SANA; *Ghulami ka Zeher* [The Poison of Slavery] (San Francisco: Hindustan Ghadar Press, 1918), box 1:35, SANA; *Indian Peasant*, box 1:36, SANA; *Social Conquest of the Hindu Race* and *The Meaning of Equality* (San Francisco: Hindustan Ghadar Press, undated.), box 2:3, SANA.

19. Brown, *Har Dayal*, 102–3.

20. Har Dayal, *The Indian Peasant* (San Francisco: Hindustan Gadar Press, n.d.), box 1:36, SANA.

21. Ibid., 98–9.

22. Ibid., 99–100. "Karl Marx: A Modern Rishi" also appears in Dharmavira, ed., *Writings of Lala Hardayal*. As was often the case with the multivalent radicalisms of the day, one could interpret this phrase as pointing *either* to anarcho-communism a la Kropotkin or protofascist integral nationalism.

23. Lahiri had graduated from Calcutta University with a degree in chemistry and was continuing his research in explosives on the way to a master of science. As the initial organizer of Nalanda Hostel, a group house for Indian students, he had residents read

books on the revolutionary movements of the world as well as the glories of Indian history and civilization. He also had them train in self-defense, boxing, fencing, wrestling, shooting revolvers and rifles, cartridge making, and "how to recruit, organize and train terrorists." Darisi Chenchiah, "History of the Freedom Movement in India: The Ghadar Movement, 1913–1918," 4–6, box 4:3, SANA; L. P. Mathur, *Indian Revolutionary Movement in the United States of America* (Delhi: S. Chand, 1970), 21; Sareen, *Select Documents*, 72.

24. Chenchiah, "History of the Freedom Movement."

25. Lal, cited in Sareen, *Select Documents*, 31.

26. March 27, 1914, cited in Brown, *Har Dayal*, 112.

27. Lal, cited in Sareen, *Select Documents*, 30.

28. Savitri Sawhney, *I Shall Never Ask For Pardon* (New Delhi: Oxford India, 2008), 226–249.

29. Brown, *Har Dayal*, 107.

30. Brooks, *Autobiography*, 210. This description could easily evoke Nechayev or Nikolay Chernyshevsky as much as Bakunin.

31. Chenchiah, "History of the Freedom Movement," 6. See also F. C. Isemonger and J. Slattery, *An Account of the Ghadar Conspiracy, 1913–1915* (repr., Berkeley, CA: Folklore Institute, 1998), 10.

32. Brown, *Har Dayal*, 112–14.

33. Sareen, *Select Documents*, 38.

34. Har Dayal to Brooks, December 23, 1913, letter and enclosed leaflet, Van Wyck Brooks Correspondence, Van Pelt Library, Rare Documents Collection, University of Pennsylvania. Also cited in Brown, *Har Dayal*, 114–16.

35. Har Dayal to Brooks, December 23, 1913.

36. Ibid. PC meant "Post Commune," a reference to Paris 1871.

37. Ibid. See also Brown, *Har Dayal*, 116–17.

38. Chaz Bufe and Mitchell Verter, eds., *Dreams of Freedom: A Ricardo Flores Magón Reader* (Oakland, CA: AK Press, 2005), 75, 81, 357.

39. Brown, *Har Dayal*, 137.

40. Lal, cited in Sareen, *Select Documents*, 32.

41. Brown, *Har Dayal*, 129; Lal, cited in Sareen, *Select Documents*, 33. According to Lal, Har Dayal said that it was "one of our boys," meaning most likely one of his young "disciples" from the circle around Amir Chand circa 1908. Amir Chand was a major suspect, and it came out later that Har Dayal's letters to him were in the hands of the police.

42. The following Har Dayal quotations in this section are in Har Dayal, "*Shabash!* or *Yugantar* Circular" (San Francisco: Hindustan Ghadar Press, 1913), box 2:2, SANA.

43. See Benedict Anderson, *Under Three Flags: Anarchism and the Anticolonial Imagination* (New York: Verso, 2005); Mike Davis, "Heroes of Hell," *Radical History Review* 85 (2003): 227–37. The Ghadar Press later published a collection of profiles of "early anti-czarists and Russian socialists," including Perovskaya, Zasulich, Vera Figner, and Leo Deutsche.

44. Guy Aldred, "Stop This Infamy!" *Herald of Revolt* 4 (May 1914), cited in Brown, 144.

45. Brown, *Har Dayal*, 153.

46. Cited in Brown, *Har Dayal*, 209. See also Richard Drinnon and Anna Maria Drinnon, eds., *Nowhere at Home: Letters from Exile of Emma Goldman and Alexander Berkman* (New York: Schocken Books, 1975). Goldman, unlike her young acquaintance Agnes Smedley, had minimal awareness of the Indian struggle.

47. Letters contained in Record of Trial, *USA v. Bopp, Ram Chandra et al.,* U.S. Attorney, Northern District, CA, Neutrality Cases, 1913–1920, Work Papers and Evidentiary Notes, record group, 118, National Archives and Records Administration, San Bruno, CA; also cited in Brown, *Har Dayal,* 208–9.

48. Cited in Brown, *Har Dayal,* 133.

49. *San Francisco Chronicle,* March 28, 1914, cited in Brown, *Har Dayal,* 156.

50. On the succeeding exchange, see Deportation File, Interrogation Report: Proceedings against Har Dayal, Bureau of Immigration of the Department of Labor, record group 85, files 53572/92, 53572/92A, National Archives and Records Administration, San Bruno, CA.

51. Cited in Brown, *Har Dayal,* 156

52. Cited in ibid., 157.

53. Cited in ibid. The Ghadarites' experience in North America has been described as "proletarianization," in function and mentality. That is, their collective self-consciousness was modified by the conditions of a low-wage migratory labor force that were initially landless—and racialized to boot. At home in Punjab, by contrast, they could have been squarely labeled as classic middle peasants: independent smallholders rather than landless tenants of big landlords, proud of their self-sufficiency, and less interested in collectivization than in autonomy and release from land revenue.

54. Ibid.

55. Cited in Brown, *Har Dayal,* 158.

56. Cited in ibid.

57. Cited in Ved Prakash Vatuk, introduction to Isemonger and Slattery, *An Account of the Ghadar Conspiracy,* 1.

58. Cited in Brown, *Har Dayal*, 161.

59. Chenchiah, "History of the Freedom Movement," 8.

60. Brown, *Har Dayal*, 161.

61. Har Dayal to Van Wyck Brooks, April 30, 1914. Van Wyck Brooks Correspondence, Van Pelt Library, Rare Documents Collection, University of Pennsylvania.

62. John Taylor Caldwell, *Come Dungeons Dark: The Life and Times of Guy Aldred, Glasgow Anarchist* (Glasgow: Luath Press, 1988), 87–88.

63. Ibid., 88–89.

64. Lal, cited in Sareen, *Select Documents*, 12.

65. Cited in Caldwell, *Come Dungeons Dark*, 13, 14.

66. This section is drawn from Mukerji, *Caste and Outcast*, 141–210. Though somewhat fictionalized, Mukerji's story corroborates the details of contemporary accounts.

The Critical Leftists

1. C. S. Subramanyam, *M.P.T. Acharya, His Life and Times: Revolutionary Trends in the Early Anti-imperialist Movements in South India and Abroad* (Madras: Institute of South Indian Studies, 1995), 67, 77.

2. Ibid., 9–10.

3. Militant Irish republican expatriates were among Ghadar's closest allies in the United States. Much of the early Indian anti-colonial literature was printed on the *Gaelic American*'s press.

4. Subramanyam, *M.P.T. Acharya*, 11.

5. Letter from Sukh Sagar Dutt to Arun C. Bose, March 30, 1958, in Arun C. Bose, *Indian Revolutionaries Abroad, 1905–1927: Select Documents* (Delhi: Northern Book Centre, 2002), 38–39.

6. Ibid.

7. Home Political files 37–39B, March and April 1913, arrest warrants and a series of letters between Hopkinson; C. W. Bennett, British Consul General in New York; William Williams, Commissioner of Immigration, Ellis Island; William W. Cory, Canadian Deputy Minister of the Interior; all in the National Archives of India, Delhi.

8. DCI Weekly Report, Home Political files, B. April 1919, Progs. 148–52, Criminal Intelligence Department, Delhi, Archive on Contemporary History, Jawaharlal Nehru University; DCI Weekly Report, March 24, 1919, 140, Criminal Intelligence Department, Delhi, Archive on Contemporary History, Jawaharlal Nehru University.

9. Nirode K. Barooah, *Chatto: The Life and Times of an Indian Anti-imperialist in Europe* (New Delhi: Oxford University Press, 2004), 126–28. Ali was a former civil servant who at the time taught Hindustani at the London School of Oriental Studies.

10. *Afton Tidningen*, May 29, 1918, cited in Barooah, *Chatto*, 130.

11. *Talvar*, December 1909, cited in Barooah, *Chatto*, 22.

12. Muzaffar Ahmed, *Myself and the Communist Party of India, 1920–1929*, trans. Prabhas Kumar Sinha (Calcutta: National Book Agency, 1970), 51; Subramanyam, *M.P.T. Acharya*, 162–63.

13. Cited in Subramanyam, *M.P.T. Acharya*, 160–73.

14. Ahmad, *Myself*, 51–55.

15. Ibid., 52.

16. Indulal Yajnik, *Life of Ranchoddas Bhavan Lotvala* (Bombay: Libertarian Book House, 1952), 76.

17. Cited in Home Political file, 1924/10/61, Criminal Intelligence Department, Delhi.

18. Subramanyam, *M.P.T. Acharya*, 176.

19. Barooah, *Chatto*, 283–324.

20. Subramanyam, *M.P.T. Acharya*, 184–91.

21. *Harijan*, May 1, 1954, cited in Subramanyam, *M.P.T. Acharya*, 192.

22. Acharya to British consul in Berlin, February 15, 1926, cited in Subramanyam, *M.P.T. Acharya*, 185.

23. Ahmad, *Myself*, 115.

24. Yajnik, *Life of Ranchoddas Bhavan Lotvala*, 1–24.

25. Ibid., 23–24.

26. Ibid., 29.

27. Ibid., 38.

28. Ibid., 37–39.

29. Ibid., 53.

30. Ibid., 60.

31. Aijaz Ahmad, Prakash Karat, Irfan Habib, and Prabhat Patnaik, *A World to Win* (New Delhi: LeftWord, 1999), 132–33.

32. Yajnik, *Life of Ranchoddas Bhavan Lotvala*, 51. Dange, a CPI founding member, was the mainstay of the Bombay organizing base, as was Ahmad in Calcutta and Singaravelu Chettiar in Madras.

33. Ahmad et al., *A World to Win*. 12–13; this is according to Gangadhar Adhikari, Marxist theorist and documenter of the early CPI.

34. Yajnik, *Life of Ranchoddas Bhavan Lotvala*, 68.

35. Bose was at one time Nehru's main rival for INC leadership, and later head of the insurgent Indian National Army formed from the Indian prisoners of war and migrant laborers

in Southeast Asia during World War II. Because of his attempts to form strategic anti-British alliances with Germany and Japan, Bose's political ideology has been difficult to categorize.

36. Yajnik, *Life of Ranchoddas Bhavan Lotvala*, 74–75.

37. Ibid., 75.

38. Ibid., 78.

39. Ibid., 78–79.

40. Ibid., 79–80.

41. Ibid., 80.

42. Ibid., 83.

43. Ibid., 85.

44. Ibid., 86.

45. Ibid., 86–87.

46. Ibid., 82.

47. Ibid., 11.

48. Sohan Singh Josh, *My Meetings with Bhagat Singh and on Other Early Revolutionaries* (New Delhi: Communist Party of India, 1976), 19.

49. Sohan Singh Josh, *My Tryst with Secularism: An Autobiography* (New Delhi: Patriot Publishers, 1991), 143–44.

50. See, for example, Ajoy Ghosh, *Bhagat Singh and His Comrades* (New Delhi: People's Publishing House, 1979); Gopal Thakur, *Bhagat Singh: The Man and His Ideas* (1953; repr., New Delhi: People's Publishing House, 1962); Gurdev Singh Deol, *Shaheed-e-Azam Sardar Bhagat Singh: The Man and His Ideology* (Nabha: Deep Prakashan, 1978); S. R. Bakshi, *Bhagat Singh and His Ideology* (New Delhi: Capital Publishers, 1981); Josh, *My Meetings*. Note that in the following section, when I cite page numbers from one author such as Deol or Thakur, the quotations or information can usually be found in multiple sources.

51. For collections of his writings and Lahore Conspiracy Case documents, see Shiv Varma, ed., *Selected Writings of Shaheed Bhagat Singh* (New Delhi: National Book Centre, 1986); Malwinderjit Singh Waraich and Gurdev Singh Sidhu, eds., *The Hanging of Bhagat Singh: Complete Judgment and Other Documents* (Chandigarh: Unistar Books, 2005).

52. Niraja Rao, "Bhagat Singh and the Revolutionary Movement," available at http://www.revolutionarydemocracy.org/rdv3n1/bsingh.htm.

53. Cited in ibid.

54. Josh, *My Tryst*, 142–43.

55. Josh, *My Meetings*, 14, 133.

56. Ghosh, *Bhagat Singh*, 144.

57. Josh, *My Tryst*, 143.

58. Ibid., 102, 103.

59. Ibid., 101. He is referring to two articles he wrote for the December 1926 issue of *Kirti* (ibid., 99, 100).

60. Ibid., 134.

61. Ibid., 128.

62. Varma, *Selected Writings*; Deol, *Shaheed-e-Azam Sardar Bhagat Singh*, 29. See also S. K. Mittal and Irfan Habib, "Towards Independence and Socialist Republic: Naujawan Bharat Sabha," *Social Scientist* 8, no. 2 (September 1979), 18–29: parts 1 and 2; Neeti Nair, "Bhagat Singh as Satyagrahi: The Limits of Non-Violence in Late Colonial India," *Modern Asian Studies* 43, no. 3 (2009), 649–81; Shalini Sharma, "Developing a Communist Identity: The Case of the Naujavan Bharat Sabha," *Journal of Punjab Studies* 14, no. 2 (Fall 2007), 167–86.

63. Chaman Lal, ed., *Bhagat Singh: The Jail Notebook and Other Writings* (New Delhi: LeftWord, 2007), 12.

64. Its stated objects were "(a) to establish completely independent Republic of workers and peasants of the whole of India; (b) to infuse a spirit of patriotism in the youth; (c) to express sympathy with and to assist the economic, industrial and social movements, which, being free from communal sentiments, are intended to take us nearer to our ideal . . . [and] (d) to organise the workers and peasants." Josh, *My Tryst*, 135; Deol, *Shaheed-e-Azam Sardar Bhagat Singh*, 111–12, 124.

65. Deol, *Shaheed-e-Azam Sardar Bhagat Singh*, 10.

66. Mittal and Habib, "Towards Independence," 25.

67. Cited in Varma, *Selected Writings*, 44–45.

68. Cited in ibid.

69. Deol, *Shaheed-e-Azam Sardar Bhagat Singh*, 12.

70. Ibid., 32.

71. Cited in Varma, *Selected Writings*, 188. According to Varma, "Philosophy of Bomb" was written by HSRA member Vohra in consultation with Azad and approved by Singh while he was in jail. This document emphasizes a diversity of tactics in which the practice of Gandhi's soul force could include both physical and moral aspects.

72. Cited in Deol, *Shaheed-e-Azam Sardar Bhagat Singh*, 49–50.

73. Ibid., 51.

74. Varma, *Selected Writings*, 116; Lal, *Bhagat Singh*, 150.

75. Varma, *Selected Writings*, 24–25. A notice in the *Bookman Advertiser* gives an indication of why *The Spy* may have appealed to Singh: it was also known in the United States as *100%: The Story of a Patriot*. "Many letters come to us from political prisoners who have read this book in jail. 'Here is the truth!' writes one. 'If only the people would read this story!'. . . '100%' is the story of the 'White Terror,' and tells how 'big business' pulled off the

stunt of landing the 'reds' in jail. It is the inside story of a 'secret agent,' and deals with half a dozen celebrated cases concerning which you have been fooled. Louis Untermeyer writers: 'Upton Sinclair has done it again. He has loaded his Maxim (no silencer attached), taken careful aim, and—bang!—hit the bell plump in the center. First of all '100%' is a story . . . full of suspense, drama, 'heart interest,' plots, counterplots, high life, low life, humor, hate and other passions—as thrillingly as a W.S. Hart movie, as interest-crammed as (and a darned sight more truthful than) your daily newspapers'" (*Bookman: A Review of Books and Life* 13 [March 1921–August 1921]).

76. Lal, *Bhagat Singh*, 161.

77. Ibid., 159.

78. Cited in ibid., 37, 39, 29.

79. Cited in ibid., 35.

80. Figner, cited in ibid., 47–48: "During the moment which immediately follow upon his sentence, the mind of the condemned in many respects resembles that of a man on the point of death. Quiet, and as if inspired, he no longer clings to what he is about to leave, but firmly looks in front of him, fully conscious of the fact that what is coming is inevitable." And Morozov, cited in ibid., 48–49: "Naked walls, prison thoughts, / How dark and sad you are, / How heavy to be a prisoner inactive, / And dream of years of freedom"; "Entirely for our fellowmen we must live, / Our entire selves for them we must give, / And for their sakes struggle against ill fate!"

81. Cited in ibid., 39.

The Romantic Countermodernists

1. Rabindranath Tagore, *Nationalism* (New York: Macmillan,

1917), 131.

2. Ibid., 84–85.

3. Ibid., 131–33.

4. Ibid., 36–37.

5. Ibid., 23–24.

6. Ibid., 37–38.

7. Ibid., 28–29.

8. Manu Goswami, "Autonomy and Comparability: Notes on the Anticolonial and the Postcolonial," *boundary 2* 32, no. 2 (2005): 49.

9. Cited in ibid., 44.

10. Tagore, *Nationalism*, 21–22.

11. Benjamin Zachariah, *Developing India: An Intellectual and Social History* (Oxford: Oxford University Press, 2005), 192–93, 167.

12. Ibid., 191.

13. Ibid., 193.

14. Ibid., 192.

15. Ibid., 192–93.

16. Nirmal Bose, "Is Gandhi a Nationalist?" *Congress Socialist*, February 19, 1935, cited in ibid., 167.

17. It also should be noted that he was far from an antiauthoritarian personally, and his assumptions about spirituality and hierarchy, caste and gender, and asceticism and the body require a critical eye.

18. Except for the Catholic Worker movement. See also Linda D'Amico, *The Anarchist Dimension of Liberation Theology* (New York: P. Lang, 1987); Alexandre Christoyannopoulos, *Christian Anarchism: A Political Commentary on the Gospel* (Exeter: Imprint Academic, 2011).

19. Cited in Rudrangshu Mukherjee, ed., *The Penguin Gandhi Reader* (New York: Penguin Books, 1993), 37, 22, 20. See also Anthony Parel, introduction to Gandhi, *Hind Swaraj and Other Writings* (Cambridge: Cambridge University Press, 1997).

20. Cited in ibid., 79.

21. Cited in ibid., 82.

22. Cited in ibid., 83.

23. Rajat K. Ray, *The Felt Community* (New Delhi: Oxford University Press, 2003), 48.

24. Ibid., 47.

25. Ibid, 47.

26. Ibid., 50.

27. Thomas Metcalf, *Ideologies of the Raj* (Cambridge: Cambridge University Press, 1995), 68–72.

28. Surendranath Karr, "On the Village Republics of India," *Independent Hindustan*, March 1921, 52, microfilm, Nehru Memorial Museum and Library, Delhi. The following Karr quotations are also taken from this same source.

29. Radhakumud Mookerji, *Local Government in Ancient India* (Oxford: Clarendon Press, 1919), 22–23.

30. Mookerji was also the author of *The Fundamental Unity of India* (1914; repr., New Delhi: DC Publishers, 2005). While it may be possible to read this text as essentially equating Indian with Hindu culture, in the context of freedom movement discourse it was a refutation of the common argument that British rule was needed to unify a fragmentary society. Like Tagore, Mookerji saw nationalism and the nation-state principle as inimical to holism and peaceful coexistence.

31. Mookerji, *Local Government*, xi, xv.

32. Cited in ibid., 3.

33. Ibid., 3.

34. Ibid., 4.

35. Ibid., 7.

36. Ibid., 7–8.

37. Ibid., 10.

38. Ibid., 20–21.

39. Ibid., 22.

40. Har Dayal, *Writings of Lala Hardyal* (Swaraj Publishing House, 1923), 54.

41. From *Democratic Values: Selections from the Addresses of Vinoba Bhave, 1951–60* (Kashi: Sarva Seva Sangh Prakashan, 1962), cited in Richard Graham, *Anarchism: A Documentary History of Libertarian Ideas* (Montreal: Black Rose Books, 2009), 2:183–4. For detailed analysis of the Sarvodaya movement's ideology and methods, see Geoffrey Ostergaard and Melville Currell, *The Gentle Anarchists* (Oxford: Oxford University Press, 1971), 1–61.

42. Ibid., 184.

43. Ibid., 184–85.

44. Ibid., 185.

45. Ibid., 186.

46. See also Ramachandra Guha, *An Anthropologist among the Marxists and Other Essays* (Delhi: Permanent Black, 2001).

47. Cited in ibid., 174–75. Not all CSP members could be considered Marxist, although JP's influence as organizer and ideologue gave it a Marxist orientation.

48. Ibid., 176–77; see also Jayaprakash Narayan, *Towards Total Revolution* (Bombay: Popular Prakashan, 1978), 1:55–73, 126–41.

49. Cited in Prasad, *Gandhi*, 180.

50. Cited in ibid., 184–85.

51. Narayan, *Towards Total Revolution*, 56.

52. Cited in Graham, *Anarchism*, 2:185–88.

53. Prasad, *Gandhi*, 192.

54. Ibid., 185.

55. Jayaprakash Narayan, "From Socialism to Sarvodaya" (1957), in Bimal Prasad, ed., *Essential Writings, 1929–79* (New Delhi: Konark Publishers, 2002), cited in Graham, *Anarchism*, 2:188.

56. Ibid., 188.

57. Ibid., 189, 190.

58. Narayan, "From Socialism to Sarvodaya," 148.

59. Cited in Prasad, *Gandhi*, 187.

60. Cited in Prasad, *Socialism, Sarvodaya and Democracy: Selected Works of Jayaprakash Narayan* (Bombay: Asia Publishing House, 1964), 199.

61. Cited in ibid., 222–23.

62. Ibid., 222.

63. Cited in ibid., 278.

64. Cited in ibid., 224.

65. Cited in ibid., 113.

66. Chaman Lal (*Himal*, July 2010) notes that JP's Bihar-based total revolution movement in the 1970s gave birth to most of the major post-Emergency, anti-Congress figures who were not Naxalites.

67. Cited in Prasad, *Gandhi*, 170.

68. Bimal Prasad, *Gandhi, Nehru, and JP: Studies in Leadership* (Delhi: Chanakya Publications, 1985), 190.

69. See, for example, Meera Nanda, *Prophets Facing Backward: Postmodern Critiques of Science and Hindu*

Nationalism in India (New Brunswick, NJ: Rutgers University Press, 2008); Benjamin Zachariah, "Uses of Scientific Argument," *Economic and Political Weekly* 36, no. 39 (September 29–October 5, 2001).

70. For Lloyd and Susanne Hoeber Rudolph, in their book *The Postmodern Gandhi* (Oxford: Oxford University Press, 2010), "postmodern" refers to anything that is first, present during the time of post-cold war late capitalism; and second, critical of at least one of the pillars of high modernism. This includes any sort of oppositional ideas or practices facing any one of the dominant features of high modernism, lumping together all the various sorts of possible critiques from the reactionary to the progressive. This makes their argument not only anachronistic but also sloppy. For instance, among the traits they consider evidence of Gandhi's postmodernity are his conscious affinity with the critical "other west," epistemological relativism, critique of modern industrial development and positivist hegemony, dislike of the centralized and authoritarian state, spirituality, and vegetarianism (since this is countercultural in the Western context, though of course not in the Hindu Indian context, it therefore must be "postmodern").

71. Robert Young, in *Postcolonialism: An Historical Introduction* (Malden, MA: Blackwell, 2001), roots postcolonialism in third worldist socialism, defining its innovations in practice as the adaptation of Marxist thought to the anticolonial context. Similarly, in *Methodologies of the Oppressed* (Minneapolis: University of Minnesota Press, 2000), Chela Sandoval argues that the insights of poststructuralist thought and other academic forms of oppositional knowledge run parallel to movements of the oppressed against colonization.

72. The phrase was coined in Jeffrey Herf, *Reactionary Modernism: Technology, Culture, and Politics in Weimar and the Third Reich* (Cambridge: Cambridge University Press, 1984).

The New Social Movements

1. I was initially reluctant to write this more contemporary chapter, because I'm not a participant-observer in the movements in question, just a knowledgeable sympathizer with multiple points of oblique contact. Plus the topic of the book itself calls for a heightened awareness of my own practice as a writer. With the inevitable risk of misrepresentation or distortion through misplaced emphasis, this piece should be considered a friendly interpretive hypothesis.

2. Nivedita Menon and Aditya Nigam, *Power and Contestation: India Since 1989* (New York: Zed Books, 2007), 3.

3. Ibid.

4. Gail Omvedt, *Reinventing Revolution: New Social Movements and the Socialist Tradition in India* (Armonk, NY: M. E. Sharpe, 1993), 183.

5. Partha Chatterjee, "Towards a Postcolonial Modernity: AsiaSource Interview with Partha Chatterjee," available at http://www.sciy.org/2009/07/04/towards-a-postcolonial-modernity-asiasource-interview-with-partha-chatterjee/.

6. Nivedita Menon, "The Nation-state in the Mirror of Political Science" (paper presented at the National Centre for Biological Sciences, Bangalore, December 1999), available at http://criticalencounters.wordpress.com/2009/02/08/the-nation-state-in-the-mirror-of-political-science-tracking-a-discipline-in-india.

7. Omvedt, *Reinventing Revolution*, 304.

8. "'End of the Left' in India? Statement by Leftists after

Recent Election Results," May 24, 2011, available at http://kafila.org/2011/05/24/end-of-the-left-in-india-statement-after-recent-election-results/. The statement was signed by Jairus Banaji, Sukumar Muralidharan, Dilip Simeon, Satya Sivaraman, and Rohini Hensman, and endorsed by twenty-four others.

9. The Andhra Pradesh Civil Liberties Committee, like other similar regional organizations, had a genealogical link to the People's Union for Civil Liberties founded by JP in 1976, intended as nonpartisan and without specific political ideology. It later split into the People's Union for Civil Liberties and the People's Union for Democratic Rights, of which the former was more reformist, seeking redress within the system, while the latter called for a more radical, systemic transformation.

10. Kandalla Balagopal, "Developing Destruction," editorial, special issue, *Human Rights Bulletin*, 2009, available at http://balagopal.org/?p=729.

11. Nivedita Menon, "Saluting a Revolutionary," October 11, 2009, available at http://kafila.org/2009/10/11/saluting-a-revolutionary-jinee-lokaneeta.

12. Kandalla Balagopal, "Reflections on Violence and Nonviolence in Political Movements in India," January 26, 2009, available at http://www.sacw.net/article1169.html.

13. Ibid.

14. Kandalla Balagopal, "Political Violence and Human Rights: The Case of the Naxalite Movement in A.P.," *Voices for Change* 2, no. 3 (1998). The passage continues, "Which includes the need of positive discrimination by the authority of law in favour of the disadvantaged, eliminate all arbitrariness of authority, and free society totally from oppressive forms of social, political and economic power."

15. Ibid.

16. Cited in Omvedt, *Reinventing Revolution*, 170–71.

17. Shramik Mukti Dal manifesto, chapter 2, available at http://www.xa.yimg.com/kq/groups/10707696/.../ Shramik+Mukti+Dal+Manifesto.doc.

18. Cited in Omvedt, *Reinventing Revolution*, 241.

19. Shramik Mukti Dal manifesto.

20. Ibid.

21. Cited in Omvedt, *Reinventing Revolution*, 246.

22. High-profile recent examples include the farmers' movement against debt enslavement via Monsanto's genetically modified Bt cotton in central India, and villager mobilizations against Coca-Cola Company's abuse of water resources in the South. One of the most formative mobilizations for nonparty activists in recent decades was the attempt to hold Union Carbide, a subsidiary of Dow Chemical, responsible for the devastating poison gas leak that killed thousands of people in Bhopal in 1984, and continues to exact chronic damage on thousands of survivors.

23. Omvedt, *Reinventing Revolution*, 309.

24. This was initially a project of the Center for the Study of Developing Societies in Delhi, with funding from West Germany during its first few years.

25. Available at http://www.rightlivelihood.org/lokayan.html.

26. Omvedt, *Reinventing Revolution*, 192.

27. Rajni Kothari, "The Non-party Political Process," *Economic and Political Weekly* 19, no. 5 (February 4, 1984): 219.

28. Menon, "The Nation-state."

29. Rajni Kothari, "State and Statelessness in Our Time," *Economic and Political Weekly* 26, nos. 11–12 (March 1991): 554.

30. Ibid., 558.

31. Kothari, "The Non-party Political Process," 221.

32. Ibid.

33. Ibid.

34. The backlash sparked by the report's recommendations on reservations for those groups designated as "scheduled castes" and "tribes or other backward classes" in education and employment was comparable to the controversies around affirmative action in the United States.

35. Menon and Nigam, *Power and Contestation*, 7; paraphrasing Sudipta Kaviraj.

36. Gail Omvedt, "Ambedkar and After: The Dalit Movement in India," in *Social Movements and the State*, ed. Ghanshyam Shah (New Delhi: Sage Publications, 2002), 303.

37. Menon and Nigam, *Power and Contestation*, 65.

38. High-profile cases recently include health care activist Binayak Sen.

39. Archana Prasad, *Environmentalism and the Left: Contemporary Debates and Future Agendas in Tribal Areas: Signpost 8* (Delhi: LeftWord, 2004).

40. Available at http://napm-india.org/aboutus.

41. Panel, Alwan for the Arts, New York, April 23, 2011, available at http://www.youtube.com/watch?v=P_Ia93DURSY.

42. Mayur Chetia, "World Social Forum and Reactions from the Indian Left," *Critical Engagement* 5 (August 2008): 14–16.

43. Mamata Dash, "The World Social Forum through the Eyes of Movement Groups in India," *Critical Engagement* 6 (August 2008): 11–13; Susana Barria with O. J. Nelson, "Main Debates around the WSF 2004 in Mumbai," *Critical Engagement* 4 (August 2008): 25.

44. Much of this material can be found at http://www.cacim.

net; Jai Sen, Anita Anand, Arturo Escobar, and Peter Waterman, eds., *The World Social Forum: Challenging Empires* (Montreal: Black Rose Books, 2008).

45. Jai Sen, "Opening Open Space: Notes on the Grammar and Vocabulary of the Concept of Open Space," *Critical Engagement* 2 (August 2008): 5, 10–14, 18–24.

46. Menon and Nigam, *Power and Contestation*, 116.

On Solidarity

1. Ali Sardar Jafri, *Lucknow ki Panch Raaten* (1962; repr., Delhi: Rajkamal Prakashan, 1998),46; my translation.

2. Faiz Ahmad Faiz (1911–84), founding member of the Progressive Writers' movement and the Communist Party of Pakistan, is generally regarded as one of the greatest Urdu poets of all time.

3. Jafri, *Lucknow ki Panch Raaten*, 49.

4. Some important texts include Roger White, *Postcolonial Anarchism: Essays on Race, Repression, and Culture in Communities of Color, 1999–2004* (Oakland, CA: Jailbreak Press); Sureyya Evren, "Post-Anarchism and the Third World," available at http://theanarchistlibrary.org//HTML/Sureyya_ Evren__Postanarchism_and_the__3rd_World_.html; Ernesto Aguilar, ed., *Our Culture, Our Resistance: People of Color Speak Out on Anarchism, Race, Class, and Gender* (Creative Commons, 2004), available at http://zinelibrary.info/files/ocor_book_1. pdf; Revolutionary Anti-authoritarians of Color, "An Anarchist Introduction to Critical Race Theory," 2002, available at http://theanarchistlibrary.org/HTML/Revolutionary_Anti- Authoritarians_of_Color__An_Anarchist_Introduction_to_ Critical_Race_Theory.html; Kuwasi Balagoon, *A Soldier's Story:*

Writings by a Revolutionary New Afrikan Anarchist (Montreal: Kersplebedeb, 2001); Lorenzo Komboa Ervin, *Anarchism and the Black Revolution*, available at http://libcom.org/library/anarchism-black-revolution-lorenzo-ervin; Ashanti Alston, "Beyond Nationalism but Not without It," available at http://www.anarchistpanther.net/writings/writing4.html.

Credits for Anarchist Interventions

Maia Ramnath

Maia Ramnath is a teacher, writer, activist, and dancer/aerialist living in New York City. She has been involved in various manifestations of global justice, anti-imperialist, and Palestine solidarity organizing for many years. Maia attended graduate school at the University of California at Santa Cruz (UCSC), earning a PhD in history, though it appears in retrospect that she spent most of the time on a picket line. She has taught courses at UCSC and New York University on global history, modern South Asian history, and anticolonial radical movements. Maia is the author of *The Haj to Utopia: How the Ghadar Movement Charted Global Radicalism and Attempted to Overthrow the British Empire* (University of California Press, 2011)—in many ways a companion volume to this one. She was a member of the Free Radio Santa Cruz and original Bluestockings bookstore collectives, and is currently a member of the Institute for Anarchist Studies board and Historians against War steering committee. Finally, as cofounder and director of a multidisciplinary performing arts group sometimes called Constellation Moving Company, she hopes some day to "use her powers for good" like radical Left circus artists Dharamvir Singh and John S. Clarke did a century ago.

Institute for Anarchist Studies

The IAS, a nonprofit foundation established in 1996, aims to support the development of anarchism by creating spaces for independent, politically engaged scholarship that explores social domination and reconstructive visions of a free society. All IAS projects strive to encourage public intellectuals and collective self-reflection within revolutionary and/or movement contexts. To this end, the IAS awards grants twice a year to radical writers and translators worldwide, and has funded some eighty projects over the years by authors from numerous countries, including Argentina, Lebanon, Canada, Chile, Ireland, Nigeria, Germany, South Africa, and the United States. It also publishes the online and print journal *Perspectives on Anarchist Theory*, organizes the Renewing the Anarchist Tradition conference, offers the Mutual Aid Speakers List, and collaborates on this book series, among other projects. The IAS is part of a larger movement seeking to create a nonhierarchical society. It is internally democratic and works in solidarity with people around the globe who share its values. The IAS is completely supported by donations from anarchists and other antiauthoritarians—like you—and/or their projects, with any contributions exclusively funding grants and IAS operating expenses; for more information or to contribute to the work of the IAS, see http://www.anarchist-studies.org/.

AK Press

AK Press is a worker-run collective that publishes and distributes radical books, visual and audio media, and other material. We're small: a dozen people who work long hours for short money, because we believe in what we do. We're anarchists, which is reflected both in the books we provide and the way we organize our business. Decisions at AK Press are made collectively, from what we publish, to what we distribute and how we structure our labor. All the work, from sweeping floors to answering phones, is shared. When the telemarketers call and ask, "who's in charge?" the answer is: everyone. Our goal isn't profit (although we do have to pay the rent). Our goal is supplying radical words and images to as many people as possible. The books and other media we distribute are published by independent presses, not the corporate giants. We make them widely available to help you make positive (or hell, revolutionary) changes in the world. For more information on AK Press, or to place an order, see http://www.akpress.org/.

Justseeds Artists' Cooperative

Justseeds Artists' Cooperative is a decentralized community of twenty-two artists who have banded together to both sell their work, and collaborate with and support each other and social movements. Our Web site is not just a place to shop but also a destination to find out about current events in radical art and culture. We regularly collaborate on exhibitions and group projects as well as produce graphics and culture for social justice movements. We believe in the power of personal expression in concert with collective action to transform society. For more information on Justseeds Artists' Cooperative or to order work, see http://www.justseeds.org/.

Anarchist Intervention Series

Support AK Press!

AK Press is one of the world's largest and most productive anarchist publishing houses. We're entirely worker-run and demo-cratically managed. We operate without a corporate structure—no bosses, no managers, no bullshit. We publish close to twenty books every year, and distribute thousands of other titles published by other like-minded independent presses from around the globe.

The Friends of AK program is a way that you can directly contribute to the continued existence of AK Press, and ensure that we're able to keep publishing great books just like this one! Friends pay a minimum of $25 per month, for a minimum three month period, into our publishing account. In return, Friends automatically receive (for the duration of their membership), as they appear, one free copy of every new AK Press title. They're also entitled to a 20% discount on everything featured in the AK Press Distribution catalog and on the web-site, on any and every order. You or your organization can even sponsor an entire book if you should so choose!

There's great stuff in the works—so sign up now to become a Friend of AK Press, and let the presses roll!

Won't you be our friend? Email friendsofak@akpress.org for more info, or visit the Friends of AK Press website: http://www.akpress.org/programs/friendsofak

A Prisoner in Fairyland

A Prisoner in Fairyland

Algernon Blackwood

MINT EDITIONS

A Prisoner in Fairyland was first published in 1913.

This edition published by Mint Editions 2021.

ISBN 9781513283128 | E-ISBN 9781513288147

Published by Mint Editions®

 MINT
EDITIONS
minteditionbooks.com

Publishing Director: Jennifer Newens
Design & Production: Rachel Lopez Metzger
Project Manager: Micaela Clark
Typesetting: Westchester Publishing Services

Contents

I

Man is his own star; and the soul that can
Render an honest and a perfect man
Commands all light, all influence, all fate,
Nothing to him falls early, or too late.
Our acts our angels are, or good or ill,

Our fatal shadows that walk by us still.

—Beaumont and Fletcher

Minks—Herbert Montmorency—was now something more than secretary, even than private secretary: he was confidential-private-secretary, adviser, friend; and this, more because he was a safe receptacle for his employer's enthusiasms than because his advice or judgment had any exceptional value. So many men need an audience. Herbert Minks was a fine audience, attentive, delicately responsive, sympathetic, understanding, and above all—silent. He did not leak. Also, his applause was wise without being noisy. Another rare quality he possessed was that he was honest as the sun. To prevaricate, even by gesture, or by saying nothing, which is the commonest form of untruth, was impossible to his transparent nature. He might hedge, but he could never lie. And he was "friend," so far as this was possible between employer and employed, because a pleasant relationship of years' standing had established a bond of mutual respect under conditions of business intimacy which often tend to destroy it.

Just now he was very important into the bargain, for he had a secret from his wife that he meant to divulge only at the proper moment. He had known it himself but a few hours. The leap from being secretary in one of Henry Rogers's companies to being that prominent gentleman's confidential private secretary was, of course, a very big one. He hugged it secretly at first alone. On the journey back from the City to the suburb where he lived, Minks made a sonnet on it. For his emotions invariably sought the safety valve of verse. It was a wiser safety valve for high spirits than horse-racing or betting on the football results, because he always stood to win, and never to lose. Occasionally he sold these bits of joy for half a guinea, his wife pasting the results neatly in a big press album from which he often read aloud on Sunday nights when the children were in bed. They were signed "Montmorency Minks"; and bore evidence of occasional pencil corrections on the margin with a view to publication later in a volume. And sometimes there were little lyrical fragments too, in a wild, original metre, influenced by Shelley and yet entirely his own. These had special pages to themselves at the end of the big book. But usually he preferred the sonnet form; it was more sober, more dignified. And just now the bumping of the Tube train shaped his emotion into something that began with

> *Success that poisons many a baser mind*
> *With thoughts of self, may lift—*

but stopped there because, when he changed into another train, the jerkier movement altered the rhythm into something more lyrical, and he got somewhat confused between the two and ended by losing both.

He walked up the hill towards his tiny villa, hugging his secret and anticipating with endless detail how he would break it to his wife. He felt very proud and very happy. The half-mile trudge seemed like a few yards.

He was a slim, rather insignificant figure of a man, neatly dressed, the City clerk stamped plainly over all his person. He envied his employer's burly six-foot stature, but comforted himself always with the thought that he possessed in its place a certain delicacy that was more becoming to a man of letters whom an adverse fate prevented from being a regular minor poet. There was that touch of melancholy in his fastidious appearance that suggested the atmosphere of frustrated dreams. Only the firmness of his character and judgment decreed against the luxury of longish hair; and he prided himself upon remembering that although a poet at heart, he was outwardly a City clerk and, as a strong man, must permit no foolish compromise.

His face on the whole was pleasing, and rather soft, yet, owing to this warring of opposing inner forces, it was at the same time curiously deceptive. Out of that dreamy, vague expression shot, when least expected, the hard and practical judgment of the City—or vice versa. But the whole was gentle—admirable quality for an audience, since it invited confession and assured a gentle hearing. No harshness lay there. Herbert Minks might have been a fine, successful mother perhaps. The one drawback to the physiognomy was that the mild blue eyes were never quite united in their frank gaze. He squinted pleasantly, though his wife told him it was a fascinating cast rather than an actual squint. The chin, too, ran away a little from the mouth, and the lips were usually parted. There was, at any rate, this air of incompatibility of temperament between the features which, made all claim to good looks out of the question.

That runaway chin, however, was again deceptive. It did, indeed run off, but the want of decision it gave to the countenance seemed contradicted by the prominent forehead and straight eyebrows, heavily marked. Minks knew his mind. If sometimes evasive rather than outspoken, he could on occasion be surprisingly firm. He saw life very clearly. He could certainly claim the good judgment stupid people sometimes have, due perhaps to their inability to see alternatives—just as some men's claim to greatness is born of an audacity due to their total lack of humour.

Minks was one of those rare beings who may be counted on—a quality better than mere brains, being of the heart. And Henry Rogers understood him and read him like an open book. Preferring the steady devotion to the brilliance a high salary may buy, he had watched him for many years in every sort of circumstance. He had, by degrees, here and there, shown an interest in his life. He had chosen his private secretary well. With Herbert Minks at his side he might accomplish many things his heart was set upon. And while Minks bumped down in his third-class crowded carriage to Sydenham, hunting his evasive sonnet, Henry Rogers glided swiftly in a taxi-cab to his rooms in St. James's Street, hard on the trail of another dream that seemed, equally, to keep just beyond his actual reach.

It would certainly seem that thought can travel across space between minds sympathetically in tune, for just as the secretary put his latch-key into his shiny blue door the idea flashed through him, "I wonder what Mr. Rogers will do, now that he's got his leisure, with a fortune and—me!" And at the same moment Rogers, in his deep arm-chair before the fire, was saying to himself, "I'm glad Minks has come to me; he's just the man I want for my big Scheme!" And then—"Pity he's such a lugubrious looking fellow, and wears those dreadful fancy waistcoats. But he's very open to suggestion. We can change all that. I must look after Minks a bit. He's rather sacrificed his career for me, I fancy. He's got high aims. Poor little Minks!"

"I'll stand by him whatever happens," was the thought the slamming of the blue door interrupted. "To be secretary to such a man is already success." And again he hugged his secret and himself.

As already said, the new-fledged secretary was married and wrote poetry on the sly. He had four children. He would make an ideal helpmate, worshipping his employer with that rare quality of being interested in his ideas and aims beyond the mere earning of a salary; seeing, too, in that employer more than he, the latter, supposed. For, while he wrote verses on the sly, "my chief," as he now preferred to call him, lived poetry in his life.

"He's got it, you know, my dear," he announced to his wife, as he kissed her and arranged his tie in the gilt mirror over the plush mantelpiece in the "parlour"; "he's got the divine thing in him right enough; got it, too, as strong as hunger or any other natural instinct. It's almost functional with him, if I may say so"—which meant "if you can understand me"—"only, he's deliberately smothered it all these years. He thinks it wouldn't go down with other business men. And he's been in business, you see, from the word go. He meant to make money, and he couldn't do both exactly. Just like myself—"

Minks wandered on. His wife noticed the new enthusiasm in his manner, and was puzzled by it. Something was up, she divined.

"Do you think he'll raise your salary again soon?" she asked practically, helping him draw off the paper cuffs that protected his shirt from ink stains, and throwing them in the fire. "That seems to be the real point."

But Herbert evaded the immediate issue. It was so delightful to watch her and keep his secret a little longer.

"And you *do* deserve success, dear," she added; "you've been as faithful as a horse." She came closer, and stroked his thick, light hair a moment.

He turned quickly. Had he betrayed himself already? Had she read it from his eyes or manner?

"That's nothing," he answered lightly. "Duty is duty."

"Of course, dear," and she brought him his slippers. He would not let her put them on for him. It was not gallant to permit menial services to a woman.

"Success," he murmured, "that poisons many a baser mind—" and then stopped short. "I've got a new sonnet," he told her quickly, determined to prolong his pleasure, "got it in the train coming home. Wait a moment, and I'll give you the rest. It's a beauty, with real passion in it, only I want to keep it cold and splendid if I can. Don't interrupt a moment." He put the slippers on the wrong feet and stared hard into the fire.

Then Mrs. Minks knew for a certainty that something had happened. He had not even asked after the children.

"Herbert," she said, with a growing excitement, "why are you so full of poetry tonight? And what's this about success and poison all of a sudden?" She knew he never drank. "I believe Mr. Rogers has raised your salary, or done one of those fine things you always say he's going to do. Tell me, dear, please tell me." There were new, unpaid bills in her pocket, and she almost felt tempted to show them. She poked the fire fussily.

"Albinia," he answered importantly, with an expression that brought the chin up closer to the lips, and made the eyebrows almost stern, "Mr. Rogers will do the right thing always—when the right time comes. As a matter of fact"—here he reverted to the former train of thought—"both he and I are misfits in a practical, sordid age. We should have been born in Greece—"

"I simply love your poems, Herbert," she interrupted gently, wondering how she managed to conceal her growing impatience so well, "but there's not the money in them that there ought to be, and they don't pay for coals or for Ronald's flannels—"

"Albinia," he put in softly, "they relieve the heart, and so make me a happier and a better man. But—I should say he would," he added, answering her distant question about the salary.

The secret was almost out. It hung on the edge of his lips. A moment longer he hugged it deliciously. He loved these little conversations with his wife. Never a shade of asperity entered into them. And this one in particular afforded him a peculiar delight.

"Both of us are made for higher things than mere money-making," he went on, lighting his calabash pipe and puffing the smoke carefully above her head from one corner of his mouth, "and that's what first attracted us to each other, as I have often mentioned to you. But now"— his bursting heart breaking through all control—"that he has sold his interests to a company and retired into private life—er—my own existence should be easier and less exacting. I shall have less routine, be more my own master, and also, I trust, find time perhaps for—"

"Then something *has* happened!" cried Mrs. Minks, springing to her feet.

"It has, my dear," he answered with forced calmness, though his voice was near the trembling point.

She stood in front of him, waiting. But he himself did not rise, nor show more feeling than he could help. His poems were full of scenes like this in which the men—strong, silent fellows—were fine and quiet. Yet his instinct was to act quite otherwise. One eye certainly betrayed it.

"It has," he repeated, full of delicious emotion.

"Oh, but Herbert—!"

"And I am no longer that impersonal factor in City life, mere secretary to the Board of a company—"

"Oh, Bertie, dear!"

"But private secretary to Mr. Henry Rogers—private and confidential secretary at—"

"Bert, darling—!"

"At 300 pounds a year, paid quarterly, with expenses extra, and long, regular holidays," he concluded with admirable dignity and self-possession.

There was a moment's silence.

"You splendour!" She gave a little gasp of admiration that went straight to his heart, and set big fires alight there. "Your reward has come at last! My hero!"

This was as it should be. The beginning of an epic poem flashed with tumult through his blood. Yet outwardly he kept his admirable calm.

"My dear, we must take success, like disaster, quietly." He said it gently, as when he played with the children. It was mostly put on, of course, this false grandiloquence of the prig. His eyes already twinkled more than he could quite disguise.

"Then we can manage the other school, perhaps, for Frank?" she cried, and was about to open various flood-gates when he stopped her with a look of proud happiness that broke down all barriers of further pretended secrecy.

"Mr. Rogers," was the low reply, "has offered to do that for us—as a start." The words were leisurely spoken between great puffs of smoke. "That's what I meant just now by saying that he lived poetry in his life, you see. Another time you will allow judgment to wait on knowledge—"

"You dear old humbug," she cried, cutting short the sentence that neither of them quite understood, "I believe you've known this for weeks—"

"Two hours ago exactly," he corrected her, and would willingly have prolonged the scene indefinitely had not his practical better half prevented him. For she came over, dropped upon her knees beside his chair, and, putting both arms about his neck, she kissed his foolish sentences away with all the pride and tenderness that filled her to the brim. And it pleased Minks hugely. It made him feel, for the moment at any rate, that he was the hero, not Mr. Henry Rogers.

But he did not show his emotion much. He did not even take his pipe out. It slipped down sideways into another corner of his wandering lips. And, while he returned the kiss with equal tenderness and pleasure, one mild blue eye looked down upon her soft brown hair, and the other glanced sideways, without a trace of meaning in it, at the oleograph of Napoleon on Elba that hung upon the wall. . .

Soon afterwards the little Sydenham villa was barred and shuttered, the four children were sound asleep, Herbert and Albinia Minks both lost in the world of happy dreams that sometimes visit honest, simple folk whose consciences are clean and whose aims in life are commonplace but worthy.

II

When the creation was new and all the stars shone in their first splendour, the gods held their assembly in the sky and sang "Oh, the picture of perfection! the joy unalloyed!"

But one cried of a sudden—"It seems that somewhere there is a break in the chain of light and one of the stars has been lost."

The golden string of their harp snapped, their song stopped, and they cried in dismay—"Yes, that lost star was the best, she was the glory of all heavens!"

From that day the search is unceasing for her, and the cry goes on from one to the other that in her the world has lost its one joy!

Only in the deepest silence of night the stars smile and whisper among themselves—"Vain is this seeking! Unbroken perfection is over all!"

RABINDRANATH TAGORE. (Prose translation by Author from his original Bengali.)

It was April 30th and Henry Rogers sat in his rooms after breakfast, listening to the rumble of the traffic down St. James's Street, and found the morning dull. A pile of letters lay unopened upon the table, waiting the arrival of the discriminating Mr. Minks with his shorthand note-book and his mild blue eyes. It was half-past nine, and the secretary was due at ten o'clock.

He smiled as he thought of this excellent fellow's first morning in the promoted capacity of private secretary. He would come in very softly, one eye looking more intelligent than the other; the air of the City clerk discarded, and in its place the bearing that belonged to new robes of office worn for the first time. He would bow, say "Good morning, Mr. Rogers," glance round with one eye on his employer and another on a possible chair, seat himself with a sigh that meant "I have written a new poem in the night, and would love to read it to you if I dared," then flatten out his oblong note-book and look up, expectant and receptive. Rogers would say "Good morning, Mr. Minks. We've got a busy day before us. Now, let me see—" and would meet his glance with welcome. He would look quickly from one eye to the other-to this day he did not know which one was right to meet-and would wonder for the thousandth time how such an insignificant face could go with such an honest, capable mind. Then he smiled again as he remembered Frank, the little boy whose schooling he was paying for, and realised that

Minks would bring a message of gratitude from Mrs. Minks, perhaps would hand him, with a gesture combining dignity and humbleness, a little note of thanks in a long narrow envelope of pale mauve, bearing a flourishing monogram on its back.

And Rogers scowled a little as he thought of the air of gruffness he would assume while accepting it, saying as pleasantly as he could manage, "Oh, Mr. Minks, that's nothing at all; I'm only too delighted to be of service to the lad." For he abhorred the expression of emotion, and his delicate sense of tact would make pretence of helping the boy himself, rather than the struggling parents.

Au fond he had a genuine admiration for Minks, and there was something lofty in the queer personality that he both envied and respected. It made him rely upon his judgment in certain ways he could not quite define. Minks seemed devoid of personal ambition in a sense that was not weakness. He was not insensible to the importance of money, nor neglectful of chances that enabled him to do well by his wife and family, but—he was after other things as well, if not chiefly. With a childlike sense of honesty he had once refused a position in a company that was not all it should have been, and the high pay thus rejected pointed to a scrupulous nicety of view that the City, of course, deemed foolishness. And Rogers, aware of this, had taken to him, seeking as it were to make this loss good to him in legitimate ways. Also the fellow belonged to leagues and armies and "things," quixotic some of them, that tried to lift humanity. That is, he gave of his spare time, as also of his spare money, to help. His Saturday evenings, sometimes a whole bank holiday, he devoted to the welfare of others, even though the devotion Rogers thought misdirected.

For Minks hung upon the fringe of that very modern, new-fashioned, but almost freakish army that worships old, old ideals, yet insists upon new-fangled names for them. Christ, doubtless, was his model, but it must be a Christ properly and freshly labelled; his Christianity must somewhere include the prefix "neo," and the word "scientific" must also be dragged in if possible before he was satisfied. Minks, indeed, took so long explaining to himself the wonderful title that he was sometimes in danger of forgetting the brilliant truths it so vulgarly concealed. Yet never quite concealed. He must be up-to-date, that was all. His attitude to the world scraped acquaintance with nobility somewhere. His gift was a rare one. Out of so little, he gave his mite, and gave it simply, unaware that he was doing anything unusual.

This attitude of mind had made him valuable, even endeared him, to the successful business man, and in his secret heart Rogers had once or twice felt ashamed of himself. Minks, as it were, knew actual achievement because he was, forcedly, content with little, whereas he, Rogers, dreamed of so much, yet took twenty years to come within reach of what he dreamed. He was always waiting for the right moment to begin.

His reflections were interrupted by the sunlight, which, pouring in a flood across the opposite roof, just then dropped a patch of soft April glory upon the black and yellow check of his carpet slippers. Rogers got up and, opening the window wider than before, put out his head. The sunshine caught him full in the face. He tasted the fresh morning air. Tinged with the sharp sweetness of the north it had a fragrance as of fields and gardens. Even St. James's Street could not smother its vitality and perfume. He drew it with delight into his lungs, making such a to-do about it that a passer-by looked up to see what was the matter, and noticing the hanging tassel of a flamboyant dressing-gown, at once modestly lowered his eyes again.

But Henry Rogers did not see the passer-by in whose delicate mind a point of taste had thus vanquished curiosity, for his thoughts had flown far across the pale-blue sky, behind the cannon-ball clouds, up into that scented space and distance where summer was already winging her radiant way towards the earth. Visions of June obscured his sight, and something in the morning splendour brought back his youth and boyhood. He saw a new world spread about him—a world of sunlight, butterflies, and flowers, of smooth soft lawns and shaded gravel paths, and of children playing round a pond where rushes whispered in a wind of long ago. He saw hayfields, orchards, tea-things spread upon a bank of flowers underneath a hedge, and a collie dog leaping and tumbling shoulder high among the standing grass. . . It was all curiously vivid, and with a sense of something about it unfading and delightfully eternal. It could never pass, for instance, whereas. . .

"Ain't yer forgotten the nightcap?" sang out a shrill voice from below, as a boy with a basket on his arm went down the street. He drew back from the window, realising that he was a sight for all admirers. Tossing the end of his cigarette in the direction of the cheeky urchin, he settled himself again in the arm-chair before the glowing grate-fire.

But the fresh world he had tasted came back with him. For Henry Rogers stood this fine spring morning upon the edge of a new life. A long chapter had just closed behind him. He was on the threshold of another. The time to begin had come. And the thrill of his freedom now at hand was very stimulating to his imagination. He was forty, and a rich man. Twenty years of incessant and intelligent labour had brought him worldly success. He admitted he had been lucky, where so many toil on and on till the gates of death stand up and block their way, fortunate if they have earned a competency through years where hope and disappointment wage their incessant weary battle. But he, for some reason known only to the silent Fates, had crested the difficult hill and now stood firm upon the top to see the sunrise, the dreadful gates not even yet in sight. At yesterday's Board meeting, Minks had handed him the papers for his signature; the patents had been transferred to the new company; the cheque had been paid over; and he was now a gentleman of leisure with a handsome fortune lying in his bank to await investment. He was a director in the parent, as well as the subsidiary companies, with fees that in themselves alone were more than sufficient for his simple needs.

For all his tastes *were* simple, and he had no expensive hobbies or desires; he preferred two rooms and a bath to any house that he had ever seen; pictures he liked best in galleries; horses he could hire without the trouble of owning; the few books worth reading would go into a couple of shelves; motors afflicted, even confused him—he was old-fashioned enough to love country and walk through it slowly on two vigorous legs; marriage had been put aside with a searing disappointment years ago, not forgotten, but accepted; and of travel he had enjoyed enough to realise now that its pleasures could be found reasonably near home and for very moderate expenditure indeed. And the very idea of servants was to him an affliction; he loathed their prying closeness to his intimate life and habits, destroying the privacy he loved. Confirmed old bachelor his friends might call him if they chose; he knew what he wanted. Now at last he had it. The ambition of his life was within reach.

For, from boyhood up, a single big ambition had ever thundered through his being—the desire to be of use to others. To help his fellow-kind was to be his profession and career. It had burned and glowed in him ever since he could remember, and what first revealed it in him was the sight—common enough, alas—of a boy with one leg hobbling along on crutches down the village street. Some deep power in his youthful heart, akin to the wondrous sympathy of women, had been touched. Like a shock of fire it came home to him. He, too, might lose his dearest possession thus, and be unable to climb trees, jump ditches, risk his neck along the edge of the haystack or the roof. "*That might happen to me too!*" was the terrible thing he realised, and had burst into tears. . .

Crutches at twelve! And the family hungry, as he later learned! Something in the world was wrong; he thought every one had enough to eat, at least, and only the old used crutches. The Poor was a sort of composite wretch, half criminal, who deserved to be dirty, suffering, punished; but this boy belonged to a family that worked and did its best. Something in the world-machinery had surely broken loose and caused violent disorder. For no one cared particularly. The "'thorities," he heard, looked after the Poor—"'thorities in law," as he used to call the mysterious Person he never actually saw, stern, but kindly in a grave impersonal way; and asked once if some relation-in-law or other, who was mentioned often but never seen, had, therefore, anything to do with the poor.

Dropping into his heart from who knows what far, happy star, this passion had grown instead of faded: to give himself for others, to help afflicted folk, to make the world go round a little more easily. And he had never forgotten the deep thrill with which he heard his father tell him of some wealthy man who during his lifetime had given away a million pounds—anonymously. . . His own pocket-money just then was five shillings a week, and his expectations just exactly—nothing.

But before his dreams could know accomplishment, he must have means. To be of use to anybody at all he must make himself effective. The process must be reversed, for no man could fight without weapons, and weapons were only to be had as the result of steady, concentrated effort—selfish effort. A man must fashion himself before he can be effective for others. Self-effacement, he learned, was rather a futile virtue after all.

As the years passed he saw his chances. He cut short a promising University career and entered business. His talents lay that way, as his friends declared, and unquestionably he had a certain genius for invention; for, while scores of futile processes he first discovered remained mere clever solutions of interesting problems, he at length devised improvements in the greater industries, and, patenting them wisely, made his way to practical results.

But the process had been a dangerous one, and during the long business experience the iron had entered his soul, and he had witnessed at close quarters the degrading influence of the lust of acquisition. The self-advertising humbug of most philanthropy had clouded something in him that he felt could never again grow clear and limpid as before, and a portion of his original zest had faded. For the City hardly encouraged it. One bit of gilt after another had been knocked off his brilliant dream, one jet of flame upon another quenched. The single eye that fills the body full of light was a thing so rare that its possession woke suspicion. Even of money generously given, so little reached its object; gaping pockets and grasping fingers everywhere lined the way of safe delivery. It sickened him. So few, moreover, were willing to give without acknowledgment in at least one morning paper. "Bring back the receipt" was the first maxim even of the office-boys; and between the right hand and the left of every one were special "private wires" that flashed the news as quickly as possible about the entire world.

Yet, while inevitable disillusion had dulled his youthful dreams, its glory was never quite destroyed. It still glowed within. At times, indeed, it ran into flame, and knew something of its original splendour. Women, in particular, had helped to keep it alive, fanning its embers bravely. For many women, he found, dreamed his own dream, and dreamed it far more sweetly. They were closer to essential realities than men were. While men bothered with fuss and fury about empires, tariffs, street-cars, and marvellous engines for destroying one another, women, keeping close to the sources of life, knew, like children, more of its sweet, mysterious secrets—the things of value no one yet has ever put completely into words. He wondered, a little sadly, to see them battling now to scuffle with the men in managing the gross machinery, cleaning the pens and regulating ink-pots. Did they really think that by helping to decide whether rates should rise or fall, or how many buttons a factory-inspector should wear upon his uniform, they more nobly helped the world go round? Did they never pause to reflect who would fill the places they thus vacated? With something like melancholy he saw them stepping down from their thrones of high authority, for it seemed to him a prostitution of their sweet prerogatives that damaged the entire sex.

"Old-fashioned bachelor, no doubt, I am," he smiled quietly to himself, coming back to the first reflection whence his thoughts had travelled so far—the reflection, namely, that now at last he possessed the freedom he had longed and toiled for.

And then he paused and looked about him, confronted with a difficulty. To him it seemed unusual, but really it was very common.

For, having it, he knew not at first what use to make of it. This dawned upon him suddenly when the sunlight splashed his tawdry slippers with its gold. The movement to the open window was really instinctive beginning of a search, as though in the free, wonderful spaces out of doors he would find the thing he sought to do. Now, settled back in the deep arm-chair, he realised that he had not found it. The memories of childhood had flashed into him instead. He renewed the search before the dying fire, waiting for the sound of Minks' ascending footsteps on the stairs. . .

And this revival of the childhood mood was curious, he felt, almost significant, for it was symbolical of so much that he had deliberately, yet with difficulty, suppressed and put aside. During these years of concentrated toil for money, his strong will had neglected of set purpose the call of a robust imagination. He had stifled poetry just as he had stifled play. Yet really that imagination had merely gone into other channels—scientific invention. It was a higher form, married at least with action that produced poetry in steel and stone instead of in verse. Invention has ever imagination and poetry at its heart.

The acquirement of wealth demanded his entire strength, and all lighter considerations he had consistently refused to recognise, until he thought them dead. This sudden flaming mood rushed up and showed him otherwise. He reflected on it, but clumsily, as with a mind too long trained in the rigid values of stocks and shares, buying and selling, hard figures that knew not elasticity. This softer subject led him to no conclusion, leaving him stranded among misty woods and fields of flowers that had no outlet. He realised, however, clearly that this side of him was not atrophied as he thought. Its unused powers had merely been accumulating—underground.

He got no further than that just now. He poked the fire and lit another cigarette. Then, glancing idly at the paper, his eye fell upon the list of births, and by merest chance picked out the name of Crayfield. Some nonentity had been "safely delivered of a son" at Crayfield, the village where he had passed his youth and childhood. He saw the Manor House where he was born, the bars across the night-nursery windows, the cedars on the lawn, the haystacks just beyond the stables, and the fields where the rabbits sometimes fell asleep as they sat after enormous meals too stuffed to move. He saw the old gravel-pit that led, the gardener told him, to the centre of the earth. A whiff of perfume from the laurustinus in the drive came back, the scent of hay, and with it the sound of the mowing-machine going over the lawn. He saw the pony in loose flat leather shoes. The bees were humming in the lime trees. The rooks were cawing. A blackbird whistled from the shrubberies where he once passed an entire day in hiding, after emptying an ink-bottle down the German governess's dress. He heard the old family butler in his wheezy voice calling in vain for "Mr. 'Enery" to come in. The tone was respectful, seductive as the man could make it, yet reproachful. He remembered throwing a little stone that caught him just where the Newgate fringe met the black collar of his coat, so that his cry of delight betrayed his hiding-place. The whacking that followed he remembered too, and how his brother emerged suddenly from behind the curtain with, "Father, may I have it instead of Henry, please?" That spontaneous offer of sacrifice, of willingness to suffer for another, had remained in his mind for a long time as a fiery, incomprehensible picture.

More dimly, then, somewhere in mist behind, he saw other figures moving—the Dustman and the Lamplighter, the Demon Chimneysweep in black, the Woman of the Haystack—outposts and sentries of a larger fascinating host that gathered waiting in the shadows just beyond. The creations of his boy's imagination swarmed up from their temporary graves, and made him smile and wonder. After twenty years of strenuous business life, how pale and thin they seemed. Yet at the same time how extraordinarily alive and active! He saw, too, the huge Net of Stars he once had made to catch them with from that night-nursery window, fastened by long golden nails made out of meteors to the tops of the cedars. . . There had been, too, a train—the Starlight Express. It almost seemed as if *they* knew, too, that a new chapter had begun, and that they called him to come back and play again. . .

Then, with a violent jump, his thoughts flew to other things, and he considered one by one the various philanthropic schemes he had cherished against the day when he could realise them. That day had come. But the schemes seemed one and all wild now, impracticable, already accomplished by others better than he could hope to accomplish them, and none of them fulfilling the first essential his practical mind demanded—knowing his money spent precisely as he wished. Dreams, long cherished, seemed to collapse one by one before him just when he at last came up with them. He thought of the woman who was to have helped him, now married to another who had money without working for it. He put the thought back firmly in its place. He knew now a greater love than that—the love for many. . .

He was embarking upon other novel schemes when there was a ring at the bell, and the charwoman, who passed with him for servant, ushered in his private secretary, Mr. Minks. Quickly readjusting the machinery of his mind, Rogers came back to the present,

"Good morning, Mr. Rogers. I trust I am punctual."

"Good morning, Minks; yes, on the stroke of ten. We've got a busy day. Let's see now. How are you, by the by?" he added, as an afterthought, catching first one eye, then the other, and looking finally between the two.

"Very well, indeed, thank you, Mr. Rogers." He was dressed in a black tail-coat, with a green tie neatly knotted into a spotless turn-down collar. He glanced round him for a chair, one hand already in his pocket for the note-book.

"Good," said Rogers, indicating where he might seat himself, and reaching for the heap of letters.

The other sighed a little and began to look expectant and receptive.

"If I might give you this first, please, Mr. Rogers," he said, suddenly pretending to remember something in his breast-pocket and handing across the table, with a slight flush upon his cheeks, a long, narrow, mauve envelope with a flourishing address. "It was a red-letter day for Mrs. Minks when I told her of your kindness. She wished to thank you in person, but—I thought a note—I knew," he stammered, "you would prefer a letter. It is a tremendous help to both of us, if I may say so again."

"Yes, yes, quite so," said Rogers, quickly; "and I'm glad to be of service to the lad. You must let me know from time to time how he's getting on."

Minks subsided, flattening out his oblong notebook and examining the points of his pencil sharpened at both ends as though the fate of Empires depended on it. They attacked the pile of correspondence heartily, while the sun, watching them through the open window, danced gorgeously upon the walls and secretly put the fire out.

In this way several hours passed, for besides letters to be dictated, there were careful instructions to be given about many things. Minks was kept very busy. He was now not merely shorthand clerk, and he had to be initiated into the inner history of various enterprises in which his chief was interested. All Mr. Rogers's London interests, indeed, were to be in his charge, and, obviously aware of this, he bore himself proudly with an air of importance that had no connection with a common office. To watch him, you would never have dreamed that Herbert Minks had ever contemplated City life, much less known ten years of drudgery in its least poetic stages. For him, too, as for his employer, anew chapter of existence had begun—"commenced" he would have phrased it—and, as confidential adviser to a man of fortune whose character he admired almost to the point of worship, he was now a person whose importance it was right the world should recognise. And he meant the world to take this attitude without delay. He dressed accordingly, knowing that of every ten people nine judge value from clothes, and hat, and boots— especially boots. His patent leather, buttoned boots were dazzling, with upper parts of soft grey leather. And his shiny "topper" wore a band of black. Minks, so far as he knew, was not actually in mourning, but somebody for whom he ought to be in mourning might die any day, and meanwhile, he felt, the band conveyed distinction. It suited a man of letters. It also protected the hat.

"Thank'ee," said his chief as luncheon time drew near; "and now, if you'll get those letters typed, you might leave 'em here for me on your way home to sign. That's all we have today, isn't it?"

"You wanted, I think, to draft your Scheme for Disabled—" began the secretary, when the other cut him short.

"Yes, yes, but that must wait. I haven't got it clear yet in my own mind. You might think it out a bit yourself, perhaps, meanwhile, and give me your ideas, eh? Look up what others have done in the same line, for instance, and tell me where they failed. What the weakness of their schemes was, you know—and—er—so forth."

A faint smile, that held the merest ghost of merriment, passed across the face of Minks, leaping, unobserved by his chief, from one eye to the other. There was pity and admiration in it; a hint of pathos visited those wayward lips. For the suggestion revealed the weakness the secretary had long ago divined—that the practical root of the matter did not really lie in him at all, and Henry Rogers forever dreamed of "Schemes" he was utterly unable and unsuited to carry out. Improvements in a silk machine was one thing, but improvements in humanity was another. Like the poetry in his soul they could never know fulfilment. He had inspiration, but no constructive talent. For the thousandth time Minks wondered, glancing at his employer's face, how such calm and gentle features, such dreamy eyes and a Vandyke beard so neatly trimmed, could go with ambitions so lofty and so unusual. This sentence he had heard before, and was destined often to hear again, while achievement came no nearer.

"I will do so at the first opportunity." He put the oblong note-book carefully in his pocket, and stood by the table in an attitude of "any further instructions, please?" while one eye wandered to the unopened letter that was signed "Albinia Minks, with heartfelt gratitude."

"And, by the by, Minks," said his master, turning as though a new idea had suddenly struck him and he had formed a hasty plan, "you might kindly look up an afternoon train to Crayfield. Loop line from Charing Cross, you know. Somewhere about two o'clock or so. I have to—er—I think I'll run down that way after luncheon."

Whereupon, having done this last commission, and written it down upon a sheet of paper which he placed with care against the clock, beside the unopened letter, the session closed, and Minks, in his mourning hat and lavender gloves, walked up St. James's Street apparently *en route* for the Ritz, but suddenly, as with careless unconsciousness, turning into an A.B.C. Depot for luncheon, well pleased with himself and with the world, but especially with his considerate employer.

Ten minutes later Mr. Rogers followed him on his way to the club, and just when Minks was reflecting with pride of the well-turned phrases he had dictated to his wife for her letter of thanks, it passed across the mind of its recipient that he had forgotten to read it altogether. And, truth to tell, he never yet has read it; for, returning late that evening from his sentimental journey down to Crayfield, it stood no longer where he had left it beside the clock, and nothing occurred to remind him of its existence. Apart from its joint composers, no one can ever know its contents but the charwoman, who, noticing the feminine writing, took it back to Lambeth and pored over it with a candle for full half an hour, greatly disappointed. "Things like that," she grumbled to her husband, whose appearance suggested that he went for bigger game, "ain't worth the trouble of taking at all, whichever way you looks at it." And probably she was right.

III

And what if All of animated nature
Be but as Instruments diversely framed
That tremble into thought, as o'er them sweeps
One infinite and intellectual Breeze,
At once the Soul of each, and God of all?

—*The Æolian Harp*, S. T. COLERIDGE

I n the train, even before St. John's was passed, a touch of inevitable reaction had set in, and Rogers asked himself why he was going. For a sentimental journey was hardly in his line, it seemed. But no satisfactory answer was forthcoming—none, at least, that a Board or a Shareholders' Meeting would have considered satisfactory.

There was an answer in him somewhere, but he couldn't quite get down to it. The spring glory had enticed him back to childhood. The journey was symbolical of escape. That was the truth. But the part of him that knew it had lain so long in abeyance that only a whisper flitted across his mind as he sat looking out of the carriage window at the fields round Lee and Eltham. The landscape seemed hauntingly familiar, but what surprised him was the number of known faces that rose and smiled at him. A kind of dream confusion blurred his outer sight;

At Bexley, as he hurried past, he caught dimly a glimpse of an old nurse whom he remembered trying to break into bits with a hop-pole he could barely lift; and, most singular thing, on the Sidcup platform, a group of noisy schoolboys, with smudged faces and ridiculously small caps stuck on the back of their heads, had scrambled viciously to get into his compartment. They carried brown canvas satchels full of crumpled books and papers, and though the names had mostly escaped him, he remembered every single face. There was Barlow—big, bony chap who stammered, bringing his words out with a kind of whistling sneeze. Barlow had given him his first thrashing for copying his stammer. There was young Watson, who funked at football and sneaked to a master about a midnight supper. He stole pocket-money, too, and was expelled. Then he caught a glimpse of another fellow with sly face and laughing eyes; the name had vanished, but he was the boy who put jalap in the music-master's coffee, and received a penny from five or six others who thus escaped a lesson. All waved their hands to him as the train hurried away, and the last thing he saw was the station lamp where he had lit the cigar that made three of them, himself included, deadly sick. Familiar woods and a little blue-eyed stream then hid the vision. . . and a moment later he was standing on the platform of his childhood's station, giving up his first-class ticket (secretly ashamed that it was not third) to a station-master-ticket-collector person who simply was not real at all.

For he had no beard. He was small, too, and insignificant. The way he had dwindled, with the enormous station that used to be a mile or so in length, was severely disappointing. That STATION-MASTER with the beard ought to have lived for ever. His niche in the Temple of Fame was sure. One evening he had called in full uniform at the house and asked to see Master Henry Rogers, the boy who had got out "WHILE-THE-TRAIN-WAS-STILL-IN-MOTION," and had lectured him gravely with a face like death. Never again had he left a train "whilestillinmotion," though it was years before he discovered how his father had engineered that awful, salutary visit.

He asked casually, in a voice that hardly seemed his own, about the service back to town, and received the answer with a kind of wonder. It was so respectful. The porters had not found him out yet; but the moment they did so, he would have to run. He did not run, however. He walked slowly down the Station Road, swinging the silver-knobbed cane the office clerks had given him when he left the City. Leisurely, without a touch of fear, he passed the Water Works, where the huge iron crank of the shaft rose and fell with ominous thunder against the sky. It had once been part of that awful hidden Engine which moved the world. To go near it was instant death, and he always crossed the road to avoid it; but this afternoon he went down the cinder pathway so close that he could touch it with his stick. It was incredible that so terrible a thing could dwindle in a few years to the dimensions of a motor piston. The crank that moved up and down like a bending, gigantic knee looked almost flimsy now. . .

Then the village street came into view and he suddenly smelt the fields and gardens that topped the hill beyond. The world turned gold and amber, shining beneath a turquoise sky. There was a rush of flaming sunsets, one upon another, followed by great green moons, and hosts of stars that came twinkling across barred windows to his very bedside. . . that grand old Net of Stars he made so cunningly. Cornhill and Lombard Street flashed back upon him for a second, then dived away and hid their faces for ever, as he passed the low grey wall beside the church where first he had seen the lame boy hobbling, and had realised that the whole world suffered.

A moment he stood here, thinking. He heard the wind sighing in the yew trees beside the dark brown porch. Rooks were cawing among the elms across the churchyard, and pigeons wheeled and fluttered about the grey square tower. The wind, the tower, the weather-stained old porch—these had not changed. This sunshine and this turquoise sky were still the same.

The village stopped at the churchyard—significant boundary. No single building ventured farther; the houses ran the other way instead, pouring down the steep hill in a cataract of bricks and roofs towards the station. The hill, once topped, and the churchyard left behind, he entered the world of fields and little copses. It was just like going through a gateway. It was a Gateway. The road sloped gently down for half-a-mile towards the pair of big iron gates that barred the drive up to the square grey house upon whose lawns he once had chased butterflies, but from whose upper windows he once had netted—stars.

The spell came over him very strongly then as he went slowly down that road. The altered scale of distance confused him; the road had telescoped absurdly; the hayfields were so small. At the turn lay the pond with yellow duckweed and a bent iron railing that divided it to keep the cows from crossing. Formerly, of course, that railing had been put to prevent children drowning in its bottomless depths; all ponds had been bottomless then, and the weeds had spread to entice the children to a watery death. But now he could have jumped across it, weed and railing too, without a run, and he looked in vain for the shores that once had been so seductively far away. They were mere dirty, muddy edges.

This general shrinkage in space was very curious. But a similar contraction, he realised, had taken place in time as well, for, looking back upon his forty years, they seemed such a little thing compared to the enormous stretch they offered when he had stood beside this very pond and looked ahead. He wondered vaguely which was the reality and which the dream. But his effort was not particularly successful, and he came to no conclusion. Those years of strenuous business life were like a few weeks, yet their golden results were in his pockets. Those years of childhood had condensed into a jumble of sunny hours, yet their golden harvest was equally in his heart. Time and space were mere bits of elastic that could stretch or shrink as thought directed, feeling chose. And now both thought and feeling chose emphatically. He stepped back swiftly. His mind seemed filled with stars and butterflies and childhood's figures of wonder. Childhood took him prisoner.

It was curious at first, though, how the acquired nature made a struggle to assert itself, and the practical side of him, developed in the busy markets of the world, protested. It was automatic rather, and at best not very persistent; it soon died away. But, seeing the gravel everywhere, he wondered if there might not be valuable clay about, what labour cost, and what the nearest stations were for haulage; and, seeing the hop-poles, he caught himself speculating what wood they were made of, and what varnish would best prevent their buried points from going rotten in this particular soil. There was a surge of practical considerations, but quickly fading. The last one was stirred by the dust of a leisurely butcher's cart. He had visions of a paste for motor-roads, or something to lay dust. . . but, before the dust had settled again through the sunshine about his feet, or the rumble of the cart died away into distance, the thought vanished like a nightmare in the dawn. It ran away over the switchback of the years, uphill to Midsummer, downhill to Christmas, jumping a ditch at Easter, and a hedge at that terrible thing known as "'Clipse of the Moon." The leaves of the elm trees whispered overhead. He was moving through an avenue that led towards big iron gates beside a little porter's lodge. He saw the hollies, and smelt the laurustinus. There lay the triangle of uncut grass at the cross-roads, the long, grey, wooden palings built upon moss-grown bricks; and against the sky he just caught a glimpse of the feathery, velvet cedar crests, crests that once held nails of golden meteors for his Net of Stars.

Determined to enjoy his cake and eat it at the same time as long as possible, he walked down the road a little distance, eyeing the lawns and windows of the house through narrow gaps between the boarding of the fence. He prolonged the pleasures of anticipation thus, and, besides, he wished to see if the place was occupied or empty. It looked unkempt rather, the gardens somewhat neglected, and yet there hung an air of occupancy about it all. He had heard the house had changed hands several times. But it was difficult to see clearly; the sunshine dazzled; the lilac and laburnum scattered sheets of colour through which the shadows wove themselves an obscuring veil, He kept seeing butterflies and chasing them with his sight.

"Can you tell me if this house is occupied?" he asked abruptly of an old gentleman who coughed suddenly behind him.

It was an explanation as well as a question, for the passer-by had surprised him in a remarkable attitude. He was standing on tiptoe upon the parapet of brick, pulling himself up above the fence by his hands, and his hat had fallen into the road.

"The shrubberies are so dense I can't see through them," he added, landing upon his feet with a jump, a little breathless. He felt rather foolish. He was glad the stranger was not Minks or one of his fellow directors. "The fact is I lived here as a boy. I'm not a burglar."

But the old gentleman—a clergyman apparently—stood there smiling without a word as he handed him the fallen hat. He was staring rather intently into his eyes.

"Ahem!" coughed Mr. Rogers, to fill an awkward gap. "You're very kind, sir," and he took the hat and brushed the dust off. Something brushed off his sight and memory at the same time.

"Ahem" coughed the other, still staring. "Please do not mention it—" adding after a second's pause, to the complete amazement of his listener, "Mr. Rogers."

And then it dawned upon him. Something in the charming, peace-lit face was strangely familiar.

"I say," he exclaimed eagerly, "this is a pleasure," and then repeated with even greater emphasis, "but this is a pleasure, indeed. Who ever would have thought it?" he added with delicious ambiguity. He seized the outstretched hand and shook it warmly—the hand of the old vicar who had once been his tutor too.

"You've come back to your boyhood, then. Is that it? And to see the old place and—your old friends?" asked the other with his beautiful, kindly smile that even false quantities had never been able to spoil. "We've not forgotten you as you've forgotten us, you see," he added; "and the place, though empty now for years, has not forgotten you either, I'll be bound."

They stood there in the sunshine on the dusty road talking of a hundred half-forgotten things, as the haze of memory lifted, and scenes and pictures, names and faces, details of fun and mischief rained upon him like flowers in a sudden wind of spring. The voice and face of his old tutor bridged the years like magic. Time had stood still here in this fair Kentish garden. The little man in black who came every Saturday morning with his dingy bag had forgotten to wind the clocks, perhaps. . .

"But you will like to go inside and see it all for yourself—alone," the Vicar said at length. "My housekeeper has the keys. I'll send a boy with them to the lodge. It won't take five minutes. And then you must come up to the Vicarage for tea—or dinner if you're kept—and stay the night. My married daughter-you remember Joan and May, of course?—is with us just now; she'll be so very glad to see you. You know the way."

And he moved off down the country road, still vigorous at seventy, with his black straw hat and big square-toed boots, his shoulders hardly more bent than when his mischievous pupil had called every morning with Vergil and Todhunter underneath one arm, and in his heart a lust to hurry after sleepy rabbits in the field.

"My married daughter—you remember May?"

The blue-eyed girl of his boyhood passion flitted beside his disappearing figure. He remembered the last time he saw her—refusing to help her from a place of danger in the cedar branches—when he put his love into a single eloquent phrase: "You silly ass!" then cast her adrift for ever because she said "Thanks awfully," and gave him a great wet kiss. But he thought a lot of her all the same, and the thoughts had continued until the uproar in the City drowned them.

Thoughts crowded thick and fast.

How vital thinking was after all! Nothing seemed able to kill its eternal pictures. The coincidence of meeting his old tutor again was like a story-book, though in reality likely enough; for his own face was not so greatly altered by the close brown beard perhaps; and the Vicar had grown smaller, that was all. Like everything else, he had shrunk, of course-like road and station-master and water-works. He had almost said, "You, too, have shrunk"—but otherwise was the same old fluffy personality that no doubt still got sadly muddled in his sermons, gave out wrong hymns, and spent his entire worldly substance on his scattered parish. His voice was softer too. It rang in his ears still, as though there had been no break of over two decades. The hum of bees and scythes was in it just as when it came through the open study window while he construed the *Georgics*. . . But, most clearly of all, he heard two sentences—

"You have come back to your boyhood," and "The empty place has not forgotten you, I'll be bound." Both seemed significant. They hummed and murmured through his mind. That old net of starlight somehow caught them in its golden meshes.

IV

A Spirit gripped him by the hair and carried him far away,
Till he heard as the roar of a rain-fed ford the roar of the Milky Way:
Till he heard the roar of the Milky Way die down and drone
and cease.

—Tomlinson, R. KIPLING

The boy presently came up in a cloud of dust with the key, and ran off again with a shilling in his pocket, while Henry Rogers, budding philanthropist and re-awakening dreamer, went down the hill of memories at high speed that a doctor would have said was dangerous, a philosopher morbid, and the City decreed unanimously as waste of time.

He went over the house from cellar to ceiling. . .

And finally he passed through a back door in the scullery and came out upon the lawn. With a shock he realised that a long time had intervened. The dusk was falling. The rustle of its wings was already in the shrubberies. He had missed the tea hour altogether. And, as he walked there, so softly that he hardly disturbed the thrushes that busily tapped the dewy grass for supper, he knew suddenly that he was not alone, but that shadowy figures hid everywhere, watching, waiting, wondering like himself. They trooped after him, invisible and silent, as he went about the old familiar garden, finding nothing changed. They were so real that once he stopped beneath the lime trees, where afternoon tea was served in summer, and where the Long Walk began its haunted, shadowy existence—stood still a moment and called to them—

"Is any one there? Come out and show yourselves. . . !"

And though his voice fell dead among the foliage, winning echoes from spots whence no echoes possibly could come, and rushing back upon him like a boomerang, he got the curious impression that it had penetrated into certain corners of the shrubberies where it had been heard and understood. Answers did not come. They were no more audible than the tapping of the thrushes, or the little feet of darkness that ran towards him from the eastern sky. But they were there. The troop of Presences drew closer. They had been creeping on all fours. They now stood up. The entire garden was inhabited and alive.

"He has come back!"

It ran in a muted whisper like a hush of wind. The thrill of it passed across the lawn in the dusk. The dark tunnel of the Long Walk filled suddenly to the brim. The thrushes raised their heads, peeping sideways to listen, on their guard. Then the leaves opened a little and the troop ventured nearer. The doors and windows of the silent, staring house had also opened. From the high nursery windows especially, queer shapes of shadow flitted down to join the others. For the sun was far away behind the cedars now, and that Net of Starlight dropped downwards through the air. So carefully had he woven it years ago that hardly a mesh was torn. . .

"*He has come back again. . . !*" the whisper ran a second time, and he looked about him for a place where he could hide.

But there was no place. Escape from the golden net was now impossible. . .

Then suddenly, looming against the field that held the Gravel-Pit and the sleeping rabbits, he saw the outline of the Third Class Railway Carriage his father bought as a Christmas present, still standing on the stone supports that were borrowed from a haystack.

That Railway Carriage had filled whole years with joy and wonder. They had called it the Starlight Express. It had four doors, real lamps in the roof, windows that opened and shut, and big round buffers. It started without warning. It went at full speed in a moment. It was never really still. The footboards were endless and very dangerous.

He saw the carriage with its four compartments still standing there in the hay field. It looked mysterious, old, and enormous as ever. There it still stood as in his boyhood days, but stood neglected and unused.

The memory of the thrilling journeys he had made in this Starlight Express completed his recapture, for he knew now who the troop of Presences all about him really were. The passengers, still waiting after twenty years' delay, thinking perhaps the train would never start again, were now impatient. They had caught their engine-driver again at last. Steam was up. Already the blackbirds whistled. And something utterly wild and reckless in him passionately broke its bonds with a flood of longings that no amount of years or "Cities" could ever subdue again. He stepped out from the dozing lime trees and held his hat up like a flag.

"Take your seats," he cried as of old, "for the Starlight Express. Take your seats! No luggage allowed! Animals free! Passengers with special tickets may drive the engine in their turn! First stop the Milky Way for hot refreshments! Take your seats, or stay at home for ever!"

It was the old cry, still remembered accurately; and the response was immediate. The rush of travellers from the Long Walk nearly took him off his feet. From the house came streams of silent figures, families from the shrubberies, tourists from the laurels by the scullery windows, and throngs of breathless oddities from the kitchen-garden. The lawn was littered with discarded luggage; umbrellas dropped on flower-beds, where they instantly took root and grew; animals ran scuttling among them—birds, ponies, dogs, kittens, donkeys, and white mice in trailing swarms. There was not a minute to spare. One big Newfoundland brought several Persian kittens on his back, their tails behind them in the air like signals; a dignified black retriever held a baby in his mouth; and fat children by the score, with unfastened clothes and smudged faces, many of them in their nightclothes, poured along in hurrying, silent crowds, softer than clouds that hide a crescent moon in summer.

"But this is impossible," he cried to himself. "The multiplication tables have gone wrong. The City has driven me mad. No shareholder would stand such a thing for a minute!"

While, at the same time, that other voice in him kept shouting, ever more loudly—

"Take your seats! Take your seats! The Starlight Express is off to Fairyland! Show your tickets! Show your tickets!"

He laughed with happiness.

The throng and rush were at first so great that he recognised hardly any of the passengers; but, the first press over, he saw several bringing up the rear who were as familiar as of yesterday. They nodded kindly to him as they passed, no sign of reproach for the long delay in their friendly eyes. He had left his place beside the lime trees, and now stood at the carriage door, taking careful note of each one as he showed his ticket to the Guard. And the Guard was the blue-eyed girl. She did not clip the tickets, but merely looked at them. She looked, first at the ticket, then into the face of the passenger. The glance of the blue eyes was the passport. Of course, he remembered now—both guard and engine-driver were obliged to have blue eyes. Blue eyes furnished the motor-power and scenery and everything. It was the spell that managed the whole business—the Spell of the Big Blue eyes—blue, the colour of youth and distance, of sky and summer flowers, of childhood.

He watched these last passengers come up one by one, and as they filed past him he exchanged a word with each. How pleased they were to see him! But how ashamed he felt for having been so long away. Not one, however, reminded him of it, and—what touched him most of all—not one suspected he had nearly gone for good. All knew he would come back.

What looked like a rag-and-bone man blundered up first, his face a perfect tangle of beard and hair, and the eyebrows like bits of tow stuck on with sealing-wax. It was The Tramp—Traveller of the World, the Eternal Wanderer, homeless as the wind; his vivid personality had haunted all the lanes of childhood. And, as Rogers nodded kindly to him, the figure waited for something more.

"Ain't forgot the rhyme, 'ave yer?" he asked in a husky voice that seemed to issue from the ground beneath his broken boots. "The rhyme we used to sing together in the Noight-Nursery when I put my faice agin' the bars, after climbin' along 'arf a mile of slippery slaites to git there."

And Rogers, smiling, found himself saying it, while the pretty Guard fixed her blue eyes on his face and waited patiently:—

> *I travel far and wide,*
> *But in my own inside!*
> *Such places*
> *And queer races!*
> *I never go to them, you see,*
> Because they always come to me!

"Take your seat, please," cried the Guard. "No luggage, you know!" She pushed him in sideways, first making him drop his dirty bundle.

With a quick, light step a very thin man hurried up. He had no luggage, but carried on his shoulder a long stick with a point of gold at its tip.

"Light the lamps," said the Guard impatiently, "and then sit on the back buffers and hold your pole out to warn the shooting stars."

He hopped in, though not before Rogers had passed the time of night with him first:—

> *I stand behind the sky, and light the stars,—*
> *Except on cloudy nights;*
> *And then my head*

Remains in bed,
And takes along the ceiling—easier flights!

Others followed quickly then, too quickly for complete recognition. Besides, the Guard was getting more and more impatient.

"You've clean forgotten *me*," said one who had an awful air of darkness about him; "and no wonder, because you never saw me properly. On Sundays, when I was nicely washed up you couldn't 'ardly reckernise me. Nachural 'nuff, too!"

He shot by like a shadow, then pulled up a window with a rattle, popped his dirty head out, and called back thickly as if his mouth was full of smoke or pudding:—

The darkness suits me *best,*
For my old face
Is out of place,
Except in chimney stacks!
Upon my crown
The soot comes down
Filling my eyes with blacks.
Don't light the fire,
Or I'd—.

"Stop it!" cried the Guard, shutting the window with a snap, so that Rogers never knew whether the missing word used to be "expire" or "perspire"; "and go on to your proper place on the tender." Then she turned quickly to fix her big blue eyes upon the next comer. And how they did come, to be sure! There was the Gypsy, the Creature of the Gravel-Pit, the long-legged, long-armed thing from the Long Walk—she could make her arm stretch the whole length like elastic— the enormous Woman of the Haystack, who lived beneath the huge tarpaulin cover, the owner of the Big Cedar, and the owner of the Little Cedar, all treading fast upon one another's heels.

From the Blue Summer-house came the Laugher. Rogers remembered pretending once that he was going to faint. He had thrown himself upon the summer-house floor and kicked, and the blue-eyed girl, instead of being thrilled as both anticipated, had laughed abominably.

"Painters don't kick!" she had said with scorn, while he had answered, though without conviction, "Men-fainters do—kick dreadfully." And she had simply laughed till her sides ached, while he lay there kicking till his muscles were sore, in the vain hope of winning her belief.

He exchanged a glance with her now, as the Laugher slipped in past them. The eyes of the Guard were very soft. He was found out and forgiven at the same time.

Then came the very mysterious figure of authority—the Head Gardener, a composite being who included all the lesser under-gardeners as well. His sunburned face presented a resume of them all. He was the man who burned the hills of dead leaves in autumn.

"Give me of your fire, please," whispered Rogers, something between joy and sadness in his heart, "for there are hills of leaves that I would burn up quickly—" but the man hurried on, tossing his trowel over the Guard's head, and nearly hitting another passenger who followed too close. This was the Woman of the Haystack, an enormous, spreading traveller who utterly refused to be hurried, and only squeezed through the door because Rogers, the Guard, and several others pushed behind with all their might, while the Sweep, the Tramp, and those already in tugged breathlessly at the same time. . .

Last of all, just as the train was starting, came a hurrying shadowy thing with dreamy eyes, long hair like waving grass, and open hands that he spread like wings, as though he were sowing something through the air. And he was singing softly as he came fumbling along the byeways of the dusk.

"Oh, but I know *you* well," cried Rogers, watching him come with a thrill of secret wonder, "and I love you better than all the rest together."

The face was hidden as he wafted silently past them. A delicious odour followed him. And something, fine as star-dust, as he scattered it all about him, sifted down before the other's sight. The Dustman entered like a ghost.

"Oh, give me of your dust!" cried Rogers again, "for there are eyes that I would blind with it—eyes in the world that I would blind with it—your dust of dreams and beauty. . . !"

The man waved a shadowy hand towards him, and his own eyes filled. He closed the lids a moment; and when he opened them again he saw two monster meteors in the sky. They crossed in two big lines of glory above the house, dropping towards the cedars. The Net of Stars was being fastened. He remembered then his old Star Cave—cave where lost starlight was stored up by these sprites for future use.

He just had time to seize the little hand the Guard held out, and to drop into a seat beside her, when the train began to move. It rose soundlessly with lightning speed. It shot up to a tremendous height, then paused, hovering in the night.

The Guard turned her big blue eyes upon him.

"Where to?" she whispered. And he suddenly remembered that it was always he who decided the destination, and that this time he was at a loss what to say.

"The Star Cave, of course," he cried, "the cave where the lost starlight gathers."

"Which direction?" she asked, with the yellow whistle to her lips ready to signal the driver.

"Oh, out there—to the north-west," he answered, "to the mountains of—across the Channel."

But this was not precise enough. Formerly he had always given very precise directions.

"Name, please," she urged, "but quickly. The Interfering Sun, you know—there's no time to lose. We shall be meeting the Morning Spiders soon."

The Morning Spiders! How it all came back! The Morning Spiders that fly over the fields in the dawn upon their private threads of gossamer and fairy cotton.

He remembered that, as children, they had never actually found this Star Cave, for the Interfering Sun had always come too soon and spoilt it all.

"Name, please, and do hurry up. We can't hover here all night," rang in his ears.

And he made a plunge. He suddenly thought of Bourcelles, the little village in the Jura mountains, where he and his cousin had spent a year learning French. The idea flashed into him probably because it contained mountains, caves, and children. His cousin lived there now to educate his children and write his books. Only that morning he had got a letter from him.

"Bourcelles, of course, Bourcelles!" he cried, "and steer for the slopes of Boudry where the forests dip towards the precipices of the Areuse. I'll send word to the children to meet us."

"Splendid!" cried the Guard, and kissed him with delight. The whistle shrieked, the train turned swiftly in a tremendous sweeping curve, and vanished along the intricate star-rails into space, humming and booming as it went. It flew a mane of stars behind it through the sky.

V

Oh! thou art fairer than the evening air
Clad in the beauty of a thousand stars.

—Doctor Famtus, CHRISTOPHER MARLOWE

The plop of a water-rat in the pond that occupied the rock-garden in the middle of the lawn brought him back to earth, and the Vicar's invitation to tea flashed across his mind.

"Stock Exchange and typewriters!" he exclaimed, "how rude he'll think me!" And he rubbed something out of his eyes. He gave one long, yearning glance at the spangled sky where an inquisitive bat darted zigzag several times between himself and the Pleiades, that bunch of star-babies as yet unborn, as the blue-eyed guard used to call them.

"And I shall miss my supper and bed into the bargain!"

He turned reluctantly from his place beside the lime trees, and crossed the lawn now wet with dew. The whole house seemed to turn its hooded head and watch him go, staring with amusement in its many lidless eyes. On the front lawn there was more light, for it faced the dying sunset. The Big and Little Cedar rose from their pools of shadow, beautifully poised. Like stately dowagers in voluminous skirts of velvet they seemed to curtsey to him as he passed. Stars like clusters of sprinkled blossoms hung upon their dignified old heads. The whole place seemed aware of him. Glancing a moment at the upper nursery windows, he could just distinguish the bars through which his little hands once netted stars, and as he did so a meteor shot across the sky its flashing light of wonder. Behind the Little Cedar it dived into the sunset afterglow. And, hardly had it dipped away, when another, coming crosswise from the south, drove its length of molten, shining wire straight against the shoulder of the Big Cedar.

The whole performance seemed arranged expressly for his benefit. The Net was loosed—this Net of Stars and Thoughts—perhaps to go elsewhere. For this was taking out the golden nails, surely. It would hardly have surprised him next to see the Starlight Express he had been dreaming about dart across the heavens overhead. That cool air stealing towards him from the kitchen-garden might well have been the wind of its going. He could almost hear the distant rush and murmur of its flying mass.

"How extraordinarily vivid it all was!" he thought to himself, as he hurried down the drive. "What detail! What a sense of reality! How carefully I must have *thought* these creatures as a boy! How thoroughly! And what a good idea to go out and see Jack's children at Bourcelles. They've never known these English sprites. I'll introduce 'em!"

He thought it out in detail, very vividly indeed. His imagination lingered over it and gave it singular reality.

Up the road he fairly ran. For Henry Rogers was a punctual man; these last twenty years he had never once been late for anything. It had been part of the exact training he had schooled himself with, and the Vicar's invitation was not one he desired to trifle with. He made his peace, indeed, easily enough, although the excuses sounded a little thin. It was something of a shock, too, to find that the married daughter after all was not the blue-eyed girl of his boyhood's passion. For it was Joan, not May, who came down the gravel path between the roses to greet him.

On the way up he had felt puzzled. Yet "bemused," perhaps, is the word that Herbert Minks would have chosen for one of his poems, to describe a state of mind he, however, had never experienced himself. And he would have chosen it instinctively—for onomatopoeic reasons— because it hums and drones and murmurs dreamily. "Puzzled" was too sharp a word.

Yet Henry Rogers, who felt it, said "puzzled" without more ado, although mind, imagination, memory all hummed and buzzed pleasantly about his ears even while he did so.

"A dream is a dream," he reflected as he raced along the familiar dusty road in the twilight, "and a reverie is a reverie; but that, I'd swear, went a bit further than either one or t'other. It puzzles me. Does vivid thinking, I wonder, make pictures everywhere? . . . And—can they last?"

For the detailed reality of the experience had been remarkable, and the actuality of those childhood's creations scarcely belonged to dream or reverie. They were certainly quite as real as the sleek Directors who sat round the long Board Room table, fidgeting with fat quill pens and pewter ink-pots; more alive even than the Leading Shareholder who rose so pompously at Annual Meetings to second the resolution that the "Report and Balance Sheet be adopted without criticism."

And he was conscious that in himself rose, too, a deep, passionate willingness to accept the whole experience, also "without criticism."

Those picturesque passengers in the Starlight Express he knew so intimately, so affectionately, that he actually missed them. He felt that he had said good-bye to genuine people. He regretted their departure, and was keenly sorry he had not gone off with them—such a merry, wild, adventurous crew! He must find them again, whatever happened. There was a yearning in him to travel with that blue-eyed guard among the star-fields. He would go out to Bourcelles and tell the story to the children. He thought very hard indeed about it all.

And now, in the Vicarage drawing-room after dinner, his bemusement increased rather than grew less. His mind had already confused a face and name. The blue-eyed May was not, after all, the girl of his boyhood's dream. His memory had been accurate enough with the passengers in the train. There was no confusion there. But this gentle married woman, who sang to her own accompaniment at her father's request, was not the mischievous, wilful creature who had teased and tortured his heart in years gone by, and had helped him construct the sprites and train and star-trips. It was, surely, the other daughter who had played that delicious role. Yet, either his memory was at fault, or the Vicar had mixed the names up. The years had played this little unimportant trick upon him anyhow. And that was clear.

But if with so-called real people such an error was possible, how could he be sure of anything? Which after all, he asked himself, was real? It was the Vicar's mistake, he learned later, for May was now a teacher in London; but the trivial incident served to point this confusion in his mind between an outer and an inner world—to the disadvantage, if anything, of the former.

And over the glass of port together, while they talked pleasantly of vanished days, Rogers was conscious that a queer, secret amusement sheltered in his heart, due to some faint, superior knowledge that this Past they spoke of had not moved away at all, but listened with fun and laughter just behind his shoulder, watching them. The old gentleman seemed never tired of remembering his escapades. He told them one after another, like some affectionate nurse or mother, Rogers thought, whose children were—to her—unique and wonderful. For he had really loved this good-for-nothing pupil, loved him the more, as mothers and nurses do, because of the trouble he had given, and because of his busy and fertile imagination. It made Rogers feel ridiculously young again as he listened. He could almost have played a trick upon him then and there, merely to justify the tales. And once or twice he actually called him "Sir." So that even the conversation helped to deepen this bemusement that gathered somewhat tenderly about his mind. He cracked his walnuts and watched the genial, peace-lit eyes across the table. He chuckled. Both chuckled. They spoke of his worldly success too—it seemed unimportant somehow now, although he was conscious that something in him expected, nay demanded tribute—but the former tutor kept reverting to the earlier days before achievement.

"You were indeed a boy of mischief, wonder, and mystery," he said, his eyes twinkling and his tone almost affectionate; "you made the whole place alive with those creatures of your imagination. How Joan helped you too—or was it May? I used to wonder sometimes—" he glanced up rather searchingly at his companion a moment—"whether the people who took the Manor House after your family left did not encounter them sometimes upon the lawn or among the shrubberies in the dusk—those sprites of yours. Eh?" He passed a neatly pared walnut across the table to his guest. "These ghosts that people nowadays explain scientifically—what are they but thoughts visualised by vivid thinking such as yours was—creative thinking? They may be just pictures created in moments of strong passionate feeling that persist for centuries and reach other minds direct. They're not seen with the outer eye; that's certain, for no two people ever see them together. But I'm sure these pictures flame up through the mind sometimes just as clearly as some folk see Grey Ladies and the rest flit down the stairs at midnight."

They munched their walnuts a moment in silence. Rogers listened very keenly. How curious, he reflected, that the talk should lie this way. But he said nothing, hoping that the other would go on.

"And if you really believed in your things," the older man continued presently, "as I am sure you did believe, then your old Dustman and Sweep and Lamplighter, your Woman of the Haystack and your Net of Stars and Star Train—all these, for instance, must still be living, where you left them, waiting perhaps for your return to lead their fresh adventures."

Rogers stared at him, choking a little over a nut he had swallowed too hurriedly.

"Yet," mused on the other, "it's hardly likely the family that succeeded you met them. There were no children!"

"Ah," exclaimed the pupil impulsively, "that's significant, yes—no children." He looked up quickly, questioningly.

"Very, I admit."

"Besides, the chief Magician had gone away into the City. They wouldn't answer to anybody's call, you know."

"True again. But the Magician never forgot them quite, I'll be bound," he added. "They're only in hiding till his return, perhaps!" And his bright eyes twinkled knowingly.

"But, Vicar, really, you know, that is an extraordinary idea you have there-a wonderful idea. Do you really think—?"

"I only mean," the other replied more gravely, "that what a man thinks, and makes with thinking, is the real thing. It's in the heart that sin is first real. The act is the least important end of it—grave only because it is the inevitable result of the thinking. Action is merely delayed thinking, after all. Don't think ghosts and bogeys, I always say to children, or you'll surely see them."

"Ah, in *that* sense—!"

"In any sense your mind and intuition can grasp. The thought that leaves your brain, provided it be a real thought strongly fashioned, goes all over the world, and may reach any other brain tuned to its acceptance. *You* should understand that!" he laughed significantly.

"I do," said Rogers hastily, as though he felt ashamed of himself or were acknowledging a fault in his construing of Homer. "I understand it perfectly. Only I put all those things—imaginative things—aside when I went into business. I had to concentrate my energies upon making money."

"You did, yes. Ah!" was the rejoinder, as though he would fain have added, "And was that wise?"

"And I made it, Vicar; you see, I've made it." He was not exactly nettled, but he wanted a word of recognition for his success. "But you know why, don't you?" he added, ashamed the same moment. There was a pause, during which both looked closely at their broken nuts. From one of the men came a sigh.

"Yes," resumed the older man presently, "I remember your great dream perfectly well, and a noble one it was too. Its fulfilment now, I suppose, lies well within your reach? You have the means to carry it out, eh? You have indeed been truly blessed." He eyed him again with uncommon keenness, though a smile ran from the eyes and mouth even up to the forehead and silvery hair. "The world, I see, has not yet poisoned you. To carry it out as you once explained it to me would be indeed success. If I remember rightly," he added, "it was a—er—a Scheme for Disabled—"

Rogers interrupted him quickly. "And I am full of the same big dream still," he repeated almost shyly. "The money I have made I regard as lent to me for investment. I wish to use it, to give it away as one gives flowers. I feel sure—"

He stopped abruptly, caught by the glow of enthusiasm that had leaped into the other's face with a strangely beautiful expression.

"You never did anything by halves, I remember," the Vicar said, looking at him proudly. "You were always in earnest, even in your play, and I don't mind telling you that I've often prayed for something of that zeal of yours—that zeal for others. It's a remarkable gift. You will never bury it, will you?" He spoke eagerly, passionately, leaning forward a little across the table. "Few have it nowadays; it grows rarer with the luxury and self-seeking of the age. It struck me so in you as a boy, that even your sprites worked not for themselves but for others—your Dustman, your Sweep, your absurd Lamplighter, all were busy doing wonderful things to help their neighbours, all, too, without reward."

Rogers flushed like a boy. But he felt the thrill of his dream course through him like great fires. Wherein was any single thing in the world worth doing, any object of life worth following, unless as means to an end, and that end helping some one else. One's own little personal dreams became exhausted in a few years, endeavours for self smothered beneath the rain of disappointments; but others, and work for others, this was endless and inexhaustible.

"I've sometimes thought," he heard the older man going on, "that in the dusk I saw"—his voice lowered and he glanced towards the windows where the rose trees stood like little figures, cloaked and bonneted with beauty beneath the stars—"that I saw your Dustman scattering his golden powder as he came softly up the path, and that some of it reached my own eyes, too; or that your swift Lamplighter lent me a moment his gold-tipped rod of office so that I might light fires of hope in suffering hearts here in this tiny world of my own parish. Your dreadful Head Gardener, too! And your Song of the Blue-Eyes Fairy," he added slyly, almost mischievously, "you remember that, I wonder?"

"H'm—a little, yes—something," replied Rogers confusedly. "It was a dreadful doggerel. But I've got a secretary now," he continued hurriedly and in rather a louder voice, "a fellow named Minks, a jewel really of a secretary he is—and he, I believe, can write real—"

"It was charming enough for us all to have remembered it, anyhow," the Vicar stopped him, smiling at his blushes, "and for May—or was it Joan? dear me, how I do forget names!—to have set it to music. She had a little gift that way, you may remember; and, before she took up teaching she wrote one or two little things like that."

"Ah, did she really?" murmured the other. He scarcely knew what he was saying, for a mist of blue had risen before his eyes, and in it he was seeing pictures. "The Spell of Blue, wasn't it, or something like that?" he said a moment later, "blue, the colour of beauty in flowers, sea, sky, distance—the childhood colour par excellence?"

"But chiefly in the eyes of children, yes," the Vicar helped him, rising at the same time from the table. "It was the spell, the passport, the open sesame to most of your adventures. Come now, if you won't have another glass of port, and we'll go into the drawing-room, and Joan, May I mean—no, Joan, of course, shall sing it to you. For this is a very special occasion for us, you know," he added as they passed across the threshold side by side. "To see you is to go back with you to Fairyland."

The piano was being idly strummed as they went in, and the player was easily persuaded to sing the little song. It floated through the open windows and across the lawn as the two men in their corners listened. She knew it by heart, as though she often played it. The candles were not lit. Dusk caught the sound and muted it enchantingly. And somehow the simple melody helped to conceal the meagreness of the childish words. Everywhere, from sky and lawn and solemn trees, the Past came softly in and listened too.

There's a Fairy that hides in the beautiful eyes
Of children who treat her well;
In the little round hole where the eyeball lies
She weaves her magical spell.

Oh, tell it to me,
Oh, how can it be,
This Spell of the Blue-Eyes Fairy.

Well,—the eyes must be blue,
And the heart must be true,
And the child must be better *than gold;*
And then, if you'll let her,
The quicker the better,

She'll make you forget that you're old,
That you're heavy and stupid, and—old!

So, if such a child you should chance to see,
Or with such a child to play,
No matter how weary and dull you be,
Nor how many tons you weigh;
You will suddenly find that you're young again,
And your movements are light and airy,
And you'll try to be solemn and stiff in vain—
It's the Spell of the Blue-Eyes Fairy!

Now I've told it to you,
And you know *it is true—*
It's the Spell of the Blue-Eyes Fairy!

"And it's the same spell," said the old man in his corner as the last notes died away, and they sat on some minutes longer in the fragrant darkness, "that you cast about us as a boy, Henry Rogers, when you made that wonderful Net of Stars and fastened it with your comets' nails to the big and little cedars. The one catches your heart, you see, while the other gets your feet and head and arms till you're a hopeless prisoner—a prisoner in Fairyland."

"Only the world today no longer believes in Fairyland," was the reply, "and even the children have become scientific. Perhaps it's only buried though. The two ought to run in harness really—opposite interpretations of the universe. One might revive it—here and there perhaps. Without it, all the tenderness seems leaking out of life—"

Joan presently said good-night, but the other two waited on a little longer; and before going to bed they took a turn outside among the flower-beds and fruit-trees that formed the tangled Vicarage garden at the back. It was uncommonly warm for a night in early spring. The lilacs were in bud, and the air most exquisitely scented.

Rogers felt himself swept back wonderfully among his early years. It seemed almost naughty to be out at such an hour instead of asleep in bed. It was quite ridiculous—but he loved the feeling and let himself go with happy willingness. The story of "Vice Versa," where a man really became a boy again, passed through his mind and made him laugh.

And the old Vicar kept on feeding the semi-serious mood with what seemed almost intentional sly digs. Yet the digs were not intentional, really; it was merely that his listener, already prepared by his experience with the Starlight Express, read into them these searching meanings of his own. Something in him was deeply moved.

"You might make a great teacher, you know," suggested his companion, stooping to sniff a lilac branch as they paused a moment. "I thought so years ago; I think so still. You've kept yourself so simple."

"How not to do most things," laughed the other, glad of the darkness.

"How to do the big and simple things," was the rejoinder; "and do them well, without applause. You have Belief."

"Too much, perhaps. I simply can't get rid of it."

"Don't try to. It's belief that moves the world; people want teachers— that's my experience in the pulpit and the parish; a world in miniature, after all—but they won't listen to a teacher who hasn't got it. There are no great poets today, only great discoverers. The poets, the interpreters of discovery, are gone—starved out of life by ridicule, and by questions to which exact answers are impossible. With your imagination and belief you might help a world far larger than this parish of mine at any rate. I envy you."

Goodness! how the kind eyes searched his own in this darkness. Though little susceptible to flattery, he was aware of something huge the words stirred in the depths of him, something far bigger than he yet had dreamed of even in his boyhood, something that made his cherished Scheme seem a little pale and faded.

"Take the whole world with you into fairyland," he heard the low voice come murmuring in his ear across the lilacs. And there was starlight in it—that gentle, steady brilliance that steals into people while they sleep and dream, tracing patterns of glory they may recognise when they wake, yet marvelling whence it came. "The world wants its fairyland back again, and won't be happy till it gets it."

A bird listening to them in the stillness sang a little burst of song, then paused again to listen.

"Once give them of your magic, and each may shape his fairyland as he chooses. . ." the musical voice ran on.

The flowers seemed alive and walking. This was a voice of beauty. Some lilac bud was singing in its sleep. Sirius had dropped a ray across its lips of blue and coaxed it out to dance. There was a murmur and a stir among the fruit-trees too. The apple blossoms painted the darkness with their tiny fluttering dresses, while old Aldebaran trimmed them silently with gold, and partners from the Milky Way swept rustling down to lead the violets out. Oh, there was revelry tonight, and the fairy spell of the blue-eyed Spring was irresistible. . .

"But the world will never dance," he whispered sadly, half to himself perhaps; "it's far too weary."

"It will follow a leader," came the soft reply, "who dances well and pipes the true old music so that it can hear. Belief inspires it always. And that Belief you have." There was a curious vibration in his voice; he spoke from his heart, and his heart was evidently moved.

"I wonder when it came to me, then, and how?"

The Vicar turned and faced him where they stood beneath the lime trees. Their scent was pouring out as from phials uncorked by the stars.

"It came," he caught the answer that thrilled with earnestness, "when you saw the lame boy on the village hill and cried. As long ago as that it came."

His mind, as he listened, became a plot of fresh-turned earth the Head Gardener filled with flowers. A mass of covering stuff the years had laid ever thicker and thicker was being shovelled away. The flowers he saw being planted there were very tiny ones. But they would grow. A leaf from some far-off rocky mount of olive trees dropped fluttering through the air and marvellously took root and grew. He felt for a moment the breath of night air that has been tamed by an eastern sun. He saw a group of men, bare-headed, standing on the slopes, and in front of them a figure of glory teaching little, simple things they found it hard to understand. . .

"You have the big and simple things alive in you," the voice carried on his pictured thought among the flowers. "In your heart they lie all waiting to be used. Nothing can smother them. Only-you must give them out."

"If only I knew how—!"

"Keep close to the children," sifted the strange answer through the fruit-trees; "the world is a big child. And catch it when it lies asleep—not thinking of itself," he whispered.

"The time is so short—"

"At forty you stand upon the threshold of life, with values learned and rubbish cleared away. So many by that time are already dead—in heart. I envy your opportunities ahead. You have learned already one foundation truth—the grandeur of toil and the insignificance of acquisition. The other foundation thing is even simpler—you have a neighbour. Now, with your money to give as flowers, and your Belief to steer you straight, you have the world before you. And—keep close to the children."

"Before there are none left," added Rogers under his breath. But the other heard the words and instantly corrected him—

"Children of any age, and wherever you may find them."

And they turned slowly and made their way in silence across the soaking lawn, entering the house by the drawing-room window.

"Good-night," the old man said, as he lit his candle and led him to his room; "and pleasant, happy, inspiring dreams."

He seemed to say it with some curious, heartfelt meaning in the common words. He disappeared slowly down the passage, shading the candle with one hand to pick his way, and Rogers watched him out of sight, then turned and entered his own room, closing the door as softly as possible behind him.

It had been an astonishing conversation. All his old enthusiasm was stirred. Embers leaped to flame. No woman ever had done as much. This old fellow, once merely respected tutor, had given him back his first original fire and zeal, yet somehow cleansed and purified. And it humbled him at the same time. Dead leaves, dropped year by year in his City life, were cleared away as though a mighty wind had swept him. The Gardener was burning up dead leaves; the Sweep was cleaning out the flues; the Lamplighter waving his golden signal in the sky—far ahead, it is true, but gleaming like a torch and beacon. The Starlight Express was travelling at top speed among the constellations. He stood at the beginning of the important part of life. . .

And now, as he lay in bed and heard the owls hooting in the woods, and smelt the flowers through the open window, his thoughts followed strongly after that old Star Train that he used to drive about the sky. He was both engine-driver and passenger. He fell asleep to dream of it.

And all the vital and enchanting thoughts of his boyhood flowed back upon him with a rush, as though they had never been laid aside. He remembered particularly one singular thing about them—that they had never seemed quite his own, but that he had either read or heard them somewhere else. As a child the feeling was always strong that these "jolly thoughts," as he called them, were put into him by some one else—some one who whispered to him—some one who lived close behind his ears. He had to listen very hard to catch them. It was *not* dreams, yet all night long, especially when he slept tightly, as he phrased it, this fairy whispering continued, and in the daytime he remembered what he could and made up his stories accordingly. He stole these ideas about a Star Net and a Starlight Express. One day he would be caught and punished for it. It was trespassing upon the preserves of some one else.

Yet he could never discover who this some one else was, except that it was a "she" and lived among the stars, only coming out at night. He imagined she hid behind that little dusty constellation called the Pleiades, and that was why the Pleiades wore a veil and were so dim— lest he should find her out. And once, behind the blue gaze of the guard-girl, who was out of his heart by this time, he had known a moment of thrilling wonder that was close to awe. He saw another pair of eyes gazing out at him They were ambery eyes, as he called them— just what was to be expected from a star. And, so great was the shock, that at first he stood dead still and gasped, then dashed up suddenly close to her and stared into her face, frightening her so much that she fell backwards, and the amber eyes vanished instantly. It was the "some one else" who whispered fairy stories to him and lived behind his ear. For a second she had been marvellously close. And he had lost her!

From that moment, however, his belief in her increased enormously, and he never saw a pair of brown-ambery eyes without feeling sure that she was somewhere close about him. The lame boy, for instance, had the same delicate tint in his sad, long, questioning gaze. His own collie had it too! For years it was an obsession with him, haunting and wonderful—the knowledge that some one who watched close beside him, filling his mind with fairy thoughts, might any moment gaze into his face through a pair of ordinary familiar eyes. And he was certain that all his star-imagination about the Net, the Starlight Express, and the Cave of Lost Starlight came first into him from this hidden "some one else" who brought the Milky Way down into his boy's world of fantasy.

"If ever I meet her in real life," he used to say, "I'm done for. She is my Star Princess!"

And now, as he fell asleep, the old atmosphere of that Kentish garden drew thickly over him, shaking out clusters of stars about his bed. Dreams usually are determined by something more remote than the talk that has just preceded going to bed, but tonight it was otherwise. And two things the old Vicar had let fall—two things sufficiently singular, it seemed, when he came to think about them—influenced his night adventures. "Catch the world when it's asleep," and "Keep close to the children"—these somehow indicated the route his dream should follow. For he headed the great engine straight for the village in the Jura pine woods where his cousin's children lived. He did not know these children, and had seen his cousin but rarely in recent years; yet, it seemed, they came to meet the train up among the mountain forests somewhere. For in this village, where he had gone to study French, the moods of his own childhood had somehow known continuation and development. The place had once been very dear to him, and he had known delightful adventures there, many of them with this cousin. Now he took all his own childhood's sprites out in this Starlight Express and introduced them to these transplanted children who had never made acquaintance with the English breed. They had surprising, wild adventures all together, yet in the morning he could remember very little of it all. The interfering sun melted them all down in dew. The adventures had some object, however; that was clear; though what the object was, except that it did good somewhere to. some one, was gone, lost in the deeps of sleep behind him. They scurried about the world. The sprites were very active indeed—quite fussily energetic. And his Scheme for Disabled Something-or other was not anywhere discoverable in these escapades. That seemed forgotten rather, as though they found bigger, more important things to do, and nearer home too. Perhaps the Vicar's hint about the "Neighbour" was responsible for that. Anyhow, the dream was very vivid, even though the morning sun melted it away so quickly and completely. It seemed continuous too. It filled the entire night.

Yet the thing that Rogers took off with him to town next morning was, more than any other detail, the memory of what the old tutor had said about the living reality and persistence of figures that passionate thinking has created—that, and the value of Belief.

VI

*Be thou my star, and thou in me be seen
To show what source divine is, and prevails.
I mark thee planting joy in constant fire.*

—*To Sirius*, G. MEREDITH

And he rather astonished the imperturbable Minks next day by the announcement that he was thinking of going abroad for a little holiday. "When I return, it will be time enough to take up the Scheme in earnest," he said. For Minks had brought a sheaf of notes embodying the results of many hours' labour, showing what others had already done in that particular line of philanthropy.

"Very good indeed, Minks, very good. I'll take 'em with me and make a careful study of the lot. I shall be only gone a week or so," he added, noticing the other's disappointment. For the secretary had hoped to expound these notes himself at length. "Take a week's holiday yourself," he added. "Mrs. Minks might like to get to the sea, perhaps. There'll only be my letters to forward. I'll give you a little cheque." And he explained briefly that he was going out to Bourcelles to enjoy a few days' rest before they attacked great problems together. After so many years of application to business he had earned it. Crayfield, it seemed, had given him a taste for sentimental journeys. But the fact was, too, the Tramp, the Dustman, the Lamplighter, and the Starlight Express were all in his thoughts still.

And it was spring. He felt this sudden desire to see his cousin again, and make the acquaintance of his cousin's children. He remembered how the two of them had tramped the Jura forests as boys. They had met in London at intervals since. He dictated a letter to him then and there—Minks taking it down like lightning—and added a postscript in his own handwriting:—

"I feel a longing," he wrote, "to come out and see the little haven of rest you have chosen, and to know your children. Our ways have gone very far apart—too far—since the old days when we climbed out of the windows of *la cure* with a sheet, and tramped the mountains all night long. Do you remember? I've had my nose on the grindstone ever since, and you've worked hard too, judging by your name in publishers' lists.

I hope your books are a great success. I'm ashamed I've never any time to read now. But I'm 'retired' from business at last and hope to do great things. I'll tell you about a great Scheme I have in hand when we meet. I should like your advice too.

"Any room will do—sunny aspect if possible. And please give my love to your children in advance. Tell them I shall come out in the Starlight Express. Let me have a line to say if it's all right."

In due course the line—a warm-hearted one—arrived. Minks came to Charing Cross to see him off, the gleam of the sea already in his pale-blue eyes.

"The Weather Report says 'calm,' Mr. Rogers," he kept repeating. "You'll have a good crossing, I hope and trust. I'm taking Mrs. Minks myself—"

"Yes, yes, that's good," was the quick reply. "Capital. And—let me see-I've got your notes with me, haven't I? I'll draft out a general plan and send it to you as soon as I get a moment. You think over it too, will you, while I'm away. And enjoy yourself at the same time. Put your children in the sea—nothing like the sea for children—sea and sun and sand and all that sort of thing."

"Thank you very much, Mr. Rogers, and I trust—"

Somebody bumped against him, cutting short a carefully balanced sentence that was intended to be one-third good wishes, one-third weather remark, and the last third Mrs. Minks. Her letter of thanks had never been referred to. It rankled, though very slightly.

"What an absurd-looking person!" exclaimed the secretary to himself, following the aggressor with one eye, and trying to recapture the lost sentence at the same time. "They really should not allow such people in a railway terminus," he added aloud. The man was ragged and unkempt to the last degree—a sort of tramp; and as he bought a ticket at the third-class wicket, just beyond, he kept looking up slyly at Minks and his companion. "The way he knocked against me almost seemed intentional," Minks thought. The idea of pickpockets and cleverly disguised detectives ran confusedly in his mind. He felt a little flustered for some reason.

"I beg your pardon," Mr. Rogers was saying to a man who tried to push in front of him. "But we *must* each take our turn, you know." The throng of people was considerable. This man looked like a dustman. He, too, was eagerly buying a ticket, but had evidently mistaken the window. "Third-class is lower down I think," Mr. Rogers suggested with a touch of authority.

"What a lot of foreigners there are about," remarked Minks. "These stations are full of suspicious characters." The notice about loitering flashed across him.

He took the ticket Mr. Rogers handed to him, and went off to register the luggage, and when later he joined his chief at the carriage door he saw him talking to a couple of strangers who seemed anxious to get in.

"I took *this* corner seat for you, Mr. Rogers," he explained, both to prove his careful forethought and to let the strangers know that his master was a person of some importance. They were such an extraordinary couple too! Had there been hop-pickers about he could have understood it. They were almost figures of masquerade; for while one resembled more than anything else a chimney-sweep who had forgotten to wash his face below the level of the eyes, the other carried a dirty sack across his shoulders, which apparently he had just been trying to squeeze into the rack.

They moved off when they saw Minks, but the man with the sack made a gesture with one hand, as though he scattered something into the carriage through the open door.

The secretary threw a reproachful look at a passing guard, but there was nothing he could do. People with tickets had a right to travel. Still, he resented these crowding, pushing folk. "I'm sorry, Mr. Rogers," he said, as though he had chosen a poor train for his honoured chief; "there must be an excursion somewhere. There's a big fete of Vegetarians, I know, at Surbiton today, but I can hardly think these people—"

"Don't wait, Minks," said the other, who had taken his seat. "I'll let you hear from me, you know, about the Scheme and—other things. Don't wait." He seemed curiously unobservant of these strange folk, almost absent-minded.

The guard was whistling. Minks shut the door and gave the travelling-rug a last tuck-in about his feet. He felt as though he were packing off a child. The mother in him became active. Mr. Rogers needed looking after. Another minute and he would have patted him and told him what to eat and wear. But instead he raised his hat and smiled. The train moved slowly out, making a deep purring sound like flowing water. The platform had magically thinned. Officials stood lonely among the scattered wavers of hats and handkerchiefs. As he stepped backwards to keep the carriage window in sight until the last possible moment, Minks was nearly knocked over by a man who hurried along the platform as if he still had hopes of catching the train.

"Really, sir!" gasped the secretary, stooping to pick up his newspaper and lavender glove—he wore one glove and carried the other—the collision had sent flying. But the man was already far beyond the reach of his voice. "He must be an escaped lamplighter, or something," he laughed good-naturedly, as he saw the long legs vanish down the platform. He leaped on to the line. Evidently he was a railway employe. He seemed to be vainly trying to catch the departing buffers. An absurd and reckless fellow, thought Minks.

But what caught the secretary's attention last, and made him wonder a little if anything unusual was happening to the world, was the curious fact that, as the last carriage glided smoothly past, he recognised four figures seated comfortably inside. Their feet were on the cushions—disgracefully. They were talking together, heads forward, laughing, even—singing. And he could have sworn that they were the two men who had watched himself and Mr. Rogers at the ticket window, and the strangers who had tried to force their way into Mr. Rogers's carriage when he came up just in time to interfere.

"They got in somehow after all, then," he said to himself. "Of course, I had forgotten. The Company runs third-class carriages on the continental trains now. Odd!" He mentally rubbed his eyes.

The train swept round the corner out of sight, leaving a streaming cloud of smoke and sparks behind it. It went out with a kind of rush of delight, glad to be off, and conscious of its passengers' pleasure.

"Odd." This was the word that filled his mind as he walked home. "Perhaps—our minds are in such intimate sympathy together—perhaps he was thinking of—of that kind of thing—er—and some of his thoughts got into my own imagination. Odd, though, very, *very* odd."

He had once read somewhere in one of his new-fangled books that "thoughts are things." It had made a great impression on him. He had read about Marconi too. Later he made a more thorough study of this "thinking business."

And soon afterwards, having put his chief's papers in order at the flat, he went home to Mrs. Minks and the children with this other thought—that he had possibly been overworking himself, and that it was a good thing he was going to have a holiday by the sea.

He liked to picture himself as an original thinker, not afraid of new ideas, but in reality he preferred his world sober, ordinary, logical. It was merely big-sounding names he liked. And this little incident was somewhere out of joint. It was—odd.

Success that poisons many a baser mind
May lift—

But the sonnet had never known completion. In the space it had occupied in his mind another one abruptly sprouted. The first subject after all was banal. A better one had come to him—

Strong thoughts that rise in a creative mind
May flash about the world, and carry joy—

Then it stuck. He changed "may" to "shall," but a moment later decided that "do" was better, truer than either. After that inspiration failed him. He retired gracefully upon prose again.

"Odd," he thought, "very odd!"

And he relieved his mind by writing a letter to a newspaper. He did not send it in the end, for his better judgment prevented, but he had to do something by way of protest, and the only alternative was to tell his wife about it, when she would look half puzzled, half pained, and probably reply with some remark about the general cost of living. So he wrote the letter instead.

For Herbert Minks regarded himself as a man with the larger view of citizenship, a critic of public affairs, and, in a measure, therefore, an item of that public opinion which moulded governments. Hence he had a finger, though but a little finger, in the destiny of nations and in the polity—a grand word that!—of national councils. He wrote frequent letters, thus, to the lesser weekly journals; these letters were sometimes printed; occasionally—oh, joy!—they were answered by others like himself, who referred to him as "your esteemed correspondent." As yet, however, his following letter had never got into print, nor had he experienced the importance of that editorial decision, appended between square brackets: "This correspondence must now cease"—so vital, that is, that the editor and the entire office staff might change their opinions unless it *did* cease.

Having drafted his letter, therefore, and carried it about with him for several hours in his breast pocket, he finally decided not to send it after all, for the explanation of his "odd" experience, he well knew, was hardly one that a newspaper office could supply, or that public correspondence could illuminate. His better judgment always won the day in the end. Thinking *was* creative, after all.

VII

. . . The sun,
Closing his benediction,
Sinks, and the darkening air
Thrills with a sense of the triumphing night-
Night with her train of stars
And her great gift of sleep.

—W. E. HENLEY

In a southern-facing room on the first floor of La Citadelle the English family sat after tea. The father, a spare, mild-eyed man, his thatch of brown hair well sprinkled with grey above the temples, was lighting his pipe for the tenth time-the tenth match, but the same pipeful of tobacco; and his wife, an ample, motherly woman, slightly younger than himself, was knitting on the other side of the open fireplace, in which still glowed a mass of peat ashes. From time to time she stirred them with a rickety pair of tongs, or with her foot kicked into the grate the matches he invariably threw short upon the floor. But these were adventures ill-suited to her. Knitting was her natural talent. She was always knitting.

By the open window stood two children, a boy and a girl of ten and twelve respectively, gazing out into the sunshine. It was the end of April, and though the sun was already hot, there was a sharpness in the air that told of snow still lying on the mountain heights behind the village. Across vineyard slopes and patches of agricultural land, the Lake of Neuchatel lay blue as a southern sea, while beyond it, in a line of white that the sunset soon would turn to pink and gold, stretched the whole range of Alps, from Mont Blanc to where the Eiger and the Weisshorn signalled in the east. They filled the entire horizon, already cloud-like in the haze of coming summer.

The door into the corridor opened, and a taller child came in. A mass of dark hair, caught by a big red bow, tumbled untidily down her back. She was sixteen and very earnest, but her eyes, brown like her father's, held a curious puzzled look, as though life still confused her so much that while she did her duties bravely she did not quite understand why it should be so.

"Excuse me, Mother, shall I wash up?" she said at once. She always did wash up. And "excuse me" usually prefaced her questions.

"Please, Jane Anne," said Mother. The entire family called her Jane Anne, although her baptismal names were rather fine. Sometimes she answered, too, to Jinny, but when it was a question of household duties it was Jane Anne, or even "Ria."

She set about her duties promptly, though not with any special deftness. And first she stooped and picked up the last match her father had dropped upon the strip of carpet that covered the linoleum.

"Daddy," she said reprovingly, "you do make such a mess." She brushed tobacco ashes from his coat. Mother, without looking up, went on talking to him about the bills—washing, school-books, boots, blouses, oil, and peat. And as she did so a puzzled expression was visible in his eyes akin to the expression in Jane Anne's. Both enjoyed a similar mental confusion sometimes as to words and meanings and the import of practical life generally.

"We shan't want any more now, thank goodness," he said vaguely, referring to the peat, though Mother was already far ahead, wading among boots and shirts and blouses.

"But if we get a load in now, you see, it's *cheaper*," she said with emphasis on every alternate word, slowing up the pace to suit him.

"Mother, where *did* you put the washing-up rag?" came the voice of Jinny in plaintive accents from the tiny kitchen that lay beyond the adjoining bedroom. "I can't find it anywhere," she added, poking her head round the door suddenly.

"Pet lamb," was Mother's answer, still bending over her knitting—she was prodigal of terms like this and applied them indiscriminately, for Jane Anne resembled the animal in question even less than did her father—"I saw it last on the geranium shelf—you know, where the fuchsias and the—" She hesitated, she was not sure herself. "I'll get it, my duckie, for you," she added, and began to rise. She was a voluminous, very stately woman. The operation took time.

"Let me," said Daddy, drawing his mind with difficulty from the peat, and rising too. They rose together.

"It's all right, I've got it," cried the child, who had disappeared again. "It was in the sink. That's Jimbo; he washed up yesterday."

"Pas vrai!" piped a little voice beside the open window, overhearing his name, "because I only dried. It was Monkey who washed up." They talked French and English all mixed up together.

But Monkey was too busy looking at the Alps through an old pair of opera-glasses, relic of her father's London days that served for telescope, to think reply worth while. Her baptismal names were also rather wonderful, though neither of her parents could have supplied them without a moment's reflection first. There was commotion by that window for a moment but it soon subsided again, for things that Jinny said never provoked dissension, and Jimbo and Monkey just then were busy with a Magic Horse who had wings of snow, and was making fearful leaps from the peaks of the Dent du Midi across the Blumlisalp to the Jungfrau.

"Will you please carry the samovar for me?" exclaimed Jane Anne, addressing both her parents, as though uncertain which of them would help her. "You filled it so awfully full today, I can't lift it. I advertise for help."

Her father slowly rose. "I'll do it, child," he said kindly, but with a patience, almost resignation, in his tone suggesting that it was absurd to expect such a thing of him. "Then do exactly as you think best," he let fall to his wife as he went, referring to the chaos of expenses she had been discussing with him. "That'll be all right." For his mind had not yet sorted the jumble of peat, oil, boots, school-books, and the rest. "We can manage THAT at any rate; you see it's francs, not shillings," he added, as Jane Anne pulled him by the sleeve towards the steaming samovar. He held the strings of an ever empty purse.

"Daddy, but you've *always* got a crumb in your beard," she was saying, "and if it isn't a crumb, it's ashes on your coat or a match on the floor." She brushed the crumb away. He gave her a kiss. And between them they nearly upset the old nickel-plated samovar that was a present from a Tiflis Armenian to whom the mother once taught English. They looked round anxiously as though afraid of a scolding; but Mother had not noticed. And she was accustomed to the noise and laughter. The scene then finished, as it usually did, by the mother washing up, Jane Anne drying, and Daddy hovering to and fro in the background making remarks in his beard about the geraniums, the China tea, the indigestible new bread, the outrageous cost of the necessaries of life, or the book he was at work on at the moment. He often enough gave his uncertain assistance in the little menial duties connected with the preparation or removal of the tea-things, and had even been known to dry. Only washing-up he never did. Somehow his vocation rendered him immune from that. He might bring the peat in, fill the lamps, arrange and dust the scanty furniture, but washing-up was not a possibility even. As an author it was considered beneath his dignity altogether, almost improper—it would have shocked the children. Mother could do anything; it was right and natural that she should—poor soul I But Daddy's profession set him in an enclosure apart, and there were certain things in this servantless menage he could not have done without disgracing the entire family. Washing-up was one; carrying back the empty basket of tea-things to the Pension was another. Daddy wrote books. As Jane Anne put it forcibly and finally once, "Shakespeare never washed up or carried a tea-basket in the street!"—which the others accepted as a conclusive statement of authority.

And, meantime, the two younger children, who knew how to amuse each other for hours together unaided, had left the Magic Horse in its stables for the night—an enormous snow-drift—and were sitting side by side upon the sofa conning a number of *Punch* some English aunt had sent them. The girl read out the jokes, and her brother pointed with a very dirty finger to the pictures. None of the jokes were seized by either, but Jimbo announced each one with, "Oh! I say!" and their faces were grave and sometimes awed; and when Jimbo asked, "But what does THAT mean?" his sister would answer, "Don't you see, I suppose the cabman meant—" finishing with some explanation very far from truth, whereupon Jimbo, accepting it doubtfully, said nothing, and they turned another page with keen anticipation. They never appealed for outside aid, but enjoyed it in their own dark, mysterious way. And, presently, when the washing-up was finished, and the dusk began to dim the landscape and conceal the ghostly-looking Alps, they retired to the inner bedroom—for this was Saturday and there were no school tasks to be prepared—and there, seated on the big bed in the corner, they opened a book of *cantiques* used in school, and sang one hymn and song after another, interrupting one another with jokes and laughter and French and English sentences oddly mixed together. Jimbo sang the tune, and Monkey the alto. It was by no means unpleasant to listen to. And, upon the whole, it was a very grave business altogether, graver even than their attitude to "Punch." Jane Anne considered it a foolish waste of time, but she never actually said so. She smiled her grave smile and went her own puzzled way alone.

Usually at this hour the Den presented a very different appearance, the children, with slates and *cahiers*, working laboriously round the table, Jane Anne and mother knitting or mending furiously, Mere

Riquette, the old cat, asleep before the fire, and a general schoolroom air pervading the place. The father, too, tea once finished, would depart for the little room he slept in and used as work-place over at the carpenter's house among the vineyards. He kept his books there, his rows of pipes and towering little heap of half-filled match-boxes, and there he wrote his clever studies that yet were unproductive of much gold and brought him little more than pleasant notices and occasional letters from enthusiastic strangers. It seemed very unremunerative labour indeed, and the family had done well to migrate from Essex into Switzerland, where, besides the excellent schools which cost barely two pounds annually per head, the children learned the language and enjoyed the air of forest and mountain into the bargain. Life, for all that, was a severe problem to them, and the difficulty of making both ends come in sight of each other, let alone meeting, was an ever-present one. That they jogged along so well was due more than the others realised to the untiring and selfless zeal of the Irish mother, a plucky, practical woman, and a noble one if ever such existed on this earth. The way she contrived would fill a book; her economies, so clever they hardly betrayed themselves, would supply a comic annual with material for years, though their comedy involved a pathos of self-denial and sleepless nights that only those similarly placed could have divined. Herself a silent, even inarticulate, woman, she never spoke of them, least of all to her husband, whose mind it was her brave desire to keep free from unnecessary worries for his work. His studies she did not understand, but his stories she read aloud with patient resignation to the children. She marked the place when the reading was interrupted with a crimson paper-knife, and often Jimbo would move it several pages farther on without any of them discovering the gap. Jane Anne, however, who made no pretence of listening to "Daddy's muddle-stories," was beginning to realise what went on in Mother's mind underground. She hardly seized the pathos, but she saw and understood enough to help. And she was in many ways a little second edition—a phrase the muddle-stories never knew, alas!—of her mother, with the same unselfishness that held a touch of grandeur, the same clever domestic instinct for contrivance, and the same careful ways that yet sat ill upon a boundless generosity of heart beneath. She loved to be thought older than she was, and she used the longest, biggest, grandest words she could possibly invent or find.

And the village life suited them all in all respects, for, while there was no degrading poverty anywhere, all the inhabitants, from the pasteur to the carpenter, knew the exact value of a centime; there was no question of keeping up impossible appearances, but a general frankness with regard to the fundamental values of clothing, food, and education that all shared alike and made no pretence about. Any faintest sign of snobbery, for instance, would have been drummed out of the little mountain hamlet at once by Gygi, the gendarme, who spent more time in his fields and vineyards than in his uniform. And, while every one knew that a title and large estates were a not impossible future for the famille anglaise, it made no slightest difference in the treatment of them, and indeed hardly lent them the flavour of a faintest cachet. They were the English family in La Citadelle, and that was all there was about it.

The peasants, however, rather pitied the hard-working author who "had to write all those books," than paid him honourable tribute for his work. It seemed so unnecessary. Vineyards produced wine a man could drink and pay for, but books—! Well, results spoke for themselves, and no one who lived in La Citadelle was millionaire.

Yet the reputation of John Frederic Campden stood high enough, for all his meagre earnings, and he was an ineffective author chiefly, perhaps, because he missed his audience. Somewhere, somehow, he fell between two stools. And his chagrin was undeniable; for though the poet's heart in him kept all its splendid fires alight, his failure chilled a little the intellect that should fashion them along effective moulds. Now, with advancing years, the increasing cost of the children's growing-up, and the failing of his wife's health a little, the burdens of life were heavier than he cared to think about.

But this evening, as the group sat round the wide peat fire, cheerful and jolly in the lamplight, there was certainly no sign of sadness. They were like a party of children in which the grave humour of the ever-knitting mother kept the balance true between fun and foolishness.

"Please, Daddy, a story at once," Jane Anne demanded, "but a told one, not a read-aloud one. I like a romantic effort best."

He fumbled in his pocket for a light, and Jimbo gravely produced a box he had secretly filled with matches already used, collected laboriously from the floor during the week. Then Monkey, full of mischief, came over from the window where she had been watching them with gasps of astonishment no one had heeded through the small end of the opera-glasses. There was a dancing brilliance in her movements, and her eyes, brown like her mother's, sparkled with fun and wickedness. Taking the knee Jimbo left unoccupied, and waiting till the diversion caused by the match-box had subsided, she solemnly placed a bread-crumb in his rather tangled beard.

"Now you're full-dress," she said, falling instantly so close against him that he could not tickle her, while Mother glanced up a second uncertain whether to criticise the impertinence or let it pass. She let it pass. None of the children had the faintest idea what it meant to be afraid of their father.

"People who waste bread," he began, "end by getting so thin themselves that they double up like paper and disappear."

"But *how* thin, Daddy?" asked Jane Anne, ever literal to the death. "And is it romantic or just silly?"

He was puzzled for a moment what to reply.

"He doesn't know. He's making up," piped Jimbo.

"I *do* know," came the belated explanation, as he put the crumb into the bowl of his extinguished pipe with a solemnity that delighted them, but puzzled Jane Anne, who suggested it would taste "like toast smelt." "People who take bread that doesn't belong to them end by having no dinner—"

"But that isn't anything about thinness," interrupted Jinny, still uncomforted. Some one wasted by love was in her mind perhaps.

"It is, child, because they get so frightfully thin," he went on, "that they end by getting thinner than the thin end of a wedge."

The eyes of Mother twinkled, but the children still stared, waiting. They had never heard of this phrase about the wedge. Indeed Jane Anne shared with Jimbo total ignorance of the word at all. Like the audience who read his books, or rather ought to have read them, they expected something different, yet still hoped.

"It's a rhyme, and not a story though," he added, anticipating perhaps their possible disappointment. For the recent talk about expenses had chilled his imagination too much for an instantaneous story, whereas rhymes came ever to him easily.

"All right! Let's have it anyhow," came the verdict in sentences of French and English. And in the breathless pause that followed, even Mother looking up expectantly from her busy fingers, was heard this strange fate of the Thin Child who stole another's bread-crumb:—

> *He then grew thinner than the thin,*
> *The thin end of the wedge;*

He grew so pitifully thin
It set his teeth on edge;
But the edge it set his teeth upon
Was worse than getting thinner,
For it was the edge of appetite,
And his teeth were in no dinner!

There was a deep silence. Mother looked as though she expected more,—the good part yet to come. The rhyme fell flat as a pancake, for of course the children did not understand it. Its nonsense, clever enough, escaped them. True nonsense is for grown-ups only. Jane Anne stared steadily at him with a puzzled frown. Her face wore an expression like a moth.

"Thank you, Daddy, *very* much," she said, certain as ever that the fault if any was her own, since all that Daddy said and did was simply splendid. Whereupon the others fairly screamed with delight, turning attention thereby from the dismal failure.

"She doesn't understand it, but she's always so polite!" cried Monkey.

Her mother quickly intervened. "Never mind, Jane Anne," she soothed her, lest her feelings should be ruffled; "you shall never want a dinner, lovey; and when all Monkey's teeth are gone you'll still be able to munch away at something."

But Jinny's feelings were never ruffled exactly, only confused and puzzled. She was puzzled now. Her confidence in her father's splendour was unshakable.

"And, anyhow, Mother, you'll never be a thin wedge," she answered, meaning to show her gratitude by a compliment. She joined herself as loudly as anybody in the roar that followed this sally. Obviously, she had said a clever and amusing thing, though it was not clear to her why it was so. Her flushed face was very happy; it even wore a touch of proud superiority. Her talents were domestic rather than intellectual.

"Excuse me, Daddy," she said gravely, in a pause that followed presently. "But what is a wedge, exactly? And I think I'd like to copy that poetry in my book, please." For she kept a book in which his efforts were neatly inscribed in a round copy-book handwriting, and called by Monkey "The Muddle Book." There his unappreciated doggerels found fame, though misunderstood most of all by the affectionate child who copied them so proudly.

The book was brought at once. Her father wrote out the nonsense verse on his knee and made a funny little illustration in the margin. "Oh, I say!" said Jimbo, watching him, while Monkey, lapsing into French, contributed with her usual impudence, "Pas tant mal!" They all loved the illustrations.

The general interest, then, as the way is with children, puppies, and other young Inconsistencies, centred upon the contents of the book. They eagerly turned the pages, as though they did not know its contents by heart already. They praised for the hundredth time the drawing of the Muddle Animal who

> *Hung its hopes upon a nail*
> *Or laid them on the shelf;*
> *Then pricked its conscience with its tail,*
> *And sat upon itself.*

They looked also with considerable approval upon the drawings and descriptions of the Muddle Man whose manners towards the rest of the world were cool; because

> *He saw things with his naked eye,*
> *That's why his glance was chilly.*

But the explanation of the disasters he caused everywhere by his disagreeable sharpness of speech and behaviour did *not* amuse them. They observed as usual that it was "too impossible"; the drawings, moreover, did not quite convince:—

> *So cutting was his speaking tone*
> *Each phrase snipped off a button,*
> *So sharp his words, they have been known*
> *To carve a leg of mutton;*
> *He shaved himself with sentences,*
> *And when he went to dances,*
> *He made—Oh shocking tendencies!—*
> *Deep holes with piercing glances.*

But on the last page the Muddle Man behaved so badly, was so positively indecent in his conduct, that he was persuaded to disappear altogether; and his manner of extinguishing himself in the illustration delighted the children far more than the verse whose fun again escaped them:—

> *They observed he was indecent,*
> *But he said it wasn't true,*
> *For he pronounced it "in descent"—*
> *Then disappeared from view!*

Mother's alleged "second sight" was also attributed to the fact that she "looked twice before she leaped"—and the drawing of that leap never failed to produce high spirits. For her calm and steady way of walking—sailing—had earned her the name of the frigate—and this was also illustrated, with various winds, all coloured, driving her along.

The time passed happily; some one turned the lamp out, and Daddy, regardless of expense—he had been grumbling about it ten minutes before—heaped on the bricks of peat. Riquette, a bit of movable furniture without which the room seemed incomplete, deftly slipped in between the circle of legs and feet, and curled up upon Jinny's lap. Her snoring, a wheezy noise that made Jimbo wonder "why it didn't scrape her," was as familiar as the ticking of the clock. Old Mere Riquette knew her rights. And she exacted them. Jinny's lap was one of these. She had a face like an old peasant woman, with a curious snub nose and irregular whiskers that betrayed recklessly the advance of age. Her snores and gentle purring filled the room now. A hush came over the whole party. At seven o'clock they must all troop over to the Pension des Glycines for supper, but there was still an hour left. And it was a magic hour. Sighs were audible here and there, as the exhausted children settled deeper into their chairs.

A change came over the atmosphere. Would nothing exciting ever happen?

"The stars are out," said Jimbo in his soft, gentle little voice, turning his head towards the windows. The others looked too—all except Mother, whose attitude suggested suspiciously that she slept, and Riquette, who most certainly did sleep. Above the rampart of the darkened Alps swung up the army of the stars. The brighter ones were reflected in the lake. The sky was crowded. Tiny, golden pathways slid down the purple walls of the night. "Some one in heaven is letting down the star-ladders. . ." he whispered.

Jimbo's sentence had marked the change of key. Enchantment was abroad—the Saturday evening spell was in the room.

And suddenly a new enormous thing stirred in their father's heart. Whence it came, or why, he knew not. Like a fire it rose in him deep down, from very far away, delightful. Was it an inspiration coming, he wondered? And why did Jimbo use that phrase of beauty about star-ladders? How did it come into the mind of a little boy? The phrase opened a new channel in the very depths of him, thence climbing up and outwards, towards the brain. . . And, with a thrill of curious high wonder, he let it come. It was large and very splendid. It came with a rush—as of numerous whispering voices that flocked about him, urging some exquisite, distant sweetness in him to unaccustomed delivery. A softness of ten thousand stars trooped down into his blood. Some constellation like the Pleiades had flung their fiery tackle across the dusk upon his mind. His thought turned golden. . .

VIII

We are the stars which sing.
We sing with our light.
We are the birds of fire.
We fly across the heaven.
Our light is a star.
We make a road for Spirits,
A road for the Great Spirit.
Among us are three hunters
Who chase a bear:
There never was a time
When they were not hunting;
We look down on the mountains.
This is the Song of the Mountains.

—Red Indian (Algonquin) Lyric.
Translator, J. D. PRINCE

A star-story, please," the boy repeated, cuddling up. They all drew, where possible, nearer. Their belief in their father's powers, rarely justified, was pathetic. Each time they felt sure he would make the adventures seem real, yet somehow he never quite did. They were aware that it was invention only. These things he told about he had not experienced himself. For they badly needed a leader, these children; and Daddy just missed filling the position. He was too "clever," his imagination neither wild nor silly enough, for children. And he felt it. He threw off rhymes and stories for them in a spirit of bravado rather— an expression of disappointment. Yet there was passion in them too— concealed. The public missed the heart he showed them in his books in the same way.

"The stars are listening. . ." Jimbo's voice sounded far away, almost outside the window. Mother now snored audibly. Daddy took his courage in both hands and made the plunge.

"You know about the Star Cavern, I suppose—?" he began. It was the sudden idea that had shot into him, he knew not whence.

"No."

"Never heard of it."

"Where is it, please?"

"Don't interrupt. That wasn't a *real* question. Stories always begin like that." It was Jane Anne who thus finally commanded order.

"It's not a story exactly, but a sort of adventure," he continued, hesitating yet undaunted. "Star Caverns are places where the unused starlight gathers. There are numbers of them about the world, and one I know of is up here in our mountains," he pointed through the north wall towards the pine-clad Jura, "not far from the slopes of Boudry where the forests dip towards the precipices of the Areuse—" The phrase ran oddly through him like an inspiration, or the beginning of a song he once had heard somewhere.

"Ah, beyond le Vallon Vert? I know," whispered Jimbo, his blue eyes big already with wonder.

"Towards the precipices on the farther side," came the explanation, "where there are those little open spaces among the trees."

"Tell us more exactly, please."

"Star-rays, you see," he evaded them, "are visible in the sky on their way to us, but once they touch the earth they disappear and go out like a candle. Unless a chance puddle, or a pair of eyes happens to be about to catch them, you can't tell where they've gone to. They go really into these Star Caverns."

"But in a puddle or a pair of eyes they'd be lost just the same," came the objection.

"On the contrary," he said; "changed a little—increased by reflection—but not lost."

There was a pause; the children stared, expectantly. Here was mystery.

"See how they mirror themselves whenever possible," he went on, "doubling their light and beauty by giving themselves away! What is a puddle worth until a Star's wee golden face shines out of it? And then—what gold can buy it? And what are your eyes worth until a star has flitted in and made a nest there?"

"Oh, like that, you mean—!" exclaimed Jane Anne, remembering that the wonderful women in the newspaper stories always had "starry eyes."

"Like that, yes." Daddy continued. "Their light puts sympathy in you, and only sympathy makes you lovely and—and—"

He stopped abruptly. He hesitated a moment. He was again most suddenly aware that this strange idea that was born in him came from somewhere else, almost from *some one* else. It was not his own idea, nor had he captured it completely yet. Like a wandering little inspiration from another mind it seemed passing through him on uncertain, feathery feet. He had suddenly lost it again. Thought wandered. He stared at Jimbo, for Jimbo somehow seemed the channel.

The children waited, then talked among themselves. Daddy so often got muddled and inattentive in this way. They were accustomed to it, expected it even.

"I always love being out at night," said Monkey, her eyes very bright; "it sort of excites and makes me soft and happy."

"Excuse me, Daddy, but have you been inside one? What's it like? The Cave, I mean?" Jinny stuck to the point. She had not yet travelled beyond it.

"It all collects in there and rises to the top like cream," he went on, "and has a little tiny perfume like wild violets, and by walking through it you get clothed and covered with it, and come out again all soft-shiny—"

"What's soft-shiny, please?"

"Something half-primrose and half-moon. You're like a star—"

"But how—like a star?"

"Why," he explained gently, yet a little disappointed that his adventure was not instantly accepted, "you shine, and your eyes twinkle, and everybody likes you and thinks you beautiful—"

"Even if you're not?" inquired Jinny.

"But you *are*—"

"Couldn't we go there now? Mother's fast asleep!" suggested Jimbo in a mysterious whisper. He felt a curious excitement. This, he felt, was more real than usual. He glanced at Monkey's eyes a moment.

"Another time," said Daddy, already half believing in the truth of his adventure, yet not quite sure of himself. "It collects, and collects, and collects. Sometimes, here and there, a little escapes and creeps out into yellow flowers like dandelions and buttercups. A little, too, slips below the ground and fills up empty cracks between the rocks. Then it hardens, gets dirty, and men dig it out again and call it gold. And some slips out by the roof—though very, very little—and you see it flashing back to find the star it belongs to, and people with telescopes call it a shooting star, and—" It came pouring through him again.

"But when you're in it—in the Cavern," asked Monkey impatiently; "what happens then?"

"Well," he answered with conviction, "it sticks to you. It sticks to the eyes most, but a little also to the hair and voice, and nobody loves you unless you've got a bit of it somewhere on you. A girl, before any one falls in love with her, has always been there, and people who write stories and music and things—all have got some on their fingers or else nobody cares for what they write—"

"Oh, Daddy, then why don't you go there and get sticky all over with it?" Jinny burst out with sudden eagerness, ever thinking of others before herself. "I'll go and get some for you—lots and lots."

"I *have* been there," he answered slowly, "once long, long ago. But it didn't stick very well with me. It wipes off so quickly in the day-time. The sunlight kills it."

"But you got *some*!" the child insisted. "And you've got it still, I mean?"

"A little, perhaps, a very little."

All felt the sadness in his voice without understanding it. There was a moment's pause. Then the three of them spoke in a single breath—

"Please show it to us—*now*," they cried.

"I'll try," he said, after a slight hesitation, "but—er—it's only a rhyme, you see"; and then began to murmur very low for fear of waking Mother: he almost sang it to them. The flock of tiny voices whispered it to his blood. He merely uttered what he heard:—

Starlight
Runs along my mind
And rolls into a ball of golden silk—
A little skein
Of tangled glory;
And when I want to get it out again
To weave the pattern of a verse or story,
It must unwind.

It then gets knotted, looped, and all up-jumbled,
And long before I get it straight again, unwumbled,
To make my verse or story,
The interfering sun has risen
And burst with passion through my silky prison
To melt it down in dew,
Like so much spider-gossamer or fairy-cotton.
Don't you?
I call it rotten!

ALGERNON BLACKWOOD

A hushed silence followed. Eyes sought the fire. No one spoke for several minutes. There was a faint laughter, quickly over, but containing sighs. Only Jinny stared straight into her father's face, expecting more, though prepared at any stage to explode with unfeigned admiration.

"But that 'don't you' comes in the wrong place," she objected anxiously. "It ought to come after 'I call it rotten'—" She was determined to make it seem all right.

"No, Jinny," he answered gravely, "you must always put others before yourself. It's the first rule in life and literature."

She dropped her eyes to the fire like the others. "Ah," she said, "I see; of course." The long word blocked her mind like an avalanche, even while she loved it.

"*I* call it rotten," murmured Monkey under her breath. Jimbo made no audible remark. He crossed his little legs and folded his arms. He was not going to express an opinion until he understood better what it was all about. He began to whisper to his sister. Another longish pause intervened. It was Jinny again who broke it.

"And 'wumbled,'" she asked solemnly as though the future of everybody depended on it, "what *is* wumbled, really? There's no such thing, is there?—In life, I mean?" She meant to add "and literature," but the word stopped her like a hedge.

"It's what happens to a verse or story I lose in that way," he explained, while Jimbo and Monkey whispered more busily still among themselves about something else. "The bit of starlight that gets lost and doesn't stick, you see—ineffective."

"But there *is* no such word, really," she urged, determined to clear up all she could. "It rhymes—that's all."

"And there *is* no verse or story," he replied with a sigh. "There *was*—that's all."

There was another pause. Jimbo and Monkey looked round suspiciously. They ceased their mysterious whispering. They clearly did not wish the others to know what their confabulation was about.

"That's why your books are wumbled, is it?" she inquired, proud of an explanation that excused him, yet left his glory somehow unimpaired. Her face was a map of puzzled wrinkles.

"Precisely, Jinny. You see, the starlight never gets through properly into my mind. It lies there in a knot. My plot is wumbled. I can't disentangle it quite, though the beauty lies there right enough—"

"Oh, yes," she interrupted, "the beauty lies there still." She got up suddenly and gave him a kiss.

"Never mind, Daddy," she whispered. "I'll get it straight for you one day. I'll unwumble it. I'll do it like a company promoter, I will." She used words culled from newspapers.

"Thank you, child," he smiled, returning her kiss; "I'm sure you will. Only, you'd better let me know when you're coming. It might be dangerous to my health otherwise."

She took it with perfect seriousness. "Oh, but, excuse me, I'll come when you're asleep," she told him, so low that the others could not hear. "I'll come to you when I'm dreaming. I dream all night like a busy Highlander."

"That's right," he whispered, giving her a hug. "Come when I'm asleep and all the stars are out; and bring a comb and a pair of scissors—"

"And a hay-rake," added Monkey, overhearing.

Everybody laughed. The children cuddled up closer to him. They pitied him. He had failed again, though his failure was as much a pleasure as his complete success. They sat on his knees and played with him to make up for it, repeating bits of the rhyme they could remember. Then Mother and Riquette woke up together, and the spell was broken. The party scattered. Only Jimbo and his younger sister, retiring into a corner by themselves, continued their mysterious confabulation. Their faces were flushed with excitement. There was a curious animation in their eyes—though this may have been borrowed from the embers of the peat. Or, it may have been the stars, for they were close to the open window. Both seemed soft-shiny somehow. *They*, certainly, were not wumbled.

And several hours later, when they had returned from supper at the Pension and lay in bed, exchanging their last mysterious whispers across the darkness, Monkey said in French—

"Jimbo, I'm going to find that Cavern where the star stuff lies," and Jimbo answered audaciously, "I've already been there."

"Will you show me the way, then?" she asked eagerly, and rather humbly.

"Perhaps," he answered from beneath the bedclothes, then added, "Of course I will." He merely wished to emphasise the fact that he was leader.

"Sleep quickly, then, and join me—over there." It was their game to believe they joined in one another's dreams.

They slept. And the last thing that reached them from the outer world was their mother's voice calling to them her customary warning: that the *ramoneur* was already in the chimney and that unless they were asleep in five minutes he would come and catch them by the tail. For the Sweep they looked upon with genuine awe. His visits to the village—once in the autumn and once in the spring—were times of shivery excitement.

Presently Mother rose and sailed on tiptoe round the door to peep. And a smile spread softly over her face as she noted the characteristic evidences of the children beside each bed. Monkey's clothes lay in a scattered heap of confusion, half upon the floor, but Jimbo's garments were folded in a precise, neat pile upon the chair. They looked ready to be packed into a parcel. His habits were so orderly. His school blouse hung on the back, the knickerbockers were carefully folded, and the black belt lay coiled in a circle on his coat and what he termed his "westkit." Beneath the chair the little pair of very dirty boots stood side by side. Mother stooped and kissed the round plush-covered head that just emerged from below the mountainous *duvet*. He looked like a tiny radish lying in a big ploughed field.

Then, hunting for a full five minutes before she discovered the shoes of Monkey, one beneath the bed and the other inside her petticoat, she passed on into the little kitchen where she cleaned and polished both pairs, and then replaced them by their respective owners. This done, she laid the table in the outer room for their breakfast at half-past six, saw that their school-books and satchels were in order, gave them each a little more unnecessary tucking-up and a kiss so soft it could not have waked a butterfly, and then returned to her chair before the fire where she resumed the mending of a pile of socks and shirts, blouses and stockings, to say nothing of other indescribable garments, that lay in a formidable heap upon the big round table.

This was her nightly routine. Sometimes her husband joined her. Then they talked the children over until midnight, discussed expenses that threatened to swamp them, yet turned out each month "just manageable somehow" and finally made a cup of cocoa before retiring, she to her self-made bed upon the sofa, and he to his room in the carpenter's house outside the village. But sometimes he did not come. He remained in the Pension to smoke and chat with the Russian and Armenian students, who attended daily lectures in the town, or else went over to his own quarters to work at the book he was engaged on at the moment. Tonight he did not come. A light in an attic window, just visible above the vineyards, showed that he was working.

The room was very still; only the click of the knitting needles or the soft noise of the collapsing peat ashes broke the stillness. Riquette snored before the fire less noisily than usual.

"He's working very late tonight," thought Mother, noticing the lighted window. She sighed audibly; mentally she shrugged her shoulders. Daddy had long ago left that inner preserve of her heart where she completely understood him. Sympathy between them, in the true sense of the word, had worn rather thin.

"I hope he won't overtire himself," she added, but this was the habit of perfunctory sympathy. She might equally have said, "I wish he would do something to bring in a little money instead of earning next to nothing and always complaining about the expenses."

Outside the stars shone brightly through the fresh spring night, where April turned in her sleep, dreaming that May was on the way to wake her.

IX

Wrap thy form in a mantle gray,
Star-inwrought!
Blind with thine hair the eyes of Day;
Kiss her until she be wearied out,
Then wander o'er city, and sea, and land,
Touching all with thine opiate wand–
Come, long sought!

—To *Night*, SHELLEY

N ow, cats are curious creatures, and not without reason, perhaps, are they adored by some, yet regarded with suspicious aversion by others. They know so much they never dare to tell, while affecting that they know nothing and are innocent. For it is beyond question that several hours later, when the village and the Citadelle were lost in slumber, Mère Riquette stirred stealthily where she lay upon the hearth, opened her big green eyes, and—began to wash.

But this toilette was pretence in case any one was watching. Really, she looked about her all the time. Her sleep also had been that sham sleep of cats behind which various plots and plans mature—a questionable business altogether. The washing, as soon as she made certain no one saw her, gave place to another manoeuvre. She stretched as though her bones were of the very best elastic. Gathering herself together, she arched her round body till it resembled a toy balloon straining to rise against the pull of four thin ropes that held it tightly to the ground. Then, unable to float off through the air, as she had expected, she slowly again subsided. The balloon deflated. She licked her chops, twitched her whiskers, curled her tail neatly round her two front paws—and grinned complacently. She waited before that extinguished fire of peat as though she had never harboured a single evil purpose in all her days. "A saucer of milk," she gave the world to understand, "is the only thing *I* care about." Her smile of innocence and her attitude of meek simplicity proclaimed this to the universe at large. "That's me," she told the darkness, "and I don't care a bit who knows it." She looked so sleek and modest that a mouse need not have feared her. But she did not add, "That's what I mean the world to think," for this belonged to the secret life cats never talk about. Those among humans might divine it who could, and welcome. They would be admitted. But the rest of the world were regarded with mere tolerant disdain. They bored.

Then, satisfied that she was unobserved, Mere Riquette abandoned all further pretence, and stalked silently about the room. The starlight just made visible her gliding shadow, as first she visited the made-up sofa-bed where the exhausted mother snored mildly beneath the book-shelves, and then, after a moment's keen inspection, turned back and went at a quicker pace into the bedroom where the children slept. There the night-light made her movements easily visible. The cat was excited. Something bigger than any mouse was coming into her life just now.

Riquette then witnessed a wonderful and beautiful thing, yet witnessed it obviously not for the first time. Her manner suggested no surprise. "It's like a mouse, only bigger," her expression said. And by this she meant that it was natural. She accepted it as right and proper.

For Monkey got out of herself as out of a case. She slipped from her body as a sword slips from its sheath, yet the body went on breathing in the bed just as before; the turned-up nose with the little platform at its tip did not cease from snoring, and the lids remained fastened tightly over the brilliant brown eyes, buttoned down so securely for the night. Two plaits of hair lay on the pillow; another rose and fell with the regular breathing of her little bosom. But Monkey herself stood softly shining on the floor within a paw's length.

Riquette blinked her eyes and smiled complacently. Jimbo was close behind her, even brighter than his sister, with eyes like stars.

The visions of cats are curious things, no doubt, and few may guess their furry, silent pathways as they go winding along their length of inconsequent development. For, softer than any mouse, the children glided swiftly into the next room where Mother slept beneath the book-shelves—two shining little radiant figures, hand in hand. They tried for a moment to pull out Mother too, but found her difficult to move. Somewhere on the way she stuck. They gave it up.

Turning towards the window that stood open beyond the head of the sofa-bed, they rose up lightly and floated through it out into the starry night. Riquette leaped like a silent shadow after them, but before she reached the roof of red-brown tiles that sloped down to the yard, Jimbo and Monkey were already far away. She strained her big green eyes in vain, seeing nothing but the tops of the plane trees, thick with tiny coming leaves, the sweep of vines and sky, and the tender, mothering night beyond. She pattered softly back again, gave a contemptuous glance at Mother in passing, and jumped up at once into the warm nest of sheets that gaped invitingly between the shoulder of Jimbo's body and the pillow. She shaped the opening to her taste, kneading it with both front paws, turned three times round, and then lay down. Curled in a ball, her nose buried between her back feet, she was asleep in a single moment. Her whiskers ceased to quiver.

The children were tugging at Daddy now over in the carpenter's house. His bed was short, and his body lay in a kind of knot. On the chair beside it were books and papers, and a candle that had burnt itself out. A pencil poked its nose out among the sheets, and it was clear he had fallen asleep while working.

"Wumbled!" sighed Jimbo, pointing to the scribbled notes. But Monkey was busy pulling him out, and did not answer. Then Jimbo helped her. And Daddy came out magnificently—as far as the head—then stuck like Mother. They pulled in vain. Something in his head prevented complete release.

"En voila un!" laughed Monkey. "Quel homme!" It was her natural speech, the way she talked at school. "It's a pity," said Jimbo with a little sigh. They gave it up, watching him slide slowly back again. The moment he was all in they turned towards the open window. Hand in hand they sailed out over the sleeping village. And from almost every house they heard a sound of weeping. There were sighs and prayers and pleadings. All slept and dreamed—dreamed of their difficulties and daily troubles. Released in sleep, their longings rose to heaven unconsciously, automatically as it were. Even the cheerful and the happy yearned a little, even the well-to-do whom the world judged so secure—these, too, had their burdens that found release, and so perhaps relief in sleep.

"Come, and we'll help them," Jimbo said eagerly. "We can change all that a little. Oh, I say, what a lot we've got to do tonight."

"Je crois bien," laughed Monkey, turning somersaults for joy as she followed him. Her tendency to somersaults in this condition was irresistible, and a source of worry to Jimbo, who classed it among the foolish habits of what he called "womans and things like that!"

And the sound came loudest from the huddled little building by the Church, the Pension where they had their meals, and where Jinny had her bedroom. But Jinny, they found, was already out, off upon adventures of her own. A solitary child, she always went her independent way in everything. They dived down into the first floor, and there, in a narrow bedroom whose windows stood open upon the wistaria branches, they found Madame Jequier—"Tante Jeanne," as they knew the sympathetic, generous creature best, sister-in-law of the Postmaster—not sleeping like the others, but wide awake and praying vehemently in a wicker-chair that creaked with every nervous movement that she made. All about her were bits of paper covered with figures, bills, calculations, and the rest.

"We can't get at her," said Monkey, her laughter hushed for a moment. "There's too much sadness. Come on! Let's go somewhere else."

But Jimbo held her tight. "Let's have a try. Listen, you silly, can't you!"

They stood for several minutes, listening together, while the brightness of their near approach seemed to change the woman's face a little. She looked up and listened as though aware of something near her.

"She's praying for others as well as herself," explained Jimbo.

"Ca vaut la peine alors," said Monkey. And they drew cautiously nearer. . . But, soon desisting, the children were far away, hovering about the mountains. They had no steadiness as yet.

"Starlight," Jimbo was singing to himself, "runs along my mind."

"You're all up-jumbled," Monkey interrupted him with a laugh, turning repeated somersaults till she looked like a catherine wheel of brightness.

". . . the pattern of my verse or story. . ." continued Jimbo half aloud, ". . . a little ball of tangled glory. . ."

"You must unwind!" cried Monkey. "Look out, it's the sun! It'll melt us into dew!"

But it was not the sun. Out there beyond them, towards the purple woods still sleeping, appeared a draught of starbeams like a broad, deep river of gold. The rays, coming from all corners of the sky, wove a pattern like a network.

"Jimbo!" gasped the girl, "it's like a fishing-net. We've never noticed it before."

"It *is* a net," he answered, standing still as a stone, though he had not thought of it himself until she said so. He instantly dressed himself, as he always translated *il se dressait* in his funny Franco-English. *Deja* and *comme ca*, too, appeared everywhere. "It is a net like that. I saw it already before, once."

"Monkey," he added, "do you know what it really is? Oh, I say!"

"Of course I do." She waited nevertheless for him to tell her, and he was too gallant just then in his proud excitement for personal exultation.

"It's the Star Cave—it's Daddy's Star Cave. He said it was up here 'where the Boudry forests dip below the cliffs towards the Areuse.' . . ." He remembered the very words.

His sister forgot to turn her usual somersaults. Wonder caught them both. "A pair of eyes, then, or a puddle! Quick!" she cried in a delighted whisper. She looked about her everywhere at once, making confused and rushing little movements of helplessness. "Quick, quick!"

"No," said Jimbo, with a man's calm decision, "it's when they *can't* find eyes or puddles that they go in there. Don't interfere."

She admitted her mistake. This was no time to press a petty advantage.

"I'll shut my eyes while you sponge up the puddles with a wedge of moss," she began. But her brother cut her short. He was very sure of himself. He was leader beyond all question.

"You follow me," he commanded firmly, "and you'll get in somehow. We'll get all sticky with it. Then we'll come out again and help those crying people like Tante Jeanne and. . ." A list of names poured out. "They'll think us wonderful—"

"We shall be wonderful," whispered Monkey, obeying, yet peeping with one big brown eye.

The cataract of starbeams rushed past them in a flood of gold.

They moved towards an opening in the trees where the limestone cliffs ran into rugged shapes with pinnacles and towers. They found the entrance in the rocks. Water dripped over it, making little splashes. The lime had run into hanging pillars and a fringe of pointed fingers. Past this the river of starlight poured its brilliant golden stream. Its soft brightness shone yellow as a shower of primrose dust.

"Look out! The Interfering Sun!" gasped Monkey again, awed and confused with wonder. "We shall melt in dew or fairy cotton. Don't you? . . . I call it rotten. . . !"

"You'll unwind all right," he told her, trying hard to keep his head and justify his leadership. He, too, remembered phrases here and there. "I'm a bit knotted, looped, and all up-jumbled too, inside. But the sun is miles away still. We're both soft-shiny still."

They stooped to enter, plunging their bodies to the neck in the silent flood of sparkling amber.

Then happened a strange thing. For how could they know, these two adventurous, dreaming children, that Thought makes images which, regardless of space, may flash about the world, and reach minds anywhere that are sweetly tuned to their acceptance?

"What's that? Look out! *Gare!* Hold tight!" In his sudden excitement Jimbo mixed questions with commands. He had caught her by the hand. There was a new sound in the heavens above them—a roaring, rushing sound. Like the thunder of a train, it swept headlong through the sky. Voices were audible too.

"There's something enormous caught in the star-net," he whispered.

"It's Mother, then," said Monkey.

They both looked up, trembling with anticipation. They saw a big, dark body like a thundercloud hovering above their heads. It had a line of brilliant eyes. From one end issued a column of white smoke. It settled slowly downwards, moving softly yet with a great air of bustle and importance. Was this the arrival of a dragon, or Mother coming after them? The blood thumped in their ears, their hands felt icy. The thing dipped slowly through the trees. It settled, stopped, began to purr.

"It's a railway train," announced Jimbo finally with authority that only just disguised amazement. "And the passengers are getting out." With a sigh of immense relief he said it. "You're not in any danger, Monkey," he added.

He drew his sister back quickly a dozen steps, and they hid behind a giant spruce to watch. The scene that followed was like the holiday spectacle in a London Terminus, except that the passengers had no luggage. The other difference was that they seemed intent upon some purpose not wholly for their own advantage. It seemed, too, they had expected somebody to meet them, and were accordingly rather confused and disappointed. They looked about them anxiously.

"Last stop; all get out here!" a Guard was crying in a kind of pleasant singing voice. "Return journey begins five minutes before the Interfering Sun has risen."

Jimbo pinched his sister's arm till she nearly screamed. "Hear that?" he whispered. But Monkey was too absorbed in the doings of the busy passengers to listen or reply. For the first passenger that hurried past her was no less a person than—Jane Anne! Her face was not puzzled now. It was like a little sun. She looked utterly happy and contented, as though she had found the place and duties that belonged to her.

"Jinny!" whispered the two in chorus. But Jane Anne did not so much as turn her head. She slipped past them like a shaft of light. Her hair fell loose to her waist. She went towards the entrance. The flood rose to her neck.

"Oh! there she is!" cried a voice. "She travelled with us instead of coming to meet us." Monkey smiled. She knew her sister's alien, unaccountable ways only too well.

The train had settled down comfortably enough between the trees, and lay there breathing out a peaceable column of white smoke, panting a little as it did so. The Guard went down the length of it, turning out the lamps; and from the line of open doors descended the stream of passengers, all hurrying to the entrance of the cave. Each one stopped a moment in front of the Guard, as though to get a ticket clipped, but instead of producing a piece of pasteboard, or the Guard a punching instrument, they seemed to exchange a look together. Each one stared into his face, nodded, and passed on.

"What blue eyes they've got," thought Monkey to herself, as she peered into each separate face as closely as she dared. "I wish mine were like that!" The wind, sighing through the tree-tops, sent a shower of dew about their feet. The children started. "What a lovely row!" Jimbo whispered. It was like footsteps of a multitude on the needles. The fact that it was so clearly audible showed how softly all these passengers moved about their business.

The Guard, they noticed then, called out the names of some of them; perhaps of all, only in the first excitement they did not catch them properly. And each one went on at once towards the entrance of the cave and disappeared in the pouring river of gold.

The light-footed way they moved, their swiftness as of shadows, the way they tossed their heads and flung their arms about—all this made the children think it was a dance. Monkey felt her own legs twitch to join them, but her little brother's will restrained her.

"If you turn a somersault here," he said solemnly, "we're simply lost." He said it in French; the long word had not yet dawned upon his English consciousness. They watched with growing wonder then, and something like terror seized them as they saw a man go past them with a very familiar look about him. He went in a cloud of sparkling, black dust that turned instantly into shining gold when it reached the yellow river from the stars. His face was very dirty.

"It's *not* the *ramoneur*," whispered Jimbo, uncertain whether the shiver he felt was his sister's or his own. "He's much too springy." Sweeps always had a limp.

For the figure shot along with a running, dancing leap as though he moved on wires. He carried long things over his shoulders. He flashed into the stream like a shadow swallowed by a flame. And as he went, they caught such merry words, half sung, half chanted:—,

"I'll mix their smoke with hope and mystery till they see dreams and faces in their fires—" and he was gone.

Behind him came a couple arm in arm, their movements equally light and springy, but the one behind dragging a little, as though lazily. They wore rags and torn old hats and had no collars to their shirts. The lazy one had broken boots through which his toes showed plainly. The other who dragged him had a swarthy face like the gypsies who once had camped near their house in Essex long, oh, ever so long ago.

"I'll get some too," the slow one sang huskily as he stumbled along with difficulty "but there's never any hurry. I'll fill their journeys with desire and make adventure call to them with love—"

"And I," the first one answered, "will sprinkle all their days with the sweetness of the moors and open fields, till houses choke their lungs and they come out to learn the stars by name. Ho, ho!"

They dipped, with a flying leap, into the rushing flood. Their rags and filthy slouched hats flashed radiant as they went, all bathed and cleaned in glory.

Others came after them in a continuous stream, some too outlandish to be named or recognised, others half familiar, very quick and earnest, but merry at the same time, and all intent upon bringing back something for the world. It was not for themselves alone, or for their own enjoyment that they hurried in so eagerly.

"How splendid! What a crew!" gasped Monkey. "*Quel spectacle!*" And she began a somersault.

"Be quiet, will you?" was the rejoinder, as a figure who seemed to have a number of lesser faces within his own big one of sunburned brown, tumbled by them somewhat heavily and left a smell of earth and leaves and potting-sheds about the trees behind him. "Won't my flowers just shine and dazzle 'em? And won't the dead leaves crackle as I burn 'em up!" he chuckled as he disappeared from view. There was a rush of light as an eddy of the star-stream caught him, and something certainly went up in flame. A faint odour reached the children that was like the odour of burning leaves.

Then, with a rush, came a woman whose immensely long thin arms reached out in front of her and vanished through the entrance a whole minute before the rest of her. But they could not see the face. Some one with high ringing laughter followed, though they could not see the outline at all. It went so fast, they only heard the patter of light footsteps on the moss and needles. Jimbo and Monkey felt slightly uncomfortable as they watched and listened, and the feeling became positive uneasiness the next minute as a sound of cries and banging reached them from the woods behind. There was a great commotion going on somewhere in the train.

"I can't get out, I can't get out!" called a voice unhappily. "And if I do, how shall I ever get in again? The entrance is so ridiculously small. I shall only stick and fill it up. Why did I ever come? Oh, why did I come at all?"

"Better stay where you are, lady," the Guard was saying. "You're good ballast. You can keep the train down. That's something. Steady thinking's always best, you know."

Turning, the children saw a group of figures pushing and tugging at a dark mass that appeared to have stuck halfway in the carriage door. The pressure of many willing hands gave it a different outline every minute. It was like a thing of india-rubber or elastic. The roof strained outwards with ominous cracking sounds; the windows threatened to smash; the foot-board, supporting the part of her that had emerged, groaned with the weight already.

"Oh, what's the good of *me*?" cried the queer deep voice with petulance. "You couldn't get a wisp of hay in there, much less all of me. I should block the whole cave up!"

"Come out a bit!" a voice cried.

"I can't."

"Go back then!" suggested the Guard.

"But I can't. Besides I'm upside down!"

"You haven't got any upside down," was the answer; "so that's impossible."

"Well, anyhow, I'm in a mess and muddle like this," came the smothered voice, as the figures pulled and pushed with increasing energy." And my tarpaulin skirt is all askew. The winds are at it as usual."

"Nothing short of a gale can help you now," was somebody's verdict, while Monkey whispered beneath her breath to Jimbo. "She's even bigger than Mother. Quelle masse!"

Then came a thing of mystery and wonder from the sky. A flying figure, scattering points of light through the darkness like grains of shining sand, swooped down and stood beside the group.

"Oh, Dustman," cried the guard, "give her of your dust and put her to sleep, please. She's making noise enough to bring the Interfering Sun above the horizon before his time."

Without a word the new arrival passed one hand above the part of her that presumably was the face. Something sifted downwards. There was a sound of gentle sprinkling through the air; a noise followed that was half a groan and half a sigh. Her struggles grew gradually less, then ceased. They pushed the bulk of her backwards through the door. Spread over many seats the Woman of the Haystack slept.

"Thank you," said several voices with relief. "She'll dream she's been in. That's just as good."

"Every bit," the others answered, resuming their interrupted journey towards the cavern's mouth.

"And when I come out she shall have some more," answered the Dustman in a soft, thick voice; "as much as ever she can use."

He flitted in his turn towards the stream of gold. His feet were already in it when he paused a moment to shift from one shoulder to the other a great sack he carried. And in that moment was heard a low voice singing dreamily the Dustman's curious little song. It seemed to come from the direction of the train where the Guard stood talking to a man the children had not noticed before. Presumably he was the engine-driver, since all the passengers were out now. But it may have been the old Dustman himself who sang it. They could not tell exactly. The voice made them quite drowsy as they listened:—

> *The busy Dustman flutters down the lanes,*
> *He's off to gather star-dust for our dreams.*
>
> *He dusts the Constellations for his sack,*
> *Finding it thickest on the Zodiac,*
> *But sweetest in the careless meteor's track;*
> *That he keeps only*
> *For the old and lonely,*
> *(And is very strict about it!)*
> *Who sleep so little that they need the best;*
> *The rest,—*
> *The common stuff,—*
> *Is good enough*

> *For Fraulein, or for Baby, or for Mother,*
> *Or any other*
> *Who likes a bit of dust,*
> *But yet can do without it*
> *If they* must!

> *The busy Dustman hurries through the sky*
> *The kind old Dustman's coming to* your *eye!*

By the time the song was over he had disappeared through the opening.

"I'll show 'em the real stuff!" came back a voice—this time certainly his own—far inside now.

"I simply love that man," exclaimed Monkey. "Songs are usually such twiddly things, but that was real." She looked as though a somersault were imminent. "If only Daddy knew him, he'd learn how to write unwumbled stories. Oh! we *must* get Daddy out."

"It's only the head that sticks," was her brother's reply. "We'll grease it."

They remained silent a moment, not knowing what to do next, when they became aware that the big man who had been talking to the Guard was coming towards them.

"They've seen us!" she whispered in alarm. "*He's* seen us." An inexplicable thrill ran over her.

"They saw us long ago," her brother added contemptuously. His voice quavered.

Jimbo turned to face them, getting in front of his sister for protection, although she towered above him by a head at least. The Guard, who led the way, they saw now, was a girl—a girl not much older than Monkey, with big blue eyes. "There they are," the Guard said loudly, pointing; and the big man, looking about him as though he did not see very clearly, stretched out his hands towards him. "But you must be very quick," she added, "the Interfering Sun—"

"I'm glad you came to meet us. I hoped you might. Jane Anne's gone in ages ago. Now we'll all go in together," he said in a deep voice, "and gather star-dust for our dreams. . ." He groped to find them. His hands grew shadowy. He felt the empty air.

His voice died away even as he said it, and the difficulty he had in seeing seemed to affect their own eyes as well. A mist rose. It turned to darkness. The river of starlight faded. The net had suddenly big holes in it. They were slipping through. Wind whispered in the trees. There was a sharp, odd sound like the plop of a water-rat in a pond. . .

"We must be quick," his voice came faintly from far away. They just had time to see his smile, and noticed the gleam of two gold teeth. . . Then the darkness rushed up and covered them. The stream of tangled, pouring beams became a narrow line, so far away it was almost like the streak of a meteor in the sky. . . Night hid the world and everything in it. . .

Two radiant little forms slipped past Riquette and slid feet first into the sleeping bodies on the beds.

There came soon after a curious sound from the outer room, as Mother turned upon her sofa-bed and woke. The sun was high above the Blumlisalp, spreading a sheet of gold and silver on the lake. Birds were singing in the plane trees. The roof below the open windows shone with dew, and draughts of morning air, sweet and fresh, poured into the room. With it came the scent of flowers and forests, of fields and peaty smoke from cottage chimneys. . .

But there was another perfume too. Far down the sky swept some fleet and sparkling thing that made the world look different. It was delicate and many-tinted, soft as a swallow's wing, and full of butterflies and tiny winds.

For, with the last stroke of midnight from the old church tower, May had waked April; and April had run off into the mountains with the dawn. Her final shower of tears still shone upon the ground. Already May was busy drying them.

That afternoon, when school was over, Monkey and Jimbo found themselves in the attics underneath the roof together. They had abstracted their father's opera-glasses from the case that hung upon the door, and were using them as a telescope.

"What can you see?" asked Jimbo, waiting for his turn, as they looked towards the hazy mountains behind the village.

"Nothing."

"That must be the opening, then," he suggested, "just air."

His sister lowered the glasses and stared at him. "But it can't be a real place?" she said, the doubt in her tone making her words a question. "Daddy's never been there himself, I'm sure—from the way he told it. You only dreamed it." "Well, anyhow," was the reply with conviction, "it's there, so there must be *somebody* who believes in it." And he was evidently going to add that he had been there, when Mother's voice was heard calling from the yard below, "Come down from that draughty place. It's dirty, and there are dead rats in it. Come out and play in the sunshine. Try and be sensible like Jinny."

They smuggled the glasses into their case again, and went off to the woods to play. Though their union seemed based on disagreements chiefly they were always quite happy together like this, living in a world entirely their own. Jinny went her own way apart always—ever busy with pots and pans and sewing. She was far too practical and domestic for their tastes to amalgamate; yet, though they looked down upon her a little, no one in their presence could say a word against her. For they recognised the child's unusual selflessness, and rather stood in awe of it.

And this afternoon in the woods they kept coming across places that seemed oddly familiar, although they had never visited them before. They had one of their curious conversations about the matter—queer talks they indulged in sometimes when quite alone. Mother would have squelched such talk, and Daddy muddled them with long words, while Jane Anne would have looked puzzled to the point of tears.

"I'm *sure* I've been here before," said Monkey, looking across the trees to a place where the limestone cliffs dropped in fantastic shapes of pointed rock. "Have you got that feeling too?"

Jimbo, with his hands in the pockets of his blue reefer overcoat and his feet stuck wide apart, stared hard at her a moment. His little mind was searching too.

"It's natural enough, I suppose," he answered, too honest to pretend, too proud, though, to admit he had not got it.

They were rather breathless with their climb, and sat down on a boulder in the shade.

"I know all this awfully well," Monkey presently resumed, looking about her. "But certainly we've never come as far as this. I think my underneath escapes and comes to places by itself. I feel like that. Does yours?"

He looked up from a bundle of moss he was fingering. This was rather beyond him.

"Oh, I feel all right," he said, "just ordinary." He would have given his ten francs in the savings bank, the collection of a year, to have answered otherwise. "You're always getting tummy-aches and things," he added kindly. "Girls do." It was pride that made the sharp addition. But Monkey was not hurt; she did not even notice what he said. The insult thus ignored might seem almost a compliment Jimbo thought with quick penitence.

"Then, perhaps," she continued, more than a little thrilled by her own audacity, "it's somebody else's thinking. Thinking skips about the world like anything, you know. I read it once in one of Daddy's books."

"Oh, yes—like that—"

"Thinking hard *does* make things true, of course," she insisted.

"But you can't exactly see them," he put in, to explain his own inexperience. He felt jealous of these privileges she claimed. "They can't last, I mean." "But they can't be wiped out either," she said decidedly. "I'm sure of that."

Presently they scrambled higher and found among the rocks an opening to a new cave. The Jura mountains are riddled with caves which the stalactites turn into palaces and castles. The entrance was rather small, and they made no attempt to crawl in, for they knew that coming out again was often very difficult. But there was great excitement about it, and while Monkey kept repeating that she knew it already, or else had seen a picture of it somewhere, Jimbo went so far as to admit that they had certainly found it *very* easily, while suggesting that the rare good fortune was due rather to his own leadership and skill.

But when they came home to tea, full of the glory of their discovery, they found that a new excitement made the announcement fall a little flat. For in the Den, Daddy read a telegram he had just received from England to say that Cousin Henry was coming out to visit them for a bit. His room had already been engaged at the carpenter's house. He would arrive at the end of the week.

It was the first of May!

X

One of the great facts of the world I hold to be the registration in the Universe of every past scene and thought.

—F. W. M.

No place worth knowing yields itself at sight, and those the least inviting on first view may leave the most haunting pictures upon the walls of memory.

This little village, that Henry Rogers was thus to revisit after so long an interval, can boast no particular outstanding beauty to lure the common traveller. Its single street winds below the pine forest; its tiny church gathers close a few brown-roofed houses; orchards guard it round about; the music of many fountains tinkle summer and winter through its cobbled yards; and its feet are washed by a tumbling stream that paints the fields with the radiance of countless wild-flowers in the spring. But tourists never come to see them. There is no hotel, for one thing, and ticket agents, even at the railway stations, look puzzled a moment before they realise where this place with the twinkling name can hide. . . Some consult books. Yet, once you get there, it is not easy to get away again. Something catches the feet and ears and eyes. People have been known to go with all their luggage on Gygi's handcart to the station—then turn aside at the last moment, caught back by the purple woods.

A traveller, glancing up at the little three-storey house with "Poste et Telegraphe" above the door, could never guess how busy the world that came and went beneath its red-tiled roof. In spring the wistaria tree (whence the Pension borrowed its brave name, Les Glycines) hangs its blossoms between "Poste" and "Telegraphe," and the perfume of invisible lilacs drenches the street from the garden at the back. Beyond, the road dips past the bee-hives of *la cure*; and Boudry towers with his five thousand feet of blue pine woods over the horizon. The tinkling of several big stone fountains fills the street.

But the traveller would not linger, unless he chanced to pass at twelve o'clock and caught the stream of people going into their mid-day dinner at the Pension. And even then he probably would not see the presiding genius, Madame Jequier, for as often as not she would be in her garden, busy with eternal bulbs, and so strangely garbed that if she showed herself at all, it would be with a shrill, plaintive explanation—"Mais il ne faut pas me regarder. Je suis invisible!" Whereupon, consistently, she would not speak again, but flit in silence to and fro, as though she were one of those spirits she so firmly believed in, and sometimes talked to by means of an old Planchette.

And on this particular morning the Widow Jequier was "invisible" in her garden clothes as Gygi, the gendarme, came down the street to ring the *midi* bell. Her mind was black with anxiety. She was not thinking of the troop that came to *dejeuner*, their principal meal of the day, paying a franc for it, but rather of the violent scenes with unpaid tradesmen that had filled the morning-tradesmen who were friends as well (which made it doubly awkward) and often dropped in socially for an evening's music and conversation. Her pain darkened the sunshine, and she found relief in the garden which was her passion. For in three weeks the interest on the mortgages was due, and she had nothing saved to meet it. The official notice had come that morning from the Bank. Her mind was black with confused pictures of bulbs, departed *pensionnaires*, hostile bankers, and— the ghastly *charite de la Commune* which awaited her. Yet her husband, before he went into the wine-business so disastrously, had been pasteur here. He had preached from this very church whose bells now rang out the mid-day hour. The spirit of her daughter, she firmly believed, still haunted the garden, the narrow passages, and the dilapidated little salon where the ivy trailed along the ceiling.

Twelve o'clock, striking from the church-tower clock, and the voice of her sister from the kitchen window, then brought the Widow Jequier down the garden in a flying rush. The table was laid and the soup was almost ready. The people were coming in. She was late as usual; there was no time to change. She flung her garden hat aside and scrambled into more presentable garments, while footsteps already sounded on the wooden stairs that led up from the village street.

One by one the retired governesses entered, hung their cloaks upon the pegs in the small, dark hallway, and took their places at the table. They began talking among themselves, exchanging the little gossip of the village, speaking of their books and clothes and sewing, of the rooms in which they lived, scattered down the street, of the heating, of barking dogs that disturbed their sleep, the behaviour of the postman, the fine spring weather, and the views from their respective windows across the lake and distant Alps. Each extolled her own position: one had a garden; another a balcony; a third was on the top floor and so had no noisy tenant overhead; a fourth was on the ground, and had no stairs to climb. Each had her secret romance, and her secret method of cheap feeding at home. There were five or six of them, and this was their principal meal in the day; they meant to make the most of it; they always did; they went home to light suppers of tea and coffee, made in their own *appartements*. Invitations were issued and accepted. There were some who would not speak to each other. Cliques, divisions, *societes a part*, existed in the little band. And they talked many languages, learned in many lands—Russian, German, Italian, even Armenian—for all had laboured far from their country, spending the best of their years teaching children of foreign families, many of them in important houses. They lived upon their savings. Two, at least, had less than thirty pounds a year between them and starvation, and all were of necessity careful of every centime. They wore the same dresses from one year's end to another. They had come home to die.

The Postmaster entered with the cash-box underneath one arm. He bowed gravely to the assembled ladies, and silently took his seat at the table. He never spoke; at meals his sole remarks were statements: "Je n'ai pas de pain," "Il me manque une serviette," and the like, while his black eyes glared resentfully at every one as though they had done him an injury. But his fierceness was only in the eyes. He was a meek and solemn fellow really. Nature had dressed him in black, and he respected her taste by repeating it in his clothes. Even his expression was funereal, though his black eyes twinkled.

The servant-girl at once brought in his plate of soup, and he tucked the napkin beneath his chin and began to eat. From twelve to two the post was closed; his recreation time was precious, and no minute must be lost. After dinner he took his coat off and did the heavy work of the garden, under the merciless oversight of the Widow Jequier, his sister-in-law, the cash-box ever by his side. He chatted with his tame *corbeau*, but he never smiled. In the winter he did fretwork. On the stroke of two he went downstairs again and disappeared into the cramped and stuffy bureau, whose window on the street was framed by the hanging wistaria blossoms; and at eight o'clock his day of labour ended. He carried the cash-box up to bed at 8.15. At 8.30 his wife followed him. From nine to five he slept.

Alone of all the little household the Widow Jequier scorned routine. She came and went with the uncertainty of wind. Her entrances and exits, too, were like the wind. With a scattering rush she scurried through the years—noisy, ineffective, yet somewhere fine. Her brother had finished his plate of soup, wiped his black moustaches elaborately, and turned his head towards the kitchen door with the solemn statement "Je n'ai pas de viande," when she descended upon the scene like a shrill-voiced little tempest.

"Bonjour Mesdames, bonjour Mademoiselle, bonjour, bonjour," she bowed and smiled, washing her hands in the air; "et comment allez-vous ce matin?" as the little band of hungry governesses rose with one accord and moved to take their places. Some smiled in answer; others merely bowed. She made enemies as well as friends, the Widow Jequier. With only one of them she shook hands warmly-the one whose payments were long overdue. But Madame Jequier never asked for her money; she knew the old body's tiny income; she would pay her when she could. Only last week she had sent her food and clothing under the guise of a belated little Easter present. Her heart was bigger than her body.

"La famille Anglaise n'est pas encore ici," announced the Postmaster as though it were a funeral to come. He did not even look up. His protests passed ever unobserved.

"But I hear them coming," said a governess, swallowing her soup with a sound of many waters. And, true enough, they came. There was a thunder on the stairs, the door into the hall flew open, voices and laughter filled the place, and Jimbo and Monkey raced in to take their places, breathless, rosy, voluble, and very hungry. Jane Anne followed sedately, bowing to every one in turn. She had a little sentence for all who cared for one. Smiles appeared on every face. Mother, like a frigate coming to anchor with a favourable wind, sailed into her chair; and behind her stumbled Daddy, looking absent-minded and pre-occupied. Money was uncommonly scarce just then—the usual Bourcelles complaint.

Conversation in many tongues, unmusically high-pitched, then at once broke loose, led ever by *la patronne* at the head of the table. The big dishes of meat and vegetables were handed round; plates were piled and smothered; knives and forks were laid between mouthfuls upon plate-edges, forming a kind of frieze all round the cloth; the gossip of the village was retailed with harmless gusto. *Dejeuner* at Les Glycines was in full swing. When the apples and oranges came round, most of the governesses took two apiece, slipping one or other into little black velvet bags they carried on their laps below the table.

Some, it was whispered, put bread there too to keep them company.

But this was probably a libel. Madame Jequier, at any rate, never saw it done. She looked the other way. "We all must live," was her invariable answer to such foolish stories. "One cannot sleep if one's supper is too light." Like her body, her soul was a bit untidy—careless, that is, with loose ends. Who would have guessed, for instance, the anxiety that just now gnawed her very entrails? She was a mixture of shameless egotism, and of burning zeal for others. There was a touch of grandeur in her.

At the end of the table, just where the ivy leaves dropped rather low from their trailing journey across the ceiling, sat Miss Waghorn, her vigorous old face wrapped, apparently, in many apple skins. She was well past seventy, thin, erect, and active, with restless eyes, and hooked nose, the poor old hands knotted with rheumatism, yet the voice somehow retaining the energy of forty. Her manners were charming and old-fashioned, and she came of Quaker stock. Seven years before she arrived at the Pension for the summer, and had forgotten to leave. For she forgot most things within ten minutes of their happening. Her memory was gone; she remembered a face, as most other things as well, about twenty minutes; introductions had to be repeated every day, and sometimes at supper she would say with her gentle smile, "We haven't met before, I think," to some one she had held daily intercourse with for many months. "I was born in '37," she loved to add, "the year of Queen Victoria's accession"; and five minutes later you might hear her ask, "Now, guess how old I am; I don't mind a bit." She was as proud of her load of years as an old gentleman of his thick hair. "Say exactly what you think. And don't guess too low, mind." Her numerous stories were self-repeaters.

Miss Waghorn's memory was a source of worry and anxiety to all except the children, who mercilessly teased her. She loved the teasing, though but half aware of it. It was their evil game to extract as many of her familiar stories as possible, one after another. They knew all the clues. There was the Cornishman—she came from Cornwall—who had seen a fairy; his adventure never failed to thrill them, though she used the same words every time and they knew precisely what was coming. She was particularly strong on family reminiscences:—her father was bald at thirty, her brother's beard was so long that he tied it round his neck when playing cricket; her sister "had the shortest arms you ever saw." Always of youth she spoke; it was pathetic, so determined was she to be young at seventy. Her family seemed distinguished in this matter of extremes.

But the superiority of Cornish over Devonshire cream was her *piece de resistance*. Monkey need merely whisper—Miss Waghorn's acuteness of hearing was positively uncanny—"Devonshire cream is what *I* like," to produce a spurt of explanation and defence that lasted a good ten minutes and must be listened to until the bitter end.

Jimbo would gravely inquire in a pause—of a stranger, if possible, if not, of the table in general—

"Have you ever seen a fairy?"

"No, but I've eaten Cornish cream—it's poison, you know," Monkey would reply. And up would shoot the keen old face, preened for the fray.

"We haven't been introduced, I think"—forgetting the formal introduction of ten minutes ago—"but I overheard, if you'll forgive my interrupting, and I can tell you all about Cornish cream. I was born in '37"—with her eager smile—"and for years it was on our table. I have made quantities of it. The art was brought first by the Phoenicians—"

"Venetians," said Monkey.

"No, Phoenicians, dear, when they came to Cornwall for tin—"

"To put the cream in," from the same source.

"No, you silly child, to get tin from the mines, of course, and—"

Then Mother or Daddy, noting the drift of things, would interfere, and the youngsters would be obliterated—until next time. Miss Waghorn would finish her recital for the hundredth time, firmly believing it to be the first. She was a favourite with everybody, in spite of the anxiety she caused. She would go into town to pay her bill at the bootmaker's, and order another pair of boots instead, forgetting why she came. Her income was sixty pounds a year. She forgot in the afternoon the money she had received in the morning, till at last the Widow Jequier seized it for her the moment it arrived. And at night she would doze in her chair over the paper novel she had been "at" for a year and more, beginning it every night afresh, and rarely getting beyond the opening chapter. For it was ever new. All were anxious, though, what she would do next. She was so full of battle.

Everybody talked at once, but forced conversation did not flourish. Bourcelles was not fashionable; no one ever had appendicitis there. Yet ailments of a milder order were the staple, inexhaustible subjects at meals. Instead of the weather, *mon estomac* was the inexhaustible tale. The girl brought in the little Cantonal newspaper, and the widow read out selections in a high, shrill voice, regardless who listened. Misfortunes and accidents were her preference. *Grand ciel* and *quelle horreur* punctuated the selections. "There's Tante Jeanne grand-cieling as usual," Mother would say to her husband, who, being a little deaf, would answer, "What?" and Tante Jeanne, overhearing him, would re-read the accident for his especial benefit, while the governesses recounted personal experiences among themselves, and Miss Waghorn made eager efforts to take part in it all, or tell her little tales of fairies and Cornish cream. . .

One by one the governesses rose to leave; each made a comprehensive bow that included the entire company. Daddy lit a cigarette or let Jimbo light it for him, too wumbled with his thoughts of afternoon work to notice the puff stolen surreptitiously on the way. Jane Anne folded her napkin carefully, talking with Mother in a low voice about the packing of the basket with provisions for tea. Tea was included in the Pension terms; in a small clothes-basket she carried bread, milk, sugar, and butter daily across to La Citadelle, except on Sundays when she wore gloves and left the duty to the younger children who were less particular.

The governesses, charged with life for another twenty-four hours at least, flocked down the creaking stairs. They nodded as they passed the Bureau window where the Postmaster pored over his collection of stamps, or examined a fretwork pattern of a boy on a bicycle—there was no heavy garden work that day—and went out into the street. They stood in knots a moment, discussing unfavourably the food just eaten, and declaring they would stand it no longer. "Only where else can we go?" said one, feeling automatically at her velvet bag to make sure the orange was safely in it. Upstairs, at the open window, Madame Jequier overheard them as she filled the walnut shells with butter for the birds. She only smiled.

"I wish we could help her," Mother was saying to her husband, as they watched her from the sofa in the room behind. "A more generous creature never lived." It was a daily statement that lacked force owing to repetition, yet the emotion prompting it was ever new and real.

"Or a more feckless," was his reply. "But if we ever come into our estates, we will. It shall be the first thing." His mind always hovered after those distant estates when it was perplexed by immediate financial difficulty, and just now he was thinking of various bills and payments falling due. It was his own sympathetic link with the widow—ways and means, and the remorseless nature of sheets of paper with columns of figures underneath the horrible word *doit*.

"So Monsieur 'Enry Rogairs is coming," she said excitedly, turning to them a moment on her way to the garden. "And after all these years! He will find the house the same, and the garden better—oh, wonderfully improved. But us, *helas!* he will find old, oh, how old!" She did not really mean herself, however.

She began a long "reminiscent" chapter, full of details of the days when he and Daddy had been boys together, but in the middle of it Daddy just got up and walked out, saying, "I must get over to my work, you know." There was no artificiality of manners at Bourcelles. Mother followed him, with a trifle more ceremony. "Ah, c'est partir a l'anglaise!" sighed the widow, watching them go. She was accustomed to it. She went out into her garden, full of excitement at the prospect of the new arrival. Every arrival for her meant a possible chance of help. She was as young as her latest bulb really. Courage, hope, and generosity invariably go together.

XI

The announcement of Henry Rogers's coming was received—variously, for any new arrival into the Den circle was subjected to rigorous criticism. This criticism was not intentional; it was the instinctive judgment that children pass upon everything, object or person, likely to affect themselves. And there is no severer bar of judgment in the world.

"Who *is* Cousinenry? What a name! Is he stiff, I wonder?" came from Monkey, almost before the announcement had left her father's lips. "What will he think of Tante Jeanne?" Her little torrent of questions that prejudged him thus never called for accurate answers as a rule, but this time she meant to have an answer. "What is he exaccurately?" she added, using her own invention made up of "exact" and "accurate."

Mother looked up from the typewritten letter to reply, but before she could say, "He's your father's cousin, dear; they were here as boys twenty years ago to learn French," Jinny burst in with an explosive interrogation. She had been reading *La Bonne Menagere* in a corner. Her eyes, dark with conjecture, searched the faces of both parents alternately. "Excuse me, Mother, but is he a clergyman?" she asked with a touch of alarm.

"Whatever makes you think that, child?"

"Clergymen are always called the reverundhenry. He'll wear black and have socks that want mending."

"He shouldn't punt his letters," declared Monkey. "He's not an author, is he?"

Jimbo, busy over school tasks, with a huge slate-pencil his crumpled fingers held like a walking-stick, watched and listened in silence. He was ever fearful, perhaps, lest his superior man's knowledge might be called upon and found wanting. Questions poured and crackled like grapeshot, while the truth slowly emerged from the explanations the parents were occasionally permitted to interject. The personality of Cousin Henry Rogers grew into life about them—gradually. The result was a curious one that Minks would certainly have resented with indignation. For Cousinenry was, apparently, a business man with pockets full of sovereigns; stern, clever, and important; the sort of man that gets into Governments and things, yet somewhere with the flavour of the clergyman about him. This clerical touch was Jane Anne's contribution to the picture; and she was certain that he wore silk socks of the most expensive description—a detail she had read probably in some chance fragments of a newspaper. For Jinny selected phrases in this way from anywhere, and repeated them on all occasions without the slightest relevancy. She practised them. She had a way of giving abrupt information and making startling statements *a propos* of nothing at all. Certain phrases stuck in her mind, it seemed, for no comprehensible reason. When excited she picked out the one that first presented itself and fired it off like a gun, the more inapt the better. And "busy" was her favourite adjective always.

"It's like a communication from a company," Mother was saying, as she handed back the typewritten letter.

"Is he a company promoter then?" asked Jinny like a flash, certainly ignorant what that article of modern life could mean.

"Oh, I say!" came reproachfully from Jimbo, thus committing himself for the first time to speech. He glanced up into several faces round him, and then continued the picture of Cousin Henry he was drawing on his slate. He listened all the time. Occasionally he cocked an eye or ear up. He took in everything, saying little. His opinions matured slowly. The talk continued for a long time, questions and answers.

"I think he's nice," he announced at length in French. For intimate things, he always used that language; his English, being uncertain, was kept for matters of unimportance. "A gentle man."

And it was Jimbo's verdict that the children then finally adopted. Cousin Henry was *gentil*. They laughed loudly at him, yet agreed. His influence on their little conclaves, though never volubly expressed— because of that very fact, perhaps—was usually accepted. Jimbo was so decided. And he never committed himself to impulsive judgments that later had to be revised. He listened in silence to the end, then went plump for one side or the other. "I think he'll be a nice man," was the label, therefore, then and there attached to Mr. Henry Rogers in advance of delivery. Further than that, however, they would not go. It would have been childish to commit themselves more deeply till they saw him.

The conversation then slipped beyond their comprehension, or rather their parents used long words and circumventing phrases that made it difficult to follow. Owing to lack of space, matters of importance often had to be discussed in this way under the children's eyes, unless at night, when all were safe in bed; for French, of course, was of no avail for purposes of concealment. Long words were then made use of, dark, wumbled sentences spoken very quickly, with suggestive gestures and expressions of the eyes labelled by Monkey with, "Look, Mother and Daddy are making faces—something's up!"

But, none the less, all listened, and Monkey, whose intuitive intelligence soaked up hidden meanings like a sponge, certainly caught the trend of what was said. She detailed it later to the others, when Jinny checked her exposition with a puzzled "but Mother could never have said *that*," while Jimbo looked wise and grave, as though he had understood it all along, and was even in his parents' councils.

On this occasion, however, there was nothing very vital to retail. Cousin Henry was to arrive tomorrow by the express from Paris. He was a little younger than Daddy, and would have the room above him in the carpenter's house. His meals he would take at the Pension just as they did, and for tea he would always come over to the Den. And this latter fact implied that he was to be admitted into intimacy at once, for only intimates used the Den regularly for tea, of course.

It was serious. It involved a change in all their lives. Jinny wondered if it "would cost Daddy any more money," or whether "Cousinenry would bring a lot of things with him," though not explaining whether by "things" she meant food or presents or clothes. He was not married, so he couldn't be very old; and Monkey, suggesting that he might "get to love" one of the retired governesses who came to the Pension for their mid-day dinner, was squelched by Jimbo with "old governesses *never* marry; they come back to settle, and then they just die off."

Thus was Henry Rogers predigested. But at any rate he was accepted. And this was fortunate; for a new arrival whom the children did not "pass" had been known to have a time that may best be described as not conducive to repose of body, mind, or spirit.

The arrival of Mr. Henry Rogers in the village—in La Citadelle, that is—was a red-letter day. This, however, seems a thin description of its glory. For a more adequate description a well-worn phrase must be borrowed from the poems of Montmorency Minks—a "Day of Festival," for which "coronal" invariably lay in waiting for rhyming purposes a little further down the sonnet.

Monkey that afternoon managed to get home earlier than usual from Neuchatel, a somewhat suspicious explanation as her passport. Her eyes were popping. Jimbo was always out of the village school at three. He carried a time-table in his pocket; but it was mere pretence, since he was a little walking Bradshaw, and knew every train by heart—the Geneva Express, the Paris Rapide, the "omnibus" trains, and the mountain ones that climbed the forest heights towards La Chaux de Fonds and Le Locle. Of these latter only the white puffing smoke was visible from the village, but he knew with accuracy their times of departure, their arrival, and the names of every station where they stopped. In the omnibus trains he even knew some of the guards personally, the engine-drivers too. He might be seen any day after school standing in the field beside the station, waiting for them to pass; *mecanicien* and *conducteur* were the commonest words in his whole vocabulary. When possible he passed the time of day with both of these important personages, or from the field he waved his hand and took his cap off. All engines, moreover, were "powerful locomotives." The phrase was stolen from his father—a magnificent sound it had, taking several seconds to pronounce. No day was wholly lived in vain which enabled him to turn to some one with, "There's the Paris Rapide; it's five minutes late"; or "That's the Geneva omnibus. You see, it has to have a very"—here a deep breath—"powerful locomotive."

So upon this day of festival it was quite useless to talk of common things, and even the holidays acquired a very remote importance. Everybody in the village knew it. From Gygi, the solitary gendarme, to Henri Beguin, who mended boots, but had the greater distinction that he was the only man Gygi ever arrested, for periodical wild behaviour—all knew that "Cousin Henry, father's cousin, you know," was expected to arrive in the evening, that he was an important person in the life of London, and that he was not exactly a *pasteur*, yet shared something of a clergyman's grave splendour. Clothed in a sacerdotal atmosphere he certainly was, though it was the gravity of Jane Anne's negative description that fastened this wild ecclesiastical idea upon him.

"He's not *exactly* a clergyman," she told the dressmaker, who for two francs every Monday afternoon sat in the kitchen and helped with the pile of indiscriminate mending, "because he has to do with rather big companies and things. But he is a serious man all the same—and most fearfully busy always."

"We're going to meet him in the town," said Jimbo carelessly. "You see, the Paris Rapide doesn't stop here. We shall come back with him by the 6.20. It gets here at 6.50, so he'll be in time for supper, if it's punctual. It usually is."

And accordingly they went to Neuchatel and met the Paris train. They met their Cousin Henry, too. Powerful locomotives and everything else were instantly forgotten when they saw their father go up to a tall thin man who jumped—yes, jumped—down the high steps on to the level platform and at once began to laugh. He had a beard like their father. "How *will* they know which is which?" thought Jinny. They stood in everybody's way and stared. He was so tall. Daddy looked no bigger than little Beguin beside him. He had a large, hooked nose, brown skin, and keen blue eyes that took in everything at a single glance. They twinkled absurdly for so big a man. He wore rough brown tweeds and a soft felt travelling hat. He wore also square-toed English boots. He carried in one hand a shiny brown leather bag with his initials on it like a member of the Government.

The clergyman idea was destroyed in a fraction of a second, never to revive. The company promoter followed suit. Jinny experienced an entirely new sensation in her life—something none but herself had ever felt before—something romantic. "He's like a soldier—a General," she said to anybody who cared to listen, and she said it so loudly that many did listen. But she did not care. She stood apart from the others, staring as though it were a railway accident. This tall figure of a cousin she could fit nowhere as yet into her limited scheme of life. She admired him intensely. Yet Daddy laughed and chatted with him as if he were nothing at all! She kept outside the circle, wondering about his socks and underclothes. His beard was much neater and better trimmed than her father's. At least no crumb or bit of cotton was in it.

But Jimbo felt no awe. After a moment's hesitation, during which the passers-by butted him this way and that, he marched straight up and looked him in the face. He reached to his watch-chain only.

"I'll be your sekrity, too," he announced, interrupting Daddy's foolishness about "this is my youngest lad, Rogers." Youngest lad indeed!

And Henry Rogers then stooped and kissed the lot of them. One after the other he put his big arms round them and gave them a hug that was like the hug of a bear standing on its hind legs. They took it, each in his own way, differently. Jimbo proudly; Monkey, with a smacking return kiss that somehow conveyed the note of her personality—impudence; but Jane Anne, with a grave and outraged dignity, as though in a public railway station this kind of behaviour was slightly inappropriate. She wondered for days afterwards whether she had been quite correct. He was a cousin, but still he was—a man. And she wondered what she ought to call him. "Mr. Rogers" was not quite right, yet "Mr. Cousin Henry" was equally ill-chosen. She decided upon a combination of her own, a kind of code-word that was affectionate yet distant: "Cousinenry." And she used it with an explosive directness that was almost challenge— he could accept which half he chose.

But all accepted him at once without fear. They felt, moreover, a secret and very tender thing; there was something in this big, important man that made them know he would love them for themselves; and more—that something in him had need of them. Here lay the explanation of their instant confidence and acceptance.

"What a jolly bunch you are, to be sure!" he exclaimed. "And you're to be my secretary, are you?" he added, taking Jimbo by the shoulders. "How splendid!"

"*I'm* not," said Monkey, with a rush of laughter already too long restrained. Her manner suggested a somersault, only prevented by engines and officials.

But Jimbo was a little shocked. This sort of thing disgraced them.

"Oh, I say!" he exclaimed reproachfully.

"Daddy, isn't she awful?" added Jane Anne under her breath, a sentence of disapproval in daily use. Her life seemed made up of apologising for her impudent sister.

"The 6.20 starts at 6.20, you know," Jimbo announced. "The Lausanne Express has gone. Are your 'baggages' registered?" And the party moved off in a scattered and uncertain manner to buy tickets and register the luggage. They went back second class—for the first time in their lives. It was Cousin Henry who paid the difference. That sealed his position finally in their eyes. He was a millionaire. All London people went first or second class.

But Jimbo and his younger sister had noticed something else about the new arrival besides his nose and eyes and length. Even his luxurious habit of travelling second class did not impress them half as much as this other detail in his appearance. They referred to it in a whispered talk behind the shelter of the *conducteur's* back while tickets were being punched.

"You know," whispered Monkey, her eyes popping, "I've seen Cousin Henry before somewhere. I'm certain." She gave a little gasp.

Jimbo stared, only half believing, yet undeniably moved. Even his friend, the Guard, was temporarily neglected. "Where?" he asked; "do you mean in a picture?"

"No," she answered with decision, "out here, I think. In the woods or somewhere." She seemed vague. But her very vagueness helped him to believe. She was not inventing; he was sure of that.

The *conducteur* at that moment passed away along the train, and Cousin Henry looked straight at the pair of them. Through the open window dusk fluttered down the sky with spots of gold already on its wings.

"What jolly stars you've got here," he said, pointing. "They're like diamonds. Look, it's a perfect network far above the Alps. By gum—what beauties!"

And as he said it he smiled. Monkey gave her brother a nudge that nearly made him cry out. He wondered what she meant, but all the same he returned the nudge significantly. For Cousin Henry, when he smiled, had plainly shown—two teeth of gold.

The children had never seen gold-capped teeth.

"I'd like one for my collection," thought Jimbo, meaning a drawer that included all his loose possessions of small size. But another thing stirred in him too, vague, indefinite, far away, something he had, as it were, forgotten.

XII

O star benignant and serene,
I take the good tomorrow,
That fills from verge to verge my dream,
With all its joy and sorrow!
The old sweet spell is unforgot
That turns to June December;
And, though the world remember not,
Love, we would remember.

—*Life and Death*, W. E. HENLEY

A nd Rogers went over to unpack. It was soon done. He sat at his window in the carpenter's house and enjoyed the peace. The spell of evening stole down from the woods. London and all his strenuous life seemed very far away. Bourcelles drew up beside him, opened her robe, let down her forest hair, and whispered to him with her voice of many fountains. . .

She lies just now within the fringe of an enormous shadow, for the sun has dipped behind the blue-domed mountains that keep back France. Small hands of scattered mist creep from the forest, fingering the vineyards that troop down towards the lake. A dog barks. Gygi, the gendarme, leaves the fields and goes home to take his uniform from its peg. Pere Langel walks among his beehives. There is a distant tinkling of cow-bells from the heights, where isolated pastures gleam like a patchwork quilt between the spread of forest; and farther down a train from Paris or Geneva, booming softly, leaves a trail of smoke against the background of the Alps where still the sunshine lingers.

But trains, somehow, do not touch the village; they merely pass it. Busy with vines, washed by its hill-fed stream, swept by the mountain winds, it lies unchallenged by the noisy world, remote, un-noticed, half forgotten. And on its outskirts stands the giant poplar that guards it— *la sentinelle* the peasants call it, because its lofty crest, rising to every wind, sends down the street first warning of any coming change. They see it bend or hear the rattle of its leaves. The *coup de Joran*, most sudden and devastating of mountain winds, is on the way from the precipice of the Creux du Van. It comes howling like artillery down the deep

Gorges de l'Areuse. They run to fasten windows, collect the washing from roof and garden, drive the cattle into shelter, and close the big doors of the barns. The children clap their hands and cry to Gygi, "Plus vite! Plus vite!" The lake turns dark. Ten minutes later it is raging with an army of white horses like the sea.

Darkness drapes the village. It comes from the whole long line of Jura, riding its troop of purple shadows—slowly curtaining out the world. For the carpenter's house stands by itself, apart. Perched upon a knoll beside his little patch of vineyard, it commands perspective. From his upper window Rogers saw and remembered. . .

High up against the fading sky ridges of limestone cliff shine out here and there, and upon the vast slopes of Boudry—*l'immense geant de Boudry*—lies a flung cloak of forest that knows no single seam. The smoke from *bucheron* fires, joining the scarves of mist, weaves across its shoulder a veil of lace-like pattern, and at its feet, like some great fastening button, hides the village of the same name, where Marat passed his brooding youth. Its evening lights are already twinkling. They signal across the vines to the towers of Colombier, rising with its columns of smoke and its poplars against the sheet of darkening water—Colombier, in whose castle *milord marechal Keith* had his headquarters as Governor of the Principality of Neuchatel under the King of Prussia. And, higher up, upon the flank of wooded mountains, is just visible still the great red-roofed farm of Cotendard, built by his friend Lord Wemyss, another Jacobite refugee, who had strange parties there and entertained Jean Jacques Rousseau in his exile. La Citadelle in the village was the wing of another castle he began to build, but left unfinished.

White in the gathering dusk, Rogers saw the strip of roadway where passed the gorgeous coach—*cette fameuse diligence du milord marshal Keith*—or more recent, but grimmer memory, where General Bourbaki's division of the French army, 80,000 strong, trailed in unspeakable anguish, hurrying from the Prussians. At Les Verrieres, upon the frontier, they laid down their arms, and for three consecutive days and nights the pitiful destitute procession passed down that strip of mountain road in the terrible winter of 1870–71.

Some among the peasants still hear that awful tramping in their sleep: the kindly old *vigneron* who stood in front of his chalet from dawn to sunset, giving each man bread and wine; and the woman who nursed three soldiers through black small-pox, while neighbours left food upon the wall before the house. . . Memories of his boyhood crowded thick and fast. The spell of the place deepened about him with the darkness. He recalled the village postman—fragment of another romance, though a tattered and discredited one. For this postman was the descendant of that audacious pale-frenier who married Lord Wemyss' daughter, to live the life of peasants with her in a yet tinier hamlet higher up the slopes. If you asked him, he would proudly tell you, with his bullet-shaped, close-cropped head cocked impertinently on one side, how his brother, now assistant in a Paris shop, still owned the title of baron by means of which his reconciliated lordship sought eventually to cover up the unfortunate escapade. He would hand you English letters—and Scotch ones too!—with an air of covert insolence that was the joy of half the village. And on Sundays he was to be seen, garbed in knickerbockers, gaudy stockings, and sometimes high, yellowish spats, walking with his peasant girl along the very road his more spirited forbear covered in his runaway match. . .

The night stepped down more quickly every minute from the heights. Deep-noted bells floated upwards to him from Colombier, bringing upon the evening wind some fragrance of these faded boyhood memories. The stars began to peep above the peaks and ridges, and the mountains of the Past moved nearer. A veil of gossamer rose above the tree-tops, hiding more and more of the landscape; he just could see the slim new moon dip down to drink from her own silver cup within the darkening lake. Workmen, in twos and threes, came past the little house from their toil among the vines, and fragments of the Dalcroze songs rose to his ear—songs that the children loved, and that he had not heard for nearly a quarter of a century. Their haunting refrains completed then the spell, for all genuine spells are set to some peculiar music of their own. These Dalcroze melodies were exactly right. . . The figures melted away into the single shadow of the village street. The houses swallowed them, voices, footsteps, and all.

And his eye, wandering down among the lights that twinkled against the wall of mountains, picked out the little ancient house, nestling so close beside the church that they shared a wall in common. Twenty-five years had passed since first he bowed his head beneath the wistaria that still crowned the Pension doorway. He remembered bounding up the creaking stairs. He felt he could still bound as swiftly and with as sure a step, only—he would expect less at the top now. More truly put, perhaps, he would expect less for himself. That ambition of his life was over and done with. It was for others now that his desires flowed so strongly. Mere personal aims lay behind him in a faded heap, their seductiveness exhausted. . . He was a man with a Big Scheme now—a Scheme to help the world. . .

The village seemed a dull enough place in those days, for the big Alps beckoned beyond, and day and night he longed to climb them instead of reading dull French grammar. But now all was different. It dislocated his sense of time to find the place so curiously unchanged. The years had played some trick upon him. While he himself had altered, developed, and the rest, this village had remained identically the same, till it seemed as if no progress of the outer world need ever change it. The very people were so little altered—hair grown a little whiter, shoulders more rounded, steps here and there a trifle slower, but one and all following the old routine he knew so well as a boy.

Tante Jeanne, in particular, but for wrinkles that looked as though a night of good sound sleep would smooth them all away, was the same brave woman, still "running" that Wistaria Pension against the burden of inherited debts and mortgages. "We're still alive," she had said to him, after greetings delayed a quarter of a century, "and if we haven't got ahead much, at least we haven't gone back!" There was no more hint of complaint than this. It stirred in him a very poignant sense of admiration for the high courage that drove the ageing fighter forward still with hope and faith. No doubt she still turned the kitchen saucer that did duty for planchette, unconsciously pushing its blunted pencil towards the letters that should spell out coming help. No doubt she still wore that marvellous tea-gown garment that did duty for so many different toilettes, even wearing it when she went with goloshes and umbrella to practise Sunday's hymns every Saturday night on the wheezy church harmonium. And most likely she still made underskirts from the silk of discarded umbrellas because she loved the sound of frou-frou thus obtained, while the shape of the silk exactly adapted itself to the garment mentioned. And doubtless, too, she still gave away a whole week's profits at the slightest call of sickness in the village, and then wondered how it was the Pension did not pay. . . !

A voice from below interrupted his long reverie.

"Ready for supper, Henry?" cried his cousin up the stairs. "It's past seven. The children have already left the Citadelle."

And as the two middle-aged dreamers made their way along the winding street of darkness through the vines, one of them noticed that the stars drew down their grand old network, fastening it to the heights of Boudry and La Tourne. He did not mention it to his companion, who was wumbling away in his beard about some difficult details of his book, but the thought slipped through his mind like the trail of a flying comet: "I'd like to stay a long time in this village and get the people straight a bit,"—which, had he known it, was another thought carefully paraphrased so that he should not notice it and feel alarm: "It will be difficult to get away from here. My feet are in that net of stars. It's catching about my heart."

Low in the sky a pale, witched moon of yellow watched them go. . .

"The Starlight Express is making this way, I do believe," he thought. But perhaps he spoke the words aloud instead of thinking them.

"Eh! What's that you said, Henry?" asked the other, taking it for a comment of value upon the plot of a story he had referred to.

"Oh, nothing particular," was the reply. "But just look at those stars above La Tourne. They shine like beacons burning on the trees." Minks would have called them "braziers."

"They are rather bright, yes," said the other, disappointed. "The air here is so very clear." And they went up the creaking wooden stairs to supper in the Wistaria Pension as naturally as though the years had lifted them behind the mountains of the past in a single bound—twenty-five years ago.

XIII

Near where yonder evening star
Makes a glory in the air,
Lies a land dream—found and far
Where it is light always.
There those lovely ghosts repair
Who in sleep's enchantment are,
In Cockayne dwell all things fair—
(But it is far away).

—Cockayne Country, Agnes Duclaux

The first stage in Cousinenry's introduction took place, as has been seen, at a railway station; but further stages were accomplished later. For real introductions are not completed by merely repeating names and shaking hands, still less by a hurried kiss. The ceremony had many branches too—departments, as it were. It spread itself, with various degrees, over many days as opportunity offered, and included Gygi, the gendarme, as well as the little troop of retired governesses who came to the Pension for their mid-day dinner. Before two days were passed he could not go down the village street without lifting his cap at least a dozen times. Bourcelles was so very friendly; no room for strangers there; a new-comer might remain a mystery, but he could not be unknown. Rogers found his halting French becoming rapidly fluent again. And every one knew so much about him—more almost than he knew himself.

At the Den next day, on the occasion of their first tea together, he realised fully that introduction—to the children at any rate—involved a kind of initiation.

It seemed to him that the room was full of children, crowds of them, an intricate and ever shifting maze. For years he had known no dealings with the breed, and their movements now were so light and rapid that it rather bewildered him. They were in and out between the kitchen, corridor, and bedroom like bits of a fluid puzzle. One moment a child was beside him, and the next, just as he had a suitable sentence ready to discharge at it, the place was vacant. A minute later "it" appeared through another door, carrying the samovar, or was on the roof outside struggling with Riquette.

"Oh, there you are!" he exclaimed. "How you do dart about, to be sure!"

And the answer, if any, was invariably of the cheeky order—

"One can't keep still here; there's not room enough."

Or, worse still—

"I must get past you somehow!" This, needless to say, from Monkey, who first made sure her parents were out of earshot.

But he liked it, for he recognised this proof that he was accepted and made one of the circle. These were tentative invitations to play. It made him feel quite larky, though at first he found his machinery of larking rather stiff. The wheels required oiling. And his first attempt to chase Miss Impudence resulted in a collision with Jane Anne carrying a great brown pot of home-made jam for the table. There was a dreadful sound. He had stepped on the cat at the same time.

His introduction to the cat was the immediate result, performed solemnly by Jimbo, and watched by Jinny, still balancing the jar of jam, with an expression of countenance that was half amazement and half shock. Collisions with creatures of his size and splendour were a new event to her.

"I must advertise for help if it occurs again!" she exclaimed.

"That's Mere Riquette, you know," announced Jimbo formally to his cousin, standing between them in his village school blouse, hands tucked into his belt.

"I heard her, yes." From a distance the cat favoured him with a single comprehensive glance, then turned away and disappeared beneath the sofa. She, of course, reserved her opinion.

"It didn't REALLY hurt her. She always squeals like that."

"Perhaps she likes it," suggested Rogers.

"She likes better tickling behind the ear," Jimbo thought, anxious to make him feel all right, and then plunged into a description of her general habits—how she jumped at the door handles when she wanted to come in, slept on his bed at night, and looked for a saucer in a particular corner of the kitchen floor. This last detail was a compliment. He meant to imply that Cousin Henry might like to see to it himself sometimes, although it had always been his own special prerogative hitherto.

"I shall know in future, then," said Rogers earnestly, showing, by taking the information seriously, that he possessed the correct instinct.

"Oh yes, it's quite easy. You'll soon learn it," spoken with feet wide apart and an expression of careless importance, as who should say,

"What a sensible man you are! Still, these *are* little things one has to be careful about, you know."

Mother poured out tea, somewhat laboriously, as though the exact proportions of milk, hot water, and sugar each child took were difficult to remember. Each had a special cup, moreover. Her mind, ever crammed with a thousand domestic details which she seemed to carry all at once upon the surface, ready for any sudden question, found it difficult to concentrate upon the teapot. Her mind was ever worrying over these. Her husband was too vague to be of practical help. When any one spoke to her, she would pause in the middle of the operation, balancing a cup in one hand and a milk jug in the other, until the question was properly answered, every t crossed and every i dotted. There was no mistaking what Mother meant—provided you had the time to listen. She had that careful thoroughness which was no friend of speed. The result was that hands were stretched out for second cups long before she had completed the first round. Her own tea began usually when everybody else had finished—and lasted—well, some time.

"Here's a letter I got," announced Jimbo, pulling a very dirty scrap of paper from a pocket hidden beneath many folds of blouse. "You'd like to see it." He handed it across the round table, and Rogers took it politely. "Thank you very much; it came by this morning's post, did it?"

"Oh, no," was the reply, as though a big correspondence made the date of little importance. "Not by *that* post." But Monkey blurted out with the jolly laughter that was her characteristic sound, "It came ages ago. He's had it in his pocket for weeks."

Jimbo, ignoring the foolish interruption, watched his cousin's face, while Jinny gave her sister a secret nudge that every one could see.

"Darling Jimbo," was what Rogers read, "I have been to school, and did strokes and prickings and marched round. I am like you now. A fat kiss and a hug, your loving—" The signature was illegible, lost amid several scratchy lines in a blot that looked as if a beetle had expired after violent efforts in a pool of ink.

"Very nice indeed, very well put," said Rogers, handing it gravely back again, while some one explained that the writer, aged five, had just gone to a kindergarten school in Geneva. "And have you answered it?"

"Oh, yes. I answered it the same day, you see." It was, perhaps, a foolish letter for a man to have in his pocket. Still—it was a letter.

"Good! What a capital secretary you'll make me." And the boy's flush of pleasure almost made the dish of butter rosy.

"Oh, take another; take a lot, please," Jimbo said, handing the cakes that Rogers divined were a special purchase in his honour; and while he did so, managed to slip one later on to the plates of Monkey and her sister, who sat on either side of him. The former gobbled it up at once, barely keeping back her laughter, but Jinny, with a little bow, put hers carefully aside on the edge of her plate, not knowing quite the "nice" thing to do with it. Something in the transaction seemed a trifle too familiar perhaps. She stole a glance at mother, but mother was filling the cups and did not notice. Daddy could have helped her, only he would say "What?" in a loud voice, and she would have to repeat her question for all to hear. Later, she ate the cake in very small morsels, a little uncomfortably.

It was a jolly, merry, cosy tea, as teas in the Den always were. Daddy wumbled a number of things in his beard to which no one need reply unless they felt like it. The usual sentences were not heard today: "Monkey, what a mouthful! You *must* not shovel in your food like that!" or, "Don't *gurgle* your tea down; swallow it quietly, like a little lady"; or, "How often have you been told *not* to drink with your mouth full; this is not the servants' hall, remember!" There were no signs of contretemps of any kind, nothing was upset or broken, and the cakes went easily round, though not a crumb was left over.

But the entire time Mr. Rogers was subjected to the keenest scrutiny imaginable. Nothing he did escaped two pairs of eyes at least. Signals were flashed below as well as above the table. These signals were of the kind birds know perhaps—others might be aware of their existence if they listened very attentively, yet might not interpret them. No Comanche ever sent more deft communications unobserved to his brother across a camp fire.

Yet nothing was done visibly; no crumb was flicked; and the table hid the pressure of the toe which, fortunately, no one intercepted. Monkey, at any rate, had eyes in both her feet, and Jimbo knew how to keep his counsel without betrayal. But inflections of the voice did most of the work—this, with flashes of brown and blue lights, conveyed the swift despatches.

"My underneath goes out to him," Monkey telegraphed to her brother while she asked innocently for "jam, please, Jimbo"; and he replied, "Oh, he's all right, I think, but better not go too fast," as he wiped the same article from his chin and caught her big brown eye upon him. "He'll be our Leader," she conveyed later by the way she stirred her cup of tea-hot-water-milk, "when once we've got him 'out' and taught him"; and Jimbo offered and accepted his own resignation of the coveted, long-held post by the way he let his eyelid twiddle in answer to her well-directed toe-nudge out of sight.

This, in a brief resume, was the purport of the give and take of numerous despatches between them during tea, while outwardly Mother—and Father, too, when he thought about it—were delighted with their perfect company manners.

Jane Anne, outside all this flummery, went her own way upon an even keel. She watched him closely too, but not covertly. She stared him in the face, and imitated his delicate way of eating. Once or twice she called him "Mr. Rogers," for this had a grown-up flavour about it that appealed to her, and "Cousin Henry" did not come easily to her at first. She could not forget that she had left the *ecole secondaire* and was on her way to a Geneva Pension where she would attend an *ecole menagere*. And the bursts of laughter that greeted her polite "Mr. Rogers, did you have a nice journey, and do you like Bourcelles?"—in a sudden pause that caught Mother balancing cup and teapot in mid-air—puzzled her a good deal. She liked his quiet answer though—"Thank you, Miss Campden, I think both quite charming." He did not laugh. He understood, whatever the others might think. She had wished to correct the levity of the younger brother and sister, and he evidently appreciated her intentions. He seemed a nice man, a very nice man.

Tea once over, she carried off the loaded tray to the kitchen to do the washing-up. Jimbo and Monkey had disappeared. They always vanished about this time, but once the unenvied operation was safely under way, they emerged from their hiding-places again. No one ever saw them go. They were gone before the order, "Now, children, help your sister take the things away," was even issued. By the time they re-appeared Jinny was halfway through it and did not want to be disturbed.

"Never mind, Mother," she said, "they're chronic. They're only little busy Highlanders!" For "chronic" was another catch-word at the moment, and sometimes by chance she used it appropriately. The source of "busy Highlanders" was a mystery known only to herself. And resentment, like jealousy, was a human passion she never felt and did not understand. Jane Anne was the spirit of unselfishness incarnate. It was to her honour, but made her ineffective as a personality.

Daddy lit his big old meerschaum—the "squelcher" Jinny called it, because of its noise—and mooned about the room, making remarks on literature or politics, while Mother picked a work-basket cleverly from a dangerously overloaded shelf, and prepared to mend and sew. The windows were wide open, and framed the picture of snowy Alps, now turning many-tinted in the slanting sunshine. (Riquette, gorged with milk, appeared from the scullery and inspected knees and chairs and cushions that seemed available, selecting finally the best arm-chair and curling up to sleep. Rogers smoked a cigarette, pleased and satisfied like the cat.) A hush fell on the room. It was the hour of peace between tea and the noisy Pension supper that later broke the spell. So quiet was it that the mouse began to nibble in the bedroom walls, and even peeped through the cracks it knew between the boards. It came out, flicked its whiskers, and then darted in again like lightning. Jane Anne, rinsing out the big teapot in the scullery, frightened it. Presently she came in softly, put the lamp ready for her mother's needle, in case of need later, gave a shy queer look at "Mr. Rogers" and her father, both of whom nodded absent-mindedly to her, and then went on tip-toe out of the room. She was bound for the village shop to buy methylated spirits, sugar, blotting-paper, and—a "plaque" of Suchard chocolate for her Cousinenry. The forty centimes for this latter was a large item in her savings; but she gave no thought to that. What sorely perplexed her as she hurried down the street was whether he would like it "milk" or "plain." In the end she bought both.

Down the dark corridor of the Citadelle, before she left, she did not hear the muffled laughter among the shadows, nor see the movement of two figures that emerged together from the farther end.

"He'll be on the sofa by now. Shall we go for him?" It was the voice of Monkey.

"Leave it to me." Jimbo still meant to be leader so far as these two were concerned at any rate. Let come later what might.

"Better get Mother out of the way first, though."

"Mother's nothing. She's sewing and things," was the reply. He understood the conditions thoroughly. He needed no foolish advice.

"He's awfully easy. You saw the two gold teeth. It's him, I'm sure."

"Of course he's easy, only a person doesn't want to be pulled about after tea," in the tone of a man who meant to feel his way a bit.

Clearly they had talked together more than once since the arrival at the station. Jimbo made up for ignorance by decision and sublime self-confidence. He answered no silly questions, but listened, made up his mind, and acted. He was primed to the brim—a born leader.

"Better tell him that we'll come for him tonight," the girl insisted. "He'll be less astonished then. You can tell he dreams a lot by his manner. Even now he's only half awake."

The conversation was in French—school and village French. Her brother ignored the question with "va te cacher!" He had no doubts himself.

"Just wait a moment while I tighten my belt," he observed. "You can tell it by his eyes," he added, as Monkey urged him forward to the door. "I know a good dreamer when I see one."

Then fate helped them. The door against their noses opened and Daddy came out, followed by his cousin. All four collided.

"Oh, is the washing-up finished?" asked Monkey innocently, quick as a flash.

"How you startled me!" exclaimed Daddy. "You really must try to be less impetuous. You'd better ask Mother about the washing," he repeated, "she's in there sewing." His thoughts, it seemed, were just a trifle confused. Plates and linen both meant washing, and sometimes hair and other stuff as well.

"There's no light, you see, yet," whispered Jimbo. A small lamp usually hung upon the wall. Jane Anne at that moment came out carrying it and asking for a match.

"No starlight, either," added Monkey quickly, giving her cousin a little nudge. "It's all upwumbled, or whatever Daddy calls it."

The look he gave her might well have suppressed a grown-up person—"grande personne," as Jimbo termed it, translating literally— but on Monkey it had only slight effect. Her irrepressible little spirit concealed springs few could regulate. Even avoir-dupois increased their resiliency the moment it was removed. But Jimbo checked her better than most. She did look a trifle ashamed—for a second.

"Can't you wait?" he whispered. "Daddy'll spoil it if you begin it here. How you do fidget!"

They passed all together out into the yard, the men in front, the two children just behind, walking warily.

Then came the separation, yet none could say exactly how it was accomplished. For separations are curious things at the best of times, the forces that effect them as mysterious as wind that blows a pair of butterflies across a field. Something equally delicate was at work. One minute all four stood together by the fountain, and the next Daddy was walking downhill towards the carpenter's house alone, while the other three were already twenty metres up the street that led to the belt of forest.

Jimbo, perhaps, was responsible for the deft manoeuvring. At any rate, he walked beside his big cousin with the air of a successful aide-de-camp. But Monkey, too, seemed flushed with victory, rolling along—her rotundity ever suggested rolling rather than the taking of actual steps—as if she led a prisoner.

"Don't bother your cousin, children," their father's voice was heard again faintly in the distance. Then the big shoulder of La Citadelle hid him from view and hearing. .

And so the sight was seen of these three, arm in arm, passing along the village street in the twilight. Gygi saw them go and raised his blue, peaked cap; and so did Henri Favre, standing in the doorway of his little shop, as he weighed the possible value of the new customer for matches, chocolate, and string—the articles English chiefly bought; and likewise Alfred Sandoz, looking a moment through the window of his cabaret, the Guillaume Tell, saw them go past like shadows towards the woods, and observed to his carter friend across the table, "They choose queer times for expeditions, these English, *ouah!*"

"It's their climate makes them like that," put in his wife, a touch of pity in her voice. Her daughter swept the Den and lit the *fourneau* for *la famille anglaise* in the mornings, and the mother, knowing a little English, spelt out the weather reports in the *Daily Surprise* she sometimes brought.

Meanwhile the three travellers had crossed the railway line, where Jimbo detained them for a moment's general explanation, and passed the shadow of the sentinel poplar. The cluster of spring leaves rustled faintly on its crest. The village lay behind them now. They turned a moment to look back upon the stretch of vines and fields that spread towards the lake. From the pool of shadow where the houses nestled rose the spire of the church, a strong dark line against the fading sunset. Thin columns of smoke tried to draw it after them. Lights already twinkled on the farther shore, five miles across, and beyond these rose dim white forms of the tremendous ghostly Alps. Dusk slowly brought on darkness.

Jimbo began to hum the song of the village he had learned in school—

> *P'tit Bourcelles sur sa colline*
> *De partout a gentille mine;*
> *On y pratique avec success*
> *L'exploitation du francais,*

and the moment it was over, his sister burst out with the question that had been buzzing inside her head the whole time—

"How long are you going to stay?" she said, as they climbed higher along the dusty road.

"Oh, about a week," he told her, giving the answer already used a dozen times. "I've just come out for a holiday—first holiday I've had for twenty years. Fancy that! Pretty long time, eh?"

They simply didn't believe that; they let it pass—politely.

"London's stuffy, you know, just now," he added, aware that he was convicted of exaggeration. "Besides, it's spring."

"There are millions of flowers here," Jimbo covered his mistake kindly, "millions and millions. Aren't there, Monkey?"

"Oh, billions."

"Of course," he agreed.

"And more than anywhere else in the whole world."

"It looks like that," said Cousin Henry, as proudly as they said it themselves. And they told him how they picked clothes-baskets full of the wild lily of the valley that grew upon the Boudry slopes, hepaticas, periwinkles, jonquils, blue and white violets, as well as countless anemones, and later, the big yellow marguerites.

"Then how long are you going to stay—*really?*" inquired Monkey once again, as though the polite interlude were over. It was a delicate way of suggesting that he had told an untruth. She looked up straight into his face. And, meeting her big brown eyes, he wondered a little— for the first time—how he should reply.

"Daddy came here meaning to stay only six months—first."

"When I was littler," Jimbo put in.

"—and stayed here all this time—four years."

"I hope to stay a week or so—just a little holiday, you know," he said at length, giving the answer purposely. But he said it without conviction, haltingly. He felt that they divined the doubt in him. They guessed his thought along the hands upon his arm, as a horse finds out its rider from the touch upon the reins. On either side big eyes watched and judged him; but the brown ones put a positive enchantment in his blood. They shone so wonderfully in the dusk.

"Longer than that, I think," she told him, her own mind quite made up. "It's not so easy to get away from."

"You mean it?" he asked seriously. "It makes one quite nervous."

"There's such a lot to do here," she said, still keeping her eyes fixed upon his face till he felt the wonder in him become a little unmanageable. "You'll never get finished in a week."

"My secretary," he stammered, "will help me," and Jimbo nodded, fastening both hands upon his arm, while Monkey indulged in a little gust of curious laughter, as who should say "He who laughs last, laughs best."

They entered the edge of the forest. Hepaticas watched them with their eyes of blue. Violets marked their tread. The frontiers of the daylight softly closed behind them. A thousand trees opened a way to let them pass, and moss twelve inches thick took their footsteps silently as birds. They came presently to a little clearing where the pines stood in a circle and let in a space of sky. Looking up, all three saw the first small stars in it. A wild faint scent of coming rain was in the air—those warm spring rains that wash the way for summer. And a signal flashed unseen from the blue eyes to the brown.

"This way," said Jimbo firmly. "There's an armchair rock where you can rest and get your wind a bit," and, though Rogers had not lost his wind, he let himself be led, and took the great grey boulder for his chair. Instantly, before he had arranged his weight among the points and angles, both his knees were occupied.

"By Jove," flashed through his mind. "They've brought me here on purpose. I'm caught!"

A tiny pause followed.

"Now, look here, you little Schemers, I want to know what—"

But the sentence was never finished. The hand of Monkey was already pointing upwards to the space of sky. He saw the fringe of pine tops fencing it about with their feathery, crested ring, and in the centre shone faint, scattered stars. Over the fence of mystery that surrounds common objects wonder peeped with one eye like a star.

"Cousinenry," he heard close to his ear, so soft it almost might have been those tree-tops whispering to the night, "do you know anything about a Star Cave—a place where the starlight goes when there are no eyes or puddles about to catch it?"

A Star Cave! How odd! His own boyhood's idea. He must have mentioned it to his cousin perhaps, and *he* had told the children. And all that was in him of nonsense, poetry, love rose at a bound as he heard it. He felt them settle themselves more comfortably upon his knees. He forgot to think about the points and angles. Here surely a gateway was opening before his very feet, a gateway into that world of fairyland the old clergyman had spoken about. A great wave of tenderness swept him—a flood strong and deep, as he had felt it long ago upon the hill of that Kentish village. The golden boyhood's mood rushed over him once more with all its original splendour. It took a slightly different form, however. He knew better how to direct it for one thing. He pressed the children closer to his side.

"A what?" he asked, speaking low as they did. "Do I know a what?"

"A cave where lost starlight collects," Monkey repeated, "a Star Cave."

And Jimbo said aloud the verses he had already learned by heart. While his small voice gave the words, more than a little mixed, a bird high up among the boughs woke from its beauty sleep and sang. The two sounds mingled. But the singing of the bird brought back the scenery of the Vicarage garden, and with it the strange, passionate things the old clergyman had said. The two scenes met in his mind, passed in and out of one another like rings of smoke, interchanged, and finally formed a new picture all their own, where flowers danced upon a carpet of stardust that glittered in mid-air.

He knew some sudden, deep enchantment of the spirit. The Fairyland the world had lost spread all about him, and—he had the children close. The imaginative faculty that for years had invented ingenious patents, woke in force, and ran headlong down far sweeter channels—channels that fastened mind, heart, and soul together in a single intricate network of soft belief. He remembered the dusk upon the Crayfield lawns.

"Of course I know a Star Cave," he said at length, when Jimbo had finished his recitation, and Monkey had added the details their father had told them. "I know the very one your Daddy spoke about. It's not far from where we're sitting. It's over there." He pointed up to the mountain heights behind them, but Jimbo guided his hand in the right direction—towards the Boudry slopes where the forests dip upon the precipices of the Areuse.

"Yes, that's it—exactly," he said, accepting the correction instantly; "only *I* go to the top of the mountains first so as to slide down with the river of starlight."

"We go straight," they told him in one breath.

"Because you've got more star-stuff in your eyes than I have, and find the way better," he explained.

That touched their sense of pity. "But you can have ours," they cried, "we'll share it."

"No," he answered softly, "better keep your own. I can get plenty now. Indeed, to tell the truth—though it's a secret between ourselves, remember—that's the real reason I've come out here. I want to get a fresh supply to take back to London with me. One needs a fearful lot in London—"

"But there's no sun in London to melt it," objected Monkey instantly.

"There's fog though, and it gets lost in fog like ink in blotting-paper. There's never enough to go round. I've got to collect an awful lot before I go back."

"That'll take more than a week," she said triumphantly.

They fastened themselves closer against him, like limpets on a rock.

"I told you there was lots to do here," whispered Monkey again. "You'll never get it done in a week."

"And how will you take it back?" asked Jimbo in the same breath. The answer went straight to the boy's heart.

"In a train, of course. I've got an express train here on purpose—"

"The 'Rapide'?" he interrupted, his blue eyes starting like flowers from the earth.

"Quicker far than that. I've got—"

They stared so hard and so expectantly, it was almost like an interruption. The bird paused in its rushing song to listen too.

"—a Starlight Express," he finished, caught now in the full tide of fairyland. "It came here several nights ago. It's being loaded up as full as ever it can carry. I'm to drive it back again when once it's ready."

"Where is it now?"

"Who's loading it?"

"How fast does it go? Are there accidents and collisions?"

"How do you find the way?"

"May I drive it with you?"

"Tell us exactly everything in the world about it—at once!"

Questions poured in a flood about him, and his imagination leaped to their answering. Above them the curtain of the Night shook out her million stars while they lay there talking with bated breath together. On every single point he satisfied them, and himself as well. He told them all—his visit to the Manor House, the sprites he found there still alive and waiting as he had made them in his boyhood, their songs and characters, the Dustman, Sweep, and Lamplighter, the Laugher, and the Woman of the Haystack, the blue-eyed Guard—

"But now her eyes are brown, aren't they?" Monkey asked, peering very close into his face. At the same moment she took his heart and hid it deep away among her tumbling hair.

ALGERNON BLACKWOOD

"I was coming to that. They're brown now, of course, because in this different atmosphere brown eyes see better than blue in the dark. The colours of signals vary in different countries.

"And I'm the *mecanicien*," cried Jimbo. "I drive the engine."

"And I'm your stoker," he agreed, "because here we burn wood instead of coal, and I'm director in a wood-paving company and so know all about it."

They did not pause to dissect his logic—but just tore about full speed with busy plans and questionings. He began to wonder how in the world he would satisfy them—and satisfy himself as well!— when the time should come to introduce them to Express and Cave and Passengers. For if he failed in that, the reality of the entire business must fall to the ground. Yet the direct question did not come. He wondered more and more. Neither child luckily insisted on immediate tangible acquaintance. They did not even hint about it. So far the whole thing had gone splendidly and easily, like floating a new company with the rosiest prospectus in the world; but the moment must arrive when profits and dividends would have to justify mere talk. Concrete results would be demanded. If not forthcoming, where would his position be?

Yet, still the flood of questions, answers, explanations flowed on without the critical sentence making its appearance. He had led them well—so far. How in the world, though, was he to keep it up, and provide definite result at the end?

Then suddenly the truth dawned upon him. It was not he who led after all; it was they. He was being led. They knew. They understood. The reins of management lay in their small capable hands, and he had never really held them at all. Most cleverly, with utmost delicacy, they had concealed from him his real position. They were Directors, he the merest shareholder, useful only for "calls." The awkward question that he feared would never come, but instead he would receive instructions. "Keep close to the children; they will guide you." The words flashed back. He was a helpless prisoner; but had only just discovered the fact. He supplied the funds; they did the construction. Their plans and schemes netted his feet in fairyland just as surely as the weight of their little warm, soft bodies fastened him to the boulder where he sat. He could not move. He could not go further without their will and leadership.

But his captivity was utterly delightful to him. . .

The sound of a deep bell from the Colombier towers floated in to them between the trees. The children sprang from his knees. He rose slowly, a little cramped and stiff.

"Half-past six," said Jimbo. "We must go back for supper."

He stood there a moment, stretching, while the others waited, staring up at him as though he were a tree. And he felt like a big tree; they were two wild-flowers his great roots sheltered down below.

And at that moment, in the little pause before they linked up arms and started home again, the Question of Importance came, though not in the way he had expected it would come.

"Cousinenry, do you sleep very tightly at night, please?" Monkey asked it, but Jimbo stepped up nearer to watch the reply.

"Like a top," he said, wondering.

Signals he tried vainly to intercept flashed between the pair of them.

"Why do you ask?" as nothing further seemed forthcoming.

"Oh, just to know," she explained. "It's all right."

"Yes, it's quite all right like that," added Jimbo. And without more ado they took his arms and pulled him out of the forest.

And Henry Rogers heard something deep, deep down within himself echo the verdict.

"I think it is all right."

On the way home there were no puddles, but there were three pairs of eyes—and the stars were uncommonly thick overhead. The children asked him almost as many questions as there were clusters of them between the summits of Boudry and La Tourne. All three went floundering in that giant Net. It was so different, too, from anything they had been accustomed to. Their father's stories, answers, explanations, and the like, were ineffective because they always felt he did not quite believe them himself even while he gave them. He did not think he believed them, that is. But Cousin Henry talked of stars and star-stuff as though he had some in his pocket at the moment. And, of course, he had. For otherwise they would not have listened. He could not have held their attention.

They especially liked the huge, ridiculous words he used, because such words concealed great mysteries that pulsed with wonder and exquisitely wound them up. Daddy made things too clear. The bones of impossibility were visible. They saw thin nakedness behind the explanations, till the sense of wonder faded. They were not babies to be fed with a string of one-syllable words!

Jimbo kept silence mostly, his instinct ever being to conceal his ignorance; but Monkey talked fifteen to the dozen, filling the pauses with long "ohs" and bursts of laughter and impudent observations. Yet her cheeky insolence never crossed the frontier where it could be resented. Her audacity stopped short of impertinence.

"There's a point beyond which——" her cousin would say gravely, when she grew more daring than usual; and, while answering "It'll stick into you, then, not into me," she yet withdrew from the borders of impertinence at once.

"What is star-stuff really then?" she asked.

"The primordial substance of the universe," he answered solemnly, no whit ashamed of his inaccuracy.

"Ah yes!" piped Jimbo, quietly. *Ecole primaire* he understood. This must be something similar.

"But what does it do, I mean, and why is it good for people to have it in them—on them—whatever it is?" she inquired.

"It gives sympathy and insight; it's so awfully subtle and delicate," he answered. "A little of it travels down on every ray and soaks down into you. It makes you feel inclined to stick to other people and understand them. That's sympathy."

"*Sympathie*," said Jimbo for his sister's benefit apparently, but in reality because he himself was barely treading water.

"But sympathy," the other went on, "is no good without insight—which means seeing things as others see them—from inside. That's insight——"

"Inside sight," she corrected him.

"That's it. You see, the first stuff that existed in the universe was this star-stuff—nebulae. Having nothing else to stick to, it stuck to itself, and so got thicker. It whirled in vortices. It grew together in sympathy, for sympathy brings together. It whirled and twirled round itself till it got at last into solid round bodies—worlds—stars. It passed, that is, from mere dreaming into action. And when the rays soak into you, they change your dreaming into action. You feel the desire to do things—for others."

"Ah! yes," repeated Jimbo, "like that."

"You must be full of vorty seas, then, because you're so long," said Monkey, "but you'll never grow into a solid round body——"

He took a handful of her hair and smothered the remainder of the sentence.

"The instant a sweet thought is born in your mind," he continued, "the heavenly stables send their starry messengers to harness it for use. A ray, perhaps, from mighty Sirius picks it out of your heart at birth."

"Serious!" exclaimed Jimbo, as though the sun were listening.

"Sirius—another sun, that is, far bigger than our own—a perfect giant, yet so far away you hardly notice him."

The boy clasped his dirty fingers and stared hard. The sun *was* listening.

"Then what I *think* is known—like that—all over the place?" he asked. He held himself very straight indeed.

"Everywhere," replied Cousinenry gravely. "The stars flash your thoughts over the whole universe. None are ever lost. Sooner or later they appear in visible shape. Some one, for instance, must have thought this flower long ago"—he stooped and picked a blue hepatica at their feet—"or it couldn't be growing here now."

Jimbo accepted the statement with his usual gravity.

"Then I shall always think enormous and tremendous things—powerful locomotives, like that and—and—"

"The best is to think kind little sweet things about other people," suggested the other. "You see the results quicker then."

"Mais oui," was the reply, "je pourrai faire ca au meme temps, n'est-ce pas?"

"Parfaitemong," agreed his big cousin.

"There's no room in her for inside sight," observed Monkey as a portly dame rolled by into the darkness. "You can't tell her front from her back." It was one of the governesses.

"We'll get her into the cave and change all that," her cousin said reprovingly. "You must never judge by outside alone. Puddings should teach you that."

But no one could reprove Monkey without running a certain risk.

"We don't have puddings here," she said, "we have dessert—sour oranges and apples."

She flew from his side and vanished down the street and into the Citadelle courtyard before he could think of anything to say. A shooting star flashed at the same moment behind the church tower, vanishing into the gulf of Boudry's shadow. They seemed to go at the same pace together.

"Oh, I say!" said Jimbo sedately, "you must punish her for that, you know. Shall I come with you to the carpenter's?" he added, as they stood a moment by the fountain. "There's just ten minutes to wash and brush your hair for supper."

"I think I can find my way alone," he answered, "thank you all the same."

"It's nothing," he said, lifting his cap as the village fashion was, and watching his cousin's lengthy figure vanish down the street.

"We'll meet at the Pension later," the voice came back, "and in the morning I shall have a lot of correspondence to attend to. Bring your shorthand book and lots of pencils, mind."

"How many?"

"Oh, half a dozen will do."

The boy turned in and hurried after his sister. But he was so busy collecting all the pencils and paper he could find that he forgot to brush his hair, and consequently appeared at the supper table with a head like a tangled blackberry bush. His eyes were bright as stars.

XIV

O pure one, take thy seat in the barque of the Sun,
And sail thou over the sky.
Sail thou with the imperishable stars,
Sail thou with the unwearied stars.

—Pyramid Texts, Dynasty VI

B ut Henry Rogers ran the whole two hundred yards to his lodgings in the carpenter's house. He ran as though the entire field of brilliant stars were at his heels. There was bewilderment, happiness, exhilaration in his blood. He had never felt so light-hearted in his life. He felt exactly fifteen years of age—and a half. The half was added to ensure a good, safe margin over the other two.

But he was late for supper too—later than the children, for first he jotted down some notes upon the back of an envelope. He wrote them at high speed, meaning to correct them later, but the corrections were never made. Later, when he came to bed, the envelope had been tidied away by the careful housewife into the dustbin. And he was ashamed to ask for them. The carpenter's wife read English.

"Pity," he said to himself. "I don't believe Minks could have done it better!"

The energy that went to the making of those "notes" would have run down different channels a few years ago. It would have gone into some ingenious patent. The patent, however, might equally have gone into the dustbin. There is an enormous quantity of misdirected energy pouring loose about the world!

The notes had run something like this—

O children, open your arms to me,
Let your hair fall over my eyes;
Let me sleep a moment—and then awake
In your Gardens of sweet Surprise!
For the grown-up folk
Are a wearisome folk,
And they laugh my fancies to scorn,
My fun and my fancies to scorn.

O children, open your hearts to me,
And tell me your wonder-thoughts;
Who lives in the palace inside your brain?
Who plays in its outer courts?
Who hides in the hours Tomorrow holds?
Who sleeps in your yesterdays?
Who tiptoes along past the curtained folds
Of the shadow that twilight lays?

O children, open your eyes to me,
And tell me your visions too;
Who squeezes the sponge when the salt tears flow
To dim their magical blue?
Who draws up their blinds when the sun peeps in?
Who fastens them down at night?
Who brushes the fringe of their lace-veined lids?
Who trims their innocent light?

Then, children, I beg you, sing low to me,
And cover my eyes with your hands;
O kiss me again till I sleep and dream
That I'm lost in your fairylands;
For the grown-up folk
Are a troublesome folk,
And the book of their childhood is torn,
Is blotted, and crumpled, and torn!

Supper at the Pension dissipated effectively the odd sense of enchantment to which he had fallen a victim, but it revived again with a sudden rush when Jimbo and his sister came up at half-past eight to say good-night. It began when the little fellow climbed up to plant a resounding kiss upon his lips, and it caught him fullest when Monkey's arms were round his neck, and he heard her whisper in his ear—

"Sleep as tightly as you can, remember, and don't resist. We'll come later to find you." Her brown eyes were straight in front of his own. Goodness, how they shone! Old Sirius and Aldebaran had certainly left a ray in each.

"Hope you don't get any longer when you're asleep!" she added, giving him a sly dig in the ribs—then was gone before he could return it, or ask her what she meant by "we'll find you later."

"And don't say a word to Mother," was the last thing he heard as she vanished down the stairs.

Slightly confused, he glanced down at the aged pumps he happened to have on, and noticed that one bow was all awry and loose. He stooped to fidget with it, and Mother caught him in the act.

"I'll stitch it on for you," she said at once. "It won't take a minute. One of the children can fetch it in the morning."

But he was ashamed to add to her endless sewing. Like some female Sisyphus, she seemed always pushing an enormous needle through a mountain of clothes that grew higher each time she reached the top.

"I always wear it like that," he assured her gravely, his thoughts still busy with two other phrases—"find you" and "sleep tightly." What in the world could they mean? Did the children really intend to visit him at night? They seemed so earnest about it. Of course it was all nonsense. And yet—!

"You mustn't let them bother you too much," he heard their mother saying, her voice sounding a long way off. "They're so wildly happy to have some one to play with."

"That's how I like them," he answered vaguely, referring half to the pumps and half to the children. "They're no trouble at all, believe me."

"I'm afraid we've spoilt them rather—"

"But—not at all," he murmured, still confused. "They're only a little loose—er—lively, I mean. That's how they should be."

And outside all heard their laughing voices dying down the street as they raced along to the Citadelle for bed. It was Monkey's duty to see her brother safely in. Ten minutes later Mother would follow to tell them tuck-up stories and hear their prayers.

"Excuse me! Have you got a hot-water bottle?" asked a sudden jerky voice, and he turned with a start to see Jane Anne towering beside him.

"I'm sorry," he answered, "but I don't carry such things about with me." He imagined she was joking, then saw that it was very serious.

She looked puzzled a moment. "I meant—would you like one? Everybody uses them here." She thought all grown-ups used hot-water bottles.

He hesitated a second. The child looked as though she would produce one from her blouse like any conjurer. As yet, however, the article in question had not entered his scheme of life. He declined it with many thanks.

"I can get you a big one," she urged. But even that did not tempt him.

"Will you have a cold-water bandage then—for your head—or anything?"

She seemed so afflicted with a desire to do something for him that he almost said "Yes"; only the fear that she might offer next a beehive or a gramophone restrained him.

"Thank you *so* much, but really I can manage without it—tonight."

Jane Anne made no attempt to conceal her disappointment. What a man he was, to be sure! And what a funny place the world was!

"It's Jinny's panacea," said Mother, helping herself with reckless uncertainty to a long word. "She's never happy unless she's doing for somebody," she added ambiguously. "It's her *metier* in life."

"Mother, what *are* you saying?" said the child's expression. Then she made one last attempt. She remembered, perhaps, the admiring way he had watched her brother and sister's antics in the Den before. She was not clever on her feet, but at least she could try.

"Shall I turn head over heels for you, then?"

He caught her mother's grave expression just in time to keep his laughter back. The offer of gymnastics clearly involved sacrifice somewhere.

"Tomorrow," he answered quickly. "Always put off till tomorrow what you're too old to do today."

"Of course; I see—yes." She was more perplexed than ever, as he meant that she should be. His words were meaningless, but they helped the poignant situation neatly. She could not understand why all her offers were refused like this. There must be something wrong with her selection, perhaps. She would think of better ones in future. But, oh, what a funny place the world was!

"Good-night, then, Mr.—Cousin Rogers," she said jerkily with resignation. "Perhaps tomorrow—when I'm older—"

"If it comes." He gravely shook the hand she held out primly, keeping a certain distance from him lest he should attempt to kiss her.

"It always comes; it's a chronic monster," she laughed, saying the first thing that came into her queer head. They all laughed. Jane Anne went out, feeling happier. At least, she had amused him. She marched off with the air of a grenadier going to some stern and difficult duty. From the door she flung back at him a look of speechless admiration, then broke into a run, afraid she might have been immodest or too forward. They heard her thumping overhead.

And presently he followed her example. The Pension sitting-room emptied. Unless there was something special on hand—a dance, a romp, a game, or some neighbours who dropped in for talk and music—it was rarely occupied after nine o'clock. Daddy had already slipped home—he had this mysterious way of disappearing when no one saw him go. At this moment, doubtless, a wumbled book absorbed him over at the carpenter's. Old Miss Waghorn sat in a corner nodding over her novel, and the Pension cat, Borelle, was curled up in her sloping, inadequate lap.

The big, worn velvet sofa in the opposite corner was also empty. On romping nights it was the *train de Moscou*, where Jimbo sold tickets to crowded passengers for any part of the world. Tonight it was a mere dead sofa, uninviting, dull.

He went across the darkened room, his head scraping acquaintance with the ivy leaves that trailed across the ceiling. He slipped through the little hall. In the kitchen he heard the shrill voice of Mme. Jequier talking very loudly about a dozen things at once to the servant-girl, or to any one else who was near enough to listen. Luckily she did not see him. Otherwise he would never have escaped without another offer of a hot-water bottle, a pot of home-made marmalade, or a rug and pillow for his bed. He made his way downstairs into the street unnoticed; but just as he reached the bottom his thundering tread betrayed him. The door flew open at the top.

"Bon soir, bonne nuit," screamed the voice; "wait a moment and I'll get the lamp. You'll break your neck. Is there anything you want—a hot-water bottle, or a box of matches, or some of my marmalade for your breakfast? Wait, and I'll get it in a moment—" She would have given the blouse off her back had he needed, or could have used it.

She flew back to the kitchen to search and shout. It sounded like a quarrel; but, pretending not to hear, he made good his escape and passed out into the street. The heavy door of the Post Office banged behind him, cutting short a stream of excited sentences. The peace and quiet of the night closed instantly about his steps.

By the fountain opposite the Citadelle he paused to drink from the pipe of gushing mountain water. The open courtyard looked inviting, but he did not go in, for, truth to tell, there was a curious excitement in him—an urgent, keen desire to get to sleep as soon as possible. Not that he felt sleepy—quite the reverse in fact, but that he looked forward to his bed and to "sleeping tightly."

The village was already lost in slumber. No lights showed in any houses. Yet it was barely half-past nine. Everywhere was peace and stillness. Far across the lake he saw the twinkling villages. Behind him dreamed the forests. A deep calm brooded over the mountains; but within the calm, and just below the surface in himself, hid the excitement as of some lively anticipation. He expected something. Something was going to happen. And it was connected with the children. Jimbo and Monkey were at the bottom of it. They had said they would come for him—to "find him later." He wondered—quite absurdly he wondered.

He passed his cousin's room on tiptoe, and noticed a light beneath the door. But, before getting into bed, he stood a moment at the open window and drew in deep draughts of the fresh night air. The world of forest swayed across his sight. The outline of the Citadelle merged into it. A point of light showed the window where the children already slept. But, far beyond, the moon was loading stars upon the trees, and a rising wind drove them in glittering flocks along the heights. . .

Blowing out the candle, he turned over on his side to sleep, his mind charged to the brim with wonder and curious under-thrills of this anticipation. He half expected—what? Reality lay somewhere in the whole strange business; it was not merely imaginative nonsense. Fairyland was close.

And the moment he slept and began to dream, the thing took a lively and dramatic shape. A thousand tiny fingers, soft and invisible, drew him away into the heart of fairyland. There was a terror in him lest he should—stick. But he came out beautifully and smoothly, like a thread of summer grass from its covering sheath.

"I *am* slippery after all, then—slippery enough," he remembered saying with surprised delight, and then—

XV

Look how the floor of heaven
Is thick inlaid with patines of bright gold.
There's not the smallest orb which thou beholdest
But in his motion like an angel sings,
Still quiring to the young-eyed cherubims.

—*Merchant of Venice*

—there came to him a vivid impression of sudden light in the room, and he knew that something very familiar was happening to him, yet something that had not happened consciously for thirty years and more—since his early childhood in the night-nursery with the bars across the windows.

He was both asleep and awake at the same time. Some part of him, rather, that never slept was disengaging itself—with difficulty. He was getting free. Stimulated by his intercourse with the children, this part of him that in boyhood used to be so easily detached, light as air, was getting loose. The years had fastened it in very tightly. Jimbo and Monkey had got at it. And Jimbo and Monkey were in the room at this moment. They were pulling him out.

It was very wonderful; a glory of youth and careless joy rushed through him like a river. Some sheath or vesture melted off. It seemed to tear him loose. How in the world could he ever have forgotten it—let it go out of his life? What on earth could have seemed good enough to take its place? He felt like an eagle some wizard spell had imprisoned in a stone, now released and shaking out its crumpled wings. A mightier spell had set him free. The children stood beside his bed!

"I can manage it alone," he said firmly. "You needn't try to help me."

No sound was audible, but they instantly desisted. This thought, that took a dozen words to express ordinarily, shot from him into them the instant it was born. A gentle pulsing, like the flicker of a flame, ran over their shining little forms of radiance as they received it. They shifted to one side silently to give him room. Thus had he seen a searchlight pass like lightning from point to point across the sea.

Yet, at first, there was difficulty; here and there, in places, he could not get quite loose and free.

"He sticks like Daddy," he heard them think. "In the head it seems, too."

There was no pain in the sensation, but a certain straining as of unaccustomed muscles being stretched. He felt uncomfortable, then embarrassed, then—exhilarated. But there were other exquisite sensations too. Happiness, as of flooding summer sunshine, poured through him.

"He'll come with a rush. Look out!" felt Jimbo—"felt" expressing "thought" and "said" together, for no single word can convey the double operation thus combined in ordinary life.

The reality of it caught him by the throat.

"This," he exclaimed, "is real and actual. It is happening to me now!"

He looked from the pile of clothes taken off two hours ago—goodness, what a mass!—to the children's figures in the middle of the room. And one was as real as the other. The moods of the day and evening, their play and nonsense, had all passed away. He had crossed a gulf that stood between this moment and those good-nights in the Pension. This was as real as anything in life; more real than death. Reality—he caught the obvious thought pass thickly through the body on the bed—is what has been experienced. Death, for that reason, is not real, not realised; dinner is. And this was real because he had been through it, though long forgotten it. Jimbo stood aside and "felt" directions.

"Don't push," he said.

"Just think and wish," added Monkey with a laugh.

It was her laugh, and perhaps the beauty of her big brown eyes as well, that got him finally loose. For the laughter urged some queer, deep yearning in him towards a rush of exquisite accomplishment. He began to slip more easily and freely. The brain upon the bed, oddly enough, remembered a tradition of old Egypt—that Thoth created the world by bursting into seven peals of laughter. It touched forgotten springs of imagination and belief. In some tenuous, racy vehicle his thought flashed forth. With a gliding spring, like a swooping bird across a valley, he was suddenly—out.

"I'm out!" he cried.

"All out!" echoed the answering voices.

And then he understood that first vivid impression of light. It was everywhere, an evenly distributed light. He saw the darkness of the night as well, the deep old shadows that draped the village, woods, and mountains. But in themselves was light, a light that somehow enabled them to see everything quite clearly. Solid things were all transparent.

Light even radiated from objects in the room. Two much-loved books upon the table shone beautifully—his Bible and a volume of poems; and, fairer still, more delicate than either, there was a lustre on the table that had so brilliant a halo it almost corruscated. The sparkle in it was like the sparkle in the children's eyes. It came from the bunch of violets, gentians, and hepaticas, already faded, that Mother had placed there days ago on his arrival. And overhead, through plaster, tiles, and rafters he saw—the stars.

"We've already been for Jinny," Jimbo informed him; "but she's gone as usual. She goes the moment she falls asleep. We never can catch her up or find her."

"Come on," cried Monkey. "How slow you both are! We shan't get anywhere at this rate." And she made a wheel of coloured fire in the air. "I'm ready," he answered, happier than either. "Let's be off at once."

Through his mind flashed this explanation of their elder sister's day-expression—that expression of a moth she had, puzzled, distressed, only half there, as the saying is. For if she went out so easily at night in this way, some part of her probably stayed out altogether. She never wholly came back. She was always dreaming. The entire instinct of the child, he remembered, was for others, and she thought of herself as little as did the sun—old tireless star that shines for all.

"She's soaked in starlight," he cried, as they went off headlong. "We shall find her in the Cave. Come on, you pair of lazy meteors."

He was already far beyond the village, and the murmur of the woods rose up to them. They entered the meshes of the Star Net that spun its golden threads everywhere about them, linking up the Universe with their very hearts.

"There are no eyes or puddles tonight. Everybody sleeps. Hooray, hooray!" they cried together.

There were cross-currents, though. The main, broad, shining stream poured downwards in front of them towards the opening of the Cave, a mile or two beyond, where the forests dipped down among the precipices of the Areuse; but from behind—from some house in the slumbering village—came a golden tributary too, that had a peculiar and astonishing brightness of its own. It came, so far as they could make out, from the humped outline of La Citadelle, and from a particular room there, as though some one in that building had a special source of supply. Moreover, it scattered itself over the village in separate swift rivulets that dived and dipped towards particular houses here and there. There seemed a constant coming and going, one stream driving straight into the Cave, and another pouring out again, yet neither mingling. One stream brought supplies, while the other directed their distribution. Some one, asleep or awake—they could not tell—was thinking golden thoughts of love and sympathy for the world.

"It's Mlle. Lemaire," said Jimbo. "She's been in bed for thirty years—" His voice was very soft.

"The Spine, you know," exclaimed Monkey, a little in the rear.

"—and even in the daytime she looks white and shiny," added the boy. "I often go and talk with her and tell her things." He said it proudly. "She understands everything—better even than Mother." Jimbo had told most. It was all right. His leadership was maintained and justified. They entered the main stream and plunged downwards with it towards the earth—three flitting figures dipped in this store of golden brilliance.

A delicious and wonderful thing then happened. All three remembered.

"This was where we met you first," they told him, settling down among the trees together side by side. "We saw your teeth of gold. You came in that train—"

"I was thinking about it—in England," he exclaimed, "and about coming out to find you here."

"The Starlight Express," put in Jimbo.

"—and you were just coming up to speak to us when we woke, or you woke, or somebody woke—and it all went," said Monkey.

"That was when I stopped thinking about it," he explained.

"It all vanished anyhow. And the next time was"—she paused a moment—"you—we saw your two gold teeth again somewhere, and half recognised you—"

It was the daylight world that seemed vague and dreamlike now, hard to remember clearly.

"In another train—" Jimbo helped her, "the Geneva omnibus that starts at—at—" But even Jimbo could not recall further details.

"You're wumbled," said Rogers, helping himself and the others at the same time. "You want some starlight to put you in touch again. Come on; let's go in. We shall find all the others inside, I suspect, hard at it."

"At what?" asked two breathless voices.

"Collecting, of course—for others. Did you think they ate the stuff, just to amuse themselves?"

"They glided towards the opening, cutting through the little tributary stream that was pouring out on its way down the sky to that room in La Citadelle. It was brighter than the main river, they saw, and shone with a peculiar brilliance of its own, whiter and swifter than the rest. Designs, moreover, like crystals floated on the crest of every wave.

"That's the best quality," he told them, as their faces shone a moment in its glory. "The person who deserves it must live entirely for others. That he keeps only for the sad and lonely. The rest, the common stuff, is good enough for Fraulein or for baby, or for mother, or any other—" The words rose in him like flowers that he knew.

"Look out, *mon vieux*!" It was Monkey's voice. They just had time to stand aside as a figure shot past them and disappeared into the darkness above the trees. A big bundle, dripping golden dust, hung down his back.

"The Dustman!" they cried with excitement, easily recognising his energetic yet stooping figure; and Jimbo added, "the dear old Dustman!" while Monkey somersaulted after him, returning breathless a minute later with, "He's gone; I couldn't get near him. He went straight to La Citadelle—"

And then collided violently with the Lamplighter, whose pole of office caught her fairly in the middle and sent her spinning like a conjurer's plate till they feared she would never stop. She kept on laughing the whole time she spun—like a catherine wheel that laughs instead of splutters. The place where the pole caught her, however—it was its lighted end—shines and glows to this day: the centre of her little heart.

"Do let's be careful," pleaded Jimbo, hardly approving of these wild gyrations. He really did prefer his world a trifle more dignified. He was ever the grave little gentleman.

They stooped to enter by the narrow opening, but were stopped again—this time by some one pushing rudely past them to get in. From the three points of the compass to which the impact scattered them, they saw a shape of darkness squeeze itself, sack and all, to enter. An ordinary man would have broken every bone in his body, judging by the portion that projected into the air behind. But he managed it somehow, though the discomfort must have been intolerable, they all thought. The darkness dropped off behind him in flakes like discarded clothing; he turned to gold as he went in; and the contents of his sack—he poured it out like water—shone as though he squeezed a sponge just dipped in the Milky Way.

"What a lot he's collected," cried Rogers from his point of vantage where he could see inside. "It all gets purified and clean in there. Wait a moment. He's coming out again—off to make another collection."

And then they knew the man for what he was. He shot past them into the night, carrying this time a flat and emptied sack, and singing like a blackbird as he went:—

> *Sweeping chimneys and cleaning flues,*
> *That is the work I love;*
> *Brushing away the blacks and the blues,*
> *And letting in light from above!*
> *I twirl my broom in your tired brain*
> *When you're tight in sleep up-curled,*
> *Then scatter the stuff in a soot-like rain*
> *Over the edge of the world.*

The voice grew fainter and fainter in the distance—

> *For I'm a tremendously busy Sweep,*
> *Catching the folk when they're all asleep,*
> *And tossing the blacks on the Rubbish Heap*
> *Over the edge of the world. . . !*

The voice died away into the wind among the high branches, and they heard it no more.

"There's a Sweep worth knowing," murmured Rogers, strong yearning in him.

"There are no blacks or blues in *my* brain," exclaimed Monkey, "but Jimbo's always got some on his face."

The impudence passed ignored. Jimbo took his cousin's hand and led him to the opening. The "men" went in first together; the other sex might follow as best it could. Yet somehow or other Monkey slipped between their legs and got in before them. They stood up side by side in the most wonderful place they had ever dreamed of.

And the first thing they saw was—Jane Anne.

"I'm collecting for Mother. Her needles want such a chronic lot, you see." Her face seemed full of stars; there was no puzzled expression in the eyes now. She looked beautiful. And the younger children stared in sheer amazement and admiration.

"I have no time to waste," she said, moving past them with a load in her spread apron that was like molten gold; "I have to be up and awake at six to make your porridge before you go to school. I'm a busy monster, I can tell you!" She went by them like a flash, and out into the night.

Monkey felt tears in her somewhere, but they did not fall. Something in her turned ashamed—for a moment. Jimbo stared in silence. "What a girl!" he thought. "I'd like to be like that!" Already the light was sticking to him.

"So this is where she always comes," said Monkey, soon recovering from the temporary attack of emotion. "She's better out than in; she's safest when asleep! No wonder she's so funny in the daytime."

Then they turned to look about them, breathing low as wild-flowers that watch a rising moon.

The place was so big for one thing—far bigger than they had expected. The storage of lost starlight must be a serious affair indeed if it required all this space to hold it. The entire mountain range was surely hollow. Another thing that struck them was the comparative dimness of this huge interior compared with the brilliance of the river outside. But, of course, lost things are ever dim, and those worth looking for dare not be too easily found.

A million tiny lines of light, they saw, wove living, moving patterns, very intricate and very exquisite. These lines and patterns the three drew in with their very breath. They swallowed light—the tenderest light the world can know. A scent of flowers—something between a violet and a wild rose—floated over all. And they understood these patterns while they breathed them in. They read them. Patterns in Nature, of course, are fairy script. Here lay all their secrets sweetly explained in golden writing, all mysteries made clear. The three understood beyond their years; and inside-sight, instead of glimmering, shone. For, somehow or other, the needs of other people blazed everywhere, obliterating their own. It was most singular.

Monkey ceased from somersaulting and stared at Jimbo.

"You've got two stars in your face instead of eyes. They'll never set!" she whispered. "I love you because I understand every bit of you."

"And you," he replied, as though he were a grande personne, "have got hair like a mist of fire. It will never go out!"

"Every one will love me now," she cried, "my underneath is gold."

But her brother reproved her neatly:—

"Let's get a lot—simply an awful lot"—he made a grimace to signify quantity—"and pour it over Daddy's head till it runs from his eyes and beard. He'll write real fairy stories then and make a fortune."

And Cousin Henry moved past them like a burning torch. They held their breath to see him. Jane Anne, their busy sister, alone excelled him in brightness. Her perfume, too, was sweeter.

"He's an old hand at this game," Monkey said in French.

"But Jinny's never done anything else since she was born," replied her brother proudly.

And they all three fell to collecting, for it seemed the law of the place, a kind of gravity none could disobey. They stooped—three semi-circles of tender brilliance. Each lost the least desire to gather for himself; the needs of others drove them, filled them, made them eager and energetic.

"Riquette would like a bit," cried Jimbo, almost balancing on his head in his efforts to get it all at once, while Monkey's shining fingers stuffed her blouse and skirts with sheaves of golden gossamer that later she meant to spread in a sheet upon the pillow of Mademoiselle Lemaire.

"She sleeps so little that she needs the best," she sang, realising for once that her own amusement was not the end of life. "I'll make her nights all wonder."

Cousinenry, meanwhile, worked steadily like a man who knows his time is short. He piled the stuff in heaps and pyramids, and then compressed it into what seemed solid blocks that made his pockets bulge like small balloons. Already a load was on his back that bent him double.

"Such a tiny bit is useful," he explained, "if you know exactly how and where to put it. This compression is my own patent."

"Of course," they echoed, trying in vain to pack it up as cleverly as he did.

Nor were these three the only gatherers. The place was full of movement. Jane Anne was always coming back for more, deigning no explanations. She never told where she had spent her former loads. She gathered an apron full, sped off to spend and scatter it in places she knew of, and then came bustling in again for more. And they always knew her whereabouts because of the whiter glory that she radiated into the dim yellow world about them.

And other figures, hosts of them, were everywhere—stooping, picking, loading one another's backs and shoulders. To and fro they shot and glided, like Leonids in autumn round the Earth. All were collecting, though the supply seemed never to grow less. An inexhaustible stream poured in through the narrow opening, and scattered itself at once in all directions as though driven by a wind. How could the world let so much escape it, when it was what the world most needed every day. It ran naturally into patterns, patterns that could be folded and rolled up like silken tablecloths. In silence, too. There was no sound of drops falling. Sparks fly on noiseless feet. Sympathy makes no bustle.

"Even on the thickest nights it falls," a voice issued from a robust patch of light beside them that stooped with huge brown hands all knotted into muscles; "and it's a mistake to think different." His voice rolled on into a ridiculous bit of singing:—

> *It comes down with the rain drops,*
> *It comes down with the dew,*
> *There's always 'eaps for every one—*
> *For 'im and me and you.*

They recognised his big face, bronzed by the sun, and his great neck where lines drove into the skin like the rivers they drew with blunt pencils on their tedious maps of Europe. It was several faces in one. The Head Gardener was no stranger to their imaginations, for they remembered him of old somewhere, though not quite sure exactly where. He worked incessantly for others, though these "others" were only flowers and cabbages and fruit-trees. He did his share in the world, he and his army of queer assistants, the under-gardeners.

Peals of laughter, too, sounded from time to time in a far away corner of the cavern, and the laughter sent all the stuff it reached into very delicate, embroidered patterns. For it was merry and infectious laughter, joy somewhere in it like a lamp. It bordered upon singing; another touch would send it rippling into song. And to that far corner, attracted by the sound, ran numberless rivulets of light, weaving a lustrous atmosphere about the Laugher that, even while it glowed, concealed the actual gatherer from sight. The children only saw that the patterns were even more sweet and dainty than their own. And they understood. Inside-sight explained the funny little mystery. Laughter is magical—brings light and help and courage. They laughed themselves then, and instantly saw their own patterns wave and tremble into tiny outlines that they could squeeze later even into the darkest, thickest head.

Cousinenry, meanwhile, they saw, stopped for nothing. He was singing all the time as he bent over his long, outstretched arms. And it was the singing after all that made the best patterns—better even than the laughing. He knew all the best tricks of this Star Cave. He remained their leader.

And the stuff no hands picked up ran on and on, seeking a way of escape for itself. Some sank into the ground to sweeten the body of the old labouring earth, colouring the roots of myriad flowers; some soaked into the rocky walls, tinting the raw materials of hills and woods and mountain tops. Some escaped into the air in tiny drops that, meeting in moonlight or in sunshine, instantly formed wings. And people saw a brimstone butterfly—all wings and hardly any body. All went somewhere for some useful purpose. It was not in the nature of star-stuff to keep still. Like water that must go down-hill, the law of its tender being forced it to find a place where it could fasten on and shine. It never could get wholly lost; though, if the place it settled on was poor, it might lose something of its radiance. But human beings were obviously what most attracted it. Sympathy must find an outlet; thoughts are bound to settle somewhere.

And the gatherers all sang softly—"Collect for others, never mind yourself!"

Some of it, too, shot out by secret ways in the enormous roof. The children recognised the exit of the separate brilliant stream they had encountered in the sky—the one especially that went to the room of pain and sickness in La Citadelle. Again they understood. That unselfish thinker of golden thoughts knew special sources of supply. No wonder that her atmosphere radiated sweetness and uplifting influence. Her patience, smiles, and courage were explained. Passing through the furnace of her pain, the light was cleansed and purified. Hence the delicate, invariable radiation from her presence, voice, and eyes. From the bed of suffering she had not left for thirty years she helped the world go round more sweetly and more easily, though few divined those sudden moments of beauty they caught flashing from her halting words, nor guessed their source of strength.

"Of course," thought Jimbo, laughing, "I see now why I like to go and tell her everything. She understands all before I've said it. She's simply stuffed with starlight—bursting with inside-sight."

"That's sympathy," his cousin added, hearing the vivid thought. And he worked away like an entire ant-heap. But he was growing rather breathless now. "There's too much for me," he laughed as though his mouth were full. "I can't manage it all!" He was wading to the waist, and his coat and trousers streamed with runnels of orange-coloured light.

"Swallow it then!" cried Monkey, her hair so soaked that she kept squeezing it like a sponge, both eyes dripping too.

It was their first real experience of the joy of helping others, and they hardly knew where to begin or end. They romped and played in the stuff like children in sand or snow—diving, smothering themselves, plunging, choking, turning somersaults, upsetting each other's carefully reared loads, and leaping over little pyramids of gold. Then, in a flash, their laughter turned the destroyed heaps into wonderful new patterns again; and once more they turned sober and began to work.

But their cousin was more practical. "I've got all I can carry comfortably," he sang out at length. "Let's go out now and sow it among the sleepers. Come on!"

A field of stars seemed to follow him from the roof as he moved with difficulty towards the opening of the cave.

Some one shot out just in front of him. "My last trip!" The words reached them from outside. His bulging figure squeezed somehow through the hole, layers of light scraping off against the sides. The children followed him. But no one stuck. All were beautifully elastic; the starlight oiled and greased their daring, subtle star-bodies. Laden to the eyes, they sped across the woods that still slept heavily. The tips of the pines, however, were already opening a million eyes. There was a faint red glimmer in the east. Hours had passed while they were collecting.

"The Interfering Sun is on the way. Look out!" cried some one, shooting past them like an unleashed star. "I must get just a little more—my seventeenth journey tonight!" And Jane Anne, the puzzled look already come back a little into her face, darted down towards the opening. The waking of the body was approaching.

"What a girl!" thought Jimbo again, as they hurried after their grown-up cousin towards the village.

And here, but for the leadership of Cousin Henry, they must have gone astray and wasted half their stores in ineffective fashion. Besides, the east was growing brighter, and there was a touch of confusion in their little star-bodies as sleep grew lighter and the moment of the body's waking drew nearer.

Ah! the exquisite adjustment that exists between the night and day bodies of children! It is little wonder that with the process of growing-up there comes a coarsening that congeals the fluid passages of exit, and finally seals the memory centres too. Only in a few can this delicate adjustment be preserved, and the sources of inspiration known to children be kept available and sweet—in the poets, dreamers, and artists of this practical, steel-girdled age.

"This way," called Cousinenry. "Follow me." They settled down in a group among Madame Jequier's lilacs. "We'll begin with the Pension des Glycines. Jinny is already busy with La Citadelle."

They perched among the opening blossoms. Overhead flashed by the Sweep, the Dustman, and the Laugher, bound for distant ports, perhaps as far as England. The Head Gardener lumbered heavily after them to find his flowers and trees. Starlight, they grasped, could be no separate thing. The rays started, indeed, from separate points, but all met later in the sky to weave this enormous fairy network in which the currents and cross-currents and criss-cross-currents were so utterly bewildering. Alone, the children certainly must have got lost in the first five minutes.

Their cousin gathered up the threads from Monkey's hair and Jimbo's eyes, and held them in one hand like reins. He sang to them a moment while they recovered their breath and forces:—

> *The stars in their courses*
> *Are runaway horses*
> *That gallop with Thoughts from the Earth;*
> *They collect them, and race*
> *Back through wireless space,*
> *Bringing word of the tiniest birth;*
> *Past old Saturn and Mars,*
> *And the hosts of big stars,*
> *Who strain at their leashes for joy.*
> *Kind thoughts, like fine weather,*
> *Bind sweetly together*

God's suns—with the heart of a boy.
So, beware what you think;
It is written in ink
That is golden, and read by His Stars!

"Hadn't we better get on?" cried Monkey, pulling impatiently at the reins he held.

"Yes," echoed Jimbo. "Look at the sky. The 'rapide' from Paris comes past at six o'clock."

XVI

Aus den Himmelsaugen droben
Fallen zitternd goldne Funken
Durch die Nacht, und meine Seele
Dehnt sich liebeweit und weiter.

O ihr Himmelsaugen droben,
Weint euch aus in meine Seele,
Dass von lichten Sternentranen
Uberfliesset meine Seele!

—Heine

They rose, fluttered a moment above the lilac bushes, and then shot forward like the curve of a rainbow into the sleeping house. The next second they stood beside the bed of the Widow Jequier.

She lay there, so like a bundle of untidy sticks that, but for the sadness upon the weary face, they could have burst out laughing. The perfume of the wistaria outside the open window came in sweetly, yet could not lighten the air of heavy gloom that clothed her like a garment. Her atmosphere was dull, all streaked with greys and black, for her mind, steeped in anxiety even while she slept, gave forth cloudy vapours of depression and disquietude that made impossible the approach of— light. Starlight, certainly, could not force an entrance, and even sunlight would spill half its radiance before it reached her heart. The help she needed she thus deliberately shut out. Before going to bed her mood had been one of anxious care and searching worry. It continued, of course, in sleep.

"Now," thought their leader briskly, "we must deal with this at once"; and the children, understanding his unspoken message, approached closer to the bed. How brilliant their little figures were—Jimbo, a soft, pure blue, and Monkey tinged faintly here and there with delicate clear orange. Thus do the little clouds of sunset gather round to see the sun get into bed. And in utter silence; all their intercourse was silent— thought, felt, but never spoken.

For a moment there was hesitation. Cousinenry was uncertain exactly how to begin. Tante Jeanne's atmosphere was so very thick he hardly knew the best way to penetrate it. Her mood had been so utterly black and rayless. But his hesitation operated like a call for help that flew instantly about the world and was communicated to the golden threads that patterned the outside sky. They quivered, flashed the message automatically; the enormous network repeated it as far as England, and the answer came. For thought is instantaneous, and desire is prayer. Quick as lightning came the telegram. Beside them stood a burly figure of gleaming gold.

"I'll do it," said the earthy voice. "I'll show you 'ow. For she loves 'er garden. Her sympathy with trees and flowers lets me in. Always send for *me* when she's in a mess, or needs a bit of trimmin' and cleanin' up."

The Head Gardener pushed past them with his odour of soil and burning leaves, his great sunburned face and his browned, stained hands. These muscular, big hands he spread above her troubled face; he touched her heart; he blew his windy breath of flowers upon her untidy hair; he called the names of lilac, wistaria, roses, and laburnum. . .

The room filled with the little rushing music of wind in leaves; and, as he said "laburnum," there came at last a sudden opening channel through the fog that covered her so thickly. Starlight, that was like a rivulet of laburnum blossoms melted into running dew, flowed down it. The Widow Jequier stirred in her sleep and smiled. Other channels opened. Light trickled down these, too, drawn in and absorbed from the store the Gardener carried. Then, with a rush of scattering fire, he was gone again. Out into the enormous sky he flew, trailing golden flame behind him. They heard him singing as he dived into the Network— singing of buttercups and cowslips, of primroses and marigolds and dandelions, all yellow flowers that have stored up starlight.

And the atmosphere of Tante Jeanne first glowed, then shone; it changed slowly from gloom to glory. Golden channels opened everywhere, making a miniature network of their own. Light flashed and corruscated through it, passing from the children and their leader along the tiny pipes of sympathy the Gardener had cleared of rubbish and decay. Along the very lines of her face ran tiny shining rivers; flooding across her weary eyelids, gilding her untidy hair, and pouring down into her heavy heart. She ceased fidgeting; she smiled in her sleep; peace settled on her face; her fingers on the coverlet lost their touch of strain. Finally she turned over, stretched her old fighting body into a more comfortable position, sighed a moment, then settled down into a deep and restful slumber. Her atmosphere was everywhere "soft-shiny" when they left her to shoot next into the attic chamber above, where

Miss Waghorn lay among her fragments of broken memory, and the litter of disordered images that passed with her for "thinking."

And here, again, although their task was easier, they needed help to show the right way to begin. Before they reached the room Jimbo had wondered how they would "get at" her. That wonder summoned help. The tall, thin figure was already operating beside the bed as they entered. His length seemed everywhere at once, and his slender pole, a star hanging from the end, was busy touching articles on walls and floor and furniture. The disorder everywhere was the expression of her dishevelled mind, and though he could not build the ruins up again, at least he could trace the outlines of an ordered plan that she might use when she left her body finally and escaped from the rebellious instrument in death. And now that escape was not so very far away. Obviously she was already loose. She was breaking up, as the world expresses it.

And the children, watching with happy delight, soon understood his method. Each object that he touched emitted a tiny light. In her mind he touched the jumble of wandering images as well. On waking she would find both one and the other better assorted. Some of the lost things her memory ever groped for she would find more readily. She would see the starlight on them.

"See," said their leader softly, as the long thin figure of the Lamplighter shot away into the night, "she sleeps so lightly because she is so old—fastened so delicately to the brain and heart. The fastenings are worn and loose now. Already she is partly out!"

"That's why she's so muddled in the daytime," explained Jimbo, for his sister's benefit.

"Exaccurately, I knew it already!" was the reply, turning a somersault like a wheel of twirling meteors close to the old lady's nose.

"Carefully, now!" said their leader. "And hurry up! There's not much we can do here, and there's heaps to do elsewhere. We must remember Mother and Daddy—before the Interfering Sun is up, you know."

They flashed about the attic chamber, tipping everything with light, from the bundle of clothes that strewed the floor to the confused interior of the black basket-trunk where she kept her money and papers. There were no shelves in this attic chamber; no room for cupboards either; it was the cheapest room in the house. And the old woman in the bed sometimes opened her eyes and peered curiously, expectantly, about her. Even in her sleep she looked for things. Almost, they felt, she seemed aware of their presence near her, she knew that they were there; she smiled.

A moment later they were in mid-air on their way to the Citadelle, singing as they went:—

> *He keeps that only*
> *For the old and lonely,*
> *Who sleep so little that they need the best.*
> *The rest—*
> *The common stuff—*
> *Is good enough*
> *For Fraulein, or for baby, or for mother,*
> *Or any other*
> *Who likes a bit of dust,*
> *And yet can do without it—*
> *If they must. . .*

Already something of the Dawn's faint magic painting lay upon the world. Roofs shone with dew. The woods were singing, and the flowers were awake. Birds piped and whistled shrilly from the orchards. They heard the Mer Dasson murmuring along her rocky bed. The rampart of the Alps stood out more clearly against the sky.

"We must be *very* quick," Cousin Henry flashed across to them, "quicker than an express train."

"That's impossible," cried Jimbo, who already felt the call of waking into his daily world. "Hark! There's whistling already. . ."

The next second, in a twinkling, he was gone. He had left them. His body had been waked up by the birds that sang and whistled so loudly in the plane tree outside his window. Monkey and her guide raced on alone into the very room where he now sat up and rubbed his eyes in the Citadelle. He was telling his mother that he had just been "dreaming extraordinary." But Mother, sleeping like a fossil monster in the Tertiary strata, heard him not.

"He often goes like that," whispered Monkey in a tone of proud superiority. "He's only a little boy really, you see."

But the sight they then witnessed was not what they expected.

For Mademoiselle Lemaire herself was working over Mother like an engine, and Mother was still sleeping like the dead. The radiance that emanated from the night-body of this suffering woman, compared to their own, was as sunlight is to candle-light. Its soft glory was indescribable, its purity quite unearthly, and the patterns that it wove lovely beyond all telling. Here they surprised her in the act, busy with her ceaseless activities for others, working for the world by *thinking* beauty. While her pain-racked body lay asleep in the bed it had not left for thirty years, nor would ever leave again this side of death, she found her real life in loving sympathy for the pain of others everywhere. For thought is prayer, and prayer is the only true effective action that leaves no detail incomplete. She *thought* light and glory into others. Was it any wonder that she drew a special, brilliant supply from the Starlight Cavern, when she had so much to give? For giving-out involved drawing-in to fill the emptied spaces. Her pure and endless sources of supply were all explained.

"I've been working on her for years," she said gently, looking round at their approach, "for her life is so thickly overlaid with care, and the care she never quite knows how to interpret. We were friends, you see, in childhood. . . You'd better hurry on to the carpenter's house. You'll find Jinny there doing something for her father." She did not cease her working while she said it, this practical mind so familiar with the methods of useful thinking, this loving heart so versed in prayer while her broken body, deemed useless by the world, lay in the bed that was its earthly prison-house. "*He* can give me all the help I need," she added.

She pointed, and they saw the figure of the Sweep standing in the corner of the room among a pile of brimming sacks. His dirty face was beaming. They heard him singing quietly to himself under his breath, while his feet and sooty hands marked time with a gesture of quaintest dancing:—

> Such *a tremendously busy Sweep,*
> *Catching the world when it's all asleep,*
> *And tossing the blacks on the Rubbish Heap*
> *Over the edge of the world!*

"Come," whispered Cousin Henry, catching at Monkey's hair, "we can do something, but we can't do *that*. She needs no help from us!"

They sped across to the carpenter's house among the vineyards.

"What a splendour!" gasped the child as they went. "My starlight seems quite dim beside hers."

"She's an old hand at the game," he replied, noticing the tinge of disappointment in her thought. "With practice, you know—"

"And Mummy must be pretty tough," she interrupted with a laugh, her elastic nature recovering instantly.

"—with practice, I was going to say, your atmosphere will get whiter too until it simply shines. That's why the saints have halos."

But Monkey did not hear this last remark, she was already in her father's bedroom, helping Jinny.

Here there were no complications, no need for assistance from a Sweep, or Gardener, or Lamplighter. It was a case for pulling, pure and simple. Daddy was wumbled, nothing more. Body, mind, and heart were all up-jumbled. In making up the verse about the starlight he had merely told the truth—about himself. The poem was instinctive and inspirational confession. His atmosphere, as he lay there, gently snoring in his beauty sleep, was clear and sweet and bright, no darkness in it of grey or ugliness; but its pattern was a muddle, or rather there were several patterns that scrambled among each other for supremacy. Lovely patterns hovered just outside him, but none of them got really in. And the result was chaos. Daddy was not clear-headed; there was no concentration. Something of the perplexed confusion that afflicted his elder daughter in the daytime mixed up the patterns inextricably. There was no main pathway through his inner world.

And the picture proved it. It explained why Jinny pulled in vain. His night-body came out easily as far as the head, then stuck hopelessly. He looked like a knotted skein of coloured wools. Upon the paper where he had been making notes before going to sleep—for personal atmosphere is communicated to all its owner touches—lay the same confusion. Scraps of muddle, odds and ends of different patterns, hovered in thick blots of colour over the paragraphs and sentences. His own uncertainty was thus imparted to what he wrote, and his stories brought no conviction to his readers. He was too much the Dreamer, or too much the Thinker, which of the two was not quite clear. Harmony was lacking.

"That's probably what I'M like, too," thought his friend, but so softly that the children did not hear it. That Scheme of his passed vaguely through his mind.

Then he cried louder—a definite thought:—

"There's no good tugging like that, my dears. Let him slip in again. You'll only make him restless, and give him distorted dreams."

"I've tugged like this every night for months," said Jinny, "but the moment I let go he flies back like elastic."

"Of course. We must first untie the knots and weave the patterns into one. Let go!"

Daddy's night-body flashed back like a sword into its sheath. They stood and watched him. He turned a little in his sleep, while above him the lines twined and wriggled like phosphorus on moving water, yet never shaped themselves into anything complete. They saw suggestions of pure beauty in them here and there that yet never joined together into a single outline; it was like watching the foam against a steamer's sides in moonlight—just failing of coherent form.

"They want combing out," declared Jane Anne with a brilliant touch of truth. "A rake would be best."

"Assorting, sifting, separating," added Cousinenry, "but it's not easy." He thought deeply for a moment. "Suppose you two attend to the other things," he said presently, "while I take charge of the combing-out."

They knew at once his meaning; it was begun as soon as thought, only they could never have thought of it alone; none but a leader with real sympathy in his heart could have discovered the way.

Like Fairies, lit internally with shining lanterns, they flew about their business. Monkey picked up his pencils and dipped their points into her store of starlight, while Jinny drew the cork out of his ink-pot and blew in soft-shiny radiance of her own. They soaked his books in it, and smoothed his paper out with their fingers of clean gold. His note-books, chair, and slippers, his smoking-coat and pipes and tobacco-tins, his sponge, his tooth-brush and his soap—everything from dressing-gown to dictionary, they spread thickly with their starlight, and continued until the various objects had drunk in enough to make them shine alone.

Then they attacked the walls and floor and ceiling, sheets and bed-clothes. They filled the tin-bath full to the very brim, painted as well the windows, door-handles, and the wicker chair in which they knew he dozed after dejeuner. But with the pencils, pens, and ink-pots they took most trouble, doing them very thoroughly indeed. And his enormous mountain-boots received generous treatment too, for in these he went for his long lonely walks when he thought out his stories among the woods and valleys, coming home with joy upon his face—"I got a splendid idea today—a magnificent story—if only I can get it on to paper before it's gone. . . !" They understood his difficulty now: the "idea" was wumbled before he could fashion it. He could not get the pattern through complete.

And his older friend, working among the disjointed patterns, saw his trouble clearly too. It was not that he lacked this sympathy that starlight brings, but that he applied it without discernment. The receiving instrument was out of order, some parts moving faster than others. Reason and imagination were not exaccurately adjusted. He gathered plenty in, but no clear stream issued forth again; there was confusion in delivery. The rays were twisted, the golden lines caught into knots and tangles. Yet, ever just outside him, waiting to be taken in, hovered these patterns of loveliness that might bring joy to thousands. They floated in beauty round the edges of his atmosphere, but the moment they sank in to reach his mind, there began the distortion that tore their exquisite proportions and made designs mere disarrangement. Inspiration, without steady thought to fashion it, was of no value.

He worked with infinite pains to disentangle the mass of complicated lines, and one knot after another yielded and slipped off into rivulets of gold, all pouring inwards to reach heart and brain. It was exhilarating, yet disappointing labour. New knots formed themselves so easily, yet in the end much surely had been accomplished. Channels had been cleared; repetition would at length establish habit.

But the line of light along the eastern horizon had been swiftly growing broader meanwhile. It was brightening into delicate crimson. Already the room was clearer, and the radiance of their bodies fading into a paler glory. Jane Anne grew clumsier, tumbling over things, and butting against her more agile sister. Her thoughts became more muddled. She said things from time to time that showed it—hints that waking was not far away.

"Daddy's a wumbled Laplander, you know, after all. Hurry up!" The foolish daylight speech came closer.

"Give his ink-pot one more blow," cried Monkey. Her body always slept at least an hour longer than the others. She had more time for work.

Jane Anne bumped into the washhand-stand. She no longer saw quite clearly.

"I'm a plenipotentiary, that's what I am. I'm afraid of nothing. But the porridge has to be made. I must get back. . ."

She vanished like a flash, just as her brother had vanished half an hour before.

"We'll go on with it tomorrow night," signalled Cousin Henry to his last remaining helper. "Meet me here, remember, when. . . the moon. . . is high enough to. . . cast. . . a. . . shadow. . ."

The opening and shutting of a door sounded through his sleep. He turned over heavily. Surely it was not time to get up yet. That could not be hot water coming! He had only just fallen asleep. He plunged back again into slumber.

But Monkey had disappeared.

"What a spanking dream I've had. . .!" Her eyes opened, and she saw her school-books on the chair beside the bed. Mother was gently shaking her out of sleep. "Six o'clock, darling. The bath is ready, and Jinny's nearly got the porridge done. It's a lovely morning!"

"Oh, Mummy, I—"

But Mummy lifted her bodily out of bed, kissed her sleepy eyes awake, and half carried her over to the bath. "You can tell me all about that later," she said with practical decision; "when the cold water's cleared your head. You're always fuzzy when you wake."

Another day had begun. The sun was blazing high above the Blumlisalp. The birds sang in chorus. Dew shone still on the fields, but the men were already busy in the vineyards.

And presently Cousin Henry woke too and stared lazily about his room. He looked at his watch.

"By Jove," he murmured. "How one does sleep in this place! And what a dream to be sure—I who never dream!"

He remembered nothing more. From the moment he closed his eyes, eight hours before, until this second, all was a delicious blank. He felt refreshed and wondrously light-hearted, at peace with all the world. There was music in his head. He began to whistle as he lay among the blankets for half an hour longer. And later, while he breakfasted alone downstairs, he remembered that he ought to write to Minks. He owed Minks a letter. And before going out into the woods he wrote it. "I'm staying on a bit," he mentioned at the end. "I find so much to do here, and it's such a rest. Meanwhile I can leave everything safely in your hands. But as soon as I get a leisure moment I'll send you the promised draft of my Scheme for Disabled, etc., etc."

But the Scheme got no further somehow. New objections, for one thing, kept cropping up in his mind. It would take so long to build the place, and find the site, satisfy County Councils, and all the rest. The Disabled, moreover, were everywhere; it was invidious to select one group and leave the others out. Help the world, yes—but what was "the world"? There were so many worlds. He touched a new one every day and every hour. Which needed his help most? Bourcelles was quite as important, quite as big and hungry as any of the others. "That old Vicar knew a thing or two," he reflected later in the forest, while he gathered a bunch of hepaticas and anemones to take to Mlle. Lemaire. "There are 'neighbours' everywhere, the world's simply chock full of 'em. But what a pity that we die just when we're getting fit and ready to begin. Perhaps we go on afterwards, though. I wonder. . . !"

XVII

The stars ran loose about the sky,
Wasting their beauty recklessly,
Singing and dancing,
Shooting and prancing,
Until the Pole Star took command,
Changing each wild, disordered band
Into a lamp to guide the land—
A constellation.

And so, about my mind and yours,
Thought dances, shoots, and wastes its powers,
Coming and going,
Aimlessly flowing,
Until the Pole Star of the Will
Captains them wisely, strong, and still,
Some dream for others to fulfil
With consecration.

—Selected Poems, Montmorency Minke

There was a certain air of unreality somewhere in the life at Bourcelles that ministered to fantasy. Rogers had felt it steal over him from the beginning. It was like watching a children's play in which the scenes were laid alternately in the Den, the Pension, and the Forest. Side by side with the grim stern facts of existence ran the coloured spell of fairy make-believe. It was the way they mingled, perhaps, that ministered to this spirit of fantasy.

There were several heroines for instance—Tante Jeanne, Mademoiselle Lemaire, and Mother; each played her role quite admirably. There were the worthy sterling men who did their duty dumbly, regardless of consequences—Daddy, the Postmaster, and the picturesque old clergyman with failing powers. There was the dark, uncertain male character, who might be villain, yet who might prove extra hero—the strutting postman of baronial ancestry; there was the role of quaint pathetic humour Miss Waghorn so excellently filled, and there were the honest rough-and-tumble comedians—half mischievous, half malicious—the retired governesses. Behind them all, brought on chiefly in scenes of dusk and moonlight, were the Forest Elves who, led by Puck, were responsible for the temporary confusion that threatened disaster, yet was bound to have a happy ending—the children. It was all a children's play set in the lovely scenery of mountain, forest, lake, and old-world garden.

Numerous other characters also flitted in and out. There was the cat, the bird, the donkey as in pantomime; goblin caves and haunted valleys and talking flowers; and the queer shadowy folk who came to the Pension in the summer months, then vanished into space again. Links with the outside world were by no means lacking. As in the theatre, one caught now and again the rumble of street traffic and the roar of everyday concerns. But these fell in by chance during quiet intervals, and served to heighten contrast only.

And so many of the principal roles were almost obviously assumed, interchangeable almost; any day the players might drop their wigs, rub off the paint, and appear otherwise, as they were in private life. The Widow Jequier's husband, for instance, had been a *pasteur* who had gone later into the business of a wine-merchant. She herself was not really the keeper of a Pension for Jeune Filles, but had drifted into it owing to her husband's disastrous descent from pulpit into cellar—understudy for some one who had forgotten to come on. The Postmaster, too, had originally been a photographer, whose funereal aspect had sealed his failure in that line. His customers could never smile and look pleasant. The postman, again, was a baron in disguise—in private life he had a castle and retainers; and even Gygi, the gendarme, was a make-believe official who behind the scenes was a *vigneron* and farmer in a very humble way. Daddy, too, seemed sometimes but a tinsel author dressed up for the occasion, and absurdly busy over books that no one ever saw on railway bookstalls. While Mademoiselle Lemaire was not in fact and verity a suffering, patient, bed-ridden lady, but a princess who escaped from her disguise at night into glory and great beneficent splendour.

Mother alone was more real than the other players. There was no make-believe about Mother. She thundered across the stage and stood before the footlights, interrupting many a performance with her stubborn common-sense and her grip upon difficult grave issues. "This performance will finish at such and such an hour," was her cry. "Get your wraps ready. It will be cold when you go out. And see that you have money handy for your 'bus fares home!" Yes, Mother was real. She knew some facts of life at least. She knitted the children's stockings and did the family mending.

Yet Rogers felt, even with her, that she was merely waiting. She knew the cast was not complete as yet. She waited. They all waited—for some one. These were rehearsals; Rogers himself had dropped in also merely as an understudy. Another role was vacant, and it was the principal role. There was no one in the company who could play it, none who could understudy it even. Neither Rogers nor Daddy could learn the lines or do the "business." The part was a very important one, calling for a touch of genius to be filled adequately. And it was a feminine role. For here was a Fairy Play without a Fairy Queen. There was not even a Fairy Princess!

This idea of a representation, all prepared specially for himself, induced a very happy state of mind; he felt restful, calm, at peace with all the world. He had only to sit in his stall and enjoy. But it brought, too, this sense of delicate bewilderment that was continually propounding questions to which he found no immediate answer. With the rest of the village, he stood still while Time flowed past him. Later, with Minks, he would run after it and catch it up again. Minks would pick out the lost clues. Minks stood on the banks—in London—noting the questions floating by and landing them sometimes with a rod and net. His master would deal with them by and by; but just now he could well afford to wait and enjoy himself. It was a holiday; there was no hurry; Minks held the fort meanwhile and sent in reports at intervals.

And the sweet spring weather continued; days were bright and warm; the nights were thick with stars. Rogers postponed departure on the flimsiest reasons. It was no easy thing to leave Bourcelles. "Next week the muguet will be over in the vallon vert. We must pick it quickly together for Tante Anna." Jinny brought every spring flower to Mademoiselle Lemaire in this way the moment they appeared. Her room was a record of their sequence from week to week. And Jimbo knew exactly where to find them first; his mind was a time-table of flowers as well as of trains, dates of arrival, and stations where they grew. He knew it all exaccurately. This kind of fact with him was never wumbled. "Soon the sabot de Venus will be in flower at the Creux du Van, but it takes time to find it. It's most awfully rare, you see. You'll have to climb beyond the fontaine froide. That's past the Ferme Robert, between Champ du Moulin and Noiraigue. The snow ought to be gone by now. We'll go and hunt for it. I'll take you in—oh, in about deux semaines—comme ca." Alone, those dangerous cliffs were out of bounds for him, but if he went with Cousinenry, permission could not be refused. Jimbo knew what he was about. And he took for granted that his employer would never leave Bourcelles again. "Thursday and Saturday would be the best days," he added. They were his half-holidays, but he did not say so. Secretaries, he knew, did not have half-holidays comme ca. "Je suis son vrai secretaire," he had told Mademoiselle Lemaire, who had confirmed it with a grave mais oui. No one but Mother heard the puzzled question one night when he was being tucked into bed; it was asked with just a hint of shame upon a very puckered little face—"But, Mummy, what really *is* a sekrity?"

And so Rogers, from day to day, stayed on, enjoying himself and resting. The City would have called it loafing, but in the City the schedule of values was a different one. Meanwhile the bewilderment he felt at first gradually disappeared. He no longer realised it, that is. While still outside, attacked by it, he had realised the soft entanglement. Now he was in it, caught utterly, a prisoner. He was no longer mere observer. He was part and parcel of it. "What does a few weeks matter out of a whole strenuous life?" he argued. "It's all to the good, this holiday. I'm storing up strength and energy for future use. My Scheme can wait a little. I'm thinking things out meanwhile."

He often went into the forest alone to think his things out, and "things" always meant his Scheme. . . but the more he thought about it the more distant and impracticable seemed that wondrous Scheme. He had the means, the love, the yearning, all in good condition, waiting to be put to practical account. In his mind, littered more and more now with details that Minks not infrequently sent in, this great Scheme by which he had meant to help the world ran into the confusion of new issues that were continually cropping up. Most of these were caused by the difficulty of knowing his money spent exactly as he wished, not wasted, no pound of it used for adornment, whether salaries, uniforms, fancy stationery, or unnecessary appearances, whatever they might be. Whichever way he faced it, and no matter how carefully thought out were the plans that Minks devised, these leakages cropped up and mocked him. Among a dozen propositions his original clear idea went lost, and floundered. It came perilously near to wumbling itself away altogether.

For one thing, there were rivals on the scene—his cousin's family, the education of these growing children, the difficulties of the Widow Jequier, some kind of security he might ensure to old Miss Waghorn, the best expert medical attendance for Mademoiselle Lemaire. . . and his fortune was after all a small one as fortunes go. Only his simple scale of personal living could make these things possible at all. Yet here, at least, he would know that every penny went exaccurately where it was meant to go, and accomplished the precise purpose it was intended to accomplish.

And the more he thought about it, the more insistent grew the claims of little Bourcelles, and the more that portentous Scheme for Disabled Thingumabobs faded into dimness. The old Vicar's words kept singing in his head: "The world is full of Neighbours. Bring them all back to Fairyland." He thought things out in his own way and at his leisure. He loved to wander alone among the mountains. . . thinking in this way. His thoughts turned to his cousin's family, their expenses, their difficulties, the curious want of harmony somewhere. For the conditions in which the *famille anglaise* existed, he had soon discovered, were those of muddle pure and simple, yet of muddle on so large a scale that it was fascinating and even exhilarating. It must be lovely, he reflected, to live so carelessly. They drifted. Chance forces blew them hither and thither as gusts of wind blow autumn leaves. Five years in a place and then—a gust that blew them elsewhere. Thus they had lived five years in a London suburb, thinking it permanent; five years in a lonely Essex farm, certain they would never abandon country life; and five years, finally, in the Jura forests.

Neither parent, though each was estimable, worthy, and entirely of good repute, had the smallest faculty for seeing life whole; each studied closely a small fragment of it, the fragment limited by the Monday and the Saturday of next week, or, in moments of optimistic health, the fragment that lies between the first and thirty-first of a single month. Of what lay beyond, they talked; oh, yes, they talked voluminously and with detail that sounded impressive to a listener, but somehow in circles that carried them no further than the starting-point, or in spirals that rose higher with each sentence and finally lifted them bodily above the solid ground. It was merely talk—ineffective—yet the kind that makes one feel it has accomplished something and so brings the false security of carelessness again. Neither one nor other was head of the house. They took it in turns, each slipping by chance into that onerous position, supported but uncoveted by the other. Mother fed the children, mended everything, sent them to the dentist when their teeth ached badly, but never before as a preventative, and—trusted to luck.

"Daddy," she would say in her slow gentle way, "I do wish we could be more practical sometimes. Life is such a business, isn't it?" And they would examine in detail the grain of the stable door now that the horse had escaped, then close it very carefully.

"I really must keep books," he would answer, "so that we can see exactly how we stand," having discovered at the end of laborious calculation concerning the cost of the proposed Geneva schooling for Jinny that they had reckoned in shillings instead of francs. And then, with heads together, they selected for their eldest boy a profession utterly unsuited to his capacities, with coaching expenses far beyond their purses, and with the comforting consideration that "there's a pension attached to it, you see, for when he's old."

Similarly, having planned minutely, and with personal sacrifice, to save five francs in one direction, they would spend that amount unnecessarily in another. They felt they had it to spend, as though it had been just earned and already jingled in their pockets. Daddy would announce he was walking into Neuchatel to buy tobacco. "Better take the tram," suggested Mother, "it's going to rain. You save shoe leather, too," she added laughingly. "Will you be back to tea?" He thought not; he would get a cup of tea in town. "May I come, too?" from Jimbo. "Why not?" thought Mother. "Take him with you, he'll enjoy the trip." Monkey and Jane Ann, of course, went too. They *all* had tea in a shop, and bought chocolate into the bargain. The five francs melted into—nothing, for tea at home was included in their Pension terms. Saving is in the mind. There was no system in their life.

"It would be jolly, yes, if you could earn a little something regular besides your work," agreed Mother, when he thought of learning a typewriter to copy his own books, and taking in work to copy for others too.

"I'll do it," he decided with enthusiasm that was forgotten before he left the room ten minutes later.

It was the same with the suggestion of teaching English. He had much spare time, and could easily have earned a pound a week by giving lessons, and a pound a week is fifty pounds a year—enough to dress the younger children easily. The plan was elaborated laboriously. "Of course," agreed Daddy, with genuine interest. "It's easily done. I wonder we never thought of it before." Every few months they talked about it, but it never grew an inch nearer to accomplishment. They drifted along, ever in difficulty, each secretly blaming the other, yet never putting their thoughts into speech. They did not quite understand each other's point of view.

"Mother really might have foreseen *that*!" when Jimbo, growing like a fairy beanstalk, rendered his recent clothes entirely useless. "Boys must grow. Why didn't she buy the things a size or two larger?"

"It's rather thoughtless, almost selfish, of Daddy to go on writing these books that bring in praise without money. He could write anything if he chose. At least, he might put his shoulder to the wheel and teach, or something!"

And so, not outwardly in spoken words or quarrels, but inwardly, owing to that deadliest of cancers, want of sympathy, these two excellent grown-up children had moved with the years further and further apart. Love had not died, but want of understanding, not attended to in time, had frayed the edges so that they no longer fitted well together. They have blown in here, thought Rogers as he watched them, like seeds the wind has brought. They have taken root and grown a bit. They think they're here for ever, but presently a wind will rise and blow them off again elsewhere. And thinking it is their own act, they will look wisely at each other, as children do, and say, "Yes, it *is* time now to make a move. The children are getting big. Our health, too, needs a change." He wondered, smiling a little, in what vale or mountain top the wind would let them down. And a big decision blazed up in his heart. "I'm not very strong in the domestic line," he exclaimed, "but I think I can help them a bit. They're neighbours at any rate. They're all children too. Daddy's no older than Jimbo, or Mother than Jane Anne!"

IN THE SPACES OF THE forest there was moss and sunshine. It was very still. The primroses and anemones had followed the hepaticas and periwinkles. Patches of lily of the valley filled the air with fragrance. Through openings of the trees he caught glimpses of the lake, deep as the Italian blue of the sky above his head. White Alps hung in the air beyond its farther shore line. Below him, already far away, the village followed slowly, bringing its fields and vineyards with it, until the tired old church called halt. And then it lay back, nestling down to sleep, very small, very cosy, mere handful of brown roofs among the orchards. Only the blue smoke of occasional peat fires moved here and there, betraying human occupation.

The peace and beauty sank into his heart, as he wandered higher across Mont Racine's velvet shoulder. And the contrast stirred memories of his recent London life. He thought of the scurrying busy-bodies in the "City," and he thought of the Widow Jequier attacking life so restlessly in her garden at that very minute. That other sentence of the old Vicar floated though his mind: "the grandeur of toil and the insignificance of acquisition." . . . Far overhead two giant buzzards circled quietly, ceaselessly watching from the blue. A brimstone butterfly danced in random flight before his face. Two cuckoos answered one another in the denser forest somewhere above him. Bells from distant village churches boomed softly through the air, voices from a world forgotten.

And the contrast brought back London. He thought of the long busy chapter of his life just finished. The transition had been so abrupt. As a rule periods fade into one another gradually in life, easily, divisions blurred; it is difficult on looking back to say where the change began. One is well into the new before the old is realised as left behind. "How did I come to this?" the mind asks itself. "I don't remember any definite decision. Where was the boundary crossed?" It has been imperceptibly accomplished.

But here the change had been sudden and complete, no shading anywhere. He had leaped a wall. Turmoil and confusion lay on that side; on this lay peace, rest and beauty. Strain and ugliness were left behind, and with them so much that now seemed false, unnecessary, vain. The grandeur of toil, and the insignificance of acquisition—the phrase ran through his mind with the sighing of the pine trees; it was like the first line of a song. The Vicar knew the song complete. Even Minks, perhaps, could pipe it too. Rogers was learning it. "I must help them somehow," he thought again. "It's not a question of money merely. It's that they want welding together more—more harmony—more sympathy. They're separate bits of a puzzle now, whereas they might be a rather big and lovely pattern. . ."

He lay down upon the moss and flung his hat away. He felt that Life stood still within him, watching, waiting, asking beautiful, deep, searching questions. It made him slightly uncomfortable. Henry Rogers, late of Threadneedle Street, took stock of himself, not of set intention, yet somehow deliberately. He reviewed another Henry Rogers who had been unable to leap that wall. The two peered at one another gravely.

The review, however, took no definite form; precise language hardly came to help with definite orders. A vague procession of feelings, half sad, half pleasurable, floated past his closing eyes. . . Perhaps he slept a moment in the sunshine upon that bed of moss and pine needles. . .

Such curious thoughts flowed up and out and round about, dancing like the brimstone butterflies out of reach before he could seize them, calling with voices like the cuckoos, themselves all the time just out of sight. Who ever saw a cuckoo when it's talking? Who ever foretold the instant when a butterfly would shoot upwards and away? Such darting, fragile thoughts they were, like hints, suggestions. Still, they *were* thoughts.

Minks, dragging behind him an enormous Scheme, emerged from the dark vaults of a Bank where gold lay piled in heaps. Minks was looking for him, yet smiling a little, almost pityingly, as he strained beneath the load. It was like a comic opera. Minks was going down the noisy, crowded Strand. Then, suddenly, he paused, uncertain of the way. From an upper window a shining face popped out and issued clear directions—as from a pulpit. "That way—towards the river," sang the voice—and far down the narrow side street flashed a gleam of flowing water with orchards on the farther bank. Minks instantly turned and went down it with his load so fast that the scenery changed before the heavy traffic could get out of the way. Everything got muddled up with fields and fruit-trees; the Scheme changed into a mass of wild-flowers; a lame boy knocked it over with his crutch; gold fell in a brilliant, singing shower, and where each sovereign fell there sprang up a buttercup or dandelion. Rogers rubbed his eyes... and realised that the sun was rather hot upon his face. A dragon fly was perched upon his hat three feet away...

The tea hour at the Den was close, and Jimbo, no doubt, was already looking for him at the carpenter's house. Rogers hurried home among the silent forest ways that were sweet with running shadows and slanting sunshine. Oh, how fragrant was the evening air! And how the lily of the valley laughed up in his face! Normally, at this time, he would be sitting in a taxi, hurrying noisily towards his Club, thoughts full of figures, politics, philanthropy cut to line and measure—a big Scheme standing in squares across the avenue of the future. Now, moss and flowers and little children took up all the available space... How curiously out of the world Bourcelles was, to be sure. Newspapers had no meaning any longer. Picture-papers and smart weekly Reviews, so necessary and important in St. James's Street, here seemed vulgar, almost impertinent— ridiculous even. Big books, yes; but not pert, topical comments issued with an absurd omnipotence upon things merely ephemeral. How the mind accumulated rubbish in a city! It seemed incredible. He surely had climbed a wall and dropped down into a world far bigger, though a world the "city" would deem insignificant and trivial. Yet only because it had less detail probably! A loved verse flashed to him across the years:—

"O to dream, O to awake and wander
There, and with delight to take and render,
Through the trance of silence,
Quiet breath!

Lo! for there among the flowers and grasses,
Only the mightier movement sounds and passes;
Only winds and rivers,
Life and death."

Bourcelles was important as London, yes, while simple as the nursery. The same big questions of life and death, of battle, duty, love, ruled the peaceful inhabitants. Only the noisy shouting, the clatter of superfluous chattering and feverish striving had dropped away. Hearts and minds wore fewer clothes among these woods and vineyards. There was no nakedness though. . . there were flowers and moss, blue sky and peace and beauty. . . Thought ran into confused, vague pictures. He could not give them coherence, shape, form. . .

He crossed the meadows and entered the village through the Pension garden. The Widow Jequier gave him a spray of her Persian lilac on the way. "It's been growing twenty-five years for you," she said, "only do not look at *me*. I'm in my garden things—invisible." He remembered with a smile Jane Anne's description—that "the front part of the house was all at the back."

Tumbling down the wooden stairs, he crossed the street and made for the Citadelle, where the children opened the door for him even before he rang. Jimbo and Monkey, just home from school, pulled him by both arms towards the tea-table. They had watched for his coming.

"The samovar's just boiling," Mother welcomed him. Daddy was on the sofa by the open window, reading manuscript over to himself in a mumbling voice; and Jane Anne, apron on, sleeves tucked up, face flushed, poked her head in from the kitchen:

"Excuse me, Mother, the cupboard's all in distress. I can't find the marmalade anywhere."

"But it's already on the table, child."

She saw her Cousin and popped swiftly back again from view. One heard fragments of her sentences—"wumbled. . . chronic. . . busy monster. . ." And two minutes later *la famille anglaise* was seriously at tea.

XVIII

What art thou, then? I cannot guess;
But tho' I seem in star and flower
To feel thee some diffusive power,
I do not therefore love thee less.

—*Love and Death*, TENNYSON

In the act of waking up on the morning of the Star Cave experience, Henry Rogers caught the face of a vivid dream close against his own—but in rapid motion, already passing. He tried to seize it. There was a happy, delightful atmosphere about it. Examination, however, was impossible; the effort to recover the haunting dream dispersed it. He saw the tip, like an express train flying round a corner; it flashed and disappeared, fading into dimness. Only the delightful atmosphere remained and the sense that he had been somewhere far away in very happy conditions. People he knew quite well, had been there with him; Jimbo and Monkey; Daddy too, as he had known him in his boyhood. More than this was mere vague surmise; he could not recover details. Others had been also of the merry company, familiar yet unrecognisable. Who in the world were they? It all seemed oddly real.

"How I do dream in this place, to be sure," he thought; "I, who normally dream so little! It was like a scene of my childhood—Crayfield or somewhere." And he reflected how easily one might be persuaded that the spirit escaped in sleep and knew another order of experience. The sense of actuality was so vivid.

He lay half dozing for a little longer, hoping to recover the adventures. The flying train showed itself once or twice again, but smaller, and much, much farther away. It curved off into the distance. A deep cutting quickly swallowed it. It emerged for the last time, tiny as a snake upon a chess-board of far-off fields. Then it dipped into mist; the snake shot into its hole. It was gone. He sighed. It had been so lovely. Why must it vanish so entirely? Once or twice during the day it returned, touched him swiftly on the heart and was gone again. But the waking impression of a dream is never the dream itself. Sunshine destroys the sense of enormous wonder.

"I believe I've been dreaming all night long, and going through all kinds of wild adventures."

He dressed leisurely, still hunting subconsciously for fragments of that happy dreamland. Its aroma still clung about him. The sunshine poured into the room. He went out on to the balcony and looked at the Alps through his Zeiss field-glasses. The brilliant snow upon the Diablerets danced and sang into his blood; across the broken teeth of the Dent du Midi trailed thin strips of early cloud. Behind him rose great Boudry's massive shoulders, a pyramid of incredible deep blue. And the limestone precipices of La Tourne stood dazzlingly white, catching the morning sunlight full in their face.

The air had the freshness of the sea. Men were singing at their work among the vineyards. The tinkle of cow-bells floated to him from the upper pastures upon Mont Racine. Little sails like sea-gulls dipped across the lake. Goodness, how happy the world was at Bourcelles! Singing, radiant, careless of pain and death. And, goodness, how he longed to make it happier still!

Every day now this morning mood had been the same. Desire to do something for others ran races with little practical schemes for carrying it out. Selfish considerations seemed to have taken flight, all washed away while he slept. Moreover, the thought of his Scheme had begun to oppress him; a touch of shame came with it, almost as though an unworthy personal motive were somewhere in it. Perhaps after all—he wondered more and more now—there had been an admixture of personal ambition in the plan. The idea that it would bring him honour in the eyes of the world had possibly lain there hidden all along. If so, he had not realised it; the depravity had been unconscious. Before the Bourcelles standard of simplicity, artificial elements dropped off automatically, ashamed. . . And a profound truth, fished somehow out of that vanished dreamland, spun its trail of glory through his heart. Kindness that is thanked-for surely brings degradation—a degradation almost as mean as the subscription acknowledged in a newspaper, or the anonymous contribution kept secret temporarily in order that its later advertisement may excite the more applause. Out flashed this blazing truth: kind acts must be instinctive, natural, thoughtless. One hand must be in absolute ignorance of the other's high adventures. . . And when the carpenter's wife brought up his breakfast tray, with the bunch of forest flowers standing in a tumbler of water, she caught him pondering over another boyhood's memory—that friend of his father's who had given away a million anonymously.

. . . In his heart plans shaped themselves with soft, shy eyes and hidden faces. . . He longed to get *la famille anglaise* straight. . . for one thing. . .

It was an hour later, while he still sat dreaming in the sunshine by the open window, that a gentle tap came at the door, and Daddy entered. The visit was a surprise. Usually, until time for *dejeuner*, he kept his room, busily unwumbling stories. This was unusual. And something had happened to him; he looked different. What was it that had changed? Some veil had cleared away; his eyes were shining. They greeted one another, and Rogers fell shyly to commonplaces, while wondering what the change exactly was.

But the other was not to be put off. He was bursting with something. Rogers had never seen him like this before.

"You've stopped work earlier than usual," he said, providing the opening. He understood his diffidence, his shyness in speaking of himself. Long disappointments lay so thinly screened behind his unfulfilled enthusiasm.

But this time the enthusiasm swept diffidence to the winds. It had been vitally stirred.

"Early indeed," he cried. "I've been working four hours without a break, man. Why, what do you think?—I woke at sunrise, a thing I never do, with—with a brilliant idea in my head. Brilliant, I tell you. By Jove, if only I can carry it out as I see it—!"

"You've begun it already?"

"Been at it since six o'clock, I tell you. It was in me when I woke— idea, treatment, everything complete, all in a perfect pattern of Beauty."

There was a glow upon his face, his hair was untidy; a white muffler with blue spots was round his neck instead of collar. One end stuck up against his chin. The safety pin was open.

"By Jove! I am delighted!" Rogers had seen him excited before over a "brilliant idea," but the telling of it always left him cold. It touched the intellect, yet not the heart. It was merely clever. This time, however, there was a new thing in his manner. "How did you get it?" he repeated. Methods of literary production beyond his own doggerels were a mystery to him. "Sort of inspiration, eh?"

"Woke with it, I tell you," continued his cousin, twisting the muffler so that it tickled his ear now instead of his chin. "It must have come to me in sleep—" "In sleep," exclaimed the other; "you dreamt it, then?"

"Kind of inspiration business. I've heard of that sort of thing, but never experienced it—" The author paused for breath.

"What is it? Tell me." He remembered how ingenious details of his patents had sometimes found themselves cleared up in the morning after refreshing slumber. This might be something similar. "Let's hear it," he added; "I'm interested."

His cousin's recitals usually ended in sad confusion, so that all he could answer by way of praise was—"You ought to make something good out of that. I shall like to read it when you've finished it." But this time, he felt, there was distinctly a difference. There were new conditions.

The older man leaned closer, his face alight, his manner shyly, eagerly confidential. The morning sunshine blazed upon his untidy hair. A bread crumb from breakfast still balanced in his beard.

"It's difficult to tell in a few words, you see," he began, the enthusiasm of a boy in his manner, "but—I woke with the odd idea that this little village might be an epitome of the world. All the emotions of London, you see, are here in essence—the courage and cowardice, the fear and hope, the greed and sacrifice, the love and hate and passion—everything. It's the big world in miniature. Only—with one difference."

"That's good," said Rogers, trying to remember when it was he had told his cousin this very thing. Or had he only *thought* it? "And what *is* the difference?"

"The difference," continued the other, eyes sparkling, face alight, "that here the woods, the mountains and the stars are close. They pour themselves in upon the village life from every side—above, below, all round. Flowers surround it; it dances to the mountain winds; at night it lies entangled in the starlight. Along a thousand imperceptible channels an ideal simplicity from Nature pours down into it, modifying the human passions, chastening, purifying, uplifting. Don't you see? And these sweet, viewless channels—who keeps them clean and open? Why, God bless you—. The children! *My* children!"

"By Jingo, yes; *your* children."

Rogers said it with emphasis. But there was a sudden catch at his heart; he was conscious of a queer sensation he could not name. This was exactly what he had felt himself—with the difference that his own thought had been, perhaps, emotion rather than a reasoned-out idea. His cousin put it into words and gave it form. A picture—had he seen it in a book perhaps?—flashed across his mind. A child, suspiciously like

Monkey, held a pen and dipped it into something bright and flowing. A little boy with big blue eyes gathered this shining stuff in both hands and poured it in a golden cataract upon the eyelids of a sleeping figure. And the figure had a beard. It was a man. . . familiar. . . A touch of odd excitement trembled through his undermind. . . thrilled. . . vanished. . .

All dived out of sight again with the swiftness of a darting swallow. His cousin was talking at high speed. Rogers had lost a great deal of what he had been saying.

". . . it may, of course, have come from something you said the other night as we walked up the hill to supper—you remember?—something about the brilliance of our stars here and how they formed a shining network that hung from Boudry and La Tourne. It's impossible to say. The germ of a true inspiration is never discoverable. Only, I remember, it struck me as an odd thing for *you* to say. I was telling you about my idea of the scientist who married—no, no, it wasn't that, it was my story of the materialist doctor whom circumstances compelled to accept a position in the Community of Shakers, and how the contrast produced an effect upon his mind of—of—you remember, perhaps? It was one or the other; I forget exactly,"—then suddenly—"No, no, I've got it—it was the analysis of the father's mind when he found—"

"Yes, yes," interrupted Rogers. "We were just passing the Citadelle fountain. I saw the big star upon the top of Boudry, and made a remark about it." His cousin was getting sadly wumbled. He tried to put severity and concentration into his voice.

"That's it," the other cried, head on one side and holding up a finger, "because I remember that my own thought wandered for a moment—thought will, you know, in spite of one's best effort sometimes—and you said a thing that sent a little shiver of pleasure through me for an instant—something about a Starlight Train—and made me wonder where you got the idea. That's it. I do believe you've hit the nail on the head. Isn't it curious sometimes how a practical mind may suggest valuable material to the artist? I remember, several years ago—"

"Starlight Express, wasn't it?" said his friend with decision in his voice. He thumped the table vigorously with one fist. "Keep to the point, old man. Follow it out. Your idea is splendid."

"Yes, I do believe it is." Something in his voice trembled.

One sentence in particular Rogers heard, for it seemed plucked out of the talk he had with the children in the forest that day two weeks ago.

"You see, all light meets somewhere. It's all one, I mean. And so with minds. They all have a common meeting-place. Sympathy is the name for that place—that state—they feel with each other, see flash-like from the same point of view for a moment. And children are the conduits. They do not think things out. They feel them, eh?" He paused an instant.

"For you see, along these little channels that the children—my children, as I think I mentioned—keep sweet and open, there might troop back into the village—Fairyland. Not merely a foolish fairyland of make-believe and dragons and princesses imprisoned in animals, but a fairyland the whole world needs—the sympathy of sweet endeavour, love, gentleness and sacrifice for others. The stars would bring it—starlight don't you see? One might weave starlight in and out everywhere—use it as the symbol of sympathy—and—er—so on—"

Rogers again lost the clue. Another strangely familiar picture, and then another, flashed gorgeously before his inner vision; his mind raced after them, yet never caught them up. They were most curiously familiar. Then, suddenly, he came back and heard his cousin still talking. It was like a subtle plagiarism. Too subtle altogether, indeed, it was for him. He could only stare and listen in amazement.

But the recital grew more and more involved. Perhaps, alone in his work-room, Daddy could unwumble it consistently. He certainly could not tell it. The thread went lost among a dozen other things. The interfering sun had melted it all down in dew and spider gossamer and fairy cotton. . .

"I must go down and work," he said at length, rising and fumbling with the door handle. He seemed disappointed a little. He had given out his ideas so freely, perhaps too freely. Rogers divined he had not sympathised enough. His manner had been shamefully absent-minded. The absent-mindedness was really the highest possible praise, but the author did not seem to realise it.

"It's glorious, my dear fellow, glorious," Rogers added emphatically. "You've got a big idea, and you can write it too. You will." He said it with conviction. "You touch my heart as you tell it. I congratulate you. Really I do."

There was no mistaking the sincerity of his words and tone. The other came back a step into the room again. He stroked his beard and felt the crisp, hard crumb. He picked it out, examining it without surprise. It was no unfamiliar thing, perhaps; at any rate, it was an excuse to lower his eyes. Shyness returned upon him.

"Thank you," he said gently; "I'm glad you think so. You see, I sometimes feel—perhaps—my work has rather suffered from—been a little deficient in—the human touch. One must reach people's hearts if one wants big sales. So few have brains. Not that I care for money, or could ever write for money, for that brings its own punishment in loss of inspiration. But of course, with a family to support. . . I *have* a family, you see." He raised his eyes and looked out into the sunshine. "Well, anyhow, I've begun this thing. I shall send it in short form to the *X. Review*. It may attract attention there. And later I can expand it into a volume." He hesitated, examined the crumb closely again, tossed it away, and looked up at his cousin suddenly full in the face. The high enthusiasm flamed back into his eyes again. "Bring the world back to Fairyland, you see!" he concluded with vehemence, "'eh?"

"Glorious!" Surely thought ran about the world like coloured flame, if this was true.

The author turned towards the door. He opened it, then stopped on the threshold and looked round like a person who has lost his way.

"I forgot," he added, "I forgot another thing, one of the chief almost. It's this: there must be a Leader—who shall bring it back. Without the Guide, Interpreter, Pioneer, how shall the world listen or understand, even the little world of Bourcelles?"

"Of course, yes—some big figure—like a priest or prophet, you mean? A sort of Chairman, President, eh?"

"Yes," was the reply, while the eyes flashed fires that almost recaptured forgotten dreams, "but hardly in the way you mean, perhaps. A very simple figure, *I* mean, unconscious of its mighty role. Some one with endless stores of love and sympathy and compassion that have never found an outlet yet, but gone on accumulating and accumulating unexpressed."

"I see, yes." Though he really did not "see" a bit. "But who is there like that here? You'll have to invent him." He remembered his own thought that some principal role was vacant in his Children's Fairy Play. How queer it all was! He stared. "Who is there?" he repeated.

"No one—now. I shall bring her, though."

"*Her!*" exclaimed Rogers with surprise. "You mean a woman?"

"A childless woman," came the soft reply. "A woman with a million children—all unborn." But Rogers did not see the expression of the face. His cousin was on the landing. The door closed softly on the words. The steps went fumbling down the stairs, and presently he heard the door below close too. The key was turned in it.

"A childless woman!" The phrase rang on long after he had gone. What an extraordinary idea! "Bring her here" indeed! Could his cousin mean that some such woman might read his story and come to claim the position, play the vacant role? No, nothing so literal surely. The idea was preposterous. He had heard it said that imaginative folk, writers, painters, musicians, all had a touch of lunacy in them somewhere. He shrugged his shoulders. And what a job it must be, too, the writing of a book! He had never realised it before. A real book, then, meant putting one's heart into sentences, telling one's inmost secrets, confessing one's own ideals with fire and lust and passion. That was the difference perhaps between literature and mere facile invention. His cousin had never dared do this before; shyness prevented; his intellect wove pretty patterns that had no heat of life in them. But now he had discovered a big idea, true as the sun, and able, like the sun, to warm thousands of readers, all ready for it without knowing it. . .

Rogers sat on thinking in the bright spring sunshine, smoking one cigarette after another. For the idea his cousin had wumbled over so fubsily had touched his heart, and for a long time he was puzzled to find the reason. But at length he found it. In that startling phrase "a childless woman" lay the clue. A childless woman was like a vessel with a cargo of exquisite flowers that could never make a port. Sweetening every wind, she yet never comes to land. No harbour welcomes her. She sails endless seas, charged with her freight of undelivered beauty; the waves devour her glory, her pain, her lovely secret all unconfessed. To bring such a woman into port, even imaginatively in a story, or subconsciously in an inner life, was fulfilment of a big, fine, wholesome yearning, sacred in a way, too.

"By George!" he said aloud. He felt strange, great life pour through him. He had made a discovery. . . in his heart. . . deep, deep down.

Something in himself, so long buried it was scarcely recognisable, stirred out of sight and tried to rise. Some flower of his youth that time had hardened, dried, yet never killed, moved gently towards blossoming. It shone. It was still hard a little, like a crystal, glistening down there among shadows that had gathered with the years. And then it suddenly melted, running in a tiny thread of gold among his thoughts into that quiet sea which so rarely in a man may dare the relief of tears. It was a tiny yellow flower, like a daisy that had forgotten to close at night, so that some stray starbeam changed its whiteness into gold.

Forgotten passion, and yearning long denied, stirred in him with that phrase. His cousin's children doubtless had prepared the way. A faded Dream peered softly into his eyes across the barriers of the years. For every woman in the world was a mother, and a childless woman was the grandest, biggest mother of them all. And he had longed for children of his own; he, too, had remained a childless father. A vanished face gazed up into his own. Two vessels, making the same fair harbour, had lost their way, yet still sailed, perhaps, the empty seas. Yet the face he did not quite recognise. The eyes, instead of blue, were amber. . .

And did this explain a little the spell that caught him in this Jura village, perhaps? Were these children, weaving a network so cunningly about his feet, merely scouts and pilots? Was his love for the world of suffering folk, after all, but his love for a wife and children of his own transmuted into wider channels? Denied the little garden he once had planned for it, did it seek to turn the whole big world into a garden? Suppression was impossible; like murder, it must out. A bit of it had even flamed a passage into work and patents and "City" life. For love is life, and life is ever and everywhere one. He thought and thought and thought. A man begins by loving himself; then, losing himself, he loves a woman; next, that love spreads itself over a still bigger field, and he loves his family, his wife and children, and their families again in turn. But, that expression denied, his love inevitably, irrepressibly seeking an outlet, finds it in a Cause, a Race, a Nation, perhaps in the entire world. The world becomes his "neighbour." It was a great Fairy Story. . .

Again his thoughts returned to that one singular sentence. . . and he realised what his cousin meant. Only a childless Mother, some woman charged to the brim with this power of loving to which ordinary expression had been denied, could fill the vacant role in his great Children's Play. No man could do it. He and his cousin were mere "supers" on this stage. His cousin would invent her for his story. He would make her come. His passion would create her. That was what he meant.

Rogers smiled to himself, moving away from the window where the sunshine grew too fierce for comfort. What a funny business it all was, to be sure! And how curiously every one's thinking had intermingled! The children had somehow divined his own imaginings in that Crayfield garden; their father had stolen the lot for his story. It was most extraordinary. And then he remembered Minks, and all his lunatic theories about thought and thought-pictures. The garden scene at Crayfield came back vividly, the one at Charing Cross, in the orchard, too, with the old Vicar, when they had talked beneath the stars. Who among them all was the original sponsor? And which of them had set the ball a-rolling? It was stranger than the story of creation. . . It *was* the story of creation.

Yet he did not puzzle very long. Actors in a play are never puzzled; it is the bewildered audience who ask questions. And Henry Rogers was on the stage. The gauzy curtain hung between him and the outside point of view. He was already deeply involved in Fairyland. . . His feet were in the Net of Stars. . . He was a prisoner.

And that woman he had once dreamed might mother his own children—where was she? Until a few years ago he had still expected, hoped to meet her. One day they would come together. She waited somewhere. It was only recently he had let the dream slip finally from him, abandoned with many another personal ambition.

Idly he picked up a pencil, and before he was aware of it the words ran into lines. It seemed as though his cousin's mood, thought, inspiration, worked through him.

Upon what flowering shore,
'Neath what blue skies
She stands and waits,
It is not mine to know;
Only I know that shore is fair,
Those skies are blue.

Her voice I may not hear,
Nor see her eyes,
Yet there are times
When in the wind she speaks.
When stars and flowers
Tell me of her eyes.
When rivers chant her name.

If ever signs were sure,
I know she waits;
If not, what means this sweetness in the wind,
The singing in the rain, the love in flowers?

What mean these whispers in the air,
This calling from the hills and from the sea?
These tendernesses of the Day and Night?
Unless she waits!

What in the world was this absurd sweetness running in his veins?

He laughed a little. A slight flush, too, came and went its way. The tip of the pencil snapped as he pressed too heavily on it. He had drawn it through the doggerel with impatience, for he suddenly realised that he had told a deep, deep secret to the paper. It had stammered its way out before he was aware of it. This was youth and boyhood strong upon him, the moods of Crayfield that he had set long ago on one side—deliberately. The mood that wrote the Song of the Blue Eyes had returned, waking after a sleep of a quarter of a century.

"What rubbish!" he exclaimed; "I shall be an author next!" He tore it up and, rolling the pieces into a ball, played catch with it. "What waste of energy! Six months ago that energy would have gone into something useful, a patent—perhaps an improvement in the mechanism of—of—" he hesitated, then finished the sentence with a sigh of yearning and another passing flush—"a perambulator!"

He tossed it out of the window and, laughing, leaned out to watch it fall. It bounced upon a head of tousled hair beneath, then flew off sideways in the wind and rattled away faintly among the vines. The head was his cousin's.

"What are you up to?" cried the author, looking up. "I'm not a waste-paper basket." There was a cigarette ash in his beard.

"Sending you ideas," he answered. "I'm coming myself now. Look out!" He was in high spirits again. He believed in that Fairy Princess.

"All right; I've put you in already. Everybody will wonder who Cousinenry is. . ." The untidy head of hair popped in again.

"Hark!" cried Rogers, trying to look round the corner of the house. He edged himself out at a dangerous angle. His ears had caught another sound. There was music in the air.

XIX

The sweet spring winds came laughing down the street, bearing a voice that mingled with their music.

"*Daddy! Daddy! vite; il y a un paquet!*" sounded in a child's excited cry. "It arrives this afternoon. It's got the Edinburgh postmark. Here is the notice. *C'est enorme!*"

The figure of Jimbo shot round the corner, dancing into view. He waved a bit of yellow paper in his hand. A curious pang tore its way into the big man's heart as he saw him—a curious, deep, searching pain that yet left joy all along its trail. Positively moisture dimmed his eyes a second.

But Jimbo belonged to some one else.

Daddy's wumbled head projected instantly again from the window beneath.

"A box?" he asked, equally excited. "A box from Scotland? Why, we had one only last month. Bless their hearts! How little they know what help and happiness. . ." The rest of the sentence disappeared with the head; and a moment later Jimbo was heard scampering up the stairs. Both men went out to meet him.

The little boy was breathless with excitement, yet the spirit of the man of affairs worked strongly in him. He deliberately suppressed hysterics. He spoke calmly as might be, both hands in his trouser-pockets beneath the blouse of blue cotton that stuck out like a ballet skirt all round. The belt had slipped down. His eyes were never still. He pulled one hand out, holding the crumpled paper up for inspection.

"It's a *paquet*," he said, "*comme ca.*" He used French and English mixed, putting the latter in for his cousin's benefit. He had little considerate ways like that. It's coming from Scotland, *et puis ca pese soixante-quinze kilos.* "Oh, it's big. It's enormous. The last one weighed," he hesitated, forgetful, "much, much less," he finished. He paused, looking like a man who has solved a problem by stating it.

"One hundred and fifty pounds," exclaimed his father, just as eager as the boy. "Let me look," and he held his hand out for the advice from the railway. "What *can* be in it?"

"Something for everybody," said Jimbo decidedly. "All the village knows it. It will come by the two o'clock train from Bale, you know."

He gave up the paper unwillingly. It was his badge of office. "That's the paper about it," he added again.

Daddy read out slowly the advice of consignment, with dates and weights and address of sender and recipient, while Jimbo corrected the least mistake. He knew it absolutely by heart.

"There'll be dresses and boots for the girls this time," he announced, "and something big enough for Mother to wear, too. You can tell—"

"How can you tell?" asked Daddy, laughing slyly, immensely pleased about it all.

"Oh, by the weight of the *paquet, comme ca*," was the reply. "It weighs 75 kilos. That means there must be something for Mummy in it."

The author turned towards his cousin, hiding his smile. "It's a box of clothes," he explained, "from my cousins in Scotland, Lady X you know, and her family. Things they give away—usually to their maids and what-not. Awfully good of them, isn't it? They pay the carriage too," he added. It was an immense relief to him.

"Things they can't wear," put in Jimbo, "but *very* good things—suits, blouses, shirts, collars, boots, gloves, and—oh, *toute sorte de choses comme ca*."

"Isn't it nice of 'em," repeated Daddy. It made life easier for him—ever so much easier. "A family like that has such heaps of things. And they always pay the freight. It saves me a pretty penny I can tell you. Why, I haven't bought the girls a dress for two years or more. And Edward's dressed like a lord, I tell you," referring to his eldest boy now at an expensive tutor's. "You can understand the excitement when a box arrives. We call it the Magic Box."

Rogers understood. It had puzzled him before why the children's clothes, Daddy's and Mummy's as well for that matter, were such an incongruous assortment of village or peasant wear, and smart, well-cut garments that bore so obviously the London mark.

"They're very rich indeed," said Jimbo. "They have a motor car. These are the only things that don't fit them. There's not much for me usually; I'm too little yet. But there's lots for the girls and the others." And "the others," it appeared, included the Widow Jequier, the Postmaster and his wife, the carpenter's family, and more than one household in the village who knew the use and value of every centimetre of ribbon. Even the retired governesses got their share. No shred or patch was ever thrown away as useless. The assortment of cast-off clothing furnished Sunday Bests to half the village for weeks to come. A consignment of bullion could not have given half the pleasure and delight that the arrival of a box produced.

But *midi* was ringing, and *dejeuner* had to be eaten first. Like a meal upon the stage, no one ate sincerely; they made a brave pretence, but the excitement was too great for hunger. Every one was in the secret—the Postmaster (he might get another hat out of it for himself) had let it out with a characteristic phrase: "Il y a un paquet pour la famille anglaise!" Yet all feigned ignorance. The children exchanged mysterious glances, and afterwards the governesses hung about the Post Office, simulating the purchase of stamps at two o'clock. But every one watched Daddy's movements, for he it was who would say the significant words.

And at length he said them. "Now, we had better go down to the station," he observed casually, "and see if there is anything for us." His tone conveyed the impression that things often arrived in this way; it was an everyday affair. If there was nothing, it didn't matter much. His position demanded calmness.

"Very well," said Jimbo. "I'll come with you." He strutted off, leading the way.

"And I, and I," cried Monkey and Jane Anne, for it was a half-holiday and all were free. Jimbo would not have appeared to hurry for a kingdom.

"I think I'll join you, too," remarked Mother, biting her lips, "only please go slowly." There were hills to negotiate.

They went off together in a party, and the governesses watched them go. The Widow Jequier put her head out of the window, pretending she was feeding the birds. Her sister popped out opportunely to post a letter. The Postmaster opened his *guichet* window and threw a bit of string into the gutter; and old Miss Waghorn, just then appearing for her daily fifteen minutes' constitutional, saw the procession and asked him, "Who in the world all those people were?" She had completely forgotten them. "Le barometre a monte," he replied, knowing no word of English, and thinking it was her usual question about the weather. He reported daily the state of the barometer. "Vous n'aurez pas besoin d'un parapluie." "Mercy," she said, meaning *merci*.

The train arrived, and with it came the box. They brought it up themselves upon the little hand-cart—*le char*. It might have weighed a ton and contained priceless jewels, the way they tugged and pushed, and the care they lavished on it. Mother puffed behind, hoping there would be something to fit Jimbo this time.

"Shall we rest a moment?" came at intervals on the hill, till at last Monkey said, "Sit on the top, Mummy, and we'll pull you too." And during the rests they examined the exterior, smelt it, tapped it, tried to see between the cracks, and ventured endless and confused conjectures as to its probable contents.

They dragged the hand-cart over the cobbles of the courtyard, and heaved the box up the long stone staircase. It was planted at length on the floor beside the bed of Mlle. Lemaire, that she might witness the scene from her prison windows. Daddy had the greatest difficulty in keeping order, for tempers grow short when excitement is too long protracted. The furniture was moved about to make room. Orders flew about like grape-shot. Everybody got in everybody else's way. But finally the unwieldy packing-case was in position, and a silence fell upon the company.

"My gum, we've put it upside down," said Daddy, red in the face with his exertions. It was the merest chance that there was no wisp of straw yet in his beard.

"Then the clothes will all be inside out," cried Monkey, "and we shall have to stand on our heads."

"You silly," Jane Anne rebuked her, yet half believing it was true, while Jimbo, holding hammer and chisel ready, looked unutterable contempt. "Can't you be serious for a moment?" said his staring blue eyes.

The giant chest was laboriously turned over, the two men straining every muscle in the attempt. Then, after a moment's close inspection again to make quite sure, Daddy spoke gravely. Goodness, how calm he was!

"Jimbo, boy, pass me the hammer and the chisel, will you?"

In breathless silence the lid was slowly forced open and the splintered pieces gingerly removed. Sheets of dirty brown paper and bundles of odorous sacking came into view.

"Perhaps that's all there is," suggested Jinny.

"Ugh! What a whiff!" said Monkey.

"Fold them up carefully and put them in a corner," ordered Mother. Jane Anne religiously obeyed. Oh dear, how slow she was about it!

Then everybody came up very close, heads bent over, hands began to stretch and poke. You heard breathing—nothing more.

"Now, wait your turn," commanded Mother in a dreadful voice, "and let your Father try on everything first." And a roar of laughter made the room echo while Daddy extracted wonder after wonder that were packed in endless layers one upon another.

Perhaps what would have struck an observer most of all would have been the strange seriousness against which the comedy was set. The laughter was incessant, but it was a weighty matter for all that. The bed-ridden woman, who was sole audience, understood that; the parents understood it too. Every article of clothing that could be worn meant a saving, and the economy of a franc was of real importance. The struggles of *la famille anglaise* to clothe and feed and educate themselves were no light affair. The eldest boy, now studying for the consular service, absorbed a third of their entire income. The sacrifices involved for his sake affected each one in countless ways. And for two years now these magic boxes had supplied all his suits and shirts and boots. The Scotch cousins luckily included a boy of his own size who had extravagant taste in clothes. A box sometimes held as many as four excellent suits. Daddy contented himself with one a year—ordered ready-made from the place they called "Chasbakerinhighholborn." Mother's clothes were "wropp in mystery" ever. No one ever discovered where they came from or how she made them. She did. It seemed always the same black dress and velvet blouse.

Gravity and laughter, therefore, mingled in Daddy's face as he drew out one paper parcel after another, opened it, tried the article on himself, and handed it next to be tried on similarly by every one in turn.

And the first extraction from the magic box was a curious looking thing that no one recognised. Daddy unfolded it and placed it solemnly on his head. He longed for things for himself, but rarely found them. He tried on everything, hoping it might "just do," but in the end yielded it with pleasure to the others. He rarely got more than a pair of gloves or a couple of neckties for himself. The coveted suits just missed his size.

Grave as a judge he balanced the erection on his head. It made a towering heap. Every one was puzzled. "It's a motor cap," ventured some one at length in a moment of intuition.

"It's several!" cried Monkey. She snatched the bundle and handed it to Mother. There were four motor caps, neatly packed together. Mother put on each in turn. They were in shades of grey. They became her well.

"You look like a duchess," said Daddy proudly. "You'd better keep them all."

"I think perhaps they'll do," she said, moving to the glass, "if no one else can wear them." She flushed a little and looked self-conscious.

"They want long pins," suggested Jinny. "They'll keep the rain off too, like an umbrella." She laughed and clapped her hands. Mother pinned one on and left it there for the remainder of the afternoon. The unpacking of the case continued.

The next discovery was gloves. The lid of the box looked like a counter in a glove shop. There were gloves of leather and chamois, gauntlets, driving-gloves, and gloves of suede, yellow, brown, and grey. All had been used a little, but all were good. "They'll wash," said Jane Anne. They were set aside in a little heap apart. No one coveted them. It was not worth while. In the forests of Bourcelles gloves were at a discount, and driving a pleasure yet unknown. Jinny, however a little later put on a pair of ladies' suede that caught her fancy, and wore them faithfully to the end of the performance, just to keep her mother's motor cap in countenance.

The main contents of the box were as yet unbroached, however, and when next an overcoat appeared, with velvet collar and smart, turned-up cuffs, Daddy beamed like a boy and was into it before any one could prevent. He went behind a screen. The coat obviously did not fit him, but he tugged and pulled and wriggled his shoulders with an air of "things that won't fit must be made to fit."

"You'll bust the seams! You'll split the buttons! See what's in the pockets!" cried several voices, while he shifted to and fro like a man about to fight.

"It may stretch," he said hopefully. "I think I can use it. It's just what I want." He glanced up at his wife whose face, however, was relentless.

"Maybe," replied the practical mother, "but it's more Edward's build, perhaps." He looked fearfully disappointed, but kept it on. Edward got the best of every box. He went on with the unpacking, giving the coat sly twitches from time to time, as he pulled out blouses, skirts, belts, queer female garments, boots, soft felt hats—the green Homburg he put on at once, as who should dare to take it from him—black and brown Trilbys, shooting-caps, gaiters, flannel shirts, pyjamas, and heaven knows what else besides.

The excitement was prodigious, and the floor looked like a bargain sale. Everybody talked at once; there was no more pretence of keeping order Mlle. Lemaire lay propped against her pillows, watching the scene with feelings between tears and laughter. Each member of the family tried on everything in turn, but yielded the treasures instantly at a word from Mother—"That will do for so and so; this will fit Monkey; Jimbo, you take this," and so on.

The door into the adjoining bedroom was for ever opening and shutting, as the children disappeared with armfuls and reappeared five minutes later, marvellously apparelled. There was no attempt at sorting yet. Blouses and flannel trousers lay upon the floor with boots and motor veils. Every one had something, and the pile set aside for Edward grew apace. Only Jimbo was disconsolate. He was too small for everything; even the ladies' boots were too narrow and too pointed for his little feet. From time to time he rummaged with the hammer and chisel (still held *very* tightly) among the mass of paper at the bottom. But, as usual, there was nothing but gaudy neckties that he could use. And these he did not care about. He said no word, but stood there watching the others and trying to laugh, only keeping the tears back with the greatest difficulty.

From his position in the background Rogers took it all in. He moved up and slipped a ten-franc piece into the boy's hand. "Secretaries don't wear clothes like this," he whispered. "We'll go into town tomorrow and get the sort of thing you want."

Jimbo looked up and stared. He stood on tip-toe to kiss him. "Oh, thank you so much," he said, fearful lest the others should see; and tucked the coin away into a pocket underneath his cotton blouse. A moment later he came back from the corner where he had hid himself to examine it. "But, Cousin Henry," he whispered, utterly astonished, "it's gold." He had thought the coin was a ten-centime piece such as Daddy sometimes gave him. He could not believe it. He had never seen gold before. He ran up and told his parents. His sisters were too excited to be told just then. After that he vanished into the passage without being noticed, and when he returned five minutes later his eyes were suspiciously red. But no one heard him say a word about getting nothing out of the box. He stood aside, with a superior manner and looked quietly on. "It's very nice for the girls," his expression said. His interest in the box had grown decidedly less. He could buy an entire shop for himself now.

"Mother, Daddy, everybody," cried an excited voice, "will you look at me a minute, please! It all fits me perfectly," and Jinny emerged from the bedroom door. She had been trying on. A rough brown dress of Harris tweed became her well; she wore a motor veil about her head, and another was tied round her neck; a white silk blouse, at least one size too large for her, bulged voluminously from beneath the neat tweed jacket. She wore her suede gloves still. "And there's an outside pocket in the skirt, you see." She pulled it up and showed a very pointed pair of brown boots; they were much too long; they looked ridiculous after her square village boots. "I can waggle my toes in them," she explained, strutting to and fro to be admired. "I'm a fashionable monster now!"

But she only held the centre of the stage a minute, for Monkey entered at her heels, bursting with delight in a long green macintosh thrown over another tweed skirt that hid her feet and even trailed behind. A pair of yellow spats were visible sometimes that spread fan-shaped over her boots and climbed half-way up the fat legs.

"It all fits me exaccurately," was her opinion. The sisters went arm in arm about the room, dancing and laughing.

"We're busy blackmailers," cried Jinny, using her latest acquisition which she practised on all possible occasions. "We're in Piccadilly, going to see the Queen for tea."

They tripped over Monkey's train and one of the spats came off in the struggle for recovery. Daddy, in his Homburg hat, looked round and told them sternly to make less noise. Behind a screen he was getting surreptitiously into a suit that Mother had put aside for Edward. He tried on several in this way, hopeful to the last.

"I think this will fit me all right," he said presently, emerging with a grave expression on his puckered face. He seemed uncertain about it. He was solemn as a judge. "You could alter the buttons here and there, you know," and he looked anxiously at his wife. The coat ran up behind, the waistcoat creased badly owing to the strain, and the trousers were as tight as those of a cavalry officer. Anywhere, and any moment, he might burst out into unexpected revelation. "A little alteration," he suggested hopefully, "and it would be all right—don't you think?" And then he added "perhaps."

He turned and showed himself. Even the roar of laughter that greeted his appearance did not quite convince him. He looked like a fat, impoverished bookmaker.

"I think it will fit Edward better," said Mother again without pity, for she did not like to see her husband look foolish before the children. He disappeared behind the screen, but repeated the performance with two other suits. "This striped one seems a little looser," he said; or, "If you'd let out the trousers at the bottom, I think they would do." But in the end all he got from the box was two pairs of pink silk pyjamas, the Homburg hat, several pairs of gloves, spats, and gaiters, and half a dozen neckties that no one else would wear. He made his heap carefully in the corner of the room, and later, when the mess was all cleared up and everybody went off with their respective treasures, he entirely forgot them in his pleasure and admiration of the others. He left them lying in the corner. Riquette slept on them that night, and next morning Jimbo brought them over for him to the carpenter's house. And Edward later magnanimously yielded up two flannel shirts because he had so many left over from the previous box. Also a pair of pumps.

"I've not done so badly after all," was his final matured opinion. "Poor mother! She got nothing but motor caps." Jimbo, however, had made a final discovery of value for himself—of some value, at least. When the empty case was overturned as a last hope, he rummaged among the paper with his hammer and chisel, and found four pairs of golf stockings! The legs fitted him admirably, but the feet were much too big. There was some discussion as to whether they had belonged to a very thin-legged boy with big feet or to a girl who had no calves. Luckily, the former was decided upon, for otherwise they would have given no pleasure to Jimbo. Even as it was, he adopted them chiefly because it pleased his parents. Mother cut off the feet and knitted new ones a little smaller. But there was no mystery about those stockings. No special joy went with them. He had watched Mother knitting too often for that; she could make stockings half asleep.

Two hours later, while Jane Ann and Mother prepared the tea in the Den, Daddy, Jimbo, and Cousin Henry went in a procession to the carpenter's house carrying the piles of clothing in their arms to the astonishment of half the village. They were to be re-sorted there in privacy by the "men," where the "children" could not interfere. The things they could not use were distributed later among the governesses; the Pension and the village also, got their share. And the Postmaster got his hat—a black Trilby. He loved its hue.

And for days afterwards the children hoarded their treasures with unholy joy. What delighted them as much as anything, perhaps, were the coronets upon the pyjamas and the shirts. They thought it was a London or Edinburgh laundry mark. But Jimbo told them otherwise: "It means that Daddy's Cousin is a Lord-and-Waiting, and goes to see the King." This explanation was generally accepted.

The relief to the parents, however, as they sat up in the Den that night and discussed how much this opportune Magic Box had saved them, may be better imagined than described. The sum ran into many,

many francs. Edward had suits now for at least two years. "He's stopped growing," said his mother; "thank goodness," said his father.

And to the long list he prayed for twice a day Jimbo added of his accord, "Ceux qui ont envoye la grosse caisse."

XX

Break up the heavens, O Lord! and far,
Thro' all yon starlight keen,
Draw me, thy bride, a glittering star,
In raiment white and clean.

He lifts me to the golden doors;
The flashes come and go;
All heaven bursts her starry floors,
And strews her lights below.

—St. Agnes' Eve, Tennyson

Miss Waghorn, of late, had been unusually trying, and especially full of complaints. Her poor old memory seemed broken beyond repair. She offered Madame Jequier her weekly payment twice within ten minutes, and was quite snappy about it when the widow declined the second tender.

"But you had the receipt in your hand wizin ten minutes ago, Mees Wag'orn. You took it upstairs. The ink can hardly be now already yet dry." But nothing would satisfy her that she had paid until they went up to her room together and found it after much searching between her Bible and her eternal novel on the writing-table.

"Forgive me, Madame, but you do forget sometimes, don't you?" she declared with amusing audacity. "I like to make quite sure—especially where money is concerned." On entering the room she had entirely forgotten why they came there. She began complaining, instead, about the bed, which had not yet been made. A standing source of grumbling, this; for the old lady would come down to breakfast many a morning, and then go up again before she had it, thinking it was already late in the day. She worried the *pensionnaires* to death, too. It was their duty to keep the salon tidy, and Miss Waghorn would flutter into the room as early as eight o'clock, find the furniture still unarranged, and at once dart out again to scold the girls. These interviews were amusing before they became monotonous, for the old lady's French was little more than "nong pas" attached to an infinitive verb, and the girls' Swiss-German explanations of the alleged neglect of duty only confused her. "Nong pas faire la chambre," she would say, stamping her foot with vexation. "You haven't done the room, though it's nearly dejooner time!" Or else— "Ten minutes ago it was tidy. Look at it now!" while she dragged them in and forced them to put things straight, until some one in authority came and explained gently her mistake. "Oh, excuse me, Madame," she would say then, "but they do forget *so* often." Every one was very patient with her as a rule.

And of late she had been peculiarly meddlesome, putting chairs straight, moving vases, altering the lie of table-cloths and the angle of sofas, opening windows because it was "so stuffy," and closing them a minute later with complaints about the draught, forcing occupants of arm-chairs to get up because the carpet was caught, fiddling with pictures because they were crooked either with floor or ceiling, and never realising that in the old house these latter were nowhere parallel. But her chief occupation was to prevent the children crossing their legs when they sat down, or pulling their dresses lower, with a whispered, "You *must* not cross your legs like that; it isn't ladylike, dear."

She had been very exasperating and interfering. Tempers had grown short. Twice running she had complained about the dreadful noise the *pensionnaires* made at seven o'clock in the morning. "Nong pas creer comme ca!" she called, running down the passage in her dressing-gown and bursting angrily into their rooms without knocking—to find them empty. The girls had left the day before.

But today (the morning after the Star Cave adventure) the old lady was calmer, almost soothed, and at supper she was composed and gentle. Sleep, for some reason, had marvellously refreshed her. Attacks that opened as usual about Cornish Cream or a Man with a long Beard, she repelled easily and quietly. "I've told you that story before, my dear; I know I have." It seemed her mind and memory were more orderly somehow. And the Widow Jequier explained how sweet and good-natured she had been all day—better than for years. "When I took her drops upstairs at eleven o'clock I found her tidying her room; she was sorting her bills and papers. She read me a letter she had written to her nephew to come out and take her home— well written and quite coherent. I've not known her mind so clear for months. Her memory, too. She said she had slept so well. If only it would last, *helas*!"

"There *are* days like that," she added presently, "days when everything goes right and easily. One wakes up happy in the morning and sees only the bright side of things. Hope is active, and one has new courage somehow." She spoke with feeling, her face was brighter, clearer, her mind less anxious. She had planned a visit to the Bank Manager about the mortgages. It had come as an inspiration. It might be fruitless, but she was hopeful, and so knew a little peace. "I wonder why it is," she added, "and what brings these changes into the heart so suddenly."

"Good sleep and sound digestion," Mrs. Campden thought. She expressed her views deliberately like this in order to counteract any growth of fantasy in the children.

"But it is strange," her husband said, remembering his new story; "it may be much deeper than that. While the body sleeps the spirit may get into touch with helpful forces—" His French failed him. He wumbled painfully.

"Thought-forces possibly from braver minds," put in Rogers. "Who knows? Sleep and dreaming have never really been explained." He recalled a theory of Minks.

"*I* dream a great deal," Miss Waghorn observed, eager to take part. "It's delightful, dreaming—if only one could remember!" She looked round the table with challenge in her eager old eyes. But no one took her up. It involved such endless repetition of well-known stories. The Postmaster might have said a word—he looked prepared—but, not understanding English, he went on with his salad instead.

"Life is a dream," observed Monkey, while Jinny seemed uncertain whether she should laugh or take it seriously.

The Widow Jequier overheard her. There was little she did not overhear.

"Coquine!" she said, then quoted with a sentimental sigh:—

La vie est breve,
Un peu d'amour.
Un peu de rive
Et puis—bonjour!

She hung her head sideways a moment for effect. There was a pause all down the long table.

"I'm sure dreams have significance," she went on. "There's more in dreaming than one thinks. They come as warnings or encouragement. All the saints had dreams. I always pay attention to mine."

"Madame, *I* dream a great deal," repeated Miss Waghorn, anxious not to be left out of a conversation in which she understood at least the key-word *reve*; "a very great deal, I may say."

Several looked up, ready to tell nightmares of their own at the least sign of encouragement. The Postmaster faced the table, laying down his knife and fork. He took a deep breath. This time he meant to have his say. But his deliberation always lost him openings.

"*I* don't," exclaimed Jinny, bluntly, five minutes behind the others. "When I'm in bed, I sleep." The statement brought laughter that confused her a little. She loved to define her position. She had defined it. And the Postmaster had lost his chance. Mlle. Sandoz, a governess who was invited to supper as payment for a music lesson given to his boy, seized the opening.

"Last night I dreamed that a bull chased me. Now what did *that* mean, I wonder?"

"That there was no danger since it was only a dream!" said the Postmaster sharply, vexed that he had not told his own.

But no one applauded, for it was the fashion to ignore his observations, unless they had to do with stamps and weights of letters, parcels, and the like. A clatter of voices rose, as others, taking courage, decided to tell experiences of their own; but it was the Postmaster's wife in the hall who won. She had her meals outside with the kitchen maid and her niece, who helped in the Post Office, and she always tried to take part in the conversation from a distance thus. She plunged into a wordy description of a lengthy dream that had to do with clouds, three ravens, and a mysterious face. All listened, most of them in mere politeness, for as cook she was a very important personage who could furnish special dishes on occasion—but her sister listened as to an oracle. She nodded her head and made approving gestures, and said, "Aha, you see," or "Ah, voila!" as though that helped to prove the importance of the dream, if not its actual truth. And the sister came to the doorway so that no one could escape. She stood there in her apron, her face hot and flushed still from the kitchen.

At length it came to an end, and she looked round her, hoping for a little sympathetic admiration, or at least for expressions of wonder and interest. All waited for some one else to speak. Into the pause came her husband's voice, "Je n'ai pas de sel."

There was no resentment. It was an everyday experience. The spell was broken instantly. The cook retired to her table and told the dream all over again with emphatic additions to her young companions. The Postmaster got his salt and continued eating busily as though dreams were only fit for women and children to talk about. And the English group began whispering excitedly of their Magic Box and all it had contained. They were tired of dreams and dreaming.

Tante Jeanne made a brave effort to bring the conversation back to the key of sentiment and mystery she loved, but it was not a success.

"At any rate I'm certain one's mood on going to bed decides the kind of dream that comes," she said into the air. "The last thought before going to sleep is very important. It influences the adventures of the soul when it leaves the body every night."

For this was a tenet of her faith, although she always forgot to act upon it. Only Miss Waghorn continued the train of ideas this started, with a coherence that surprised even herself. Somehow the jabber about dreams, though in a language that only enabled her to catch its general drift, had interested her uncommonly. She seemed on the verge of remembering something. She had listened with patience, a look of peace upon her anxious old face that was noticed even by Jane Anne. "It smoothed her out," was her verdict afterwards, given only to herself though. "Everything is a sort of long unfinished dream to her, I suppose, at *that* age."

While the *famille anglaise* renewed noisily their excitement of the Magic Box, and while the talk in the hall went on and on, re-hashing the details of the cook's marvellous experience, and assuming entirely new proportions, Miss Waghorn glanced about her seeking whom she might devour—and her eye caught Henry Rogers, listening as usual in silence.

"Ah," she said to him, "but *I* look forward to sleep. I might say I long for it." She sighed very audibly. It was both a sigh for release and a faint remembrance that last night her sleep had been somehow deep and happy, strangely comforting.

"It is welcome sometimes, isn't it?" he answered, always polite and rather gentle with her.

"Sleep unravels, yes," she said, vaguely as to context, yet with a querulous intensity. It was as if she caught at the enthusiasm of a connected thought somewhere. "I might even say it unties," she added, encouraged by his nod, "unties knots—if you follow me."

"It does, Miss Waghorn. Indeed, it does." Was this a precursor of the Brother with the Beard, he wondered? "Untied knots" would inevitably start her off. He made up his mind to listen to the tale with interest for the twentieth time if it came. But it didn't come.

"I am very old and lonely, and *I* need the best," she went on happily, half saying it to herself.

Instantly he took her up—without surprise too. It was like a dream.

"Quite so. The rest, the common stuff—"

"Is good enough—" she chimed in quickly—

"For Fraulein, or for baby, or for mother," he laughed.

"Or any other," chuckled Miss Waghorn.

"Who needs a bit of sleep—"

"But yet can do without it—" she carried it on.

Then both together, after a second's pause—

"If they must—" and burst out laughing.

Goodness, how did *she* know the rhyme? Was it everywhere? Was thought running loose like wireless messages to be picked up by all who were in tune for acceptance?

"Well, I never!" he heard her exclaim, "if that's not a nursery rhyme of my childhood that I've not heard for sixty years and more! I declare," she added with innocent effrontery, "I've not heard it since I was ten years old. And I was born in '37—the year—"

"Just fancy!" he tried to stop her.

"Queen Victoria came to the throne."

"Strange," he said more to himself than to any one else. She did not contradict him.

"You or me?" asked Monkey, who overheard.

"All of us," he answered. "We all think the same things. It's a dream, I believe; the whole thing is a dream."

"It's a fact though," said Miss Waghorn with decision, "and now I must go and write my letters, and then finish a bit of lace I'm doing. You will excuse me?" She rose, made a little bow, and left the table.

Mother watched her go. "What *has* come over the old lady?" she thought. "She seems to be getting back her mind and memory too. How very odd!"

In the afternoon Henry Rogers had been into Neuchatel. It seemed he had some business there of a rather private nature. He was very mysterious about it, evading several offers to accompany him, and after supper he retired early to his own room in the carpenter's house. And, since he now was the principal attraction, a sort of magnet that drew the train of younger folk into his neighbourhood, the Pension emptied, and the English family, deprived of their leader, went over to the Den.

"Partir a l'anglaise," laughed the Widow Jequier, as she saw them file away downstairs; and then she sighed. Some day, when the children were older and needed a different education, they would all go finally. Down these very stairs they would go into the street. She loved them for themselves, but, also, the English family was a permanent source of income to her, and the chief. They stayed on in the winter, when boarders were few and yet living expenses doubled. She sighed, and fluttered into her tiny room to take her finery off, finery that had once been worn in Scotland and had reached her by way of Cook and *la petite vitesse* in the Magic Box.

And presently she fluttered out again and summoned her sister. The Postmaster had gone to bed; the kitchen girl was washing up the last dishes; Miss Waghorn would hardly come down again. The salon was deserted.

"Come, Anita," she cried, yet with a hush of excitement in her voice, "we will have an evening of it. Bring the *soucoupe* with you, while I prepare the little table." In her greasy kitchen apron Anita came. Zizi, her boy, came with her. Madame Jequier, with her flowing garment that was tea-gown, garden-dress, and dressing-gown all in one, looked really like a witch, her dark hair all askew and her eyes shining with mysterious anticipation. "We'll ask the spirits for help and guidance," she said to herself, lest the boy should overhear. For Zizi often helped them with their amateur planchette, only they told him it was electricity: *le magnetisme*, *le fluide*, was the term they generally made use of. Its vagueness covered all possible explanations with just the needed touch of confusion and suggestion in it.

They settled down in a corner of the room, where the ivy from the ceiling nearly touched their heads. The small round table was produced; the saucer, with an arrow pencilled on its edge, was carefully placed upon the big sheet of paper which bore the letters of the alphabet and the words *oui* and *non* in the corners. The light behind them was half veiled by ivy; the rest of the old room lay in comparative darkness; through the half-opened door a lamp shone upon the oil-cloth in the hall, showing the stains and the worn, streaked patches where the boards peeped through. The house was very still.

They began with a little prayer—to *ceux qui ecoutent*,—and then each of them placed a finger on the rim of the upturned saucer, waiting in silence. They were a study in darkness, those three pointing fingers.

"Zizi, tu as beaucoup de fluide ce soir, oui?" whispered the widow after a considerable interval.

"Oh, comme d'habitude," he shrugged his shoulders. He loved these mysterious experiments, but he never claimed much *fluide* until the saucer moved, jealous of losing his reputation as a storehouse of this strange, human electricity.

Yet behind this solemn ritual, that opened with prayer and invariably concluded with hope renewed and courage strengthened, ran the tragic element that no degree of comedy could kill. In the hearts of the two old women, ever fighting their uphill battle with adversity, burned the essence of big faith, the faith that plays with mountains. Hidden behind the curtain, an indulgent onlooker might have smiled, but tears would have wet his eyes before the smile could have broadened into laughter. Tante Jeanne, indeed, *had* heard that the subconscious mind was held to account for the apparent intelligence that occasionally betrayed itself in the laboriously spelled replies; she even made use of the word from time to time to baffle Zizi's too importunate inquiries. But after *le subconscient* she always tacked on *fluide*, *magnetisme*, or *electricite* lest he should be frightened, or she should lose her way. And of course she held to her belief that spirits produced the phenomena. A subconscious mind was a cold and comfortless idea.

And, as usual, the saucer told them exactly what they had desired to know, suggested ways and means that hid already in the mind of one or other, yet in stammered sentences that included just enough surprise or turn of phrase to confirm their faith and save their self-respect. It was their form of prayer, and with whole hearts they prayed. Moreover, they acted on what was told them. Had they discovered that it was merely the content of their subconscious mind revealing thus its little hopes and fears, they would have lost their chief support in life. God and religion would have suffered a damaging eclipse. Big scaffolding in their lives would have collapsed.

Doubtless, Tante Jeanne did not knowingly push the saucer, neither did the weighty index finger of the concentrated cook deliberately exert muscular pressure. Nor, similarly, was Zizi aware that the weight of his entire hand helped to urge the dirty saucer across the slippery surface of the paper in whatever direction his elders thus indicated. But one and all knew "subconsciously" the exact situation of consonants and vowels—

that *oui* lay in the right-hand corner and *non* in the left. And neither Zizi nor his mother dared hint to their leader not to push, because she herself monopolised that phrase, saying repeatedly to them both, "mais il ne faut *pas* pousser! Legerement avec les doigts, toujours tres legerement! Sans ca il n'y a pas de valeur, tu comprends!" Zizi inserted an occasional electrical question. It was discreetly ignored always.

They asked about the Bank payments, the mortgages, the future of their much-loved old house, and of themselves; and the answers, so vague concerning any detailed things to come, were very positive indeed about the Bank. They were to go and interview the Manager three days from now. They had already meant to go, only the date was undecided; the corroboration of the spirits was required to confirm it. This settled it. Three days from tonight!

"Tu vois!" whispered Tante Jeanne, glancing mysteriously across the table at her sister. "Three days from now! That explains your dream about the three birds. Aha, tu vois!" She leaned back, supremely satisfied. And the sister gravely bowed her head, while Zizi looked up and listened intently, without comprehension. He felt a little alarm, perhaps, tonight.

For this night there *was* indeed something new in the worn old ritual. There was a strange, uncalculated element in it all, unexpected, and fearfully thrilling to all three. Zizi for the first time had his doubts about its being merely electricity.

"C'est d'une puissance extraordinaire," was the widow's whispered, eager verdict.

"C'est que j'ai enormement de fluide ce soir," declared Zizi, with pride and confidence, yet mystified. The other two exchanged frequent glances of surprise, of wonder, of keen expectancy and anticipation. There was certainly a new "influence" at work tonight. They even felt a touch of faint dread. The widow, her ruling passion strong even before the altar, looked down anxiously once or twice at her disreputable attire. It was vivid as that—this acute sense of another presence that pervaded the room, not merely hung about the little table. She could be "invisible" to the Pension by the magic of old-established habit, but she could not be so to the true Invisibles. And they saw her in this unbecoming costume. She forgot, too, the need of keeping Zizi in the dark. He must know some day. What did it matter when?

She tidied back her wandering hair with her free hand, and drew the faded garment more closely round her neck.

"Are you cold?" asked her sister with a hush in her voice; "you feel the cold air—all of a sudden?"

"I do, *maman*," Zizi answered. "It's blowing like a wind across my hand. What is it?" He was shivering. He looked over his shoulder nervously.

There was a heavy step in the hall, and a figure darkened the doorway. All three gave a start.

"J'ai sommeil," announced the deep voice of the Postmaster. This meant that the boy must come to bed. It was the sepulchral tone that made them jump perhaps. Zizi got up without a murmur; he was glad to go, really. He slept in the room with his parents. His father, an overcoat thrown over his night things, led him away without another word. And the two women resumed their seance. The saucer moved more easily and swiftly now that Zizi had gone. "C'est done *toi* qui as le fluide," each said to the other.

But in the excitement caused by this queer, new element in the proceedings, the familiar old routine was forgotten. Napoleon and Marie Antoinette were brushed aside to make room for this important personage who suddenly descended upon the saucer from an unknown star with the statement—it took half an hour to spell—"Je viens d'une etoile tres eloignee qui n'a pas encore de nom."

"There *is* a starry light in the room. It was above your head just now," whispered the widow, enormously excited. "I saw it plainly." She was trembling.

"That explains the clouds in my dream," was the tense reply, as they both peered round them into the shadows with a touch of awe. "Now, give all your attention. This has an importance, but, you know, an importance—" She could not get the degree of importance into any words. She looked it instead, leaving the sentence eloquently incomplete.

For, certainly, into the quaint ritual of these two honest, troubled old women there crept then a hint of something that was uncommon and uplifting. That it came through themselves is as sure as that it spelt out detailed phrases of encouragement and guidance with regard to their coming visit to the Bank. That they both were carried away by it into joy and the happiness of sincere relief of mind is equally a fact. That their receptive mood attuned them to overhear subconsciously messages of thought that flashed across the night from another mind in sympathy with their troubles—a mind hard at work that very moment in the carpenter's house—was not known to them; nor would it have brought the least explanatory comfort even if they had been told of it. They picked up these starry telegrams of unselfish thinking that flamed towards them through the midnight sky from an eager mind elsewhere busily making plans for their benefit. And, reaching them subconsciously, their deep subconsciousness urged the dirty saucer to the spelling of them, word by word and letter by letter. The flavour of their own interpretation, of course, crept in to mar, and sometimes to obliterate. The instruments were gravely imperfect. But the messages came through. And with them came the great feeling that the Christian calls answered prayer. They had such absolute faith. They had belief.

"Go to the Bank. Help awaits you there. And I shall go with you to direct and guide." This was the gist of that message from "une etoile tres eloignee."

They copied it out in violet ink with a pen that scratched like the point of a pin. And when they stole upstairs to bed, long after midnight, there was great joy and certainty in their fighting old hearts. There was a perfume of flowers, of lilacs and wistaria in the air, as if the whole garden had slipped in by the back door and was unable to find its way out again. They dreamed of stars and starlight.

XXI

La vie est un combat qu'ils ont change en fete.

—*Lei Elus*, E. VERHAIREN

The excitement a few days later spread through the village like a flame. People came out of their way to steal a glance at the Pension that now, for the first time in their—memory, was free of debt. Gygi, tolling the bell at *midi*, forgot to stop, as he peered through the narrow window in the church tower and watched the Widow Jequier planting and digging recklessly in her garden. Several came running down the street, thinking it was a warning of fire.

But the secret was well kept; no one discovered who had worked the miracle. Pride sealed the lips of the beneficiaries themselves, while the inhabitants of the Citadelle, who alone shared the knowledge, kept the facts secret, as in honour bound. Every one wondered, however, for every one knew the sum ran into several thousand francs; and a thousand francs was a fortune; the rich man in the corner house, who owned so many vineyards, and was reputed to enjoy an income of ten thousand francs a year, was always referred to as "le million naire." And so the story spread that Madame Jequier had inherited a fortune, none knew whence. The tradespeople treated her thereafter with a degree of respect that sweetened her days till the end of life.

She had come back from the Bank in a fainting condition, the sudden joy too much for her altogether. A remote and inaccessible air pervaded her, for all the red of her inflamed eyes and tears. She was aloof from the world, freed at last from the ceaseless, gnawing anxiety that for years had eaten her life out. The spirits had justified themselves, and faith and worship had their just reward. But this was only the first, immediate effect: it left her greater than it found her, this unexpected, huge relief—brimming with new sympathy for others. She doubled her gifts. She planned a wonderful new garden. That very night she ordered such a quantity of bulbs and seedlings that to this day they never have been planted.

Her interview with Henry Rogers, when she called at the carpenter's house in all her finery, cannot properly be told, for it lay beyond his powers of description. Her sister accompanied her; the Postmaster, too, snatched fifteen minutes from his duties to attend. The ancient tall hat, worn only at funerals as a rule, was replaced by the black Trilby that had been his portion from the Magic Box, as he followed the excited ladies at a reasonable distance. "You had better show yourself," his wife suggested; "Monsieur Rogairs would like to see you with us—to know that you are there." Which meant that he was not to interfere with the actual thanksgiving, but to countenance the occasion with his solemn presence. And, indeed, he did not go upstairs. He paced the road beneath the windows during the interview, looking exactly like a professional mourner waiting for the arrival of the hearse.

"My dear old friend—friends, I mean," said Rogers in his fluent and very dreadful French, "if you only knew what a pleasure it is to *me*—It is *I* who should thank you for giving me the opportunity, not you who should thank me." The sentence broke loose utterly, wandering among intricacies of grammar and subjunctive moods that took his breath away as he poured it out. "I was only afraid you would think it unwarrantable interference. I am delighted that you let me do it. It's such a little thing to do."

Both ladies instantly wept. The Widow came closer with a little rush. Whether Rogers was actually embraced, or no, it is not stated officially.

"It is a loan, of course, it is a loan," cried the Widow.

"It is a present," he said firmly, loathing the scene.

"It's a part repayment for all the kindness you showed me here as a boy years and years ago." Then, remembering that the sister was not known to him in those far-away days, he added clumsily, "and since—I came back. . . And now let's say no more, but just keep the little secret to ourselves. It is nobody's business but our own."

"A present!" gasped both ladies to one another, utterly overcome; and finding nothing else to embrace, they flung their arms about each other's necks and praised the Lord and wept more copiously than ever. . . "Grand ciel" was heard so frequently, and so loudly, that Madame Michaud, the carpenter's wife, listening on the stairs, made up her mind it was a quarrel, and wondered if she ought to knock at the door and interfere.

"I see your husband in the road," said Rogers, tapping at the window. "I think he seems waiting for you. Or perhaps he has a telegram for me, do you think?" He bowed and waved his hand, smiling as the Postmaster looked up in answer to the tapping and gravely raised his Trilby hat.

"There now, he's calling for you. Do not keep him waiting—I'm sure—" he didn't know what to say or how else to get them out. He opened the door. The farewells took some time, though they would meet an hour later at *dejeuner* as usual.

"At least you shall pay us no more *pension*," was the final sentence as they flounced downstairs, so happy and excited that they nearly tumbled over each other, and sharing one handkerchief to dry their tears.

"Then I shall buy my own food and cook it here," he laughed, and somehow managed to close his door upon the retreating storm. Out of the window he saw the procession go back, the sombre figure of the Postmaster twenty yards behind the other two.

And then, with joy in his heart, though a sigh of relief upon his lips—there may have been traces of a lump somewhere in his throat as well, but if so, he did not acknowledge it—he turned to his letters, and found among them a communication from Herbert Montmorency Minks, announcing that he had found an ideal site, and that it cost so and so much per acre—also that the County Council had made no difficulties. There was a hint, moreover—a general flavour of resentment and neglect at his master's prolonged absence—that it would not be a bad thing for the great Scheme if Mr. Rogers could see his way to return to London "before very long."

"Bother the fellow!" thought he; "what a nuisance he is, to be sure!"

And he answered him at once. "Do not trouble about a site just yet," he wrote; "there is no hurry for the moment." He made a rapid calculation in his head. He had paid those mortgages out of capital, and the sum represented just about the cost of the site Minks mentioned. But results were immediate. There was no loss, no waste in fees and permits and taxes. Each penny did its work.

"There's the site gone, anyhow," he laughed to himself. "The foundation will go next, then the walls. But, at any rate, they needed it. The Commune Charity would have had 'em at the end of the month. They're my neighbours after all. And I must find out from them who else in the village needs a leg up. For these people are worth helping, and I can see exactly where every penny goes."

Bit by bit, as it would seem, the great Scheme for Disabled Thingumagigs was being undermined.

XXII

And those who were good shall be happy.
They shall sit in a golden chair;
They shall splash at a ten-league canvas
With brushes of comets' hair.
They shall have real saints to paint from—
Magdalene, Peter, and Paul;
They shall work for an age at a sitting
And never get tired at all.

And only the Master shall praise them,
And only the Master shall blame;
And no one shall work for money,
And no one shall work for fame;
But each for the joy of the working,
And each in his separate star,
Shall draw the thing as he sees it
For the God of things as they are,

—R. KIPLING

And meanwhile, as May ran laughing to meet June, an air of coloured wonder spread itself about the entire village. Rogers had brought it with him from that old Kentish garden somehow. His journey there had opened doors into a region of imagination and belief whence fairyland poured back upon his inner world, transfiguring common things. And this transfiguration he unwittingly put into others too. Through this very ordinary man swept powers that usually are left behind with childhood. The childhood aspect of the world invaded all who came in contact with him, enormous, radiant, sparkling, charged with questions of wonder and enchantment. And every one felt it according to their ability of reconstruction. Yet he himself had not the least idea that he did it all. It was a reformation, very tender, soft, and true.

For wonder, of course, is the basis of all inquiry. Interpretation varies, facts remain the same; and to interpret is to recreate. Wonder leads to worship. It insists upon recreation, prerogative of all young life. The Starlight Express ran regularly every night, Jimbo having constructed a perfect time-table that answered all requirements, and was sufficiently elastic to fit instantly any scale that time and space demanded. Rogers and the children talked of little else, and their adventures in the daytime seemed curiously fed by details of information gleaned elsewhere.

But where? The details welled up in one and all, though whence they came remained a mystery. "I believe we dream a lot of it," said Jimbo. "It's a lot of dreams we have at night, comme fa." He had made a complete map of railway lines, with stations everywhere, in forests, sky, and mountains. He carried stations in his pocket, and just dropped one out of the carriage window whenever a passenger shouted, "Let's stop here." But Monkey, more intellectual, declared it was "all Cousinenry's invention and make-up," although she asked more questions than all the others put together. Jinny, her sister, stared and listened with her puzzled, moth-like expression, while Mother watched and marvelled cautiously from a distance. In one and all, however, the famished sense of wonder interpreted life anew. It named the world afresh—the world of common things. It subdued the earth unto itself. What a mind creates it understands. Through the familiar these adventurers trace lines of discovery into the unfamiliar. They understood. They were up to their waists in wonder. There was still disorder, of course, in their great reconstruction, but that was where the exciting fun came in; for disorder involves surprise. Any moment out might pop the unexpected—event or person.

Cousin Henry was easily leader now. While Daddy remained absorbed with his marvellous new story, enthusiastic and invisible, they ran about the world at the heels of this "busy engineer," as Jane Ann entitled him. He had long ago told them, with infinite and exaccurate detail, of his journey to the garden and his rediscovery of the sprites, forgotten during his twenty years of business life. And these sprites were as familiar to them now as those of their own childhood. They little knew that at night they met and talked with them. Daddy had put them all into the Wumble Book, achieving mediocre success with the rhymes, but amply atoning with the illustrations. The Woman of the Haystack was evidently a monster pure and simple, till Jinny announced that she merely had "elephantitis," and thus explained her satisfactorily. The Lamplighter, with shining feet, taking enormous strides from Neuchatel to a London slum, putting fire into eyes and hearts *en route*, thrilled them by his radiant speed and ubiquitous activity, while his doggerel left them coldly questioning. For the rhymes did *not* commend themselves to their sense of what was proper in the use of words. His natural history left them unconvinced, though the anatomy of the drawing fascinated them.

> *He walked upon his toes*
> *As softly as a saying does,*
> *For so the saying goes.*

That he "walked upon his toes" was all right, but that he "walked softly as a saying" meant nothing, even when explained that "thus the saying goes."

"Poor old Daddy," was Jinny's judgment; "he's got to write something. You see, he is an author. Some day he'll get his testimonial."

It was Cousin Henry who led them with a surer, truer touch. He always had an adventure up his sleeve—something their imaginations could accept and recreate. Each in their own way, they supplied interpretations as they were able.

Every walk they took together furnished the germ of an adventure.

"But I'm not exciting today," he would object thirsting for a convincing compliment that should persuade him to take them out. Only the compliment never came quite as he hoped.

"Everybody's exciting somewhere," said Monkey, leading the way and knowing he would follow. "We'll go to the Wind Wood."

Jimbo took his hand then, and they went. Corners of the forest had names now, born of stories and adventures he had placed there—the Wind Wood, the Cuckoo Wood, where Daddy could not sleep because "the beastly cuckoo made such a noise"; the Wood where Mother Fell, and so on. No walk was wholly unproductive.

And so, one evening after supper, they escaped by the garden, crossed the field where the standing hay came to their waists, and climbed by forest paths towards the Wind Wood. It was a spot where giant pines stood thinly, allowing a view across the lake towards the Alps. The moss was thick and deep. Great boulders, covered with lichen, lay about, and there were fallen trees to rest the back against. Here he had told them once his vision of seeing the wind, and the name had stuck; for the story had been very vivid, and every time they felt the wind or heard it stirring in the tree-tops, they expected to see it too. There were blue winds, black winds, and winds—violent these—of purple and flaming scarlet.

They lay down, and Cousinenry made a fire. The smoke went up in thin straight lines of blue, melting into the sky. The sun had set half an hour before, and the flush of gold and pink was fading into twilight. The glamour of Bourcelles dropped down upon all three. They ought to have been in bed—hence the particular enjoyment.

"Are you getting excited now?" asked Monkey, nestling in against him.

"Hush!" he said, "can't you hear it coming?"

"The excitement?" she inquired under her breath.

"No, the Night. Keep soft and silent—if you can."

"Tell us, please, at once," both children begged him instantly, for the beauty of the place and hour demanded explanation, and explanation, of course, must be in story or adventure form. The fire crackled faintly; the smell crept out like incense; the lines of smoke coiled upwards, and seemed to draw the tree-stems with them. Indeed they formed a pattern together, big thick trunks marking the uprights at the corners, and wavy smoke lines weaving a delicate structure in between them. It was a kind of growing, moving scaffolding. Saying nothing, Cousin Henry pointed to it with his finger. He traced its general pattern for them in the air.

"That's the Scaffolding of the Night beginning," he whispered presently, feeling adventure press upon him.

"Oh, I say," said Jimbo, sitting up, and pretending as usual more comprehension than he actually possessed. But his sister instantly asked, "What is it—the Scaffolding of the Night? A sort of cathedral, you mean?"

How she divined his thought, and snatched it from his mind always, this nimble-witted child! His germ developed with a bound at once.

"More a palace than a cathedral," he whispered. "Night is a palace, and has to be built afresh each time. Twilight rears the scaffolding first, then hangs the Night upon it. Otherwise the darkness would simply fall in lumps, and lie about in pools and blocks, unfinished—a ruin instead of a building. Everything must have a scaffolding first. Look how beautifully it's coming now," he added, pointing, "each shadow in its place, and all the lines of grey and black fitting exaccurately together like a skeleton. Have you never noticed it before?"

Jimbo, of course, *had* noticed it, his manner gave them to understand, but had not thought it worth while mentioning until his leader drew attention to it.

"Just as trains must have rails to run on," he explained across Cousinenry's intervening body to Monkey, "or else there'd be accidents and things all the time."

"And night would be a horrid darkness like a plague in Egypt," she supposed, adroitly defending herself and helping her cousin at the same time. "Wouldn't it?" she added, as the shadows drew magically nearer from the forest and made the fire gradually grow brighter. The children snuggled closer to their cousin's comforting bulk, shivering a little. The woods went whispering together. Night shook her velvet skirts out.

"Yes, everything has its pattern," he answered, "from the skeleton of a child or a universe to the outline of a thought. Even a dream must have its scaffolding," he added, feeling their shudder and leading it towards fun and beauty. "Insects, birds, and animals all make little scaffoldings with their wee emotions, especially kittens and butterflies. Engine-drivers too," for he felt Jimbo's hand steal into his own and go to sleep there, "but particularly little beasties that live in holes under stones and in fields.

> When a little mouse in wonder
> Flicks its whiskers at the thunder,

it makes a tiny scaffolding behind which it hides in safety, shuddering. Same with Daddy's stories. Thinking and feeling does the trick. Then imagination comes and builds it up solidly with bricks and wall-papers. . ."

He told them a great deal more, but it cannot be certain that they heard it all, for there were other Excitements about besides their cousin—the fire, the time, the place, and above all, this marvellous coming of the darkness. They caught words here and there, but Thought went its own independent way with each little eager mind. He had started the machinery going, that was all. Interpretation varied; facts remained the same. And meanwhile twilight brought the Scaffolding of Night before their eyes.

"You can see the lines already," he murmured sleepily, "like veins against the sunset. . . Look!"

All saw the shadowy slim rafters slip across the paling sky, mapping its emptiness with intricate design. Like an enormous spider's web of fine dark silk it bulged before the wind. The trellis-work, slung from the sky, hung loose. It moved slowly, steadily, from east to west, trailing grey sheets of dusk that hung from every filament. The maze of lines bewildered sight. In all directions shot the threads of coming darkness, spun from the huge body of Night that still hid invisible below the horizon.

"They're fastening on to everything... look!" whispered Cousin Henry, kicking up a shower of sparks with his foot. "The Pattern's being made before your eyes! Don't you see the guy ropes?"

And they saw it actually happen. From the summits of the distant Alps ran filmy lines of ebony that knotted themselves on to the crests of the pines beside them. There were so many no eye could follow them. They flew and darted everywhere, dropping like needles from the sky itself, sewing the tent of darkness on to the main supports, and threading the starlight as they came. Night slowly brought her beauty and her mystery upon the world. The filmy pattern opened. There was a tautness in the lines that made one feel they would twang with delicate music if the wind swept its hand more rapidly across them. And now and again all vibrated, each line making an ellipse between its fastened ends, then gradually settling back to its thin, almost invisible bed. Cables of thick, elastic darkness steadied them.

How much of it all the children realised themselves, or how much flashed into them from their cousin's mind, is of course a thing not even a bat can tell.

"Is that why bats fly in such a muddle? Like a puzzle?"

"Of course," he said. The bats were at last explained.

They built their little pictures for themselves. No living being can lie on the edge of a big pine forest when twilight brings the darkness without the feeling that everything becomes too wonderful for words. The children as ever fed his fantasy, while he thought he did it all himself. Dusk wore a shroud to entangle the too eager stars, and make them stay.

"I never noticed it before," murmured Monkey against his coat sleeve. "Does it happen every night like this?"

"You only see it if you look very closely," was the low reply. "You must think hard, very hard. The more you think, the more you'll see."

"But really," asked Jimbo, "it's only—*crepuscule, comme ca,* isn't it?" And his fingers tightened on his leader's hand.

"Dusk, yes," answered Cousin Henry softly, "only dusk. But people everywhere are watching it like ourselves, and thinking feather thoughts. You can see the froth of stars flung up over the crest of Night. People are watching it from windows and fields and country roads everywhere, wondering what makes it so beautiful. It brings yearnings and long, long desires. Only a few like ourselves can see the lines of scaffolding, but everybody who thinks about it, and loves it, makes it more real for others to see, too. Daddy's probably watching it too from his window."

"I wonder if Jinny ever sees it," Monkey asked herself.

But Jimbo knew. "She's in it," he decided. "She's always in places like that; that's where she lives."

The children went on talking to each other under their breath, and while they did so Cousin Henry entered their little wondering minds. Or, perhaps, they entered his. It is difficult to say. Not even an owl, who is awfully wise about everything to do with night and darkness, could have told for certain. But, anyhow, they all three saw more or less the same thing. The way they talked about it afterwards proves that. Their minds apparently merged, or else there was one big mirror and two minor side-reflections of it. It was their cousin's interpretation, at any rate, that they remembered later. They brought the material for his fashioning.

"Look!" cried Monkey, sitting up, "there are millions and millions now—lines everywhere—pillars and squares and towers. It's like a city. I can see lamps in every street—"

"That's stars," interrupted Jimbo. The stars indeed were peeping here and there already. "I feel up there," he added, "my inside, I mean—up among the stars and lines and sky-things."

"That's the mind wandering," explained the eldest child of the three. "Always follow a wandering mind. It's quite safe. Mine's going presently too. We'll all go off together."

Several little winds, released by darkness, passed them just then on their way out of the forest. They gathered half a dozen sparks from the fire to light them on their way, and brought cool odours with them from the deepest recesses of the trees—perfumes no sunlight ever finds. And just behind them came a big white moth, booming and whirring softly. It darted to and fro to find the trail, then vanished, so swiftly that no one saw it go.

"He's pushing it along," said Jimbo.

"Or fastening the lines," his sister thought, "you see he hovers in one place, then darts over to another."

"That's fastening the knots," added Jimbo.

"No; he's either an Inspector or a Pathfinder," whispered Cousin Henry, "I don't know exactly which. They show the way the scaffolding goes. Moths, bats, and owls divide the work between them somehow." He sat up suddenly to listen, and the children sat up with him. "Hark!" he added, "do you hear that?"

Sighings and flutterings rose everywhere about them, and overhead the fluffy spires of the tree-tops all bent one way as the winds went foraging across the night. Majestically the scaffolding reared up and towered through the air, while sheets of darkness hung from every line, and trailed across the earth like gigantic sails from some invisible vessel. Loose and enormous they gradually unfolded, then suddenly swung free and dropped with a silent dip and rush. Night swooped down upon the leagues of Jura forest. She spread her tent across the entire range.

The threads were fastened everywhere now, and the uprights all in place. Moths were busy in all directions, showing the way, while bats by the dozen darted like black lightning from corner to corner, making sure that every spar and beam was fixed and steady. So exquisitely woven was the structure that it moved past them overhead without the faintest sound, yet so frail and so elastic that the whirring of the moths sent ripples of quivering movement through the entire framework.

"Hush!" murmured Rogers, "we're properly inside it now. Don't think of anything in particular. Just follow your wandering minds and wait." The children lay very close against him. He felt their warmth and the breathing of their little bosoms. All three moved sympathetically within the rhythm of the dusk. The "inside" of each went floating up into the darkening sky.

The general plan of the scaffolding they clearly made out as they passed among its myriad, mile-long rafters, but the completed temple, of course, they never saw. Black darkness hides that ever. Night's secret mystery lies veiled finally in its innermost chamber, whence it steals forth to enchant the mind of men with its strange bewilderment. But the Twilight Scaffolding they saw clearly enough to make a map of it. For Daddy afterwards drew it from their description, and gave it an entire page in the Wumble Book, Monkey ladling on the colour with her camel's-hair brush as well as she could remember.

It was a page to take the breath away, the big conception blundering clumsily behind the crude reconstruction. Great winds formed the base, winds of brown and blue and purple, piled mountainously upon each other in motionless coils, and so soft that the upright columns of the structure plunged easily and deeply into them. Thus the framework could bend and curve and sway, moving with steady glide across the landscape, yet never collapsing nor losing its exquisite proportions. The forests shored it up, its stays and bastions were the Jura precipices; it rested on the shoulders of the hills. From vineyard, field, and lake vast droves of thick grey shadows trooped in to curtain the lower halls of the colossal edifice, as chamber after chamber disappeared from view and Night clothed the structure from the ground-floors upwards. And far overhead a million tiny scarves, half sunset and half dusk, wove into little ropes that lashed the topmost spars together, dovetailing them neatly, and fastening them at last with whole clusters of bright thin stars.

"Ohhhhh!" breathed Jimbo with a delicious shudder of giddiness. "Let's climb to the very tip and see all the trains and railway stations in the world!"

"Wait till the moon comes up and puts the silver rivets in," the leader whispered. "It'll be safer then. My weight, you know—"

"There she is!" interrupted Monkey with a start, "and there's no such thing as weight—"

For the moon that instant came up, it seemed with a rush, and the line of distant Alps moved forward, blocked vividly against the silvery curtain that she brought. Her sight ran instantly about the world. Between the trees shot balls of yellowish white, unfolding like ribbon as they rolled. They splashed the rocks and put shining pools in the hollows among the moss. Spangles shone on Monkey's hair and eyes; skins and faces all turned faintly radiant. The lake, like a huge reflector, flashed its light up into the heavens. The moon laid a coating of her ancient and transfiguring paint upon the enormous structure, festooning the entire sky. "She's put the silver rivets in," said Jimbo.

"Now we can go," whispered Rogers, "only, remember, it's a giddy business, rather."

All three went fluttering after it, floating, rising, falling, like fish that explore a sunken vessel in their own transparent medium. The elastic structure bore them easily as it swung along. Its enormous rhythm lulled their senses with a deep and drowsy peace, and as they climbed from storey to storey it is doubtful if the children caught their leader's words at all. There were no echoes—the spaces were too vast for that—and they swung away from spar to spar, and from rafter to rafter, as easily as acrobats on huge trapezes. Jimbo and Monkey shot upwards into space.

"I shall explore the lower storeys first," he called after them, his words fluttering in feathers of sound far up the vault. "Keep the fire in sight to guide you home again. . ." and he moved slowly towards the vast ground-floor chambers of the Night. Each went his independent way along the paths of reverie and dream. He found himself alone.

For he could not soar and float as they did; he kept closer to the earth, wandering through the under chambers of the travelling building that swung its way over vineyards, woods, and village roofs. He kept more in touch with earth than they did. The upper sections where the children climbed went faster than those lower halls and galleries, so that the entire framework bent over, breaking ever into a crest of foaming stars. But in these under halls where he stood and watched there was far less movement. From century to century these remained the same. Between the bases of the mighty columns he watched the wave of darkness drown the world, leading it with a rush of silence towards sleep. For the children Night meant play and mischief; for himself it meant graver reverie. . .

These were the chambers, clearly, of ancestral sleep and dream: they seemed so familiar and well known. Behind him blinked the little friendly fire in the forest, link with the outer world he must not lose. He would find the children there when he went back, lively from their scamper among the stars; and, meanwhile, he was quite content to wander down these corridors in the floor of Night and taste their deep repose. For years he had not visited or known them. The children had led him back, although he did not realise it. He believed, on the contrary, that it was he who led and they who followed. For true leadership is ever inspired, making each follower feel that he goes first and of his own free will. . .

"Jimbo, you flickery sprite, where are you now?" he called, suddenly noticing how faint the little fire had grown with distance.

A lonely wind flew down upon him with a tiny shout:

"Up here, at the very top, with Daddy. He's making notes in a tower-room all by himself!"

Rogers could not believe his ears. Daddy indeed!

"Is Monkey with you? And is she safe?"

"She's helping Daddy balance. The walls aren't finished, and he's on a fearful ledge. He's after something or other for his story, he says."

It seemed impossible. Daddy skylarking on the roof of Night, and making notes! Yet with a moment's reflection the impossibility vanished; surprise went after it; it became natural, right, and true. Daddy, of course, sitting by his window in the carpenter's house, had seen the Twilight Scaffolding sweep past and had climbed into it. Its beauty had rapt him out and away. In the darkness his mind wandered, too, gathering notes subconsciously for his wonderful new story.

"Come down here to me," he cried, as a man cries in his sleep, making no audible sound. "There's less risk among the foundations." And down came Daddy with an immediate rush. He arrived in a bundle, then straightened up. The two men stood side by side in these subterraneans of the night.

"You!" whispered Rogers, trying to seize his hand, while the other evaded him, hiding behind a shadow.

"Don't touch me," he murmured breathlessly. "You'll scatter my train of thought. Think of something else at once, please. . ." He moved into thicker shadows, half disappearing. "I'm after something that suddenly occurred to me for my story."

"What is it? I'll think it with you," his cousin called after him. "You'll see it better if I do. Tell me."

"A train that carries Thought, as this darkness carries stars—a starlight express," was the quick reply, "and a cavern where lost starlight gathers till it's wanted-sort of terminus of the railway. They belong to the story somewhere if only I can find them and fit them in. Starlight binds all together as thought and sympathy bind minds. . ."

Rogers thought hard about them. Instantly his cousin vanished.

"Thank you," ran a faint whisper among the pillars; "I'm on their trail again now. I must go up again. I can see better from the top," and the voice grew fainter and higher and further off with each word till it died away completely into silence. Daddy went chasing his inspiration through the scaffolding of reverie and dream.

"We did something for him the other night after all, then," thought Rogers with delight.

"Of course," dropped down a wee, faint answer from above, as the author heard him thinking; "you did a lot. I'm partly out at last. This is where all the Patterns hide. Awake, I only get their dim reflections, broken and distorted. This is reality, not that. Ha, ha! If only I can get it through, my lovely, beautiful pattern—"

"You will, you will," cried the other, as the voice went fluttering through space. "Ask the children. Jimbo and Monkey are up there somewhere. They're the safest guides."

Rogers gave a gulp and found that he was coughing. His feet were cold. A shudder ran across the feathery structure, making it tremble from the foundations to the forest of spires overhead. Jimbo came sliding down a pole of gleaming ebony. In a hammock of beams and rafters, swinging like a network of trapezes, Monkey swooped down after him, head first as usual. For the moon that moment passed behind a cloud, and the silver rivets started from their shadowy sockets.

Clusters of star nails followed suit. The palace bent and tottered like a falling wave. Its pillars turned into trunks of pine trees; its corridors were spaces through the clouds; its chambers were great dips between the mountain summits.

"It's going too fast for sight," thought Rogers; "I can't keep up with it. Even the children have toppled off." But he still heard Daddy's laughter echoing down the lanes of darkness as he chased his pattern with yearning and enthusiasm.

The huge structure with its towers and walls and platforms slid softly out of sight. The moonlight sponged its outlines from the sky. The scaffolding melted into darkness, moving further westwards as night advanced. Already it was over France and Italy, sweeping grandly across the sea, bewildering the vessels in its net of glamour, and filling with wonder the eyes of the look-out men at the mast heads.

"The fire's going out," a voice was saying. Rogers heard it through a moment's wild confusion as he fell swiftly among a forest of rafters, beams, and shifting uprights.

"I'll get more wood."

The words seemed underground. A mountain wind rose up and brought the solid world about him. He felt chilly, shivered, and opened his eyes. There stood the solemn pine trees, thick and close; moonlight flooded the spaces between them and lit their crests with silver.

"This is the Wind Wood," he remarked aloud to reassure himself.

Jimbo was bending over the fire, heaping on wood. Flame leaped up with a shower of sparks. He saw Monkey rubbing her eyes beside him.

"I've had a dream of falling," she was saying, as she snuggled down closer into his side.

"*I* didn't," Jimbo said. "I dreamed of a railway accident, and everybody was killed except one passenger, who was Daddy. It fell off a high bridge. We found Daddy in the *fourgon* with the baggages, writing a story and laughing—making an awful row."

"What did *you* dream, Cousinenry?" asked Monkey, peering into his eyes in the firelight.

"That my feet were cold, because the fire had gone out," he answered, trying in vain to remember whether he had dreamed anything at all. "And—that it's time to go home. I hear the curfew ringing."

Some one whistled softly. They ought to have been in bed an hour ago.

It was ten o'clock, and Gygi was sounding the *couvre feu* from the old church tower. They put the fire out and walked home arm in arm, separating with hushed good-nights in the courtyard of the Citadelle. But Rogers did not hear the scolding Mother gave them when they appeared at the Den door, for he went on at once to his own room in the carpenter's house, with the feeling that he had lived always in Bourcelles, and would never leave it again. His Scheme had moved bodily from London to the forest.

And on the way upstairs he peeped a moment into his cousin's room, seeing a light beneath the door. The author was sitting beside the open window with the lamp behind him and a note-book on his knees. Moonlight fell upon his face. He was sound asleep.

"I won't wake him," thought his cousin, going out softly again. "He's dreaming—dreaming of his wonderful new story probably."

XXIII

Even as a luminous haze links star to star,
I would supply all chasms with music, breathing
Mysterious motions of the soul, no way
To be defined save in strange melodies.

—*Paracelsus*, R. BROWNING

D addy's story, meanwhile, continued to develop itself with wonder and enthusiasm. It was unlike anything he had ever written. His other studies had the brilliance of dead precious stones, perhaps, but this thing moved along with a rushing life of its own. It grew, fed by sources he was not aware of. It developed of itself—changed and lived and flashed. Some creative fairy hand had touched him while he slept perhaps. The starry sympathy poured through him, and he thought with his feelings as well as with his mind.

At first he was half ashamed of it; the process was so new and strange; he even attempted to conceal his method, because he could not explain or understand it. "This is emotional, not intellectual," he sighed to himself; "it must be second childhood. I'm old. They'll call it decadent!" Presently, however, he resigned himself to the delicious flow of inspiration, and let it pour out till it flowed over into his daily life as well. Through his heart it welled up and bubbled forth, a thing of children, starlight, woods, and fairies.

Yet he was shy about it. He would talk about the story, but would not read it out. "It's a new *genre* for me," he explained shyly, "an attempt merely. We'll see what comes of it. My original idea, you see, has grown out of hand rather. I wake every morning with something fresh, as though"—he hesitated a moment, glancing towards his wife—"as if it came to me in sleep," he concluded. He felt her common sense might rather despise him for it.

"Perhaps it does," said Rogers.

"Why not?" said Mother, knitting on the sofa that was her bed at night.

She had put her needles down and was staring at her husband; he stared at Rogers; all three stared at each other. Something each wished to conceal moved towards utterance and revelation. Yet no one of them wished to be the first to mention it. A great change had come of late upon Bourcelles. It no longer seemed isolated from the big world outside as before; something had linked it up with the whole surrounding universe, and bigger, deeper currents of life flowed through it. And with the individual life of each it was the same. All dreamed the same enormous, splendid dream, yet dared not tell it—yet.

Both parents realised vaguely that it was something their visitor had brought, but what could it be exactly? It was in his atmosphere, he himself least of all aware of it; it was in his thought, his attitude to life, yet he himself so utterly unconscious of it. It brought out all the best in everybody, made them feel hopeful, brighter, more courageous. Yes, certainly, *he*, brought it. He believed in them, in the best of them—they lived up to it or tried to. Was that it? Was it belief and vision that he brought into their lives, though unconsciously, because these qualities lay so strongly in himself? Belief is constructive. It is what people *are* rather than what they preach that affects others. Two strangers meet and bow and separate without a word, yet each has changed; neither leaves the other quite as he was before. In the society of children, moreover, one believes everything in the world—for the moment. Belief is constructive and creative; it is doubt and cynicism that destroy. In the presence of a child these latter are impossible. Was this the explanation of the effect he produced upon their little circle—the belief and wonder and joy of Fairyland?

For a moment something of this flashed through Daddy's mind. Mother, in her way, was aware of something similar. But neither of them spoke it. The triangular staring was its only evidence. Mother resumed her knitting. She was not given to impulsive utterance. Her husband once described her as a solid piece of furniture. She was.

"You see," said Daddy bravely, as the moment's tension passed, "my original idea was simply to treat Bourcelles as an epitome, a miniature, so to speak, of the big world, while showing how Nature sweetened and kept it pure as by a kind of alchemy. But that idea has grown. I have the feeling now that the Bourcelles we know is a mere shadowy projection cast by a more real Bourcelles behind. It is only the dream village we know in our waking life. The real one—er—we know only in sleep." There!—it was partly out!

Mother turned with a little start. "You mean when we sleep?" she asked. She knitted vigorously again at once, as though ashamed of this sudden betrayal into fantasy. "Why not?" she added, falling back upon her customary non-committal phrase. Yet this was not the superior attitude he had dreaded; she was interested. There was something she wanted to confess, if she only dared. Mother, too, had grown softer in some corner of her being. Something shone through her with a tiny golden radiance.

"But this idea is not my own," continued Daddy, dangerously near to wumbling. "It comes *through* me only. It develops, apparently, when I'm asleep," he repeated. He sat up and leaned forward. "And, I believe," he added, as on sudden reckless impulse, "it comes from you, Henry. Your mind, I feel, has brought this cargo of new suggestion and discharged it into me—into every one—into the whole blessed village. Man, I think you've bewitched us all!"

Mother dropped a stitch, so keenly was she listening. A moment later she dropped a needle too, and the two men picked it up, and handed it back together as though it weighed several pounds.

"Well," said Rogers slowly, "I suppose all minds pour into one another somewhere—in and out of one another, rather—and that there's a common stock or pool all draw upon according to their needs and power to assimilate. But I'm not conscious, old man, of driving anything deliberately into you—"

"Only you think and feel these things vividly enough for me to get them too," said Daddy. Luckily "thought transference" was not actually mentioned, or Mother might have left the room, or at least have betrayed an uneasiness that must have chilled them.

"As a boy I imagined pretty strongly," in a tone of apology, "but never since. I was in the City, remember, twenty years—"

"It's the childhood things, then," Daddy interrupted eagerly. "You've brought the great childhood imagination with you—the sort of gorgeous, huge, and endless power that goes on fashioning of its own accord just as dreams do—"

"I *did,* indulge in that sort of thing as a boy, yes," was the half-guilty reply; "but that was years and years ago, wasn't it?"

"They have survived, then," said Daddy with decision. "The sweetness of this place has stimulated them afresh. The children"—he glanced suspiciously at his wife for a moment—"have appropriated them too. It's a powerful combination." After a pause he added, "I might develop that idea in my story—that you've brought back the sweet creations of childhood with you and captured us all—a sort of starry army."

"Why not?" interpolated Mother, as who should say there was no harm in *that*. "They certainly have been full of mischief lately."

"Creation *is* mischievous," murmured her husband. "But since you have come," he continued aloud,—"how can I express it exactly?—the days have seemed larger, fuller, deeper, the forest richer and more mysterious, the sky much closer, and the stars more soft and intimate. I dream of them, and they all bring me messages that help my story. Do you know what I mean? There were days formerly, when life seemed empty, thin, peaked, impoverished, its scale of values horribly reduced, whereas now—since you've been up to your nonsense with the children—some tide stands at the full, and things are always happening."

"Well, really, Daddy!" said the expression on Mother's face and hands and knitting-needles, "you *are* splendid today"; but aloud she only repeated her little hold-all phrase, "Why not?"

Yet somehow he recognised that she understood him better than usual. Her language had not changed—things in Mother worked slowly, from within outwards as became her solid personality—but it held new meaning. He felt for the first time that he could make her understand, and more—that she was ready to understand. That is, he felt new sympathy with her. It was very delightful, stimulating; he instantly loved her more, and felt himself increased at the same time.

"I believe a story like that might even sell," he observed, with a hint of reckless optimism. "People might recognise a touch of their own childhood in it, eh?"

He longed for her to encourage him and pat him on the back.

"True," said Mother, smiling at him, "for every one likes to keep in touch with their childhood—if they can. It makes one feel young and hopeful—jolly; doesn't it? Why not?"

Their eyes met. Something, long put aside and buried under a burden of exaggerated care, flashed deliciously between them. Rogers caught it flying and felt happy. Bridges were being repaired, if not newly built.

"Nature, you see, is always young really," he said; "it's full of children. The very meaning of the word, eh, John?" turning to his cousin as who should say, "We knew our grammar once."

"*Natura*, yes—something about to produce." They laughed in their superior knowledge of a Latin word, but Mother, stirred deeply though she hardly knew why, was not to be left out. Would the bridge bear her, was perhaps her thought.

"And of the feminine gender," she added slyly, with a touch of pride. The bridge creaked, but did not give way. She said it very quickly. She had suddenly an air of bouncing on her sofa.

"Bravo, Mother," said her husband, looking at her, and there was a fondness in his voice that warmed and blessed and melted down into her. She had missed it so long that it almost startled her. "There's the eternal old magic, Mother; you're right. And if I had more of you in me—more of the creative feminine—I should do better work, I'm sure. You must give it to me."

She kept her eyes upon her needles. The others, being unobservant "mere men," did not notice that the stitches she made must have produced queer kind of stockings if continued. "We'll be collaborators," Daddy added, in the tone of a boy building on the sands at Margate.

"I will," she said in a low voice, "if only I know how."

"Well," he answered enthusiastically, looking from one to the other, delighted to find an audience to whom he could talk of his new dream, "you see, this is really a great jolly fairy-tale I'm trying to write. I'm blessed if I know where the ideas come from, or how they pour into me like this, but—anyhow it's a new experience, and I want to make the most of it. I've never done imaginative work before, and—though it is a bit fantastical, mean to keep in touch with reality and show great truths that emerge from the commonest facts of life. The critics, of course, will blame me for not giving 'em the banal thing they expect from me, but what of that?" He was dreadfully reckless.

"I see," said Mother, gazing open-mindedly into his face; "but where does *my* help come in, please?"

She leaned back, half-sighing, half-smiling. "Here's my life"—she held up her needles—"and that's the soul of prosaic dulness, isn't it?"

"On the contrary," he answered eagerly, "it's reality. It's courage, patience, heroism. You're a spring-board for my fairy-tale, though I'd never realised it before. I shall put you in, just as you are. You'll be one of the earlier chapters."

"Every one'll skip me, then, I'm afraid."

"Not a bit," he laughed gaily; "they'll feel you all through the book. Their minds will rest on you. You'll be a foundation. 'Mother's there,' they'll say, 'so it's all right. This isn't nonsense. We'll read on.' And they will read on."

"I'm all through it, then?"

"Like the binding that mothers the whole book, you see," put in

Rogers, delighted to see them getting on so well, yet amazed to hear his cousin talk so openly with her of his idea.

Daddy continued, unabashed and radiant. Hitherto, he knew, his wife's attitude, though never spoken, had been very different. She almost resented his intense preoccupation with stories that brought in so little cash. It would have been better if he taught English or gave lessons in literature for a small but regular income. He gave too much attention to these unremunerative studies of types she never met in actual life. She was proud of the reviews, and pasted them neatly in a big book, but his help and advice on the practical details of the children's clothing and education were so scanty. Hers seemed ever the main burden.

Now, for the first time, though she distrusted fantasy and deemed it destructive of action, she felt something real. She listened with a kind of believing sympathy. She noticed, moreover, with keen pleasure, that her attitude fed him. He talked so freely, happily about it all. Already her sympathy, crudely enough expressed, brought fuel to his fires. Some one had put starlight into her.

"He's been hungry for this all along," she reflected; "I never realised it. I've thought only of myself without knowing it."

"Yes, I'll put you in, old Mother," he went on, "and Rogers and the children too. In fact, you're in it already," he chuckled, "if you want to know. Each of you plays his part all day long without knowing it." He changed his seat, going over to the window-sill, and staring down upon them as he talked on eagerly. "Don't you feel," he said, enthusiasm growing and streaming from him, "how all this village life is a kind of dream we act out against the background of the sunshine, while our truer, deeper life is hidden somewhere far below in half unconsciousness? Our daily doings are but the little bits that emerge, tips of acts and speech that poke up and out, masquerading as complete? In that vaster sea of life we lead below the surface lies my big story, my fairy-tale—when we sleep." He paused and looked down questioningly upon them. "When we sleep," he repeated impressively, struggling with his own thought. "You, Mother, while you knit and sew, slip down into that enormous under-sea and get a glimpse of the coloured pictures that pass eternally behind the veil. I do the same when I watch the twilight from my window in reverie. Sunshine obliterates them, but they go just the same. *You* call it day-dreaming. Our waking hours are the clothes we dress the spirit in after its nightly journeys and activities. Imagination does not create so much as remember. Then, by transforming, it reveals."

Mother sat staring blankly before her, utterly lost, while her husband flung these lumps of the raw material of his story at her—of its atmosphere, rather. Even Rogers felt puzzled, and hardly followed what he heard. The intricacies of an artistic mind were indeed bewildering. How in the world would these wild fragments weave together into any intelligible pattern?

"You mean that we travel when we sleep," he ventured, remembering a phrase that Minks had somewhere used, "and that our real life is out of the body?" His cousin was taking his thought—or was it originally Minks's?—wholesale.

Mother looked up gratefully. "I often dream I'm flying," she put in solemnly. "Lately, in particular, I've dreamed of stars and funny things like that a lot."

Daddy beamed his pleasure. "In my fairy-tale we shall all see stars," he laughed, "and we shall all get 'out.' For our thoughts will determine the kind of experience and adventure we have when the spirit is free and unhampered. And contrariwise, the kind of things we do at night—in sleep, in dream—will determine our behaviour during the day. There's the importance of thinking rightly, you see. Out of the body is eternal, and thinking is more than doing—it's more complete. The waking days are brief intervals of test that betray the character of our hidden deeper life. We are judged in sleep. We last for ever and ever. In the day, awake, we stand before the easel on which our adventures of the night have painted those patterns which are the very structure of our outer life's behaviour. When we sleep again we re-enter the main stream of our spirit's activity. In the day we forget, of course—as a rule, and most of us—but we follow the pattern just the same, unwittingly, because we can't help it. It's the mould we've made."

"Then your story," Rogers interrupted, "will show the effect in the daytime of what we do at night? Is that it?" It amazed him to hear his cousin borrowing thus the entire content of his own mind, sucking it out whole like a ripe plum from its skin.

"Of course," he answered; "and won't it be a lark? We'll all get out in sleep and go about the village together in a bunch, helping, soothing, cleaning up, and putting everybody straight, so that when they wake up they'll wonder why in the world they feel so hopeful, strong, and happy all of a sudden. We'll put thoughts of beauty into them—beauty, you remember, which 'is a promise of happiness.'"

"Ah!" said Mother, seizing at his comprehensible scrap with energy. "That *is* a story."

"If I don't get it wumbled in the writing down," her husband continued, fairly bubbling over. "You must keep me straight, remember, with your needles—your practical aspirations, that is. I'll read it out to you bit by bit, and you'll tell me where I've dropped a stitch or used the wrong wool, eh?"

"Mood?" she asked.

"No, wool," he said, louder.

There was a pause.

"But you see my main idea, don't you—that the sources of our life lie hid with beauty very very far away, and that our real, big, continuous life is spiritual—out of the body, as I shall call it. The waking-day life uses what it can bring over from this enormous under-running sea of universal consciousness where we're all together, splendid, free, untamed, and where thinking is creation and we feel and know each other face to face? See? Sympathy the great solvent? All linked together by thought as stars are by their rays. Ah! You get my idea—the great Network?"

He looked straight into his wife's eyes. They were opened very wide. Her mouth had opened a little, too. She understood vaguely that he was using a kind of shorthand really. These cryptic sentences expressed in emotional stenography mere odds and ends that later would drop into their proper places, translated into the sequence of acts that are the scaffolding of a definite story. This she firmly grasped—but no more.

"It's grand-a wonderful job," she answered, sitting back upon the sofa with a sigh of relief, and again bouncing a little in the process, so that Rogers had a horrible temptation to giggle. The tension of listening had been considerable. "People, you mean, will realise how important thinking is, and that sympathy—er—" and she hesitated, floundering.

"Is the great way to grow," Rogers quickly helped her, "because by feeling with another person you add his mind to yours and so get bigger. And"—turning to his cousin—"you're taking starlight as the symbol of sympathy? You told me that the other day, I remember." But the author did not hear or did not answer; his thought was far away in his dream again.

The situation was saved. All the bridges had borne well. Daddy, having relieved his overcharged mind, seemed to have come to a full stop. The Den was full of sunlight. A delightful feeling of intimacy wove the three humans together. Mother caught herself thinking of the far-off courtship days when their love ran strong and clear. She felt at one with her husband, and remembered him as lover. She felt in touch with him all over. And Rogers was such a comfortable sort of person. Tact was indeed well named—sympathy so delicately adjusted that it involved feeling-with to the point of actual touch.

Daddy came down from his perch upon the window-sill, stretched his arms, and drew a great happy sigh.

"Mother," he added, rising to go out, "you shall help me, dearie. We'll write this great fairy-tale of mine together, eh?" He stooped and kissed her, feeling love and tenderness and sympathy in his heart.

"You brave old Mother!" he laughed; "we'll send Eddie to Oxford yet, see if we don't. A book like that might earn 100 pounds or even 200 pounds."

Another time she would have answered, though not bitterly, "Meanwhile I'll go on knitting stockings," or "Why not? we shall see what we shall see"—something, at any rate, corrective and rather sober, quenching. But this time she said nothing. She returned the kiss instead, without looking up from her needles, and a great big thing like an unborn child moved near her heart. He had not called her "dearie" for so long a time, it took her back to their earliest days together at a single, disconcerting bound. She merely stroked his shoulder as he straightened up and left the room. Her eyes then followed him out, and he turned at the door and waved his hand. Rogers, to her relief, saw him to the end of the passage, and her handkerchief was out of sight again before he returned. As he came in she realised even more clearly than before that he somehow was the cause of the changing relationship. He it was who brought this something that bridged the years—made old bridges safe to use again. And her love went out to him. He was a man she could open her heart to even.

Patterns of starry beauty had found their way in and were working out in all of them. But Mother, of course, knew nothing of this. There was a tenderness in him that won her confidence. That was all she felt. "Oh, dear," she thought in her odd way, "what a grand thing a man is to be sure, when he's got that!" It was like one of Jane Anne's remarks.

As he came in she had laid the stocking aside and was threading a needle for darning and buttons, and the like.

"'Threading the eye of a yellow star,' eh?" he laughed, "and always at it. You've stirred old Daddy up this time. He's gone off to his story, simply crammed full. What a help and stimulus you must be to him!"

"I," she said, quite flabbergasted; "I only wish it were true—again." The last word slipped out by accident; she had not meant it.

But Rogers ignored it, even if he noticed it.

"I never can help him in his work. I don't understand it enough. I don't understand it at all." She was ashamed to hedge with this man. She looked him straight in the eye.

"But he feels your sympathy," was his reply. "It's not always necessary to understand. That might only muddle him. You help by wishing, feeling, sympathising—believing."

"You really think so?" she asked simply. "What wonderful thoughts you have I One has read, of course, of wives who inspired their husbands' work; but it seemed to belong to books rather than to actual life."

Rogers looked at her thoughtful, passionate face a moment before he answered. He realised that his words would count with her. They approached delicate ground. She had an absurd idea of his importance in their lives; she exaggerated his influence; if he said a wrong thing its effect upon her would be difficult to correct.

"Well," he said, feeling mischief in him, "I don't mind telling *you* that I should never have understood that confused idea of his story but for one thing."

"What was that?" she asked, relieved to feel more solid ground at last.

"That I saw the thing from his own point of view," he replied; "because I have had similar thoughts all my life. I mean that he's bagged it all unconsciously out of my own mind; though, of course," he hastened to add, "I could never, never have made use of it as he will. I could never give it shape and form."

Mother began to laugh too. He caught the twinkle in her eyes. She bounced again a little on the springy sofa as she turned towards him, confession on her lips at last.

"And I do believe you've felt it too, haven't you?" he asked quickly, before she could change her mind.

"I've felt something—yes," she assented; "odd, unsettled; new things rushing everywhere about us; the children mysterious and up to all sorts of games and wickedness; and bright light over everything, like-like a scene in a theatre, somehow. It's exhilarating, but I can't quite make it out. It can't be right to feel so frivolous and jumpy-about at my age, can it?"

"You feel lighter, eh?

She burst out laughing. Mother was a prosaic person; that is, she had strong common-sense; yet through her sober personality there ran like a streak of light some hint of fairy lightness, derived probably from her Celtic origin. Now, as Rogers watched her, he caught a flash of that raciness and swift mobility, that fluid, protean elasticity of temperament which belonged to the fairy kingdom. The humour and pathos in her had been smothered by too much care. She accepted old age before her time. He saw her, under other conditions, dancing, singing, full of Ariel tricks and mischief—instead of eternally mending stockings and saving centimes for peat and oil and washerwomen. He even saw her feeding fantasy—poetry—to Daddy like a baby with a spoon. The contrast made him laugh out loud.

"You've lived here five years," he went on, "but lived too heavily. Care has swamped imagination. I did the same-in the City-for twenty years. It's all wrong. One has to learn to live carelessly as well as carefully. When I came here I felt all astray at first, but now I see more clearly. The peace and beauty have soaked into me." He hesitated an instant, then continued. Even if she didn't grasp his meaning now with her brains, it would sink down into her and come through later.

"The important things of life are very few really. They stand out vividly here. You've both vegetated, fossilised, atrophied a bit. I discovered it in my own case when I went back to Crayfield and—"

He told her about his sentimental journey, and how he found all the creations of his childhood's imagination still so alive and kicking in a forgotten backwater of his mind that they all hopped out and took objective form—the sprites, the starlight express, the boundless world of laughter, fun and beauty.

"And, without exactly knowing it, I suppose I've brought them all out here," he continued, seeing that she drank it in thirstily, "and—somehow or other—you all have felt it and responded. It's not my doing, of course," he added; "it's simply that I'm the channel as it were, and Daddy, with his somewhat starved artist's hunger of mind, was the first to fill up. It's pouring through him now in a story, don't you see; but we're all in it—"

"In a way, yes, that's what I've felt," Mother interrupted. "It's all a kind of dream here, and I've just waked up. The unchanging village, the forests, the Pension with its queer people, the Magic Box—"

"Like a play in a theatre," he interrupted, "isn't it?"

"Exactly," she laughed, yet half-seriously.

"While your husband is the dramatist that writes it down in acts and scenes. You see, his idea is, perhaps, that life as we know it is never a genuine story, complete and leading to a climax. It's all in disconnected fragments apparently. It goes backwards and forwards, up and down, in and out in a wumbled muddle, just anyhow, as it were. The fragments seem out of their proper place, the first ones often last, and *vice versa*. It seems inconsequential, because we only see the scraps that break through from below, from the true inner, deeper life that flows on steadily and dramatically out of sight. That's what he means by 'out of the body' and 'sleep' and 'dreaming.' The great pattern is too big and hidden for us to see it whole, just as when you knit I only see the stitches as you make them, although the entire pattern is in your mind complete. Our daily, external acts are the stitches we show to others and that everybody sees. A spiritual person sees the whole."

"Ah!" Mother interrupted, "I understand now. To know the whole pattern in my mind you'd have to get in sympathy with my thought below. Is that it?"

"Sometimes we look over the fence of mystery, yes, and see inside— see the entire stage as it were."

"It *is* like a great play, isn't it?" she repeated, grasping again at the analogy with relief. "We give one another cues, and so on—"

"While each must know the whole play complete in order to act his part properly—be in sympathy, that is, with all the others. The tiniest details so important, too," he added, glancing significantly at the needles on her lap. "To act your own part faithfully you must carry all the others in your mind, or else—er—get your own part out of proportion."

"It will be a wonderful story, won't it?" she said, after a pause in which her eyes travelled across the sunshine towards the carpenter's house where her husband, seen now in a high new light, laboured steadily.

There was a clatter in the corridor before he could reply, and Jimbo and Monkey flew in with a rush of wings and voices from school. They were upon him in an instant, smelling of childhood, copy-books, ink, and rampagious with hunger. Their skins and hair were warm with sunlight. "After tea we'll go out," they cried, "and show you something in the forest—oh, an enormous and wonderful thing that nobody knows of but me and Jimbo, and comes over every night from France and hides inside a cave, and goes back just before sunrise with a sack full of thinkings—"

"Thoughts," corrected Jimbo.

"—that haven't reached the people they were meant for, and then—"

"Go into the next room, wash yourselves and tidy up," said Mother sternly, "and then lay the table for tea. Jinny isn't in yet. Put the charcoal in the samovar. I'll come and light it in a moment."

They disappeared obediently, though once behind the door there were sounds that resembled a pillow-fight rather than tidying-up; and when Mother presently went after them to superintend, Rogers sat by the window and stared across the vineyards and blue expanse of lake at the distant Alps. It was curious. This vague, disconnected, rambling talk with Mother had helped to clear his own mind as well. In trying to explain to her something he hardly understood himself, his own thinking had clarified. All these trivial scenes were little bits of rehearsal. The Company was still waiting for the arrival of the Star Player who should announce the beginning of the real performance. It was a woman's role, yet Mother certainly could not play it. To get the family really straight was equally beyond his powers. "I really must have more common-sense," he reflected uneasily; "I am getting out of touch with reality somewhere. I'll write to Minks again."

Minks, at the moment, was the only definite, positive object in the outer world he could recall. "I'll write to him about—" His thought went wumbling. He quite forgot what it was he had to say to him— "Oh, about lots of things," he concluded, "his wife and children and—and his own future and so on."

The Scheme had melted into air, it seemed. People lost in Fairyland, they say, always forget the outer world of unimportant happenings. They live too close to the source of things to recognise their clownish reflections in the distorted mirrors of the week-day level.

Yes, it was curious, very curious. Did Thought, then, issue primarily from some single source and pass thence along the channels of men's minds, each receiving and interpreting according to his needs and powers? Was the Message—the Prophet's Vision—merely the more receipt of it than most? Had, perhaps, this whole wonderful story his cousin wrote originated, not in his, Rogers's mind, nor in that of Minks, but in another's altogether—the mind of her who was destined for the principal role? Thrills of absurd, electric anticipation rushed through him—very boyish, wildly impossible, yet utterly delicious.

Two doors opened suddenly—one from the kitchen, admitting Monkey with a tray of cups and saucers, steam from the hissing samovar

ALGERNON BLACKWOOD

wrapping her in a cloud, the other from the corridor, letting in Jane Anne, her arms full of packages. She had been shopping for the family in Neuchatel, and was arrayed in garments from the latest Magic Box. She was eager and excited.

"Cousinenry," she cried, dropping half the parcels in her fluster, "I've had a letter!" It was in her hand, whereas the parcels had been merely under her arms. "The postman gave it me himself as I came up the steps. I'm a great correspondencer, you know." And she darted through the steam to tell her mother. Jimbo passed her, carrying the tea-pot, the sugar-basin dangerously balanced upon spoons and knives and butter-dish. He said nothing, but glanced at his younger sister significantly. Rogers saw the entire picture through the cloud of steam, shot through with sunlight from the window. It was like a picture in the clouds. But he intercepted that glance and knew then the writer of the letter.

"But did you get the mauve ribbon, child?" asked Mother.

Instead of answer, the letter was torn noisily open. Jinny never had letters. It was far more important than ribbons.

"And how much change have you left out of the five francs? Daddy will want to know."

Jimbo and Monkey were listening carefully, while pretending to lay the table. Mother's silence betrayed that she was reading the letter with interest and curiosity equal to those of its recipient. "Who wrote it? Who's it from? I must answer it at once," Jinny was saying with great importance. "What time does the post go, I wonder? I mustn't miss it."

"The post-mark," announced Mother, "is Bourcelles. It's very mysterious." She tapped the letter with one hand, like the villain in the theatre. Rogers heard her and easily imagined the accompanying stage gesture. "The handwriting on the envelope is like Tante Anna," he heard, "but the letter itself is different. It's all capitals, and wrongly spelt." Mlle. Lemaire was certainly not the writer.

Jimbo and Monkey were busy hanging the towel out of the window, signal to Daddy that tea was ready. But as Daddy was already coming down the street at a great pace, apparently excited too, they waved it instead. Rogers suddenly remembered that Jimbo that morning had asked him for a two-centime stamp. He made no remark, however, merely wondering what was in the letter itself.

"It's a joke, of course," Mother was heard to say in an odd voice.

"Oh no, Mother, for how could anybody know? It's what I've been dreaming about for nights and nights. It's so aromantic, isn't it?"

The louder hissing of the samovar buried the next words, and at that moment Daddy came into the room. He was smiling and his eyes were bright. He glanced at the table and sat down by his cousin on the sofa.

"I've done a lot of work since you saw me," he said happily, patting him on the knee, "although in so short a time. And I want my cup of tea. It came so easily and fluently for a wonder; I don't believe I shall have to change a word—though usually I distrust this sort of rapid composition."

"Where are you at now?" asked Rogers. "We're all 'out,'" was the reply, "and the Starlight Express is just about to start and—Mother, let me carry that for you," he exclaimed, turning round as his wife appeared in the doorway with more tea-things. He got up quickly, but before he could reach her side Jinny flew into his arms and kissed him.

"Did you get my tobacco, Jinny?" he asked. She thrust the letter under his nose. What was tobacco, indeed, compared to an important letter! "You can keep the change for yourself."

He read it slowly with a puzzled expression, while Mother and the children watched him. Riquette jumped down from her chair and rubbed herself against his leg while he scratched himself with his boot, thinking it was the rough stocking that tickled him.

"Eh? This is very queer," he muttered, slapping the open sheet just as his wife had done, and reading it again at arm's-length. "Somebody"— he looked suspiciously round the room—"has been reading my notes or picking out my thoughts while I'm asleep, eh?"

"But it's a real letter," objected Jinny; "it's correspondence, isn't it, Daddy?"

"It is certainly a correspondence," he comforted her, and then, reading it aloud, he proceeded to pin it on the wall above the mantelpiece:—

"The Starlight Xpress starts tonight, Be reddy and punctuel. Sleep titely and get out."

That was all. But everybody exchanged glances.

"Odd," thought Mother, again remembering her dreams.

Jimbo upset the milk-jug. Usually there would have been a rumpus over this. Today it seemed like something happening far away— something that had not really happened at all.

"We must all be ready then," said Rogers, noticing vaguely that Mother's sleeve had smeared the butter as she mopped up the mess.

Daddy was making a note on his shirt sleeve:—

The Sweep, the Laugher and the Tramp,
The running man who lights the lamp,
The Woman of the Haystack, too,
The Gardener and Man of Dust
Are passengers because they must
Follow the Guard with eyes of blue.
Over the forests and into the Cave
That is the way we must all behave—

"Please, Daddy, will you move? It's dripping on to your boot."

They all looked down; the milk had splashed from the cloth and fallen upon the toe of his big mountain boots. It made a pretty, white star. Riquette was daintily lapping it up with her long pink Tongue. Ray by ray the star set in her mysterious interior.

"Riquette must come too," said Rogers gravely. "She's full of white starlight now."

And Jimbo left his chair and went seriously over to the bookshelf above Mother's sofa-bed to arrange the signals. For between the tightly-wedged books he had inserted all the available paper-knives and book-markers he could find to represent railway-signals. They stuck out at different angles. He altered several, putting some up, some down, and some at right angles.

"The line's all clear for tonight," he announced to Daddy with a covert significance he hardly grasped himself, then coming back to home-made jam and crusty village bread.

Jane Anne caught her father's answering glance-mysterious, full of unguessed meanings. "Oh, excuse me, Mother," she said, feeling the same thing in herself and a little frightened; "but I do believe they're conspiring, aren't they?"

And Mother gave a sudden start, whose cause she equally failed to analyse. "Hush, dear," she said. "Don't criticise your elders, and when you do, don't use long words you cannot possibly understand."

And everybody understood something none of them understood-while tea went on as usual to the chatter of daily details of external life.

XXIV

All we have willed or hoped or dreamed of good shall exist;
Not its semblance, but itself; no beauty, nor good, nor power
Whose voice has gone forth, but each survives for the melodist
When eternity affirms the conception of an hour.
The high that proved too high, the heroic for earth too hard,
The passion that left the ground to lose itself in the sky,
Are music sent up to God by the lover and the bard;
Enough that he heard it once: we shall hear it by and by.

—*Abt Vogler*, R. BROWNING

S ome hours later, as Rogers undressed for bed in his room beneath the roof, he realised abruptly that the time had come for him to leave. The weeks had flown; Minks and the Scheme required him; other matters needed attention too. What brought him to the sudden decision was the fact that he had done for the moment all he could find to do, beginning with the Pension mortgages and ending with little Edouard Tissot, the *vigneron's* boy who had curvature of the spine and could not afford proper treatment. It was a long list. He was far from satisfied with results, yet he had done his best, in spite of many clumsy mistakes. In the autumn he might return and have a further try. Finances were getting muddled, too, and he realised how small his capital actually was when the needs of others made claims upon it. Neighbours were as plentiful as insects.

He had made all manner of schemes for his cousin's family as well, yet seemed to have accomplished little. Their muddled life defied disentanglement, their difficulties were inextricable. With one son at a costly tutor, another girl in a Geneva school, the younger children just outgrowing the local education, the family's mode of living so scattered, meals in one place, rooms in several others,—it was all too unmethodical and dispersed to be covered by their small uncertain income. Concentration was badly needed. The endless talks and confabulations, which have not been reported here because their confusion was interminable and unreportable, landed every one in a mass of complicated jumbles. The solution lay beyond his power, as equally beyond the powers of the obfuscated parents. He would return to England, settle his own affairs, concoct some practical scheme with the aid of Minks, and return later to discuss its working out. The time had come for him to leave.

And, oddly enough, what made him see it were things the children had said that very evening when he kissed them all good-night. England had been mentioned.

"You're here for always now," whispered Monkey, "because you love me and can't get away. I've tied you with my hair, you know."

"You'll have no sekrity in London," said Jimbo. "Who'll stick your stamps on?"

"The place will seem quite empty if you go," Jane Anne contributed, not wishing to make her contribution too personal, lest she should appear immodest. "You've made a memorandum of agreement." This meant he had promised rashly once to stay for ever. The phrase lent an official tone besides.

He fell asleep, devising wonderful plans, as usual, for the entire world, not merely a tiny section of it. The saviour spirit was ever in his heart. It failed to realise itself because the mind was unequal to the strain of wise construction; but it was there, as the old vicar had divined. He had that indestructible pity to which no living thing is outcast.

But tonight he fell asleep so slowly, gradually, that he almost watched the dissolving of consciousness in himself. He hovered a long time about the strange, soft frontiers. He saw the barriers lower themselves into the great dim plains. Inch by inch the outer world became remote, obscure, lit dubiously by some forgotten sun, and inch by inch the profound recesses of nightly adventure coaxed him down. He realised that he swung in space between the two. The room and house were a speck in the universe above him, his brain the mere outlet of a tunnel up which he climbed every morning to put his horns out like a snail, and sniff the outer world. Here, in the depths, was the workroom where his life was fashioned. Here glowed the mighty, hidden furnaces that shaped his tools. Drifting, glimmering figures streamed up round him from the vast under-world of sleep, called unconscious. "I *am* a spirit," he heard, not said or thought, "and no spirit can be unconscious for eight hours out of every twenty-four. . . !"

Slowly the sea of dreamless sleep, so-called, flowed in upon him, down, round, and over; it submerged the senses one by one, beginning with hearing and ending with sight. But, as each physical sense was closed, its spiritual counterpart—the power that exists apart from its limited organ-opened into clear, divine activity, free as life itself. . .

How ceaseless was this movement of Dreams, never still, always changing and on the dance, incessantly renewing itself in kaleidoscopic patterns. There was perpetual metamorphosis and rich transformation; many became one, one many; the universe was a single thing, charged with stimulating emotional shocks as each scrap of interpretation passed in and across the mind. . .

He was falling into deeper and deeper sleep, into that eternal region where he no longer thought, but knew. . . Immense processions of shifting imagery absorbed him into themselves, spontaneous, unfamiliar, self-multiplying, and as exquisitely baffling as God and all His angels. . .

The subsidence of the external world seemed suddenly complete.

So deeply was he sunk that he reached that common pool of fluid essence upon which all minds draw according to their needs and powers. Relations were established, wires everywhere connected. The central switchboard clicked all round him; brains linked with brains, asleep or not asleep. He was so deep within himself that, as the children and the Story phrased it, he was "out." The air grew light and radiant.

"Hooray! I'm out!" and he instantly thought of his cousin.

"So am I!" That wumbled author shot immediately into connection with him. "And so is Mother—for the first time. Come on: we'll all go together."

It was unnecessary to specify where, for that same second they found themselves in the room of Mlle. Lemaire. At this hour of the night it was usually dark, except for the glimmer of the low-turned lamp the sufferer never quite extinguished.

From dusk till dawn her windows in La Citadelle shone faintly for all to see who chanced to pass along the village street. "There she lies, poor aching soul, as she has lain for twenty years, thinking good of some one, or maybe praying!" For the glimmer was visible from very far, and familiar as a lighthouse to wandering ships at sea. But, had they known her inner happiness, they would not have said "poor soul!" They would have marvelled. In a Catholic canton, perhaps, they would have crossed themselves and prayed. Just now they certainly would have known a singular, exalted joy. Caught in fairyland, they would have wondered and felt happy.

For the room was crowded to the doors. Walls, windows, ceiling, had melted into transparency to let in the light of stars; and, caught like gold-fish in the great network of the rays, shone familiar outlines everywhere—Jimbo, Monkey, Jinny, the Sweep, the Tramp, the Gypsy, the Laugher up against the cupboard, the Gardener by the window where the flower-pots stood, the Woman of the Haystack in the corridor, too extensive to slip across the threshold, and, in the middle of the room, motionless with pleasure-Mother!

"Like gorgeous southern butterflies in a net, I do declare!" gasped Daddy, as he swept in silently with his companion, their colours mingling harmoniously at once with the rest.

And Mother turned.

"You're out, old girl, at last!" he cried.

"God bless my soul, I am!" she answered. Their sentences came both together, and their blues and yellows swam into each other and made a lovely green. "It's what I've been trying to do all these years without knowing it. What a glory! I understand now—understand myself and you. I see life clearly as a whole. Hooray, hooray!" She glided nearer to him, her face was beaming.

"Mother's going to explode," said Monkey in a whisper. But, of course, everybody "heard" it; for the faintest whisper of thought sent a ripple through that sea of delicate colour. The Laugher bent behind the cupboard to hide her face, and the Gardener by the window stooped to examine his flower-pots. The Woman of the Haystack drew back a little into the corridor again, preparatory to another effort to squeeze through. But Mother, regardless of them all, swam on towards her husband, wrapped in joy and light as in a garment. Hitherto, in her body, the nearest she had come to coruscating was once when she had taken a course of sulphur baths. This was a very different matter. She fairly glittered.

"We'll never go apart again," Daddy was telling her. "This inner sympathy will last, you know. *He* did it. It's him we have to thank," and he pointed at his cousin. "It's starlight, of course, he has brought down into us."

But Rogers missed the compliment, being busy in a corner with Monkey and Jimbo, playing at mixing colours with startling results. Mother swam across to her old friend, Mlle. Lemaire. For a quarter of a century these two had understood one another, though never consciously been "out" together. She moved like a frigate still, gliding and stately, but a frigate that has snapped its hawsers and meant to sail the skies.

"Our poor, stupid, sleeping old bodies," she smiled.

But the radiant form of the other turned to her motionless cage upon the bed behind her. "Don't despise them," she replied, looking down upon the worn-out prison-house, while a little dazzle of brilliance flashed through her atmosphere. "They are our means of spreading this starlight about the world and giving it to others. Our brains transmit it cunningly; it flashes from our eyes, and the touch of our fingers passes it on. We gather it here, when we are 'out,' but we can communicate it best to others when we are 'in.'"

There was sound of confusion and uproar in the room behind as some one came tumbling in with a rush, scattering the figures in all directions as when a gust of wind descends upon a bed of flowers.

"In at last!" cried a muffled voice that sounded as though a tarpaulin smothered it, and the Woman of the Haystack swept into the room with a kind of clumsy majesty. The Tramp and Gypsy, whose efforts had at length dislodged her awkward bulk, came rolling after. They had been pushing steadily from behind all this time, though no one had noticed them slip out.

"*We* can do more than the smaller folk," she said proudly, sailing up to Mother. "We can't be overlooked, for one thing"; and arm-in-arm, like a pair of frigates then, they sailed about the room, magnificent as whales that swim in a phosphorescent sea. The Laugher straightened up to watch them, the Gardener turned his head, and Rogers and the children paused a moment in their artificial mixing, to stare with wonder.

"I'm in!" said the Woman.

"I'm out!" said Mother.

And the children felt a trifle envious. Instantly their brilliance dimmed a little. The entire room was aware of it.

"Think always of the world in gold and silver," shot from Mile. Lemaire. The dimness passed as she said it.

"It was my doing," laughed Monkey, turning round to acknowledge her wickedness lest some one else should do it for her and thus increase her shame.

"Sweep! Sweep!" cried Rogers.

But this thought-created sprite was there before the message flashed. With his sack wide open, he stood by Monkey, full of importance. A moment he examined her. Then, his long black fingers darting like a shuttle, he discovered the false colouring that envy had caused, picked it neatly out—a thread of dirty grey—and, winding it into a tiny ball, tossed it with contempt into his sack.

> *"Over the edge of the world you go,*
> *With the mud and the leaves and the dirty snow!"*

he sang, skipping off towards the door. The child's star-body glowed and shone again, pulsing all over with a shimmering, dancing light that was like moonshine upon running water.

"Isn't it time to start now?" inquired Jinny; and as she said it all turned instinctively towards the corner of the room where they were assembled. They gathered round Mlle. Lemaire. It was quite clear who was leader now. The crystal brilliance of her whiteness shone like a little oval sun. So sparkling was her atmosphere, that its purity scarcely knew a hint of colour even. Her stream of thought seemed undiluted, emitting rays in all directions till it resembled a wheel of sheer white fire. The others fluttered round her as lustrous moths about an electric light.

"Start where?" asked Mother, new to this great adventure.

Her old friend looked at her, so that she caught a darting ray full in the face, and instantly understood.

"First to the Cave to load up," flashed the answer; "and then over the sleeping world to mix the light with everybody's dreams. Then back again before the morning spiders are abroad with the interfering sun."

She floated out into the corridor, and all the others fell into line as she went. The draught of her going drew Mother into place immediately behind her. Daddy followed close, their respective colours making it inevitable, and Jinny swept in after him, bright and eager as a little angel. She tripped on the edge of something he held tightly in one hand, a woven maze of tiny glittering lines, exquisitely inter-threaded—a skeleton of beauty, waiting to be filled in and clothed, yet already alive with spontaneous fire of its own. It was the Pattern of his story he had been busy with in the corner.

"I won't step on it, Daddy," she said gravely.

"It doesn't matter if you do. You're in it," he answered, yet lifted it higher so that it flew behind him like a banner in the night.

The procession was formed now. Rogers and the younger children came after their sister at a little distance, and then, flitting to and fro in darker shades, like a fringe of rich embroidery that framed the moving picture, came the figures of the sprites, born by Imagination out of

Love in an old Kentish garden years and years ago. They rose from the tangle of the ancient building. Climbing the shoulder of a big, blue wind, they were off and away!

It was a jolly night, a windy night, a night without clouds, when all the lanes of the sky were smooth and swept, and the interstellar spaces seemed close down upon the earth.

> *"Kind thoughts, like fine weather,*
> *Link sweetly together God's stars*
> *With the heart of a boy,"*

sang Rogers, following swiftly with Jimbo and his sister. For all moved along as easily as light across the surfaces of polished glass. And the sound of Rogers's voice seemed to bring singing from every side, as the gay procession swept onwards. Every one contributed lines of their own, it seemed, though there was a tiny little distant voice, soft and silvery, that intruded from time to time and made all wonder where it came from. No one could see the singer. At first very far away, it came nearer and nearer.

DADDY: "The Interfering Sun has set!
GARDENER: Now Sirius flings down the Net!
LAMPLIGHTER: See, the meshes flash and quiver,
   As the golden, silent river
SWEEP: Clears the dark world's troubled dream.
DUSTMAN: Takes it sleeping,
   Gilds its weeping
   With a star's mysterious beam.
TINY, DISTANT VOICE: Oh, think Beauty!
   It's your duty!
   In the Cave you work for others,
   All the stars are little brothers;
ROGERS: Think their splendour,
   Strong and tender;
DADDY: Think their glory
   In the Story
MOTHER: Of each day your nights redeem?
VOICE (nearer): Every loving, gentle thought
   Of this fairy brilliance wrought,

JANE ANNE: Every wish that you surrender,
MONKEY: Every little impulse tender,
JIMBO: Every service that you render
TANTE ANNA: Brings its tributary stream!
TRAMP AND GYPSY: In the fretwork
    Of the network
  Hearts lie patterned and a-gleam!
WOMAN OF THE HAYSTACK: Think with passion
  That shall fashion
  Life's entire design well-planned;
VOICE (still nearer): While the busy Pleiades,
ROGERS: Sisters to the Hyades,
VOICE (quite close): Seven by seven,
    Across the heaven,
ROGERS: Light desire
  With their fire!
VOICE (in his ear): Working cunningly together in a soft and
  tireless band,
    Sweetly linking
    All our thinking,
  In the Net of Sympathy that brings back
    Fairyland!"

Mother kept close to her husband; she felt a little bewildered, and uncertain in her movements; it was her first conscious experience of being out. She wanted to go in every direction at once; for she knew everybody in the village, knew all their troubles and perplexities, and felt the call from every house.

"Steady," he told her; "one thing at a time, you know." Her thoughts, he saw, had turned across the sea to Ireland where her strongest ties were. Ireland seemed close, and quite as accessible as the village. Her friend of the Haystack, on the other hand, seemed a long way off by comparison.

"That's because Henry never realised her personality very clearly," said Daddy, seeing by her colour that she needed explanation. "When creating all these Garden Sprites, he didn't *think* her sharply, vividly enough to make her effective. He just felt that a haystack suggested the elderly spread of a bulky and untidy old woman whose frame had settled beneath too many clothes, till she had collapsed into a field and stuck there. But he left her where he found her. He assigned no duties to her. She's only half alive. As a rule, she merely sits—just 'stays put'—until some one moves her."

Mother turned and saw her far in the rear, settling down comfortably upon a flat roof near the church. She rather envied her amiable disposition. It seemed so safe. Every one else was alive with such dangerous activity.

"Are we going *much* further—?" she began, when Monkey rushed by, caught up the sentence, and discharged herself with impudence into Daddy.

"Which is right, 'further' or 'farther'?" she asked with a flash of light.

"Further, of course," said unsuspecting Mother.

"But 'further' sounds 'farther,'" she cried, with a burst of laughter that died away with her passage of meteoric brilliance—into the body of the woods beyond.

"But the other Sprites, you see, are real and active," continued Daddy, ignoring the interruption as though accustomed to it, because he thought out clearly every detail. "They're alive enough to haunt a house or garden till sensitive people become aware of them and declare they've seen a ghost."

"And *we?*" she asked. "Who thought us out so wonderfully?"

"That's more than I can tell," he answered after a little pause. "God knows that, for He thought out the entire universe to which we belong. I only know that we're real, and all part of the same huge, single thing." He shone with increased brightness as he said it. "There's no question about *our* personalities and duties and the rest. Don't you feel it too?"

He looked at her as he spoke. Her outline had grown more definite. As she began to understand, and her bewilderment lessened, he noted that her flashing lines burned more steadily, falling into a more regular, harmonious pattern. They combined, moreover, with his own, and with the starlight too, in some exquisite fashion he could not describe. She put a hand out, catching at the flying banner of his Story that he trailed behind him in the air. They formed a single design, all three. His happiness became enormous.

"I feel joined on to everything," she replied, half singing it in her joy. "I feel tucked into the universe everywhere, and into you, dear. These rays of starlight have sewn us together." She began to tremble, but it was the trembling of pure joy and not of alarm. . .

"Yes," he said, "I'm learning it too. The moment thought gets away from self it lets in starlight and makes room for happiness. To think with sympathy of others is to grow: you take in their experience and add it to your own—development; the heart gets soft and deep and wide till you feel the entire universe buttoning its jacket round you. To think of self means friction and hence reduction."

"And your Story," she added, glancing up proudly at the banner that they trailed. "I have helped a little, haven't I?"

"It's nearly finished," he flashed back; "you've been its inspiration and its climax. All these years, when we thought ourselves apart, you've been helping really underground—that's true collaboration."

"Our little separation was but a *reculer pour mieux sauter*. See how we've rushed together again!"

A strange soft singing, like the wind in firs, or like shallow water flowing over pebbles, interrupted them. The sweetness of it turned the night alive.

"Come on, old Mother. Our Leader is calling to us. We must work."

They slid from the blue wind into a current of paler air that happened to slip swiftly past them, and went towards the forest where Mlle. Lemaire waited for them. Mother waved her hand to her friend, settled comfortably upon the flat roof in the village in their rear. "We'll come back to lean upon you when we're tired," she signalled. But she felt no envy now. In future she would certainly never "stay put." Work beckoned to her—and such endless, glorious work: the whole Universe.

"What life! What a rush of splendour!" she exclaimed as they reached the great woods and heard them shouting below in the winds. "I see now why the forest always comforted me. There's strength here I can take back into my body with me when I go."

"The trees, yes, express visibly only a portion of their life," he told her. "There is an overflow we can appropriate."

Yet their conversation was never audibly uttered. It flashed instantaneously from one to the other. All they had exchanged since leaving La Citadelle had taken place at once, it seemed. They were awake in the region of naked thought and feeling. The dictum of the materialists that thought and feeling cannot exist apart from matter did not trouble them. Matter, they saw, was everywhere, though too tenuous for any measuring instrument man's brain had yet invented.

"Come on!" he repeated; "the Starlight Express is waiting. It will take you anywhere you please—Ireland if you like!"

They found the others waiting on the smooth layer of soft purple air that spread just below the level of the tree-tops. The crests themselves tossed wildly in the wind, but at a depth of a few feet there was peace and stillness, and upon this platform the band was grouped. "The stars are caught in the branches tonight," a sensitive walker on the ground might have exclaimed. The spires rose about them like little garden trees of a few years' growth, and between them ran lanes and intricate, winding thoroughfares Mother saw long, dark things like thick bodies of snakes converging down these passage-ways, filling them, all running towards the centre where the group had established itself. There were lines of dotted lights along them. They did not move with the waving of the tree-tops. They looked uncommonly familiar.

"The trains," Jimbo was crying. He darted to and fro, superintending the embarking of the passengers.

All the sidings of the sky were full of Starlight Expresses.

The loading-up was so quickly accomplished that Mother hardly realised what was happening. Everybody carried sacks overflowing with dripping gold and bursting at the seams. As each train filled, it shot away across the starry heavens; for everyone had been to the Cave and gathered their material even before she reached the scene of action. And with every train went a *mecanicien* and a *conducteur* created by Jimbo's vivid and believing thought; a Sweep, a Lamplighter, and a Head Gardener went, too, for the children's thinking multiplied these, too, according to their needs. They realised the meaning of these Sprites so clearly now—their duties, appearance, laws of behaviour, and the rest-that their awakened imaginations thought them instantly into existence, as many as were necessary. Train after train, each with its full complement of passengers, flashed forth across that summer sky, till the people in the Observatories must have thought they had miscalculated strangely and the Earth was passing amid the showering Leonids before her appointed time.

"Where would you like to go first?" Mother heard her friend ask softly. "It's not possible to follow all the trains at once, you know."

"So I see," she gasped. "I'll just sit still a moment, and think."

The size and freedom of existence, as she now saw it, suddenly overwhelmed her. Accustomed too long to narrow channels, she found space without railings and notice-boards bewildering. She had never dreamed before that thinking can open the gates to heaven and bring the Milky Way down into the heart. She had merely knitted stockings. She had been practical. At last the key to her husband's being was in her hand. That key at the same time opened a door through him, into her own. Hitherto she had merely criticised. Oh dear! Criticism, when she might have created!

She turned to seek him. But only her old friend was there, floating beside her in a brilliant mist of gold and white that turned the tree-tops into rows of Burning Bushes.

"Where is he?" she asked quickly.

"Hush!" was the instant reply; "don't disturb him. Don't think, or you'll bring him back. He's filling his sack in the Star Cave. Men have to gather it,—the little store they possess is soon crystallised into hardness by Reason,—but women have enough in themselves usually to last a lifetime. They are born with it."

"Mine crystallised long ago, I fear."

"Care and anxiety did that. You neglected it a little. But your husband's cousin has cleaned the channels out. He does it unconsciously, but he does it. He has belief and vision like a child, and therefore turns instinctively to children because they keep it alive in him, though he hardly knows why he seeks them. The world, too, is a great big child that is crying for its Fairyland. . ."

"But the practical—" objected Mother, true to her type of mind-an echo rather than an effort.

"—is important, yes, only it has been exaggerated out of all sane proportion in most people's lives. So little is needed, though that little of fine quality, and ever fed by starlight. Obeyed exclusively, it destroys life. It bricks you up alive. But now tell me," she added, "where would you like to go first? Whom will you help? There is time enough to cover .the world if you want to, before the interfering sun gets up."

"*You!*" cried Mother, impulsively, then realised instantly that her friend was already developed far beyond any help that she could give. It was the light streaming from the older, suffering woman that was stimulating her own sympathies so vehemently. For years the process had gone on. It was at last effective.

"There are others, perhaps, who need it more than I," flashed forth a lovely ray.

"But I would repay," Mother cried eagerly, "I would repay." Gratitude for life rushed through her, and her friend must share it.

"Pass it on to others," was the shining answer. "That's the best repayment after all." The stars themselves turned brighter as the thought flashed from her.

Then Ireland vanished utterly, for it had been mixed, Mother now perceived, with personal longings that were at bottom selfish. There were indeed many there, in the scenes of her home and childhood, whose lives she might ease and glorify by letting in the starlight while they slept; but her motive, she discerned, was not wholly pure. There was a trace in it, almost a little stain, of personal gratification—she could not analyse it quite—that dimmed the picture in her thought. The brilliance of her companion made it stand out clearly. Nearer home was a less heroic object, a more difficult case, some one less likely to reward her efforts with results. And she turned instead to this.

"You're right," smiled the other, following her thought; "and you couldn't begin with a better bit of work than that. Your old mother has cut herself off so long from giving sympathy to her kind that now she cannot accept it from others without feeling suspicion and distrust. Ease and soften her outlook if you can. Pour through her gloom the sympathy of stars. And remember," she added, as Mother rose softly out of the trees and hovered a moment overhead, "that if you need the Sweep or the Lamplighter, or the Gardener to burn away her dead leaves, you have only to summon them. Think hard, and they'll be instantly beside you."

Upon an eddy of glowing wind Mother drifted across the fields to the corner of the village where her mother occupied a large single room in solitude upon the top floor, a solitude self-imposed and rigorously enforced.

"Use the finest quality," she heard her friend thinking far behind her, "for you have plenty of it. The Dustman gave it to you when you were not looking, gathered from the entire Zodiac. . . and from the careless meteor's track. . ."

The words died off into the forest.

"That he keeps only
For the old and lonely,
(And is very strict about it)
Who sleep so little that they need the best—"

The words came floating behind her. She felt herself brimful—charged with loving sympathy of the sweetest and most understanding quality. She looked down a moment upon her mother's roof. Then she descended.

XXV

And also there's a little star—
So white, a virgin's it must be;—
Perhaps the lamp my love in heaven
Hangs out to light the way for me.

—*Song*, THEOPHILE MARZIALS

In this corner of Bourcelles the houses lie huddled together with an air of something shamefaced; they dare not look straight at the mountains or at the lake; they turn their eyes away even from the orchards at the back. They wear a mysterious and secret look, and their shoulders have a sly turn, as though they hid their heads in the daytime and stirred about their business only after dark.

They lie grouped about a cobbled courtyard that has no fountain in it. The fair white road goes quickly by outside, afraid to look in frankly; and the entrance to the yard is narrow. Nor does a single tree grow in it. If Bourcelles could have a slum, this would be it.

Why the old lady had left her cosy quarters in Les Glycines and settled down in this unpleasant corner of the village was a puzzle to everybody. With a shrug of the shoulders the problem was generally left unsolved. Madame Jequier discussed it volubly a year ago when the move took place, then dismissed it as one of those mysteries of old people no one can understand. To the son-in-law and the daughter, who got nearer the truth, it was a source of pain and sadness beyond their means of relief. Mrs. "Plume"—it was a play in French upon her real name,—had been four years in the Pension, induced to come from a lonely existence in Ireland by her daughter and throw in her lot with the family, and at first had settled down comfortably enough. She was over seventy, and possessed 80 pounds a year—a dainty, witty, amusing Irish lady, with twinkling eyes and a pernicketty strong will, and a brogue she transferred deliciously into her broken French. She loved the children, yet did not win their love in return, because they stood in awe of her sarcastic criticisms. Life had gone hardly with her; she had lost her fortune and her children, all but this daughter, with whose marriage she was keenly disappointed. An aristocrat to the finger-tips, she could not accept the change of circumstances; distress had soured her; the transplanting hastened her decline; there was no sweetness left in her. She turned her heart steadily against the world.

The ostensible cause of this hiding herself away with her sorrow and disappointment was the presence of Miss Waghorn, with whom she disagreed, and even quarrelled, from morning till night. They formed a storm-centre that moved from salon to dining-room, and they squabbled acutely about everything—the weather, the heating, the opening or shutting of windows, the details of the food, the arrangement of the furniture, even the character of the cat. Miss Waghorn loved. The bickerings were incessant. They only had to meet for hot disagreement to break out. Mrs. Plume, already bent with age, would strike the floor with the ebony stick she always carried, and glare at the erect, defiant spinster—"That horrud, dirrty cat; its always in the room!" Then Miss Waghorn: "It's a very nice cat, Madame"—she always called her Madame—"and when *I* was a young girl I was taught to be kind to animals."—"The drawing-room is *not* the place for animals," came the pricking answer. And then the scuffle began in earnest.

Miss Waghorn, owing to her want of memory, forgot the squabble five minutes afterwards, and even forgot that she knew her antagonist at all. She would ask to be introduced, or even come up sweetly and introduce herself within half an hour of the battle. But Madame Plume forgot nothing; her memory was keen and accurate. She did not believe in the other's failing. "That common old woman!" she exclaimed with angry scorn to her daughter.

"It's deliberate offensiveness, that's all it is at all!" And she left the Pension.

But her attitude to the harmless old Quaker lady was really in small her attitude to humanity at large. She drew away in disgust from a world that had treated her so badly. Into herself she drew, growing smaller every day, more sour, more suspicious, and more averse to her own kind. Within the restricted orbit of her own bitter thoughts she revolved towards the vanishing point of life which is the total loss of sympathy. She felt *with* no one but herself. She belonged to that, alas, numerous type which, with large expectations unrealised, cannot accept disillusionment with the gentle laughter it deserves. She resented the universe. Sympathy was dead.

And she had chosen this unsavoury corner to dwell in because "the poor" of the village lived there, and she wished to count herself among them. It emphasised the spite, the grudge, she felt against humanity. At first she came into *dejeuner* and *souper*, but afterwards her meals were sent over twice a day from the Pension. She discovered so many reasons for not making the little journey of a hundred yards. On Sunday the "common people" were in the streets; on Saturday it was cleaning-day and the Pension smelt of turpentine; Monday was for letter-writing, and other days were too hot or too cold, too windy or too wet. In the end she accomplished her heart's desire. Madame Cornu, who kept the grocer's shop, and lived on the floor below with her husband, prepared the two principal meals and brought them up to her on a tray. She ate them alone. Her breakfast cup of tea she made herself, Mme. Cornu putting the jug of milk outside the door. She nursed her bitter grievance against life in utter solitude. Acidity ate its ugly pattern into her heart.

The children, as in duty bound, made dolorous pilgrimages to that upper floor from time to time, returning frightened, and Mother went regularly twice a week, coming home saddened and distressed. Her husband rarely went at all now, since the time when she told him to his face he came to taunt her. She spent her time, heaven only knows how, for she never left the building. According to Mother she was exceedingly busy doing nothing. She packed, unpacked, and then repacked all her few belongings. In summer she chased bees in her room with a wet towel; but with venom, not with humour. The Morning Post came daily from London. "I read my paper, write a letter, and the morning's gone," she told her daughter, by way of complaint that time was so scanty. Mme. Cornu often heard her walking up and down the floor, tapping her ebony stick and talking softly to herself. Yet she was as sane as any old body living in solitude with evil thinking well can be. She starved-because she neither gave nor *asked*.

As Mother thought of her, thus finding the way in instantly, the church clock sounded midnight. She entered a room that was black as coal and unsweetened as an airless cellar. The fair rays that had been pouring out of her returned with a little shock upon themselves— repulsed. She felt herself reduced, and the sensation was so unpleasant at first that she almost gasped. It was like suffocation. She felt enclosed with Death. That her own radiance dimmed a moment was undeniable, but it was for a moment only, for, thinking instantly of her friend, she drew upon that woman's inexhaustible abundance, and found her own stores replenished.

Slowly, as a wintry sun pierces the mist in some damp hollow of the woods, her supply of starlight lit up little pathways all about her, and she saw the familiar figure standing by the window. The figure was also black; it stood like an ebony statue in an atmosphere that was thick with gloom, turgid, sinister, and wholly rayless. It was like a lantern in a London fog. A few dim lines of sombre grey issued heavily from it, but got no farther than its outer surface, then doubled back and plunged in again. They coiled and twisted into ugly knots. Her mother's atmosphere was opaque, and as dismal as a November fog. There was a speck of light in the room, however, and it came, the visitor then perceived, from a single candle that stood beside the bed. The old lady had been reading; she rarely slept before two o'clock in the morning.

And at first, so disheartening, so hopeless seemed the task, that Mother wavered in her mission; a choking, suffocating sensation blocked all her channels of delivery. The very flowers on the window-sill, she noted, drooped in a languishing decline; they had a lifeless air as of flowers that struggle for existence in deep shadow and have never known the kiss of sunshine. Through the inch of opened window stole a soft breath of the night air, but it turned black and sluggish the moment it came in. And just then, as Mother hovered there in hesitating doubt, the figure turned and moved across to the bed, supporting herself with the ebony cane she always used. Stiffly she sank upon her knees. The habit was as strong as putting her shoes outside the door at night to be cleaned,-those shoes that never knew the stain of roadway dust-and equally devoid of spiritual significance. Yet, for a moment, as the embittered mind gabbled through the string of words that long habit had crystallised into an empty formula, Mother noticed that the lines of grey grew slightly clearer; the coil and tangle ceased; they even made an effort to emerge and leave the muddy cloud that obscured their knotted, intricate disorder.

The formula Mother recognised; it had hardly changed, indeed, since she herself had learned it at those very knees when days were brighter; it began with wholesale and audacious requests for self, then towards the end passed into vague generalities for the welfare of others. And just here it was that the lines of grey turned brighter and tried to struggle out of the murky atmosphere. The sight was pathetic, yet deeply significant. Mother understood its meaning. There was hope. Behind the prayer for others still shone at least an echo of past meaning.

"I believe in you, old, broken, disappointed heart," flashed through her own bright atmosphere, "and, believing, I can help you!"

Her skill, however, was slight, owing to lack of practice and experience.

She moved over to the bed, trying first to force her own darting rays into the opaque, dull cloud surrounding the other; then seeking a better way-for this had no results—she slipped somehow inside the mist, getting behind it, down at the very source. From here she forced her own light through, mixing her beams of coloured radiance with the thick grey lines themselves. She tried to feel and think as her mother felt and thought, moving beside her mind's initial working, changing the gloom into something brighter as she moved along. This was the proper way, she felt-to clean the source itself, rather than merely untie knots at the outer surface. It was a stifling business, but she persisted. Tiny channels cleared and opened. A little light shone through. She felt-with her mother, instead of arguing, as it were. . .

The old lady presently blew the candle out and composed herself to sleep. Mother laboured on. . .

"Oh dear," she sighed, "oh dear!" as she emerged from the gloom a moment to survey her patient and note results. To her amazement she saw that there was a change indeed, though a very curious one. The entire outer surface of the cloud seemed in commotion, with here and there a glimmering lustre as if a tiny lamp was at last alight within. She felt herself swell with happiness. Instantly, then, the grey lines shot out, fastening with wee loops and curves among her own. Some links evidently had been established. She had imparted something.

"She's dreaming! I do believe I've sown some dream of beauty in her!" she beamed to herself.

Some golden, unaccustomed sleep had fallen over the old lady. Stray shreds of darkness loosened from the general mass and floated off, yet did not melt entirely from sight. She was shedding some of her evil thoughts.

"The Sweep!" thought Mother, and turning, found him beside her in the room. Her husband, to her astonishment, was also there.

"But I didn't think of *you*!" she exclaimed.

"Not a definite thought," he answered, "but you needed me. I felt it. We're so close together now that we're practically one, you see." He trailed his Pattern behind him, clothed now with all manner of rich new colouring, "I've collected such heaps of new ideas," he went on, "and now I want her too. She's in the Story. I'll transfigure her as well." He was bright as paint, and happy as a sand-boy. "Well done, old Mother," he added, "you've done a lot already. See, she's dreaming small, soft, tender things of beauty that your efforts have let through."

He glided across and poured from his own store of sympathy into that dry, atrophied soul upon the bed. "It's a question how much she will be able to transmit, though," he said doubtfully. "The spiritual machinery is so stiff and out of gear from long disuse. In Miss Waghorn's case it's only physical—I've just been there—but this is spiritual blackness. We shall see tomorrow. Something will get through at any rate, and we must do this every night, you know."

"Rather!" echoed Mother.

"Her actual self, you see, has dwindled so that one can hardly find it. It's smaller than a flea, and as hard and black." They smiled a little sadly.

The Sweep, rushing out of the window with his heavy sack loaded to the brim, interrupted their low laughter. He was no talker, but a man of action. Busily all this time he had been gathering up the loose, stray fragments that floated off from the cloud, and stuffing them into the sack. He now flew, singing, into the night, and they barely caught the last words of his eternal song:—

> "... a tremendously busy Sweep,
> Tossing the blacks in the Rubbish Heap
> Over the edge of the world."

"Come," whispered Daddy. "It's getting late. The interfering sun is on the way, and you've been hours here already. All the trains are back, and every one is waiting for us." Yet it had seemed so short a time really.

Wrapped together in the beauty of his Pattern, they left the old lady peacefully asleep, and sped across the roofs towards the forest.

But neither of them noticed, it seemed, the lovely little shining figure that hovered far in the air above and watched them go. It followed them all the way, catching even at the skirts of the flying Pattern as they went. Was it the Spirit of some unknown Star they had attracted from beyond the Milky Way? Or was it, perhaps, a Thought from some fair, exquisite heart that had been wakened by the rushing of the Expresses, and had flashed in to take a place in the wonderful story Daddy wove?

It had little twinkling feet, and its eyes were of brown flame and amber.

"No, they did not notice the starry, fluttering figure. It overtook them none the less, and with a flying leap was into the Pattern of his story—in the very centre, too!—as quickly as lightning passes through the foliage of the tree it strikes. Only the lightning stayed. The figure remained caught. The entire Pattern shivered to its outer fringes, then began to glow and shine all over. As the high harmonic crowns the end of a long cadenza on a violin, fulfilling bars of difficult effort, this point of exquisite beauty flashed life into the Pattern of the story, consummating the labour of construction with the true, inevitable climax. There was something of fairy insolence, both cheeky and delicious, in the proprietary way it chose the principal place, yet the only place still unoccupied, and sang "I'm here. I've come!" It calmly fashioned itself a nest, as it were, curled up and made itself at home. It *was* at home. The audacity was justified. The Pattern seemed at last complete. Beauty and Truth shone at its centre. And the tiny voice continued singing, though no one seemed to know exactly whence the sound proceeded:—

"While the busy Pleiades,
Sisters to the Hyades,
Seven by seven,
Across the heaven,
Light desire
With their fire,

Flung from huge Orion's hand,
Sweetly linking
All our thinking
In the Net of Sympathy that brings back Fairyland!"

No—neither Mother nor Daddy were aware of what had happened thus in the twinkling of an eye. Certainly neither guessed that another heart, far distant as the crow flies, had felt the stream of his vital, creative thinking, and had thus delicately responded and sent out a sympathetic message of belief. But neither did Adams and Leverrier, measuring the heavens, and calculating through years of labour the delicate interstellar forces, know that each had simultaneously caught Neptune in their net of stars—three thousand million miles away. Had they been "out," these two big, patient astronomers, they might have realised that they really worked in concert every night. But history does not relate that they slept well or ill; their biographies make no mention of what their "Underneaths" were up to while their brains lay resting on the pillow; and private confession, if such exists, has never seen the light of print as yet. In that region, however, where Thinking runs and plays, thought dancing hand in hand with thought that is akin to it, the fact must surely have been known and recognised. They, too, travelled in the Starlight Express.

Mother and Daddy realised it just then as little as children are aware of the loving thoughts of the parent that hovers protectingly about them all day long. They merely acknowledged that a prodigious thrill of happiness pulsed through both of them at once, feeling proud as the group in the tree-tops praised their increased brightness and admired the marvellous shining of the completed Pattern they trailed above their heads. But more than that they did not grasp. Nor have they ever grasped it perhaps. That the result came through later is proved, however, by the published story, and by the strange, sweet beauty its readers felt all over the world. But this belongs to the private working of inspiration which can never be explained, not even by the artist it has set on fire. He, indeed, probably understands it least of all.

"Where are the trains, the Starlight Expresses?" asked Mother.

"Gone!" answered Jimbo. "Gone to Australia where they're wanted. It's evening now down there."

He pointed down, then up. "Don't you see? We must hurry." She looked across the lake where the monstrous wall of Alps was dimly visible. The sky was brightening behind them. Long strata of thin cloud glimmered with faintest pink. The stars were rapidly fading. "What ages you've been!" he added.

"And where's Tante Anna?" she inquired quickly, looking for her brilliant friend.

"She's come and gone a dozen times while you've been skylarking somewhere else," explained Monkey with her usual exaggeration. "She's gone for good now. She sleeps so badly. She's always waking up, you know." Mother understood. Only too well she knew that her friend snatched sleep in briefest intervals, incessantly disturbed by racking pain.

A stream of light flashed past her, dashing like a meteor towards the village and disappearing before she could see the figure.

"There goes Jinny," cried some one, "always working to the very last. The interfering sun'll catch her if she doesn't look out!"

There was movement and hurry everywhere. Already the world ran loose and soft in colour. Birds, just awake, were singing in the trees below. Several passed swiftly overhead, raking the sky with a whirring rush of wings. Everybody was asking questions, urging return, yet lingering as long as possible, each according to his courage. To be caught "out" by the sun meant waking with a sudden start that made getting out of bed very difficult and might even cause a headache.

Rogers alone seemed unperturbed, unhurried, for he was absorbed in a discovery that made him tremble. Noting the sudden perfection of his cousin's Pattern, he had gone closer to examine it, and had—seen the starry figure. Instantly he forgot everything else in the world. It seemed to him that he had suddenly found all he had ever sought. He gazed into those gentle eyes of amber and felt that he gazed into the eyes of the Universe that had taken shape in front of him. Floating up as near as he could, he spoke—

"Where do you come from—from what star?" he asked softly in an ecstasy of wonder.

The tiny face looked straight at him and smiled.

"From the Pleiades, of course,—that little group of star-babies as yet unborn."

"I've been looking for you for ever," he answered.

"You've found me," sang the tiny voice. "This is our introduction. Now, don't forget. There was a lost Pleiad, you know. Try to remember me when you wake."

"Then why are you here?" He meant in the Pattern.

The star-face rippled with laughter.

"It's yours—your Scheme. He's given it perfect shape for you, that's all. Don't you recognise it? But it's my Story as well. . ."

A ray with crimson in it shot out just then across the shoulder of the Blumlisalp, and, falling full upon the tiny face, it faded out; the Pattern faded with it; Daddy vanished too. On the little azure winds of dawn they flashed away. Jimbo, Monkey, and certain of the Sprites alone held on, but the tree-tops to which they clung were growing more and more slippery every minute. Mother, loth to return, balanced bravely on the waving spires of a larch. Her sleep that night had been so deep and splendid, she struggled to prolong it. She hated waking up too early.

"The Morning Spiders! Look out!" cried a Sprite, as a tiny spider on its thread of gossamer floated by. It was the Dustman's voice. Catching the Gypsy with one arm and the Tramp with the other, all three instantly disappeared.

"But where's my Haystack friend?" called Mother faintly, almost losing her balance in the attempt to turn round quickly.

"Oh, she's all right," the Head Gardener answered from a little distance where he was burning something. "She just 'stays put' and flirts with every wind that comes near her. She loves the winds. They know her little ways." He went on busily burning up dead leaves he had been collecting all night long—dead, useless thoughts he had found clogging a hundred hearts and stopping outlets.

"Look sharp!" cried a voice that fell from the sky above them.

> *"Here come the Morning Spiders,*
> *On their gossamer outriders!"*

This time it was the Lamplighter flashing to and fro as he put the stars out one by one. He was in a frantic hurry; he extinguished whole groups of them at once. The Pleiades were the last to fade.

Rogers heard him and came back into himself. For his ecstasy had carried him even beyond the region of the freest "thinking." He could give no account or explanation of it at all. Monkey, Jimbo, Mother, and he raced in a line together for home and safety. Above the fields they met the spiders everywhere, the spiders that bring the dawn and ride off into the Star Cave on lost rays and stray thoughts that careless minds have left scattered about the world.

And the children, as they raced and told their mother to "please move a little more easily and slipperily," sang together in chorus:—

> *"We shall meet the Morning Spiders,*
> *The fairy-cotton riders,*
> *Each mounted on a star's rejected ray;*
> *With their tiny nets of feather*
>
> *They collect our thoughts together,*
> *And on strips of windy weather*
> *Bring the Day. . ."*

"That's stolen from you or Daddy," Mother began to say to Rogers— but was unable to complete the flash. The thought lay loose behind her in the air.

A spider instantly mounted it and rode it off.

Something brushed her cheek. Riquette stood rover her, fingering her face with a soft extended paw.

"But it surely can't be time yet to get up!" she murmured. "I've only just fallen asleep, it seems." She glanced at her watch upon the chair beside the bed, saw that it was only four o'clock, and then turned over, making a space for the cat behind her shoulder. A tremendous host of dreams caught at her sliding mind. She tried to follow them. They vanished. "Oh dear!" she sighed, and promptly fell asleep again. But this time she slept lightly. No more adventures came. She did not dream. And later, when Riquette woke her a second time because it was half-past six, she remembered as little of having been "out" as though such a thing had never taken place at all.

She lit the fire and put the porridge saucepan on the stove. It was a glorious July morning. She felt glad to be alive, and full of happy, singing thoughts. "I wish I could always sleep like that!" she said. "But what a pity one has to wake up in the end!"

And then, as she turned her mind toward the coming duties of the day, another thought came to her. It was a very ordinary, almost a daily thought, but there seemed more behind it than usual. Her whole heart was in it this time—

"As soon as the children are off to school I'll pop over to mother, and see if I can't cheer her up a bit and make her feel more happy. Oh dear!" she added, "life is a bag of duties, whichever way one looks at it!" But she felt a great power in her that she could face them easily and turn each one into joy. She could take life more bigly, carelessly, more as a whole somehow. She was aware of some huge directing power in her "underneath." Moreover, the "underneath" of a woman like Mother was not a trifle that could be easily ignored. That great Under Self, resting in the abysses of being, rose and led. The pettier Upper Self withdrew ashamed, passing over the reins of conduct into those mighty, shadowy hands.

XXVI

Canst thou bind the sweet influences of Pleiades,
Or loose the bands of Orion?

—*Book of Job*

The feeling that something was going to happen—that odd sense of anticipation—which all had experienced the evening before at tea-time had entirely vanished, of course, next morning. It was a mood, and it had passed away. Every one had slept it off. They little realised how it had justified itself. Jane Anne, tidying the Den soon after seven o'clock, noticed the slip of paper above the mantelpiece, read it over—"The Starlight Express will start tonight. Be reddy!"—and tore it down. "How could that. have amused us!" she said aloud, as she tossed it into the waste-paper basket. Yet, even while she did so, some stray sensation of delight clutched at her funny little heart, a touch of emotion she could not understand that was wild and very sweet. She went singing about her work. She felt important and grown-up, extraordinarily light-hearted too. The things she sang made up their own words—such odd snatches that came she knew not whence. An insect clung to her duster, and she shook it out of the window with the crumbs and bits of cotton gathered from the table-cloth.

"Get out, you Morning Spider,
You fairy-cotton rider!"

she sang, and at the same minute Mother opened the bedroom door and peeped in, astonished at the unaccustomed music. In her voluminous dressing-gown, her hair caught untidily in a loose net, her face flushed from stooping over the porridge saucepan, she looked, thought Jinny, "like a haystack somehow." Of course she did not say it. The draught, flapping at her ample skirts, added the idea of a covering tarpaulin to the child's mental picture. She went on dusting with a half-offended air, as though Mother had no right to interrupt her with a superintending glance like this.

"You won't forget the sweeping too, Jinny?" said Mother, retiring again majestically with that gliding motion her abundant proportions achieved so gracefully.

"Of course I won't, Mother," and the instant the door was closed she fell into another snatch of song, the words of which flowed unconsciously into her mind, it seemed—

> *"For I'm a tremendously busy Sweep,*
> *Dusting the room while you're all asleep,*
> *And shoving you all in the rubbish heap,*
> *Over the edge of the tiles"*

—a little wumbled, it is true, but its source unmistakable.

And all day long, with every one, it was similar, this curious intrusion of the night into the day, the sub-conscious into the conscious—a kind of subtle trespassing. The flower of forgotten dreams rose so softly to the surface of consciousness that they had an air of sneaking in, anxious to be regarded as an integral part of normal waking life. Like bubbles in water they rose, discharged their puff of fragrant air, and disappeared again. Jane Anne, in particular, was simply radiant all day long, and more than usually clear-headed. Once or twice she wumbled, but there was big sense in her even then. It was only the expression that evaded her. Her little brain was a poor transmitter somehow.

"I feel all endowed today," she informed Rogers, when he congratulated her later in the day on some cunning act of attention she bestowed upon him. It was in the courtyard where they all sat sunning themselves after *dejeuner*, and before the younger children returned to afternoon school.

"I feel emaciated, you know," she added, uncertain whether emancipated was the word she really sought.

"You'll be quite grown-up," he told her, "by the time I come back to little Bourcelles in the autumn." Little Bourcelles! It sounded, the caressing way he said it, as if it lay in the palm of his big brown hand.

"But you'll never come back, because you'll never go," Monkey chimed in. "My hair, remember—"

"*My* trains won't take you," said Jimbo gravely.

"Oh, a train may *take* you," continued Monkey, "but you can't leave. Going away by train isn't leaving."

"It's only like going to sleep," explained her brother. You'll come back every night in a Starlight Express—"

"Because a Starlight Express takes passengers—whether they like it or not. You take an ordinary train, but a starlight train takes you!" added Monkey.

Mother heard the words and looked up sharply from her knitting. Something, it seemed, had caught her attention vividly, though until now her thoughts had been busy with practical things of quite another order. She glanced keenly round at the faces, where all sat grouped upon the stone steps of La Citadelle. Then she smiled curiously, half to herself. What she said was clearly not what she had first meant to say.

"Children, you're not sitting on the cold stone, are you?" she inquired, but a little absent-mindedly.

"We're quite warm; we've got our thick under-neathies on," was the reply. They realised that only part of her mind was in the, question, and that any ordinary answer would satisfy her.

Mother resumed her knitting, apparently satisfied.

But Jinny, meanwhile, had been following her own train of thought, started by her cousin's description of her as "grown-up." The picture grew big and gracious in her mind.

"I wonder what I shall do when my hair goes up?" she observed, apparently *a propos de bottes*. It was the day, of course, eagerly, almost feverishly, looked forward to.

"Hide your head in a bag probably," laughed her sister. Jinny flushed; her hair was not abundant. Yet she seemed puzzled rather than offended.

"Never mind," Rogers soothed her. "The day a girl puts up her hair, a thousand young men are aware of it,—and one among them trembles." The idea of romance seemed somehow in the air.

"Oh, Cousinenry!" She was delighted, comforted, impressed; but perplexity was uppermost. Something in his tone of voice prevented impudent comment from the others.

"And all the stars grow a little brighter," he added. "The entire universe is glad."

"I shall be a regular company promoter!" she exclaimed, nearer to wit than she knew, yet with only the vaguest inkling of what he really meant.

"And draw up a Memorandum of Agreement with the Milky Way," he added, gravely smiling.

He had just been going to say "with the Pleiades," when something checked him. A wave of strange emotion swept him. It rose from the depths within, then died away as mysteriously as it came. Like exquisite music heard from very far away, it left its thrill of beauty and of wonder, then hid behind the breath of wind that brought it. "The whole world, you see, will know," he added under his breath to the delighted child. He looked into her queer, flushed face. The blue eyes for a moment had, he thought, an amber tinge. It was a mere effect of light, of course; the sun had passed behind a cloud. Something that he ought to have known, ought to have remembered, flashed mockingly before him and was gone. "One among them trembles," he repeated in his mind. He himself was trembling.

"The Morning Spiders," said some one quietly and softly, "are standing at their stable doors, making faces at the hidden sun."

But he never knew who said it, or if it was not his own voice speaking below his breath. He glanced at Jimbo. The small grave face wore an air of man-like preoccupation, as was always the case when he felt a little out of his depth in general conversation. He assumed it in self-protection. He never exposed himself by asking questions. The music of that under-voice ran on:—

> *"Sweet thoughts, like fine weather,*
> *Bind closely together*
> *God's stars with the heart of a boy."*

But he said it aloud apparently this time, for the others looked up with surprise. Monkey inquired what in the world he was talking about, only, not quite knowing himself, he could not answer her. Jimbo then, silent and preoccupied, found his thoughts still running on marriage. The talk about his sister's hair going up no doubt had caused it. He remembered the young schoolmistress who had her meals at the Pension, and the Armenian student who had fallen in love with, and eventually married, her. It was the only courtship he had ever witnessed. Marriage and courtship seemed everywhere this morning.

"I saw it all with Mlle. Perette," he informed the party. "It began already by his pouring out water for her and passing the salt and things. It *always* begins like that. He got shawls even when she was hot."

He looked so wise and grave that nobody laughed, and his sisters even seemed impressed rather. Jinny waited anxiously for more. If Mother did make an odd grimace, it was not noticed, and anyhow was cleverly converted into the swallowing of a yawn. There was a moment's silence. Jimbo, proudly conscious that more was expected of him, provided it in his solemn little voice.

"But it must be horrid," he announced, "to be married—always sticked to the same woman, like that." No sentence was complete without the inevitable "already" or "like that," translated from the language he was more at home in. He thought in French. "I shall never marry myself (*me marier*) he decided, seeing his older sister's eyes upon him wonderingly. Then, uncertain whether he had said an awfully wise or an awfully foolish thing, he added no more. Anyhow, it was the way a man should talk—with decision.

"It's bad enough to be a wife," put in Monkey, "but it must be worse still to have one!"

But Jane Anne seemed shocked. A man, Jimbo reflected, can never be sure how his wisdom may affect the other sex; women are not meant to know everything. She rose with dignity and went upstairs towards the door, and Monkey, rippling with laughter, smacked her as she went. This only shocked her more.

"That was a slight mistake behind," she said reprovingly, looking back; "you should have more reserve, I think," then firmly shut the door.

All of which meant—so far as Jane Anne was concerned—that an important standard of conduct—grown-up, dignified, stately in a spiritual sense—was being transferred to her present behaviour, but transferred ineffectively. Elsewhere Jane Anne lived it, *was* it. She knew it, but could not get at the part of her that knew it. The transmitting machinery was imperfect. Connecting links and switches were somehow missing. Yearning was strong in her, that yearning which is common to all the world, though so variously translated. Once out of the others' sight, she made a curious face. She went into her room between the kitchen and the Den, flung herself on the bed, and burst into tears. And the fears brought relief. They oiled the machinery perhaps. At any rate, she soon felt better.

"I felt so enormous and unsettled," she informed Mother later, when the redness of her eyes was noticed and she received breathlessly a great comforting hug. "I never get anything right."

"But you *are* right, darling," Mother soothed her, little guessing that she told the perfect truth. "You are all right, only you don't know it. Everybody's wumbled somewhere." And she advised her—ah, Mother was profoundly wise instinctively—not to think so much, but just go ahead as usual and do her work.

For Mother herself felt a little queer that day, as though something very big and splendid lay hiding just beyond her reach. It surged up, vanished, then surged up again, and it came closest when she was not thinking of it. The least effort of the mind to capture it merely plunged her into an empty gulf where she could not touch bottom. The glorious thing ran instantly underground. She never ceased to be aware of it, but any attempt to focus resulted in confusion. Analysis was beyond her powers, yet the matter was very simple really, for only when thought is blank, and when the mind has forgotten to think, can inspiration come through into the heart. The intellect interprets afterwards, sets in order, regulates, examines the wonder and beauty the heart distils alchemically out of the eternal stream in which life everywhere dips its feet. If Reason interferes too soon, or during transmission, it only muddles and destroys. And Mother, hitherto, had always been so proud of being practical, prosaic, reasonable. She had deliberately suppressed the other. She could not change in a single day just because she had been "out" and made discoveries last night. Oh, how simple it all was really, and yet how utterly most folk convert the wonder of it into wumbling!

Like Jane Anne, her miniature, she felt splendid all day long, but puzzled too. It was almost like those religious attacks she had experienced in early youth. She had no definite creed by which she could explain it. Though nominally Christian, like her husband, she could not ascribe her joy to a "Holy Spirit," or to a "God" working in her. But she was reminded of her early "religious attacks" because she now experienced that large sensation of glorious peace and certainty which usually accompanies the phenomenon in the heart called "conversion." She saw life whole. She rested upon some unfailing central Joy. Come what might, she felt secure and "saved." Something everlasting lay within call, an ever-ready help in trouble; and all day she was vaguely conscious that her life lay hid with—with what? She never found the word exactly, for "Joy" was but one aspect of it. She fell back upon the teachings of the big religions which are the police regulations of the world. Yet all creeds shared these, and her feeling was far deeper than mere moral teachings. And then she gave up thinking about it. Besides, she had much knitting to do.

"It's come to stay anyhow; I feel in sympathy with everybody," she said, and so dismissed vain introspection, keeping the simple happiness and peace. That was her strength, as it was also Jinny's. A re-formation had begun.

Jimbo, too, felt something in his microcosmic way, only he said little and asked no single question. It betrayed itself, however, to his Mother's widened vision. He was all stirred up. He came back again from school at three o'clock—for it was Thursday and he did not take the singing lesson from three to four—put down his books with a very business-like air, forgot to kiss his Mother—and went out.

"Where are you off to, Jimbo?" She scented mischief. He was so *affaire*.

He turned obediently at once, the face grave and puckered.

"Going over to the carpenter's house, Mummy."

"What for, dear? Why don't you stay and play here?" She had the feeling that her husband was absorbed in his work and would not like to be disturbed.

The boy's reply was evasive too. "I want to have a long discuss with Daddy," he said.

"Can't you have your long discuss with me instead?" she asked.

He shook his head. "You see," he answered solemnly, "it's about things."

"But Daddy's working just now; he'll be over to tea at four. Can't it wait till then?"

She understood too well to inquire what "things" might be. The boy wished to speak with one of his own sex—as one man to another man.

"When a man's at work," she added, "he doesn't like to be disturbed."

"All right," was the reply. "We can wait a little," and he settled down to other things in a corner by himself. His mind, clearly, was occupied with grave considerations he could not discuss with anybody, least of all with women and children. But, of course, busy men must not be interrupted. For a whole hour in his corner he made no sound, and hardly any movement.

But Daddy did not come at four o'clock. He was evidently deep in work. And Mother did not send for him. The carpenter's wife, she knew, would provide a cup of tea.

He came late to supper, too, at the Pension, nodded to Mother with an expression which plainly said, "I've finished the story at last"; winked to his cousin, meaning, "It came out all right, I'm satisfied," and took his seat between Jinny and Mlle. Vuillemot, the governess who had earned her meal by giving a music lesson that afternoon to a *pensionnaire*. Jinny looked sideways at him in a spirit of examination, and picked the inevitable crumb deftly from his beard.

"Reminiscences!" she observed slyly. "You did have some tea, then." Her long word was well chosen for once; her mind unusually logical, too.

But Daddy made no reply; he went on eating whatever was set before him with an air of complete detachment; he devoured cold ham and salad automatically; and the children, accustomed to this absorption, ignored his presence. He was still in the atmosphere of his work, abstracted, lost to the outer world. They knew they would only, get wumbled answers to their questions and remarks, and they did not dare to tease him. From time to time he lifted his eyes—very bright they were—and glanced round the table, dimly aware that he was in the midst of a stream of noisy chatter, but unable to enter it successfully at any point. Mother, watching him, thought, "He's sitting on air, he's wrapped in light, he's very happy"; and ate an enormous supper, as though an insatiable hunger was in her.

The governess, Mlle. Vuillemot, who stood in awe of the "author" in him, seized her opportunity. She loved to exchange a *mot* with a real writer, reading all kinds of unintended subtlety into his brief replies in dreadful French. Tonight she asked him the meaning of a word, title of a Tauchnitz novel she had been reading—Juggernaut; but, being on his deaf side, he caught "Huguenot" instead, and gave her a laboured explanation, strangled by appalling grammar.

The historical allusions dazed her; the explanation ended on a date. She was sorry she had ventured, for it made her feel so ignorant.

"Shuggairnort," she repeated bravely. She had a vague idea he had not properly heard before.

But this time he caught "Argonaut," and swamped her then with classical exposition, during which she never took her eyes off him, and decided that he was far more wonderful than she had ever dreamed. He was; but not for the reasons she supposed.

"Thank you," she said with meek gratitude at the end, "I thank you."

"Il n'y a pas de quar," replied Daddy, bowing; and the adventure came to an end. The others luckily had not heard it in full swing; they only caught the final phrase with which he said adieu. But it served its unwitting purpose admirably. It brought him back to the world about him. The spell was broken. All turned upon him instantly.

"Snay pas un morsow de bong." Monkey copied his accent, using a sentence from a schoolboy's letter in *Punch*. "It's not a bit of good." Mother squelched her with a look, but Daddy, even if he noticed it, was not offended. Nothing could offend him tonight. Impertinence turned silvery owing to the way he took it. There was a marvellous light and sweetness about him. "He *is* on air," decided Mother finally. "He's written his great Story—our story. It's finished!"

"I don't know," he said casually to the others, as they stood talking a few minutes in the salon before going over to the Den, "if you'd like to hear it; but I've got a new creature for the Wumble Book. It came to me while I was thinking of something else—"

"Thinking of one thing while you were thinking of another!" cried Monkey. It described exaccurately his state of mind sometimes.

"—and I jotted down the lines on my cuff. So it's not very perfect yet."

Mother had him by the arm quickly. Mlle. Vuillemot was hovering in his neighbourhood, for one thing. It seemed to her they floated over, almost flew.

"It's a Haystack Woman," he explained, once they were safely in the Den grouped about him. "A Woman of the Haystack who is loved by the Wind. That is to say, the big Wind loves her, but she prefers the younger, handsomer little Winds, and—"

He was not allowed to finish. The children laid his cuff back in a twinkling, drawing up the coat sleeve.

"But surely I know that," Mother was saying. "I've heard of her before somewhere. I wonder where?" Others were saying the same thing. "It's not new."

"Impossible," said Daddy, "for the idea only came to me this morning while I was—"

"Thinking of something else," Monkey again finished the sentence for him.

Mother felt that things were rushing about her from another world. She was vaguely conscious—deliciously, bewilderingly—of having heard this all before. Imaginative folk have built the certainty of a previous existence upon evidence as slight; for actual scenery came with it, and she saw dim forest trees, and figures hovering in the background, and bright atmosphere, and fields of brilliant stars. She felt happy and shining, light as a feather, too. It all was just beyond her reach, though; she could not recover it properly. "It must have been a dream *she* told me," was her conclusion, referring to Mlle. Lemaire. Her old friend was in it somewhere or other. She felt sure of that.

She hardly heard, indeed, the silly lines her husband read aloud to the children. She liked the sound of his voice, though; it suggested music she had known far away—in her childhood.

"It's high spirits really," whispered Rogers, sitting beside her in the window. "It's a sort of overflow from his story. He can't do that kind of rhyme a bit, but it's an indication—"

"You think he's got a fine big story this time?" she asked under her breath; and Cousin Henry's eyes twinkled keenly as he gave a significant nod and answered: "Rather! Can't you feel the splendour all about him, the strength, the harmony!"

She leaped at the word. Harmony exactly described this huge new thing that had come into the family, into the village, into the world. The feeling that they all were separate items, struggling for existence one against the other, had gone for ever. Life seemed now a single whole, an enormous pattern. Every one fitted in. There was effort—wholesome jolly effort, but no longer the struggle or fighting that were ugly. To "live carelessly" was possible and right because the pattern was seen entire. It was to live in the whole.

"Harmony," she repeated to herself, with a great swelling happiness in her heart, "that's the nunculus of the matter."

"The what?" he asked, overhearing her.

"The nunculus," she repeated bravely, seeing the word in her mind, yet unable to get it quite. Rogers did not correct her.

"Rather," was all he said. "Of course it is." What did the pronunciation of a word matter at such a time? Her version even sounded better than the original. Mother saw things bigger! Already she was becoming creative!

"And you're the one who brought it," she continued, but this time so low that he did not catch the words. "It's you, your personality, your thinking, your atmosphere somehow that have brought this gigantic sense of peace and calm security which are *au fond* nothing but the consciousness of harmony and the power of seeing ugly details in their proper place—in a single *coup d'oeil*—and understanding them as parts of a perfect whole."

It was her thought really running on; she never could have found the words like that. She thought in French, too, for one thing. And, in any case, Rogers could not have heard her, for he was listening now to the uproar of the children as they criticised Daddy's ridiculous effusion. A haystack, courted in vain by zephyrs, but finally taken captive by an equinoctial gale, strained nonsense too finely for their sense of what was right and funny. It was the pictures he now drew in the book that woke their laughter. He gave the stack a physiognomy that they recognised.

"But, Mother, he's making it look like you!" cried Monkey—only Mother was too far away in her magnificent reverie to reply intelligently.

"I know her; she's my friend," she answered vaguely. "So it's all right."

"Majestic Haystack"—it was the voice of the wind addressing her:—

"*Majestic Haystack, Empress of my life,*
Your ample waist
Just fits the gown I fancy for my wife,
And suits my taste;
Yet there you stand, flat-footed, square and deep,
An unresponsive, elephantine heap,
Coquetting with the stars while I'm asleep,
O cruel Stack!

Coy, silent Monster, Matron of the fields,
I sing to you;
And all the fondest love that summer yields
I bring to you;
Yet there you squat, immense in your disdain,
Heedless of all the tears of streaming rain
My eyes drip over you—your breathless swain;
O stony Stack!

Stupendous Maiden, sweetest when oblong,
Does inner flame
Now smoulder in thy soul to hear my song
Repeat thy name?
Or does thy huge and ponderous heart object
The advances of my passion, and reject
My love because it's airy and elect?
O wily Stack!

O crested goddess, thatched and top-knotted,
O reckless Stack!
Of wives that to the Wind have been allotted
There is no lack;
You've spurned my love as though I were a worm;
But next September when I see thy form,
I'll woo thee with an equinoctial storm!
I have that knack!"

"Far less wumbled than usual," thought Rogers, as the children danced about the room, making up new ridiculous rhymes, of which "I'll give you a whack" seemed the most popular. Only Jane Anne was quiet. A courtship even so remote and improbable as between the Wind and a Haystack sent her thoughts inevitably in the dominant direction.

"It must be nice when one is two," she whispered ambiguously to Mother with a very anxious face, "but I'm sure that if a woman can't cook, love flies out of the window. It's a positive calamity, you know."

But it was Cousin Henry's last night in Bourcelles, and the spirit of pandemonium was abroad. Neither parent could say no to anything, and mere conversation in corners was out of the question. The door was opened into the corridor, and while Mother played her only waltz, Jimbo and Monkey danced on the splintery boards as though it were a parquet floor, and Rogers pirouetted somewhat solemnly with Jane Anne. She enjoyed it immensely, yet rested her hand very gingerly upon his shoulder. "Please don't hold me *quite* so tight," she ventured. "I've never danced with a strange man before, you see"; and he no more laughed at her than he had laughed at Mother's "nunculus." Even Jane Anne, he knew, would settle down comfortably before long into the great big pattern where a particular nook awaited—aye, needed—her bizarre, odd brilliance. The most angular fragments would nest softly, neatly in. A little filing, a little polishing, and all would fit together. To force would only be to break. Hurry was of the devil. And later, while Daddy played an ancient tune that was written originally as a mazurka yet did duty now for a two-step, he danced with Mother too, and the children paused to watch out of sheer admiration.

"Fancy, Mother dancing!" they exclaimed with glee—except Jinny, who was just a little offended and went to stand by the piano till it was over. For Mother danced as lightly as a child for all her pride of measurement, and no frigate ever skimmed the waves more gracefully than Mother glided over those uneven boards.

"The Wind and the Haystack" of course, was Monkey's description.

"You'll wind and haystack to bed now," was the reply, as Mother sat and fanned herself in the corner. The "bed-sentence" as the children called it, was always formed in this way. Whatever the child was saying when the moment came, Mother adopted as her verb. "Shall I put some peat on, Mother?" became "Peat yourself off to bed-it's nine o'clock"—and the child was sorry it had spoken.

Good-byes had really been said at intervals all day long, and so tonight were slight enough; the children, besides, were so "excitey-tired," as Monkey put it, that they possessed no more emotion of any kind. There were various disagreeable things in the immediate future of Tomorrow—getting up early, school, and so forth; and Cousin Henry's departure they lumped in generally with the mass, accepted but unrealised. Jimbo could hardly keep his eyes alight, and Monkey's hair was like a baby haystack the wind had treated to an equinoctial storm. Jinny, stiff, perplexed, and solemn with exhaustion, yet dared not betray it because she was older, in measurable distance of her hair going up.

"Why don't you play with the others, child?" asked Mother, finding her upright on a sofa while the romp went on.

"Oh, tonight," Jinny explained, "I sit indifferent and look on. I don't always feel like skedivvying about!"

To skedivvy was to chivvy and skedaddle—its authority not difficult to guess.

"Good-bye, Cousinenry," each gasped, as his big arms went round them and squeezed out the exclamation. "Oh, thank you most awfully," came next, with another kiss, produced by his pressing something hard and round and yellow into each dirty little hand. "It's only a bit of crystallised starlight," he explained, "that escaped long ago from the Cave. And starlight, remember, shines for everybody as well as for yourselves. You can buy a stamp with it occasionally, too," he added, "and write to me."

"We will. Of course!"

Jimbo straightened up a moment before the final collapse of sleep.

"Your train leaves at 6.23," he said, with the authority of exclusive information. "You must be at the station at six to get the *bagages enregistrees*. It's a slow train to Pontarlier, but you'll find a *wagon direct* for Paris in front, next to the engine. I shall be at the station to see you off."

"*I* shan't," said Monkey.

Rogers realised with delight the true meaning of these brief and unemotional good-byes. "They know I'm coming back; they feel that the important part of me is not going away at all. My thinking stays here with them."

Jinny lingered another ten minutes for appearance's sake. It was long past her bed-time, too, but dignity forbade her retiring with the others. Standing by the window she made conversation a moment, feeling it was the proper, grown-up thing to do. It was even expected of her.

"Look! It's full moon," she observed gravely, as though suggesting that she could, if she liked, go out and enjoy the air. "Isn't it lovely?"

"No, yesterday was full moon," Rogers corrected her, joining her and looking out. "Two nights ago, to be exact, I think."

"Oh," she replied, as solemnly as though politics or finance were under discussion, "then it's bigger than full moon now. It goes on, does it, getting fuller and fuller, till—"

"Now, Jinny dear, it's very late, and you'd better full-moon off to bed," Mother interrupted gently.

"Yes, Mother; I'm just saying good-night." She held her hand out, as though she was afraid he might kiss her, yet feared he would not. "Good-bye, Mr. Cousin Henry, and I hope you'll have an exceedingly happy time in the train and soon come back and visit us again."

"Thank you," he said, "I'm sure I shall." He gave her a bit of solid starlight as he said it, then suddenly leaned forward and kissed her on the cheek. Making a violent movement like an experienced boxer who dodges an upper cut, Jinny turned and fled precipitately from the room, forgetting her parents altogether. That kiss, she felt, consumed her childhood in a flash of fiery flame. In bed she decided that she must lengthen her skirts the very next day, and put her hair up too. She must do something that should give her protection and yet freedom. For a long time she did not sleep. She lay thinking it over. She felt supremely happy—wild, excited, naughty. "A man has kissed me; it was a man; it was Mr. Rogers, Daddy's cousin. . . He's not *my* cousin exactly, but just 'a man.'" And she fell asleep, wondering how she ought to begin her letter to him when she wrote, but, more perplexing still, how she ought to—end it! That little backward brain sought the solution of the problem all night long in dreams. She felt a criminal, a dare-devil caught in the act, awaiting execution. Light had been flashed cruelly upon her dark, careful secret—the greatest and finest secret in the world. The child lay under sentence indeed, only it was a sentence of life, and not of death.

XXVII

ASIA: . . . *I feel, I see*
Those eyes which burn through smiles that fade in tears,
Like stars half quenched in mists of silver dew.

—Prometheus Unbound, SHELLEY

It was only ten o'clock, really, and the curfew was ringing from every village on the mountain-side. The sound of the bells, half musical, half ominous, was borne by the bise across the vineyards, for the easterly wind that brings fine weather was blowing over lake and forest, and seemed to drive before it thin sheets of moonlight that turned the whole world soft. The village lay cosily dreaming beneath the sky. Once the curfew died away there was only the rustling of the plane trees in the old courtyard. The great Citadelle loomed above the smaller houses, half in shadow half in silver, nodding heavily to the spire of the Church, and well within sight of the sentinelle poplar that guarded the village from the forest and the mountains. Far away, these mountains now lowered their enormous shoulders to let night flow down upon the sleeping world. The Scaffolding that brought it had long since sailed over France towards the sea. . .

Mother, still panting from the ritual of fastening the younger children into bed, had gone a moment down the passage to say good-night to Mlle. Lemaire, and when she returned, the three of them—herself, her husband, and Cousin Henry—dropped into chairs beside the window and watched the silvery world in silence for a time. None felt inclined to speak. There was drama somehow in that interval of silence—that drama which lurks everywhere and always behind life's commonest, most ordinary moments. Actions reveal it—sometimes—but it mostly lies concealed, and especially in deep silences like this, when the ticking of a cuckoo clock upon the wall may be the sole hint of its presence.

It was not the good-byes that made all three realise it so near, though good-byes are always solemn and momentous things; it was something that stirred and rose upon them from a far deeper strata of emotion than that caused by apparent separation. For no pain lay in it, but a power much more difficult to express in the sounds and syllables of speech—Joy. A great joy, creative and of big significance, had known accomplishment. Each felt it, knew it, realised it. The moonlit night was aware of it. The entire universe knew it, too. The drama lay in that. There had been creation—of more light. . . The world was richer than it had been. Some one had caught Beauty in a net, and to catch Beauty is to transform and recreate all common things. It is revelation.

Through the mind of each of these three flowed the stream of casual thinking—images, reflections, and the shadowy scaffoldings of many new emotions—sweeping along between the banks of speech and silence. And this stream, though in flood, did not overflow into words for a long time. With eyes turned inwards, each watched the current pass. Clear and deep, it quietly reflected—stars. Each watched the same stream, the same calm depths, the same delicate reflections. They were in harmony with themselves, and therefore with the universe. . .

Then, suddenly, one of the reflections—it was the Pleiades—rose to the surface to clasp its lovely original. It was the woman who netted the golden thought and drew it forth for all to see.

"Couldn't you read it to us, Daddy?" she whispered softly across the silence.

"If it's not too long for you." He was so eager, so willing to comply.

"We will listen till the Morning Spiders take us home," his cousin said.

"It's only the shorter version," Daddy agreed shiningly, "a sketch for the book which, of course, will take a year to write. I might read *that*, perhaps."

"Do," urged Mother. "We are all in it, aren't we? It's our story as well as yours."

He rose to get the portfolio from the shelf where he had laid it, and while Rogers lit the lamp, Riquette stole in at the window, picking her way daintily across the wet tiles. She stood a moment, silhouetted against the sky; then shaking her feet rapidly each in turn like bits of quivering wire, she stepped precisely into the room. "I am in it too," she plainly said, curling herself up on the chair Daddy had just vacated, but resigning herself placidly enough to his scanty lap when he came back again and began to read. Her deep purring, while he stroked her absent-mindedly, became an undercurrent in the sound of his voice, then presently ceased altogether. . .

On and on he read, while the moon sailed over La Citadelle, bidding the stars hush to listen too. She put her silvery soft hands across their eyes that they might hear the better. The blue wind of night gathered up the meaning and spread it everywhere. The forest caught the tale from the low laughter in the crest of the poplar, and passed it on to the leagues of forest that bore it in turn across the frontiers into France. Thence snowy Altels and the giant Blumlisalp flashed it south along the crowding peaks and down among the Italian chestnut woods, who next sent it coursing over the rustling waves of the Adriatic and mixed it everywhere with the Mediterranean foam. In the morning the shadows upon bare Grecian hills would whisper it among the ancient islands, and the East catch echoes of it in the winds of dawn. The forests of the North would open their great gloomy eyes with wonder, as though strange new wild-flowers had come among them in the night. All across the world, indeed, wherever there were gardened minds tender enough to grow fairy seed, these flakes of thought would settle down in sleep, and blossom in due season into a crop of magic beauty.

He read on and on. . . The village listened too, the little shadowy street, the familiar pine woods, the troubled Pension, each, as its image was evoked in the story, knew its soul discovered, and stirred in its sleep towards the little room to hear. And the desolate ridges of La Tourne and Boudry, the clefts where the wild lily of the valley grew unknown, high nooks and corners where the buzzards nested, these also knew and answered to the trumpet summons of the Thought that made them live. A fire of creation ran pulsing from this centre. All were in the Pattern of the Story.

To the two human listeners it seemed as familiar as a tale read, in childhood long ago, and only half forgotten. They always knew a little of what was coming next. Yet it spread so much further than mere childhood memories, for its golden atmosphere included all countries and all times. It rose and sang and sparkled, lighting up strange deep recesses of their unconscious and half-realised life, and almost revealing the tiny silver links that joined them on to the universe at large. The golden ladders from the Milky Way were all let down. They climbed up silvery ropes into the Moon. . .

"It's not my own idea," he said; "I'm convinced of that. It's all flocked into me from some other mind that thought it long ago, but could not write it, perhaps. No thought is lost, you see—never can be lost. Like this, somehow, I feel it:—

Now sinks to sleep the clamour of the day,
And, million-footed, from the Milky Way,

Falls shyly on my heart the world's lost Thought—
Shower of primrose dust the stars have taught
To haunt each sleeping mind,
Till it may find

A garden in some eager, passionate brain
That, rich in loving-kindness as in pain,
Shall harvest it, then scatter forth again
It's garnered loveliness from heaven caught.

Oh, every yearning thought that holds a tear,
Yet finds no mission,
And lies untold,

Waits, guarded in that labyrinth of gold,—
To reappear
Upon some perfect night,
Deathless—not old—
But sweet with time and distance,
And clothed as in a vision
Of starry brilliance
For the world's delight."

In the pauses, from time to time, they heard the distant thunder of the Areuse as it churned and tumbled over the Val de Travers boulders. The Colombier bells, as the hours passed, strung the sentences together; moonlight wove in and out of every adventure as they listened; stars threaded little chapters each to each with their eternal golden fastenings. The words seemed written down in dew, but the dew crystallised into fairy patterns that instantly flew about the world upon their mission of deliverance. In this ancient Network of the Stars the universe lay fluttering; and they lay with it, all prisoners in Fairyland.

For the key of it all was sympathy, and the delicate soul of it was tender human love. Bourcelles, in this magic tale, was the starting-point whence the Starlight Expresses flashed into all the world, even unto unvisited, forgotten corners that had known no service hitherto. It was so adaptable and searching, and knew such tiny, secret ways of entrance. The thought was so penetrating, true, and simple. Even old Mother Plume would wake to the recovery of some hitherto forgotten fragrance in her daily life. . . just as those Northern forests would wake to find new wild-flowers. For all fairytales issue first from the primeval forest, thence undergoing their protean transformation; and in similar fashion this story, so slight but so tremendous, issued from the forest of one man's underthinking—one deep, pure mind, wumbled badly as far as external things were concerned, yet realising that Bourcelles contained the Universe, and that he, in turn contained Bourcelles. Another, it is true, had shown it to him, though all unwittingly, and had cleaned in his atmosphere the channels for the entrance of the glorious pattern. But the result was the same. In his brain—perhaps by Chance, perhaps by God—lay the machinery which enabled him to give it out to others—the power and ability to transmit. It was a fairy-tale of the world, only the world had forgotten it. He brought back its fairyland again.

And this fairyland, what and where was it? And how could this tale of its recovery bring into his listeners' hearts such a sense of peace and joy that they felt suddenly secure in the world and safe mid all the confusion of their muddled lives? That there were tears in Mother's eyes seems beyond question, because the moonlight, reflected faintly from a wet cobble in the yard below, glistened like a tiny silver lantern there. They betrayed the fact that something in her had melted and flowed free. Yet there was no sadness in the fairy-tale to cause it; they were tears of joy.

Surely it was that this tale of Starlight, Starlight Expresses and Star Caves, told as simply as running water, revealed the entire Universe—as One, and that in this mighty, splendid thing each of them nested safe and comfortable. The world was really *thinking*, and all lay fluttering in the grand, magnificent old Net of Stars. What people think, they are. All can think Beauty. And sympathy—to feel with everything—was the clue; for sympathy is love, and to love a star was to love a neighbour. To be without sympathy was to feel apart, and to think apart was to cut oneself off from life, from the Whole, from God and joy—it was Death. To work at commonplace duties because they were duties to the Universe at large, this was the way to find courage, peace, and happiness, because this was genuine and successful work, no effort lost, and the most distant star aware of it. Thinking was living, whether material results were visible or not; yearning was action, even though no accomplishment was apparent; thought and sympathy, though felt but for a passing moment, sweetened the Pleiades and flashed along the Milky Way, and so-called tangible results that could prove it to the senses provided no adequate test of accomplishment or success. In the knowledge of belonging to this vast underlying unity was the liberation that brings courage, carelessness, and joy, and to admit failure in anything, by thinking it, was to weaken the entire structure which binds together the planets and the heart of a boy. Thoughts were the fairies that the world believed in when it was younger, simpler, less involved in separation; and the golden Fairyland recovered in this story was the Fairyland of lovely thinking. . .

In this little lamp-lit room of the Citadelle, the two listeners were conscious of this giant, delicate network that captured every flying thought and carried it streaming through the world. God became a simple thing: He fashioned Rogers's Scheme, even though it never materialised in bricks and mortar. God was behind Mother, even when she knitted or lit the fire in the Den. All were prisoners in His eternal Fairyland. . .

And the symbolism of the story, the so-called fantasy, they also easily understood, because they felt it true. To be "out" of the body was merely to think and feel away from self. As they listened they realised themselves in touch with every nation and with every time, with all possible beliefs and disbeliefs, with every conceivable kind of thinking, that is, which ever has existed or ever shall exist. . .

The heat and radiance given out by the clear delivery of this "inspirational" fairy-tale must have been very strong; far-reaching it certainly was. . .

"Ah!" sighed Rogers to himself, "if only I could be like that!" not realising that he was so.

"Oh dear!" felt the Woman, "that's what I've felt sometimes. I only wish it were true of me!" unaware that it could be, and even by the fact of her yearning, *was* so.

"If only I could get up and help the world!" passed like a flame across the heart of the sufferer who lay on her sleepless bed next door, listening to the sound of the droning voice that reached her through the wall, yet curiously ignorant that this very longing was already majestically effective in the world of definite action.

And even Mother Plume, pacing her airless room at the further end of the village and tapping her ebony stick upon the floor, turned suspiciously, as at a passing flash of light that warmed her for a sudden instant as it went.

"Perhaps, after all, they don't mean all these unkind things they do to me!" she thought; "I live so much alone. Possibly I see things less clearly than I used to do!"

The spell was certainly very potent, though Daddy himself, reading out the little shining chapters, guessed as little as the rest of them how strong. So small a part of what he meant to say, it seemed, had been transferred to the paper. More than he realised, far, far more, lay between the lines, of course. There was conviction in it, because there was vision and belief. Not much was said when he put his roll of paper down and leaned back in his chair. Riquette opened her eyes and blinked narrowly, then closed them again and began to purr. The ticking of the cuckoo clock seemed suddenly very loud and noticeable.

"Thank you," said Mother quietly in an uncertain kind of voice. "The world seems very wonderful now—quite different."

She moved in her chair—the first movement she had made for over two hours. Daddy rubbed his eyes, stroked his beard, and lit a cigarette; it went out almost immediately, but he puffed on at it just the same, till his cousin struck a match and stood over him to see it properly alight.

"You have caught Beauty naked in your net of stars," he murmured; "but you have left her as you found her—shining, silvery, unclothed. Others will see her, too. You have taken us all back into Fairyland, and I, for one, shall never get out again."

"Nor I," breathed some one in the shadows by the window. . .

The clock struck two. "Odd," said Mother, softly, "but I never heard it strike once while you were reading!"

"We've all been out," Rogers laughed significantly, "just as you make them get out in the story"; and then, while Riquette yawned and turned a moment from the window-sill to say thank you for her long, warm sleep, Mother lit the spirit-lamp and brewed the cups of chocolate. She tiptoed in next door, and as she entered the sick-room she saw through the steam rising from the cup she carried a curious thing—an impression of brilliance about the bed, as though shafts of light issued from it. Rays pulsed and trembled in the air. There was a perfume of flowers. It seemed she stepped back into the atmosphere of the story for an instant.

"Ah, you're not asleep," she whispered. "We've brewed some chocolate, and I thought you might like a cup."

"No, I'm not asleep," answered the other woman from the bed she never would leave until she was carried from it, "but I have been dreaming. It seemed the stars came down into my room and sang to me; this bed became a throne; and some power was in me by which I could send my thoughts out to help the world. I sent them out as a king sends messengers—to people everywhere—even to people I've never heard of. Isn't it wonderful?"

"You've had no pain?" For Mother knew that these sleepless hours at night brought usually intense suffering. She stared at her, noting how the eyes shone and glistened with unshed moisture.

"None," was the answer, "but only the greatest joy and peace I've ever known." The little glass of *calmant* was untouched; it was not a drug that had soothed the exhausted nerves. In this room at any rate the spell was working still. "I was carried through the air by stars, as though my ceaseless yearning to get up and work in the world for once was realised."

"You can do everything from your bed," her friend murmured, sitting down beside her. "You do. Your thoughts go out so strongly. I've often felt them myself. Perhaps that's why God put you here in bed like this," she added, surprised at the power in herself that made her say such things—"just to think and pray for the world."

"I do pray sometimes for others," the tortured woman answered modestly, "but this time I was not conscious of praying at all. It all swept out of me of its own accord. The force in me seemed so free and inexhaustible that it overflowed. It was irresistible. I felt able to save the world."

"You were out," said Mother softly, "out of yourself, I mean," she corrected it. "And your lovely thoughts go everywhere. You do save the world."

There fell a long silence then between them.

"You've been reading aloud," Mlle. Lemaire said presently. "I heard the drone of the voice through the wall—"

"Daddy was reading his new story to us," the other said. "It didn't disturb you?"

"On the contrary. I think it was the voice somehow that brought the vision. I listened vaguely at first, trying to sleep; then, opening my eyes suddenly, the room, as I told you, was full of stars. Their rays caught hold of me and drew these forces out of my very heart. I yielded, giving and giving and giving. . . such life flowed from me, and they carried it away in streams. . . Oh, it was really like a divine sensation." "It was divine," said Mother, but whether she meant the story or her friend's experience, she hardly knew herself.

"And the story—was it not about our little Bourcelles?" asked the other.

Mother held her hands up as though words failed her. She opened her arms wide. She was not quite sure of her voice.

"It was," she said at length, "but Bourcelles had grown into the universe. It's a fairy-tale, but it's like a great golden fire. It warmed my heart till my whole body seemed all heart, and I didn't know whether to laugh or cry. It makes you see that the whole world is *one*, and that the sun and moon and stars lie in so small and unimportant a thing as, say, Jimbo's mischief, or Monkey's impudence, or Jinny's backwardness and absurdity. All are in sympathy together, as in a network, and to feel sympathy with anything, even the most insignificant, connects you instantly with the Whole. Thought and sympathy *are* the Universe— they are life."

While Mother paused for breath, her old friend smiled a curious, meaning smile, as though she heard a thing that she had always known.

"And all of us are in the story, and all the things we *think* are alive and active too, because we have created them. Our thoughts populate the world, flying everywhere to help or hinder others, you see."

The sound of a door opening was heard. Mother got up to go. Shafts of light again seemed to follow her from the figure in the bed.

"Good-night," she whispered with a full heart, while her thought ran suddenly—"You possess the secret of life and of creation, for suffering has taught it to you, and you have really known it always. But Daddy has put it into words for everybody." She felt proud as a queen.

There were whispered good-nights then in the corridor, for Rogers and her husband were on their way home to bed.

"Your chocolate is getting cold," said Daddy kindly.

"We thought you would probably stay in there. We're going over now. It's very late," Rogers added. They said good-night again.

She closed and locked the great door of the Citadelle behind them, hearing their steps upon the cobbles in the yard, and for some time afterwards upon the road. But their going away seemed the same as coming nearer. She felt so close to everything that lived. Everything did live. Her heart included all that existed, that ever had existed, that ever could exist. Mother was alive all over. "I have just been created," she laughed, and went back into the Den to drink her cup of tepid chocolate.

XXVIII

See, the busy Pleiades,
Sisters to the Hyades,
Seven by seven
Across the heaven,
Light desire
With their fire,
Working cunningly together in a soft and tireless band,

Sweetly linking
All our thinking
In the Net of Sympathy that brings back Fairyland.

—A Voice

The prophecy of the children that Bourcelles was a difficult place to get away from found its justification next morning, for Rogers slept so heavily that he nearly missed his train. It was six o'clock when he tumbled downstairs, too late for a real breakfast, and only just in time to get his luggage upon the little char that did duty for all transport in this unsophisticated village. The carpenter pulled it for him to the station.

"If I've forgotten anything, my cousin will send it after me," he told Mme. Michaud, as he gulped down hot coffee on the steps.

"Or we can keep it for you," was the answer. "You'll be coming back soon." She knew, like the others, that one always came back to Bourcelles. She shook hands with him as if he were going away for a night or two. "Your room will always be ready," she added. "Ayez la bonte seulement de m'envoyer une petite ligne d'avance."

"There's only fifteen minutes," interrupted her husband, "and it's uphill all the way."

They trundled off along the dusty road, already hot in the early July sun. There was no breath of wind; swallows darted in the blue air; the perfume of the forests was everywhere; the mountains rose soft and clear into the cloudless sky. They passed the Citadelle, where the awning was already being lowered over the balcony for Mlle. Lemaire's bed to be wheeled out a little later. Rogers waved his handkerchief, and saw the answering flutter inside the window. Riquette, on her way in, watched him from the tiles. The orchards then hid the lower floors; he passed the tinkling fountain; to the left he saw the church and the old Pension, the wistaria blossoms falling down its walls in a cascade of beauty.

The Postmaster put his head out and waved his Trilby hat with a solemn smile. "Le barometre est tres haut. . ." floated down the village street, instead of the sentence of good-bye. Even the Postmaster took it for granted that he was not leaving. Gygi, standing in the door of his barn, raised his peaked hat and smiled. "Fait beau, ce matin," he said, "plus tard il fera rudement chaud." He spoke as if Rogers were off for a walk or climb. It was the same everywhere. The entire village saw him go, yet behaved as if he was not really leaving. How fresh and sweet the morning air was, keen mountain fragrance in it, and all the delicious, delicate sharpness of wet moss and dewy fields.

As he passed the courtyard near the Guillaume Tell, and glanced up at the closed windows of Mother Plume's apartment, a pattering step startled him behind, and Jimbo came scurrying up. Rogers kissed him and lifted him bodily upon the top of his portmanteau, then helped the carpenter to drag it up the hill. "The barriers at the level crossing are down, the warning gongs are ringing. It's signalled from Auvernier." They were only just in time. The luggage was registered and the train panting up the steep incline, when Monkey, sleep still thick in her eyes, appeared rolling along the white road. She was too breathless to speak; she stood and stared like a stuffed creature in a Museum. Jimbo was beside the engine, having a word with the *mecanicien*.

"Send a telegram, you know—like that," he shouted, as the carriage slid past him, "and we'll bring the *char*." He knew his leader would come back. He took his cap off politely, as a man does to a lady— the Bourcelles custom. He did not wave his handkerchief or make undignified signs. He stood there, watching his cousin to the last, and trying to see the working of the engine at the same time. He had already told him the times and stopping places, and where he had to change; there was nothing more for a man to say.

Monkey, her breath recovered now, shouted something impudent from the road. "The train will break down with you in it before it gets to Pontarlier, and you'll be back for tea—worse luck!" He heard it faintly, above the grinding of the wheels. She blew him a kiss; her hair flew out in a cloud of brown the sunshine turned half golden. He almost saw the shining of her eyes. And then the belt of the forest hid her from view, hid Jimbo and the village too. The last thing he saw of Bourcelles was the top of the church spire and the red roof of the towering Citadelle. The crest of the sentinel poplar topped them both for a minute longer, waved a slight and stately farewell, then lowered itself into the forest and vanished in its turn.

And Rogers came back with a start and a bump to what is called real life.

He closed his eyes and leaned back in his corner, feeling he had suddenly left his childhood behind him for the second time, not gradually as it ought to happen, but all in one dreadful moment. A great ache lay in his heart. The perfect book of fairy-tales he had been reading was closed and finished. Weeks had passed in the delicious reading, but now the last page was turned; he came back to duty—duty in London—great, noisy, overwhelming London, with its disturbing bustle, its feverish activities, its complex, artificial, unsatisfying amusements, and its hosts of frantic people. He grew older in a moment; he was forty again now; an instant ago, just on the further side of those blue woods, he had been fifteen. Life shrank and dwindled in him to a little, ugly, unattractive thing. He was returning to a flat in the dolorous edifice of civilisation. A great practical Scheme, rising in sombre bricks and mortar through a disfiguring fog, blocked all the avenues of the future.

The picture seemed sordid somewhere, the contrast was so striking. In a great city was no softness; hard, sharp angles everywhere, or at best an artificial smoothness that veiled ugliness and squalor very thinly. Human relationship worked like parts of a machine, cramped into definite orbits, each wheel, each pulley, the smallest deviation deemed erratic. In Bourcelles, the mountain village, there was more latitude, room for expansion, space. The heart leaped up spontaneously like a spring released. In the city this spring was held down rigidly in place, pressed under as by a weight; and the weight, surely, was that one for ever felt compelled to think of self—self in a rather petty, shameful way—personal safety. In the streets, in the houses, in public buildings, shops, and railway stations, even where people met to eat and drink in order to keep alive, were Notice Boards of caution and warning against their fellow kind. Instead of the kindly and unnecessary, even ridiculous little Gygi, there were big, grave policemen by the score, a whole army of them; and everywhere grinned the Notice Boards, like automatic, dummy policemen, mocking joy with their insulting warnings. The heart was oppressed with this constant reminder that safety could only be secured by great care and trouble—safety for the little personal self; protection from all kinds of robbery, depredation, and attack; beware of pickpockets, the proprietor is not responsible for overcoats and umbrellas even! And burglar alarms and doors of steel and iron everywhere—an organised defence from morning till night—against one's own kind.

He had lived among these terrible conditions all his life, proud of the personal security that civilisation provided, but he had never before viewed it from outside, as now he suddenly did. A spiritual being, a man, lives in a city as in a state of siege among his own kind. It was deplorable, it was incredible. In little Bourcelles, a mountain village most would describe pityingly as half civilised and out of the world, there was safety and joy and freedom as of the universe... His heart contracted as he thus abruptly realised the distressing contrast. Although a city is a unit, all classes neatly linked together by laws and by-laws, by County Councils, Parliaments, and the like, the spirit of brotherhood was a mockery and a sham. There is organised charity, but there is not—Charity. In a London Square he could not ring the bell and ask for a glass of milk... In Bourcelles he would walk into any house, since there were no bells, and sit down to an entire meal!

He laughed as the absurd comparison darted across his mind, for he recognised the foolish exaggeration in it; but behind the laughter flamed the astonishing truth. In Bourcelles, in a few weeks, he had found a bigger, richer life than all London had supplied to him in twenty years; he had found wings, inspiration, love, and happiness; he had found the universe. The truth of his cousin's story blazed upon him like an inner sun. In this new perspective he saw that it was a grander fairy-tale than he had guessed even when close to it. What was a Scheme for Disabled Thingumabobs compared to the endless, far-reaching schemes that life in Bourcelles suggested to him! There was the true centre of life; cities were accretions of disease upon the surface merely! He was leaving Fairyland behind him.

In sudden moments like this, with their synthetic bird's-eye view, the mind sometimes sees more clearly than in hours of careful reflection and analysis. And the first thing he saw now was Minks, his friendly, ridiculous little confidential secretary. From all the crowds of men and women he knew, respected, and enjoyed in London, as from the vast deluge of human mediocrity which for him *was* London, he picked out suddenly—little Minks—Herbert Montmorency Minks. His mind, that is, darting forward in swift, comprehensive survey, and searching automatically for some means whereby it might continue the happiness and sweetness recently enjoyed, selected Minks. Minks was a clue. Minks possessed—no matter how absurd the proportions of their mixing—three things just left behind: Vision, Belief, Simplicity, all products of a spiritual imagination.

And at first this was the single thought sent forward into the future. Rogers saw the fact, flash-like and true-then let it go, yielding to the greater pull that drew reflection back into the past.

And he found it rather dislocating, this abrupt stepping out of his delightful forest Fairyland. . . Equilibrium was not recovered for a long time, as the train went thundering over the Jura Mountains into France, Only on the other side of Pontarlier, when the country grew unfamiliar and different, did harmony return. Among the deep blue forests he was still in Fairyland, but at Mouchard the scenery was already changing, and by the time Dole was reached it had completely changed. The train ran on among the plains and vineyards of the Burgundy country towards Laroche and Dijon. The abrupt alteration, however, was pain. His thoughts streamed all backwards now to counteract it. He roamed again among the star fields above the Bourcelles woods. It was true— he had not really left Bourcelles. His body was bumping into Dijon, but the important part of him—thought, emotion, love—lingered with the children, hovered above the Citadelle, floated through the dusky, scented forests.

And the haunting picture was ever set in its framework of old burning stars. He could not get the Pleiades in particular out of his mind. The pictures swarmed past him as upon a boy returning to school after the holidays, and each one had a background of sky with stars behind it; the faces that he knew so well had starry eyes; Jimbo flung handfuls of stars loose across the air, and Monkey caught them, fastening them like golden pins into her hair. Glancing down, he saw a long brown hair upon his sleeve. He picked it off and held his finger and thumb outside the window till the wind took it away. Some Morning Spider would ride it home—perhaps past his cousin's window while he copied out that wonderful, great tale. But, instead—how in the world could it happen in clear daylight?—a little hand shot down from above and gathered it in towards the Pleiades.

The Pleiades—the Seven Sisters—that most exquisite cluster of the eastern sky, soft, tender, lovely, clinging close together always like a group of timid children, who hide a little dimly for fear of being surprised by bolder stars upon their enormous journey—they now shone down upon all he thought and remembered. They seemed always above the horizon of his mind. They never set. In them lay souls of unborn children, children waiting to be born. He could not imagine why this particular constellation clung with such a haunting touch of beauty about his mind, or why some passion of yearning unconfessed and throbbing hid behind the musical name. Stars and unborn children had got strangely mixed!

He tried to recall the origin of the name—he had learned it once in the old Vicar's study. The Pleiades were attendants upon Artemis, the huntress moon, he recalled vaguely, and, being pursued by Orion, were set for safety among the stars. He even remembered the names of some of them; there was Maia, Tagete, Alcyone, but the other four lay in his mental lumber room, whence they could not be evoked, although Merope, he felt sure, was one of them. Of Maia, however, he felt positive. . . How beautiful the names were!

Then, midway, in thinking about them, he found himself, as Monkey said, thinking of something else: of his weeks at Bourcelles again and what a long holiday it had been, and whether it was wasted time or well-used time-a kind of general stock-taking, as it were, but chiefly of how little he had accomplished after all, down in black and white. He had enjoyed himself and let himself go, rather foolishly perhaps, but how much after all had he actually accomplished? He remembered pleasant conversations with Mother that possibly cheered and helped her—or possibly were forgotten as soon as ended. He remembered his cousin's passing words of gratitude—that he had helped him somehow with his great new story: and he remembered—this least of all-that his money had done something to relieve a case or two of suffering. And this was all! The net result so insignificant! He felt dissatisfied, eager already to make new plans, something definite and thorough that should retrieve the wasted opportunities. With a little thought and trouble, how easily he might have straightened out the tangle of his cousin's family, helped with the education of the growing children, set them all upon a more substantial footing generally. It was possible still, of course, but such things are done best on the spot, the personal touch and presence of value; arranged by correspondence it becomes another thing at once and loses spontaneity. The accent lies on the wrong details. Sympathy is watered by the post. . . Importance lodges in angles not intended for it. Master of his time, with certain means at his disposal, a modicum of ability as well, he was free to work hard on the side of the angels wherever opportunity might offer; yet he had wasted all these weeks upon an unnecessary holiday, frittering the time away in enjoyment with the children. He felt ashamed and mortified as the meagre record stared him in the face.

Yet, curiously enough, when Reason had set down the figures accurately, as he fancied, and totted up the trifling totals, there flitted before him something more that refused to be set down upon the paper. The Ledger had no lines for it. What was it? Why was it pleasant, even flattering? Why did it mitigate his discontent and lessen the dissatisfied feeling? It passed hovering in and about his thoughts, though uncaught by actual words; and as his mind played with it, he felt more hopeful. He searched in vain for a definition, but, though fruitless, the search brought comfort somehow. Something *had* been accomplished and it was due to himself, because without his presence it would never have been done. This hint slipped into desire, yearning, hope—that, after all, a result *had* perhaps been achieved, a result he himself was not properly aware of—a result of that incalculable spiritual kind that escapes the chains of definite description. For he recalled—yet mortified a little the memory should flatter—that his cousin had netted Beauty in his story, and that Mother had spoken of living with greater carelessness and peace, and that each had thanked him as though he were the cause.

And these memories, half thought, half feeling, were comforting and delicious, so that he revelled in them lingeringly, and wished that they were really true. For, if true, they were immensely significant. Any one with a purse could build a hospital or pay an education fee, but to be helpful because of being oneself was a vast, incalculable power, something direct from God. . . and his thoughts, wandering on thus between fact and fantasy, led him back with a deep inexplicable thrill again to—the Pleiades, whose beauty, without their being aware of it, shines nightly for all who can accept it. Here was the old, old truth once more-that the left hand must not know what the right is doing, and that to be is of greater importance than to do. Here was Fairyland once more, the Fairyland he had just left. To think beauty and love is to become them, to shed them forth without realising it. A Fairy blesses because she is a Fairy, not because she turns a pumpkin into a coach and four. . . The Pleiades do not realise how their loveliness may. . .

Rogers started. For the thought had borrowed a tune from the rhythm of the wheels and sleepers, and he had uttered the words aloud in his corner. Luckily he had the carriage to himself. He flushed. Again a tender and very exquisite thing had touched him somewhere. . . It was in that involuntary connection his dreaming had found between a Fairy and the Pleiades. Wings of gauzy gold shone fluttering a moment before his inner sight, then vanished. He was aware of some one very dear and wild and tender, with amber eyes and little twinkling feet—some one whom the Great Tale brought almost within his reach. . . He literally had seen stars for an instant—*a* star! Its beauty brimmed him up. He laughed in his corner. This thing, whatever it was, had been coming nearer for some time. These hints of sudden joy that breathe upon a sensitive nature, how mysterious, how wildly beautiful, how stimulating they are! But whence, in the name of all the stars, do they come? A great happiness passed flaming through his heart, an extraordinary sense of anticipation in it—as though he were going to meet some one who—who—well, what?—who was a necessity and a delight to him, the complement needed to make his life effective—some one he loved abundantly—who would love him abundantly in return. He recalled those foolish lines he had written on sudden impulse once, then thrown away. . .

Thought fluttered and went out. He could not seize the elusive cause of this delicious joy. It was connected with the Pleiades, but how, where, why? Above the horizon of his life a new star was swimming into glory. It was rising. The inexplicable emotion thrilled tumultuously, then dived back again whence it came. . . It had to do with children and with a woman, it seemed, for the next thing he knew was that he was thinking of children, children of his own, and of the deep yearning Bourcelles had stirred again in him to find their Mother. . . and, next, of his cousin's story and that wonderful detail in it that the principal role was filled at last, the role in the great Children's Play he himself had felt was vacant. It was to be filled by that childless Mother the writer's imagination had discovered or created. And again the Pleiades lit up his inner world and beckoned to him with their little fingers of spun gold; their eyes of clouded amber smiled into his own. It was most extraordinary and delightful. There was something—come much closer this time, almost within reach of discovery—something he ought to remember about them, something he had promised to remember, then stupidly forgotten. The lost, hidden joy was a torture. Yet, try as he would, no revelation came to clear the matter up. Had he read it somewhere perhaps? Or was it part of the Story his cousin had wumbled into his ear when he only partly listened?

"I believe I dreamed it," he smiled to himself at last in despair. "I do believe it was a dream—a fragment of some jolly dream I had in my Fairyland of little Bourcelles!"

Children, stars, Fairyland, dreams—these brought it somehow. His cousin's story also had to do with it, chiefly perhaps after all—this great story.

"I shall have to go back there to get hold of it completely," he added with conviction. He almost felt as if some one were thinking hard about him—one of the characters in the story, it seemed. The mind of some one far away, as yet unknown, was searching for him in thought, sending forth strong definite yearnings which came to rest of their own accord in his own being, a garden naturally suited to their growth. The creations of his boyhood's imagination had survived, the Sweep, the Dustman, and the Lamplighter, then why not the far more powerful creations in the story. . . ? Thought was never lost!

"But no man in his senses can believe such a thing!" he exclaimed, as the train ran booming through the tunnel.

"That's the point," whispered a voice beside him. "You are *out* of your senses. Otherwise you could not feel it!"

He turned sharply. The carriage was empty; there was no one there. It was, of course, another part of himself that supplied the answer; yet it startled him. The blurred reflection of the lamp, he noticed, cast a picture against the black tunnel wall that was like a constellation. The Pleiades again! It almost seemed as if the voice had issued from that false reflection in the shaking window-pane. . .

The train emerged from the tunnel. He rushed out into the blaze of the Interfering Sun. The lovely cluster vanished like a dream, and with it the hint of explanation melted down in dew. Fields sped past with a group of haystacks whose tarpaulin skirts spread and lifted in the gust of wind the train made. He thought abruptly of Mother. . . Perhaps, after all, he had taught her something, shown her Existence as a big, streaming, endless thing in which months and years, possibly even life itself, were merely little sections, each unintelligible unless viewed as portions of the Whole, and not as separate, difficult, puzzling items set apart. Possibly he had drawn her map to bigger scale, increased her faith, given her more sense of repose and peace, more courage therefore. She thought formerly of a day, but not of its relation to all days before and behind. She stuck her husband's "reviews" in the big book, afflicted by the poor financial results they represented, but was unable to think of his work as a stage in a long series of development and progress, no effort lost, no single hope mislaid. And that was something—*if* he had accomplished it. Only, he feared he had not. There was the trouble. There lay the secret of a certain ineffectiveness in his character. For he did not realise that fear is simply suppressed desire, vivid signs of life, and that desire is the ultimate causative agent everywhere and always. "Behind Will stands Desire," and Desire is Action.

And if he *had* accomplished this, how was it done? Not by preaching, certainly. Was it, then, simply by being, thinking, feeling it? A glorious thought, if true! For assuredly he had this faculty of seeing life whole, and even in boyhood he had looked ahead over its entire map. He had, indeed, this way of relating all its people, and all its parts together, instead of seeing them separate, unintelligible because the context was left out. He lived intensely in the present, yet looked backwards and forwards too at the same time. This large sympathy, this big comforting vision was his gift. Consequently he believed in Life. Had he also, then, the gift of making others feel and believe it too. . . ?

There he was again, thinking in a circle, as Laroche flew past with its empty platforms, and warned him that Paris was getting close. He bumped out of Fairyland, yet tumbled back once more for a final reverie before the long ugly arms of the city snatched him finally out. "To see life whole," he reflected, "is to see it glorious. To think one's self part of humanity at large is to bring the universe down into the heart. But to see life whole, a whole heart is necessary. . . He's done it in that splendid story, and he bagged the raw idea somehow from me. That's something at any rate. . . So few think Beaaty. . . But will others see it? That's the point!"

"No, it isn't," answered the voice beside him. "The point is that he has thought it, and the universe is richer. Even if others do not read or understand, what he has thought *is there now*, for ever and ever."

"True," he reflected, "for that Beauty may float down and settle in other minds when they least are looking for it, and ignoring utterly whence comes the fairy touch. Divine! Delicious! Heavenly!"

"The Beauty he has written came through you, yet was not yours," the voice continued very faintly. "A far more beautiful mind first projected it into that network which binds all minds together. 'Twas thence you caught it flying, and, knowing not how to give it shape, transferred it to another—who could use it—for others. . . Thought is Life, and Sympathy is living. . ."

The voice died away; he could not hear the remainder clearly; the passing scenery caught his attention again; during his reverie it had been unnoticed utterly. "Thought is Life, but Sympathy is living—" it rolled and poured through him as he repeated it. Snatches of another sentence then came rising into him from an immense distance, falling upon him from immeasurable heights—barely audible:-

". . . from a mind that so loved the Pleiades she made their loveliness and joy her own. . . Alcyone, Merope, Maia. . ." It dipped away into silence like a flower closing for the night, and the train, he realised, was slackening speed as it drew into the hideous Gare de Lyon.

"I'll talk to Minks about it, perhaps," he thought, as he stood telling the Customs official that he had no brandy, cigarettes, or lace. "He knows about things like that. At any rate, he'll sympathise."

He went across Paris to the Gare du Nord, and caught the afternoon boat train to London. The sunshine glared up from the baking streets, but he never forgot that overhead, though invisible, the stars were shining all the time—Starlight, the most tender and least suspected light in all the world, shining bravely even when obscured by the Interfering Sun, and the Pleiades, softest, sweetest little group among them all.

And when at eleven o'clock he entered his St. James's flat, he took a store of it shining in his heart, and therefore in his eyes. Only that was no difficult matter, for all the lamps far up the heights were lit and gleaming, and caught old mighty London in their gorgeous net.

XXIX

Think with passion
That shall fashion
Life's entire design, well planned.

—*Woman of the Haystack*

Y ou are looking so wonderfully well, Mr. Rogers," Minks observed at Charing Cross Station, "the passage across the Channel, I trust, was calm."

"And yourself and Mrs. Minks?" asked Rogers, looking into the equally sunburned face of his secretary, remembering suddenly that he had been to the sea with his family; "Frank, too, and the other children? All well, I hope?"

"All in excellent health, Mr. Rogers, thanks to your generous thought. My wife—"

"These are the small bags," the other interrupted, "and here are the keys for my portmanteaux. There's nothing dutiable. You might bring them on to the flat while I run over to the Club for a bit of supper, Minks."

"Certainly, with pleasure, Mr. Rogers," was the beaming reply. "And Mrs. Minks begged me to tell you—"

Only Rogers was already in his taxi-cab and out of ear-shot.

"How well he looks!" reflected Minks, dangling the keys, accustomed to these abrupt interruptions, and knowing that his message had been understood and therefore duly delivered. These cut-off sentences were like a secret code between them. "And ten years younger! Almost like a boy again. I wonder if—" He did not permit himself to finish the thought. He tried to remember if he himself had looked like that perhaps in the days of long ago when he courted Albinia Lucy—an air of joy and secrecy and an absent-minded manner that might any moment flame into vehement, concentrated action. For this was the impression his employer had made upon him. Only he could not quite remember those far-off, happy days. There was ecstasy in them; that he knew. And there was ecstasy in Henry Rogers now; that he divined.

"He oughtn't to," he reflected, as he hurried in another taxi with the luggage. "All his yearnings would be satisfied if he did, his life flow into a single channel instead of into many."

He did not think about his own position and his salary.

"He won't," he decided as the cab stopped at the door; "he's not that kind of man." Minks had insight; he knew men. "No artist ever ought to. We are so few, and the world has need of us." His own case was an exception that had justified itself, for he was but a man of talent, and talent did not need an exclusive asceticism; whereas his employer was a man of genius, and no one woman had the right to monopolise what was intended to sweeten the entire universe.

By the time the luggage had been taken up, he had missed the last tram home, and his sleep that night must in any case be short. Yet he took no note of that. One must live largely. A small sacrifice for such a master was nothing at all. He lingered, glancing now and again at the heap of correspondence that would occupy them next morning, and sorting once more the little pile that would need immediate personal attention. He was picking a bit of disfiguring fluff from his coat sleeve when the door opened and Henry Rogers came upon him.

"Ah! I waited a moment, Mr. Rogers. I thought you might have something to say before I went, perhaps."

"I hoped you would, Minks. I have a great deal to say. It can wait till tomorrow, really—only I wanted—but, there now, I forgot; you have to get down to Sydenham, haven't you? And it's late already—"

"That's nothing, Mr. Rogers. I can easily sleep in town. I came prepared, indeed, to do so—" as though he, too, had his Club and would take a bedroom in it.

"Clever and thoughtful of you, Minks!"

"Only you must be tired after your journey," suggested the secretary.

"Tired!" exclaimed the other vigorously, "not a bit! I'm as fresh as a st—a daisy, I mean. Come, draw your chair up; we'll have a smoke and a little chat. I'm delighted to see you again. How are you? And how's everything?"

Goodness! How bright his eyes were, how alert his manner! He looked so young, almost springy, thought Minks, as he obeyed decorously, feeling flattered and pleased, yet at the same time uneasy a little. Such spirits could only proceed, he feared, from one cause. He was a close observer, as all poets had need to be. He would discover some clue before he went to bed, something that should betray the true state of affairs. In any case sleep would be impossible unless he did.

"You stayed away somewhat longer than you originally intended," he ventured at length, having briefly satisfied his employer's question. "You found genuine recreation. You needed it, I'm sure." He glanced with one eye at the letters.

"Re-creation, yes; the very word. It was difficult to leave. The place was so delightful," said Rogers simply, filling his pipe and lighting it. "A wonderful mountain village, Minks," he added, between puffs of smoke, while the secretary, who had been waiting for the sign, then lit his own Virginian and smoked it diffidently, and with just the degree of respect he felt was becoming. He never presumed upon his master's genial way of treating him. He made little puffs and was very careful with the ashes.

"Ah, yes," he said; "I am sure it must have been—both delightful and—er—difficult to leave." He recalled the Margate sands, bathing with Albinia and digging trenches with the children. He had written many lyrics during those happy weeks of holiday.

"Gave one, in fact, quite a new view of life—and work. There was such space and beauty everywhere. And my cousin's children simply would not let me go."

There was a hint of apology and excuse in the tone and words—the merest hint, but Minks noticed it and liked the enthusiasm. "He's been up to some mischief; he feels a little ashamed; his work—his Scheme—has been so long neglected; conscience pricks him. Ha, ha!" The secretary felt his first suspicion confirmed. "Cousin's children," perhaps! But who else?

"He made a tactful reference—oh, very slight and tentative—to the data he had collected for the Scheme, but the other either did not hear it, or did not wish to hear it. He brushed it aside, speaking through clouds of tobacco smoke. Minks enjoyed a bigger, braver puff at his own. Excitement grew in him.

"Just the kind of place you would have loved, Minks," Rogers went on with zeal. "I think you really must go there some day; cart your family over, teach the children French, you know, and cultivate a bit of vineyard. Such fine big forests, too, full of wild flowers and things—O such lovely hand-made things—why, you could almost see the hand that made 'em." The phrase had slipped suddenly into his mind.

"Really, really, Mr. Rogers, but how very jo—delightful it sounds." He thought of the stubble fields and treeless sea-coast where he had been. The language, however, astonished him. Enthusiasm like this could only spring from a big emotion. His heart sank a little.

"And the people all so friendly and hospitable and simple that you could go climbing with your bootmaker or ask your baker in to dine and sleep. No snobbery! Sympathy everywhere and a big free life flowing in your veins." This settled it. Only a lover finds the whole world lovable.

"One must know the language, though," said Minks, "in order to enjoy the people and understand them, I suppose?"

"Not a bit, not a bit! One *feels* it all, you see; somehow one feels it and understands. A few words useful here and there, but one gets along without even these. I never knew such a place. Every one seemed to be in sympathy together. They think it, as it were. It was regular fairyland, I tell you."

"Which means that *you* felt and thought it," said Minks to himself. Aloud he merely remarked, though with conviction, for he was getting interested, "Thinking is important, I know."

Rogers laid his pipe aside and suddenly turned upon him—so abruptly that Minks started. Was this the confession coming? Would he hear now that his chief was going to be married? His wandering eyes almost drew level in the excitement that he felt. He knocked a tiny ash from his cigarette and waited. But the expected bomb did not explode. He heard instead this curious question:—

"And that's something—it reminds me now—something I particularly wanted to ask you about, my dear fellow. You are familiar, I know, with such things and theories—er—speculations, as it were. You read that sort of stuff. You are in touch with the latest ideas, I mean, and up-to-date. You can tell me, if any one can."

He paused, hesitating a moment, as Minks, listening in some bewilderment, gazed into his eager face. He said nothing. He only committed himself to a deprecating gesture with his hands, letting his cigarette slip from his fingers on to the carpet.

"About *thought*," continued Rogers, keeping his eyes fixed upon him while he rose with flushed face from the search to find the stump. "What do you know about thought? Tell me what you hear about *that*—what theories are held—what people believe about it. I mean thought-transference, telepathy, or whatever it is called. Is it proved? Is it a fact?"

His voice had lowered. There was mystery in his manner. He sat back in his chair, picked up his pipe, replaced it in his mouth unlighted, and waited.

Minks pulled himself together. His admirable qualities as a private secretary now came in. Putting excitement and private speculations of his own aside, he concentrated his orderly mind upon replies that should be models of succinct statement. He had practised thought-control, and prided himself upon the fact. He could switch attention instantly from one subject to another without confusion. The replies, however, were, of course, drawn from his own reading. He neither argued nor explained. He merely stated.

"Those who have taken the trouble to study the evidence believe," he began, "that it is established, though its laws are as yet unknown. Personally, if I may quote myself, I do believe it."

"Quite so, quite so. Do quote yourself—that's what I want—facts. But you refer to deliberate experiments, don't you?"

"In my own case, yes, Mr. Rogers, although the most successful thought-transference is probably unconscious and not deliberate—"

"Such as, for instance—"

"Public opinion," replied Minks, after a moment's search, "which is the result of waves of thought sent out by everybody—by a community; or by the joint thinking of a nation, again, which modifies every mind born into that nation, the result of centuries of common thinking along definite familiar channels. Thought-currents rush everywhere about the world, affecting every one more or less, and—er—particularly lodging in minds receptive to them."

"Thought is dynamic, then, they hold?"

"An actual force, yes; as actual as electricity, and as little understood," returned the secretary, proud that he had read these theories and remembered them. "With every real thought a definite force goes forth from you that modifies every single person, and probably every single object as well, in the entire world. Thought is creative according to its intensity. It links everybody in the world with everybody else—"

"Objects too, you say?" Rogers questioned.

Minks glanced up to make sure there was no levity in the question, but only desire for knowledge.

"Objects too," he replied, apparently satisfied, "for science tells us that the movement of a body here affects the farthest star. A continuous medium—ether—transmits the vibrations without friction—and thought-force is doubtless similarly transmitted—er—"

"So that if I think of a flower or a star, my thought leaps into them and affects them?" the other interrupted again.

"More, Mr. Rogers," was the reply, "for your thought, being creative, enriches the world with images of beauty which may float into another mind across the sea, distance no obstacle at all. You make a mental image when you think. There's imagination in all real thinking—if I make myself clear. 'Our most elaborate thoughts,' to quote for a moment, 'are often, as I think, not really ours, but have on a sudden come up, as it were, out of hell or down out of heaven.' So what one thinks affects everybody in the world. The noble thinkers lift humanity, though they may never tell their thoughts in speech or writing."

His employer stared at him in silence through the cloud of smoke. The clock on the mantelpiece struck half-past twelve.

"That is where the inspiration of the artist comes in," continued the secretary after a moment's hesitation whether he should say it or not, "for his sensitive soul collects them and gives them form. They lodge in him and grow, and every passionate longing for spiritual growth sets the whole world growing too. Your Scheme for Disabled—"

"Even if it never materialises—" Rogers brusquely interposed.

"Sweetens the world—yes—according to this theory," continued Minks, wondering what in the world had come over his chief, yet so pleased to state his own views that he forgot to analyse. "A man in a dungeon earnestly praying would accomplish more than an active man outside who merely lived thoughtlessly, even though beneficently—if I make myself clear."

"Yes, yes; you make yourself admirably clear, Minks, as I knew you would." Rogers lit his pipe again and puffed hard through a minute's silence. The secretary held his peace, realising from the tone of the last sentence that he had said enough. Mr. Rogers was leading up to other questions. Hitherto he had been clearing the ground.

It came then, through the clouds of smoke, though Minks failed to realise exactly why it was—so important:

"So that if I thought vividly of anything, I should. actually create a mental picture which in turn might slip into another's mind, while that other would naturally suppose it was his own?"

"Exactly, Mr. Rogers; exactly so." Minks contrived to make the impatience in his voice sound like appreciation of his master's quickness. "Distance no obstacle either," he repeated, as though fond of the phrase.

"And, similarly, the thought I deemed my own might have come in its turn from the mind of some one else?"

"Precisely; for thought binds us all together like a network, and to think of others is to spread oneself about the universe. When we think thus we get out—as it were—into that medium common to all of us where spirit meets spirit—"

"Out!" exclaimed Rogers, putting down his pipe and staring keenly, first into one eye, then into the other. "Out?"

"Out—yes," Minks echoed faintly, wondering why that particular word was chosen. He felt a little startled. This earnest talk, moreover, stirred the subconsciousness in him, so that he remembered that unfinished sonnet he had begun weeks ago at Charing Cross. If he were alone now he could complete it. Lines rose and offered themselves by the dozen. His master's emotion had communicated itself to him. A breath of that ecstasy he had already divined passed through the air between them.

"It's what the Contemplative Orders attempt—" he continued, yet half to himself, as though a little bemused.

"Out, by George! Out!" Rogers said again.

So emphatic was the tone that Minks half rose from his chair to go.

"No, no," laughed his chief; "I don't mean that you're to get out. Forgive my abruptness. The fact is I was thinking aloud a moment. I meant—I mean that you've explained a lot to me I didn't understand before—had never thought about, rather. And it's rather wonderful, you see. In fact, it's *very* wonderful. Minks," he added, with the grave enthusiasm of one who has made a big discovery, "this world *is* a very wonderful place."

"It is simply astonishing, Mr. Rogers," Minks answered with conviction, "astonishingly beautiful."

"That's what I mean," he went on. "If I think beauty, that beauty may materialise—"

"Must, will, does materialise, Mr. Rogers, just as your improvements in machinery did. You first thought them out!"

"Then put them into words; yes, and afterwards into metal. Strong thought is bound to realise itself sooner or later, eh? Isn't it all grand and splendid?"

They stared at one another across the smoky atmosphere of the London flat at the hour of one in the morning in the twentieth century.

"And when I think of a Scaffolding of Dusk that builds the Night," Rogers went on in a lower tone to himself, yet not so low that Minks, listening in amazement, did not catch every syllable, "or of a Dustman, Sweep, and Lamplighter, of a Starlight Express, or a vast Star Net that binds the world in sympathy together, and when I weave all these into a story, whose centre somehow is the Pleiades—all this is real and actual, and—and—"

"May have been projected by another mind before it floated into your own," Minks suddenly interposed almost in a whisper, charmed wholly into the poet's region by these suggestive phrases, yet wondering a little why he said it, and particularly how he dared to say it.

His chief turned sharply upon him.

"My own thought exactly!" he exclaimed; "but how the devil did you guess it?"

Minks returned the stare with triumph.

"Unconscious transference!" he said.

"You really think *that*?" his master asked, yet not mockingly.

Minks turned a shade pinker.

"I do, indeed, sir," he replied warmly. "I think it probable that the thoughts of people you have never seen or heard of drop into your mind and colour it. They lodge there, or are rejected, according to your mood and the texture of your longings—what you want to be, that is. What you want, if I may say so, is emptiness, and that emptiness invites. The flying thought flits in and makes itself at home. Some people overflow with thoughts of kindness and beauty that radiate from them, of love and tenderness and desire to help. These thoughts, it may be, find no immediate object; but they are not lost. They pour loose about the world of men and women, and sooner or later find the empty heart that needs them. I believe, sir, that to sit in a chair and think such things strongly brings comfort to thousands who have little idea whence comes the sudden peace and happiness. And any one who happens to be praying for these things at the moment attracts them instantly. The comfort, the joy, the relief come—"

"What a good idea, Minks," said Rogers gently, "and how helpful if we all believed it. No one's life need be a failure then. Those who want love, for instance, need it, crave it, just think what an army they are!"

He stared thoughtfully a moment at his little secretary.

"You might write a book about it, you know—try and make people believe it—convince them. Eh? Only, you'd have to give your proofs, you know. People want proofs."

Minks, pinker than before, hesitated a moment. He was not sure how far he ought to, indulge his private theories in words. The expression in his chief's blue eyes apparently encouraged him.

"But, indeed, Mr. Rogers, the proofs are there. Those moments of sudden strength and joy that visit a man, catching him unawares and unexplained—every solitary man and woman knows them, for every solitary man and woman in the world craves first of all—to *be* loved. To love another, others, an impersonal Cause, is not enough. It is only half of life; to *be* loved is the other half. If every single person—I trust, sir, I do not tire you?—was loved by some one, the happiness of life would be enormously greater than it is, for each one loved would automatically then give out from his own store, and to receive love makes one overflow with love for every one else. It is so, is it not, sir?"

Rogers, an odd thrill catching him unawares, nodded. "It is, Minks, it is," he agreed. "To love one person makes one half prepared to love all, and to be loved in turn may have a similar effect. It is nice to think so anyhow."

"It is true, sir—" and Minks sat up, ready with another deluge.

"But you were saying something just now," interrupted the other, "about these sudden glimpses of joy and beauty that—er—come to one—er—inexplicably. What d'ye mean by that precisely?"

Minks glowed. He was being listened to, and understood by his honoured chief, too!

"Simply that some one, perhaps far away—some sweet woman probably—has been thinking love," he replied with enthusiasm, yet in a low and measured voice, "and that the burning thoughts have rushed into the emptiness of a heart that needs them. Like water, thought finds its level. The sudden gush—all feel it more or less at times, surely!—may rise first from her mind as she walks lonely upon the shore, pacing the decks at sea, or in her hillside rambles, thinking, dreaming, hoping, yearning—to pour out and find the heart that needs these very things, perhaps far across the world. Who knows? Heart thrills in response to heart secretly in every corner of the globe, and when these tides flood unexplained into your soul—"

"Into *my* soul—!" exclaimed his chief.

"I beg your pardon, sir," Minks hurried to explain; "I mean to any lonely soul that happens to crave such comfort with real longing—it implies, to my mind at least, that these two are destined to give and take from one another, and that, should they happen to meet in actual life, they will rush together instantly like a pair of flames—"

"And if they never—meet?" asked Rogers slowly, turning to the mantel-piece for the matches.

"They will continue to feed each other in this delicious spiritual way from a distance, sir. Only—the chances are—that they will meet, for their thought already connects them vitally, though as yet unrealised."

There was a considerable pause. Rogers lit his pipe. Minks, feeling he ought to stand while his master did so, also rose from his chair. The older man turned; they faced each other for a moment, Rogers putting smoke violently into the air between them.

"Minks, my dear fellow," he observed, "you are, as I have always thought, a poet. You have ideas, and, whether true or not, they are rather lovely. Write them out for others to read. Use your spare time writing them out. I'll see to it that you have more leisure."

With a laugh the big man moved abruptly past his chair and knocked his pipe on the edge of the ash-bowl. His eye, as he did so, fell upon the pile of letters and papers arranged so neatly on the table. He remembered the lateness of the hour—and other things besides.

"Well, well," he said vaguely with a sigh; "so here we are again back at work in London."

Minks had turned, too, realising that the surprising conversation was over. A great excitement was in him. He did not feel in the least tired. An unusual sense of anticipation was in the air. He could not make it out at all. Reviewing a dozen possibilities at once, he finally rejected the romantic one he had first suspected, and decided that the right moment had at last come to say something of the Scheme. He had worked so hard to collect data. All was in perfect order. His chief could not feel otherwise than pleased.

"Then I'll be saying good-night, Mr. Rogers," he began, "for you must be very tired, and I trust you will enjoy a long night's rest. Perhaps you would like me to come a little later in the morning than usual."

He stood looking affectionately at the formidable pile of correspondence, and, as his chief made no immediate reply, he went on, with more decision in his voice:

"Here," he said, touching the papers he had carefully set on one side, "are all the facts you wanted referring to your great Scheme—"

He jumped. His master's fist had come down with a bang upon the table. He stepped back a pace. They stared at one another.

"Damn the Scheme!" cried Rogers. "have done and finished with it. Tear up the papers. Cancel any arrangements already made. And never mention the thing again in my hearing. It's all unreal and wrong and unnecessary!"

Minks gasped. The man was so in earnest. What could it mean?

"Wrong—unnecessary—done with!" he faltered. Then, noticing the flashing eyes that yet betrayed a hint of merriment in their fire, he added quickly, "Quite so, Mr. Rogers; I understand. You've got an improvement, you mean?"

It was not his place to ask questions, but he could not contain himself. Curiosity and disappointment rushed over him.

"A bigger and a better one altogether, Minks," was the vehement reply. He pushed the heap of papers towards the secretary. Minks took them gingerly, reluctantly.

"Burn 'em up," Rogers went on, "and never speak to me again about the blessed thing. I've got a far bigger Scheme than that."

Minks slowly gathered the papers together and put them in his biggest pocket. He knew not what to think. The suddenness of the affair dazed him. Thought-transference failed this time; he was too perturbed, indeed, to be in a receptive state at all. It seemed a catastrophe, a most undesirable and unexpected climax. The romantic solution revived in him—but only for a passing moment. He rejected it. Some big discovery was in the air. He felt that extraordinary sense of anticipation once again.

"Look here, my dear fellow, Minks," said Rogers, who had been watching his discomfiture with amusement, "you may be surprised, but you need not be alarmed. The fact is, this has been coming for a long time; it's not an impulsive decision. You must have felt it— from my letters. That Scheme was all right enough, only I am not the right man for it. See? And our work," he added laughingly, "won't go for nothing either, because our thought will drop into another mind somewhere that will accomplish the thing far better than I could have accomplished it."

Minks made an odd gesture, as who should say this might not be true. He did not venture upon speech, however. This new plan must be very wonderful, was all he thought just then. His faith in his employer's genius was complete.

"And in due time you shall hear all about it. Have a little patience. Perhaps you'll get it out of my thoughts before I tell it to you," he smiled, "but perhaps you won't. I can only tell you just now that it has beauty in it—a beauty of the stars."

Yet what his bigger Scheme was he really had no clear idea. He felt it coming-that was all!

And with that Minks had to be content. This was dismissal. Good-nights were said, and the secretary went out into the street.

"Go to a comfortable hotel," was the last thing he heard, "and put it down to me, of course. Sleep well, sleep well. Tomorrow at two o'clock will do."

Minks strolled home, walking upon air. The sky was brilliant with its gorgeous constellations—the beauty of the stars. Poems blazed upon him. But he was too excited to compose. Even first lines evaded capture. "Stars," besides, was a dreadful word to rhyme with, for all its charm and loveliness. He knew of old that the only word was "wars," most difficult to bring in naturally and spontaneously, and with the wrong sound in any case.

"He must have been writing poetry out there," he reflected finally, "or else living it. Living it, probably. He's a grand fellow anyhow, grand as a king." Stars, wars, kings, thrones—the words flew in and out among a maze of unaccomplished lines.

But the last thing in his mind as he curled up to sleep in the strange bed was that he had delivered his wife's message, but that he could not tell her about this sudden collapse of the great, long-talked-of Scheme. Albinia would hardly understand. She might think less of his chief. He would wait until the new one dawned upon the horizon with its beauty of the stars. Then he would simply overwhelm her with it, as his temperament loved to do.

XXX

Lo, every yearning thought that holds a tear,
Yet finds no mission
And lies untold,
Waits, guarded in that labyrinth of gold,—
To reappear
Upon some perfect night,
Deathless—not old—
But sweet with time and distance,
And clothed as in a vision
Of starry brilliance
For the world's delight.

—JOHN HENRY CAMPDEN

Then, as the days passed, practical life again caught Henry Rogers in its wholesome grip. Fairyland did not fade exactly, but it dipped a little below the horizon. Like hell and heaven, it was a state of mind, open potentially to all, but not to be enjoyed merely for the asking. Like other desirable things, it was to be "attained." Its remoteness and difficulty of access lent to it a haunting charm; for though its glory dimmed a little, there was a soft afterglow that shed its radiance even down Piccadilly and St. James's Street. He was always conscious of this land beyond the sunset; the stars shone brightly, though clouds or sunlight interfered to blur their message.

London life, however, by the sheer weight of its grinding daily machinery, worked its slow effect upon him. He became less sensitive to impressions. These duller periods were interrupted sometimes by states of brilliant receptiveness, as at Bourcelles; but there was a fence between the two—a rather prickly frontier, and the secret of combining them lay just beyond his reach. For his London mind, guided by reason, acted in a logical plane of two dimensions, while imagination, captained by childhood's fairy longings, cantered loose in all directions at once—impossibly. The first was the world; the second was the universe. As yet, he was unable to co-ordinate them. Minks, he was certain, could—and did, sailing therefore upon an even keel. There was this big harmony in little Minks that he envied. Minks had an outlet. Sydenham, and even the City, for him were fairyland; a motor-bus fed his inspiration as surely as a starlit sky; moon always rhymed with June, and forget with regret. But the inner world of Henry Rogers was not yet properly connected with the outer. Passage from one to the other was due to chance, it seemed, not to be effected at will. Moods determined the sudden journey. He rocked. But for his talks with little Minks, he might have wrecked.

And the talks with Minks were about—well, he hardly knew what, but they all played round this map of fairyland he sought to reduce to the scale of everyday life. They discussed thought, dreams, the possibility of leaving the body in sleep, the artist temperament, the source of inspiration as well as the process of the imaginative faculty that created. They talked even of astronomy. Minks held that the life of practical, daily work was the bed-rock of all sane production, yet while preaching this he bubbled over with all the wild, entrancing theories that were in the air today. They were comical, but never dangerous—did not upset him. They were almost a form of play.

And his master, listening, found these conversations an outlet somehow for emotions in himself he could not manage—a scaffolding that provided outlines for his awakening dreams to build upon. He found relief. For Minks, with his delightful tact, asked no awkward questions. He referred neither to the defunct Scheme, nor mentioned the new one that held "a beauty of the stars." He waited. Rogers also waited.

And, while he waited, he grew conscious more and more of an enormous thing that passed, driving behind, *below*, his daily external life. He could never quite get at it. In there, down out of sight somewhere, he knew everything. His waking existence was fed invisibly from below. In the daytime he now frequently caught himself attempting to recover the memory of things that went on elsewhere, things he was personally involved in, vital things. This daylight effort to recover them was as irksome as the attempt to draw a loose hair that has wound about the tongue. He spoke at length to Minks about it.

"Some part of you," replied the imperturbable secretary, after listening carefully to his master's vague description of the symptoms, "is being engaged elsewhere—very actively engaged—"

"Eh?" asked Rogers, puzzled.

"Probably at night, sir, while your brain and body sleep," Minks elaborated, "your energetic spirit is out—on the plane of causes—"

The other gasped slightly, "While my body lies unconscious?"

"Your spirit may be busy at all kinds of things. *That* can never be unconscious," was the respectful answer. "They say—"

"Yes, what do they say?" He recognised a fairy theory, and jumped at it.

"That in sleep," continued the other, encouraged, "the spirit knows a far more concentrated life—dips down into the deep sea of being—our waking life merely the froth upon the shore."

Rogers stared at him. "Yes, yes," he answered slowly, "that's very pretty, very charming; it's quite delightful. What ideas you have, my dear Minks! What jolly, helpful ideas!"

Minks beamed with pleasure.

"Not my own, Mr. Rogers, not my own," he said, with as much pride as if they *were* his own, "but some of the oldest in the world, just coming into fashion again with the turn of the tide, it seems. Our daily life—even the most ordinary—is immensely haunted, girdled about with a wonder of incredible things. There are hints everywhere today, though few can read the enormous script complete. Here and there one reads a letter or a word, that's all. Yet the best minds refuse to know the language, not even the ABC of it; they read another language altogether—"

"The best minds!" repeated Rogers. "What d'you mean by that!" It sounded, as Minks said it, so absurdly like best families.

"The scientific and philosophical minds, sir. They think it's not worth learning, this language. That's the pity of it—ah, the great pity of it!" And he looked both eager and resentful—his expression almost pathetic. He turned half beseechingly to his employer, as though *he* might alter the sad state of things. "As with an iceberg, Mr. Rogers," he added, "the greater part of everything—of ourselves especially—is invisible; we merely know the detail banked against an important grand Unseen."

The long sentence had been suffered to its close because the audience was busy with thoughts of his own instead of listening carefully. Behind the wild language stirred some hint of meaning that, he felt, held truth. For a moment, it seemed, his daylight searching was explained—almost.

"Well and good, my dear fellow, and very picturesque," he said presently, gazing with admiration at his secretary's neat blue tie and immaculate linen; "but thinking, you know, is not possible without matter." This in a tone of "*Do* talk a little sense." "Even if the spirit does go out, it couldn't think apart from the brain, could it now, eh?"

Minks took a deep breath and relieved himself of the following:

"Ah, Mr. Rogers"—as much as to say "Fancy *you* believing that!"—"but it can experience and know *direct*, since it passes into the region whence the material that feeds thought issues in the first instance—causes, Mr. Rogers, causes."

"Oho!" said his master, "oho!"

"There is no true memory afterwards," continued the little dreamer, "because memory depends upon how much the spirit can bring back into the brain, you see. We have vague feelings, rather than actual recollection—feelings such as you were kind enough to confess to me you had been haunted by yourself—"

"All-overish feelings," Rogers helped him, seeing that he was losing confidence a little, "vague sensations of joy and wonder and—well—in a word, strength."

"Faith," said Minks, with a decision of renewed conviction, "which is really nothing but unconscious knowledge—knowledge unremembered. And it's the half-memory of what you do at night that causes this sense of anticipation you now experience; for what is anticipation, after all, but memory thrown forward?"

There was a pause then, during which Rogers lit a cigarette, while Minks straightened his tie several times in succession.

"You are a greater reader than I, of course," resumed his employer presently; "still, I have come across one or two stories which deal with this kind of thing. Only, in the books, the people always remember what they've done at night, out of the body, in the spirit, or whatever you like to call it. Now, *I* remember nothing whatever. How d'you account for that, pray?"

Minks smiled a little sadly. "The books," he answered very softly, "are wrong there—mere inventions—not written from personal experience. There can be no detailed memory unless the brain has been 'out' too—which it hasn't. That's where inaccuracy and looseness of thought come in. If only the best minds would take the matter up, you see, we might—"

Rogers interrupted him. "We shall miss the post, Minks, if we go on dreaming and talking like this," he exclaimed, looking at his watch and then at the pile of letters waiting to be finished. "It is very delightful indeed, very—but we mustn't forget to be practical, too."

And the secretary, not sorry perhaps to be rescued in time from the depths he had floundered in, switched his mind in concentration upon the work in hand again. The conversation had arisen from a chance coincidence in this very correspondence—two letters that had crossed after weeks of silence.

Work was instantly resumed. It went on as though it had never been interrupted. Pride and admiration stirred the heart of Minks as he noticed how keenly and accurately his master's brain took up the lost threads again. "A grand fellow!" he thought to himself, "a splendid man! He lives in both worlds at once, yet never gets confused, nor lets one usurp his powers to the detriment of the other. If only I were equally balanced and effective. Oh dear!" And he sighed.

And there were many similar conversations of this kind. London seemed different, almost transfigured sometimes. Was this the beginning of that glory which should prove it a suburb of Bourcelles?

Rogers found his thoughts were much in that cosy mountain village: the children capered by his side all day; he smelt the woods and flowers; he heard the leaves rustle on the poplar's crest; and had merely to think of a certain room in the tumble-down old Citadelle for a wave of courage and high anticipation to sweep over him like a sea. A new feeling of harmony was taking him in hand. It was very delightful; and though he felt explanation beyond his reach still, his talks with Minks provided peep-holes through which he peered at the enormous thing that brushed him day and night.

A great settling was taking place inside him. Thoughts certainly began to settle. He realised, for one thing, that he had left the theatre where the marvellous Play had been enacted. He stood outside now, able to review and form a judgment. His mind loved order. Undue introspection he disliked, as a form of undesirable familiarity; a balanced man must not be too familiar with himself; it endangered self-respect.

He had been floundering rather. After years of methodical labour the freedom of too long a holiday was disorganising. He tried to steady himself. And the Plan of Life, answering to control, grew smaller instantly, reduced to proportions he could examine reasonably. This was the beginning of success. The bewildering light of fairyland still glimmered, but no longer so diffused. It focused into little definite kernels he could hold steady while he scrutinised them.

And these kernels he examined carefully as might be: in the quiet, starry evenings usually, while walking alone in St. James's Park after his day of board meetings, practical work with Minks, and the like.

Gradually then, out of the close survey, emerged certain things that seemed linked together in an intelligible sequence of cause and effect.

There was still mystery, for subconscious investigation ever involves this background of shadow. Question and Wonder watched him. But the facts emerged.

He jotted them down on paper as best he could. The result looked like a Report drawn up by Minks, only less concise and—he was bound to admit it—less intelligible. He smiled as he read them over. . .

"My thoughts and longings, awakened that night in the little Crayfield garden," he summed it up to himself, having read the Report so far, "went forth upon their journey of realisation. I projected them—according to Minks—vividly enough for that! I thought Beauty—and this glorious result materialised! More—my deepest, oldest craving of all has come to life again—the cry of loneliness that yearns to—that seeks—er—"

At this point, however, his analysis grew wumbled; the transference of thought and emotion seemed comprehensible enough; though magical, it was not more so than wireless telegraphy, or that a jet of steam should drive an express for a hundred miles. It was conceivable that Daddy had drawn thence the inspiration for his wonderful story. What baffled him was the curious feeling that another was mixed up in the whole, delightful business, and that neither he nor his cousin were the true sponsors of the fairy fabric. He never forgot the description his cousin read aloud that night in the Den—how the Pattern of his Story reached its climax and completeness when a little starry figure with twinkling feet and amber eyes had leaped into the centre and made itself at home there. From the Pleiades it came. The lost Pleiad was found. The network of thought and sympathy that contained the universe had trembled to its uttermost fastenings. The principal role was filled at last.

It was here came in the perplexing thing that baffled him. His mind sat down and stared at an enormous, shadowy possibility that he was unable to grasp. It brushed past him overhead, beneath, on all sides. He peered up at it and marvelled, unconvinced, yet knowing himself a prisoner. Something he could not understand was coming, was already close, was watching him, waiting the moment to pounce out, like an invisible cat upon a bewildered mouse. The question he flung out brought no response, and he recalled with a smile the verse that described his absurd position:—

Like a mouse who, lost in wonder,
Flicks its whiskers at the thunder!

For, while sprites and yearning were decidedly his own, the interpretation of them, if not their actual origin, seemed another's. This other, like some dear ideal on the way to realisation, had taken him prisoner. The queer sense of anticipation Bourcelles had fostered was now actual expectation, as though some Morning Spider had borne his master-longing, exquisitely fashioned by the Story, across the Universe, and the summons had been answered-from the Pleiades. The indestructible threads of thought and feeling tightened. The more he thought about his cousin's interpretation the more he found in it a loveliness and purity, a crystal spiritual quality, that he could credit neither to the author's mind nor to his own. This soft and starry brilliance was another's. Up to a point the interpretation came through Daddy's brain, just as the raw material came through his own; but thereafter this other had appropriated both, as their original creator and proprietor. Some shining, delicate hand reached down from its starry home and gathered in this exquisite form built up from the medley of fairy thought and beauty that were first its own. The owner of that little hand would presently appear to claim it.

"We were but channels after all then—both of us," was the idea that lay so insistently in him. "The sea of thought sends waves in all directions. They roll into different harbours. I caught the feeling, he supplied the form, but this other lit the original fire!"

And further than this wumbled conclusion he could not get. He went about his daily work. however, with a secret happiness tugging at his mind all day, and a sense of expectant wonder glancing brightly over everything he thought or did. He was a prisoner in fairyland, and what he called his outer and his inner world were, after all, but different ways of looking at one and the same thing. Life everywhere was one.

XXXI

Es stehen unbeweglich
Die Sterne in der Höh'
Viel tausend Jahr', und schauen
Sich an mit Liebesweh.

Sie sprechen eine Sprache,
Die ist so reich, so schön;
Doch keiner der Philologen
Kann diese Sprache verstehen.

Ich aber hab' sie gelernet,
Und ich vergesse sie nicht;
Mir diente als Grammatik
Der Herzallerliebsten Gesicht.

—HEINE

O ne evening in particular the sense of expectation in him felt very close upon delivery. All day he had been aware of it, and a letter received that morning from his cousin seemed the cause. The story, in its shorter version, had been accepted. Its reality, therefore, had already spread; one other mind, at least, had judged it with understanding. Two months from now, when it appeared in print, hundreds more would read it. Its beauty would run loose in many hearts. And Rogers went about his work that day as though the pleasure was his own. The world felt very sweet. He saw the good in every one with whom he came in contact. And the inner excitement due to something going to happen was continuous and cumulative.

Yet London just then—it was August—was dull and empty, dusty, and badly frayed at the edges. It needed a great cleaning; he would have liked to pour sea water over all its streets and houses, bathed its panting parks in the crystal fountains of Bourcelles. All day long his thoughts, indeed, left London for holidays in little Bourcelles. He was profoundly conscious that the Anticipation he first recognised in that forest village was close upon accomplishment now. On the journey back to England he recalled how urgent it had been. In London, ever since, it had never really left him. But today it now suddenly became more than expectation—he felt it in him as a certainty that approached fulfilment. It was strange, it was bewildering; it seemed to him as though something from that under-self he could never properly reach within him, pushed upwards with a kind of aggressive violence towards the surface. It was both sweet and vital. Behind the "something" was the "some one" who led it into action.

At half-past six he strolled down a deserted St. James's Street, passed the door of his club with no temptation to go in, and climbed the stairs slowly to his rooms. His body was languid though his mind alert. He sank into an arm-chair beside the open window. "I must *do* something tonight," he thought eagerly; "mere reading at the club is out of the question. I'll go to a theatre or—or—." He considered various alternatives, deciding finally upon Richmond Park. He loved long walks at night when his mind was restless thus; the air in Richmond Park was peculiarly fresh and scented after dark. He knew the little gate that was never closed. He would dine lightly, and go for a ten-mile stretch among the oaks, surprise the deer asleep, listen to the hum of distant London, and watch the fairy battle between the lurid reflection of its million lights and the little stars. . . There were places in the bracken where. . .

The rumbling clatter of a railway van disturbed the picture. His mind followed the noise instead. Thought flashed along the street to a station. He saw trains. . .

"Come at once! You're wanted here—some one calls you!" sounded a breathless merry voice beside him. "Come quickly; aussi schnell que moglich!"

There was a great gulp of happiness in him; his spirit plunged in joy. He turned and looked about him swiftly. That singing voice, with its impudent mingling of languages was unmistakable.

"From the Pleiades. Look sharp! You've been further off than ever lately, and further is further than farther—much! Over the forests and into the cave, that is the way we must all behave—!"

He opened an eye.

Between him and a great gold sunset ran the wind. It was a slender violet wind. The sunset, however, was in the act of disappearing for the Scaffolding of Dusk was passing through the air—he saw the slung trellis-work about him, the tracery of a million lines, the guy-ropes, uprights, and the feathery threads of ebony that trailed the Night behind them like a mighty cloth. There was a fluttering as of innumerable wings.

ALGERNON BLACKWOOD

"You needn't tug like that," he gasped. "I'm coming all right. I'm out!"

"But you're so slow and sticky," she insisted. "You've been sticky like this for weeks now!"

He saw the bright brown eyes and felt the hair all over his face like a bath of perfume. They rushed together. His heart beat faster. . .

"Who wants me in such a hurry?" he cried, the moment he was disentangled. Laughter ran past him on every side from the world of trees.

"As if you didn't know! What *is* the good of pretending any longer! You're both together in the Network, and you know it just as well as she does!"

Pretending! Just as well as *she* does!

As though he had eyes all over his body he saw the Net of Stars above him. Below were forests, vineyards, meadows, and the tiny lights of houses. In the distance shimmered the waters of a familiar lake. Great purple mountains rolled against the sky line. But immediately over his head, close yet also distant, filling the entire heavens, there hung a glittering Pattern that he knew, grown now so vast that at first he scarcely recognised its dazzling loveliness. From the painted western horizon it stretched to other fastenings that dipped below the world, where the East laid its gulfs of darkness to surprise the sun. It swung proudly down, as though hung from the Pole Star towards the north, and while the Great Bear "pointers" tossed its embroidery across Cassiopeia, the Pleiades, just rising, flung its further fringes down to Orion, waiting in wonder to receive them far below the horizon. Old Sirius wore one breadth of it across his stupendous shoulder, and Aldebaran, with fingers of bronze and fire, drew it delicately as with golden leashes over the sleeping world.

When first he saw it, there was this gentle fluttering as of wings through all its intricate parts, but the same moment four shooting stars pierced its outlying edges with flying nails of gold. It steadied and grew taut.

"There she is!" cried Monkey, flashing away like a comet towards the Cave. "You'll catch it now—and you deserve to!" She turned a brilliant somersault and vanished.

Then, somehow, the vast Pattern settled into a smaller scale, so that he saw it closer, clearer, and without confusion. Beauty and wonder focused for his sight. The perfected design of Daddy's fairy story floated down into his heart without a hint of wumbling. Never had he seen it so luminous and simple. For others, of course, meanwhile had known and understood it. Others believed. Its reality was more intense, thus, than before.

He rose from the maze of tree-tops where he floated, and stretched his arms out, no fear or hesitation in him anywhere. Perched in the very centre of the Pattern, seated like a new-born star upon its throne, he saw that tiny figure who had thrilled him months ago when he caught it in a passing instant, fluttering in the web of Daddy's story,—both its climax and its inspiration. The twinkling feet were folded now. He saw the soft little eyes that shone like starlight through clear amber. The hands, palms upwards, were stretched to meet his own.

"You, of course, must come up—to me," he heard.

And climbing the lace-like tracery of the golden web, he knelt before her. But, almost before both knees were bent, her hands had caught him—the touch ran like a sheath of fire through every nerve—and he was seated beside her in that shining centre.

"But why did it suddenly grow small?" he asked at once. He felt absolutely at home. It was like speaking to a child who loved him utterly, and whom he, in his turn, knew intimately inside out.

"Because you suddenly understood," was the silvery, tiny answer. "When you understand, you bring everything into yourself, small as a toy. It is size that bewilders. Men make size. Fairy things, like stars and tenderness, are always small."

"Of course," he said; "as if I didn't know it already!"

"Besides," she laughed, half closing her brilliant eyes and peering at him mischievously, "I like everything so tiny that you can find it inside a shell. That makes it possible to do big things."

"Am *I* too big—?" he exclaimed, aware of clumsiness before this exquisite daintiness.

"A little confused, that's all," her laughter rippled. "You want smoothing down. I'll see to that."

He had the feeling, as she said it, that his being included the entire Pattern, even to its most distant edges where it fastened on to the rim of the universe. From this huge sensation, he came back swiftly to its tiny correspondence again. His eyes turned to study her. But she seemed transparent somehow, so that he saw the sky behind her, and in it, strangely enough—just behind her face—the distant Pleiades, shining faintly with their tender lustre. They reached down into her little being, it seemed, as though she emanated from them. Big Aldebaran guided strongly from behind. For an instant he lost sight of the actual figure, seeing in its place a radiant efflorescence, purified as by some spiritual fire—the Spirit of a Star.

"I'm here, quite close beside you," whispered the tiny voice. "Don't let your sight get troublesome like your size. Inside-sight, remember, is the thing!"

He turned, or rather he focused sight again to find her. He was startled a little. For a moment it seemed like his own voice speaking deep down within himself.

"Make yourself at home," it continued, "you belong here—almost as much as I do." And at the sound of her voice all the perplexities of his life lay down. It brushed him smooth, like a wind that sets rough feathers all one way,

He remembered again where he was, and what was going on.

"I do," he answered, happy as a boy. "I am at home. It is perfect."

"Do you, indeed! You speak as though this story were your own!"

And her laugh was like the tinkle of hare-bells in the wind.

"It is," he said; "at least I had—I *have*, rather, a considerable hand in the making of it."

"Possibly," she answered, "but the story belongs to the person who first started it. And that person is myself. The story is mine really!"

"Yours!" he gasped.

"Because—I am the story!"

He stared hard to find the face that said this thing. Thought stopped dead a moment, blocked by a marvel that was impossible, yet true.

"You mean—?" he stammered.

"You heard perfectly what I said; you understood it, too. There's no good pretending," impatience as well as laughter in the little voice. "I am the story,—the story that you love."

A sudden joy burst over him in a flood. Struggle and search folded their wings and slept. An immense happiness wrapped him into the very woof of the pattern wherein they sat. A thousand loose and ineffective moods of his life found coherence, as a thousand rambling strands were gathered home and fastened into place.

And the Pattern quivered and grew brighter.

"I am the story because I thought of it first. You, as a version of its beauty—a channel for its delivery—belong utterly to me. You can no more resist me than a puddle can resist the stars' reflection. You increase me. We increase each other."

"You say you thought it first," he cried, feeling the light he radiated flow in and mingle with her own. "But who are you? Where do you come from?"

"Over there somewhere, I think," she laughed, while a ray like fire flashed out in the direction of the Pleiades that climbed the sky towards the East. "You ought to know. You've been hunting for me long enough!"

"But who *are* you?" he insisted again, "for I feel it's you that have been looking for me—I've so often heard you calling!"

She laughed again till the whole web quivered. Through her eyes the softness of all the seven Pleiades poured deliciously into him.

"It's absurd that such a big thing as you could hide so easily," she said. "But you'll never hide again. I've got you fast now. And you've got me! It's like being reflected together in the same puddle, you see!"

The dazzling radiance passed as she said it into a clearer glow, and across the fire of it he caught her eyes steadily a moment, though he could not see the face complete. Two brilliant points of amber shone up at him, as stars that peep from the mirror of a forest pool. That mental daylight-searching seemed all explained, only he could not remember now that there was any such thing at all as either searching or daylight. When "out" like this, waking was the dream—the sunlight world forgotten.

"This Pattern has always been my own," she continued with infinite softness, yet so clearly that his whole body seemed a single ear against her lips, "for I've thought it ever since I can remember. I've lived it. This Network of Stars I made ages ago in a garden among far bigger mountains than these hills, a garden I knew vividly, yet could not always find—almost as though I dreamed it. The Net included the—oh, included everything there is, and I fastened it to four big pines that grew on the further side of the torrent in that mountain garden of my dream—fastened it with nails of falling stars. And I made the Pleiades its centre because I loved them best of all. Oh! Orion, Orion, how big and comforting your arms are! Please hold me tight for ever and ever!"

"But I know it, too, that lovely dream," he cried. "It all comes back to me. I, too, have dreamed it with you then somewhere—somewhere—!" His voice choked. He had never known that life could hold such sweetness, wonder, joy. The universe lay within his arms.

"All the people I wanted to help I used to catch in my Net of Stars," she went on. "There was a train that brought them up to its edges, and once I got the passengers into the web, and hung them loose in it till they were soaked with starlight, I could send them back happier and braver than they came. It's been my story ever since I can remember anything—my adventure, my dream, my life. And when the great Net faded a little and wanted brightening, we knew an enormous cavern in the mountains where lost starlight collected, and we used to gather this in thousands of sacks, and wash and paint the entire web afresh. That made it sticky, so that the passengers hung in it longer. Don't you remember?

They came back with starlight in their hair and eyes and voices—and in their hearts."

"And the way you—*we* got them into the Net," he interrupted excitedly, "was by understanding them—by feeling with them—"

"Sympathy," she laughed, "of course! Only there were so many I could not reach and could not understand, and so could never get in. In particular there was some one who ought to have been there to help me. If I could find that some one I could do twice as much. I searched and searched. I hunted through every corner of the garden, through forest, cavern, sky, but never with success. Orion never overtook me! My longing cried every where, but in vain. Oh, Orion, my lost Orion, I have found you now at last! . . . The Net flashed messages in all directions, but without response. This some one who could make my work complete existed—that I *knew*—only he was hidden somewhere out of sight—concealed in some corner or other, veiled by a darkness that he wove about himself—as though by some funny kind of wrong thinking that obscured the light I searched for and made it too dim to reach me properly. His life or mind—his thought and feeling, that is—were wumbled—"

"*Wumbled!*" he cried, as the certainty burst upon him with the password. He stood close to her, opening his arms.

Instantly she placed her golden palm upon his mouth, with fingers that were like soft star-rays. Her words, as she continued, were sweeter than the footfalls of the Pleiades when they rise above the sea.

"Yet there were times when we were so close that we could feel each other, and each wondered why the other did not actually appear. I have been trying," she whispered, oh so dearly, "to find you always. And you knew it, too, for I've felt you searching too. . ."

The outlying skirts of the Pattern closed in a little, till the edges gathered over them like a tent of stars. Alone in the heart of the universe they told their secret very softly. . .

"There are twin-stars, you know," she whispered, when he released her, "that circle so close about each other that they look like one. I wonder, oh, I wonder, do they ever touch!"

"They are apart in order to see one another better," he murmured. "They watch one another more sweetly so. They play at separation for the joy of coming together again."

And once more the golden Pattern hid them for a moment from the other stars. . . The shafts of night-fire played round and above their secret tent in space. . . Most marvellously their beings found each other in the great whispering galleries of the world where Thought and Yearning know that first fulfilment which is the source of action later. . .

"So, now that I have found you," her voice presently went on, "our Network shall catch everybody everywhere. For the Pattern of my story, woven so long ago, has passed through you as through a channel—to another who can give it forth. It will spread across every sky. All, all will see it and climb up."

"My scheme—" he cried, with eager delight, yet not quite certain what he meant, nor whence the phrase proceeded.

"Was my thought first," she laughed, "when you were a little boy and I was a little girl—somewhere in a garden very long ago. A ray from its pattern touched you into beauty. Though I could do nothing with it myself, one little ray shot into the mirror of your mind and instantly increased itself. But then, you hid yourself; the channel closed—"

"It never died, though," he interrupted; "the ray, I mean."

"It waited," she went on, "until you found children somewhere, and the channel cleared instantly. Through you, opened up and cleaned by them, my pattern rushed headlong into another who can use it. It could never die, of course. And the long repression—I never ceased to live it—made its power irresistible."

"Your story!" he cried. "It *is* indeed your story."

The eyes were so close against his own that he made a movement that was like diving into a deep and shining sea to reach them. . . The Pleiades rushed instantly past his face. . . Soft filaments of golden texture stroked his very cheeks. That slender violet wind rose into his hair. He saw other larger winds behind it, deeply coloured. . . Something made him tremble all over like a leaf in a storm. He saw, then, the crest of the sentinel poplar tossing between him and the earth far, far below. A mist of confusion caught him, so that he knew not where he was. . . He made an effort to remember. . . a violent effort. . . Some strange sense of heaviness oppressed him. . . He was leaving her.

"Quick!" he tried to cry; "be quick! I am changing. I am drowsy with your voice and beauty. Your eyes have touched me, and I am—falling asleep!" His voice grew weaker as he said it.

Her answer sounded faint, and far above him:

"Give me. . . your. . . hand. Touch me. Come away with me. . . to. . . my. . . garden. . . in the mountains. . . We may wake together. . . You are waking now. . . !"

He made an effort to find her little palm. But the wind swept coldly between his opened fingers.

"Waking!—what is it?" he cried thinly. He thought swiftly of something vague and muddy—something dull, disordered, incomplete. Here it was all glass-clear. "Where are you? I can't find you. I can't see!"

A dreadful, searching pain shot through him. He was losing her, just when he had found her. He struggled, clung, fought frantically to hold her. But his fingers seized the air.

"Oh, I shall find you—even when you wake," he heard far away among the stars. "Try and remember me—when I come. *Try and remember. . .*"

It dipped into the distance. He had lost her. He caught a glimpse of the Pleiades as he fell at a fearful speed. Some one behind them picked up stars and tossed them after him. They dimmed as they shot by—from gold to white, from white to something very pale. Behind them rose a wave of light that hurt his eyes.

"Look out! The Interfering Sun!" came a disappearing voice that was followed by a peal of laughter. "I hope you found her, and I hope you caught it well. You deserved to. . ."

There was a scent of hair that he loved, a vision of mischievous brown eyes, an idea that somebody was turning a somersault beside him—and then he landed upon the solid earth with a noise like thunder.

The room was dark. At first he did not recognise it. Through the open window came the clatter of lumbering traffic that passed heavily down St. James's Street. He rose stiffly from his chair, vexed with himself for having dozed. It was more than a doze, though; he had slept some thirty minutes by his watch. No memory of any dreams was in him—nothing but a feeling of great refreshing lightness and peace. . .

It was wonderful, he reflected, as he changed into country clothes for his walk in Richmond Park, how even the shortest nap revives the brain and body. There was a sense that an immense interval had elapsed, and that something very big had happened or was going to happen to him very soon. . .

And an hour later he passed through the Richmond Gate and found the open spaces of the Park deserted, as they always were. The oaks and bracken rustled in a gentle breeze. The swishing of his boots through the wet grass was the only sound he heard, for the boom and purr of distant London reached him more as touch than as something audible. Seated on a fallen tree, he watched the stars and listened to the wind. That hum and boom of the city seemed underground, the flare it tossed into the sky rose from vast furnaces below the world. The stars danced lightly far beyond its reach, secure and unafraid. He thought of children dancing with twinkling feet upon the mountains. . .

And in himself there was hum and light as well. Too deep, too far below the horizon for full discovery, he caught the echo, the faint, dim flashings of reflection that are called by men a Mood. These, rising to the surface, swept over him with the queer joy of intoxicating wonder that only children know. Some great Secret he had to tell himself, only he had kept it so long and so well that he could not find it quite. He felt the thrill, yet had forgotten what it was.

Something was going to happen. A new footfall was coming across the world towards him. He could almost hear its delicate, swift tread. Life was about to offer him this delicious, thrilling secret—very soon. Looking up he saw the Pleiades, and the single footfall became many. He remembered that former curious obsession of the Pleiades. . . and as Thought and Yearning went roaming into space, they met Anticipation, who took them by the hand. It seemed, then, that children came flocking down upon him from the sky, led by a little figure with starry eyes of clearest amber, a pair of tiny twinkling feet, and a voice quite absurdly soft and tender.

"Your time is coming," he heard behind the rustling of the oak leaves overhead, "for the children are calling to you—children of your own. And this is the bravest Scheme in all the world. There is no bigger. How can there be? For all the world is a child that goes past your windows crying for its lost Fairyland. . . !"

It was after midnight when at length he slipped through the Robin Hood Gate, passed up Priory Lane, and walked rapidly by the shuttered houses of Roehampton. And, looking a moment over Putney Bridge; he saw the reflections of the stars in the muddy, dawdling Thames. Nothing anywhere was thick enough to hide them. The Net of Stars, being in his heart, was everywhere. No prisoner could be more securely caught than he was.

XXXII

ASIA: *The point of one white star is quivering still*
Deep in the orange light of widening morn
Beyond the purple mountains: through a chasm
Of wind-divided mist the darker lake
Reflects it: now it wanes: it gleams again
As the waves fade, and as the burning threads
Of woven cloud unravel in the pale air:
'Tis lost! and through yon peaks of cloud-like snow
The roseate sunlight quivers: hear I not
The AEolian music of her sea-green plumes
Winnowing the crimson dawn?

—*Prometheus Unbound*, SHELLEY

August had blazed its path into September, and September had already trimmed her successor's gown with gold and russet before Henry Rogers found himself free again to think of holidays. London had kept its grip upon him all these weeks while the rest of the world was gay and irresponsible. He was so absurdly conscientious. One of his Companies had got into difficulties, and he was the only man who could save the shareholders' money. The Patent Coal Dust Fuel Company, Ltd., had bought his invention for blowing fine coal dust into a furnace whereby an intense heat was obtainable in a few minutes. The saving in material, time, and labour was revolutionary. Rogers had received a large sum in cash, though merely a nominal number of the common shares. It meant little to him if the Company collapsed, and an ordinary Director would have been content with sending counsel through the post in the intervals of fishing and shooting. But Henry Rogers was of a different calibre. The invention was his child, born by hard labour out of loving thought. The several thousand shareholders believed in him: they were his neighbours. Incompetence and extravagance threatened failure. He took a room in the village near the Essex factories, and gave his personal energy and attention to restoring economical working of every detail. He wore overalls. He put intelligence into hired men and foremen; he spent his summer holiday turning a system of waste into the basis of a lucrative industry. The shareholders would never know whose faithfulness had saved them loss, and at the most his thanks would be a formal paragraph in the Report at the end of the year. Yet he was satisfied, and worked as though his own income depended on success. For he knew—of late this certainty had established itself in him, influencing all he did—that faithful labour, backed by steady thinking, must reach ten thousand wavering characters, merge with awakening tendencies in them, and slip thence into definite daily action. Action was thought materialised. He helped the world. A copybook maxim thus became a weapon of tempered steel. His Scheme was bigger than any hospital for disabled bodies. It would still be cumulative when bodies and bricks were dust upon the wind. It must increase by geometrical progression through all time.

It was largely to little Minks that he owed this positive conviction and belief, to that ridiculous, high-souled Montmorency Minks, who, while his master worked in overalls, took the air himself on Clapham Common, or pored with a wet towel round his brow beneath the oleograph of Napoleon in the attempt to squeeze his exuberant emotion into tripping verse. For Minks admired intensely from a distance. He attended to the correspondence in the flat, and made occasional visits down to Essex, but otherwise enjoyed a kind of extra holiday of his own. For Minks was not learned in coal dust. The combustion was in his eager brain. He produced an amazing series of lyrics and sonnets, though too high-flown, alas, to win a place in print. Love and unselfishness, as usual, were his theme, with a steady sprinkling of "the ministry of Thought," "true success, unrecognised by men, yet noted by the Angels," and so forth. His master's labour seemed to him a "brilliant form of purity," and "the soul's security" came in admirably to close the crowded, tortuous line. "Beauty" and "Duty" were also thickly present, both with capitals, but the verse that pleased him most, and even thrilled Albinia to a word of praise, was one that ended—"Those active powers which are the Doves of Thought." It followed "neither can be sold or bought," and Mrs. Minks approved, because, as she put it, "there, now, is something you can *sell*; it's striking and original; no editor could fail to think so." The necessities of Frank and Ronald were ever her standard of praise or blame.

Thus, it was the first week in October before Rogers found himself free to leave London behind him and think of a change of scene. No planning was necessary. . . Bourcelles was too constantly in his mind all these weary weeks to admit of alternatives. Only a few days ago a letter had come from Jinny, saying she was going to a Pension in Geneva after Christmas, and that unless he appeared soon he would not see her again as she "was," a qualification explained by the postscript, "My hair will be up by that time. Mother says I can put it up on Xmas Day. So please hurry up, Mr. Henry Rogers, if you want to see me as I am."

But another thing that decided him was that the great story was at last in print. It was published in the October number of the Review, and the press had already paid considerable attention to it. Indeed, there was a notice at the railway bookstall on the day he left, to the effect that the first edition was exhausted, and that a large second edition would be available almost immediately. "Place your orders at once" was added in bold red letters. Rogers bought one of these placards for his cousin.

"It just shows," observed Minks, whom he was taking out with him.

"Shows what?" inquired his master.

"How many more thoughtful people there are about, sir, than one had any idea of," was the reply. "The public mind is looking for something of that kind, expecting it even, though it hardly knows what it really wants. That's a story, Mr. Rogers, that must change the point of view of all who read it—with understanding. It makes the commonest man feel he is a hero."

"You've put our things into a non-smoker, Minks," the other interrupted him. "What in the world are you thinking about?"

"I beg your pardon, I'm sure, sir; so I have," said Minks, blushing, and bundling the bags along the platform to another empty carriage, "but that story has got into my head. I sat up reading it aloud to Mrs. Minks all night. For it says the very things I have always longed to say. Sympathy and the transference of thought—to say nothing of the soul's activity when the body is asleep—have always seemed to me—"

He wandered on while his companion made himself comfortable in a corner with his pipe and newspaper. But the first thing Rogers read, as the train went scurrying through Kent, was a summary of the contents of this very Review. Two-thirds of the article was devoted to the "Star Story" of John Henry Campden, whose name "entitled his work to a high standard of criticism." The notice was well written by some one evidently of intelligence and knowledge; sound judgment was expressed on style and form and general execution, but when it came to the matter itself the criticism was deplorably misunderstanding. The writer had entirely missed the meaning. While praising the "cleverness" he asked plainly between the lines of his notice "What does it mean?"

This unconscious exposure of his own ignorance amused his reader while it also piqued him. The critic, expert in dealing with a political article, was lamentably at sea over an imaginative story.

"Inadequate receiving instrument," thought Rogers, smiling audibly.

Minks, deep in a mysterious looking tome in the opposite corner, looked up over his cigarette and wondered why his employer laughed. He read the article the other handed to him, thinking how much better he could have done it himself. Encouraged by the expression in Mr. Rogers's eyes, he then imparted what the papers call "a genuine contribution to the thought upon the subject."

"The writer quarrels with him," he observed, "for not giving what is expected of him. What he has thought he must go on thinking, or be condemned. He must repeat himself or be uncomprehended."

Hitherto—Minks prided himself upon the knowledge—"he has written studies of uncommon temperaments. Therefore to indulge in fantasy now is wrong."

"Ah, you take it that way, do you?"

"Experience justifies me, Mr. Rogers," the secretary continued. "A friend of mine, or rather of Mrs. Minks's, once wrote a volume of ghost stories that, of course, were meant to thrill. His subsequent book, with no such intention, was judged by the object of the first—as a failure. It must make the flesh creep. Everything he wrote must make the flesh creep. One of the papers, the best—a real thunderer, in fact—said 'Once or twice the desired thrill comes close, but never, alas, quite comes off.'"

"How wumbled," exclaimed his listener.

"It is indeed," said Minks, "in fact, one of the thorns in the path of literature. The ordinary clever mind is indeed a desolate phenomenon. And how often behind the 'Oxford manner' lurks the cultured prig, if I may put it so."

"Indeed you may," was the other's rejoinder, "for you put it admirably."

They laughed a little and went on with their reading in their respective corners. The journey to Paris was enlivened by many similar discussions, Minks dividing his attentions between his master, his volume of philosophy, and the needs of various old ladies, to whom such men attach themselves as by a kind of generous, manly instinct. Minks was always popular and inoffensive. He had such tact.

"Ah! and that reminds me, Minks," said Rogers, as they paced the banks of the Seine that evening, looking at the starry sky over Paris. "What do you know about the Pleiades? Anything—eh?"

Minks drew with pride upon his classical reading.

"The seven daughters of Atlas, Mr. Rogers, if I remember correctly, called therefore the Atlantides. They were the virgin companions of Artemis. Orion, the great hunter, pursued them in Boeotia, and they called upon the gods for help."

"And the gods turned 'em into stars, wasn't it?"

"First into doves, sir—Peleiades means doves—and then set them among the Constellations, where big Orion still pursues, yet never overtakes them."

"Beautiful, isn't it? What a memory you've got, Minks. And isn't one of 'em lost or something?"

"Merope, yes," the delighted Minks went on. He knew it because he had looked it up recently for his lyric about "the Doves of Thought." "She married a mortal, Sisyphus, the son of Aeolus, and so shines more dimly than the rest. For her sisters married gods. But there is one who is more luminous than the others—"

"Ah! and which was that?" interrupted Rogers.

"Maia," Minks told him pat. "She is the most beautiful of the seven. She was the Mother, too, of Mercury, the Messenger of the gods. She gave birth to him in a cave on Mount Cyllene in Arcadia. Zeus was the father—"

"Take care; you'll get run over," and Rogers pulled him from the path of an advancing taxi-cab, whose driver swore furiously at the pair of them. "Charming, all that, isn't it?"

"It is lovely, sir. It haunts the mind. I suppose," he added, "that's why your cousin, Mr. Campden, made the Pleiades the centre of his Star Net in the story—a cluster of beautiful thoughts as it were."

"No doubt, no doubt," his tone so brusque suddenly that Minks decided after all not to mention his poem where the Pleiades made their appearance as the "doves of thought."

"What a strange coincidence," Rogers said as they turned towards the hotel again.

"Subconscious knowledge, probably, sir," suggested the secretary, scarcely following his meaning, if meaning indeed there was.

"Possibly! One never knows, does one?"

"Never, Mr. Rogers. It's all very wonderful."

And so, towards six o'clock in the evening of the following day, having passed the time pleasantly in Paris, the train bore them swiftly beyond Pontarlier and down the steep gradient of the Gorges de l'Areuse towards Neuchatel. The Val de Travers, through which the railway slips across the wooded Jura into Switzerland, is like a winding corridor cleft deep between savage and precipitous walls. There are dizzy glimpses into the gulf below. With steam shut off and brakes partly on, the train curves sharply, hiding its eyes in many tunnels lest the passengers turn giddy. Strips of bright green meadow-land, where the Areuse flows calmly, alternate with places where the ravine plunges into bottomless depths that have been chiselled out as by a giant ploughshare. Rogers pointed out the chosen views, while his secretary ran from window to window, excited as a happy child. Such scenery he had never known. It changed the entire content of his mind. Poetry he renounced finally before the first ten minutes were past. The descriptions that flooded his brain could be rendered only by the most dignified and stately prose, and he floundered among a welter of sonorous openings that later Albinia would read in Sydenham and retail judiciously to the elder children from "Father's foreign letters."

"We shall pass Bourcelles in a moment now! Look out! Be ready with your handkerchief!" Rogers warned him, as the train emerged from the final tunnel and scampered between thick pine woods, emblazoned here and there with golden beeches. The air was crystal, sparkling. They could smell the forests.

They took their places side by side at the windows. The heights of Boudry and La Tourne, that stand like guardian sentries on either side of the mountain gateway, were already cantering by. The precipices flew past. Beyond lay the smiling slopes of vineyard, field, and orchard, sprinkled with farms and villages, of which Bourcelles came first. The Areuse flowed peacefully towards the lake. The panorama of the snowy Alps rolled into view along the farther horizon, and the slanting autumn sunshine bathed the entire scene with a soft and ruddy light. They entered the Fairyland of Daddy's story.

"Voila la sentinelle deja!" exclaimed Rogers, putting his head out to see the village poplar. "We run through the field that borders the garden of the Pension. They'll come out to wave to us. Be ready."

"Ah, oui," said Minks, who had been studying phrase books, "je vwa." But in reality he saw with difficulty, for a spark had got into his eye, and its companion optic, wandering as usual, was suffused with water too.

The news of their arrival had, of course, preceded them, and the row of waving figures in the field gave them a welcome that went straight to Minks's heart. He felt proud for his grand employer. Here was a human touch that would modify the majesty of the impersonal mountain scenery in his description. He waved his handkerchief frantically as the train shot past, and he hardly knew which attracted him most—the expression of happiness on Mr. Rogers's face, or the line of nondescript humanity that gesticulated in the field as though they wished to stop the Paris "Rapide."

For it was a *very* human touch; and either Barnum's Circus or the byeways and hedges of Fairyland had sent their picked representatives with a dance seen usually only in shy moonlit glades. His master named them as the carriage rattled by. The Paris Express, of course, did not stop at little Bourcelles. Minks recognised each one easily from the descriptions in the story.

The Widow Jequier, with garden skirts tucked high, and wearing big gauntlet gloves, waved above her head a Union Jack that knocked her bonnet sideways at every stroke, and even enveloped the black triangle of a Trilby hat that her brother-in-law held motionless aloft as though to test the wind for his daily report upon the condition of le barometre. The Postmaster never waved. He looked steadily before him at the passing train, his small, black figure more than usually dwarfed by a stately outline that rose above the landscape by his side, and was undoubtedly the Woman of the Haystack. Telling lines from the story's rhymes flashed through Minks's memory as, chuckling with pleasure, he watched the magnificent, ample gestures of Mother's waving arms. She seemed to brush aside the winds who came a-courting, although wide strokes of swimming really described her movements best. A little farther back, in the middle distance, he recognised by his peaked cap the gendarme, Gygi, as he paused in his digging and looked up to watch the fun; and beyond him again, solid in figure as she was unchanging in her affections, he saw Mrs. Postmaster, struggling with a bed sheet the *pensionnaires des Glycines* helped her shake in the evening breeze. It was too close upon the hour of *souper* for her to travel farther from the kitchen. And beside her stood Miss Waghorn, waving an umbrella. She was hatless. Her tall, thin figure, dressed in black, against the washing hung out to dry, looked like a note of exclamation, or, when she held the umbrella up at right angles, like a capital L the fairies had set in the ground upon its head.

And the fairies themselves, the sprites, the children! They were everywhere and anywhere. Jimbo flickered, went out, reappeared, then flickered again; he held a towel in one hand and a table napkin in the other. Monkey seemed more in the air than on the solid earth, for one minute she was obviously a ball, and the next, with a motion like a somersault, her hair shot loose across the sunlight as though she flew. Both had their mouths wide open, shouting, though the wind carried their words all away unheard. And Jane Anne stood apart. Her welcome, if the gesture is capable of being described at all, was a bow. She moved at the same time sedately across the field, as though she intended to be seen separately from the rest. She wore hat and gloves. She was evidently in earnest with her welcome. But Mr. John Henry Campden, the author and discoverer of them all, Minks did not see.

"But I don't see the writer himself!" he cried. "I don't see Mr. Campden."

"You can't," explained Rogers, "he's standing behind his wife."

And the little detail pleased the secretary hugely. The true artist, he reflected, is never seen in his work.

It all was past and over—in thirty seconds. The spire of the church, rising against a crimson sky, with fruit trees in the foreground and a line of distant summits across the shining lake, replaced the row of wonderful dancing figures. Rogers sank back in his corner, laughing, and Minks, saying nothing, went across to his own at the other end of the compartment. It all had been so swift and momentary that it seemed like the flash of a remembered dream, a strip of memory's pictures, a vivid picture of some dazzling cinematograph. Minks felt as if he had just read the entire story again from one end to the other—in thirty seconds. He felt different, though wherein exactly the difference lay was beyond him to discover. "It must be the spell of Bourcelles," he murmured to himself. "Mr. Rogers warned me about it. It is a Fairyland that thought has created out of common things. It is quite wonderful!" He felt a glow all over him. His mind ran on for a moment to another picture his master had painted for him, and he imagined Albinia and the family out here, living in a little house on the borders of the forest, a strip of vineyards, sunlight, mountains, happy scented winds, and himself with a writing-table before a window overlooking the lake. . . writing down Beauty.

XXXIII

We never meet; yet we meet day by day
Upon those hills of life, dim and immense:
The good we love, and sleep-our innocence.
O hills of life, high hills! And higher than they,

Our guardian spirits meet at prayer and play.
Beyond pain, joy, and hope, and long suspense,
Above the summits of our souls, far hence,
An angel meets an angel on the way.

Beyond all good I ever believed of thee
Or thou of me, these always love and live.
And though I fail of thy ideal of me,

My angel falls not short. They greet each other.
Who knows, they may exchange the kiss we give,
Thou to thy crucifix, I to my mother.

—ALICE MCYNELL

The arrival at the station interrupted the reverie in which the secretary and his chief both were plunged.

"How odd," exclaimed Minks, ever observant, as he leaped from the carriage, "there are no platforms. Everything in Switzerland seems on one level, even the people—everything, that is, except the mountains."

"Switzerland *is* the mountains," laughed his chief.

Minks laughed too. "What delicious air!" he added, filling his lungs audibly. He felt half intoxicated with it.

After some delay they discovered a taxi-cab, piled the luggage on to it, and were whirled away towards a little cluster of lights that twinkled beneath the shadows of La Tourne and Boudry. Bourcelles lay five miles out.

"Remember, you're not my secretary here," said Rogers presently, as the forests sped by them. "You're just a travelling companion."

"I understand," he replied after a moment's perplexity. "You have a secretary here already."

"His name is Jimbo."

The motor grunted its way up the steep hill above Colombier. Below them spread the vines towards the lake, sprinkled with lights of farms and villages. As the keen evening air stole down from forest and mountain to greet them, the vehicle turned into the quiet village street. Minks saw the big humped shoulders of La Citadelle, the tapering church spire, the trees in the orchard of the Pension. Cudrefin, smoking a cigar at the door of his grocery shop, recognised them and waved his hand. A moment later Gygi lifted his peaked hat and called "bon soir, bonne nuit," just as though Rogers had never gone away at all. Michaud, the carpenter, shouted his welcome as he strolled towards the Post Office farther down to post a letter, and then the motor stopped with a jerk outside the courtyard where the fountain sang and gurgled in its big stone basin. Minks saw the plane tree. He glanced up at the ridged backbone of the building. What a portentous looking erection it was. It seemed to have no windows. He wondered where the famous Den was. The roof overlapped like a giant hood, casting a deep shadow upon the cobbled yard. Overhead the stars shone faintly.

Instantly a troop of figures shot from the shadow and surrounded them. There was a babel of laughter, exclamations, questions. Minks thought the stars had fallen. Children and constellations were mingled all together, it seemed. Both were too numerous to count. All were rushing with the sun towards Hercules at a dizzy speed.

"And this is my friend, Mr. Minks," he heard repeated from time to time, feeling his hand seized and shaken before he knew what he was about. Mother loomed up and gave him a stately welcome too.

"He wears gloves in Bourcelles!" some one observed audibly to some one else.

"Excuse me! This is Riquette!" announced a big girl, hatless like the rest, with shining eyes. "It's a she."

"And this is my secretary, Mr. Jimbo," said Rogers, breathlessly, emerging from a struggling mass. Minks and Jimbo shook hands with dignity.

"Your room is over at the Michauds, as before."

"And Mr. Mix is at the Pension—there was no other room to be had—"

"Supper's at seven—"

"Tante Jeanne's been *grand-cieling* all day with excitement. She'll burst when she sees you!"

"She's read the story, too. Elle dit que c'est le bouquet!"

"There's new furniture in the salon, and they've cleaned the sink while you've been away! . . ."

The author moved forward out of the crowd. At the same moment another figure, slight and shadowy, revealed itself, outlined against the white of the gleaming street. It had been hidden in the tangle of the stars. It kept so quiet.

"Countess, may I introduce him to you," he said, seizing the momentary pause. There was little ceremony in Bourcelles. "This is my cousin I told you about—Mr. Henry Rogers. You must know one another at once. He's Orion in the story."

He dragged up his big friend, who seemed suddenly awkward, difficult to move. The children ran in and out between them like playing puppies, tumbling against each in turn.

"They don't know which is which," observed Jinny, watching the introduction. Her voice ran past him like the whir of a shooting star through space—far, far away. "Excuse me!" she cried, as she cannoned off Monkey against Cousinenry. "I'm not a terminus! This is a regular shipwreck!"

The three elder ones drew aside a little from the confusion.

"The Countess," resumed Daddy, as soon as they were safe from immediate destruction, "has come all the way from Austria to see us. She is staying with us for a few days. Isn't it delightful? We call her the little Grafin." His voice wumbled a trifle thickly in his beard. "She was good enough to like the story—our story, you know—and wrote to me—"

"My story," said a silvery, laughing voice.

And Rogers bowed politely, and with a moment's dizziness, at two bright smiling eyes that watched him out of the little shadow standing between him and the children. He was aware of grandeur.

He stood there, first startled, then dazed. She was so small. But something about her was so enormous. His inner universe turned over and showed its under side. The hidden thing that so long had brushed his daily life came up utterly close and took him in its gigantic arms. He stared like an unmannered child.

Something had lit the world . . .

"This *is* delicious air," he heard Minks saying to his cousin in the distance—to his deaf side judging by the answer:

"Delicious here—yes, isn't it?"

Something had lit the stars. . .

Minks and his cousin continued idly talking. Their voices twittered like birds in empty space. The children had scattered like marbles from a spinning-top. Their voices and footsteps sounded in the cobbled yard of La Citadelle, as they scampered up to prepare for supper. Mother sailed solemnly after them, more like a frigate than ever. The world, on fire, turned like a monstrous Catherine wheel within his brain.

Something had lit the universe. . .

He stood there in the dusk beneath the peeping stars, facing the slender little shadow. It was all he saw at first—this tiny figure. Demure and soft, it remained motionless before him, a hint of childhood's wonder in its graceful attitude. He was aware of something mischievous as well—that laughed at him. . . He realised then that she waited for him to speak. Yet, for the life of him, he could find no words, because the eyes, beneath the big-brimmed hat with its fluttering veil, looked out at him as though some formidable wild creature watched him from the opening of its cave. There was a glint of amber in them. The heart in him went thumping. He caught his breath. Out, jerked, then, certain words that he tried hard to make ordinary—

"But surely—we have met before—I think I know you—"

He just said it, swallowing his breath with a gulp upon the unfinished sentence. But he said it—somewhere else, and not here in the twilight street of little Bourcelles. For his sight swam somehow far away, and he was giddy with the height. The roofs of the houses lay in a sea of shadow below him, and the street wound through them like a ribbon of thin lace. The tree-tops waved very softly in a wind that purred and sighed beneath his feet, and this wind was a violet little wind, that bent them all one way and set the lines and threads of gold a-quiver to their fastenings. For the fastenings were not secure; any minute he might fall. And the threads, he saw, all issued like rays from two central shining points of delicate, transparent amber, radiating forth into an exquisite design that caught the stars. Yet the stars were not reflected in them. It was they who lit the stars. . .

He *was* dizzy. He tried speech again.

"I told you I *should*—" But it was not said aloud apparently.

Two little twinkling feet were folded. Two hands, he saw, stretched down to draw him close. These very stars ran loose about him in a cloud of fiery sand. Their pattern danced in flame. He picked out Sirius, Aldebaran—the Pleiades! There was tumult in his blood, a wild and exquisite confusion. What in the world had happened to him that he should behave in this ridiculous fashion? Yet he was doing nothing. It was only that, for a passing instant, the enormous thing his life had been dimly conscious of so long, rose at last from its subterranean hiding-place and overwhelmed him. This picture that came with it was like some far-off dream he suddenly recovered. A glorious excitement caught him. He felt utterly bewildered.

"Have we?" he heard close in front of him. "I do not think I have had the pleasure"—it was with a slightly foreign accent—"but it is so dim here, and one cannot see very well, perhaps."

And a ripple of laughter passed round some gigantic whispering gallery in the sky. It set the trellis-work of golden threads all trembling. He felt himself perched dizzily in this shaking web that swung through space. And with him was some one whom he knew. . . He heard the words of a song:

"Light desire With their fire."

Something had lit his heart. . .

He lost himself again, disgracefully. A mist obscured his sight, though with the eyes of his mind he still saw crystal-clear. Across this mist fled droves and droves of stars. They carried him out of himself—out, out, out! . . . His upper mind then made a vehement effort to recover equilibrium. An idea was in him that some one would presently turn a somersault and disappear. The effort had a result, it seemed, for the enormous thing passed slowly away again into the caverns of his under-self, . . . and he realised that he was conducting himself in a foolish and irresponsible manner, which Minks, in particular, would disapprove. He was staring rudely—at a shadow, or rather, at two eyes in a shadow. With another effort—oh, how it hurt!—he focused sight again upon surface things. It seemed his turn to say something.

"I beg your pardon," he stammered, "but I thought—it seemed to me for a moment—that I—remembered."

The face came close as he said it. He saw it clear a moment. The figure grew defined against the big stone fountain—the little hands in summer cotton gloves, the eyes beneath the big brimmed hat, the streaming veil. Then he went lost again—more gloriously than before. Instead of the human outline in the dusky street of Bourcelles, he stared at the host of stars, at the shimmering design of gold, at the Pleiades, whose fingers of spun lustre swung the Net loose across the world. . .

"Flung from huge Orion's hand. . ."

he caught in a golden whisper,

"Sweetly linking
All our thinking. . ."

His cousin and Minks, he was aware vaguely, had left him. He was alone with her. A little way down the hill they turned and called to him. He made a frantic effort—there seemed just time—to plunge away into space and seize the cluster of lovely stars with both his hands. Headlong, he dived off recklessly. . . driving at a fearful speed, . . . when—the whole thing vanished into a gulf of empty blue, and he found himself running, not through the sky to clutch the Pleiades, but heavily downhill towards his cousin and Minks.

It was a most abrupt departure. There was a curious choking in his throat. His heart ran all over his body. Something white and sparkling danced madly through his brain. What must she think of him?

"We've just time to wash ourselves and hurry over to supper," his cousin said, as he overtook them, flustered and very breathless. Minks looked at him—regarded him, rather—astonishment, almost disapproval, in one eye, and in the other, apparently observing the vineyards, a mild rebuke.

He walked beside them in a dream. The sound of Colombier's bells across Planeyse, men's voices singing fragments of a Dalcroze song floated to him, and with them all the dear familiar smells:—

Le coeur de ma mie
Est petit, tout petit petit,
J'en ai l'ame ravie. . .

It was Minks, drawing the keen air noisily into his lungs in great draughts, who recalled him to himself.

"I could find my way here without a guide, Mr. Campden," he was saying diffidently, burning to tell how the Story had moved him. "It's all so vivid, I can almost see the Net. I feel in it," and he waved one hand towards the sky.

The other thanked him modestly. "That's your power of visualising then," he added. "My idea was, of course, that every mind in the world is related with every other mind, and that there's no escape—we are all prisoners. The responsibility is vast."

"Perfectly. I've always believed it. Ah! if only one could *live* it!"

Rogers heard this clearly. But it seemed that another heard it with him. Some one very close beside him shared the hearing. He had recovered from his temporary shock. Only the wonder remained. Life was sheer dazzling glory. The talk continued as they hurried along the road together. Rogers became aware then that his cousin was giving information—meant for himself.

". . . A most charming little lady, indeed. She comes from over there," and he pointed to where the Pleiades were climbing the sky towards the East, "in Austria somewhere. She owns a big estate among the mountains. She wrote to me—I've had *such* encouraging letters, you know, from all sorts of folk—and when I replied, she telegraphed to ask if she might come and see me. She seems fond of telegraphing, rather." And he laughed as though he were speaking of an ordinary acquaintance.

"Charming little lady!" The phrase was like the flick of a lash. Rogers had known it applied to such commonplace women.

"A most intelligent face," he heard Minks saying, "quite beautiful, *I* thought—the beauty of mind and soul."

". . . Mother and the children took to her at once," his cousin's voice went on. "She and her maid have got rooms over at the Beguins. And, do you know, a most singular coincidence," he added with some excitement, "she tells me that ever since childhood she's had an idea like this—like the story, I mean—an idea of her own she always wanted to write but couldn't—"

"Of course, of course," interrupted Rogers impatiently; and then he added quickly, "but how *very* extraordinary!"

"The idea that Thought makes a network everywhere about the world in which we all are caught, and that it's a positive duty, therefore, to think beauty—as much a duty as washing one's face and hands, because what you think *touches* others all day long, and all night long too—in sleep."

"Only she couldn't write it?" asked Rogers. His tongue was like a thick wedge of unmanageable wood in his mouth. He felt like a man who hears another spoil an old, old beautiful story that he knows himself with intimate accuracy.

"She can telegraph, she says, but she can't write!"

"An expensive talent," thought the practical Minks.

"Oh, she's very rich, apparently. But isn't it odd? You see, she thought it vividly, played it, lived it. Why, she tells me she even had a Cave in her mountains where lost thoughts and lost starlight collected, and that she made a kind of Pattern with them to represent the Net. She showed me a drawing of it, for though she can't write, she paints quite well. But the odd thing is that she claims to have thought out the main idea of my own story years and years ago with the feeling that some day her idea was bound to reach some one who *would* write it—"

"Almost a case of transference," put in Minks.

"A fairy tale, yes, isn't it!"

"Married?" asked Rogers, with a gulp, as they reached the door. But apparently he had not said it out loud, for there was no reply.

He tried again less abruptly. It required almost a physical effort to drive his tongue and frame the tremendous question.

"What a fairy story for her children! How *they* must love it!" This time he spoke so loud that Minks started and looked up at him.

"Ah, but she has no children," his cousin said.

They went upstairs, and the introductions to Monsieur and Madame Michaud began, with talk about rooms and luggage. The mist was over him once more. He heard Minks saying:—

"Oui, je comprongs un poo," and the clatter of heavy boots up and down the stairs, . . . and then found himself washing his hands in stinging hot water in his cousin's room.

"The children simply adore her already," he heard, "and she won Mother's confidence at the very start. They can't manage her long name. They just call her the Little Countess—die kleine Gräfin. She's doing a most astonishing work in Austria, it seems, with children. . . the Montessori method, and all that. . ."

"By George, now; is it possible? Bourcelles accepted her at once then?"

"She accepted Bourcelles rather—took it bodily into herself—our poverty, our magic boxes, our democratic intimacy, and all the rest; it was just as though she had lived here with us always. And she kept asking who Orion was—that's you, of course—and why you weren't here—"

"And the Den too?" asked Rogers, with a sudden trembling in his heart, yet knowing well the answer.

"Simply appropriated it—came in naturally without being asked;

Jimbo opened the door and Monkey pushed her in. She said it was her Star Cave. Oh, she's a remarkable being, you know, rather," he went on more gravely, "with unusual powers of sympathy. She seems to feel at once what you are feeling. Takes everything for granted as though she knew. I think she *does* know, if you ask me—"

"Lives the story in fact," the other interrupted, hiding his face rather in the towel, "lives her belief instead of dreaming it, eh?"

"And, fancy this!" His voice had a glow and softness in it as he said it, coming closer, and almost whispering, "she wants to take Jinny and Monkey for a bit and educate them." He stood away to watch the effect of the announcement. "She even talks of sending Edward to Oxford, too!" He cut a kind of wumbled caper in his pleasure and excitement.

"She loves children then, evidently?" asked the other, with a coolness that was calculated to hide other feelings. He rubbed his face in the rough towel as though the skin must come off. Then, suddenly dropping the towel, he looked into his cousin's eyes a moment to ensure a proper answer.

"Longs for children of her own, I think," replied the author; "one sees it, feels it in all she says and does. Rather sad, you know, that! An unmarried mother—"

"In fact," put in Rogers lightly, "the very character you needed to play the principal role in your story. When you write the longer version in book form you'll have to put her in."

"And find her a husband too—which is a bore. I never write love stories, you see. She's finer as she is at present—mothering the world."

Rogers's face, as he brushed his hair carefully before the twisted mirror, was not visible.

There came a timid knock at the door.

"I'm ready, gentlemen, when you are," answered the voice of Minks outside.

They went downstairs together, and walked quickly over to the Pension for supper. Rogers moved sedately enough so far as the others saw, yet inwardly he pranced like a fiery colt in harness. There were golden reins about his neck. Two tiny hands directed him from the Pleiades. In this leash of sidereal fire he felt as though he flew. Swift thought, flashing like a fairy whip, cut through the air from an immense distance, and urged him forwards. Some one expected him and he was late—years and years late. Goodness, how his companions crawled and dawdled!

". . . she doesn't come over for her meals," he heard, "but she'll join us afterwards at the Den. You'll come too, won't you, Mr. Minks?"

"Thank you, I shall be most happy—if I'm not intruding," was the reply as they passed the fountain near the courtyard of the Citadelle. The musical gurgle of its splashing water sounded to Rogers like a voice that sang over and over again, "Come up, come up, come up! You must come up to me!"

"How brilliant your stars are out here, Mr. Campden," Minks was saying when they reached the door of La Poste. He stood aside to let the others pass before him. He held the door open politely. "No wonder you chose them as the symbol for thought and sympathy in your story." And they climbed the narrow, creaking stairs and entered the little hall where the entire population of the Pension des Glycines awaited them with impatience.

The meal dragged out interminably. Everybody had so much to say. Minks, placed between Mother and Miss Waghorn, talked volubly to the latter and listened sweetly to all her stories. The excitement of the Big Story, however, was in the air, and when she mentioned that she looked forward to reading it, he had no idea, of course, that she had already done so at least three times. The Review had replaced her customary Novel. She went about with it beneath her arm. Minks, feeling friendly and confidential, informed her that he, too, sometimes wrote, and when she noted the fact with a deferential phrase about "you men of letters," he rose abruptly to the seventh heaven of contentment. Mother meanwhile, on the other side, took him bodily into her great wumbled heart. "Poor little chap," her attitude said plainly, "I don't believe his wife half looks after him." Before the end of supper she knew all about Frank and Ronald, the laburnum tree in the front garden, what tea they bought, and Albinia's plan for making coal last longer by mixing it with coke.

Tante Jeanne talked furiously and incessantly, her sister-in-law told her latest dream, and the Postmaster occasionally cracked a solemn joke, laughing uproariously long before the point appeared. It was a merry, noisy meal, and Henry Rogers sat through it upon a throne that was slung with golden ropes from the stars. He was in Fairyland again. Outside, the Pleiades were rising in the sky, and somewhere in Bourcelles—in the rooms above Beguin's shop, to be exact—some one was waiting, ready to come over to the Den. His thoughts flew wildly. Passionate longing drove behind them. "You must come up to me," he heard. They all were Kings and Queens.

He played his part, however; no one seemed to notice his preoccupation. The voices sounded now far, now near, as though some wind made sport with them; the faces round him vanished and reappeared; but he contrived cleverly, so that none remarked upon his absent-mindedness. Constellations do not stare at one another much.

"Does your Mother know you're 'out'?" asked Monkey once beside him—it was the great joke now, since the Story had been read—and as soon as she was temporarily disposed of, Jimbo had serious information to impart from the other side. "She's a real Countess," he said, speaking as man to man. "I suppose if she went to London she'd know the King—visit him, like that?"

Bless his little heart! Jimbo always knew the important things to talk about.

There were bursts of laughter sometimes, due usually to statements made abruptly by Jane Anne—as when Mother, discussing the garden with Minks, reviled the mischievous birds:—

"They want thinning badly," she said.

"Why don't they take more exercise, then?" inquired Jinny gravely.

And in these gusts of laughter Rogers joined heartily, as though he knew exactly what the fun was all about. In this way he deceived everybody and protected himself from discovery. And yet it seemed to him that he shouted his secret aloud, not with his lips indeed, but with his entire person. Surely everybody knew it. . . ! He was self-conscious as a schoolgirl.

"You must come up—to me," rang continuously through his head like bells. "You must come up to me."

XXXIV

How many times do I love thee, dear?
Tell me how many thoughts there be
In the atmosphere
Of a new fall'n year,
Whose white and sable hours appear
The latest flake of Eternity:—
So many times do I love thee, dear.

How many times do I love again?
Tell me how many beads there are
In a silver chain
Of evening rain,
Unravelled from the tumbling main,
And threading the eye of a yellow star:—
So many times do I love again.

—THOMAS LOVELL BEDDOES

A curious deep shyness settled upon Henry Rogers as they all trooped over to the Den. The others gabbled noisily, but to him words came with difficulty. He felt like a boy going up for some great test, examination, almost for judgment. There was an idea in him that he must run and hide somewhere. He saw the huge outline of Orion tilting up above the Alps, slanting with the speed of his eternal hunt to seize the Pleiades who sailed ever calmly just beyond his giant arms. Yet what that old Hunter sought was at last within his reach. He knew it, and felt the awe of capture rise upon him.

"You've eaten so much supper you can't speak," said Monkey, whose hand was in his coat-pocket for loose chicken-feed, as she called centimes. "The Little Countess will *regler ton affaire* all right. Just wait till she gets at you."

"You love her?" he asked gently, feeling little disposed to play.

The child's reply was cryptic, yet uncommonly revealing:—

"She's just like a relation. It's so funny she didn't know us long, long ago—find us out, I mean."

"Mother likes her awfully," added Jimbo, as though that established the matter of her charm for ever. "It's a pity she's not a man"—just to show that Cousinenry's position was not endangered.

They chattered on. Rogers hardly remembers how he climbed the long stone steps. He found himself in the Den. It came about with a sudden jump as in dreams. *She* was among them before the courtyard was crossed; she had gone up the steps immediately in front of him. . . Jinny was bringing in the lamp, while Daddy struggled with a load of peat for the fire, getting in everybody's way. Riquette stood silhouetted against the sky upon the window sill. Jimbo used the bellows. A glow spread softly through the room. He caught sight of Minks standing rather helplessly beside the sofa talking to Jane Anne, and picking at his ear as he always did when nervous or slightly ill at ease. He wondered vaguely what she was saying to him. He looked everywhere but at the one person for whose comfort the others were so energetic.

His eyes did not once turn in her direction, yet he knew exactly how she was dressed, what movements she made, where she stood, the very words, indeed, she used, and in particular the expression of her face to each in turn. For he was guilty of a searching inner scrutiny he could not control. And, above all, he was aware, with a divine, tumultuous thrill, that she, for her part, also neither looked at him nor uttered one sentence that he could take as intended for himself.

Because, of course, all she said and did and looked *were* meant for him, and her scrutiny was even closer and more searching than his own.

In the Den that evening there was one world within another, though only these two, and probably the intuitive and diabolically observant Minks, perceived it. The deep furnaces of this man's inner being, banked now so long that mere little flames had forgotten their way out, lay open at last to that mighty draught before whose fusing power the molten, fluid state becomes inevitable.

"You must come up to me" rang on in his head like a chime of bells. "O think Beauty: it's your duty. . ."

The chairs were already round the open fireplace, when Monkey pushed him into the big one with the broken springs he always used, and established herself upon his knee. Jimbo was on the other in a twinkling. Jane Anne plumped down upon the floor against him. Her hair was up, and grown-ups might sit as they pleased. Minks in a hard, straight-backed chair, firmly assured everybody that he was exceedingly comfortable and really preferred stiff chairs. He found safety next to Mother who, pleased and contented, filled one corner of the sofa and looked as though she occupied a pedestal. Beyond her perched Daddy, on the music stool, leaning his back against the unlighted fourneau. The Wumble Book was balanced on his knees, and beside him sat the little figure of the visitor who, though at the end, was yet somehow the true centre of the circle. Rogers saw her slip into her unimportant place. She took her seat, he thought, as softly as a mouse. For no one seemed to notice her. She was so perfectly at home among them. In her little folded hands the Den and all its occupants seemed cared for beyond the need of words or definite action. And, although her place was the furthest possible remove from his own, he felt her closer to him than the very children who nestled upon his knees.

Riquette then finally, when all were settled, stole in to complete the circle. She planted herself in the middle of the hearth before them all, looked up into their faces, decided that all was well, and began placidly to wash her face and back. A leg shot up, from the middle of her back apparently, as a signal that they might talk. A moment later she composed herself into that attitude of dignified security possible only to the feline species. She made the fourth that inhabited this world within a world. Rogers, glancing up suddenly from observing her, caught— for the merest fraction of an instant—a flash of starfire in the air. It darted across to him from the opposite end of the horse-shoe. Behind it flickered the tiniest smile a human countenance could possibly produce.

> "Little mouse who, lost in wonder,
> Flicks its whiskers at the thunder."

It was Jane Anne repeating the rhyme for Minks's benefit. How appropriately it came in, he thought. And voices were set instantly in motion; it seemed that every one began to speak at once.

Who finally led the conversation, or what was actually said at first, he has no more recollection than the man in the moon, for he only heard the silvery music of a single voice. And that came rarely. He felt washed in glory from head to foot. In a dream of happy starlight he swam and floated. He hid his face behind the chair of Monkey, and his eyes were screened below the welcome shelter of Jimbo's shoulder.

The talk meanwhile flowed round the horse-shoe like a river that curves downhill. Life ran past him, while he stood on the banks and watched. He reconstructed all that happened, all that was said and done, each little movement, every little glance of the eye. These common things he recreated. For, while his body sat in the Den before a fire of peat, with children, a cat, a private secretary, three very ordinary people and a little foreign visitor, his spirit floated high above the world among the immensities of suns and starfields. He was in the Den, but the Den was in the universe, and to the scale of the universe he set the little homely, commonplace picture. Life, he realised, *is* thought and feeling; and just then he thought and felt like a god. He was Orion, and Orion had at last overtaken the Pleiades. The fairest of the cluster lay caught within his giant arms. The Enormous Thing that so long had haunted him with hints of its approach, rose up from his under-self, and possessed him utterly. And, oh, the glory of it, the splendour, the intoxication!

In the dim corner where *she* sat, the firelight scarcely showed her face, yet every shade of expression that flitted across her features he saw unobscured. The sparkling, silvery sentences she spoke from time to time were volumes that interpreted life anew. For years he had pored over these thick tomes, but heavily and without understanding. The little things she said now supplied the key. Mind and brain played no part in this. It was simply that he heard—and knew. He re-discovered her from their fragments, piece by piece. . .

The general talk flowed past him in a stream of sound, cut up into lengths by interrupting consonants, and half ruined by this arbitrary division; but what *she* said always seemed the living idea that lay behind the sound. He could not explain it otherwise. With herself, and with Riquette, and possibly with little, dreaming Minks, he sat firmly at the centre of this inner world. The others, even the children, hovered about its edges, trying to get in. That tiny smile had flashed its secret, ineffable explanation into him. Starlight was in his blood. . .

Mother, for instance, he vaguely knew, was speaking of the years they all had lived in Bourcelles, of the exquisite springs, of the fairy, gorgeous summers. It was the most ordinary talk imaginable, though it came sincerely from her heart.

"If only you had come here earlier," she said, "when the forest was so thick with flowers." She enumerated them one by one. "Now, in the autumn, there are so few!"

The little sparkling answer lit the forest glades afresh with colour, perfume, wonder:—

"But the autumn flowers, I think, are the sweetest; for they have the beauty of all the summer in them."

A slight pause followed, and then all fell to explaining the shining little sentence until its lustre dimmed and disappeared beneath the smother of their words. In himself, however, who heard them not, a new constellation swam above the horizon of his inner world. Riquette looked slyly up and blinked. She purred more deeply, but she made no stupid sign. . .

And Daddy mentioned then the forest spell that captured the entire village with its peace and softness—"all so rough and big and tumbled, and yet every detail so exquisitely finished and thought out, you know."

Out slipped the softest little fairy phrase imaginable from her dim corner then:—

"Yes, like hand-made things—you can almost see the hand that made them."

And Rogers started so perceptibly that Jimbo shifted his weight a little, thinking he must be uncomfortable. He had surely used that very phrase himself! It was familiar. Even when using it he remembered wondering whence its sweetness had dropped into his clumsier mind. Minks uncrossed his legs, glanced up at him a moment, then crossed them again. He made this sign, but, like Riquette, he said nothing. . .

The stream flowed on and on. Some one told a story. There was hushed attentive listening, followed suddenly by bursts of laughter and delight. Who told it, or what it was about, Rogers had no notion. Monkey dug him in the ribs once because apparently he grunted at the wrong moment, and Jimbo chided her beneath his breath—"Let him have a nap if he wants to; a man's always tired after a long journey like that. . . !" Some one followed with another story—Minks, was it, this time?—for Rogers caught his face, as through a mist, turning constantly to Mother for approval. It had to do with a vision of great things that had come to a little insignificant woman on a bed of sickness. He recognised the teller because he knew the tale of old. The woman, he remembered, was Albinia's grandmother, and Minks was very proud of it.

"That's a *very* nice story," rippled from the dim corner when it was over. "For I like everything so tiny that you can find it inside a shell. That's the way to understand big things and to do them."

And again the phrase was as familiar to him as though he had said it himself—heard it, read it, dreamed it, even. Whatever its fairy source, he knew it. His bewilderment increased absurdly. The things she said were so ordinary, yet so illuminating, though never quite betraying their secret source. Where had he heard them? Where had he met this little foreign visitor? Whence came the singular certainty that she shared this knowledge with him, and might presently explain it, all clear as daylight and as simple? He had the odd impression that she played with him, delayed purposely the moment of revelation, even expected that *he* would be the first to make it known. The disclosure was to come from himself! She provided him with opportunities—these little sparkling sentences! But he hid in his corner, silent and magically excited, afraid to take the lead. These sentences were addressed to him. There was conversation thus between the two of them; but his replies remained inaudible. Thought makes no sound; its complete delivery is ever wordless. . . He felt very big, and absurdly shy.

It was gesture, however, that infallible shorthand of the mind, which seemed the surest medium of this mute delightful intercourse. For each little gesture that she made—unconsciously, of course—expressed more than the swiftest language could have compassed in an hour. And he noted every one: the occasional flourish of the little hands, the bending of the graceful neck, the shadowy head turned sideways, the lift of one shoulder, almost imperceptible, and sometimes the attitude of the entire body. To him they were, one and all, eloquently revealing. Behind each little gesture loomed a yet larger one, the scale increasing strangely, till his thoughts climbed up them as up a ladder into the region where her ideas lay naked before casual interpretation clothed them. Those, he reflected, who are rich in ideas, but find words difficult, may reveal themselves prodigally in gesture. Expression of one kind or another there must be; yet lavish action, the language of big souls, seems a man's expression rather than a woman's. . . He built up swiftly, surely, solidly his interpretation of this little foreign visitor who came to him thus suddenly from the stars, whispering to his inmost thought, "You must come up to me." The whole experience dazed him. He sat in utter dumbness, shyer than a boy, but happier than a singing star! . . . The Joy in his heart was marvellous.

Yet how could he know all this?

In the intervals that came to him like breathing spaces he asked himself this childish question. How could he tell that this little soft being with the quiet unobtrusive manners had noble and great beauty of action in her anywhere? A few pretty phrases, a few significant gestures, these were surely a slight foundation to build so much upon! Was there, then, some absolute communion of thought between the two of them such as his cousin's story tried to show? And had their intercourse been running on for years, neither of them aware of it in the daytime? Was this intimate knowledge due to long acquaintance? Had her thought been feeding him perhaps since childhood even?

In the pause of his temporary lunacy he asked himself a dozen similar questions, but before the sign of any answer came he was off again, sweeping on outstretched wings among the stars. He drank her in. He knew. What was the good of questions? A thirsty man does not stop midway in his draught to ask when his thirst began, its cause, or why the rush of liquid down his throat is satisfying. He knows, and drinks. It seemed to Henry Rogers, ordinary man of business and practical affairs, that some deep river which so long had flowed deep out of sight, hidden below his daily existence, rose now grandly at the flood. He had heard its subterranean murmurs often. Here, in the Den, it had reached his lips at last. And he quenched his thirst. . . His thought played round her without ceasing, like flowing water. . .

This idea of flux grew everywhere about him. There was fluid movement in this world within a world. All life was a flowing past of ceaseless beauty, wonder, splendour; it was doubt and question that dammed the rush, causing that stoppage which is ugly, petty, rigid. His being flowed out to mingle with her own. It was all inevitable, and he never really doubted once. Only before long he would be compelled to act—to speak—to tell her what he felt, and hear her dear, dear answer. . . The excitement in him became more and more difficult to control. Already there was strain and tension below his apparent outer calmness. Life in him burst forward to a yet greater life than he had ever known. . .

The others—it was his cousin's voice this time—were speaking of the Story, and of his proposed treatment of it in its larger version as a book. Daddy was saying, apparently, that it must fail because he saw no climax for it. The public demanded a cumulative interest that worked up to some kind of thrilling denouement that they called a climax, whereas his tale was but a stretch of life, and of very ordinary life. And Life, for the majority, knew no such climax. How could he manage one without inventing something artificial?

"But the climax of life comes every day and every minute," he heard her answer—and how her little voice rang out above the others like a bell!—"when you deny yourself for another, and that other does not even know it. A day is lost that does not pin at least one sweet thought against each passing hour."

And his inner construction took a further prodigious leap, as the sentence showed him the grand and simple motive of her being. It had been his own as well, though he had stupidly bungled it in his search to find something big enough to seem worth doing. She, he divined, found neighbours everywhere, losing no time. He had known a few rare, exquisite souls who lived for others, but here, close beside him at last, was one of those still rarer souls who seem born to—die for others. . . They give so unsparingly of their best. . . To his imaginative interpretation of her he gave full rein. . . And it was instantaneous as creation. . .

The voices of Minks and Mother renewed the stream of sound that swept by him then, though he caught no words that were comparable in value to these little singing phrases that she used from time to time. Jimbo, bored by the grown-up talk that took the place of expected stories, had fallen asleep upon his shoulder; Monkey's hair, as usual, was in his eyes; he sat there listening and waiting with a heart that beat so loudly he thought the children must feel it and ask him what was the matter. Jinny stirred the peat from time to time. The room was full of shadows. But, for him, the air grew brighter every minute, and in this steady brilliance he saw the little figure rise and grow in grandeur till she filled all space.

"You called it 'getting out' while the body is asleep," came floating through the air through the sound of Jimbo's breathing, "whereas *I* called it getting away from self while personal desire is asleep. But the idea is the same. . ."

His cousin's words that called forth this criticism he had not heard. It was only her sentence that seemed to reach him.

From the river of words and actions men call life she detained, it seemed to him, certain that were vital and important in some symbolical sense; she italicised them, made them her own—then let them go to join the main stream again. This selection was a kind of genius. The river did not overwhelm her as it overwhelms most, because the part of it she did not need for present action she ignored, while yet she swam in the whole of it, shirking nothing.

This was the way he saw her—immediately. And, whether it was his own invention, or whether it was the divination of a man in the ecstasy of sudden love, it was vital because he felt it, and it was real because he believed it. Then why seek to explain the amazing sense of intimacy, the certainty that he had known her always? The thing was *there*; explanation could bring it no nearer. He let the explanations go their way; they floated everywhere within reach; he had only to pocket them and take them home for study at his leisure afterwards—with her.

"But, we *shall* come to it in time," he caught another flying sentence that reached him through the brown tangle of Monkey's hair. It was spoken with eager emphasis. "Does not every letter you write begin with *dear*? . . ."

All that she said added something to life, it seemed, like poetry which, he remembered, "enriches the blood of the world." The selections were not idle, due to chance, but belonged to some great Scheme, some fairy edifice she built out of the very stuff of her own life. Oh, how utterly he understood and knew her. The poison of intellectuality, thank heaven, was not in her, yet she created somehow; for all she touched, with word or thought or gesture, turned suddenly alive in a way he had never known before. The world turned beautiful and simple at her touch. . .

Even the commonest things! It was miraculous, at least in its effect upon himself. Her simplicity escaped all signs of wumbling. She had no favourite and particular Scheme for doing good, but did merely what was next her at the moment to be done. She *was* good. In her little person glowed a great enthusiasm for life. She created neighbours. And, as the grandeur of her insignificance rose before him, his own great Scheme for Disabled Thingumabobs that once had filled the heavens, shrank down into the size of a mere mouse-trap that would go into his pocket. In its place loomed up another that held the beauty of the Stars. How little, when announcing it to Minks weeks and weeks ago, had he dreamed the form it was to take!

And so, wrapped in this glory of the stars, he dreamed on in his corner, fashioning this marvellous interpretation of a woman he had never seen before, and never spoken with. It was all so different to ordinary falling in love at sight, that the phrase never once occurred to him. It was consummated in a moment—out there, beside the fountain when he saw her first, shadowy, with brilliant, peering eyes. It seemed perfect instantly, a recovery of something he had always known. And who shall challenge the accuracy of his vision, or call its sudden maturity impossible? For where one sees the surface only, another sees the potentialities below. To believe in these is to summon them into activity, just as to think the best of a person ever brings out that best. Are we not all potential splendours?

Swiftly, in a second, he reviewed the shining sentences that revealed her to him: The "autumn flowers"—she lived, then, in the Present, without that waste of energy which is regret! In "a little shell" lay the pattern of all life,—she saw the universe in herself and lived, thus, in the Whole! To be "out" meant forgetting self; and life's climax is at every minute of the day—she understood, that is, the growth of the soul, due to acceptance of what every minute brings, however practical, dull, uninteresting. By recreating the commonest things, she found a star in each. And her world was made up of neighbours—for "every letter that one writes begins with *dear!*"

The Pattern matured marvellously before his eyes; and its delicate embroideries, far out of sight, seemed the arabesques that yearnings, hitherto unfulfilled, had traced long long ago with the brush of tender thinking. Together, though at opposite ends of the world, these two had woven the great Net of sympathy, thought, and longing in which at last they both were prisoners. . . and with them all the earth.

The figure of Jane Anne loomed before him like an ogress suddenly.

"Cousinenry, *will* you answer or will you *not*? Daddy's already asked you twenty times at least!" Then, below her breath, as she bent over him, "The Little Countess will think you awf'ly rude if you go to sleep and snore like this."

He looked up. He felt a trifle dazed. For a moment he had forgotten where he was. How dark the room had grown! Only—he was sure he had not snored.

"I beg your pardon," he stammered, "but I was only thinking—how wonderful you—how wonderful it all is, isn't it? I was listening. I heard perfectly."

"You were dozing," whispered Monkey. "Daddy wants the Countess to tell you how she knew the story long ago, or something. *Ecoute un peu, man vieux!*"

"I should love to hear it," he said, louder, sitting up so abruptly in his chair that Jimbo tilted at a dangerous angle, though still without waking. "Please, please go on."

And he listened then to the quiet, silvery language in which the little visitor described the scenery of her childhood, when, without brothers or sisters, she was forced to play alone, and had amused herself by imagining a Net of Constellations which she nailed by shooting stars to four enormous pine trees that grew across the torrent. She described the great mountains that enclosed her father's estate, her loneliness in this giant garden, due to his morose severity of character, her yearnings to escape and see the big world beyond the ridges. All her thought and longing went to the fashioning of this Net, and every night she flung it far across the peaks and valleys to catch companions with whom she might play. The characters in her fairy books came out of the pages to help her, and sometimes when they drew it in, it was so heavy with the people entangled in its meshes that they could scarcely move it. But the moment all were out, the giant Net, relieved of their weight, flew back into the sky. The Pleiades were its centre, because she loved the Pleiades best of all, and Orion pursued its bright shape with passion, yet could never quite come up with it.

"And these people whom you caught," whispered Rogers from his corner, listening to a tale he knew as well as she did, "you kept them prisoners?"

"I first put into them all the things I longed to do myself in the big world, and then flung them back again into their homes and towns and villages—"

"Excepting one," he murmured.

"Who was so big and clumsy that he broke the meshes and so never got away." She laughed, while the children stared at their cousin, wondering how he knew as much as she did. "He stayed with me, and showed me how to make our prisoners useful afterwards by painting them all over with starlight which we collected in a cave. Then they went back and dazzled others everywhere by their strange, alluring brilliance. We made the whole world over in this way—"

"Until you lost him."

"One cloudy night he disappeared, yes, and I never found him again. There was a big gap between the Pleiades and Orion where he had tumbled through. I named him Orion after that; and I would stand at night beneath the four great pine trees and call and call, but in vain. 'You must come up to me! You must come up to me!' I called, but got no answer—"

"Though you knew quite well where he had fallen to, and that he was only hiding—"

"Excuse me, but *how* did she know?" inquired Jinny abruptly.

The Little Countess laughed. "I suppose—because the threads of the Net were so sensitive that they went on quivering long after he tumbled out, and so betrayed the direction—"

"And afterwards, when you got older, Gräfin," interrupted Daddy, who wished his cousin to hear the details of the extraordinary coincidence, "you elaborated your idea—"

"Yes, that thought and yearning always fulfil themselves somewhere, somehow, sooner or later," she continued. "But I kept the imagery of my Star Net in which all the world lies caught, and I used starlight as the symbol of that sympathy which binds every heart to every other heart. At my father's death, you see, I inherited his property. I escaped from the garden which had been so long my prison, and I tried to carry out in practical life what I had dreamed there as a child. I got people together, where I could, and formed Thinkers' Guilds—people, that is, who agreed to think beauty, love, and tolerance at given hours in the day, until the habit, once formed, would run through all their lives, and they should go about as centres of light, sweetening the world. Few have riches, fewer still have talent, but all can think. At least, one would *think* so, wouldn't one?"—with a smile and a fling of her little hands.

She paused a moment, and then went on to describe her failure. She told it to them with laughter between her sentences, but among her listeners was one at least who caught the undertone of sadness in the voice.

"For, you see, that was where I made my mistake. People would do anything in the world rather than think. They would work, give money, build schools and hospitals, make all manner of sacrifices—only—they would not think; because, they said, there was no visible result." She burst out laughing, and the children all laughed too.

"I should think not indeed," ventured Monkey, but so low that no one heard her.

"And so you went on thinking it all alone," said Rogers in a low voice.

"I tried to write it first as a story," she answered softly, "but found that was beyond me; so I went on thinking it all alone, as you say—"

"Until the Pattern of your thought floated across the world to me," said Daddy proudly. "I imagined I was inspired; instead I was a common, unoriginal plagiarist!"

"Like all the rest of us," she laughed.

"Mummie, what *is* a plagiarist?" asked Jinny instantly; and as Rogers, her husband, and even Minks came hurriedly to her aid, the spell of the strange recital was broken, and out of the turmoil of voices the only thing distinctly heard was Mother exclaiming with shocked surprise:—

"Why, it's ten o'clock! Jimbo, Monkey, please plagiarise off to bed at once!"—in a tone that admitted of no rejoinder or excuses.

"A most singular thing, isn't it, Henry?" remarked the author, coming across to his side when the lamp was lit and the children had said their good-nights.

"I really think we ought to report it to the Psychical Society as a genuine case of thought-transference. You see, what people never properly realise is—"

But Henry Rogers lost the remainder of the sentence even if he heard the beginning, for his world was in a state of indescribable turmoil, one emotion tumbling wildly upon the heels of another. He was elated to intoxication. The room spun round him. The next second his heart sank down into his boots. He only caught the end of the words she was saying to Mother across the room:—

". . . but I must positively go tomorrow, I've already stayed too long. So many things are waiting at home for me to do. I must send a telegram and. . ."

His cousin's wumbling drowned the rest. He was quite aware that Rogers was not listening to him.

". . . your great kindness in writing to him, and then coming yourself," Mother was saying. "It's such an encouragement. I can't tell you how much he—we—"

"And you'll let me write to you about the children," she interrupted, "the plans we discussed, you know. . ."

Rogers broke away from his cousin with a leap. It felt at least like a leap. But he knew not where to go or what to say. He saw Minks standing with Jane Anne again by the fourneau, picking at his ear. By the open window with Mother stood the little visitor. She was leaving tomorrow. A torturing pain like twisting knives went through him. The universe was going out! . . . He saw the starry sky behind her. Daddy went up and joined them, and he was aware that the three of them talked all at once for what seemed an interminable time, though all he heard was his cousin's voice repeating at intervals, "But you *can't* send a telegram before eight o'clock tomorrow morning in any case; the post is closed. . ."

And then, suddenly, the puzzle reeled and danced before his eyes. It dissolved into a new and startling shape that brought him to his senses with a shock. There had been a swift shuffling of the figures.

Minks and his cousin were helping her into her cloak. She *was* going.

One of them—he knew not which—was offering politely to escort her through the village.

It sounded like his own sentence of exile, almost of death. Was he forty years of age, or only fifteen? He felt awkward, tongue-tied, terrified.

They were already in the passage. Mother had opened the door into the yard.

"But your way home lies down the hill," he heard the silver voice, "and to go with me you must come up. I can easily—"

Above the leaves of the plane tree he saw the stars. He saw Orion and the Pleiades. The Fairy Net flung in and caught him. He found his voice.

In a single stride he was beside her. Minks started at his sudden vehemence and stepped aside.

"*I* will take you home, Countess, if I may," and his tone was so unnecessarily loud and commanding that Mother turned and stared. "Our direction lies together. I will come up—with you."

.She did not even look at him. He saw that tiny smile that was like the flicker of a star—no more. But he heard her answer. It seemed to fill the sky.

"Thank you. I might lose my way alone."

And, before he realised how she managed it, they had crossed the cobbled yard, Daddy was swinging away downhill towards the carpenter's, and Minks behind them, at the top of the stone steps, was saying his last good-night to Mother. With the little visitor beside him, he passed the singing fountain and led her down the deserted village street beneath the autumn stars.

Three minutes later they were out of sight. . . when Minks came down the steps and picked his way among the shadows after Daddy, who had the latch-key of the carpenter's house. He ran to overtake him.

> *And he ran upon his toes*
> *As softly as a saying does,*
> *For so the saying goes!*

His thoughts were very active, but as clear as day. He was thinking whether German was a difficult language to acquire, and wondering whether a best man at a wedding ought to wear white gloves or not. He decided to ask Albinia. He wrote the letter that very night before he went to sleep.

And, while he slept, Orion pursued the Pleiades across the sky, and numerous shooting stars fastened the great Net of thought and sympathy close over little Bourcelles.

THE END

A Note About the Author

Algernon Blackwood (1869–1951) was an English journalist, novelist, and short story writer. Born in Shooter's Hill, he developed an interest in Hinduism and Buddhism at a young age. After a youth spent travelling and taking odd jobs—Canadian dairy farmer, bartender, model, violin teacher—Blackwood returned to England and embarked on a career as a professional writer. Known for his connection to the Hermetic Order of the Golden Dawn, Blackwood gained a reputation as a master of occult storytelling, publishing such popular horror stories as "The Willows" and "The Wendigo." He also wrote several novels, including *Jimbo: A Fantasy* (1909) and *The Centaur* (1911). Throughout his life, Blackwood was a passionate outdoorsman, spending much of his time skiing and mountain climbing. Recognized as a pioneering writer of ghost stories, Blackwood influenced such figures as J. R. R. Tolkien, H. P. Lovecraft, and Henry Miller.

A Note from the Publisher

Spanning many genres, from non-fiction essays to literature classics to children's books and lyric poetry, Mint Edition books showcase the master works of our time in a modern new package. The text is freshly typeset, is clean and easy to read, and features a new note about the author in each volume. Many books also include exclusive new introductory material. Every book boasts a striking new cover, which makes it as appropriate for collecting as it is for gift giving. Mint Edition books are only printed when a reader orders them, so natural resources are not wasted. We're proud that our books are never manufactured in excess and exist only in the exact quantity they need to be read and enjoyed. To learn more and view our library, go to minteditionbooks.com